NATIVE NORTH AMERICAN CULTURES: FOUR CASES

THE HANO TEWA / THE KWAKIUTL / THE BLACKFEET / THE MENOMINEE

edited by GEORGE AND LOUISE SPINDLER

Stanford University

HOLT, RINEHART AND WINSTON New York Chicago San Francisco Atlanta
Dallas Montreal Toronto London Sydney

Library of Congress Cataloging in Publication Data

Main entry under title:

Native North American cultures.

    Bibliography: p. 499
    Includes index.
    CONTENTS: Spindler, G. and Spindler, L. Intro-
duction.—Dozier, E. P. Hano.—Rohner, R. P. and
Rohner, E. C. The Kwakiutl Indians of British Co-
lumbia. [etc.]
    1. Indians of North America. 2. Tewa Indians.
3. Kwakiutl Indians. 4. Menominee Indians.
I. Spindler, George Dearborn. II. Spindler, Louise S.
E77.N36   970'.004'97   76–23178
ISBN 0–03–018401–0

CONTENTS

Introduction
The editors, G. and L. Spindler   1

HANO: A TEWA INDIAN COMMUNITY IN ARIZONA
Edward T. Dozier   5

THE KWAKIUTL: INDIANS OF BRITISH COLUMBIA
Ronald P. Rohner and Evelyn C. Rohner   113

MODERN BLACKFEET: MONTANANS
ON A RESERVATION
Malcolm McFee   225

THE MENOMINEE
George and Louise Spindler   361

Further Reading on Each Culture   499

Useful General Reading   502

Index   504

Introduction

Since 1959 over a million students of anthropology have learned about cultures around the world by reading case studies from the series Case Studies in Cultural Anthropology. For the first time we have brought together in this volume several studies on native North American cultures. Until now they have only been available in single copy editions.

There is no part of the world's culture areas of greater importance to American students of anthropology than native North America. It is in this geographical space, occupied and used for many thousands of years before the coming of Europeans by human communities of great diversity and complexity, that the confrontation between the West and the tribal world appears, for many of us, in most dramatic and understandable form.

The culture cases in this volume have been carefully selected to represent four of the most important culture areas of native North America: the Pueblo Southwest; the Northwest Coast; the Plains; and the Northeastern Woodlands. The Hano-Tewa, Kwakiutl, Blackfeet, and Menominee cases represent these areas well. They cannot, of course, represent all significant aspects of the cultural profiles of these areas, but they are close to being prototypical. Although the traditional cultures are given attention in each case, these are described in the modern setting, in today's world. A student reading these four studies will understand much about the great diversity of native North America. No outline of culture patterns alone can do this. The studies included in this collection are complete enough so that one is not left with that unsatisfied feeling that one has gotten only the formal, surface features. Each study is written with attention to living detail. Students reading these studies will also understand some of the great conflicts and problems inherent in the native American situation in twentieth century America.

We suggest that you read these case studies, the first time, as though you were reading a novel. You should get the feel of the way of life without getting bogged down in details. The second time you can go over the studies for a better understanding of the ways in which each of the cultures works as a system and how it works in the modern environment, how it survives against great odds. You may find it useful to do some systematic comparing among the four cases. Keith Otterbein's book *Comparative Cultural Analysis* could be helpful, for it

1

lays out explicitly just how a comparison can be made. Another useful aid to getting the most out of this volume is to relate each of the four culture cases to the culture area in which it is found. Most good textbooks on native North America provide descriptions of these areas. In this and other ways the textbook should provide a conceptual order for the student. Questions formulated on the basis of reading and lectures can be pursued through *Native North American Cultures*, using the four culture case studies as primary sources. To this purpose we have furnished an index to the four cultures in this volume. Subentries indicate the individual case studies for which page references are provided. This will make it easier to use *Native North American Cultures* for comparative exercises and problems, preparation of reports, discussion, term papers, and, of course, exams.

Highly selected lists of reading on each culture and on American Indians in general are included at the end of this volume. Any reading from these lists will expand one's knowledge and understanding of native North American cultures.

Hano

This first culture case study, on Hano, a Tewa community in the midst of the Hopi country between Winslow and Flagstaff, Arizona, is written by a native American, Edward Dozier, who was born in the Tewa pueblo of Santa Clara. His mother, a full-blooded Tewa, was a student of his father, an American school teacher in the pueblo, when they married. Dozier's early life and schooling were in the pueblo. The study is therefore written from a somewhat different vantage point than most ethnographies. This position has great advantages, but it also has disadvantages. There were aspects of Tewa life that Dozier did not feel free to write about. But what he does write about is direct, clear, and intimate without being personal, and the description has a fullness to it that is unusual in a short ethnography.

This case study is also notable because the adaptation of one way of life and one people to another non-Western society as well as to Western culture is described. This is rare in anthropological literature.

Dozier gives us an understanding of the historical forces shaping so much of what we see today in the pueblo communities of which he writes. He also gives us a succinct description of the network of social relationships in the pueblo. His analysis is particularly notable for the clarity with which the behaviors and expectations connected with kinship terminology and group membership are described. Religious and ritual associations and activities and the way the people earn their living and share the products of their labors are described.

The Kwakiutl

Ronald and Evelyn Rohner, the authors of *The Kwakiutl: Indians of British Columbia*, state, "Part One [pp. 117–188] is written in the ethnographic present even though we lived in the Kwakiutl village on Gilford Island from September 1962 through August 1963, and again during June and July 1964. Our effort has been to describe the distinctive quality of human life within the village of Gilford as it was when we lived there. Even though our presentation in Part One relates explicitly to one unique village among a series of unique villages, Gilford is nonetheless representative of Kwakiutl communities. Most of what we write, therefore, can be generalized to the Kwakiutl rather than simply to Gilford Island Kwakiutl" (Rohner and Rohner 1970: xiii).

In Part Two (pp. 189–222) they describe some of the major features of the traditional Kwakiutl social system including the rank-class structure, potlatches, and the impressive winter ceremonial. They point out basic alterations that have occurred in this system from the turn of the century to the present.

Despite the fact that to a casual observer there might be little to distinguish the people of Gilford from a non-Indian population, they have actually retained much of their social and cultural identity. The current revitalization of certain aspects of Kwakiutl life suggests that this identity will not soon disappear.

The Blackfeet

This case study makes it clear that acculturation is not simply a one-way cultural adaptation to the impact of Euro-American culture. Malcolm McFee's careful analysis shows that although there are many subvarieties, there are essentially two major types of coping strategy represented among the contemporary Blackfeet: The Indian-oriented and the white-oriented. These two adaptations are quite different and have quite different consequences for the people involved.

For the Blackfeet of the prereservation days the buffalo was the major source of food, shelter, clothing, tools, and ornamentation. They were, of course prime users of the horse, which assumed great importance among them after its introduction sometime between 1725 and 1750. The Blackfeet represent in substantial, though of course never in perfect, degree the major features of the way of life created out of the use of the horse, buffalo hunting, and nomadism, with a high development of military institutions and values characteristic of a vast area of the high plains during the eighteenth and nineteenth centuries.

They also represent in many ways the results of the confrontation between Euro-Americans and native populations. McFee tells this story with a compassionate objectivity that furthers understanding.

The Menominee*

This is a study of two kinds of adaptation by the Menominee of Wisconsin to the results of the confrontation between their way of life and the ways of the

---

* Though the tribe is most often referred to in the literature as Menomini, the spelling Menominee has become customary recently.

Whiteman. It is the story of a people who existed in a world of thought and belief radically different from that of the Euro-Americans. The Menominee were dreamers and people of power. Their religious associations, rituals, witch bags, and medicine bundles were all devices for acquiring and maintaining sacred power. Their dreams told them of the future, instructed them about the meaning of events, gave them roles and purposes in life, and provided them with access to power.

The original case study by George and Louise Spindler tells the story of five different adaptive, or coping, strategies the Menominee used to get along in a conflicted world. For the purposes of this volume we have included only the adaptive strategies termed "native-oriented" and Peyotism. The first term calls attention to the fact that the members of this group were oriented toward keeping many of their traditions, particularly in the sphere of religious belief and behavior. In fact they worked very hard at it and were quite successful. The Peyotists adopted a different strategy. They reduced culture conflict not so much by reaffirming traditions but rather by synthesizing elements from both Indian and Anglo-American culture.

The first chapter, rewritten for this volume, describes briefly the "confrontation" between the Menominee and the Anglo-American people and their cultures. The second chapter concentrates on the native-oriented group as it was in the decade between 1951 and 1961, the date when federal control and support were withdrawn and the tribe was "terminated." Since then the Menominee have regained something resembling their former position through formal legislation restoring the reservation. A whole new complex of adaptations and conflicts were set in motion. But that is another story that someday must be told.

The chapters describing the native-oriented and Peyote ways of life are quite different from anything else included in this collection of case studies. Much is said in the people's own words. Also, the words of people who studied the Menominee way of life in the past are quoted to demonstrate the cultural continuity that we believe to be present.

Groups of the kind described here are not present, as groups, in all reservation communities. However, the tendency to assert identity through symbols and behavior patterns relating to the past is very widespread not only in reservation communities but also in cities, in fact any place where there is a sizable number of native Americans. Assertions of identity may take many specific forms. The native-oriented Menominee represent one, the Peyotists another.

The Peyotists described in Chapter 3 are surprisingly different from the native oriented. Their adaptive strategy is described in detail, and again much of the text is in the people's own words. Vision, conversion, and curing experiences are presented in this manner.

George and Louise Spindler
General Editors

HANO: A TEWA INDIAN COMMUNITY IN ARIZONA

Edward T. Dozier

Edward T. Dozier, born in a Tewa pueblo, became interested in anthropology early. He took both his B.A. and M.A. in anthropology at the University of New Mexico. He then attended the University of California at Los Angeles, where he obtained a Ph.D. degree in 1952. He taught at the University of Oregon and at the University of Tucson, Arizona. In 1958–1959 he was a Fellow at the Center for Advanced Studies in the Behavioral Sciences at Stanford, California. He did fieldwork in the southwestern United States and among the Kalinga people of northern Luzon, Philippines.

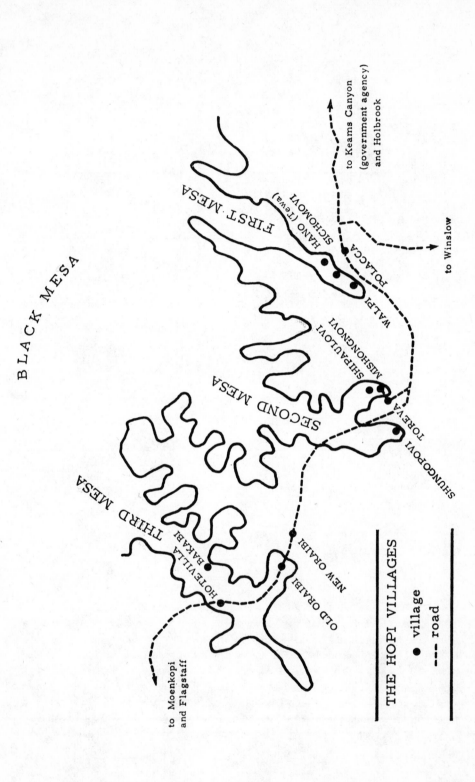

BLACK MESA

FIRST MESA

HANO (Tewa)
SICHOMOVI
POLACCA
WALPI

SHIPAULOVI
MISHONGNOVI
SECOND MESA

SHUNGOPOVI
TOREVA

THIRD MESA

HOTEVILLA
BAKABI
NEW ORAIBI
OLD ORAIBI

to Keams Canyon
(government agency)
and Holbrook

to Winslow

to Moenkopi
and Flagstaff

THE HOPI VILLAGES

● village
--- road

Contents

Introduction   11

1. Rio Grande Homeland   13

     Exploring Expeditions, 14
     Colonization, 15
     Missionary Activities, 16
     Secular Authorities, 17
     Effects of Spanish Rule, 21

2. At Hopi   23

     Traditional History, 27

3. Hano—The Tewa Community   30

     Tewa and Hopi Relations, 33
     Relations with Navaho and Other Indians, 41
     Relations with Whites, 42
     Misisonaries, 42
     Traders, 44
     Tourists, 45
     United States Indian Service, 45
     The Yearly Round of Activities, 47

4. The Social Network   49

     The Household, 50
     Lineage and Clan, 51
     The Kinship System, 58
       The Nature of the Terminology, 58
       Kinship Behavior, 58
       Mother's Lineage, 59
       Father's Lineage, 63
       Mother's Father's Matrilineal Lineage, 66
     Life Cycle, 67
     Key Features of the Kinship System and Life Cycle, 75

Social Control, 76
Hopi Tribal Council and Tribal Court, 79
Summary, 80

5. Religion and Ritual   82

Kiva Organization, 83
Associations and Ceremonies, 86
  The Kachina Cult, 86
  The Clown Association, 88
  The Curing Association, 88
  Recruitment of Association Members, 88
  Other Ceremonial Activities, 88
Initiation, 89
Social Dances, 90
Beliefs and Values, 91
Ritual Activities, 93
Summary, 94

6. Livelihood   95

Economic Pursuits, 95
Land, 96
Ownership and Inheritance, 96
Wage Work, Livestock, and Horticulture, 97
Cooperative Enterprises, 98
Summary, 106

7. Perspective and Outlook   107

Orthographic Note   110

References   111

Niman Kachina Dance. (Courtesy of Smithsonian Office of Anthropology, Bureau of American Ethnology Collection)

Left: Hano Tewa woman in ceremonial dress standing in front of Kiva. Right: Buffalo Dance at Santa Clara Pueblo, Rio Grande Tewa. (Courtesy of the Arizona State Museum)

Air view of First Mesa—showing all three villages—Hano in the foreground, then Sichomovi, and Walpi at the far tip of the mesa. (Photograph by Milton Snow, Bureau of Indian Affairs)

Introduction

THE HOPI AND TEWA INDIANS living in the *mesa* country of Arizona are of two different cultural and linguistic traditions and have lived together for more than 250 years in close contact with one another, yet only in recent years have barriers fallen and the two groups begun to live harmoniously together.

The ancestors of the Hopi have been residents of the mesa-top villages for many centuries, but the Tewa are newcomers; they are the descendants of refugees from New Mexico who fled from Spanish oppression in the seventeenth century. The coming of the Spaniards was a major catastrophe to the peaceful Pueblo Indians residing along the Rio Grande and its tributaries in New Mexico. White man's diseases and the fanatical pogroms of the Spaniards to Christianize and "civilize" the Indians took a large toll of Pueblo lives. Many of these Indians fled their villages and joined the nomadic Apachean tribes, while others sought refuge amoung the sedentary Hopi.

First Mesa, the easternmost escarpment of the Hopi mesas, contains three villages: one of them is the Tewa community of Hano; the other two villages are Hopi. Further west on similar mesa-tops are other Hopi villages; only First Mesa, however, harbors a community different in speech and customs from the others.

The traditions of the Hopi and the Tewa indicate that the community of Hano remained in a minority status for a long time. Tewa inhabitants were denied full participation in Hopi ceremonies, and only the poorer plots of land were made available for them to farm. Hano, in return, clung tenaciously to its own cultural forms and carefully prevented the diffusion of its language and customs to its neighbors. In comparatively recent years this mutual pattern of resistance has broken down. The change appears to coincide with accelerated American activities, such as the establishment of the government agency and schools, the dissemination of stock-raising information, trading-post activities, the employment of Indians for wage work, and the influx of tourists.

11

The introduction of new activities alone has not produced the changes discussed in this report. The crucial factor appears to be a reorientation of the value system on First Mesa—a reorientation more compatible with Tewa values. There is abundant evidence that the Tewa demonstrated very early in the American period a willingness to cooperate with Americans and to participate in American activities. The personality of the Tewa proved congenial to Americans, and the Indians adjusted remarkably well to the changing situation brought about by American contact. The success of the Tewa in American activities seems to have resulted in reduced tensions and in emulation of the Tewa by their Hopi neighbors. This, in turn, paved the way for greater interdependence and cooperation among the three villages on First Mesa. As a consequence, the minority status of the Tewa began to dissolve, and the present trend toward an integrated First Mesa society commenced.

This report is based on field studies carried out on the Hopi reservation (which includes the Hano Tewa) over a number of years. I have also drawn from previous studies among the Tewa and Hopi, particularly those of Fred Eggan, Mischa Titiev, and Barbara Aitken. For the support of my fieldwork, I am indebted to the Social Science Research Council, the Wenner-Gren Foundation, and to an Opportunity Fellowship from the John Hay Whitney Foundation. This report also owes much to many Hopi and Tewa friends who gave generously of their time to give me deeper insight and understanding of Pueblo culture.

1

Rio Grande Homeland

AT THE TIME the first Spanish expedition entered the Rio Grande Pueblo
country in 1540 the Tewa represented one of the largest language
groups in the Southwest. The first census report of the Pueblos contained in the Memorial of Alonzo de Benavides 1634 (Hodge, Hammond, and
Rey 1945) reported the population of the Tewa at 10,000 The Pueblo villages
of the Tanoan linguistic group, of which the Tewa were a member (along with
the Tiwa, Towa, and Piro), extended southward from Taos to near the present
site of El Paso. They formed a barrier to the Plains Indians' encroachment from
the east, and served as a buffer zone to the Keresan Pueblo communities farther
west. The Tewa, divided into a northern and southern group, lived in the vicinity of Santa Fe. The Northern Tewa resided just north of the capital in what is
now the Espanola Valley. Some of these villages have survived to the present
time, and the pueblos of Tesuque, Nambe, San Ildefonso, Santa Clara, and San
Juan carry many of the traditional Tewa cultural and social characteristics.
Southward, including Santa Fe itself, were the pueblos of the Southern Tewa,
designated in the early Spanish accounts as *Thano* or *Tano*. Historical and ethnological data indicate that there was little difference linguistically and culturally
between the two Tewa groups. The early Spanish authorities separated the
groups administratively, however, and apparently the southern branch gave the
Spaniards the most trouble. After the Pueblo Indian revolt of 1680–1692, these
Indians were dispersed among some of the more peaceful pueblos in order to
quell their rebellious nature. For a brief period some of the Southern Tewa were
resettled near the present site of Chimayo in the Northern Tewa country.
Troubles with the Spaniards persisted, however, and in 1696 this group, the ancestors of the present Hano Tewa, fled to the Hopi country to escape Spanish
oppression.

The kind of relations that existed between the Rio Grande Pueblos and
the Spaniards during the early periods of contact is important in understanding
the cultural conservatism of these Pueblos today. It is, therefore, germane to review these relations in greater detail.

13

Exploring Expeditions

The expedition of Francisco Vasquez de Coronado in 1540 brought the first white men seen by the Rio Grande Pueblo Indians. Coronado's party was a spectacular group of several hundred mailed and armed horsemen accompanied by Mexican Indian servants. The party crossed and recrossed the Tewa country several times during the two years they remained in the Pueblo country. From the beginning the Spaniards made themselves feared and distrusted. The expedition made incessant demands for food and other supplies, and in Coronado's headquarters at Tiguex (a Tiwa village), a lieutenant of Coronado executed several hundred Indians for a minor rebellion. The news of Spanish cruelty spread rapidly throughout the pueblos, and the seed of resentment and hatred for the white man had been sown.

The next expedition into the Pueblo country forty years later was a small one. The party was under the command of Francisco Sanchez Chamuscado, and included besides Chamuscado, a Franciscan priest (Father Augustin Rodriguez), two Franciscan brothers, and twelve soldiers. The party visited the Tewa pueblos, and upon its departure, left the friars among the pueblos, apparently in Tiwa pueblos.

A third expedition led by Antonio de Espejo was sent out in 1582 to find out the fate of the friars left by the Chamuscado expedition. The party included one Franciscan priest and fourteen soldiers. No evidence of the missionaries was found; obviously the friars had been put to death, but the Indians would not implicate anyone. Espejo explored the regions already visited by Coronado; he found nothing new, but he has left us probably the best detailed description of early Pueblo village life. It is interesting that with a few minor additions and deletions Espejo's account could serve as a description of Tewa pueblo life at the beginning of the present century, more than three hundred years later. The last sixty to seventy years has, of course, brought about tremendous material changes, but changes in the socio-cultural domain have been comparatively slight. The following excerpts from Espejo's report might be compared with a contemporary description of the villages and life-way of the Pueblos in order to comprehend Pueblo conservatism:

> As we were going through this province [the Piro country], from each pueblo the people came out to receive us, taking us to their pueblos and giving us a great quantity of turkeys, maize, beans, tortillas, and other kinds of bread. . . . They grind on very large stones. Five or six women together grind raw corn . . . and from this flour they make many different kinds of bread. They have houses of two, three, and four stories, with many rooms in each house . . . in each plaza of the towns they have two *estufas* [kivas], which are houses built underground, very well sheltered and closed, with seats of stone against the walls to sit on. Likewise, they have at the door of each *estufa* a ladder on which to descend, and a great quantity of community wood, so that strangers may gather there.
>
> In this province some of the natives wear cotton, cow hides [buffalo],

and dressed deerskin. . . . The women wear cotton skirts, many of them being embroidered with colored thread, and on top a *manta* like those worn by the Mexican Indians, tied around the waist with a cloth like an embroidered towel with a tassel . . . and all, men as well as women, dress their feet in shoes and boots, the soles being of cowhide and the uppers of dressed deerskin. The women wear their hair carefully combed and nicely kept in place by the moulds that they wear on their heads, one on each side, on which the hair is arranged very neatly, though they wear no headdress. In each pueblo they have their caciques. . . . These caciques have under them . . . *tequitatos*, who are like alguaciles [policemen], and who execute in the pueblo the cacique's orders. . . . And when the Spaniards ask the caciques of the pueblos for anything, they call the *tequitatos*, who cry it through the pueblo in a loud voice . . .

. . . In each one of these pueblos they have a house to which they carry food for the devil, and they have small stone idols which they worship. Just as the Spaniards have crosses along the roads, they have between the pueblos, in the middle of the road, small caves or grottoes, like shrines, built of stones, where they place painted sticks and feathers, saying that the devil goes there to rest and speak with them.

They have fields of maize, beans, gourds, and *piciete* [tobacco] in large quantities. . . . Some of the fields are under irrigation, possessing very good diverting ditches, while others are dependent upon the weather. Each one has in his field a canopy with four stakes . . . where he takes his siesta, for ordinarily they are in their fields from morning until night. . . . Their arms consist of bows and arrows, *macanas* and *chimales;* the arrows have fire-hardened shafts, the heads being pointed flint, with which they easily pass through a coat of mail. The *chimales* are made of cowhide, like leather shields; and the *macanas* consist of rods half a vara long, with very thick heads. With them they defend themselves within their houses. It was not learned that they were at war with any other province. . . . (Bolton 1916:177–179)

Colonization

For more than a decade after Espejo's return to Mexico, he, as well as others, attempted to secure royal permission to colonize the Pueblo country. The contract for colonization was eventually awarded to Don Juan de Oñate in 1595. Oñate spent three years recruiting colonists and organizing an expeditionary force. The colonizing party consisting of several hundred Spaniards and Mexican Indians finally departed from southern Chihuahua in January 15, 1598, and entered the Pueblo country late that same year. Oñate established his headquarters near the Tewa Pueblo of San Juan, and by the end of the century had obtained the submission of all the major Pueblo groups. The seat of the provincial government was moved in 1610 to Santa Fe, the site of a former Southern Tewa village. From this headquarters the Christianizing and "civilizing" program was carried forth rapidly and energetically. Father Alonzo de Benavides, who came to implement the missionary program early in the century, reported in his *Memorial* of 1630 that 60,000 Pueblo Indians had been converted and ninety chapels built in as many villages.

From 1620 to the end of the century there were three main areas of Spanish colonization in the Pueblo country: (1) Santa Fe, (2) La Canada, near present Santa Cruz in the Tewa Basin, and (3) the southern district from Santo Domingo south to approximately the position of modern Socorro. In addition to these settlements, the more populous Pueblo villages had resident priests and sometimes a small guard of soldiers. The construction of ninety chapels by 1630 reported in Benavides' *Memorial* is probably correct, but only a few of these had resident missionaries. Most of the chapels were *visitas* to which a priest resident in another pueblo journeyed once a month to conduct Mass and other church services. All of the Pueblo villages, regardless of whether they had a resident missionary or not, however, became involved in the concerns and activities of the newcomers. Both civil authorities and missionaries abused the Indians either by exacting tribute or labor from them. Indeed, the competition for the services of the Indians resulted in a continuous conflict between civil and missionary authorities. This was a factor which contributed to the demoralization and disorganization of the New Mexico colony, and in part, at least, paved the way for the Pueblo Revolt of 1680.

Missionary Activities

In the initial period of colonization the missionaries were engaged in enormous construction programs. The mission buildings were large walled compounds within or just outside the Pueblo villages. They were constructed entirely by Indian labor under supervision of the friars. They were structures of adobe, or, in the case of the Eastern Tiwa and Piro Pueblos, of sandstone slabs set in adobe mud. Beams, doors, and window frames were of timber cut on steep mountain sides and brought a distance of twenty-five to thirty miles to mission sites by the Indians.

Within the mission compound lived one or two missionaries and a number of Indian workers and servants. Although the missions were supposed to be training centers for Indians, they served primarily as a place where the friars could live in comfort. Indians were employed at leatherwork, weaving, blacksmithing, and as cooks and servants. The mission also had grazing lands outside the compound where they kept sheep and cattle under the care of Indian herdsmen. Gardens and orchards were also a regular feature of the mission compound.

The religious responsibilities of the missionaries consisted of saying Mass, conducting burial services, performing baptisms and marriages, and conducting vesper services. A few Indians were taught prayers and made responsible for making the villagers attend church services.

The following description of church services are excerpted from a statement by the resident priest of Jemez Pueblo. Although the statement is contained in a report of conditions in the missions of New Mexico after the Pueblo Revolt of 1680, the description is probably valid for the period before the revolt as well:

The bell is rung at sunrise. The married men enter, each one with his wife, and they kneel together in a row on each side of the nave of the church. Each couple has its own place designated in accordance with the census list. When there are many, the married couples make two rows on each side, the two men in the middle and the women on the sides. This may seem a superficial matter, but it is not, for experience has taught me [the resident priest] that when these women are together they spend all the time dedicated to prayer and Mass in gossip, showing one another their glass beads, ribbons, medals, etc., telling who gave them or how they obtained them, and other mischief. Therefore the religious who has charge of the administration must have a care in this regard. After all, it is a house of prayer, not of chitchat. . . .

The petty governor and his lieutenant [Indians] have their places at the door so that the people may not leave during the hour of prayer and Mass.

When all are in their places, the fiscal mayor [an Indian] notifies the father, who comes down with his census lists and takes attendance to see whether everyone is there, whether they are in their proper places, and whether their hair is unbound. If anyone is missing, the petty governor goes to fetch him. If he is not in the pueblo, it is indicated by the thong [i.e., he is whipped] and he is punished on the following Sunday or holy day of obligation. If the truant is a woman, her husband is sent to fetch her. . . .

After Mass is over, if the minister thinks that some have left, he summons them in accordance with the list and punishes anyone who does such a thing. He severely reprimands the petty governor who permits it. . . .

The lists of married men and widowers are so arranged that if anyone is guilty of absence, this is indicated by the thong. . . . (Adams and Chavez 1956:308–15)

In addition to forcing attendance at Mass and other church services, the missionaries concentrated on the eradication of Pueblo customs and beliefs. Kivas were raided periodically and masks and prayer sticks burned. Pueblo religious leaders were whipped and hanged as witches if their activities became known to church and civil authorities. In the process the missionaries incurred the resentment of all the Indians, who, instead of giving up their beliefs and customs, went "underground" but lost none of their fervor for the native religion.

Secular Authorities

The supreme authority in the Spanish province of New Mexico was the governor and captain-general. He was appointed by the viceroy in Mexico City. The governors were supposed to promote the general welfare of the province: they were charged with the administration of justice, responsible for the protection of the settlers and Pueblos from outside enemies, and required to support the missionary program. Actually, however, the governors rarely complied with these duties. Almost all the governors during the seventeenth century engaged in various types of economic ventures for their own profit. In these ventures the labor and products of the Indian were used. Indians were made to spend long hours weaving cloth and blankets in workshops set up for the purpose in the pueblos and in Santa Fe. Other Indians were made to collect large quantities of piñon nuts, which brought a handsome price in Mexico. Still other Indians were employed to build wagons and carts for special caravans to Mexico. In the caravan trains Pueblo Indians were pressed into service as servants and muleteers.

The soldier-citizens, or *encomenderos,* were usually family heads whose responsibilities entailed the protection of the province from internal revolt and from attack by nomadic Indians. In fact, however, they were but instruments of the governors and served their interests more than the responsibilities they were supposed to fulfill. They received no pay, but the *encomiendas* which they received were far more profitable than salaries. The governor allocated the encomiendas to each soldier and determined the revenues to be derived from them. An encomienda in New Mexico entitled a soldier-citizen to the services of a number of Indians. Some of these Indians were household servants, but the main service they performed was the maintenance of farms and livestock for the benefit of the encomenderos.

In addition to the governor and encomenderos, the Spanish civil government system of the province included a secretary of government and war, a lieutenant governor, and *alcaldes mayores.* All were appointed by the governor and held office at his pleasure. The secretary was the governor's adviser and constant companion; he was in charge of all documents and papers issued in the governor's name. The lieutenant governors performed services and activities which the governor could not perform, represented the governor in his absence, and during the latter part of the century assumed control over the southern district. The *alcaldes mayores* administered subdivisions of the province. During the seventeenth century there were six or eight such units in New Mexico. These people dealt directly with the settlers and the Indians. They were perhaps without exception instruments of the governor and carried out his explicit orders. They and the soldier-citizens kept the recruitment of Indians for labor and the flow of tribute going. None of the officials below the governor received direct pay, but they all profited from the collection of tribute and from the labor of the Indians.

As the missionaries and colonial officials began to see the system of exploitation bearing fruit, they made more and more demands on the Indians. The Pueblos, by nature peaceful and unaggressive, were slow to react to the injustices and abuses to which they were subjected. Yet no people, no matter how passive or submissive, can remain completely unmoved when confronted by such oppression. The relations between the colonists and the Pueblos were, by the middle of the seventeenth century, at the danger point of eruption. The case of the Pueblos is admirably presented by Scholes:

> By 1650 the Indians were fully aware of the meaning and implications of Spanish supremacy and the mission system. Spanish supremacy had brought a heavy burden of labor and tribute and encroachment on the lands of the Pueblos. The mission system added to the burden of labor, but the most important phase of the program of Christianization was its effect on the old folk customs.
>
> The friars sought not only to teach a new faith, but they zealously tried also to put an end to the practice of native religious ceremonial, to destroy the influence of the traditional leaders of the Indians, and to impose rigid

monogamy on a people whose code of marital and sexual relationship was fairly flexible and elastic. In order to maintain mission discipline the friars often resorted to the imposition of physical punishment for such offenses as failure to attend religious services, sexual immorality, and participation in the native ceremonial dances.

But drastic disciplinary measures . . . could not force full allegiance to the new order. The efforts of the clergy to abolish the old ceremonial forms and to set up new standards of conduct merely caused greater resentment on the part of the Indians. . . . The Pueblos were not unwilling to accept externals of the new faith, but they found it difficult to understand the deeper spiritual values of Christianity. Pueblo religion served definite material and social ends, viz., the propitiation of those supernatural forces which they believed controlled their daily existence. They expected the same results from the Christian faith. But they soon realized that the new ways were no more successful in obtaining a good harvest than the old, and they realized too that the efforts to abolish their traditional ceremonials and destroy the influence of the old native leaders whose functions were both social and religious, raised serious problems concerning the entire fund of Pueblo civilization. Bewilderment soon turned into resentment, and resentment into a resurgence of loyalty to the traditional norms of folk-culture. The burden of labor and tribute might have been tolerated if offset by recognized advantages, but if the new was no more efficient in guaranteeing a harvest or success in the hunt, what had been gained by accepting Spanish overlordship? (Scholes 1942:11, 15–16)

A number of minor and local revolts were repressed, but in 1680 the Pueblos successfully carried out a general revolt under the leadership of the San Juan Tewa Indian, Popé. Popé had been one of forty-seven Pueblo religious leaders given a public whipping in Santa Fe by Spanish authorities in 1675. Smarting under the punishment, Popé planned a general revolt from his headquarters which he established in Taos Pueblo. The news of the uprising leaked out before the day planned for its execution, and the revolt had to be put into effect prematurely. The rebellion lasted for only about three weeks, but for battles fought with the crude firearms of the Spanish settlers and the bows and arrows of the Indians, it was a ferocious and bloody one. At the end of the revolt, 21 missionaries and 375 colonists were dead, while another 2000 settlers had been driven out of the Pueblo country. The Tewa and the Northern Tiwa Pueblos were the most active in the revolt and suffered the most casualties. In two skirmishes alone, 300 Southern Tewa besieging Santa Fe were killed and 47 others captured and executed. The Piro Pueblos and the Pueblo of Isleta did not take part in the revolt, but all the other Pueblos aided the general revolt by killing their resident missionaries and other colonists living in or near these pueblos. The Apaches apparently did not participate actively, but the Spaniards were led to believe they were in the revolt pact and therefore succumbed more readily. Mission establishments were destroyed everywhere, and their furnishings and records burned. Much of the destruction occurred after the colonists had quit the Pueblo country. Statements issued by Indians captured in an abortive reconquest attempt in 1681–1682 by Governor Antonio de Otermin uniformly attested that the leaders of the rebellion wanted to wipe out every vestige of

Catholic religion. The declaration of two brothers from the pueblo of San Felipe is typical of the statements recorded by Otermin:

> Asked what happened after the said rebellion [the two brothers] said they saw that the said Indian, Popé, came down to the pueblo of San Felipe accompanied by many captains from the pueblos and by other Indians and ordered the churches burned and the holy images broken up and burned. They took possession of everything in the sacristy pertaining to divine worship, and said that they were weary of putting in order, sweeping, heating, and adorning the church; and that they proclaimed both in the said pueblo and in the others that he who should utter the name of Jesus would be killed immediately; and that they [the Indians] were not to pray or to live with the wives whom they had taken in holy matrimony, all under the said penalty of death; and that thereupon they could live contentedly, happy in their freedom, living according to their ancient custom. . . .
>
> They declared further that by order of the said Popé and of Alonso Catiti, governor and head of the Queres nation, they were commanded to place in the pueblo and its environs piles of stones on which they could offer ground corn and other cereals and tobacco, they saying that the stones were their God, and that they were to observe this, even to the children, giving them to understand that thereby they would have everything they might desire. They say that they have passed over many other things that they do not recall, but they saw that as soon as the señor governor and the rest of the Spaniards had left, the Indians erected many estufas in the pueblos and danced the dances of the cazina and of losse [masked Kachina and the clown or Koshare dances], which are dances instituted by the devil. . . . (Hackett and Shelby 1942:251)

Each pueblo community is an independent social and political entity; even those villages of the same language group lack an over-all political organization. Until the Pueblos were confronted by the superior arms and tactical skills of the Spaniards their pattern of resistance had been in the form of small and brief offensive and defensive encounters with other Indian enemies no better organized or equipped than they were. It was the recognition of a common grievance—the abuses and injustices suffered by the oppressive acts of Spanish religious and civil authorities—which brought the Pueblos together temporarily. As soon as the Spaniards were out of the area, the temporary unity dissolved. Controversy and dissension broke loose, and the Pueblos began to bicker among themselves, and refuse to listen to their temporary leaders. To make matters worse, the Apaches, realizing that Spanish intervention had been removed, stepped up their raids on the marginal pueblo villages. To escape the ravages of the Apaches and apprehensive of a returning Spanish punitive or reconquest expedition, the Pueblo Indians retreated into more defensible areas in the mountains and mesas. The Southern Tewa abandoned their pueblos and part of them moved into Santa Fe, while the rest established settlements near the present site of Santa Cruz among their northern linguistic relatives.

Governor Otermin attempted an unsuccessful reconquest in the winter of 1681–1682, and there were two other unsuccessful forays by Governor Pedro Reneros de Posada in 1688 and Governor Cruzate in 1689. It was Don Diego de Vargas under a well-equipped army who finally reestablished Spanish control of the Pueblos in 1693. The Tiwa and Keresan Pueblos submitted without a struggle, and they were persuaded by De Vargas to return to their pueblos peaceably. The Southern Tewa group entrenched in Santa Fe at first threatened to fight, but De Vargas took the city without firing a shot. Indians were given to soldiers and colonists as slaves, while others were settled among the Northern Tewa villages. Those Southern Tewa who had established settlements near Santa Cruz refused to surrender, however. These Tewa carried on a hit and run warfare with De Vargas from the top of Black Mesa near San Ildefonso. They withstood the attacks of Spanish soldiers for nine months, but were finally compelled to sue for peace and return to their villages.

De Vargas quickly resettled the areas formerly occupied by Spanish and Mexican colonists and founded a new villa (Santa Cruz) in the heart of the Northern Tewa country. The new settlement took in the pueblos and lands occupied by the Southern Tewa who were resettled in a single village in the vicinity of what is now Chimayo. By repossessing the lands of the Pueblos and by reintroducing some of the abuses of the prerevolt period, De Vargas again brought general discontentment among the Pueblos. Early in June of 1696, the Tewa (including the resettled Southern Tewa) together with the Indians of Taos, Picuris, Santa Domingo, and Cochiti rose in revolt. Twenty-one Spaniards and six priests were killed. De Vargas quickly put an end to the uprising, but before he could reach the Tewa area, the entire population of the resettled Southern Tewa community had fled to the Hopi country.

By the end of the century the Pueblo area had been drastically reduced. All the Piro pueblos were uninhabited as were also the Tiwa villages east of the mountains and along the Rio Grande south of Isleta pueblo. Some of these Indians had joined the Spaniards retreating south in 1680 and founded communities below El Paso, while others migrated to the Navaho and Hopi country. The aftermath of the revolt and reconquest reduced the Pueblo communities to essentially the sites they occupy today.

The flight of the remnant Southern Tewa group to the Hopi country completes the history of this formerly significant Pueblo population in the Rio Grande area. We will resume their history in their new home shortly, but at present it is important to consider the effects of almost one hundred years of Spanish rule.

Effects of Spanish Rule

Contact with Spaniards brought about obvious changes among the pueblos. A Catholic chapel became a prominent feature of the community, and in the larger villages, a mission compound and workshops as well. These additions intended by Spanish authorities to be central features of the villages rarely became such. In all but a few pueblos the center of the community was moved away from the missionary buildings and the village courtyard, where the ceremonial chamber or chambers (the kivas) were rebuilt, continued to be the hub of social and ceremonial life.

Early in the seventeenth century Spanish authorities imposed a civil government system on the Pueblos. As an aid to the missionary program and civil administration, the pueblos were required to appoint a set of officers to meet with the Spaniards. Among the Pueblos, these officers were usually a governor, a lieutenant governor, an *alguacil,* or sheriff, a sacristan, *mayordomos,* and *fiscales.* The governor was to represent the village in all important dealings with Spanish authorities. The lieutenant governor was to serve as assistant to the governor and represent him when absent, and, in the event of the governor's death, succeed him. The sheriff was to maintain law and order within the pueblo; the sacristan was church assistant and aid to the priest; the fiscales were responsible for mission discipline, while the mayordomos were ditch superintendents. But the civil government system did not displace the native socio-political organization, and to this day the native socio-political system remains the *de facto* governmental and ceremonial organization. The Tewa migrant group apparently discarded the civil government system altogether upon reaching the Hopi country, for there is no vestige of such a system at Hano today.

The effect of Spanish indoctrination on the values and beliefs of the Pueblo Indians appears to be negligible. Undoubtedly the ancestors of the Southern Tewa in New Mexico went to Mass, confessed, received communion, attended vespers, and were baptized, married, and buried by friars for almost a century. All of these practices were abandoned at Hopi, and nothing remains to indicate that Christianity was ever a part of Hano society and culture.

The resistance to change and to adopt other than material items and surface behavioral patterns from any culture are thought by many students of Pueblo culture to be deeply rooted in the indigenous past of these people. It is not possible to demonstrate such a supposition, but the contact conditions were so oppressive that no people no matter how permissive to the acceptance of alien social and cultural items could have been expected to remain for long receptive to innovations brutally forced upon them while their own indigenous practices were being viciously suppressed. When we add to this the later coercive treatment meted out to the Pueblos by Anglo-Americans we need not seek further to explain Pueblo resistance patterns. The astute observations of John C. Bourke, an early American student of the Pueblos, is pertinent here:

> The eradication of ideas rooted in the traditions of centuries and entwined with all that a nation holds lovable and sacred is beyond the decree of a Council or the order of a military Commander. Unable to practice their ancient rites in public, the Pueblos cling to them all the more tenaciously because the double halo of danger and mystery now surrounded them. The Pueblos became hypocrites; they never became Catholics. Instances without number could possibly be adduced to those among them who sloughed off the exuviae of Paganism; or of others again who modified early teachings by ingrafting upon them the doctrines of the missionaries; but the great bulk of the population remained and today remain, Pagan and Anti-Christian. (Bloom 1936:262)

It is not surprising that the immigrant Tewa carried with them to the Hopi country the resistant patterns they had learned so well during a period of almost one hundred years of Spanish rule. We will chronicle the relations of these immigrants with their new neighbors in the next section.

2

At Hopi

THE HOPI PUEBLOS were also a part of Spain's northern province, but great distance, the lack of profitable natural resources, and the general inhospitality of the environment isolated the Hopi country from the provincial capital in Santa Fe. The major Spanish expeditions had all visited the Hopi villages, however. In 1540, a party of the Coronado expedition spent several days among the Hopi, and the Espejo expedition forty years later visited all the Hopi villages. Oñate, the colonizer of New Mexico, obtained the formal submission of the Hopi in 1598, and between 1629 and 1641 missions were established at Awatobi, Shongopovi, and Oraibi with chapels at Mishongnovi and Walpi. For a period of about fifty years the Hopi, therefore, experienced the coercive Spanish missionary program. During this period they submitted to the demands of labor and outwardly accepted Catholicism. When the Rio Grande Pueblos revolted in 1680, however, the Hopi killed their resident missionaries and destroyed the missions along with all furnishings. In 1692 realizing the futility of opposing a superior force, they submitted to De Vargas, the reconqueror of the northern province of New Spain.

The Pueblo rebellion and the abortive revolts of 1696 brought refugees from the Rio Grande. The Hopi harbored these refugees, undoubtedly in order to better resist the Spaniards and also to fight off the increasing raids of nomadic Indians. Indeed, the Tewa migration legend reports specifically that the Tewa were invited to First Mesa as mercenaries to drive off Ute Indian invaders.

The first mention of the Tewa at Hopi is made in Fray Jose Narvaez Valverde's account of the destruction of Awotovi. After the reconquest Awatovi, the most eastern of the Hopi villages, again accepted Spanish missionaries. When this news spread to the Hopi villages, the Hopi were incensed and the Tewa on First Mesa more than any of the others. Delegations from all the important villages met and decided to destroy Awatovi. Under the leadership of Espeleta, the Chief of Oraibi, warriors from all the villages, including those from Hano, fell upon Awatovi and in one night and one day of vicious fighting

23

and destruction wreaked havoc on the village. Almost the entire population of the village said to number about 800 was massacred; only a few women and children were spared and later distributed among the other Hopi villages. Awatovi was completely destroyed and since that day has remained unoccupied.

The following is excerpted from Valverde's account. The Southern Tewa are here, as in the early Spanish reports, referred to as Thanos or Tanos:

> At this time, his people being infuriated because the Indians of the pueblo of Aguatubi [Awatovi] had been reduced to our holy faith and the obedience of our king, he [Espeleta, the chief of Oraibi] came with more than one hundred of his people to the said pueblo, entered it, killed all the braves, and carried off the women, leaving the pueblo to this day desolate and unpeopled. Learning of this outrage, Governor Don Pedro Rodriguez Cubero made ready some soldiers to punish it, and in the following year of 1701 went to the said province of Moqui [Spanish designation for the Hopi], taking with him the aforesaid religious, Fray Juan Caricochea and Fray Antonio Miranda. With his armed force he killed some Indians and captured others, but not being very well prepared to face the multitudes of the enemy, he withdrew and returned without being able to reduce them, especially as the Moquis had with them the Tanos Indians, who, after committing outrages had taken refuge among them and had risen at their command. (Narváez 1937:386)

Franciscan missionaries tried unsuccessfully to convert the Hopi during the first half of the eighteenth century. A number of Spanish governors also attempted to bring back the Rio Grande Pueblo Indians who had taken refuge among the Hopi. In August 1716 an army of Spaniards and Pueblo Indians under the command of Governor Felix Martinez made a futile attempt to bring back the Tewa. Martinez described his encounter with the Tewa as follows:

> . . . I explained to them [the Tewa] the sole purpose for which I had come with the army, this is, that they should offer submission to the Divine and human Majesty and bring back all of the Indians who had rebelled, some in the year '80 [1680] and others in '96 [1696]; that they should return to their own pueblos whence they fled. . . . (Bloom 1931: 204–205)

The Tewa refused to submit, however, and Martinez fired on their village killing eight Indians and wounding many others. The Spanish governor then proposed to the Hopi on First Mesa that he be allowed to ascend the Mesa and take the Tewa prisoners. According to Martinez the Hopi Cacique at Walpi "made a proclamation":

> . . . that they [the Walpi] were already friends with the Spaniards and did not desire the friendship of the said Thanos; that they will be severely punished for the harm they have done in making war . . . that many of their people had been killed and wounded through the fault of the said Thanos. . . . (Bloom 1931:218)

The Spaniards were assured that they could ascend the Mesa without being molested by the Hopi. Martinez apparently decided the venture would be too costly, however, and instead he ordered his men to destroy Tewa crops in the fields that were ready to be harvested and to kill all their livestock. "When all but a few very insignificant fields had been destroyed," Martinez felt that "the enemies of our Holy Faith" had been effectively punished and returned to Santa Fe.

Distance, the growing hostility of the nomadic tribes, and the dwindling resources of Spain all helped to keep the Hopi country isolated for another century. Toward the close of the eighteenth century Father Silvestre Velez Escalanta, seeking a route to California, spent a few days among the Hopi. The visit was apparently a friendly one. The following excerpt from Father Escalante's report mentions the Tewa on First Mesa and gives an account of their neighbors:

> . . . On the western point of the first [mesa] and on its most narrow eminence are situated three of the pueblos. The first is that of Janos (there they say Teguas) who use a tongue different from that of the Moqui. It is an ordinary pueblo with its little plaza in the middle and will include one hundred and ten families. The second to the east [west?] about a stone's throw. It has only fifteen families because of the new settlement which the Moqui are making at Gualpi. This is within gunshot of the second. It is larger than the two preceding ones and accommodates two hundred families. . . .
>
> This province is bounded on the east by the Navajos, on the west and northwest by the Cosninas [Havasupai], on the north by the Utes, on the southwest with others whom they call here Mescaleros. . . . The Moqui are very civilized, apply themselves to weaving and cultivating the land by means of which they raise abundant crops of maize, beans and chile. They also gather cotton although not much. They suffer from scarcity of wood and good water. . . . (Thomas 1932:150–52)

Mexico gained its independence from Spain in 1823, and the former northern province of Spain became a part of the new nation. During the brief Mexican interlude from 1823 to 1848 when New Mexico was annexed by the United States there were no reports of consequence about the Tewa and their Hopi neighbors. This was a difficult period for Mexico's northern possession. Spanish civil and church authorities had their hands full serving the Rio Grande Pueblos and a growing Hispanicized mestizo population. To make matters worse the vigorous Comanche Indians of the southern Plains had begun to raid the settlers and Pueblo Indians of New Mexico. The provincial government in Santa Fe was in no position to send missionaries to the Hopi country nor to provide military aid to these Indians who were likewise being besieged by Navaho and Ute raiders.

The deplorable condition of the Hopi Indians and the Rio Grande Pueblo refugees among them was highlighted in 1850 by a delegation which came to see James C. Calhoun, the First Agent of the Indians of the Territory of New Mexico. The purpose of the visit was to ascertain the "purposes and views of the government of the United States towards them" and to complain "bitterly of the depredations of the Navajos." It is interesting that the leader of the group "the Cacique of all the [Hopi] Pueblos" was from the Tewa village of Hano. (Official correspondence of James C. Calhoun, letter dated October 12, 1850).

The first eye-witness account of the Hopi and Tewa pueblos by an American is contained in a report by Dr. P. S. G. Tenbroeck, a surgeon in the United States Army, who visited the Hopi country in 1852:

> The inhabitants [of Hopi] all speak the same language except those of Harno [Hano], the most northern town of the three [on First Mesa; Hano, Sichomovi, Walpi], which has a different language and some customs peculiar to itself. It is, however, considered one of the towns of the confedertion, and joins in all the feasts. It seems a very singular fact that, being within 150 yards of the middle town, Harno should have preserved for so long a period its own language and customs. The other Moquis say the inhabitants of this town have a great advantage over them, as they perfectly understand the common language, and none but the people of Harno understand their dialect. It is the smallest town of the three. (U.S. Department of the Interior 1894:171)

Navaho depredations finally came to an end when the Navaho were rounded up and removed to eastern New Mexico by Colonel Christopher ("Kit") Carson in 1863. The Navaho were returned to their homeland in 1868 and have since lived at peace with their Indian and white neighbors.

Contact between the Hopi and Anglo-Americans steadily increased after the pacification of the Navaho. Traders and Protestant missionaries arrived about 1870 and a mission school was established in 1875 at Keams Canyon twelve miles north of First Mesa. In 1869 a special agent for the Hopi Indians was appointed and in 1882 the Hopi Indian Reservation of 3863 square miles was set aside by executive order. A government school was opened at Keams Canyon in 1887. The First Mesa Hopi and the Tewa at Hano received the school enthusiastically, but most of the Hopi were indifferent; the Hopi community of Oraibi refused to send any children to the school.

In recent years the physical isolation of the Hopi country has almost completely dissolved. Automobile roads from Gallup, Holbrook, Winslow, and Flagstaff bring a constant stream of visitors. The colorful ceremonies of the Hopi attract large numbers of tourists; the Snake Dance ceremony alone draws a crowd of several thousand spectators annually.

A constitution was drawn up by the Hopi in 1936 with the aid of the United States government under the provisions of the Indian Reorganization Act. The Constitution was an attempt at self-government through the formation of a tribal government composed of representatives from each village. The innovation was completely unfamiliar to the Hopi, and the council has not worked out as anticipated. The Hopi villages have not functioned as a unit in the past and do not seem ready to do so at present. First Mesa has achieved a remarkable degree of social and political integration in recent years, but this is not true of the other Hopi village groups. The role of the Tewa in this integration is important and will be discussed in a subsequent section.

The externals of Hopi and Tewa society and culture have been affected profoundly by white American contact. Most of the material possessions come from the outside, and English as a secondary language is spoken by the majority

of the Hopi and Tewa. Wage work and livestock have been added to horticultural activities and are now important in the economic structure. On the other
hand, important aspects of the social and ceremonial organization and the religious concepts of the Hopi and Tewa remain unaffected.

The preceding has been a review of the historical events dealing with the
Pueblos that has been gleaned from Spanish and American historical sources. It
has not been possible to isolate the Tewa specifically in this review, for Southwestern historians tend to lump all Pueblo Indians together to present the interests and concerns primarily of the chroniclers. We hope, however, that the
struggle of a people to survive physically as a group has emerged from the account. In the next few pages the Tewa's own version of their history is briefly
reviewed. As is true with the traditions of most nonliterate peoples, the Tewa's
account of their past is largely magical and fanciful. How much of the information they have passed down by word of mouth from one generation to another is
fact and how much myth would be impossible to determine. Tewa "history" does
give us insights, however, about their persistent desire to preserve cultural identity in a situation that seems favorable to rapid and complete assimilation.

Traditional History

According to a legend that the Tewa at Hano have kept alive from generation to generation, First Mesa Hopi chiefs had specifically invited the Tewa to
come to the Hopi country. The reputation of the Tewa as relentless and fearless
warriors had reached the Hopi and they wanted the Tewa to drive off their
enemies. The invitation and rewards offered to the Tewa to persuade them to
come to Hopi is contained in the following brief excerpt from the legend:

> Four times the Walpi Bear Clan Chief and Snake Clan Chief [Hopi clans
> on First Mesa] came to our village at *Tsawadeh*[1] [former home of the
> Southern Tewa in New Mexico]. They brought with them prayer sticks that
> represented the things that would be given to us if we would come and fight
> their enemies. There was one for the women that were promised to our men;
> there was one for the village site that we would occupy; there was one for the
> springs from which we would obtain our drinking water; there was one for
> the land on which we could raise our corn and other crops. . . . They drew
> for us on the sand the large stalks of corn that were raised on the land that
> would be ours. They extended both arms to indicate the size of the ears of
> corn that grew on this land. "All this will be yours if you will come and live
> among us as our protectors," they said. "In our land you will have plenty to
> eat and your storehouses will always be full."

According to the legend the Tewa accepted the invitation as a humane
service to a Pueblo people, much like themselves, who were being besieged re-
lentlessly by their enemies. It is interesting that the legend makes no mention of
difficulties with the Spaniards as a reason for accepting the Hopi invitation. The

---

[1] See Orthographic Note on page 100.

Hano migration legend mythically recounts the journey from the Rio Grande to the Hopi country, and while references to the Spaniards and other Rio Grande Pueblo groups are made, there are no expressions of antagonistic feelings toward any of these people. Apparently the oppressive treatment suffered by the original migrants became less important and eventually forgotten by succeeding generations of the Tewa at Hano who had not actually experienced Spanish rule. Later generations found the injustices and ill-treatment directed at them by their Hopi hosts more important to record in their traditional history. The Tewa migration legend reports that upon the arrival of their ancestors at Hopi, they were treated as unwelcome intruders and none of the promises which had induced them to make the journey were forthcoming

> How pitifully ignorant must have been our ancestors to believe the Hopi! [regarding the rewards promised] Little did they know that they would be so miserably deceived. . . . Our grandmothers and grandfathers were not permitted to ascend the mesa [First Mesa] when they arrived at Hopi, but were forced to make camp below. When some of them petitioned Walpi women for food, they were told to cup their hands to receive a corn-meal gruel and boiling hot, it was poured into their hands. When the Tewa let the gruel slip to the ground and proceeded to nurse their burnt hands, the Hopi women laughed and berated them for being weak and soft.
> . . . When our ancestors had defeated the Utes and made life safe for the Hopi, they asked for the land, women, and food which had been promised to them. But the Hopi refused to give them these things. Then it was that our poor ancestors had to live like beasts, foraging on the wild plants and barely subsisting on the meager supply of food. Our ancestors lived miserably, beset by disease and starvation. The Hopi, well-fed and healthy, laughed and made fun of our ancestors.

The legend says that there were repeated attacks by the enemy for some time after their arrival in the Hopi country which were all successfully repelled by the Tewa. The reputation of the Tewa as fierce and courageous warriors spread among the nomadic tribes, however, and they stopped raiding the Hopi villages. Still the Hopi remained ill-tempered and their conduct was so ignoble and ungracious that the Tewa placed a "curse" on them:

> Our clan chiefs dug a pit between Hano and the Hopi villages [on First Mesa] and told the Hopi clan chiefs to spit into it. When they had all spat, our clan chiefs spat above the spittle of the Hopi. The pit was refilled, and then our clan chiefs declared:
> "Because you have behaved in a manner unbecoming to human beings, we have sealed knowledge of our language and our way of life from you. You and your descendants will never learn our language and our ceremonies, but we will learn yours. We will ridicule you in both your language and our own."

The particulars of the "curse" differ among Tewa story tellers, but the essential points are in all of them. Like all Pueblo traditions, those of the Tewa are couched in a mystical fanciful language; it is impossible to tell what is fact or fancy in the migration legend. No explanation, for example, is given, as to how the Hopi clan chiefs, more numerous than their Tewa counterparts, were made to spit into the pit. The implication is that Tewa magic was so powerful that the Hopi automatically followed the dictates of the Tewa clan chiefs. More difficult for practical-minded Western Europeans to understand is that the curse "worked." The Tewa were able "to sell" the curse to their neighbors and to have it work in their favor. The Hopi believe in the consequences of the curse as strongly as the Tewa. For both groups the prophecy has been fulfilled: the Hopi do not speak the Tewa language and they know little or nothing about the ceremonial life and other important customs of Tewa culture. How this may have been accomplished will be explored in the next section. Suffice to say, at present, supernatural sanctions exert a strong influence in prescribing and limiting behavior.

For the Tewa, the legend and the curse, which is perhaps the most fundamental feature of the legend, has been a kind of sacred and prophetic guide of their cultural tradition. The legend is related constantly in Hano homes; children grow up knowing it intimately, and among the stories and tales regularly recited in the kivas, the legend has a prominent place. The Hopi-Tewa delight in telling it to New Mexico Tewa visitors, thus belittling their neighbors. The legend is a kind of a model for proper behavior, as well, but perhaps its most important function has been the preservation of Tewa self-esteem. To a persecuted minority group, this function of the legend is essential to maintain group identity and pride. The survival and persistence of the Tewa cultural island in the midst of the generalized Hopi culture is undoubtedly reinforced by constant reference to it.

3

Hano—The Tewa Community

T HE HOPI MESAS on which Hano and the other villages are situated are the southern spurs of Black Mesa, a high plateau which extends northward almost to the Utah border. The elevation of the villages is about 6000 feet above the sea, while the dry washes below are about 600 feet lower. The early American travelers who entered the Hopi country from the east designated the fingerlike projections as First, Second, and Third Mesa. On First Mesa are the villages of Hano, Sichomovi, and Walpi, and below the mesa is Polacca. Twelve miles beyond is Second Mesa with Mishongnovi, Shipaulovi, and Shongopovi. Another ten miles westward is Third Mesa with Old Oraibi at its tip and a recent community, New Oraibi, at its base. A mile or so beyond Oraibi, still on top of Third Mesa, is Hotevilla and a half mile northeastward, Bakabi. Forty miles farther west is Moenkopi, a colony founded about fifty years ago by members of the Third Mesa villages.

The Hopi country is an arid but picturesque land. Several miles north of the Hopi villages, Black Mesa supports a forest of piñon and juniper, but where the Hopi live, what trees might have grown have been used long ago for firewood. Only an occasional sage or rabbit brush struggles for existence. Curiously, a few twisted, dwarfed fruit trees (peaches, apricots, pears, and apples) dot the base of the mesas at places where moisture-bearing sands or seepage from springs provide enough water. These trees are grown from seeds or cuttings taken from trees originally introduced by the Spaniards. Most impressive about the land are the vistas—perhaps nowhere in America can one see so far—across sandy plains, isolated table outcrops and isolated buttes to distant outlines of blue mountains. In winter and spring the land is barren and windswept, but in late summer and fall it can be astonishingly beautiful. At this time clouds cast shadows near and far while occasional patches of sunlight enhance the rugged topography of the land. The villages themselves appear to be a part of the mesa rock outcroppings. Only one familiar with the location of the villages can detect them from below, so much are they of the same color and outline as the mesa itself.

However picturesque the Hopi country may be, it is an inhospitable environment for subsistence farmers. Except for a small stream which provides an irregular supply of irrigation water for the Hopi farmers of Moenkopi, none of the Hopi villages have access to permanently flowing streams. The plateau of Black Mesa acts as a reservoir, however, and at the base of the Hopi mesas are numerous springs which provide drinking water for the Hopi. In some springs the flow of water is abundant enough to permit the construction of small terraced gardens. These gardens merely add to the food supply; however, they are not sufficient to furnish food to feed even a small portion of a village. The Hopi subsist by dry farming in an extremely precarious environment. Annual precipitation is only about ten inches and this falls mainly in late summer, often too late to help mature crops. Maize, beans, and melons are planted near flat washes below the mesas where sands retain moisture and flash floods may hopefully irrigate the plants without uprooting them. In good years a fairly abundant harvest is taken in and stored to tide the Hopi over the lean years. But good years are the exception rather than the rule. Often there is so little rain that plants wither and die; at other times the rain falls in such torrents that the plants are washed away. The technology of the Hopi is so simple that little can be done in a practical way to solve the subsistence problem. It is no wonder that they have turned to magic to try to offset the hazards of wresting a living from an inhospitable environment. The Hopi have an elaborate ceremonial organization and engage in complex ritualistic activities that contrast sharply with the more simple and practically oriented socio-ceremonial organization of the Tewa. These differences are perhaps most marked between the two societies, but there are other important contrasts that will become evident in this and subsequent sections.

On First Mesa Hano houses merge in with those of the middle village, Sichomovi. Walpi, the third village, is located at the very tip of the mesa and is separated from Sichomovi by a narrow neck, barely fifteen feet in width. Despite the fact that Hano is contiguous with Sichomovi, the Tewa are keenly aware of the boundary that separates the two villages. At the foot of First Mesa and running roughly parallel to the villages on top is a recently settled community of both Hopi and Tewa called Polacca. Polacca was named after a Tewa man who was one of the first to settle below the mesa. An interpreter and friend of the whites, he was persuaded by Christian missionaries to build his home away from his native village. Most of today's inhabitants at Polacca, however, are not Christians; many of them are traditionalists and own houses on top of the mesa as well. The population of Polacca is constantly shifting; its inhabitants alternate freely in residence between houses at Hano and Polacca. Much of this alternation is dictated by ceremonial activities; when ceremonies are in progress, Hopi and Tewa Indians return to residences on top of the mesa. Polacca residents identify village allegiance with respect to the communities on top; hence, an individual will say he is from Walpi, or Sichomovi, or Hano, though he may be living at Polacca.

Walpi is considered the ceremonial center of First Mesa by all three villages. In Hopi thinking, time of arrival and length of residence is considered the important measure of village status and prestige. Walpi reports long residence on First Mesa and considers itself preeminent over both Hano and Sichomovi because its settlers arrived earlier. Sichomovi adheres strictly to Walpi's socio-ceremonial calendar and is considered simply a colony of that village. Hano enjoys a certain amount of social and ceremonial independence, concessions gained over a long period of quarreling, threats, and negotiations with Walpi.

In listing the population figures for First Mesa, Polacca will be excluded since its inhabitants align themselves with one of the three villages on top of the mesa. The approximate populations for each of the three villages on First Mesa are as follows: Hano 500, Sichomovi 400, Walpi 600. About one-third of the inhabitants of First Mesa are Tewa, but compared to the total Hopi population of about 5000, the Tewa comprise only one-tenth of the whole. We have no figures for the number of Tewa who came to the Hopi country in 1696, but in 1775 Father Escalante (see Chapter 2) reported the population of Hano as 110 families. If we project the average size family of present-day Hano, five to an elementary family, the population of Hano at the time of Escalante's visit would be nearly the same as the present population. Hopi and Tewa populations today represent an increase from 2338 in 1904 when smallpox epidemics had drastically reduced the population. On this date the population of the Tewa at Hano was listed at only 160. With the control of smallpox and the introduction of modern health measures, Hopi and Tewa populations rapidly increased to the present figure of over 5000. Hopi and Tewa population increases coincide with those of the Pueblos generally and the Navaho as well. Rates of population gain among these Indians are far above the national average over the past half century.

In outward appearances Hano looks like a typical Hopi village. Its houses, like those in which the Hopi live, are constructed of stone; they are flat-roofed; and the walls on the inside and occasionally on the outside as well are plastered with mud. Doors and windows are of modern design, made from milled lumber and copied fairly faithfully from the residences of low income white homes. Most of the houses have the traditional hard-packed earth floors characteristic of the old Pueblo homes, but an increasing number of houses have added an innovation—a linoleum floor laid directly over the packed earth. Only one house block in the central courtyard of Hano retains a two-storied terraced structure, formerly a typical architectural feature of the Pueblos. Hano like most of the traditional Hopi villages is still a compact village; however, its houses run parallel to the edge of the cliff with connecting house rows to form a central courtyard or plaza. A kiva, the communal and ceremonial chamber of the Pueblos, is located just off center on the north side of the plaza. Hano has another kiva, a duplicate of the other, outside of the east row of houses and only about fifty feet from the plaza kiva. Both kivas are rectangular, partly underground structures with entrance gained from a ladder protruding from a hatchway in the roof. There is nothing unique about the external appearance of Hano; all of its architectural characteristics may be found in the other Hopi villages.

The Tewa of Hano interact with three categories of people: Hopi, Navaho, and white Americans. The most intensive and intimate relations are with

Hopi neighbors, primarily with those of First Mesa, but schools, herding activities, and ceremonies also bring the Tewa into fairly frequent interaction with the Hopi from more distant villages. Navaho come frequently to trade and attend Hopi and Tewa ceremonies, and those Navaho whose herding territories adjoin those of the Tewa are often encountered on the range or in cattle and sheep camps. Interaction with whites is primarily with government officials and employees, but in the summertime tourists literally invade the Hopi mesas to attend the colorful ceremonies. White missionaries of a number of different Christian denominations are constantly around and the white trader is an important fixture of Hopi and Tewa economy.

Tewa and Hopi Relations

The people of Hano exhibit no difference in general appearance from those of the other Hopi villages. Hano adults are uniformly short or medium statured. Children are so much alike that it is impossible to identify them as Tewa or Hopi. Clothing and hair styles have subtle differences only a Hopi or Tewa can detect, but the old dress styles are fast disappearing as Hopi and Tewa alike take on the dress patterns of white Americans.

The similarity of the two populations is understandable from a biological point of view. There are no marriage restrictions at present; Tewa and Hopi marry freely. Biologically the two populations are now completely mixed, but matrilocal residence, a rule observed by both groups, permits the socio-cultural continuity of the Tewa as a separate unit. Matrilocal residence is a custom that requires the husband to reside with his wife's family in her village. The children of a Tewa or Hopi couple are then raised as members of the wife's family and village, and while the children have intimate and frequent relations with their father and his family, affiliation and primary allegiance is with the mother's family and home.

At Hano, as among the Hopi, women are the important members of the family. They own the land and houses, dispense the food, and make the important decisions. The men perform religious rites, exercise disciplinary powers in their sisters' homes, support their own family, and teach their children "how to make a living," but they have little authority in their own homes and with their own children.

The practices outlined above are inherent in the maternal lineage system which the Hopi and Tewa have. As we shall see in a later section, the reckoning of kin along the maternal line and the custom of matrilocal residence were apparently borrowed from the Hopi, but it is clear that these practices support the Tewa determination to maintain their own society and culture. A Tewa woman never leaves Hano for long; when she marries a Hopi man, he comes to live at Hano and their children are raised as Tewa. If a Hano man marries a Hopi woman, he resides with her in her village, but while his children become Hopi, he himself never loses his Tewa affiliations. Tewa men married to Hopi women consider themselves Tewa and return to Hano to exercise ceremonial and kinship obligations. A Tewa household is impervious to Hopi influence, even in cases of intermarriage. The Hopi husband would find it extremely difficult to impose Hopi values and customs on his children, even if he were disposed to do so. Any attempt at such subversion would be countered by the mother's authority in which the latter would be supported by all the men and women of her maternal lineage.

At the present time about half of the marriages at Hano represent Tewa women married to Hopi men; the other marriages consist of couples where both partners are Tewa. Like Tewa women, approximately half of the married Tewa men have taken Hopi wives. These men reside with their Hopi wives in the latter's natal household. Most of the Tewa-Hopi marriages are with members of the First Mesa villages of Sichomovi and Walpi, but a few have been contracted with Hopi from more distant villages.

Intermarriage with the Hopi in recent years has probably made the Hano more Hopi than Tewa in blood. Yet this knowledge, if the Hopi and the Tewa wonder about it at all, appears to present no anomaly. A Tewa is a person born at Hano of a mother whose maternal lineage runs back unbrokenly to the original Tewa colony. There is no deviation from the rule: "What your mother is you are." A person born of a Tewa father and a Hopi mother is Hopi, not half Tewa and half Hopi; similarly, the child of a Tewa mother, regardless of the father's ethnic affiliation, is Tewa.

Village identity and loyalty are stronger at Hano than among the Hopi who emphasize the maternal kinship or clan bond over village membership. This difference is due in part to the fact that the body of mythological lore is handed down as a village heritage at Hano, rather than as a separate maternal lineage or clan possession as among the Hopi. The Tewa of Hano are staunch supporters and defenders of the cultural heritage of the original Tewa migrants as this body of information has been transmitted and interpreted through time. The most important part of this cultural heritage is an attitude or disposition of the Tewa to preserve their own social and cultural identity. We have noted in the historical section the resistance offered by the ancestors of Hano residents against Spanish oppression in New Mexico and later at Hopi. The struggle continued in their new home, but the resistance has been against social and cultural assimilation with the Hopi. Had the original migrant group been received more graciously they might have been absorbed in a few generations, but it is clear from Hano mythological traditions that the original Tewa group was not welcomed in the manner it wished to be received. Subsequent unfavorable relations between the two groups have produced antagonistic attitudes and negative stereotyping on both sides. Antagonism toward the Hopi is also fed by keeping the migration legend alive. The portion of the legend which tells of the inhospitable reception accorded the original migrant group (see Chapter 2) is recited annually in the Tewa kivas at the time of the Winter Solstice ceremony. In less formal settings, the tale is told in Hano homes on any occasion when feeling against Hopi neighbors runs high. Negative characterizations of the Hopi are also a favorite topic when the Tewa from New Mexico come to visit Hano.

The constant telling of the migration legend has given the Tewa

confidence as individuals and reassured them as a group of their special position
on First Mesa. The fundamental feature of the legend, the "curse" (see Chapter
2), has been a most effective instrument in keeping the Hopi, particularly those
of First Mesa, "in their place." Both groups believe that the prophecy of the
tale has been fulfilled: the Hopi do not speak the Tewa language and they know
little or nothing about Tewa society and culture. How this was accomplished is
not clear, but some reasons can be ventured. The inability of the Hopi to learn
the Tewa language in the initial contact period can probably to explained in
terms of the numbers involved. The original migrants may have totaled no more
than 400 or 500, whereas the Hopi population must have been at least ten times
as large. Under these circumstances it would have been easier for the Tewa to
learn the Hopi language. This explanation is difficult to accept for the more recent period. Intermarriages with the Hopi and the matrilocal residence custom
bring Hopi husbands to live at Hano. It is remarkable that in such unions the
Hopi husband does not speak Tewa, even though in many cases he may have
spent the major part of his life at Hano and in his Tewa wife's household
where Tewa is the preferred language. In such unions the children are, of
course, conversant in both languages since husband and wife speak to one another in Hopi and a child must respectfully speak Hopi to his Hopi father, but
Tewa to his mother and his Tewa kinfolk at Hano. The Hopi men currently
married at Hano do not speak Tewa; most of them surely understand it, but
none of them will venture to speak it. To explain this situation one can only
point to the strong influence of supernatural sanctions on nonliterate peoples
and the attendant development of "psychological sets." So firmly do these
people believe in the "curse" that although a Hopi may understand everything
said in Tewa he cannot utter a Tewa word.

The Tewa have consciously and consistently tried to maintain a separation from the Hopi in other aspects of their society and culture as well. This behavior is readily understandable. It seems reasonable for a people in a social and
numerical minority status to try to retain their own distinctive social and cultural
patterns. In this endeavor the Tewa have been highly successful—a success more
comprehensible than the provision of the "curse" that prevents the Hopi from
speaking Tewa. Specific rituals and social institutions are more tangible than
language and their contamination or diffusion can be better controlled.

Why the Tewa migrant group should not have been received with open
arms and how subsequently they should have been accorded a minority status is
understandable from the Hopi point of view. The Tewa were mercenaries
among a people who despise and scorn warriors. To the Hopi religious preoccupation is esteemed and warfare is considered uncouth and barbaric. In the traditions of the Hopi, latecomers were relegated to vulnerable and undesirable
points of the mesa in order to meet the brunt of an enemy attack. Early settlers
erected their homes in the interior portions of the mesa and when the villages
were besieged, they attempted to repel the enemy by prayer retreats in the kivas
and by performing magical ceremonies.

The strain on the land resource is another factor that would have placed
the incoming Tewa in an unfavorable position. Garden plots had to be found

near the mesas because of the constant threat of enemy raids. Good arable land was undoubtedly already appropriated, yet the Tewa had to be accommodated. It is not surprising that antagonisms developed between the two groups.

The social separation of the two societies and mutual ill-feeling throughout most of their contact history is evident in their traditions, but it is apparent in their daily lives as well. For a long time a vacant area existed between Hano and Sichomovi. Although this area was on the Tewa side, no one would build there, and children were afraid to walk over the boundary line into the territory of the other.

While intermarriages are now common, they were forbidden in the past. Marriage restrictions were lifted toward the closing decades of the last century coincident with the establishment of the United States Government Agency at Keams Canyon, the construction of schools, and the advent of white traders. The coming of white Americans brought about a series of changes that altered the former position of the Tewa as a subordinate minority group. We will discuss these interesting changes shortly, but it is important to note other factors that for a long period of time fostered the maintenance of social and cultural separation.

Both groups restricted participation of the other in certain ceremonials. Thus, the Tewa were not permitted in the important Hopi Winter Solstice ceremony at Walpi, and the Hopi were likewise refused admittance to the similar Tewa ceremony. In addition, certain ceremonial benefits were not extended to the other group. For example, at the time of tribal initiation ceremonies in October or November, when priests of participating fraternities came to bless the villages, they stopped at the edge of Sichomovi and did not proceed to Hano. Similarly, Tewa priests during the Winter Solstice ceremony blessed only their portion of First Mesa and did not go to Sichomovi and Walpi.

The Hopi were and are still denied membership in Tewa ceremonial associations despite the reduction of tension between the two groups in recent years. The reason for the restriction is the belief that some dire misfortune will occur if Hopi are permitted membership in Tewa ceremonial associations. The reverse—Tewa joining Hopi associations—is apparently not viewed with such foreboding since Tewa do become members of Hopi ceremonial associations.

Apparently to bolster their own self-importance, the Tewa make repeated references to their special position on First Mesa. They assert that they fulfilled their position as warriors so well that enemy attacks stopped completely. Their roles were then reinterpreted; they became interpreters and "speakers" for the Hopi on First Mesa. That prominent Tewa individuals did indeed operate in these positions is not simply idle boasting. Numerous references are made of Tewa leaders who functioned as spokesmen of the Hopi during the American period. The leader of the delegation which visited James S. Calhoun, the first United States Indian agent of the territory of New Mexico, was a Tewa from Hano. Calhoun spoke of him as the "*cacique* of all the [Hopi] Pueblos." The Indian agent was mistaken, of course; there has never been a "chief" of all the Hopi peoples. Furthermore the term "cacique" could not have been applicable to a Tewa since the term is usually employed among the Pueblos to refer to a religious leader. It is obvious from Calhoun's letter, however, that the man was the spokesman for the group (Calhoun 1915, letter number 82).

An American traveler who visited the Hopi villages in 1872 reports that the Walpi chief on First Mesa had a Tewa interpreter or speaker:

> At [Fort] Defiance I was told to ask for Chino [Cimo or Simo, town chief of Walpi], the *Capitan* of this *mesa* [First Mesa], before I talked to any one else; so I shouted to call out some one. . . . I was greatly relieved when a tall old fellow, with a merry twinkle in his eye, arrived, addressed me in pretty good Spanish, and intimated that he did the talking for Chino when strangers came. His name, which he had on a card written by some white man, was Misiamtewah; he had visited the Mormon settlements and Sante Fe, and could speak Spanish, Moqui [Hopi], Tegua and a little English and Navajo, besides being fluent in the sign language. I cultivated his acquaintance at once. (Beadle 1878:266–267)

About the turn of the century Tom Polacca, for whom the village at the foot of First Mesa is named, served as interpreter and speaker. Polacca learned to speak English and represented the Hopi in important conferences, accompanying in 1890 a delegation of Hopi chiefs to Washington D.C. in order to present the needs of the Hopi personally to the Indian commissioner.

During the time of my field studies, the official Hopi interpreter was Albert Yava, a Tewa Indian. The following incident indicates the importance of the Tewa interpreter on First Mesa. On one occasion, during this period, the superintendent of the Hopi Agency arranged a meeting at Walpi. He was not able to find Yava so he brought along a very able Hopi Indian interpreter to the meeting. The Hopi refused flatly to go on with the meeting unless the Tewa interpreter could be secured. The superintendent complied, but it was very late at night before he located Yava and the meeting could be resumed.

In other roles involving meetings with outsiders, or in fulfilling responsible positions distasteful to the Hopi, the Tewa have been pressed into service. The positions of policemen, for example, have also devolved to the Tewa. Leo Crane, a government Indian agent for the Hopi from 1911 to 1919, comments on Tewa policemen and makes some discerning remarks about Hopi and Tewa personality differences:

> The Hopi do not make good policemen, and certainly not in a cohort of one. Their very name implies "the peaceful ones." Their towns are ruled largely by pueblo opinion. If a resident acquires the reputation of being unreasonable and unfeeling, as a policeman often must, his standing in the outraged community may affect all other phases of his life. Therefore the Hopi is not likely to become a very zealous officer when operating alone. And too, the Hopi fear the Navajo, as it is said the Navajo fear the Ute, and are useless when removed from the neighborhood of their homes.
>
> But many years ago, when the Hopi were sorely pressed by nomad enemies and had not even the consolation of telling their woes to an Indian Agent, they sent emissaries to their cousins, the Pueblo Indians of what is now New Mexico, and begged for a colony of warriors to reside with them. In response to this plea, and looking for something to their advantage, in 1700 came a

band of Tewa. . . . To these people the Hopi granted a wide valley west of
the First Mesa, known as the Wepo Wash, providing they would stay and
lend their prowess in future campaigns. They built a village atop the First
Mesa, now called Tewa or Hano, where their descendants live today. Some
intermarried with Hopi, and a few with nearby Navajo; but they have not
been absorbed, and it is a curious fact that while all the Tewa speak Hopi and
Navajo with more or less fluency, after two centuries of living side by side
few of the Hopi can speak the Tewa dialect.

The Hopi invited warriors, and the warriors have graduated into policemen, for one learns to police the Hopi districts, and even to discipline some
of the Navajo, with Tewa officers. They are dependable and courageous, even
belligerent; that is to say, they will fight when it is necessary and, strange
thing among desert Indians, with their fists, taking a delight in blacking the
opponent's eye. But one has to learn that the Hopi as policemen are fine ceremonial dancers. (Crane 1925:136–137)

Crane's astute observations of Hopi character was underscored by Solo-
mon Asch who made a field study of Hopi attitudes in the 1940s:

All individuals must be treated alike; no one must be superior and no one
must be inferior. The person who is praised or who praises himself is automatically subject to resentment and to criticism, the object of which is to
bring him back into the slow, hard-plodding line of all Hopi. . . .

Most Hopi men refuse to be foremen on jobs which the government sponsors on the reservation. If they do, they are immediately accused of thinking
they are better than others, and are continually badgered by disparaging remarks. For example, P., an able, hard-working fellow, excels on the job and
is frequently given the position of foreman, which he accepts. He is very un-
popular. . . . A more telling bit of evidence is that they do not compare the
importance of one another's work. A highly skilled stone-cutter is perfectly
content to accept the same wages as an unskilled day laborer. (Asch, in
manuscript)

First Mesa Hopi have found the Tewa willing to perform the tasks
which the Hopi disdain. The Tewa, on the other hand, have been content to do
them for the occasional morsel of approval and appreciation they receive from
their neighbors. As one Tewa put it: "We are criticized and ridiculed for whatever we do so why not perform the work that needs to be done?" Primary reinforcement for anti-Hopi behavior comes from their own community where aggressive and individualized behavior is valued. In recent years approval has
come from another source: white Americans endorse the outgoing personality
characteristics of the Tewa. Government officials and whites generally have praised
the "progressive" Tewa and pointed to them as models of the "proper attitude" Indians should have in the modern world. In the 1880s Julian Scott, a
special agent for the Hopi tribe remarked: "They [the Tewa] show a pronounced
difference in their bearing from the pure Moqui [Hopi]. . . . They are fore-
most in all things that pertain to their future good, and were the first to leave
the mesa and build new homes more convenient to wood and water and their

fields." (U.S. Dept. Int. 1894: 190). Actually the Tewa are bound to their mesa homes as much as the Hopi. Many Tewa built additional homes below the mesa, but Hano is still a thriving community. Scott's observation on the differences in "bearing" between Hopi and Tewa, however, has been noted by many other visitors to Hano and the Hopi villages.

Two prominent Tewa highlight the individualized behavior valued by whites and Tewa alike. One is Tom Polacca already mentioned as the official interpreter of First Mesa in the 1890s; the other is Nampeyo, a Tewa woman potter. Polacca became a prosperous livestock owner and built a large house at the foot of the mesa about the beginning of the century. It was around this nucleus that the present town of Polacca was built. Polacca's influence was so strong with United States governmental officials that he was proposed by the government agent in 1891 to succeed the deceased town chief of Walpi. Since this position is a religious office and is hereditary within the Hopi Bear clan or its linked clans, the Hopi protested bitterly and were able to dissuade the agent from actually forcing Polacca into the position. The incident, however, is indicative of the man's prestige with government authorities.

Before the Spanish period pottery manufacture was an important occupation in all of the Hopi villages. The craft died out completely after the first century of Spanish rule. Some say that this was because pottery, as the chief article of tribute, was so identified with Spanish oppression that the Hopi stopped making it because it reminded them of that period of suffering. But the Hopi, at least those of First Mesa, were ready for its revival at the beginning of the century. The person who brought about the renaisssance of pottery making was a Tewa woman, Nampeyo. This woman studied the pottery excavated by an archeologist in the nearby ruins of Sikyatki, experimented with clay ingredients and firing and copied the old pottery designs. Finally she succeeded; her product had an individuality of its own, but it is just as vital and attractive as the pottery of the ancient Hopi of Sikyatki. Because of its economic importance, revitalized pottery manufacture soon spread to Sichomovi and Walpi and is now the basic craft of First Mesa.

Polacca and Nampeyo shared one important characteristic: they were both traditional Tewa, participating in the ceremonies, working parties, and food exchanges of the community. In this respect Polacca and Nampeyo were little different from other Tewa, and they were not considered to be deviants or outstanding persons by the inhabitants of Hano. The fame of these two is due almost completely to their popularization by American friends. Polacca and Nampeyo, in adhering to the traditional pattern of life, became submerged as individuals in the society. The fruit of their economic success was shared, however, by all the inhabitants of First Mesa through the system of exchange of food and services.

It is clear at present that the attitudes of hostility and antagonism discussed earlier in this section are being ameliorated. For example, resistance to the Hopi way of life is stronger with the older Tewa. At the Winter Solstice ceremony it is old men who emphasize that the Tewa must not forget Hopi injustices. Young people have much in common with the Hopi, and they tend to minimize and even laugh off these serious admonitions. Consequently, old legends tend to disappear with the passing of the aged, and young Tewa seem content to forget them. Reduced friction between the two groups in recent years seems to be directly related to white contact. The unfavorable position of the Tewa on First Mesa induced them to cooperate more readily with whites. As a result of this cooperation the Tewa became acquainted with the techniques of livestock raising and wage work. The revival of pottery making, as we have noted, started at Hano and diffused to the Hopi. Tewa successes with these new economic activities brought about reduced tensions and emulation from their Hopi neighbors on First Mesa, which in turn paved the way to greater interdependence and cooperation, particularly in social and secular activities.

A reconstruction of events as they must have happened may be briefly stated. The original Tewa group came into the profoundly religiously oriented Hopi society. The Tewa religious repertoire was less complex than the Hopi and it emphasized curing (see Chapter 5) rather than "weather control." Tewa religion was also more secular because of a politically oriented social organization (see Chapter 4) and a hundred years of Spanish influence. As newcomers, the Tewa were assigned the role of "protectors" in the traditional Hopi manner. To a religion concerned primarily with "weather control" through ritual the Tewa had little to contribute. Their curing societies may have been welcome, but they probably had no important ceremonies to appease the harsh environment. Skill as warriors was helpful, but war was despicable to the Hopi and was not a prestige-bearing activity. If the Tewa displayed the outgoing, aggressive personalities that characterize their present descendants, they were probably even less desired, for Hopi behavior is ideally passive.

Tewa values at Hopi must have taken literally a "back seat." The Hopi no doubt had little respect for this religiously poverty-stricken society. They did "use" the ancestors of the Tewa, however, in the roles that they disdained—the prestigeless positions of warriors, and later as interpreters and go-betweens. In an attempt to assert their own self-importance, the Tewa accused the Hopi of inhospitality and ungracious behavior. They bolstered their own group ego by remaining aloof, reiterating Hopi injustices, and extolling their own virtues as warriors and emissaries.

White American contact altered the value system in favor of the Tewa. Americans like the Tewa are "practical," and the aggressive and outgoing personality of the Tewa is remarkably "American." The Tewa readily and enthusiastically took to stock-raising, wage work and the white man's schools. Their children, already trained in two languages, learned English more quickly than the Hopis. Moreover, their greater motivation as a minority spurred them to excel in the classroom. In the process, the Hopi began to develop a new respect for the Tewa. The Tewa role as emissaries and interpreters to the white people grew in importance and prestige. Their value orientation, remarkably like that of the newcomers, no longer had to take a back seat. The Hopi saw that "it paid to be like the whites," and the Tewa were providing the lead to this new and positive achievement.

The Tewa have thus exerted considerable influence on First Mesa, which has diffused in weaker currents to other Hopi villages. Today there is constant interaction and cooperation between the two populations on First Mesa. Intermarriages and the acquisition of relatives on both sides have intricately related all of the people. The "healthy social climate" and a generally cooperative atmosphere with the government and outsiders, noted on First Mesa by various investigators, is attributable largely to the Tewa. (See Thompson 1950: 78–80)

Relations with Navaho and Other Indians

The Navaho have been neighbors of the Hopi villages for a long time. About 200 years prior to their removal to eastern New Mexico they constantly raided and plundered Hopi fields and threatened the lives of the villagers (Chapter 2). The Tewa and Hopi enjoyed a brief respite from the Navaho menace, but a few years after being returned to their native land, problems with the Navaho again appeared. This time Navaho cattle and sheep herds encroached on Tewa and Hopi lands. Bitter relations developed as the Hopi reservation was reduced to only about one-fourth of the area designated in the original executive order. Increase in landholdings for the rapidly increasing Navaho population was thus at the expense of the Hopi and Tewa economic activity in horticulture and livestock. These problems brought about a reconsideration of the executive order that established the Hopi reservation. The boundary dispute has not yet been settled, and at this writing it is still being argued in the courts.

Despite these difficulties, face to face contacts between the Tewa and the Navaho are usually pleasant, and visiting and trading relations have been a well-established pattern for at least a half century. During the summer, in cattle and sheep camps, prolonged social contacts with neighboring Navaho families are maintained. There is, as well, frequent attendance at one another's ceremonies. From such associations many Tewa have acquired great facility with the Navaho language. These contacts have also provided opportunity to learn Navaho songs and ceremonies as well as to make the observations necessary for burlesquing Navahos in the winter kiva dances. A form of the *Yeibichai*—part of the Navaho Night Way—is performed every winter as one of the series of night kachina dances.

Many Navaho in the lower economic levels spend weeks or even months moving from one ceremonial celebration in one part of the Navaho reservation to another. Often these Navaho include the Hopi villages and Hano on their visiting cycle. The Tewa welcome these "vagabonds," as they refer to them, but treat them condescendingly. While the best eating and sleeping accommodations are provided for visiting Pueblo Indians, these Navaho are often made to eat on the floor separately from their hosts and to sleep outdoors.

Inter-Indian affairs like the Gallup Intertribal Ceremonial and the Flagstaff Pow-wow are also bringing Tewa and Hopi Indians in contact with other Indians. More and more Tewa and Hopi now visit the Rio Grande Pueblos and meet other Indians in the urban centers of Albuquerque, Santa Fe, Gallup, and Phoenix. As the result of these contacts, a number of intermarriages have taken place. The non-Tewa, non-Hopi spouse sometimes comes to the Hopi reservation to live, but the more typical pattern is for the couple to move into an off-reservation town and for the husband to take up unskilled or semi-skilled wage work. These movements are adding a significant Indian population to off-reservation towns.

The participation of Tewa and Hopi individuals in this network of inter-Indian relations is an important stimulus to acculturation. There are greater opportunities today for the exchange of ideas and information that affect not only the groups living away from the reservation, but which also filter back to the mesa communities. Despite the efforts of the Tewa and Hopi to insulate their communities against the introduction of alien practices and ideas, these influences are modifying the traditional way of life.

Relations with Whites

The Tewa, like their Hopi neighbors, tend to separate whites into three groups: missionaries, tourists, and agency personnel. In the last category, teachers, agency employees, and medical people are all lumped together. The white trader does not fit into any of these groups. He has a personal relationship to the Indians. He is a link, primarily economic, with the outside world.

Missionaries

Missionaries are primarily members of Protestant denominations. Catholic missionaries have not been successful among the Hopi and Tewa, perhaps because of the word-of-mouth tales of the ill-treatment accorded their forefathers by Spanish priests. During my fieldwork period, the following missions were on the Hopi reservation: three Baptist missions, at Polacca, Toreva (below Second Mesa), and Keams Canyon; two Mennonite missions, at Oraibi and Bakabi; a Roman Catholic Franciscan mission at Keams Canyon serving primarily Navahos; and a Protestant mission of undetermined affiliation at Sichomovi, conducted by a native Hopi missionary. In addition to these missions, missionaries and representatives of other Protestant sects visit the Hopi villages periodically. These people hold services in Hopi and Tewa homes or simply read the Bible and sing hymns, coaxing members of the household to join in. Some Tewa women appear to enjoy the singing, but none of them participate in the services wholeheartedly.

Most of the missionaries who visit the Hopi or who have missions on the Hopi reservation disapprove of the Hopi and Tewa ceremonies. Some of the sects vehemently denounce the traditonal customs and instruct their Hopi and Tewa adherents to abandon them. The Indians attend church services or Bible readings primarily to receive the gifts and nonreligious instruction which are offered as inducements to come to the missions. One woman said she had learned to sew and to can fruit by attending the services of one sect and valued this knowledge. It is obvious that few of the Hopi or the Tewa have found spiritual satisfaction in their exposure to Christian teaching. Pueblo Indians are concerned about the problems of daily living and seek to find relief from illness, crop failure, and difficulties with Indian and white neighbors. Their own religion is organized to minimize the fears and anxieties of day to day existence. They cannot understand a religion that emphasizes the spiritual world. Sin and "being saved" are concepts that are simply not a part of their thinking. They do not believe that their ancestors have wronged anyone and hence they have no "guilt", in the sense that whites have it. But they do have apprehensions about the contemporary world and are seeking relief from them. Hopi and Tewa ceremonies, particularly those of the Hopi, are mass magical rites with an emphasis on beauty of movement and costuming. They are designed and executed to induce the universe to pour forth with the good things of life. Horticulture, the economic base of life, receives the full concentration of Hopi religious devotion and ritual. In an environment where the success or failure of the subsistence economy is always fraught with uncertainty, the religious orientation of the longer term residents like the Hopi highlights "weather control." Lean and bountiful years are explained in terms of faulty or successful observance of religious retreats and rituals.

Christianity has no solutions for such concerns or problems.

While the Tewa have a more secular orientation, their religious organization, ritual, and beliefs are closer to the Hopi than to any Christian sect. They have resisted the inroads of Christianity, particularly in the early years of forceful imposition, just as strongly and persistently as have the Hopi.

In the early 1900s the ceremonies of the Hopi, the Tewa, and other Western Indians came under severe criticism. The United States government sent investigators to study reports of immoral and anti-Christian practices among the Indians. These investigators brought back reports of customs that violated white American standards of decency and morality. Under the religious Crimes Code, Indian Service officials were instructed to stop ceremonial practices that might be contrary to accepted Christian standards. The impending suppression of native ceremonial rites caused the Hopi, the Tewa, and the Pueblos of New Mexico to entrench their native ceremonial system. The situation was like a return to the days of Spanish oppression and the Pueblos survived this period of religious persecution by the same method—by holding their ceremonies behind closed doors and disciplining themselves to reveal no information about their sacred rites to outsiders.

The Hopi and Tewa are masters at passive resistance. Numerically small and unacquainted with the legal techniques with which to fight injustices, they resist by hiding behind a wall of secrecy. Elsie Clews Parsons, an anthropologist, who edited a fascinating personal journal of a Tewa Indian (Crow-wing) remarks in her foreword to the journal:

That missionaries should come up the mesa into the plazas is greatly resented, . . . and some have wanted to put them out, forcibly, as a missionary was treated at Oraibi, tossed in a blanket, I was told with a grim laugh. But others, among them our Journalist, have counselled the pose of indifference, of suppressing by ignoring. 'Let them alone, have nothing to do with them, don't speak to them,' he advises, as determined an exponent of passive resistance as might once have been found, let us say in Germany. Even in the Journal, Crow-wing carries out his policy. Not a word about the missionaries. They are negligible and ignored. (Parsons 1925:8)

Fortunately in the early 1920s the U.S. Indian Bureau reversed itself and stressed the right of Indians to practice their own religion. The suppression of ceremonies has had a negative effect on the spread of Christianity among the Hopi and Tewa. Christian missionaries today are identified by many of the people with the onus of religious persecution. The Tewa, however, do not seem to consider the missionaries at present a serious threat to their way of life and they express no particular hostility toward them. Missionaries are received courteously in the homes of many Tewa, but the attitude toward their missionary activities is one of polite tolerance. A Tewa woman expressed in words what might be witnessed by any impartial observer:

It is best to be polite to missionaries, let them come in and preach. We will go on with what we are doing. It is not good to drive anyone away; we must be nice to people no matter who they are. But we feel that no one should disturb what we want to do. If they urge us to listen, we say nothing. Sometimes they talk a long time telling us that our dances are evil and that we must stop them. They say unless we go the "Christian Road" we will not be saved. But we just keep quiet and they get tired after a while and leave us alone.

Traders

The white trader has been an important part of the Hopi and Tewa scene since the late decades of the last century. Traders have the opportunity to acquire an intimate knowledge of the Indians rarely available to non-Indians. While the relationship is primarily an economic one, many traders have taken a personal interest in the mesa communities. Thomas V. Keam, a trader of the Hopi and Navaho, for whom Keams Canyon was named, became intimately involved in the problems of the Hopi and the Tewa. It was through his efforts that the delegation of Hopi chiefs made the trip to visit the Commissioner of Indian Affairs in 1890 to Washington, D.C., to present personally the problems of the Hopi Indians (see this Chapter, p. 27).

In 1951 white traders operated three trading posts where the Tewa did most of their buying. One trader operated two large posts, one at Polacca and one in Keams Canyon. A second trading post in Keams Canyon was perhaps most popular with the Tewa. The owner of this post, a white man, had a Tewa clerk who handled most of the sales to Tewa and Hopi customers. Prices are extremely high in the trading posts, but it is a convenient way to buy, and many Indians have charge accounts of long standing in these places. The traders are generally held in higher esteem than missionaries or many of the Indian Service personnel since traders do not try to persuade them to change their way of life.

Tourists

During the summer, and less frequently at other times, hundreds of tourists come to visit the Hopi villages and Hano. Non-Indian visitors are drawn by the unusual beauty of the mesa country and also by the esoteric and colorful ceremonies. The visits of tourists are usually transient and of short duration, but there are numerous instances of a casual first visit developing into an enduring friendship between an individual Tewa or Hopi family and a family from a distant part of the country. Such friendships stimulate repeated visits. These friends are frequently drawn into taking the side of their Indian friends in petty disputes within the community, a practice that has often aggravated the trouble rather than helped matters. In a few instances, however, these friends have helped the Indians tremendously in problems that affected them all. Thus, the friends of the Indians, particularly artists and writers, joined the Indians in fighting the suppression of native customs and ceremonies and in winning for the Indians the right to hold them.

The Tewa have coined a special term for whites who come to see their ceremonies and appear to enjoy them. They are called "unbaptized" ones to differentiate them from missionaries and other whites who have denounced their customs and ceremonies. There is no resentment toward white visitors at either Tewa or Hopi dances. Both groups feel that all share in bringing about good, the spectators as well as the dancers. Hence, as long as tourists are well behaved they are welcome. Yet, photographs of public ceremonial performances are prohibited, for the Tewa and Hopi fear that such pictures may still be used to subvert and suppress their religious activities.

United States Indian Service

The Bureau of Indian Affairs has probably affected the Tewa and Hopi more profoundly than any other source of change. Before the mid-twenties, Indian administration was committed to transforming Indian communities into variants of the dominant American culture as quickly as possible. We have noted the critical attitude of missionaries and U.S. Indian Service officials toward native Indian mores and their attempts to stop them. Indian administrators also used force in recruiting Indian children to be enrolled in boarding schools located in the eastern part of the United States. The program was designed specifically to wean Indian youngsters from their traditional culture. In these schools the use of the Indian language and all other "Indian" ways were prohibited. Infractions were dealt with brutally through a variety of physical punishments. Tewa and Hopi children were among the many Indian children affected by these activities of the Bureau of Indian Affairs.

Criticism of the Indian Bureau's policy was strong and it succeeded, as we have seen, in securing for the people the right to hold their own ceremonies.

In addition, exposure of the abuses of the earlier period brought about a change in policy. After 1928 the Bureau respected the Indian ways of life, but assisted them in improving their economic, educational, and health problems. The new regime has permitted traditional Tewa and Hopi leaders to relax controls that safeguard their ceremonial life. But they *have not abandoned* these controls; the bitter experience of two periods of religious persecution is deeply imbedded in their memory. Insistence upon the preservation of a distinctive way of life has been dramatically illustrated by the Hano Tewa, but in general, cultural self-determination is an American Indian characteristic, if indeed it is not a universal human trait.

Since the late nineteenth century, the Tewa have felt the value of cooperating with government representatives and with white people in general. These relationships have had for the most part a positive effect on Tewa culture, but certain disintegrating factors are also emerging as a result of increasing contacts with Americans and American institutions. Thus, for example, a serious incompatibility is evident between the younger, school-trained generation and the older, traditionally reared group. Off-reservation boarding schools are blamed by the Tewa for this situation. Young dissidents consist mainly of youths from seventeen to twenty-five who loiter in the trading posts and at favorite spots along the protecting eaves of the cliffs on First Mesa. Sometimes girls are drawn into the group but for the most part they are youths from First Mesa ranging in number from twenty to twenty-five—although only about six to ten ever congregate together at any one time. These are the young people who take to drinking and often get into trouble and then must appear before the tribal judge at Keams Canyon. Drinking is not a serious problem at present, however; the fact that liquor must be bought in off-reservation towns and brought seventy-five miles to the Hopi mesas has undoubtedly restricted heavy and habitual drinking. In addition, the rich ceremonial cycle provides sufficient satisfactions to discourage the use of liquor as a substitute for recreational outlets.

Not all of the young people with formal education are die-hard iconoclasts; family and community pressures bring many of them to participate in traditional activities. Still, the attitude of many young people is to look with disfavor on Hopi and Tewa ceremonies and to make carping criticisms of Hopi and Tewa life. The traditionalists feel that anyone who rejects native customs is "bad" and "mean." To effect conformity, scolding and community pressures are employed. The result is greater resentment on the part of the small but increasing group of young dissidents and a widening of the gap of misunderstanding between them and the traditionalists. The group may represent simply the usual, general differences to be found in any community; yet with Tewa and Hopi culture, nonconformance to traditional customs does signal the passing of a unique way of life since ceremonial participation is such a vital part of the social order. It would be ironic that the Tewa of Hano after resisting the corrosive and acculturative pressures of a number of different societies over such a long span of history should finally succumb to the influences of white American culture.

The Yearly Round of Activities

While the ceremonies and customs at Hano may disappear in a few generations, Tewa culture at present exhibits considerable vitality. During the winter months the ceremonial calendar is full, and cooperative activities (see Chapter 6) of all kinds bring the people together. With the harvest carefully stored away and the work of herding cattle and sheep reduced to a minimum, most of the Tewa families come back to Hano to spend the winter. Kiva dances occur weekly; in between times there are continuous rehearsals for men, while Tewa women are occupied with the preparation of food.

The winter months are the time for constant social interaction. There is visiting in the evening; stories are told and experiences recounted. Most of the talk and activities, however, center around the kiva dances; the last performances are discussed while the next one is planned and eagerly anticipated.

Early in the spring the ceremonial cycle wanes. Planning and work with sheep and cattle keep entire families away from the mesa. There are only two major ceremonies in the summertime—the Niman Kachina and the Snake Dance (or Flute Dance in alternate years). Both of these are First Mesa Hopi ceremonies, and while the Tewa do not actively participate in them, they must prepare food for their Hopi relatives gained through intermarriage. The Tewa also act as hosts to outside visitors since, in recent years, they are considered and therefore consider themselves members of First Mesa society. For these important summer events families that have been away in cattle and sheep camps return, but for only a few days. As soon as the ceremonies are over they are back at work. These two ceremonies, however, are eagerly anticipated, and they provide considerable social interaction not only among themselves but with hundreds of visitors—whites, Navaho, and Pueblo Indians.

Families living at Keams Canyon, the Hopi Agency, participate in recreational activities supplied by government supervisors and Christian missions. These consist of periodic American social dances, basketball games, and weekly movies. The Baptist church conducts a weekly sewing class, which draws a small group of irregular participants. But even these people seem to find the social interaction, ceremonies, and cooperative activities on top of the mesa more satisfying. Since the winter Kachina dances now occur regularly on Saturday nights, a concession made specifically for wage workers, some of the Tewa families living on job locations in Holbrook, Winslow, and Flagstaff also come to see them from time to time. The sacrifices that these people make to attend Tewa ceremonies and renew kinship ties are indicative of the strength of traditional Tewa culture.

For the present, Tewa society and culture persist. With the coming of white Americans a more amicable and cooperative atmosphere has been established on First Mesa which offsets the former antagonistic relations between the Hopi and Tewa. American contact has acted as a catalyst in the change by altering the value system in favor of the Tewa. Basic Hopi and Tewa social institutions and practices have not been displaced and remain strong and satisfying to the people. Social cohesion on First Mesa seems to have been achieved without leveling differences and without seriously undermining the traditional cultural core on which each society rests. Modifications brought about by modern conditions are evident, but despite these changes the vitality of Hano continues. In the chapters that follow we will examine in some detail the customs and institutions of the Tewa community.

4

The Social Network

To the ordinary American tourist on a casual visit to Hano and the Hopi villages, the differences in social life from the general American pattern may not be immediately apparent. Accustomed to his society where descent is reckoned bilaterally with an emphasis on the male line, he will naturally assume that the same conditions exist at Hano and among the Hopi. It is only after greater familiarity with the social relations and the social organizations of these people that he will be impressed by striking differences. The tourist will then begin to realize that the way in which he groups relatives and the way he regards and behaves toward his relatives and neighbors is as alien to the Tewa of Hano as the social life of Hano will be to him.

The Hano kinship system is based on unilateral descent, and the social structures given prominence in Hano life are also unilateral organizations. These units are the matrilineal, extended household, the lineage, and the clan. The nuclear or elementary family which is the basic family type in American society is a temporary unit among the Tewa and the result of acculturation to white American influences. Only the Tewa living off the mesa on cattle and sheep camps or those engaged in wage work in urban areas outside of the Hopi reservation live in nuclear families. The family organization at Hano is an extended type where relatives related along the maternal line live in rooms and houses adjacent to one another. Married men live with their wives, but look upon the households of their mothers and sisters as their real homes. These men return frequently to their natal households to participate in ceremonial life and to exercise their authority over junior members of their own lineages. Hano households are the terminal structures of a number of matrilineal lineages which in turn form the important clan structures. One household in each clan is the custodian of the ceremonial lore and the religious paraphernalia of the clan. The oldest woman of this household is the head of the clan, but the "real" clan leader is her brother or perhaps a maternal uncle. This man performs rituals periodically for the benefit of all clan members and as such he is held in high esteem.

The kinship system and the lineal structures are the most significant aspects of the Hano social system. These organizations are similar to Hopi coun-terparts, and the Tewa must have adjusted their own institutions with those of their neighbors early in the contact period. At present the survival of Hano Tewa culture depends primarily on the continuity of these institutions.

The Household

Kinship relations at Hano may be comprehended most easily by a discus-sion of the extended matrilineal household where an individual receives his ini-tial and basic cultural orientation. This unit normally consists of a woman and her husband, married daughters and their husbands, unmarried sons, and chil-dren of the daughters. The women comprise the important members of the unit; they own the house, are responsible for the preparation and distribution of food, make all the important decisions, and care for the religious paraphernalia. The oldest woman of the household enjoys the most respect, and the members of the unit look to her for instructions and seek her advice in times of trouble. Next in importance is her oldest daughter, who assumes the duties and responsibilities of the household in the absence of her mother. Men of the household and lineage leave the house when they marry, although they return frequently, consider it their home, exercise considerable authority in religious matters, and are called to exert discipline over the children in serious cases. The husbands have little au-thority in the wife's home; they contribute to its economic support, teach their children the techniques of making a livelihood, and provide warmth and real affection toward them but defer to their wives and their wives' brothers and uncles in disciplinary matters.

The extended household formerly occupied a series of adjacent rooms. With the increasing importance of wage work and livestock activities in recent years, this situation has changed. Tewa families on farms and ranches during the summer are essentially of the nuclear-family type: husband, wife, and children, and in some cases, a widowed grandmother, a divorced daughter, or other rela-tive and her children are present. For wage workers, housing limitations at Keams Canyon or off the reservation restrict the size of the household even more drastically. Although it is not uncommon to have one or even both parents of the wife living with a nuclear family on a farm or ranch, older people refuse to make their home with children who live in government quarters or off the reservation.

At Polacca and Hano the size and composition of the households vary seasonally and with the occurrence of ceremonial and social functions. During these events the households are considerably larger. Hano individuals consider the residences on farms or ranches, at Keams Canyon, or off the reservation as temporary and retain homes at Tewa Village or Polacca. Here they return fre-quently for various social and ceremonial occasions and revert to extended-household living. The structure and activities of a typical Tewa household are dis-cussed in Chapter 6.

The household in recent years has thus tended to become a less integrated unit than it was formerly; nevertheless there is keen awareness of all the relatives that comprise the household group. Modern forms of transportation afford frequent resumptions of extended-household living. The growing child still has a maximum of contact with a large number of relatives. A child soon learns to identify grandparents, parents, his mother's sisters and their husbands and children, and his own brothers and sisters. For much of the time he eats, sleeps, and plays in the company of these relatives.

Almost simultaneously with his contact with the relatives of the household group, though not with the same frequency, the child comes into contact with his father's relatives. These relatives, particularly father's mother and father's sisters, are frequent visitors to his house, and he is always welcome and treated with affection in their house. At crucial periods of his life they comfort and aid him. Thus, for example, when the *Soyoku* (bogey Kachina, see Social Control below) come at the time of the *Powamu* ceremony, these relatives intercede for him and prevent the frightening ogres from carrying him away.

The enculturation process will become more evident in the discussion of kinship behavior and the life cycle, but the initial indoctrination of a Tewa individual cannot be thoroughly understood unless the structural makeup of the household is comprehended.

Lineage and Clan

A Hano lineage is the living and functional representation of a particular clan; its members are in intimate contact with one another and bound together by deep loyalties. While marriages remove the men to the various households of their wives, they renew lineage ties frequently to exercise ceremonial responsibilities. Women of the lineage are, of course, constantly together. The lineages at Hano are small and some are simply the matrilineal members of an extended household. A senior woman of one of the lineages is the head of the clan and her brother ordinarily performs the necessary rituals for the clan. Upon the death of the clan head, the position is usually assumed by the next senior woman of the same household and lineage, but prominent members of the clan in the village may decide to designate as her successor a mature woman from another household and lineage. Formerly households of the lineage occupied a block of houses adjacent to one another, a pattern that has broken down in recent years, but the intimate kinship bond remains even though the member household may be dispersed. Since the Tewa recognize affiliation with Hopi clans having the same name, lineages of equivalent clans in the Hopi villages are also considered lineal kinfolk and the ordinary clan relations are extended to members of these lineages.

Hano lineages and clans resemble corresponding Hopi organizations in all essential features. Certain basic Hopi concepts, particularly those concerned with phratral groupings and separate clan migration legends, appear to be new to the Tewa.[1] In recent years, however, there is clearly an indication that the Tewa

---

[1] See below for a discussion of Hopi and Hano phratry organization.

are attempting to adapt and adjust their own clan concepts to correspond with those of the Hopi. These efforts of the Tewa to accommodate to Hopi clan concepts disclose subtle but important factors in the trend toward acculturation noted in Chapter 3 and discussed in this and in the following sections.

Characteristics of Hano clan organization are revealed in the following statement by a Bear clansman:

I am of the Bear clan. Our mothers' mothers' mothers and our mothers' mothers' mothers' brothers were Bear clan people. They came a long, long, time ago from *Tsawadeh,* our home in the east. Our sisters' daughters' daughters' children, as long as women of my clan have children, will be of the Bear clan. These are our clan relatives, whom we trust, work with, and confide in. My mother's older sister guards the sacred fetish which is the power and guardian of our clan and which was brought in the migration from *Tsawadeh.* My mother's older sister feeds our fetish and sees that the feathers are always properly dressed. At important ceremonies, my mother's brother, erects his altar and sets our fetish in a prominent place within the altar. My mother's older sister and my mother's brother make all the important decisions for our clan, and such decisions are accepted with respect and obedience by all Bear clan members. My mother's older sister and her brother are called upon to advise, to reprimand, and to make decisions on land and ritual affairs for all of us who are of the Bear clan. My mother's older sister's house is where our fetish is kept, and therefore it is a sacred house to us and there we go for all important matters that concern our clan.

A few additional remarks about the nature of the Tewa clan are necessary to complete the above description. Marriage between members of the same clan are strictly prohibited. In addition, marriage is forbidden with a member of an equivalent Hopi, New Mexico Pueblo, or Navaho clan; a member of father's clan or of its linked clans; and a person whose father's clan is the same as one's own. Occasionally violations of these latter restrictions have occurred, but no violation of the rule that forbids marriage with a member of one's own clan is on record at Hano.

Clans are landholding units, each clan having lands set aside for the use of its members. The control of ceremonies and their ritual paraphernalia are in the keeping of certain clans. Adopted children retain the clan of their mothers; in all cases of adoption at Hano, however, the children were adopted by members of their own clan.

The importance of the matrilineal clan among the Hano can only be attributed to borrowing from the Hopi, for the New Mexico Tewa do not have a functional clan organization. These Pueblos group themselves into "clan" names but these units have neither function nor clearly defined patterns of descent and residence. These "clans" have nothing to do with ceremonial or economic affairs, land or house control, political organization, or the regulation of marriage. New Mexico Tewa Indians report variously that one acquires such a "clan" from the father or the mother. It appears then that, among the New Mexico Tewa at least, the borrowing of the clan from some diffusing agents—

perhaps from their Keresan neighbors who have clans of the Hopi type—was arrested before it became a significant part of their social organization. Possibly Spanish influences acted as a deterrent to the diffusion of clan concepts, particularly since the Spanish colonists were strongly patrilineal. At any rate, only "clan names" exist among the New Mexico Tewa at present, and it is very probable that the migrant Tewa group at Hopi had a similar undeveloped clan organization. The idea of the clan was not foreign, however, and it is possible that this nuclear idea was developed quite early into an organization which approximated the Hopi clan. An early adaptation of the kinship and clan organizations would have facilitated the preservation of a distinctive way of life, which, as the present study indicates, the ancestors of the Tewa desired. Hopi kinship and clan organizations stress matrilineal descent and matrilocal residence, hence it is possible to isolate an intermarrying community from others if its members wanted to be alone. Hano did, in fact, maintain a separation from the Hopi for over two centuries, and, as we have noted, only in comparatively recent times have intermarriages occurred and the trend toward an integrated Hopi and Tewa community on First Mesa launched.

New Mexico Tewa visitors are fully conscious of the importance of the clan among the Hopi and at Hano. They have learned from experience, for instance, that they receive more cordial treatment in the homes of Hano Tewa whose clan corresponds to their "name clan" than they do from others; therefore they proudly announce their "clan" as soon as they arrive at Hano. A New Mexico Tewa visitor is asked: "What clan are you?" When identity is established, the visitor is supposed to stay with his clan relatives. If the Tewa visitor gives the name of a clan not represented at Hano, the answer invariably is: "They have become extinct." Hano residents believe that at one time the village had a full complement of all Tewa clans, and if the "clan name" of a Tewa visitor cannot be identified, the clan must be extinct. In the event that a clan is not found for a Tewa visitor, any Hano household will take him in and treat him with kindness and respect, just as he would be treated if he were a real member of that household and clan.

The Hano clan has apparently mirrored the Hopi clan in structure and function for a long time, but the principle of clan linkage or phratry organization appears to be new to the Tewa. Among the Hopi, all the clans are grouped into larger aggregates of phratries of two or more clans each. Eggan (1950, Table 2, pp. 65–66) gives a list of some fifty clans grouped in twelve phratries for all the Hopi villages. The phratry system appears to be an old and well-established practice among the Hopi. Eggan (1950: 78–79) reports:

> The basic phratry pattern is more clearly delimited for the Hopi than are the constituent clan patterns. . . . It is evident that the phratry grouping has exerted an enormous stabilizing influence in Hopi society. Individual clans are subject to extinction from failure of the line or lines of women. This can happen rather rapidly, as the data for the last three generations indicate, particularly where the average population per clan group is small. The Hopi villages have been in existence since before 1540, the Oraibi at least probably

before 1200. With our present knowledge of the mechanisms for clan change, the basic pattern can only be due to the importance and conservatism of the phratry pattern, unless we are willing to assume that the clan-phratry pattern is recent among the Hopi. This is denied by the central importance of the clan and the uniqueness of the phratry pattern for the Hopi. . . .

Although there are seven Hano clans—Bear, Fir, Corn, Tobacco, Earth, Cloud, and Cottonwood—only two, Bear and Fir, are grouped together. This linkage seems identical with the phratry groupings of the Hopi and fits Titiev's definition of the Hopi phratry (Titiev 1944:58):

> . . . a nameless division of kindred made up of two or more clans which share certain privileges, mainly ceremonial, in common. The outstanding feature of the phratry is that it delimits the greatest extension of kinship terms based on a given relationship, and that it marks the largest exogamic unit recognized by the Hopi . . ."

All informants agree that this linkage occurred as recently as fifty or sixty years ago. The reason for merging is familiar Hopi theorizing. According to some informants, the two clans combined because in a migration legend the Fir clan is mentioned as a "pathmaker" for the Bear clan. Members of the clan assert that partnership in the past legitimatizes the linkage. Other informants report that the Fir clan was taken as a partner by the Bear clan when the Sun clan became extinct about fifty years ago. The Sun clan, along with Bear, Corn and Tobacco clans, made up the membership of Court Kiva (see Kiva Organization, Chapter 5). According to these informants, the extinction of the Sun clan disturbed the proper performance of certain ceremonies and another clan was needed to take its place. The Fir clan was therefore brought in to fill the vacancy. Kinship terms are extended to both clans, and marriages between members of the two clans are forbidden.

Members of the Fir and Cottonwood clans also consider themselves related to one another because "Fir and Cottonwood clans are both 'wood' or 'timber' clans." This grouping appears to be based on a familiar Hopi concept that "like" objects or "like" aspects of nature "belong together." On the same basis the Tewa Cottonwood clan is equated with the Hopi Kachina clan because Kachina dolls are made from cottonwood." There are no shared privileges, ceremonial or otherwise, between Fir, Cottonwood, or Hopi Kachina clans; nor are kinship terms and behavior extended; neither is marriage restricted. My own belief is that this grouping represents the initial stages of a phratral linkage which may eventually reach the full status of a Hopi phratry. Bear and Fir are the only Tewa clans linked in the Hopi fashion at present, that is, by (1) the sharing of certain ceremonial privileges; (2) extension of kinship terms, and, at least among some members, shared behavioral patterns; and (3) restriction of marriage between members of the two clans.

In good Hopi manner, members of the Bear and Fir clans now claim relationship to a host of clans present among the Hopi and other tribes. They rationalize the relationship not only on the basis that "like objects" or "like" aspects of nature belong together, but on the following principle. Hopi clans are considered to be partners "if they have shared mutual experiences during the mythical wanderings following the emergence." Thus, for example, Hopi Parrot and Crow clans are equated because of the following migration legend:

> When the Parrot people stopped for the night they perched their guide, parrot, on the branch of a tree. On one occasion they built a fire underneath the branch of the tree where the parrot had been placed. They forgot about the bird until they were about to move again and when they looked up on the branch, they saw there a bird that looked like a crow (the pitch smoke of the fire had turned the parrot black). Some of the people said: "It is a crow, and we will take the name Crow for our people and descendants." That is why some people are Parrot clan and some Crow clan, but they are one people for they traveled together and did everything as a group.

On the basis of such theories the Hano Fir and Bear clan members claim relationship to members of the Hopi Bear, Bear's Eyeball, Bear's Bones, Carrying Strap, Spider, and Bluebird clans. In addition, they believe themselves related to strictly Hano "clans" which have developed, in name at least, independently of the Hopi: Mexican, Red Coral, Yellowwood, Aspen, Pine, Wood, and Stick. These are only alternate names for clans and do not have actual representation. They occur, however, as the names of actual clans among Navaho, New Mexico Pueblo, and other tribes and are, therefore, convenient to use for associating such clans with Hano Bear and Fir clans.

The incipient linkage between the Cottonwood and Fir clans has not been carried out as far as that between the Bear and the Fir. The other four Hano clans—Tobacco, Corn, Earth, and Cloud—are not associated with other clans. These clans are present among the Hopi, or at least are recognized as "alternate" names in phratry groupings. Among the Hopi, for example, Corn clan is associated with Cloud, Fog, Snow, and Patki (Water House). When I asked if the Hano Corn clan was also similarly related, my informant, a Corn clan woman, replied that the Tewa were not Hopi and she could not believe that a Hopi clan, even though similar in name, could be related to a Tewa clan. With regard to the association of Fir and Bear clans with certain Hopi clans, she remarked that these people "were trying to deny their Tewa heritage and wanted to be like Hopi." Yet when this same woman was on a visit to Mishongnovi in the winter of 1951, she sought out Patki households. At that time she remarked: "These are our people; they treat us kindly when we visit them, and when they come to our village they stay in our houses."

The remarks of this woman indicate the ambivalent attitude toward the Hopi already noted in Chapter 3. It is my belief that the four Hano clans which at present are still retaining their distinctiveness will soon find a reason for merging among themselves and with other Hopi clans, and will thus form phratries in the Hopi manner. This prediction is made in the view of the precedent already set by Bear and Fir clans and because the trend in other areas of Hopi and Hano culture seems to point toward social and cultural integration on First Mesa.

Hano has two kivas: Court Kiva and Outside Kiva. The seven Tewa clans are divided into these two kivas. The following are Court Kiva clans: Bear, Fir, Corn, and Tobacco. The Outside Kiva clans are Earth, Cottonwood, and Cloud. Before the Fir clan merged with the Bear clan its members belonged to the Outside Kiva; thus, while representatives of the Sun clan still lived (the Sun clan was aligned with the clans of Court Kiva), the two Hano kivas were evenly balanced, each having four clans. Today, the Cloud clan is almost extinct, since it has only one old woman of about eighty and three men left in it. About 50 years ago a Hano Tewa Cloud woman married a Shongopovi man and moved with her family to his village. The Tewa village denounced her for this violation of matrilocal residence. Shongopovi people say that the family moved out because the Tewa people were "mean" to her for marrying a Hopi man. Although the Cloud clan is extinct at Hano, the clan is represented at Shongopovi by several female members of the clan. These women speak no Tewa but proudly assert that they are Tewa and not Shongopovi Hopi. The surviving members of the Cloud clan at Hano are important, however, since they control the *Shumakoli,* the only association at Hano having the curing of illness as its sole objective (see Ceremonial Associations, Chapter 5). The fate of the Shumakoli when the present members of the Hano Cloud clan pass away will be resolved in one of three ways (if past precedent is followed): (1) One of the Shongopovi women may come with her family to live at Hano and thus reseed the clan and take over the management of the association; (2) another Hano clan may take charge of the association; or (3) the sacred fetish and masks of the curing association may be buried and the association permitted to die. Another alternative that would be employed by the Hopi is that the association could go to the lineage head of the Cloud clan at Shongopovi. This is unlikely, for the Hano do not permit the borrowing of their associations and ceremonies by the Hopi.

The division of clans in terms of the two kivas suggests the New Mexico Tewa moiety system. Indeed, some Hano individuals use the New Mexico Tewa words for summer and winter to designate the Court Kiva and Outside Kiva groups, respectively. It is possible, of course, that this usage has been borrowed in recent years from the frequent visits of the New Mexico Tewa; however there are other aspects of Hano social organization which seem to reveal a vestigial moiety organization. These aspects are most pronounced in ceremonial life and are therefore reserved for discussion in Chapter 5 under "Ceremonial Organization."

Hopi concepts of clan migrations and relative position of clans in terms of status are also beginning to influence the Hano Tewa. The migration legends of the Hopi follow a characteristic pattern (see Eggan 1950: 79). After the various Hopi clans emerged from the Underworld, they set out in various directions and ultimately arrived at one or another of the Hopi villages. When a clan arrived in a Hopi village, it secured land from the clan or clans that had preceded it. The newcomers were given the land in exchange for their performing a ceremony or providing protection from marauding enemies. The priority of arrival of clans at Hopi was thus very important in terms of prestige and status because, among other things, it determined land rights. The late arrivals were as a consequence relegated to more exposed sites in the villages and given poorer farm land. In terms of status these late arrivals occupied the lowest positions. Hopi logic is not consistent, however; it appears that certain clans, though arriving late, have elevated themselves to higher positions. Such changes appear to have taken place under certain fortuitous circumstances, perhaps with the rise of unusually capable leaders in a low-ranking clan or through the phratry pattern in which a late-arriving clan might be incorporated into a league with important clans. Eggan suggests that Hopi clan migration legends have been altered through the years to correlate *order* of arrival at Hopi with the ceremonial precedence of clans at any given time (Eggan 1950: 79).

Hano clans have developed migration legends similar to the Hopi, but with certain important differences. The Tewa of Hano believe that the migration took place in two groups, the clans of the Court Kiva coming first and those of the Outside Kiva following later. This pattern differs from that of the Hopi, who conceive of the individual clans as coming to Hopi separately.

In terms of status the Court Kiva clans claim that since they were the first to arrive on First Mesa, their position at Hano is similar to that of the original Snake and Bear clans at Walpi, whose leaders, according to tradition, asked the Tewa to come to Hopi. The role of the Court Kiva clans is sacred; they must pray and mediate for the welfare of all Tewa individuals. Among the Hopi, those clans believed to have arrived first are accorded sacred functions and carry the highest rank. In recent years, under the influence of increasing diffusion of Hopi concepts, the Court Kiva clans have begun to set themselves apart as the clans with the highest status. The fact that the Bear clan was once important at Walpi (the clan is now extinct, the Horn or Flute clan has assumed its duties and status); that the Bear clan is still important in other major Hopi villages; and that the Bear clan is one of the clans of the Court Kiva group has undoubtedly strengthened this rationalization. At present, as among other major Hopi villages, the chief of Hano comes from the Bear clan.

The following statement by a Bear clansman presents the situation as viewed by the court Kiva clans:

> Our group left *Tsawadeh* ahead of the other clans. When our clans arrived at Hopi they secured a village site and farm lands and then sent for the other clans. Because our duties are sacred, we need a warrior group to defend us. Fighting an enemy must always be done with a great deal of prayer and meditation. This is as important as the actual fighting; unless our warriors are helped by war magic they will not succeed. Sometimes our magic alone is sufficient to win a victory and we do not need to sacrifice lives.
>
> The Outside Kiva clans are subject to our dictates in all important matters. In anything that pertains to the welfare of the village these clans must meet with us before they act. Their duties are concerned primarily with outside matters [secular], whereas ours pertain to religion.

The Outside Kiva clans accept the Bear clan head as the Village Chief and also the notion that the court Kiva group of clans should devote themselves to prayer and meditation. However, they emphatically deny that they were late arrivals on First Mesa. Indeed, they report that as warriors they preceded the main migration of the entire group, clearing a path and making safe the journey. They also refuse to accept the idea that clans whose functions are devoted primarily to prayer and meditation should be regarded as "better" than other clans. The report of a Cottonwood clansman express this point of view:

> When our clans [Outside Kiva clans]left our home in the east they came directly to Hopi. This was in terms of an agreement made before the migration. Our clans were to secure a village site and farm lands and then send for the other clans. At Hopi our clans fought the enemy and then sent for the Court Kiva clans when the country had been made safe for habitation. These clans brought our sacred objects and our ceremonies, and once more we began to live as one people. There are no differences between us—we have different duties but we are the same people. We need each other to make a strong pueblo and to be effective as "protectors" of First Mesa.

It is difficult, perhaps impossible, to verify Hano—or Hopi—legends. Changes appear to be going on constantly to validate statuses, functions, or particular ceremonies. In the context in which the legends have been considered here, however, they are useful because they indicate quite clearly that the Hano are beginning to pattern their clan legends along Hopi lines.

The Kinship System

THE NATURE OF THE TERMINOLOGY   Tewa kinship terms are mostly descriptive designations, that is, almost every kinship term consists of more than one word. Hopi kinship terms, on the other hand are classificatory, a single term being applied to more than one type of relationship. Only one term, the designation for older sister, *kakah,* appears to have been borrowed from the Hopi; all other terms are native Tewa and are either identical or cognate with those used among the New Mexico Tewa. It is interesting that even in kinship the purest tendencies of the Tewa with respect to their language have been exercised. As we have noted elsewhere, the vocabulary of the Tewa is free of Hopi words with the exception of this kin term and another, the male word for "thank you." Tewa girls and women use the native Tewa word for "thank you."

Like the New Mexico Tewa, siblings and mother's sisters are distinguished on the basis of seniority and the junior reciprocal is used extensively. In spite of these similarities to the New Mexico Tewa kinship system, Hano kinship structure differs hardly at all from the Hopi. The system, like that of the Hopi, is organized on a lineage principle, quite different from the bilateral generational type of the New Mexico Tewa (*cf.* Harrington 1912: 472–498; Dozier 1955: 242–257). Thus, the Hano Tewa kinship system seems to have been reorganized along the Hopi pattern without the terms themselves being greatly modified (see Eggan 1950: 141–144; Dozier 1954: 305–310).

KINSHIP BEHAVIOR   The Tewa of Hano, like their Hopi neighbors, have most intensive relations with three lineages: the mother's, the father's, and the mother's father's matrilineal lineages (*cf.* Eggan 1950: 19–26, 141–144). Women occupy a central position in the kinship system, while men are marginal. Marriage is prohibted with anyone in the three lineages. This fact plus the custom of matrilocal residence take men away from their lineal relatives upon marriage. A married man's loyalties and responsibilities are then divided between his new household and his natal one. He assumes economic and affectional bonds in the household he enters through marriage, yet custom demands that he retain his loyalties and ceremonial duties to his lineal relatives. A Tewa man married to a Tewa woman experiences little conflict, since Hano as a village has greater unity, both social and cultural, than a Hopi village. The important cementing force at Hano is *being Tewa* and this fact tends to override other loyalties and commitments. Divided loyalties and responsibilities do arise in men married to Hopi women, however, and undoubtedly these factors have prevented large scale intermarriages with the Hopi in the past and have largely restricted Hopi-Tewa marriages in recent years to the three villages on First Mesa. A man may continue to interact frequently with Hano members if he lives at Sichomovi or Walpi, but such interaction is highly restricted if he is married into one of the more distant Hopi villages. The effect of Hopi-Tewa marriages has been a unification of the three villages on First Mesa and a greater sense of community organization. Lineal loyalties and responsibilities do not therefore result in the constant disruption of village integration so characteristic of other Hopi villages (*cf.* Eggan 1950: 118–119; Titiev 1944: 69). See Chapter 7 for a more detailed discussion of Hano, Hopi, and First Mesa integration.

In the following section, kinship behavior will be discussed in terms of the three lineages given prominence in the Hano kinship system.

MOTHER'S LINEAGE   Terminological differentiation is most complex and the relations most intense and intimate within the mother's lineage. Duties and responsibilities are also more specifically structured among these relatives. For a man these responsibilities are primarily ceremonial, especially once he has left his natal household and assumed economic duties in his wife's household. A woman's concern for her lineage is both economic and ceremonial, since she remains her entire life in her natal household and in constant association with her matrilineal relatives.

A younger sibling is called *tiye;* an older brother, *pipi,* and an older sister, *kakah.* Sex distinctions are made for older siblings but not for younger ones. It is interesting, however, that girls and women tend to refer to a brother as *pipi,* older brother, even though he may be younger than the speaker. Similarly, brothers generally refer to their sisters as *tiye,* younger sibling, regardless of age. The consideration of brothers as seniors and sisters as juniors and generally the importance given to seniority probably reflect a retention of New Mexico Tewa kinship usage. Among the latter, considerable emphasis is given to relative age, and male dominance is evident in certain patterns, such as the greater importance of the father in the household and male ownership of houses and land. The special recognition of seniority and male dominance in either terminology or behavior is not characteristic of the Hopi kinship system.

Before marriage brothers work together in common tasks, and cooperation in ceremonial activities continues after marriage even when brothers reside in separate households. A younger brother defers to an older one and the latter has the right to order, chastise, and demand obedience from a younger brother.

This is a privilege that is often exercised, and the younger brother obeys and listens attentively to an older brother's remonstrations. The older brother is also conceived of as the guardian of his younger siblings and is supposed to watch that they do not get injured or fall into mischief. When a younger sibling is hurt or gets into trouble, it is often said that it happened because the older brother was not attentive. If the discrepancy in age between a younger and an older brother is very great, the older brother may, in fact, take a position almost like that of mother's brother (see below). This is particularly true in families where the mother's brother has married into a distant household and is not always available to exercise discipline and lineage duties.

The relation of sisters to one another is very intimate and lifelong. Sisters rear and care for their children in the same household and cooperate in all household tasks. An older sister may often assume an importance equal to that of the mother in the household, particularly if she is the oldest daughter in the household and the other children are considerably younger than she. There is in Hano a special term, *kakah,* to distinguish older sister from her younger siblings.

While the terminological usage implies a deference to males, the actual behavior between a brother and a sister does not reveal patterns of subordination and superordination. There is a great deal of cooperation and exchange of confidences between brother and sister. Even though a brother and a sister are eventually separated by marriage and subsequent residence in different households, contact is still maintained. A sister often advises a brother about making a proper marriage, and frequently has much to say about whom her brother should marry. Sisters aid in the preparation of food on ceremonial occasions in which their brothers participate.

The behavior of maternal parallel cousins toward each other is comparable to that between siblings. Relative age is important, behavior and terms being adjusted accordingly. The terms used for maternal cousins are those for mother's siblings and the junior reciprocals of these terms, which are formed by adding *e,* "child" to the term. Thus, mother's sister's son if older than a male or female speaker is called *meme,* mother's brother; if younger, he is called *meme-e,* mother's brother (diminutive) by a male speaker and *ko-o-, e,* mother's younger sister (diminutive) by a female speaker. Mother's sister's daughter if older than a male or female speaker is called *ko-o;* if younger, she is called *meme-e* by a male and *ko-o-e* by a female. In behavior greater respect and obedience is consistently accorded an older maternal parallel cousin. Since these relatives ordinarily live together or in close proximity, the relations are frequent, intimate, and marked with deep attachment. In recent years, modern conditions have tended to limit the interaction of siblings and maternal parallel cousins by the necessary divisions of the extended household, but these relatives still come together frequently at social and ceremonial functions.

The mother-son (*yiyah* and *e*) relationship is deep and enduring. Even after a son leaves home at marriage, he frequently returns for aid and advice. A mother may scold and admonish her son, but this is her right as a mother, and the son is not ordinarily much disturbed by her anger. Serious advice and admonition are usually referred to the mother's brother, the disciplinarian of the household. A mother has the primary decision in the selection of her son's "ceremonial father" and gives the man who is chosen food and gifts in recompense for his services. Behavior between the mother and daughter (*yiyah* and *e*) is marked by cooperative activities and duties. The mother trains the daughter in all domestic duties: grinding corn, cooking, taking care of babies, and the like. A mother and daughter constantly confide in one another. At least in the recent past, a daughter immediately informed her mother of her first menstruation; her mother then took her to the girl's father's sister's house, and she underwent the puberty ceremony there (see Life Cycle below). Important ritual knowledge pertaining to the clan is transmitted from mother to daughter. A daughter has the deepest affection for her mother and constantly aspires to be like her.

The relation between *kaye* (mother's older sister) and her younger sister's children, *kaye-e* is different from that between *ko-o* (mother's younger sister) and the latter's older sister's children. *Kaye* demands more aid and gives more orders to her younger sister's children. In return she receives strict obedience from them. A younger sister often sends her children to be admonished or instructed in certain domestic and ritual duties by her older sister. This is particularly true if both the mother's mother (*saya*) and *saya's* sister (also called *saya*) are absent. Relations between *kaye* and her younger sister's son, *kaye-e,* are marked by the same affection and gentleness. Contacts between these two relatives are less frequent because of the difference in sex and if her nephew is married, but the relations that exist are mutually affectionate.

The position of *kaye* is superseded only by *saya* (mother's mother) in the household. She has a great deal to say about both the store of foodstuffs and ritual matters. As *saya* becomes old and less able to perform her duties, *kaye* takes on more and more authority and upon the former's death takes over her position.

It is obvious that behavioral patterns within the household are to a large extent determined by relative age. If a mother's sister is much older than her nieces and nephews though younger than their mother, she is still likely to be shown the deference and respect due a female lineal relative of mother's generation. However, if the mother's sister is approximately the same age as her nephews and nieces, the relations among all these relatives would be identical with the behavior generally exhibited among siblings. Behavior is also conditioned by the kind of relations that exist between a parent and the relative under consideration. An older maternal aunt, for example, may joke with her younger sister and order her around, and thus influence the behavior of her own children toward this relative. I recall a demonstration of this pattern of behavior in the Hano home where I made my residence during the course of fieldwork. In addition to other members the household contained an older maternal aunt, two of her grown daughters, and her younger sister who was *ko-o* to her daughters. When I asked the oldest daughter to let me take a photograph of her teen-age daughter, Josie, in the "cart-wheel" hairdress worn by girls after puberty, she called her *ko-o* to dress Josie's hair. As *ko-o* worked, the daughters joked with her. They said *ko-o* was slow and that she ought to work faster. If *ko-o* pulled on Josie's hair too hard, they laughed, much to the annoyance of both *ko-o* and little Josie. *Ko-o* remonstrated with her older sister's daughters, telling them that they were just like the girls of the younger generation, ignorant of traditional tasks, even a simple one such as dressing a girl's hair.

One of the most important of Hano kinship relationships is that of a man to his sister's children. The mother's brother, *meme,* is chief disciplinarian to his sister's children and they both respect and obey him. Usually the sister's oldest brother takes the role, but in his absence a mother's younger brother may be called to perform the function of disciplining his sister's children. The mother's brother is generally feared by the children, and often the mere mention of his name, with a threat to call him if the children do not behave, is enough to make them conform. Mother's oldest brother (if mother's mother's brother is not alive) is frequently the ritual head of the clan. He and mother are responsible for clan rituals and often get together to discuss such affairs. As a son or daughter grows up, *meme* becomes more of a confidant and a source of information, while his disciplinary functions diminish. It is true that *meme* is sometimes called to settle marital quarrels and to warn a young man not to drink, but this is infrequent as adults are expected to behave properly and generally do so.

Mother's mother and mother's mother's sister are called *saya;* the reciprocal is *saya-e,* grandmother (diminutive). The behavior of *saya* toward her *saya-e* is more indulgent and kind than that of a mother toward her child. Since a grandmother ordinarily lives in the same household as her grandchildren, she has frequent contacts with them. She rarely scolds a grandchild but provides a great deal of affection. A grandmother tells her grandchild stories and legends and instills in the young child a pride in being Tewa. A *saya* is loved dearly. A child will often seek her out in order to divulge his troubles to her, and he is always assured of a sympathetic reception and kindly counsel. While *saya* is strong and active, she is the head of the household and in charge of all foodstuffs. She possesses essential ritual knowledge and must be consulted in all important matters regarding the household and clan.

The *saya* of the household in which I lived during the course of field-work fully met these requirements and performed her duties as a good grandmother. Her grandchildren respected, obeyed, and loved her. They sought her out to confide in her and to have her arbitrate quarrels between themselves and others. One of the girls slept with her every night on a sheepskin pelt. The two youngest children in the household, a boy of two and a girl of four, always took a position beside their grandmother when visitors came. If they were teased, they hid behind her or buried their faces in her lap while *saya* spoke softly to them and stroked their hair.

The Hano Tewa recognize two relatives above the grandparent generation: *pahpa,* mother's mother's mother, and her brother, *pepe.* These relatives are usually extremely old and often are blind. Inevitably, then, the duty of their great-grandchildren and great-grandnephews and nieces is to see that they are conducted about the village and guided into the houses of their relatives. A *pahpa* or *pepe* is kindly and indulgent to all, and is respected and treated affectionately by all members of the community.

There is a wide range of individuals to whom the key relative terms of mother's lineage are extended. Extension of these terms embraces the clan and, in certain cases, linked clans of the Hopi, the Navaho, and the New Mexico Pueblo Indians. These terms incorporate the important individuals of the lineage and thus extend to those individuals designated by the terms some of the same respect accorded to members of the lineage.

The term *kaye*, mother's older sister is a general term for all senior women of one's clan. Younger women are called by the junior reciprocal, *kaye-e*, mother's older sister (diminutive). Very old women are called *saya*, mother's mother.

All older men of one's own clan are called *meme*, mother's brother; and its junior reciprocal *meme-e*, mother's brother (diminutive), is applied to all very young members of the clan.

The terms given above are applied to all equivalent Hopi, Navaho, and New Mexico Pueblo clans. The New Mexico Tewa, regardless of clan affiliation, are called by clan terms as if they were of the same clan. For showing respect to Rio Grande Tewa individuals, the senior terms are employed even though the person addressed may be considerably younger. Thus, when I brought a group of Hano Tewa to my home in Santa Clara Pueblo (New Mexico) during the course of fieldwork, the visitors all called my sister *kaye* although she was younger than most of the visitors. They also used the term *meme* for male adults obviously younger than themselves. Only for children were the junior reciprocals used. At Hano I was called *meme* by the very old as well as by the very young.

Men who marry women of one's lineage are called *soyingih* (bridegroom) and women marrying men of one's lineage are designated *sai* (bride). Again these terms are applied to all men and women married to equivalent Hopi, Navaho, and New Mexico Pueblo clans. Similarly these terms are extended to men and women of non-Tewa extraction married to New Mexico Tewa regardless of clan affiliation. At Hano, my wife, although a white woman, was called *sai* by all. The parents and relatives of a spouse are called collectively *ya-a*, in-laws. A wife's or husband's father is *ya-seno*, relative man; a wife's or husband's mother is *yakwiyoh*, relative woman. There are ritual gift exchanges between the families of a couple at marriage, but relations between in-laws is on a personal level rather than one specified by kinship.

FATHER'S LINEAGE   Relations with one's father's and one's mother's father's lineage are almost identical, although by virtue of residence, where one's father lives in the same household, opportunities for interaction with the father's matrilineal relatives are most frequent and most intense. The special relations specified in the kinship system between the father's sisters and one's natal household also bring these relatives into more intimate relationship. The term *tutun* (father's brother) or *tadah* (father) is extended to all male members of father's lineage regardless of generation. They, in return, refer to a brother's son or daughter as *tu-e*, father's brother (diminutive). These relations are free of directive or authority overtones; they are relations of companionship and genuine affection.

The most important relative in father's matrilineage is father himself. He is the only member of his lineage that is a part of one's household (unless two sisters marry two clan brothers). A Hano father is the most loved relative in the household. His behavior toward his children is in direct contrast to that of the general American and European father. He neither directs, scolds, nor punishes; these are mother's, mother's sister's, and mother's brother's prerogatives. The father and indeed all classificatory fathers are affectionate confidants and companions. In part the affectionate behavior of a father may be prompted by a desire to entrench himself in the household in which he is an outsider. A wife's and her children's loyalties are primarily with their own lineage and clan; conversely, a husband is committed to his own lineage and clan. Through the custom of matrilocal residence and duties to his wife and children, however, he has responsibilities for supporting the whole household (with the aid of unmarried men of his wife's household and the men married into it). These conflicting roles make his position insecure and the marriage bond rather unstable (about 20 percent of Hano marriages end in divorce). The affectionate tie between a father and his children helps cement his position in the household. Children, because of the warm regard they have for their father, will often arbitrate controversies and effect compromises between father and mother.

The children of classificatory fathers are called by sibling terms: *pipi* (older brother), *tiye* (younger sibling), and *kakah* (older sister). One's relations with these relatives are not intimate. Interaction is infrequent since they live in separate households.

Women of father's lineage are called *kiyu* (father's sister) regardless of generation; reciprocals are *e-sen* (man child) and *e-kwiyoh* (woman child). Father's sisters manifest a deep interest in their *e-sen* from the time of his birth (see Life Cycle below) and continue a warm relationship for life. Usually a father's sister takes upon herself to become the special guardian of one of her brother's sons. Other women of father's clan may select other sons of their clansbrother on whom to bestow special attention and affection. Such a father's clanswoman appears in her brother's house at crucial periods of her brother's son's life. If he has been injured or is ill, his *kiyu* will come immediately to console him. When the ogre Kachina come on the morning before Powamu (an annual ceremony), she is at her brother's house to "protect" her *e-sen* from the child's own clansfolk, who "pretend to give away the child" to these frightful-appearing Kachinas (see Social Control below). As the boy becomes older, *kiyu* "pretends to be jealous" of her *e-sen's* regard for his girl friends.

During a buffalo dance in January 1951 two girls and two boys danced in the middle of the village courtyard. A woman spectator suddenly ran out among the dancers, pushed out one of the girls, and took the girl's position. She danced spiritedly for about five minutes and then returned among the spectators. The onlookers roared with laughter at this performance, but the woman's expression was one of mock seriousness and anger. Another woman brandishing a rifle also ran to the dancers. She pointed the weapon at the feet of one of the girls and pretended to fire it.

One of the women of the household in which I lived explained that these women were the boy dancers' *kiyu* and that they were "publicly displaying their jealousy and anger for their *e-sen's* girl partners."

When a brother's son marries, his *kiyu*, with other women of her clan, protests the marriage by attacking the boy's mother and mother's sisters in mock play. Even after a brother's son is married, his *kiyu* visits him and teases his wife, "pretending to make love to him."

A *kiyu* is "proud" of her *e-sen's* participation in social and ceremonial dances and helps prepare food for him. In return, an *e-sen* performs various services for his *kiyu*. He may make furniture or repair household fixtures for her. One of the sons of my hosts, for example, made and installed window screens for his *kiyu*. Formerly an *e-sen* brought his *kiyu* meat from game that he had killed and salt from salt expeditions. Mutually the relations are informal, affectionate, and lifelong. In the presence of each other's spouses the two "pretend to be like lovers" and speak of their deep attachment for one another, "to make the husband or wife jealous" (see the relations between a man and the husbands of women of father's lineage below).

A father's sister's relations with her brother's daughter lacks the public display of mock behavior. She participates in the naming ceremony of her *e-kwiyoh* (woman child) and protects, aids, and provides affection at crucial periods in the girl's development. She guides her through the puberty ceremonies at the time of the girl's first menstruation. At this time the father's sister also puts up the girl's hair in "cart-wheels," the symbol signifying a girl's availability for courtship. As adults, the two visit one another frequently, confide in each other, and assist in household duties.

Father's mother is also called *kiyu*, but if she has cut the umbilical cord and conducted the naming ceremony, she is called *kuku*. The reciprocal is *ku-e*, umbilical-cord-cutter (diminutive). The relation between *kuku* and her grandchild is similar to that between *saya* and the latter's grandchild. If *kuku* is young, however, she may behave toward her grandchild very much as a *kiyu* does to her *e-sen* and *e-kwiyoh*. *Kuku* will protect and aid her grandchild during the child's growth and development. More frequently, however, the relation between *kuku* and her grandchild is kindly, indulgent, and affectionate.

The Hano Tewa select ceremonial sponsors for certain stages of the life cycle and for crises situations (see Life Cycle below). Four categories of ceremonial sponsors exist: (1) A ceremonial "father" is selected for a boy between the ages of eight and ten, and a ceremonial "mother" for a girl of similar age, when the boy or girl enters the Kachina cult. (2) A ceremonial "father" inducts a young man into the Winter Solstice ceremony when he is between twelve and sixteen years old. Women are not inducted into this ceremony, but at a comparable age they grind corn for four days and have their hair style changed to "cart-wheels" (see above). (3) A "doctor father" is selected for a man or boy who is very ill (a "doctor mother" for a woman or girl); he is supposed to cure the patient who is given to him in "adoption." (4) A ceremonial sponsor—a man for a boy and a woman for a girl—is selected for a young person about to become a member of a curing society.

The ceremonial sponsor must be from a clan other than that of the novice, but he may be of the novice's father's clan. The Hano Tewa believe that a novice becomes a member of his (or her) sponsor's clan. The relations between a novice and his ceremonial sponsor are, however, much more affectionate than that which exists between members of the same clan. These relations are indeed more like those between father and son or between father's sister and her brother's child. The term "father" is used for a male sponsor, but "mother" for a female sponsor; the reciprocal is simply *e*, "child." Thus, the father's lineage terms are not consistently applied, although the behavior shown by one toward the two sets of relatives is similar for other members of the sponsor's clan; the novice uses his own lineage terms.

Women married to men of father's lineage are referred to as *yiyah* (mother) but one has no special relations with them.

Men who marry women of father's lineage are treated as joking relatives. Such a husband is called *thete* (grandfather); the reciprocal is simply the diminutivized form *thete-e*. The term is the same used for men of mother's father's matrilineal lineage, but the behavior that exists toward the two sets of relatives is not at all comparable. The behavior toward the first set of relatives is a form of releasing aggression in a culturally approved fashion, whereas the second set are respect relatives. Sons and the husbands of father's clanswomen engage in a battle of verbal wit and may even scuffle around with each other. They constantly belittle one another. They invent uncomplimentary nicknames for each other and use them at social gatherings to provide humorous entertainment for all present. On one occasion I happened upon a spirited wrestling match between two men I knew intimately. Ordinarily, the Tewa (like the Hopi) do not fight one another, but these two actually seemed angry at each other, and they struggled earnestly for almost an hour. A group of onlookers gathered; from their laughter and comments I soon learned that these two men stood in the relationship of *thete* and *thete-e*.

Relations between a woman and her father's clanswomen's husbands also involve joking and name-calling, but no physical contacts occur between them.

MOTHER'S FATHER'S MATRILINEAL LINEAGE   Mother's father's matrilineal relatives are called *thete* (grandfather) and *thete kwiyoh* (grandfather's woman) again regardless of generation. The behavior shown to these relatives and to those of one's father's lineal kinfolk is similar. Conceptually these relatives appear to be somehow equated. Behavior of *thete* toward his grandchildren is marked by kindness and deep affection. If a grandfather is still strong and vigorous, he may take his grandchild or grandnephew with him when he goes into the fields and there teach him the simple farming techniques of the Hopi and Tewa. He will also guide him in other tasks, patiently and affectionately watching to see that the boy does a good job. If the grandfather is Tewa, he will tell his grandchild all about the Tewa migration legend and the curse on the Hopi, and he will teach him Tewa songs. Very old Tewa are extremely proud of their Tewa heritage and try under all circumstances to develop such pride in younger children.

A middle-aged, acculturated Tewa man gave me the following account of his boyhood relations with his maternal grandfather:

Whenever I went to see *thete* he made me sit beside him and told me the Tewa migration legend which I had heard countless times from his lips. I knew the story so well that I could probably relate it better than he. *Thete* would start from the beginning, repeating all important events four times, as is the traditional pattern in all legends. His voice would become charged with emotion when he spoke of the injustices the Tewa suffered from the Hopi, and he always ended the legend by telling me that we Tewa must never forget this story, but must always tell it to our children as he had related it to me. I became so tired of the story that I would try to invent some excuse so that I would not have to listen to it again. Sometimes I went to sleep while he was telling the story, and then he would shake me gently and tell me that I must not sleep, that the story was very important, and that I must learn it well. Sometimes I became angry with *thete;* surely the Hopi were not as bad as he would have me believe. My own father is Hopi and I love my father dearly and all of my *kiyu* are wonderful to me. But my grandfather was old and I did not want to offend him by telling him these things or by going away without hearing the end of the story.

The paternal grandfather is also called *thete* (grandfather) and *thete kwiyoh* (grandfather's woman), which is also applied to father's father's sisters. The maternal grandfather normally lives in one's household and hence sees his daughter's children often and the latter also interact with his sisters frequently, hence the relations among these relatives is intimate. On the other hand, the paternal grandfather lives in a different household and his sisters still in another, hence interaction is infrequent in spite of the fact that the same terms are used for these relatives.

Life Cycle

An account of the development of an individual from birth to death will clarify the relations and behavior between the various relatives already discussed and give us a better understanding of how a Tewa becomes a participating member of his culture. After presentation of the life cycle, the significant aspects of the kinship system will be summarized and discussed.

The Hano Tewa have a rather elaborate ritual at birth that differs only in minor details from the Hopi. Parsons (1921: 98–104) gives a First Mesa Hopi account with references to Hano practices. During the course of my fieldwork a number of the children were born in the hospital at Keams Canyon, and the customary ritual was not, of course, carried out completely. Even in such cases, however, the naming ceremony is performed for the child as soon as it is returned to the village. Hano women usually try to have their babies in the village in the traditional manner, but in recent years a few women have been persuaded by government employees and white friends to go to the hospital. Since men are excluded, I was not able to attend any of the native birth rites but I obtained the following brief account from the senior woman of the household in which I resided. The account is similar to the one given by Parsons (1921:98–104) for First Mesa Hopi. My hostess reported:

If my daughter is going to have a baby she will have it in this house. I will call my sister and also my sister's older daughters who have already had children. We will darken the room by hanging blankets over the door and windows. Only women will be present, none of the men. If she has trouble having the child, we may call a "doctor" [a native medicine man] to help her. After the child is born I will call my *yakwiyoh,* my daughter's husband's mother, and she will cut the umbilical cord. *Yakwiyoh* [called *kuku* by the child after it is grown] cuts the cord with an arrow shaft if the baby is a boy and with a corn-gruel stirring rod if the baby is a girl. She then places fine ashes on the navel.

After the baby is born my daughter and her baby are cared for by her *yakwiyoh* [women of her husband's clan] for twenty days. They comb and bathe my daughter and make certain that she is kept warm all of the time. She is given hot corn-meal gruel and may drink only boiled juniper water; she cannot have pure water, meat, or salt. The baby is washed right after birth by *yakwiyoh* and sprinkled with fine ashes. This is repeated every four days for the twenty days that my daughter and her baby are in confinement in the darkened room. An ear of white corn is kept next to the baby all of the time "to guard the baby."

On the nineteenth day the women of my house and my sisters' houses [women of the extended household] prepare *piki* [paper-thin bread made from blue corn meal], corn pudding, stews, and other food. Before sunrise the next day all the women of my daughter's husband's clan come to the house. Each woman dips an ear of corn in a bowl of yucca suds and touches the head of the baby four times and then with a prayer gives it a name. The name is from her clan—something which describes her clan. If the baby's father is Tobacco clan, the baby may be named tobacco blossom; or maybe yellow leaf, describing the tobacco plant when it is ripe. As the sun comes up, *yakwiyoh* takes the baby outside and utters all the names that have been given to it. Out of the many names, the baby's mother and father will decide which is the prettiest and will call the baby by that name.

The infant is nursed by the mother and is cared for primarily by her, but soon he begins to become a real part of the extended household. His brothers and sisters and his mother's sisters and their children start playing an important role in his training. *Saya* mother's mother, is also frequently on the scene. For the first six or seven years of life socialization takes place almost entirely within the confines of the extended household. At the age of seven or eight, however, the child starts to go to school at the government day school at Polacca. This takes him out of the secure and familiar surroundings of the household for the first time.

The day school can be either a relatively easy adjustment for the child or a seriously disturbing one. Under a patient and indulgent teacher the transition may even be a pleasant one, opening new experiences and new horizons for the child. Unfortunately, such teachers are in the minority. Although a teacher may sincerely wish to adjust Hopi and Tewa children comfortably into an unfamiliar situation, the teacher's own value orientation is often completely different. The ordinary American teacher on an Indian reservation tries to instill in his pupils such American principles as saving, individual responsibility, competition, and a dozen others entirely alien to the Hopi or Tewa child. In the process, the child becomes confused, and disturbance to the child's personality structure may result. Not only do the goals of his teachers conflict with those of the child's traditional cultural values and training, but the child is suddenly confronted with a puzzling and bewildering maze of new technological equipment to which he must adjust: washbasins, toilets, pencils, papers, and a myriad other new things not present in his home environment.

Hano children are perhaps more fortunate in the school situation than Hopi children. The more aggressive characteristics of the Tewa generally and the fact that they are or have been in the recent past a minority group (with respect to the Hopi) have made them more receptive to American cultural values. Moreover, the necessity of having to learn a new language is not a strange phenomenon to a Hano child. Hano children have been in a bilingual situation for more than 250 years. A Tewa child learns the Hopi language almost simultaneously with Tewa. English is not an entirely unfamiliar language either. He has heard his parents, his brothers, and his sisters use it on various occasions. I have many times observed adult Tewa teaching young relatives English words and delighting in the successful attempts of the children in mastering a few words.

When not in school Hano children learn the more traditional aspects of their culture. A boy accompanies his father to the fields and slowly learns about farming through observation and by actually doing some of the work. A girl also learns household duties in the same way, from the women of the household.

Between eight and ten years of age both boys and girls are initiated into the Kachina cult. A ceremonial father is selected for the boy and a ceremonial mother for the girl. These sponsors are from a clan other than that of the child. The initiation rites are held four days before Powamu, a Hopi ceremony in which the Hano Tewa participate. Parents, ceremonial sponsors, and all the acquaintances of a child have dramatized and made these activities extremely important in his thinking. A child who is going to be initiated exhibits tremendous excitement long before the event takes place. An adult male Tewa reported his initiation experiences as follows:

> We were told that the Kachina were beings from another world. There were some boys who said that they were not, but we could never be sure, and most of us believed what we were told. Our own parents and elders tried to make us believe that the Kachina were powerful beings, some good and some bad, and that they knew our innermost thoughts and actions. If they did not know about us through their own great power, then probably our own relatives told the Kachina about us. At any rate every time they visited us they seemed to know what we had thought and how we had acted.
>
> As the time for our initiation came closer we became more and more frightened. The ogre Kachina, the Soyoku, came every year and threatened to carry us away; now we were told that we were going to face these awful creatures and many others. Though we were told not to be afraid, we could not help ourselves. If the Kachina are really supernaturals and powerful beings, we might have offended them by some thought or act and they might punish us. They might even take us with them as the Soyoku threatened to do every year.

Four days before Powamu our ceremonial fathers and our ceremonial mothers took us to Court Kiva. The girls were accompanied by their ceremonial mothers, and we boys by our ceremonial fathers. We stood outside the kiva, and then two whipper Kachina, looking very mean, came out of the kiva. Only a blanket covered the nakedness of the boys; as the Kachina drew near our ceremonial fathers removed the blankets. The girls were permitted to keep on their dresses, however. Our ceremonial parents urged us to offer sacred corn meal to the Kachina; as soon as we did so they whipped us with their yucca whips. I was hit so hard that I defecated and urinated and I could feel the welts forming on my back and I knew that I was bleeding too. He whipped me four times, but the last time he hit me on the leg instead, and as the whipper started to strike again, my ceremonial father pulled me back and he took the blow himself. "This is a good boy, my old man," he said to the Kachina. "You have hit him enough."

For many days my back hurt and I had to sleep on my side until the wounds healed.

After the whipping a small sacred feather was tied to our hair and we were told not to eat meat or salt. Four days later we went to see the Powamu ceremony in the kiva. As babies, our mother had taken us to see this event; but as soon as we began to talk, they stopped taking us. I could not remember what had happened on Powamu night and I was afraid that another frightening ordeal awaited us. Those of us who were whipped went with our ceremonial parents. In this dance we saw that the Kachina were really our own fathers, uncles, and brothers. This made me feel strange. I felt somehow that all my relatives were responsible for the whipping we had received. My ceremonial father was kind and gentle during this time and I felt very warm toward him, but I also wondered if he was to blame for our treatment. I felt deceived and ill-treated.

After the Powamu ceremony my head was washed and I received a new name. At this time, too, the small feather was removed from my hair and the food restrictions were lifted.

The traumatic experiences of the Kachina initiation are deeply embedded in the memory of all Hano Tewa. Yet most of them felt that the whippings were not harmful but on the contrary were good for the child. Although no relative will lay a hand on a child, the whippings of the Kachina are considered to have a favorable effect on the subsequent behavior of the individual. There were similar expressions of opinion among those with whom I discussed the subject. "Hopi and Tewa children are well-behaved because they are disciplined early in life." "A human being needs to be broken, like a horse, before he can become a well-behaved individual." Many of the older Tewa ascribe the "meanness" of school trained boys and girls to the fact that they have not gone through this experience. For the same reason some parents defend the old military type of government boarding school where children were heavily disciplined. Missionary boarding schools, which follow a rather strict regime, are also preferred by some to the more informal and relaxed modern government or public boarding schools.

Tewa males are qualified to impersonate Kachina characters after the first initiation and soon assume such roles. Girls take on a more active part in household duties after this event, and boys acquire more responsibilities and heavier tasks in farming and ranching activities. Schooling provided by the day school ends about the time a boy or girl has reached the age of fourteen or fifteen. At this time another important event awaits them. For the boy the event is membership in the Hano Winter Solstice Association, and the initiation is generally simple but of great significance. After this event a boy is considered a man and is eligible for active membership in other Hano religious associations. A few Tewa men (and fewer women) also join the tribal associations of the Hopi after gaining membership in the Hano Winter Solstice Association (see Chapter 5).

Membership in the Winter Solstice Association requires the selection of another ceremonial father, generally not the same as the previous one. The ceremonial father must be a man who is not of the boy's clan, but a man whose clan belongs to the same kiva group with which the boy's clan is affiliated (see above, Lineage and Clan).

For four days before the Winter Solstice ceremony in December, the boy abstains from meat and salt. He is constantly in the care of his ceremonial father during this time; he eats his meals at the man's home and also sleeps there. Finally, on the night of the fourth day he accompanies his ceremonial father to the kiva. If his clan is affiliated with Court Kiva, he goes into that one; if he belongs to the Outside Kiva, he enters that one. The Winter Solstice ceremony is an all-night affair. To members the event is announced sixteen days before, and prayer sticks are made by the members who are in retreat there. The final night of the ceremony consists of the singing of songs and the telling of migration legends and past experiences of the Tewa by the chief of the group of clans that belong to that kiva. The novitiates sit next to their ceremonial fathers and listen attentively in order to learn the songs, legends, and stories told that night. The retreat terminates just before daybreak when the manufactured prayer sticks are taken out and deposited in the various shrines and springs surrounding Hano. The ceremony is strictly a Hano one; no Hopi are permitted to attend.

The second important event in a girl's life occurs at the time of her first menstruation. A woman keeps close watch over her daughter and instructs her to report all her physiological symptoms. When a mother is informed by her daughter that her menstrual period has begun, she brings one of her husband's sisters, the girl's *kiyu*. This woman then takes charge of the girl. She is secluded in the grinding room of *Kiyu's* house and grinds corn for four days. During this time she abstains from meat and salt and must use a scratching stick to scratch herself. In her chores she is assisted by her *Kiyu*, one of whom is constantly with her. There is a general atmosphere of good natured humor, and the conversation is informal and lively. At the end of the four days one of the *Kiyu* washes the girl's hair and fixes it in the "cart-wheel" fashion of the Hopi. The girl is also given a new name at this time.

The foregoing sketch of a girl's puberty rite was given as a definite "ideal." My Tewa informants reported that this custom was no longer consistently observed. My Hano hostess told me that her own daughter had at first objected to going through the ceremony, but had been persuaded to observe the ritual. The first initiation—the Kachina initiation—is in fact observed religiously. My hostess remarked:

> We still have control of our children when they are young, but schools and white contacts make them so independent that by the time they are twelve or fourteen they are difficult to manage. They get mad when we tell them to go through the rites. School girls hate to grind corn, and we old women have to do it all the time. The boys are better; they do not mind going to the kiva and performing their duties like their uncles and ceremonial fathers tell them to do.

Boys do not mind joining the Winter Solstice Association, actually membership into either the Outside Kiva or Court Kiva. The initiation rites are not difficult and involved, but on the contrary are even pleasurable. The twenty-six-year-old youth in the household in which I resided told me that "it was fun to attend the Winter Solstice ceremony and listen to the old Hano songs and to hear the old men tell of the experiences of our forefathers."

After a boy's initiation into the Winter Solstice Association and a girl's participation in the puberty ceremony, they are theoretically ready for marriage. Hano marriages, however, do not ordinarily take place until a youth is between twenty and twenty-five and a girl between eighteen and twenty-two. Courtship is, like that of the Hopi, strictly in the hands of the two persons concerned (cf. Eggan 1950: 54). Marriage restrictions are based on kinship and, except for the one prohibiting marriage within one's own clan, are not generally observed at present. Marriage between a couple belonging to the same clan is strictly prohibited, however, and there was not a single violation of this rule in the marriages recorded at the time of fieldwork. Although marriage is an individual matter, opinions of a person's siblings and father's sisters have an important influence in his choice of a mate.

Teen-age boys and girls have a maximum opportunity to see each other. Parents or other members of the household do not keep a check on the activities of grown children. Boys and girls meet under the protecting eaves of the cliffs, around the trading post, or in the proximity of the day school during the evenings. Although, according to reports, formerly a boy stole in late at night to a girl where she slept in her house, this is no longer a customary pattern of courtship. Premarital sexual relations are the rule, and the birth of children before marriage is common. Generally, however, a girl marries the father of her child and tries to do so before her child is born.

Marriage customs are similar to those of the Hopi as reported in the existing literature (cf. Titiev 1944: 30–43; Eggan 1950: 53–57). Marriages usually take place in January and August. According to Hano belief, marriages should not be contracted in the Kachina season, from February through July. January and August are considered the months for gaiety, the time when social dances and other happy events take place.

When a couple has decided to marry, the girl presents the boy's mother with piki (maize bread) and receives meat in exchange. Then follows a period of several weeks in which the women of the girl's household grind corn. When a large amount of corn has been ground, the girl is dressed in traditional Tewa dress and her hair is fixed in "cart-wheels." The girl is then taken to the house of the boy by her maternal and paternal kinswomen. The girl grinds corn in the boy's house for three days, and early on the fourth morning her hair is washed by the boy's maternal kinswomen.

While the girl is in her prospective husband's household, the boy's father's clanswomen may "object" to the marriage. These women descend on the boy's house and bedaub his mother and sisters with mud for letting their e-sen get away from them. They speak slightingly of the bride, saying that she does not deserve so fine a husband, and point out her flaws in personality and appearance. This is all done, however, in a spirit of fun, and any damage is later paid for.

In the meantime, the boy's male relatives on both his father's and his mother's side prepare the girl's wedding garments; these consist of belt, robe, dress, and moccasins. When the garments are completed, the girl dons the new outfit and her hair is dressed in the style of a Hano married woman. This hair style differs from that of the Hopi; it is similar to that of the New Mexico Tewa in that the sides are clipped. Hopi married women part the hair and with a string twist the locks on either side of the face.

The bride and bridegroom are then taken by his mother to her (the mother's) house. Early the next morning the boy's head is washed by the girl's clanswomen. The corn meal ground in the preceding weeks by the girl's relatives is then taken to the boy's household "as payment for depriving the family of a worker."

In addition to ground meal, enormous amounts of other food are taken to the boy's house. In this practice, Hano appears to differ from the Hopi generally. A Hopi teacher at Shongopovi told me that none of the Hopi villages matched the Tewa community in the amounts of food brought. Indeed, there is an effort on the part of the girl's relatives to bring more food and to display it more elaborately in front of the bridegroom's mother's home than was done for any previous marriage. In this respect there is a real spirit of competition.

Marriages in the traditional manner, as described above, are still popular. Couples who are married in a church or by a justice of the peace will return to have an "Indian wedding" as soon as possible. Sometimes the traditional wedding is performed first, and then the couple goes through a civil or church ceremony.

Residence is matrilocal, despite the fact that a couple may live separately in a part of the girl's mother's house or may even build a new home in another part of the village or at Polacca. The term "matrilocal residence" is justified because the new residence is built primarily with the help of the girl's extended family and on her clan lands. After the couple has started housekeeping, interaction is primarily with the wife's relatives as illustrated in the discussion of the household.

As time passes, a man becomes more and more entrenched in his new household. He forms ties that bind him ever more strongly to the relatives of his wife. The longer the two remain together, the more secure the marriage tie becomes. We have already noted that children are important in keeping a couple together; perhaps equally as important are the well-working relationships a man establishes with his wife's relatives.

A Tewa husband and wife may be very devoted to each other but they never openly demonstrate their affection. Husbands and wives are often together, however; they go to the spring, to the corrals, or to the trading posts together. A husband usually walks two or three paces in front while his wife trudges behind. This is the Hopi and Tewa manner for a husband and wife to walk, however, and is not indicative of subordinate or superordinate relationship. Hano marriages appear to be set in firmer foundations than Hopi ones, at least when compared with marriage and divorce figures obtained for the Hopi community of Oraibi. The divorce rate for Oraibi is almost 40 percent (see Titiev 1944: 34–35). The Hano Tewa figure is about half the Oraibi rate; of 144 married Tewa in 1950–1951, only 23 had been divorced previously.

The Hano Tewa believe that sickness is caused by bad thoughts, quarreling, witchcraft, and the breech of taboo. Hano ceremonialism and the admonitions of the Village Chief, Outside Chief, clan chiefs, association chiefs, and maternal uncles constantly emphasize the necessity of purging oneself and the community of these disease-producing agents. Prayer sticks and prayer feathers made by members of a ceremonial association during its retreat or by a group preparing to put on a social dance are placed in the shrines in order to induce the gods to keep the community healthy and the environment appeased (that is, to prevent inclement weather and to provide abundant moisture for crops). Social dances and repeat performances of Kachina dances are requested by individuals for advancing personal, family, and community well-being (see Chapter 5 for distinction between social and ceremonial rites). Public appearance of social dancers, ceremonial association members, and Kachina performers are made beautiful and exacting in order to impress the supernaturals and thus ensure for the people the blessings of good health and a bountiful harvest. The people must "have good thoughts and not be angry at anyone, nor quarrel with one another." This is important at all times, but it is vital during important ceremonials: "Some people are witches" and they are trying to cause illness and the failure of crops; it is therefore important to counteract these evil influences by concentrating on the proper performances of ceremonials. Ceremonial leaders warn initiates and participants in the various ceremonies to observe the exacting ritual carefully and to guard against the breaking of food restrictions and sexual-continence regulations. The Tewa believe that only by strict observance of all these rules can the community be assured of a healthy existence.

The Tewa of Hano thus attempt to appease the environment and ward off illness by ceremonial activity and through the constant vigilance and admonitions of ceremonial leaders. In addition, on an individual level, a person who has a serious ailment may be dedicated to a "doctor father" or may engage the services of a medicine man. An individual may also help cure an illness or injury by sprinkling sacred meal on the Kachina dancers in a kiva or courtyard performance. Another method, believed to be similarly efficacious, is to submit voluntarily to a whipping by the Whipper Kachina during the Kachina initiation rites in February. Injuries and the common communicable diseases are now referred to Public Health nurses and dotors, but lingering illnesses such as rheumatism and similar maladies are treated by medicine men.

The failure of the community to observe the precautions discussed above, or to prevent sickness by prescribed methods, results in drought, disease, and death. Death in old age is considered natural, but death in the prime of life is always attributed to one of the disease-producing agents already noted. No formal ceremonial wailing is practiced; the body is interred as quickly as possible. A woman is buried in her wedding outfit; a man is wrapped in a blanket. Burial grounds are at the foot of the mesa on the southeast side. After burial, the relatives of the deceased avoid mentioning his name and refrain from commenting about the circumstances surrounding his death.

Key Features of the Kinship System and Life Cycle

It is clear from the foregoing analysis that lineal relatives are emphasized in the kinship system and the life cycle. The primary relationships involving authority and control are centered in the matrilineal, matrilocal household. The women of one's lineage have the duty and responsibility of running the household; the mother's brother is charged with primary disciplinary powers. The father and his sisters and brothers, on the other hand, have a very different relationship to a person. Except for the father, these kin live in a different household. They have no authority in managing one's household or in disciplining him; they provide aid and affection.

The mother's father's matrilineal relatives keep alive the cultural heritage, teaching a child songs and telling him stories and legends. Tewa grandfathers try to instill in their Tewa grandchildren pride in being Tewa and insist that the child should always remember his distinct heritage. These relationships are unstructured; no specified duties or relationships like those which characterize relations with one's own or with one's father's matrilineal relatives.

Another set of relatives provides an interesting function in the socialization of the individual. These are the husbands of father's sisters, who tease and even engage in physical fights with a boy or man. The victim is permitted to retaliate and does so with increasing vigor and frequency as he gets older. A girl or woman may also engage in loud talk, "pretending to be angry" with her father's sisters' husbands, but does not strike them.

Thus we see that along with the emphasis of the matrilineal household and lineage the Tewa kinship system also channelizes behavior in an interesting manner among four sets of relatives. Authority and control is the prerogative of one's mother and her sisters and brothers; affection, aid, and comfort during crises periods of individual's growth is provided primarily by the father and his brothers and sisters; continuance of traditional lore is furthered by the mother's father's lineal relatives; and the release of aggression is provided in a culturally approved fashion by father's sisters' husbands. For women the customs prevalent at the time of marriage, when the bridegroom's father's clanswomen descend on his (the father's) house and vigorously protest the marriage, provide another social release of aggression.

The differences in the kinship system of the Hopi and the Hano Tewa are worth repeating. Along with the retention of their Tewa language, the Hano Tewa have also retained kinship terms that are the same or obviously cognate with New Mexico Tewa terms. The Tewa husband-wife bond appears to be more enduring. Among the Tewa the mother's sisters are differentiated terminologically as older and younger, and differential treatment is accorded them, a distinction not made by the Hopi. Similarly, older siblings are accorded greater respect and obedience by the Hano Tewa. These differences appear to be vestigial holdovers from the bilateral, generational kinship system of the New Mexico Tewa.

Changes in the kinship system as a result of modern conditions are evident primarily in the extended household. Interaction brought about by wage work and livestock activities is breaking up the household unit and dispersing its members in terms of nuclear family groups. However, since social and ceremonial functions bring about frequent resumptions of extended-household living, the integrity of the household unit still has great significance to the Tewa. The deep satisfactions derived from social interaction and ceremonies are important in this respect, and so too is the automobile, which makes it possible for members of the extended household to interact frequently.

Analysis of the life cycle has also revealed another area in which modern pressures have brought changes. Tewa girls are resisting traditional patterns of work, particularly those connected with puberty rites. Girls are doing their hair in modern style and are objecting to the tedious roles of grinding corn. The number of girls who go through the puberty ceremonies is admittedly decreasing. Changes in the roles of men with respect to the life cycle are not pronounced. We shall see, however, that there are marked changes in the ceremonial system, an area of Tewa culture in which men have a prominent role. The other significant events in a person's life—birth, marriage, and death practices—appear to be less affected by modern pressures.

In spite of changes and increasing pressures from the outside world, the Tewa kinship system is still remarkably strong and functional, at the present time.

Social Control

Social control is vested in two agencies, the matrilineal extended family and the village as a whole. Within the extended household, the mother's brother, or in his absence, any adult male of the household or clan, is responsible for the maintenance of order and the discipline of younger members. The details of this process have been discussed in the section on kinship behavior. In the village social control is exerted through gossip, public ridicule, social ostracism, and, at least in the past, by the charge of witchcraft. In addition, the Village

Chief, the Outside Kiva Chief, the War Chief, and the Kachina, particularly the Soyoku (Hopi and Hano bogeyman) have social control functions.

Gossip is the most common form of social control on the village level. During the fieldwork period, Tewa gossip denounced a man who suddenly began to take an active part in the Hopi Powamu Association. Ordinarily Tewa do not join Hopi associations, but this man through his Hopi father and Hopi ceremonial father participated enthusiastically in the association's activities. There were many phrasings of disapproval: "We have our own ceremonies; they should not be mixed with the Hopi." "If he wants to be a Hopi he should not be permitted in our kivas." "Don't let him take part in the Winter Solstice ceremony next December." Eventually gossip reaches its victim and since a Tewa values Hano approval, he will ordinarily conform. Hopi criticism is often ignored, but disapproving gossip from one's community is taken seriously.

Public ridicule of a person who behaved improperly was formerly the special prerogative of the Koyala, or clown society. At present the society is extinct, but volunteer or appointed clowns often ridicule individuals during certain plaza dances. According to informants, the antics of the clowns today are mild, and it is said "they are afraid to make fun of town members." Instead, Navaho and whites become the subjects of ridicule.

On the occasion of a Kachina dance at Hano, I was once the target of the Koyala's antics. Tewa friends had told me many times that I smoked too much, and apparently on this occasion the Koyala had been instructed "to teach me a lesson." I was with friends, sitting with my back against the wall of a house and gingerly puffing on a cigarette. The clowns climbed a house next to the one I was sitting by and then crossed over to the roof of the house directly above me. I was conscious of the presence of the clowns, but for the moment the Kachina dance in the middle of the plaza occupied my attention. Then suddenly I heard the clowns yelling, "Fire! Fire!" I turned to look up and caught a bucketful of water in my face. I was thoroughly drenched. The spectators laughed heartily at my discomfiture, and my hostess laughingly remarked: "Now maybe you will not smoke so much!"

Only one case of social ostracism and exile was related to me, but I was told that there were others in the past. This case involved the prominent and prosperous Tom Polacca whose name identifies the budding community at the foot of First Mesa. During the greater part of his life Polacca was highly respected and esteemed, but in later years he lost the good will of his community. Before his death Polacca departed from the traditional pattern of life and was converted to Mormonism. The ire of Hano was aroused, however, when the Tewa learned that Polacca had sold his house and land below the mesa to the Baptist Mission—land to which he had only use right. Polacca and his family were exiled to Sand Dunes, five miles from First Mesa and he was forever prohibited from participating and viewing Tewa ceremonies.

The Tewa are reticent to discuss witchcraft. I knew of no one who was accused or suspected of witchcraft. The following general statement was obtained from a highly acculturated Tewa man:

People are never told that they are witches to their face. But, for example, if members of a family do not participate in ceremonies or help in the cooperative enterprises of the pueblo, they are "talked about." If anything goes wrong, if many people get sick, or if it does not rain, then some people may say: "It is because that family did not help and has bad thoughts that this has happened." Soon other people will blame this family too, and then they will say about the family: "It is because they are witches and they do not want to help other people that there is so much sickness or famine." And then the family finds out about it because people "act strange." But nothing is done to the family; "they are just talked about." No one wants bad things said about him or his family, and this family will then try to help the village in work and with the ceremonies. If this family does not do this, then people will continue to think that they are witches and the family will have a hard time because "people will talk about them and act strangely toward them."

There are apparently no open accusations of witchcraft, no trials, and no executions. In this respect the Hano and the Hopi too differ radically from the Zuni and the Indians of the Rio Grande pueblos. Witchcraft lore is enormously rich among Indians in all the pueblos except Hopi. I suspect that witchcraft gained in elaboration from Spanish contacts; as for witch hunts, trials, and executions, these seem to be definitely of Spanish derivation. Witchcraft trials and executions fit into a Spanish or European pattern among Indians of the Rio Grande pueblos and at Zuni, where they have occurred until fairly recently (see Scholes 1935: 218 ff.).

At every major Hano ceremony the Village Chief admonishes the people to live properly. He may, at times of unusually bad behavior or in times of severe drought, send a special Kachina character to both kivas to plead for proper conduct and to urge everyone to keep a "good heart." Thus, for example, in February 1951 a Kachina impersonator representing a bear visited both kivas and warned the people against excessive drinking.

The Chief of the Outside Kiva clans tells his people to observe the admonitions of the Village Chief and lectures his group on proper behavior during the Winter Solstice ceremony. The War Chief (see Hano ceremonial officers, Chapter 5) in the past had the duty of maintaining order and discipline in the village. Formerly, it is reported, he had the authority to whip miscreants and often exercised this right, but today the War Chief is restricted to announcing cooperative enterprises and to taking a prominent part in social dances.

The Kachina collectively arouse fears of the supernatural and the unknown and are for children particularly, a strong force for exacting conformance to Tewa mores. Until recently, Hano had a group of masked bogeymen called *Saveyoh* different from the Hopi *Soyoku*. The War Chief designated persons to represent *Saveyoh* and visit the village at certain specified times during the year. While they were about, all children were supposed to remain indoors, for these ogres were especially "fond" of children. Parents whose children needed disciplining would threaten to feed them to the monsters and would often permit their children to get a glimpse of the frightening creatures as they walked past the house.

Hano has now adopted the Hopi bogeymen, or Soyoku, and these impersonators appear with those of the First Mesa Hopi. Thus, about midmorning of the final day of the Hopi Powamu ceremony in February, the Soyoku impersonators start to visit all the homes where there are children. The group spends about five to ten minutes in front of each house, peering inside and often going partly into the house. In homes in which there is a child whose behavior has been reported to them as being very bad, they pretend to try to carry off the frightened child. While this struggle is going on, other members of the group bargain with the family for a food ransom. When a satisfactory ransom has been obtained, the Soyoku move on to another home where they repeat the performance.

The Soyoku make only one appearance a year, but parents constantly remind their children of them in order to compel obedience. The annual visits of the ogres are exceedingly traumatic experiences for the child. An acculturated Tewa gave me the following account of his childhood recollections and reacions to the Soyoku:

When I was a little boy I wished that our house would be the first one to be visited by the Soyoku. But that never happened, for we lived almost at the other end of the village. As I heard the Soyoku coming nearer and nearer the perspiration would start running all over me. Some children cried, but I just tightened up and felt like I was going to die. My aunts (*kiyu,* father's sisters) always came to tell me that the Soyoku would not carry me away, but my mother would say that I was very bad and that she didn't care if the Soyoku took me. When the Soyoku arrived, my aunts would fight with them to keep them away from me. My mother would bring corn meal and meat to give to the Soyoku, and she would say to me: "See how bad you've been, I have to give them all the food we have so they won't take you." That would make me feel very bad, for I felt that I was responsible for my mother giving all the food away. I would then run to my mother and grasp her dress crying: "Don't let them take me; I will be a good boy; I will work hard and get back all the food you've given to the Soyoku." Even after I was initiated and knew that the Soyoku were just ordinary people I would get frightened when I heard the noises they made.

There is an increasing disapproval of the visits of the bogeymen, particularly among wage-earning families. Another acculturated Tewa, a government employee, declared that he would not permit his children to witness the activities of the Soyoku because he felt that "they were too frightening" and that his children did not need such disciplining.

Hopi Tribal Council and Tribal Court

The Hopi Tribal Council came into being as the result of the Indian Reorganization Act of 1934 which permitted and encouraged the establishment of tribal governments. In 1936 the Hopi Indians adopted a tribal constitution and bylaws, formed with the aid of government specialists. The constitution

(U.S. Department of the Interior 1937) authorized the establishment of a council and a court. Nine political units or voting districts were established, the division being based chiefly on the native feeling of unity among the villages. The four communities on First Mesa—Walpi, Sichomovi, Hano, and Polacca—decided to work together, and thus First Mesa is considered one unit. Because the other villages were unable to reach an agreement in terms of larger groupings, each is considered a separate unit. Second Mesa forms three units: Mishongnovi, Shipolovi, and Shongopovi; Third Mesa, four units: Oraibi, New Oraibi, Hotevilla, and Bakabi; and the irrigation-farming community of Moenkopi is considered another unit.

Representation in the first Tribal Council was distributed as follows: First Mesa 4, Mishongnovi 2, Shipolovi 1, Shongopovi 2, Oraibi 1, New Oraibi 2, Hotevilla 2, Bakabi 1, and Moenkopi 2. The officers consisted of a chairman, vice-chairman, secretary, treasurer, sergeant-at-arms, and interpreters. The duties of the Council include the regulation of tribal funds and tribal commercial enterprises; the maintenance of law and order on the reservation; the protection of tribal arts, crafts and ceremonies; and giving of advice to the government with regard to appropriations for the benefit of the tribe.

The council has met only sporadically since its organization and in most respects is considered a failure. Traditionally, tribal unity is foreign to the Hopi Indians. Apparently they are not ready to become organized as a tribe at the present time (see Titiev 1944: 67–68; Eggan 1950: 108–109). The council has received support primarily from the people of First Mesa. The Hano Tewa enthusiastically supported the work of government specialists who were helping to draft the Hopi constitution and were largely instrumental in "selling" the idea to the Hopi (La Farge in manuscript). The Tewa's friendly and cooperative attitude toward the government and toward whites in general and their traditional role as go-betweens have helped to unite the villages of First Mesa and to convince them of the benefits that tribal unity will bring. The assumption of secular roles is traditionally correct, for the Hano Tewa and the First Mesa Hopi in recent years have generally let the Tewa lead in matters dealing with the external affairs of the group.

The Hopi Tribal Court follows a law-and-order code established by the Secretary of the Interior (U.S. Department of the Interior 1940: 243–246). It operates independently of the Indian Service under a judge, assistant judge, and two policemen. The Hopi Tribal Court hears both Hopi and Navaho cases. Most of the cases are concerned with assaults, trespass, disorderly conduct, and driving while intoxicated. In the winter of 1950–1951 I learned of only two Tewa who appeared before the Tribal Court; they were charged with driving while intoxicated.

Summary

Analysis of Hano social organization reveals lineal kinship ties as paramount over community or village bonds. In the section that follows ceremonial organization too will be seen to depend heavily on lineal kinship relations. Historically the Tewa undoubtedly once had a stronger village organization and compared with Hopi villages, community integration at Hano is considerably stronger at present. In the kinship system there is a retention of Tewa terms, and traces of the bilateral, generational emphasis are evident in kinship behavior. Moiety rationalizations persist in the grouping of clans and in migration legends. Social control, as with the Hopi, is restricted mainly to the household and lineage, but important controls are exercised on the village level. In recent years through intermarriages with First Mesa Hopi, Hano social institutions and behavioral patterns have become adjusted to Hopi ones, but Hano has given as much as it has borrowed. The exchange has brought about a remarkably high degree of social integration on First Mesa. A tribal organization might have succeeded for the villages of First Mesa, but the strong clan system of the Hopi mitigated against an organization based on nonkinship principles for the entire Hopi tribe.

5

Religion and Ritual

H ANO RELIGIOUS ORGANIZATION and ceremonies are not as complex as the Hopi, but bear similarities to those of the latter. Yet, despite these resemblances, affinity to the New Mexico Tewa is also evident in virtually all areas of Hano religion and ritual. Basic in the organizational pattern of the religion are the two-kiva pattern and the clans associated with the kivas. The core of the ceremonial system is the Kachina cult and the ceremonial association system. Kachina performers are drawn from members of clans which belong to the kivas and the performances are fitted into the Kachina cycle of Walpi. The Kachina cycle begins with the Hopi Powamu ceremony in early or mid-February and ends with the Hopi Niman ceremony in July. No Kachina dances are given in the intervening period, but other ceremonial association events occur at this time and "social dances" may be performed during the non-Kachina season.

Ceremonial associations, as among the Hopi, are "owned" and managed by a clan. Some association ceremonies occur at fixed times during the year; others may take place at a time specified by the leaders of the clan which own and manage the association.

Kachina and ceremonial association performances have both public and private (or secret) aspects. The private portion of a ceremony involves the periodic prayer retreat of the association, the erection of an altar prior to a public ceremony in the clan house, and the costuming of the dancers and participants. The public feature of the ceremony is held either in the village courtyard or in the kiva and is open to both Indian and white visitors.

The "social dances" of the Hano are secular performances. They occur among the Hopi as well as among the New Mexico Pueblos. At Hano they may be initiated by any man or woman who will assume the responsibility of selecting the dances, arranging song and dance rehearsals, and setting the time for its public presentation. Social dances consist of small group dances and at Hano they typically consist of buffalo, deer, butterfly, and war dances. Excepting the butterfly dance, these dances reveal numerous innovations and have "Plains" or pan-Indian characteristics.

The foregoing has been an outline of Hano religious organization and ceremonies. It is important now to examine Hano religion and ritual more closely in order to understand its basic features and underlying concepts. In the analysis that follows I will attempt to present the important details of Hano religious organization and also try to indicate the changes and adaptations the Tewa of Arizona have had to make in a new social and physical environment. It is clear from even a casual study of Hano religion and ritual and an examination of the historical accounts of Hano that until recently the most pronounced difference between the Hano Tewa and their Hopi neighbors was in ceremonial organization. Both groups were reluctant to borrow or give up ceremonies and ritual activities. Although the kinship and clan systems were adapted comparatively early to approximate Hopi systems, the Hano Tewa steadfastly clung to their own unique ceremonial organization. In the past fifty or sixty years, however, there has been a pronounced breakdown of Hano ceremonial organization and a greater adaptation of the organization to that of the Hopi. The breakdown is due partly to the extinction of the Sun clan, but probably the most important factor is the growing acceptance by the Hopi of the Tewa as equals.

Kiva Organization

Hano has two kivas: Court Kiva and Outside Kiva. Clan affiliation determines kiva membership. Members of the Bear, Corn, Tobacco, and Fir clans belong to Court Kiva; members of the Earth, Cottonwood, and Cloud clans belong to Outside Kiva.

As we have previously noted, Fir clan was formerly aligned with the Outside Kiva group of clans. At the time of the extinction of the Sun clan, or when its extinction was imminent, the Fir and Bear clans apparently seized upon a casual mention of the two clans as partners in a migration legend as an excuse to merge. The merging bolstered the membership of the Bear clan, which at the time had almost died out. For the Fir clan, this linkage placed it in the prestige group of clans. The merging of the two also substituted the Fir for the Sun clan and made possible the performance of ceremonies in the Court Kiva in which four clans participated.

Formerly, the chieftainship of the village, which is also that of the chief of Court Kiva, went in turn to each of the four clans of the kiva. The last two Village Chiefs, however, have been Bear clan members; apparently their appointment was an attempt to conform to the Hopi pattern of selecting the Village Chief from that clan. Reports regarding the number of years a Village Chief is supposed to serve before relinquishing his office in favor of another clan are conflicting. Some informants reported that his term is four years, others that it is for life. All are agreed that a chief can be removed if he proves unsatisfactory; that is, if illness or drought conditions persist during his tenure. The clan chiefs would meet and arrange the removal of such a chief by simply agreeing among themselves to recognize the clan chief who would ordinarily succeed the incumbent once the latter had served his term. No other action would be taken, but public sentiment would be so strong against the chief that he would abdicate.

The Village Chief functions as the ceremonial head for all of Hano. The welfare of the Tewa of Hano is his basic concern. He is supposed to watch over his people and to succor and protect them by means of prayers for rain and for physical well-being, and he is directly responsible for the proper performance of all ceremonies. The duties of Village Chief are considered sacred, and he as a person is not supposed to take an active part in disputes or quarrels.

The Winter Solstice ceremony, the most important of the Tewa ceremonies, is under the direction of the Village Chief. This is an annual gathering of all men of the clans belonging to that kiva. Formerly an altar was erected, and considerable ritual was associated with the ceremony (Stephen 1936: 39–41; 49–51), but today the ceremony is comparatively simple. An altar is no longer erected. It is reported that the last Winter Solstice Chief requested that all the Winter Solstice paraphernalia be buried with him. Informants relate that he was disturbed by the loss of knowledge of the proper performance of the ceremony and wanted the function discontinued after his death. Since learning the legends recited in the ceremony is extremely difficult, their disappearance is easy to understand.

The Winter Solstice ceremony has been briefly described in connection with the life cycle in the preceding section. A few remarks will be added here. On the final night of the ceremony, stories and clan legends are related. These tales recount the Hopi petition for Tewa aid and tell of the hardships the Tewa encountered after their arrival at Hopi. No Hopi are admitted to this ceremony, for the stories are definitely intended to malign their hosts. Many of the legends are sung as ballads. Those recited in Court Kiva differ in certain respects from those related in the Outside Kiva. The latter kiva has a number of war ballads which are their own unique possessions as a warrior group. The most characteristic feature of the dance that accompanies these songs is that the men form a circle while they sing and slowly dance around a single drummer. The formation and tempo of the songs are similar to those of the Plains Indian "circle" or "round dance" songs. At regular intervals the singers emit war whoops. The songs contain refrains that tell of Tewa bravery against the Utes, Navahos, Paiutes, and other neighboring nomadic Indian tribes, or recounts Tewa war magic, prowess, and the like.

Before the extinction of the Sun clan, a member of that clan functioned as Sun Watcher for all of Tewa Village. He was an assistant to the Village Chief in all important ceremonies, but also had his own duties. He was responsible for setting the time of all ceremonies in the annual Tewa cycle and for announcing the ceremonial dates to the village. His position was in certain respects analogous to that of the War Chief in the Outside Kiva. Both functioned as assistants and made announcements; the Sun Watcher announced items of a ceremonial nature, and the War Chief made known secular functions or instructions pertaining to war. The Hano Tewa now look to Walpi for the announcement of all important ceremonial dates.

The group of clans belonging to the Outside Kiva, although recognizing the ceremonial preeminence of the Court Kiva clans and accepting the Bear clan head as Village Chief, functions in many respects as a separate and distinct unit. The existence of this dual division at Hano has prompted an early student of the Hopi and Tewa (Parsons 1936: xliv–xlv), to speak of the situation as a survival of the New Mexico Tewa dual division or moiety system. The Hano kiva groupings are in fact similar to the moiety divisions of the New Mexico Tewa pueblos. Each group has a chief who functions separately and is said to be independent of the other. The Hano Tewa, like the New Mexico Tewa, also conduct two separate initiation rites, one for each group or moiety. The Hano Tewa organization, however, differs in that one group of clans—the Court Kiva group—is more important than the others, and the chief of the Court Kiva clans is the head of the whole village. At present, ceremonial and secular responsibilities are no longer transferred seasonally from one group to another as among the New Mexico Tewa. Parsons (1936: xlv), however, reports that seasonal transfer ceremonies were still being conducted in 1920.

It is important to remember that the Hano are a remnant group of the Southern Tewa; the Tewa still in New Mexico are the northern branch of the tribe (see Chapter 1). Thus, the differences that we note today between the two groups of Tewa may have already existed in the past rather than changed through contact with the Hopi.

Formerly, the Outside Kiva group consisted of the following clans: Fir, Earth, Cottonwood, and Cloud. The merging of the Fir clan and its alignment with the Central Plaza Kiva, however, leaves only three clans in the Outside Kiva. The chief of this group of clans for the last fifty years has been an Earth clansman, but his predecessor was a Cottonwood clansman (Parsons 1936: xliv). The chief of this group of clans rotated in the same manner as the position of the Village Chief among the clans of the Court Kiva group.

The functions of the Outside Kiva clans are ideally concerned with war and secular affairs. In general, these clans, with respect to the Court Kiva clans, occupy a position analogous to that of the whole of Hano with respect to Walpi. Thus the Outside Kiva clans are charged with the physical protection of the Court Kiva group. Members of the latter group are supposed to pray and go into retreat for a successful victory, but the Outside Kiva group is supposed to meet the enemy and engage it in battle. The assignment of "duties" to clans mentioned in the preceding section is a familiar Hopi custom. This concept may have been borrowed by the Hano Tewa; the duties are not assigned to individual clans, however, but to the two kiva groups.

The chief of the Outside Kiva group has an assistant called simply the War Chief, who is the head of the Cottonwood clan. Whether this position, like that of the Village Chief and the Outside Chief, also went in succession to a clansman of each of the member clans could not be conclusively validated; the reports of informants regarding the rotation of this office were conflicting and uncertain. The man who at present is the War Chief has been in so long that it seems unlikely that the position ever alternated among the four clans. The Outside Kiva Chief and the War Chief were responsible for the successful operation of a war and directed battle activities. The War Chief was charged with leading and directing periodic tribal hunts, and announced all cooperative enterprises such as the cleaning of springs, spinning parties, working parties, and the like, for the Village Chief. Maintenance of order and discipline in the village were also responsibilities of the War Chief.

The main responsibility of the Outside Kiva Chief, as with the Village Chief, is the Winter Solstice ceremony. This ceremony differs little from the ceremony in Court Kiva and is held at the same time. The Outside Kiva clans sing "war ballads"; the singing of these is considered their special prerogative. The Earth clan head, who today is the chief of the Outside Kiva group of clans, still erects his altar for this ceremony. Because the former Court Kiva Chief was buried with the Winter Solstice ceremony paraphernalia, as noted previously, the present Court Kiva Chief conducts a simple ceremony without an altar.

Kiva membership in either kiva is determined by a person's clan affiliation, but for men it is confirmed at the time of the Winter Solstice ceremony. At this ceremony, boys fourteen to eighteen years of age are formally inducted into the appropriate kiva.

Ownership of Tewa kivas, like that of the Hopi kivas, is ascribed to the clans that took the initiative in building them. The use of the kivas, however, is restricted to the clans believed to belong together. The Corn clan owns Court Kiva and the Earth clan owns the Outside Kiva. In any function for which the kiva is used, a member of the clan—usually a brother or uncle of the head clanswoman—that owns the particular kiva acts as caretaker. This man is also often referrred to as Kiva Chief but his job is to take care of the structure; his position is not a ceremonial office. This man receives the gifts of food that are brought by women to ceremonial participants. During the night Kachina dances he obtains an ear of corn from every troop of dancers and sprinkles sacred corn meal on all the participants. While a dance is in progress he periodically shouts approval and encouragement and may often request a performance to be repeated.

Associations and Ceremonies

THE KACHINA CULT   At once the most arresting and the most characteristic of Pueblo ceremonies are the Kachina rites. Everywhere among the Pueblos the Kachina cult is concerned with supernatural beings somewhat vaguely connected with ancestral spirits. These supernaturals are believed to have the power of bringing rain and general well-being to Pueblo communities if properly petitioned through ceremonies made as beautiful as possible and given joyously without ill feelings toward anyone or toward any aspect of the universe. There are many types of Kachina, some of animals and birds such as owl, eagle, bear, mountain sheep; others are identified by some characteristic aspect of their appearance: the Long-Beard Kachina, the Left-Handed Kachina, and so on; still others are called by the sounds they emit. There are more than

200 Kachina types among the Hopi and Tewa, but some dozen or so appear to be the most popular and are the most frequently represented in the dances. Only men impersonate the Kachina in the ceremonies; women are not permitted to don Kachina masks and costumes. Kachina dancers may be all of one kind, paired, or of mixed types. The number of dancers usually varies with the number of men in a particular kiva, the usual number being between twenty and thirty.

Kachinas are also represented as dolls made from cottonwood root. These wooden figurines are carved and painted in the likeness of the masked and costumed impersonations. At the ceremonies these dolls are given to little girls and are generally conceived to be symbolic of life—human, animal, and plant.

Until recently, the Kachina cult of Hano was quite different from that of the Hopi. Tewa Kachinas reputedly came from a mythological lake northeast of Hopi—that is, from the "original land of the Tewa." In contrast, the "home" of the Hopi Kachinas is in the San Francisco Peaks near Flagstaff, Arizona, west of the Hopi villages. Two members of the *Koyalah,* a ceremonial clown association, participated and "brought" the Kachina impersonators to each of the Hano kivas for a one-night ceremony. There were four such Kachina night ceremonies, spaced equally throughout the year. The first ceremony occurred sometime in December or January, the second in March or April, the third in July or August, and the fourth in October or November. Apparently the Hano Kachina ceremonies have been extinct so long that the names of the ceremonies and information regarding the clans or kiva groups responsible for their performance are hopelessly confused. The December or January Kachina ceremony was called *Kavenah,* and the July or August ceremony, *Suyukukwadih.* Parsons gives *Tiyogeo* as the name for the March ceremony and equates it with the Rio Grande seasonal transfer ceremony (Parsons 1936: xliv). My informants did not recognize the name given by Parsons, nor that it had reference to a "transfer"; they did, however, remember a Kachina ceremony celebrated in March or April. Parsons also reports an October seasonal transfer ceremony but does not give a name for it (Parsons 1936: xliv). This ceremony is apparently the fourth Kachina ceremony reported by my informants. I was unable to learn the names for the second and fourth Kachina ceremonies.

The original Hano Kachina cult and ceremonies are obsolete; Hano Kachina dances now follow the pattern of First Mesa as a whole and fit into the seasonal cycle directed by the Powamu association of Walpi. The Powamu association requires each of the Hano kivas to select a group of Kachina impersonators who perform first in their own kiva and then visit in turn all the other eight kivas on First Mesa (two at Hano, two at Sichomovi, five at Walpi). The present Kachina initiation rites, although performed by the Hano Court Kiva, are identical with those of the Hopi at Walpi, as far as my informants knew. All reported that both the present cult and initiations are recent; they did not know what took place in the earlier cult initiations, although they believed that they were quite different. Initiation into the Kachina cult, as presently practiced, has been described in Chapter 4 under Life Cycle.

THE CLOWN ASSOCIATION   The *Koyalah,* or clown association, of the Hano Tewa was apparently very much like the Rio Grande Tewa clown organization, the *Kosa.* Its part in the Kachina ceremony has been mentioned. In addition, the *Koyalah* appeared in several main dances, particularly courtyard dances in which large numbers participate, such as the basket or corn-grinding dances. During such a dance the clowns carried on side exhibitions for the amusement of spectators. By previous arrangement they often sought out individuals and carried them to the center of the plaza to ridicule them in view of all the spectators. The association is now extinct. Clown impersonators today, although still referred to as *Koyalah,* are appointed only for a particular occasion and do not comprise an association.

THE CURING ASSOCIATION   The *Sumakolih* is a curing association whose members wear masks like Kachina impersonators. The *Sumakolih,* now controlled by the Cloud clan, was formerly owned and managed by the extinct Sun clan. The association cures "sore eyes"; but any Tewa or even a Hopi from First Mesa may request the association to dance, either to effect a personal cure or to secure well being for the community in general. A ceremony is held in August or September, in which the association inducts new members. Members are drawn from both Hopi and Hano. Since the Cloud clan is virtually extinct, I was told that the association will probably die out with the death of the old Cloud clansman who is at present head of the association (see The Clan, Chapter 4).

In addition to the established association for curing, there are individual Hano shamans, or doctors. These have a good practice, not only at Hano but among the Hopi of all the mesas and the Navaho as well. Hano shamans are respected and renowned for their successful healing practices. Undoubtedly they have this reputation because of their Rio Grande Pueblo ancestry. Among these Indians curing receives a major emphasis in their ceremonial ritual.

RECRUITMENT OF ASSOCIATION MEMBERS   Members for Hano ceremonial associations are recruited in the same manner as for the Rio Grande Tewa associations: by vow of parents before the birth of a child, by vow of either a severely ill person or his parents, or by trespass into an area enclosed by a line of meal where the particular association has erected its altar for its annual or major ceremony. In addition, entrance may be purely voluntary, as among the Hopi. In each case a ceremonial sponsor is selected in the manner described in the preceding section.

OTHER CEREMONIAL ACTIVITIES   The Winter Solstice ceremony has already been discussed. Actually there are two such ceremonies, one in each kiva, conducted independently of the other, although they take place on the same day and coincide as well with the final night of the *Soyala,* or Winter Solstice ceremony of the Hopi at Walpi. Before the position of Sun Watcher lapsed, it is reported, the Tewa chose their own time to hold the solstice ceremonies, and this was not necessarily the same as the final night of the Hopi *Soyala.*

At any time during the year the chief of the Court Kiva or the chief of the Outside Kiva may gather the men of his kiva to engage in prayer-stick making, but this does not occur at any specified time in the annual cycle. Prayer sticks are made and deposited in order to bring rain or to insure good health. Such activities start in early morning and are usually finished by mid-afternoon, when the prayer sticks are taken by one or two men to be deposited in the various Hano shrines and in the springs that belong to the Tewa village.

Initiation

The initiation of Hano children into the Kachina cult is almost identical with that of the Hopi. All Hano Tewa are eventually initiated into the cult (see Life Cycle in Chapter 4). Only Court Kiva is empowered to conduct Kachina initiations; members of clans of the Outside Kiva must come to Court Kiva to be initiated.

Initiation, or induction, into the kiva group is uniquely Hano; the Hopi do not have kiva initiation. The initiation is only for men and is the closest approach the Hano Tewa have to the elaborate Hopi tribal initiation (see Titiev 1944: Chapter X). Hano kiva initiations suggest the moiety initiations of the New Mexico Tewa, but differ from them in certain essential features. Thus, the New Mexico Tewa moiety initiations are elaborate affairs and induct both men and women (Hill, in manuscript), whereas the Hano Tewa rites are simple rituals and are restricted to men. All Bear, Fir, Tobacco, and Corn clansmen between fourteen and eighteen years of age are inducted into Court Kiva; young men of corresponding ages belonging to the Earth, Cottonwood, and Cloud clans are inducted into the Outside Kiva. In early times the initiation may have been more complex (see Parsons 1926: 212), but today the initiates merely attend the final night of the Winter Solstice ceremony with their ceremonial fathers. The inductees receive a new name from their ceremonial fathers and may thereafter attend all important functions of their kiva.

Kachina and kiva initiations of the Hano Tewa appear to be reversed when compared with similar New Mexico Tewa ceremonies. Kachina initiations among the New Mexico Tewa are restricted to boys and occur sometime after the boy is fourteen years of age; moiety initiations, however, which confirm membership into one of two groups, induct children of both sexes of an age comparable to those of Hano children inducted into the Kachina cult.

The present Village Chief, from whom I obtained the major part of the information presented in this chapter, made the following statement about the present status of ceremonial life at Hano:

When the Sun clan people were still with us, Hano was like a separate pueblo. We were not bound by the ceremonial dictates of the Walpi leaders. Our Sun clan determined the position of the sun and the phases of the moon. Without recourse to Walpi we started our own prayer-stick making in the kivas and celebrated our private and public ceremonies separately from Walpi. It is true that in those days there was bad feeling between Hopi and Tewa, but we were strong then and we did not mind what the Hopi thought about us. Now I have to wait until the Walpi chief has announced Soyala [the Hopi Winter Solstice ceremony] before I can go into the kiva at the Hano Tewa Winter Solstice ceremony. This is true of all other ceremonies that we have—before we start them we must consult with Walpi. When I was a youth my grandmother and my granduncles used to tell me that the Hopi did not like us to hold separate ceremonies; they accused the Tewa of "playing around with their wives" while they were in retreat. When the Sun clan became extinct and the office of Sun Watcher disappeared with it, we had to give into the Hopi. Since that time we have been slowly losing our ceremonies, and my position as Hano village chief is no longer as important as it was in my grandparents' generation. My hands are bound; I can act in ceremonial matters only with the approval of the Walpi chief. We may all become Hopi some day, but I keep telling the young men at the Hano Tewa Winter Solstice ceremony what is my responsibility as Village Chief. That is, to impress upon all of us that we are Tewa and different from the Hopi and that we must always remember this. The young people do not take these things seriously, but it is my duty to tell them.

The dates of the major Hopi and Hano Tewa ceremonies are determined eight or sixteen days before the event occurs. The Hano chief is notified by Walpi leaders when he can start his ceremonies. Hence, in ceremonial affairs he is completely subordinated to Walpi religious authorities. It would seem, therefore, that with the disappearance of Hano ceremonial life, secular positions will become increasingly important. Indeed, the respect and prestige enjoyed by the Hano Tewa interpreter, a purely secular position, seems to justify such a prediction. Hopi ceremonial organizations have already made considerable headway into Hano society and will probably eventually displace the earlier system. First Mesa appears to be moving toward an integration that will be characterized by a rich Hopi ceremonialism and a high degree of political cohesion achieved through the secular interests of the Hano Tewa.

Social Dances

A diversity of dances not part of the Kachina cult and ceremonial associations are called "social dances" by both the Hopi and the Hano Tewa. These dances are open to the public, white and Indian, and are primarily secular. In fact, however, all Pueblo ceremonies have religious overtones, but some are more religious and esoteric than others. The rites of the Kachina cult and ceremonial associations, for example, are the most sacred, while the "social dances" are the most profane. Yet no Pueblo ceremony is completely serious and austere either; even the Kachina and association rites have humorous and entertainment aspects.

Social dances are of many types, but animal and war dances probably prevail. Some of these dances are obviously very old, going back to early Tewa-Plains contacts. Social dances are performed, as we have noted, primarily for entertainment; they also differ from the more esoteric rites in that novel forms are permitted and improvisations are constantly being introduced. Thus, traditonal Pueblo costumes have been modified with the addition of mirrors, sleigh bells, and colored feathers. The songs and dance steps retain basic Indian patterns, however, and Euro-American features are absent.

For arranging all the social dances for one year, excluding those in the regular ceremonial cycle, two men are chosen from each kiva group to act as supervisors. Their duties consist of collecting all the needed paraphernalia, choosing a drummer, selecting the girls who are to dance, and assisting the dancers to put on their costumes and make-up before each appearance. In addition, they see that the kiva is in proper order and that sufficient wood is brought to keep the place warm for rehearsals and for the final day of the dance.

A dance of the New Mexico Tewa called *panchale,* "prisoner's dance," has become increasingly popular on First Mesa in recent years. *Panchale* has apparently no religious significance. It has some resemblance to white American social dancing, but the New Mexico Tewa claim that it is old and native with them. Boys choose girls (sometimes there are "lady's choice" dances as well!), and about ten or more couples dance to the beat of a drum and a chorus of singers. A song and dance has several sets similar to the Virginia reel. One complete dance with its series of variations lasts for about fifteen minutes. The tempo is lively and a round of dancing leaves the young dancers breathless and flushed.

I was told that the Hopi objected to the dance when it was introduced, about twenty years ago, on the ground that it was "not Indian!" Panchale is extremely popular on First Mesa today, however, although it is not danced during the Kachina season and, so far as I know, it is danced nowhere else on the Hopi reservation but at Hano. Young Hopi and Hano boys and girls are enthusiastic about Panchale and come from other villages to join in.

Beliefs and Values

The Hano Tewa hold a world view generally characteristic of all the Pueblos. This is the premise that man and the universe are in a kind of balance and that all things are interrelated. There is no dichotomy between good and bad; evil is simply a disturbance in the equilibrium which exists between man and the universe. The activity world of man, of the natural environment of plants and animals; the inanimate world of earth, rocks, and dead vegetable matter; the ethereal world of wind, clouds, rain, and snow; even the "thought world" of human beings are all believed to be in a state of balance. The activity world is one of cooperative helpfulness; everyone works for the good of the whole. Individual subordination to group effort is believed to be an essential part of maintaining balance in the universe. Logically the "thought world" is a happy one, free of ill feeling or hostile attitudes toward any aspect of the universe. Illness, prolonged drought conditions, famines, and all other misfortunes are believed to occur as the result of a disturbance in the orderly nature of the universe.

Unfortunate happenings come, in the Pueblo Indian's belief, not as a punishment or retaliation by a supreme being or beings, but because of a break in the interrelatedness of the universe. Man alone can disturb the orderliness and harmonious balance of the universe. He may break it by ill feeling toward another, or toward a number of individuals; indeed, even by disliking or perceiving ugliness in some aspect of the universe. He may do so by taking more food than is necessary for sustenance, or by not being generous in sharing and giving what he has, He may break the balance by killing more game than is essential to supply himself and his relatives with food or by taking more clay or more pigment than is necessary to make needed pottery vessels.

Not only must man use sparingly of the food and material resources of the universe but he is required to reciprocate by appropriate propitiatory rites. These range all the way from offering corn meal, corn pollen, prayer feathers, and prayer sticks to elaborate ceremonial dances made "as beautiful as possible" and participated in by the whole village.

The importance of ceremonies as propitiatory rites to effect well-being and bring much needed moisture to parched lands is well known to students of Pueblo culture (cf. Haeberlin 1916). The associated and essential requisites of cooperative effort and a happy state of mind, however, have generally been ignored. It is significant, therefore, that as early as 1912 an anthropologist made the following insightful observation: "The assertion is made [by the Pueblos]: 'It will rain; we are happy; it will rain; we are dancing; we are dancing; it will rain.' Cause and effect are hardly differentiated. Let us hope all people are happy, but let us make sure that they are dancing." (Aitken 1930: 382)

The Pueblo individual examines his thoughts and attitudes to make sure that he is in a "happy state of mind," but he is also concerned with the actions and thoughts of his fellow man. If he is satisfied with his actions and his state of mind and still misfortunes and illness persist, then he is ready to cast blame on someone else. Hence, the constant surveillance of the behavior of one's neighbors, even of close relatives. Since an individual's misbehavior brings misfortune not only to himself but to the group as a whole, all members of one society are suspect until the guilty one is discovered. During disease epidemics, crop failures, and drought conditions Pueblo villages are fear-ridden communities. Pueblo authorities watch closely the behavior of village members to determine the culprit or "witch." Gossip and accusations of witchcraft run rampant in the village as a whole. The lot of the individual who cannot account for curious or deviant behavior is extremely grave. If his behavior remains peculiar and misfortunes persist, he falls prey to the community. Traditional sanctions of ridicule and witchcraft accusations make his life miserable. In extreme cases he may be banished from the village (see Chapter 4, Social Control).

There is no evidence that Hano itself was ever an anxiety-ridden community or that it was ever rent with internal strife. The Tewa of Hano appear to have taken over the more positive aspects of the Pueblo world view, while their more outgoing personality characteristics and their marginal position with respect to the total Hopi society have prevented the development of intravillage suspicions and conflicts. The Hopi as convenient scapegoats also helped to drain off the hostilities that might have been turned destructively toward their fellow Tewans.

Ritual Activities

Since the Hano Tewa have permitted many of their own ritual activities to lapse, they now cooperate in various ways to keep First Mesa Hopi ceremonies operating efficiently within the annual ceremonial calendar. However, only in terms of the Kachina cult, which is organized, like that of the Hopi, in kiva groups, do the Tewa actually participate in Hopi ceremonial life. As participants in the Kachina cult, the Tewa are wholly under the direction and supervision of the Powamu association. Although the Tewa are permitted to choose the Kachina characters they impersonate, they must synchronize their performances to correspond with those of all the other kiva groups on First Mesa. There are nine kivas on First Mesa, including those of Tewa Village, and each has a Kachina group. Each kiva group presents its own dance without consulting any of the other groups; indeed, it is part of the show to keep the audience in suspense until the moment the troupe comes down the kiva ladder. Spectators go into any one of the nine First Mesa kivas—usually the one nearest to home—to see all nine performances, since each kiva group starts in its own kiva and then visits all the other eight kivas successively. In February and March, Kachina performances are held inside the kiva and occur weekly on Saturday nights. Saturday night Kachina dances are a recent adjustment made necessary by off-reservation employment and boarding schools. From April until the end of the Kachina season (in July), the dances are less frequent and are usually given outdoors in the village courtyard.

The Niman, a Hopi ceremony, occurs in mid- or late July and marks the return of the Kachina to their home in the San Francisco Mountains, according to Hopi belief. During the rest of the year until the following Powamu, no masked or Kachina dances are permitted by the Hopi. In the past the Tewa frequently violated this mandate and provoked much ill feeling. There are still occasional infractions by the Tewa, such as the appearance of the Shumakoli Kachina in August or September and an occasional "social dance" in the Kachina season, when such dances are prohibited. But such violations are becoming less frequent with the loss of strictly Tewa ceremonies and the increasing desire of the Tewa to cooperate with the Hopi and to appear favorably in their eyes.

The end of the First Mesa Kachina season terminates the direct participation of the Tewa in ceremonial activities. During the rest of the year the Tewa assist the Hopi with their ceremonies and act as hosts along with their neighbors for all visitors to First Mesa. Tewa women work industriously in the preparation of food for their Hopi husbands and for other Hopi relatives who are actively engaged in these ceremonies. The men perform various services for their Hopi kinsmen. All share in the festive occasions and open their houses to all visitors.

During that part of the year when Kachina dances are forbidden and the Kachina are reportedly away in the San Francisco Peaks, the Tewa give frequent social dances in which only a small group of unmarried men and women usually participate. Many of the dances have been borrowed from other tribes, usually from the Rio Grande Tewa, and in these the war theme is frequently introduced. As the dancers emerge from the kiva, Plains war-dance songs are sung, and the War Chief dons his best war costume and periodically emits an ear-splitting war whoop. The men also try to appear like their Rio Grande Tewa kinsmen by braiding their hair or by wearing false braids. Today, many New Mexico Tewa journey to Hopi in order to teach the Hano Tewa new songs and dances and to appear with them in the dances. The Hano Tewa in turn make frequent visits to the Rio Grande Pueblo area.

Summary

Before 1900 the Tewa and Hopi were pronouncedly distinct in ceremonial organization. The present kiva organization, association, and ceremonial ritual, despite surface similarities, indicate differences that were undoubtedly sharper at an earlier period. Initiation into the Kachina cult now, however, is almost identical with that of the Hopi. Apparently with the disappearance of their own Kachina cult, the Tewa have adopted the Kachina practices of the Hopi. Adaptation to the Hopi Kachina cycle seems to have completely replaced the earlier cult and the ceremonial cycle consonant with it. Kiva initiations, however, remain uniquely Hano. They resemble the Rio Grande Tewa moiety initiations on the one hand, and the Hopi tribal initiations on the other. The elaborate ritual practices of both New Mexico Tewa and Hopi, however, contrast sharply with the simple, one-night ceremony of the Hano Tewa.

The Hano world view is typically Pueblo, but the suspicions and intra-village bickering so characteristic of Hopi and other Pueblo Indians are virtually absent at Hano. As a minority group and with the Hopi as scapegoats Tewa hostilities have been largely directed outside the village.

The adjustment of religious institutions and concepts to Hopi counterparts appears to be the most important characteristic of the Tewa at present. Hano participates wholeheartedly in the first Mesa Kachina cycle. At other times of the year they engage enthusiastically in social dances. Although they rarely join Hopi associations, they cooperate with the Hopi in all their ceremonial activities and, with their neighbors, act as hosts to all visitors.

6

Livelihood

HE MOST CHARACTERISTIC ASPECT of Hano and Hopi economics is the exchange system—the method by which food, services, and certain types of goods are exchanged. These practices link all of the peoples on First Mesa and at times involve Hopi from more distant villages as well. The system operates within the household, clan, linked clans, kiva groups, and between the three communities on First Mesa. Exchanges occur on specific occasions in an individual's life cycle (puberty, entrance into a ceremonial association, and at marriage), and are an integral part of every ceremonial rite. These practices have prevented economic stratification; the Hopi and Tewa population is essentially on an equal economic footing. In addition to this economic leveling effect, these activities have contributed to the increasing trend toward social and cultural integration on First Mesa. This section will attempt to reveal the nature of these exchange practices and to expose the characteristics of the economic system generally.

Economic Pursuits

The Tewa of Hano, like their Hopi neighbors, are still basically horticulturists. Livestock and wage work, however, have become increasingly important in recent years. These economic activities are potential threats to the integrity of the clan structure and may eventually result in social reorganization. At present, however, the Tewa, as well as the Hopi of First Mesa generally, are handling the new economic pursuits largely in terms of traditional experience. Sharing of work and food has helped to prevent the segmentation of the society into nuclear family units. Although a family that has wage workers or sheep and cattle may live as a nuclear family for long periods, it reverts to extended-family living and assumes clan responsibilities once it is back at Hano. These fluctuations between nuclear-family and extended-household living and the participation in clan responsibilities and privileges occur with great frequency. With families owning sheep and cattle, these fluctuations are usually seasonal: nuclear-family living in the summer, extended-household living in the winter. The families who are engaged in wage work in Keams Canyon revert to extended-household living on week-ends. The rich Hopi and Tewa social and ceremonial cycle also brings back nuclear-family units to participate as extended-household units and to resume clan duties and responsibilities.

Land

Land is the most important possession of the Tewa and Hopi. The Tewa report that in exchange for the services they rendered as "warriors" and "protectors" of the Hopi on First Mesa they were given lands extending northward from this mesa. According to the Tewa, one of the primary inducements for coming to Hopi was the offer of assertedly productive land. Old men relate that their forefathers were deceived by the Hopi. The land was poor and no amount of hard work could make it produce the crops they were promised. Their storehouses were often empty, and they suffered through the drought-stricken years. But the Tewa, like the Hopi, learned to overcome the rigors of the environment.

The Hopi country poses many difficult problems for farming. Only by ingenious and ardous methods of planting and caring for their growing crops have the Hopi and Tewa garnered a living from the land (*cf.* Stewart 1940). The rainfall is scant, averaging only about ten inches per year. The altitude of 6000 to 6500 feet brings early and late frosts that limit the growing season to barely three months. In July and August sudden cloudbursts are common and cause considerable damage. To insure a crop against these odds, a Tewa or Hopi farmer plants two or three fields, which he chooses with great care. Kirk Bryan's observation of Hopi-planted fields is applicable to Tewa farming practices:

> The areas utilized are variable in size and location, but each is chosen so that the local rainfall may be reinforced by the overflow of water derived from higher ground. The selection of a field involves an intimate knowledge of local conditions. The field must be flooded, but the sheet of water must not attain such velocity as to wash out the crop nor carry such a load of detritus as to bury the growing plants. Such conditions require a nice balance of forces that occur only under special conditions. Shrewd observation and good judgment are necessary in the selection of fields. (Byron 1929: 445)

Ownership and Inheritance

There have been some changes recently in ownership and inheritance. These changes are due to modern conditions; cash income from livestock sales and wage work have increased individual property. Formerly a man had only a few possessions he could call his own; now he often has money and buys numerous articles. Property acquired by a man in this way is usually inherited by his sons or is specifically transmitted to certain persons before his death. Despite these changes, however, the basic pattern of earlier times still continues with respect to the ownership and inheritance of land and houses.

Land originally assigned to the Tewa has been divided into clan plots which are set off by stone symbols marked to represent the various clans and placed along sight lines. Within a clan plot, the mother of each family has several fields at her disposal. When her daughters marry, a woman gives each of them one or more plots of land, or parts of several. Upon her death, female matrilineal relatives assume control of the land, the direct descendants having prior claim. The question of disposal of lands to married daughters has often little practical importance, since the daughters continue to live in the house and with the family of the mother.

Men have no right to ownership or inheritance of land; they work it, however. When a man marries, he relinquishes his right to work on his own clan lands and works his wife's. Before he marries, a young man works on his own clan lands, and he may return to them in the event of a separation or divorce. The farm hands in a typical Hano extended household include a woman's father, her unmarried maternal uncles, her bachelor brothers, her husband, her unmarried sons, and the husbands of her sisters. This is, of course, not true in households where wage work and/or livestock activities are of major importance; in these the number of men engaged in horticultural activities is much smaller.

Houses and household equipment, like land, are owned and inherited in the female line within the household and lineage. A woman may give certain sections of her house for the use of one of her daughters when she marries, or, with the help of men of her family—her husband, brothers, sons—she may erect a new house for the couple, or an addition to the old one; or she may simply receive her son-in-law into her own house. All the furnishings and equipment within a house also belong to the senior woman of the household; a man owns only the clothes and jewelry that are on his person.

In contrast to the land and the houses, horses, cattle, and sheep are generally the property of men. When a man marries or divorces, he takes his own personal flock or herd with him. The care of sheep and care of cattle are male occupations. Although a woman may often inherit or acquire shares in flocks, her husband or one of her male relatives is given the task of caring for them.

Wage Work, Livestock, and Horticulture

Before wage work, livestock, and horticultural activities are discussed, it is important to realize the cooperative nature of the communities on First Mesa. Marriage and kinship ties and the economic responsibilities involved in these relationships interrelate all of the three villages. The conventional economic analysis, liberally supplied with statistical tables indicating per capita or family incomes, may have meaning in our society but blur the true economic picture of a highly cooperative society such as that of the Hopi and Tewa.

Most of the Tewa wage income derives from employment at the Hopi Agency in Keams Canyon, twelve miles from First Mesa. During the period of intensive fieldwork (1950–51) the total cash income from government employment for Hano was $58,500. Livestock sales netted another $22,100. In addition, there were other sources of cash income such as nongovernment employment, compensations to servicemen's dependents, Social Security benefits, relief obtained from the Indian Service, and arts and crafts (particularly pottery) amounting to an additional $20,000. The total annual income amounted roughly to $100,000 in 1950–1951. The table below summarizes the economic activities of persons nineteen years of age and above, and thus indicates those individuals bringing in cash income and those contributing to subsistence. The population of Hano at this time was 405 individuals including those resident on the reservation as well as the few living off the reservation (the present population is about 500; compare Dozier 1954: 287).

The cash income figures distort the true economic situation on First Mesa by de-emphasizing the role of horticulture and the importance of the economic exchange practices. As cash income horticulture is negligible, but Tewa and Hopi crops still furnish the basic subsistence for the people. In addition to its economic importance, the central position of horticulture among these three villages is revealed by the cutoms and activities of the people. Ritually, these pueblos revolve around horticulture. All ceremonies have as their main theme the propitiation of the spirits so that they will make the crops bountiful. It is not only in religion, however, but also in secular activities that horticulture is stressed. From spring to fall the Tewa and Hopi are in the fields working to produce crops from an inhospitable environment. Harvest time is a period of feasting and gaiety. Everyone is happy and all generously exchange and share in the fruits of the land.

The table shows that more than one-half of the employable persons are still engaged in horticulture or in handicrafts (115 out of 203). The 88 livestock owners and wage workers are also, of course, periodically occupied with farming, and all share in the farm produce. It is important to point out that there is a great deal of overlap in economic activity; that is, almost all men work for wages periodically and/or have sheep and cattle. All women make pottery and do housework; in addition, many of them work occasionally for the government. The table thus lists only *primary* economic activities. However, when involvement in traditional economic activities is considered, it is evident that horticulture is still basic to the Tewa.

Cooperative Enterprises

Income figures, it must be repeated, do not give us the complete economic situation at Hano or on First Mesa. It is essential to describe the intricate exchange and cooperative activities of these people in order to understand Tewa and Hopi economics.

The household functions constantly as an economic unit; its members as-

PRIMARY ECONOMIC ACTIVITIES OF EMPLOYABLE PERSONS
(Ages nineteen years and above, except the very old)

	Primary Economic Activity	Men	Women	Totals
	Livestock owners	43	0	43
Cash Operation	Government employment	25	2	27
	Employed off reservation	10	8	18
	Totals	78	10	88
	Farming at Parker*	7	6	13
	Horticulture on reservation	50	0	50
	Handicraft (pottery, tanning, weaving)	25	27	52
	Totals	82	33	115
	Total engaged			203

* Parker, Arizona—an area of irrigated farmlands on the Colorado River recently made available to Hopi, Navaho and other Southwestern Indians.

Source: Data compiled during fieldwork; see Dozier 1954:359.

sist one another in daily duties and see that all are properly fed and clothed. Food sharing and the exchange of services in larger units of the society operate in relation to the social and ceremonial functions which occur with remarkable frequency and regularity. A quick review of such functions that occurred in 1950 is worthwhile here. In the month of January there were seven weddings and two social dances; from February to May there were weekly Kachina dances. June and July were busy months in the field; but there was one social dance and a water-spring cleaning operation in June, and in mid-July the Tewa joined the Hopi with their Niman festivities. August was an occasion for another social dance, two more weddings, and the Hopi Snake Dance. In September and October the Tewa were busy with harvest; but a Shumakoli ceremony was celebrated in mid-September, and in late October the complex tribal initiation ceremonies began at Walpi.

Social and ceremonial functions have a leveling effect and prevent the segmentation of the population into rich and poor. Money as such is not contributed or divided; it is food—including tobacco and cigarettes—that is distributed. This food is either home grown (that is, farm produce and livestock products) or it is bought in trading posts or off-reservation towns for the purpose of distribution. Tewa culture prescribes that everyone should give generously, and the givers expend much effort to donate large amounts. Since production and income derived from wage work, livestock, handicrafts, and other sources vary among the households, the amount of food given is not the same from each household. Division of the food among the receivers, however is equal and this has a leveling effect. The kind of social or ceremonial function determines who is to give and who is to receive. In certain functions—a wedding, for example—those benefiting from food gifts are essentially restricted to the bridegroom's clan and linked clans, whereas the givers are mainly members of the bride's clan and linked clans. At a wedding, however, the bride's garments are woven and furnished by the groom's relatives. In a kiva group ceremony, such as a social dance or a Kachina dance, the members of the group of clans that belong to the particular kiva sponsoring the ceremony are both givers and receivers. Such a function operates in the following manner. Women belonging to these clans carry the food to the kiva, and the men of the clans receive it. The food is divided equally by the kiva chief and his assistants among all the men participating in the ceremony. When the food has been divided, it is taken by the men to their respective households. A man will thus take back some of the food contributed by members of his own household, but he will also have some of the food contributed by all the other households. Hence, a variety of food products is taken back. As a rule, those households contributing more will receive less, and those giving little will receive more.

Ceremonial functions in larger units operate in much the same manner as has been outlined above for the kiva groups, Food in cooperative operations of this sort is also contributed by women and is divided equally in the kiva or kivas by the men and taken back to their respective households when the ceremonies are over.

In connection with these cooperative enterprises, work has to be done. The givers buy groceries, butcher cattle and sheep, prepare food, and carry it to the kivas. The receivers are also constantly working either in prayer or in the many tasks required to make the particular ceremony successful. All such work is done cooperatively, with gaiety and good fellowship.

The sharing of food and exchange of services, as noted previously, operates through specific social and ceremonial customs in a hierarchy of units: household, clan, kiva group, community, and the whole of First Mesa. Illustrations of the kind of activity involved in each one of these cooperative enterprises is described in the following pages. The household, though not dependent on social and ceremonial functions, is described first because it is the crucial economic unit.

HOUSEHOLD SHARING AND EXCHANGE   I have selected one more or less typical unit to illustrate food sharing and the exchange of services within the household. This household belongs to the Corn clan and consists of an old Tewa couple, their two daughters who are married to Hopi men, and their children. The relationship is shown in the following figure; the names used are fictitious.

This extended family lives separately in three family units for indefinite periods: Paul and Edith, the old couple, live by themselves in an old house at Hano; Marie, their younger daughter, and her husband, Peter, and their children live in a separate house, also at Hano; and the older daughter, Jane, who works at the Hopi Indian Agency, lives with her husband, John, and their children in government quarters at Keams Canyon. In the summertime Paul and Edith move to their ranch house, where Paul tends his sheep and cattle, assisted

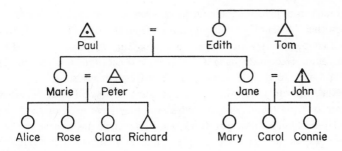

O △ Tewa Corn clan

△ A different Tewa clan

△ A Hopi clan

△ A second Hopi clan

A Tewa Household.

Tom is married to a Walpi woman and belongs to a different household; he has no economic relations in his sister's household. He frequently visits his sister, however, and she consults with him in important ritual matters and refers to him all difficult cases of disciplining her children and grandchildren.

by Edith's brother, Tom, and often by other male members of the Corn clan. Two or more of the grandchildren are usually with the old couple on the ranch.

In the summertime the nuclear family of the two daughters is thus reduced, with some of their children living on the ranch of the old couple. The younger daughter remains on the mesa top with her young children; the older daughter continues with her regular job at Keams Canyon, assisted in household chores by her older daughter, while her younger daughters spend the summer at the ranch.

During the summer months John and Peter, Jane's and Marie's husbands, respectively, farm a portion of the Corn clan lands belonging to their mother-in-law, Edith. Paul, when not busy with his cattle and sheep, gives his sons-in-law a hand with their farming activities, and in return they often help him with his livestock. John and Peter are also occasionally employed by the government and thus contribute a sporadic cash income. Both Hopi husbands also help their own Hopi clan relatives who own cattle and sheep.

In the winter the situation changes somewhat. Although Keams Canyon is twelve miles from First Mesa, Jane comes with her husband and children every week-end to spend Saturday and Sunday with her parents. Since Marie and Peter and their children live at Hano, they are constantly visiting with the old couple and exchanging services with them. In winter, as in the summer, the Hopi men are periodically on the government payroll. John works irregularly as a stonemason, and Peter occasionally works for the Indian Agency as a day laborer. John and Peter have no cattle and sheep, but some of their clansfolk have some, and John and Peter often assist them in herding activities.

Marie and Jane on their frequent visits to their parents bring food, either from their stores of garden produce or from the trading posts. Both daughters work cooperatively with their mother—cooking, grinding corn, and the like. The old couple frequently slaughter a sheep and occasionally a calf or cow, and portion the meat to their daughters on their frequent visits.

Paul, the old man, owns a wagon and a team of horses. The team and wagon are used by the sons-in-law whenever they have need of them. Recently Jane and John bought a pick-up truck, and the vehicle has to a large extent displaced the wagon and team. Since Jane is regularly employed at Keams Canyon, she made the initial down-payment on the truck, I was told, and John and Peter helped her on the monthly payments. Paul drives a car, and until he became blind about a year ago, he used the truck as much as John. At the present time the old couple ask one of their sons-in-law to drive for them whenever they wish to go anywhere. Peter uses the truck for transporting his immediate family or for performing services for the benefit of the extended household. I was told that the person using the car at a given time is supposed to pay for gas and oil and for light repairs; for major repairs a contribution is taken from all adult members of the household. Hopi and Tewa give their cars rough treatment. The farms and ranches to which they travel most frequently are situated in remote areas, and roads are extremely bad. During the initial phases of my study when I lived in one of the Tewa households, my 1949 jeep station wagon became household property, and since none of the members could drive, I was the chauffeur. I hauled sheep, calves, and wood in my car and transported members of the household to various parts of the reservation, and on several occasions to the off-reservation towns of Gallup, Holbrook, and Winslow.

The major portion of daily interaction, sharing, and cooperation goes on within the household unit. In social and ceremonial functions embracing larger units, activity is initiated within the household but is intricately fitted into the larger cooperating units, whether clan, kiva group, community, or intervillage.

CLAN AND LINKED CLAN SHARING AND EXCHANGE   The clan and its linked clans (see Chapter 5) function as economic cooperative units in many social and ceremonial functions. For an illustration of the activities in such an interacting unit, a wedding has been selected. A wedding is primarily a social event, but like all other activities of the Hopi and Tewa, it also has ceremonial features.

The Wedding to be discussed is one between a Tewa Cottonwood girl and a Hopi Butterfly boy which took place in January 1950. The boy had been secretly courting the girl, and presumably had been having sexual relations with her. (The boys sneak out together, and each meets his sweetheart at a secret rendezvous or at her house after her family is asleep.) Sanction of the marriage was obtained when the girl took up residence with the boy's family at Sichomovi and was permitted to stay. Immediately she began to grind corn in a darkened corn-grinding room. Theoretically she was supposed to grind corn for three days and four nights by herself, but actually all her clanswomen assisted. Not only did the women of her own Cottonwood clan help, but also those of the Hopi Kachina clan, which the Hopi consider related to that clan. These women ground corn in their own homes and brought it to her and also assisted her in the darkened room, in which she remained the traditional four-day and four-night period.

In the meantime the boy's male relatives on both his father's and his mother's side prepared the girl's wedding garments; these consisted of a belt, robe, dress, and moccasins. These items of clothing are the only contributions made by the boy's relatives; all of the other gifts are contributed by the girl's relatives.

While the girl was grinding corn, the men of the girl's clan and linked clans brought food to the bridegroom's house; during this four-day period they slaughtered sheep and cattle, brought firewood, and helped the women carry the food. A special room, about 15 by 20 feet, was set aside to hold the food gifts. At the end of the four days the room was entirely filled with food—basins of stew, roasted meats, stewed peaches, yellow corn-meal cakes, sugar-frosted baked cakes, pies, and other foods covered the entire floor space; sacks of wheat flour were piled almost to the ceiling against one wall; on the opposite side, piki was stacked like cordwood halfway up to the ceiling. On the last day, when most of the food was brought in, five pick-up trucks drove into the plaza in front of the bridegroom's house and unloaded enormous trays of corn meal. Each truck contained about a dozen trays, approximately fifteen to twenty inches in diameter, heaped with tightly compacted corn meal to a height of two feet or more. Large flour-sack cloths were tied about the trays to protect the corn meal. Some trays were so heavy that it required three or more men to lift and carry them.

The food brought by the girl's family was shared by the clansfolk of the bridegroom and also by those of the linked Badger clan. On the evening of the fourth day all the women of these clans visited the boy's house and were given large quantities of food to take home with them, each woman receiving an approximately equal amount.

KIVA GROUP SHARING AND EXCHANGE   In certain social and ceremonial functions the unit of cooperative activity is the kiva group, that is, the clans belonging to one of the two Hano kivas. These functions occur with less frequency than clan-phratry functions but are similar cooperative affairs, differing only in that more people take part in them. The activities that characterize kiva group enterprises will be illustrated by a discussion of a social dance.

On June 24, 1950, a *Yandewa* dance was given by members of Court Kiva at Hano. For a whole month previously, however, preparations and rehearsals had been under way. The Yandewa is a colorful dance originally borrowed from Santa Clara Pueblo. There are four dancers in each of eight courtyard appearances—two young men and two girls—thirty-two dancers in all. All the men belonging to the clans of the kiva join in the chorus and help in many other ways inside the kiva. For this occasion I made a trip to Santa Clara Pueblo (a Tewa village in New Mexico) and brought back with me three men from this village. As honored guests we were permitted to watch all the preparations for the dance inside the kiva.

Twice during the day of the dance, first at midday and again in late afternoon, all the adult women of the clans that belong to Court Kiva—Bear, Corn, Tobacco, Fir—brought in enormous quantities of food. On each occasion the kiva chief distributed the food equally among all those present in the kiva. My share was two washtubs of bread, crackers, candy, piki bread, and various other foods. In addition, there were large quantities of prepared foods in bowls and pans such as stews, roasted meats, jerky (sun-dried strips of beef), corn-meal gruel, and the like. The prepared foods were also divided as equally as possible among the men. After each "giving," the men carried their portions of the food to their respective homes. I presented my share to my hosts at Hano.

COMMUNITY SHARING AND EXCHANGE   Cooperative enterprises that are essentially communal include hunting, planting, harvesting, cleaning springs, and gathering firewood for the kivas. Such enterprises are initiated by one of the men; they are announced by the War Chief and are participated in by all able-bodied men, while the women grind corn and cook to feed the whole community. After such an enterprise, the men gather in the kiva to offer thanksgiving or to put on a social dance, and the food is given and shared, as described above, for the Yandewa. Each man, with his share of food, then returns to his own household.

The following account of the general requirements and procedure of a working party (cf. Parsons 1925: 112–115) was related to me by one of my Tewa informants:

> Whenever a man decides to have a working party he asks permission from the Village Chief. The petition is made by presenting the chief with a basket or bowl of corn meal. If the chief accepts the meal the petitioner starts preparations right away. He makes several prayer feathers and abstains from meat and salt for four days. During this time he must not sleep with his wife. At the end of four days he asks the War Chief to announce the working party to the whole village. The petitioner then supervises the work, but he is assisted by all of his clanspeople and his paternal aunts [i.e., women of his father's clan]. All those men who are not actively engaged in the work are put to other tasks. Some of the men must go for firewood, others for water and cattle. Women and girls must grind corn and prepare food to feed not only the men actively engaged in the working party but the entire village. Everyone helps to make the working party a success. While working all the people are happy; jokes and stories are told so that work becomes like play. Later there is a dance given by the kiva groups, and everyone goes home loaded with food.

INTERVILLAGE SHARING AND EXCHANGE   First Mesa Hopi ceremonies of major importance, such as the tribal initiation which occurs in certain years in November, the Powamu ceremony in February, the Niman in July, and the Snake Dance in August, are occasions in which all three villages cooperate. Only a few Tewa are active participants in Hopi ceremonies, but marriage ties with the Hopi relate them to participants in these ceremonies. Tewa women are thus as active as Hopi women in preparing and buying food to be taken to the men who are participating in the ceremonies. Tewa men are busy butchering, hauling wood, and making food supplies available for the women. Teams and wagons, and more recently, automobiles are put to use to assist in the transportation of foodstuffs. The contributed food is taken to the Walpi kivas in which these ceremonies take place; division and disposal of the food operates in the manner described for kiva group ceremonials above. The day of the dance is given over to elaborate feasting, every home setting out food for guests from other Hopi villages and for Indian visitors from other tribes. In recent years special white friends have also been honored as guests. The festive spirit and cooperative activity of the people of First Mesa in a major ceremonial is an impressive sight.

TRADING PARTIES   Another cooperative activity of First Mesa villages is the trading party. This activity is initiated by a household and is open to anyone in the three villages; indeed, visitors, Indian or white, may participate. My wife was a frequent "trader" during our residence at Polacca. Trading parties occur with great frequency, "about two or three times a month," my hostess reported.

Most of the participants are women, though men are not barred. Men are supposed to contribute game, and when I appeared for the first time at a trading party, the women greeted me in a chorus: "Where is your deer meat; where are your rabbits?" But they took the cigarettes, soft drinks, and wheat flour I brought, and I received in return hot tamales, piki, and doughnuts.

The trading party is held outdoors, in front of the house of the family that initiates it. The food, clothing, and other articles brought by those participating are spread out on the ground, while the "traders" stand around in a circle. The articles brought to be traded are extremely varied. I have seen chinaware, shoes, overalls, and toys (bought in town), along with the more common items such as Hopi pottery and baskets, piki, oven-baked bread, meat stews, cakes, pies, and wheat and corn flour.

There is very little bargaining at a trading party. Hopi and Tewa trade in a friendly, noncompetitive fashion. A "trader" walks to the article that catches his fancy, finds out who the owner is, and then trading is conducted between the two people. The food or goods traded are generally those displayed; but if a person who wishes an article does not have an item at hand which the owner wants in exchange, she may mention a number of articles at home which she is willing to give for the desired article. Exchanges are made in the most agreeable and friendly manner. I saw no attempts "to drive a hard bargain." The people seem to have no notion of getting more for an item, or one of a better quality, in exchange. When I asked my hostess why the trading parties were so popular, she replied:

Because we have a good time; we joke, laugh, and tease each other when we trade. In the evening we return home with a variety of things. Some people don't have meat, others have no flour, or piki, or cigarettes; we trade and everybody gets the things they want.

Summary

It is evident that while horticulture is still basic in Hano economy, wage work and livestock have come to form a very important part of their economic system. At present the social organization of Hano is still operating chiefly in terms of the traditional patterns of the extended-household and clan structures. A number of factors have brought about this situation. First, livestock and wage-work activities, particularly the latter, are recent innovations. Secondly, modern transportation facilities have made possible frequent resumptions of extended-household living and interaction in terms of clans and linked clans. Thirdly, the satisfaction derived from the extended household and clan and the rich ceremonial life of community living have not been matched elsewhere.

The exchange system operating in a hierarchy of social units has prevented pronounced differences in the economic standing of Tewa families and generally of the families in all three communities on First Mesa. These practices are remarkably strong and complex and indicate continuity into the future, despite modern pressures. The cooperation of Tewa and Hopi in these functions points to greater cohesion in the future, thus minimizing social barriers between the two groups and working toward a coalescence of First Mesa society.

7

Perspective and Outlook

MIGRANTS to the Hopi country, the Tewa established their village within calling distance of the nearest Hopi community. For a long time they persisted in maintaining cultural and linguistic distinction from their neighbors. Recently these barriers appear to have been lifted and a trend toward assimilation established. In this study the present community has been described in the context of Hopi society and culture and with reference to the social and cultural patterns of their ancestors, the New Mexico Tewa. The accommodating devices for and against assimilation have been explored and possible reasons for this situation have been suggested. In these final pages, I will only speculate briefly about the destiny of this Tewa community.

It is difficult to isolate aspects of Hano society and culture that may be unique to the group since affinities to both New Mexico Tewa and Hopi appear in all areas. There is one aspect, however, in which the Tewa seem to differ from both Hopi and New Mexico Tewa; this is in the realm of personality. The Hano Tewa appear to be more aggressive, and more willing to accept white ways and to cooperate with the local Indian Service. The individual Hano Tewa is friendly to whites and has little of the reticence characteristic of both the Hopi and New Mexico Tewa.

What factors are responsible for creating a personality structure at variance with that of other pueblo peoples is not clear. Certain hypotheses may be ventured, however. First, the Hano Tewa were formerly on the eastern frontier of the pueblo area, and there they interacted with Plains Indian tribes. Second, they had a history of resistance to the Spaniards but escaped to Hopi before becoming completely subdued. Third, their minority status at Hopi may well have demanded the assertion of personality traits antithetical to the Hopi. At Hopi, the aggressive, independent traits of the Tewa were encouraged by their position as warriors and protectors of the Hopi.

Any one or all of these factors may account for the formation of Hano

Tewa personality. The fact is that, at present, Hano attitudes and behavior contrast sharply with the Hopi.

In spite of Hano's friendly and cooperative relations with whites, the people have not lost their cultural identity as they have adjusted to the impact of American ways. Hano culture appears to be well integrated along traditional lines. Certain important changes have come about, however, as the result of modern pressures. The most important are the periodic reductions of the matrilineal extended household to meet demands imposed by livestock and wage-work activities. As a result of modern conditions, too, a few of the young people, particularly those who have gone to schools outside the reservation, are encountering problems of adjustment. The older people make much of this, yet these deviations from the norm may express no more than the behavior characteristic of the younger generation in any society.

Although it is possible to see both Hopi and New Mexico Tewa elements in Hano social and ceremonial organization, these have been so thoroughly integrated into Hano culture that the group differs significantly from the other two. As might be expected from the long residence of the Tewa on First Mesa, their culture more closely resembles that of the Hopi. Thus, Hano social and ceremonial organization is founded on the same principles as the Hopi: the kinship system, household, clan, ceremonial societies, and kiva groups. But in all these institutions certain similarities to the New Mexico Tewa appear—areas in which they differ from the Hopi.

The greatest difference between Hano and Hopi culture is in ceremonial organization. The dual or moiety concept is emphasized among the Tewa, not only in migration legends and myths, but in actual structural make-up. The two kiva groups at Hano function independently of each other in the performance of various ceremonials. There is a leader, or chief, for each group, as among the New Mexico Tewa. The Hano Tewa hold kiva group initiations that are suggestive of Tewa moiety initiations in New Mexico. Until recently Hano had a Kachina cult, essentially different from that of the Hopi but closely resembling the New Mexico Tewa Kachina organization. In the emphasis on curing in their ceremonies, the Hano Tewa again contrast with the Hopi and indicate retention of New Mexico Pueblo concepts.

Hano social and ceremonial organizations thus appears to be the result of (1) a core of elements indigenous to the group and bearing resemblances to the New Mexico Tewa, (2) elements borrowed from the Hopi over a period of two and a half centuries during which the two groups have lived as neighbors, and (3) a unique integration of the two that appears to be becoming progressively a new whole.

Hano economy is still to a large extent dependent on farming, handicrafts, and other traditional occupations, although wage work and livestock raising have become much more important in recent years. The economy is still functioning mainly in terms of the traditional patterns of the extended-household and clan structures. A number of factors have helped to make these patterns viable. First, livestock and wage-work activities, particularly the latter, are recent innovations. Second, modern transportation facilities have made possible frequent resumptions of extended-household living and interaction in terms of clans and groups of clans. Third, the satisfactions derived from the extended household, clan, and the rich ceremonial life of community living have not been matched elsewhere.

Potential threats to the household and clan structures are, however, clear. The Tewa's increasing relations with whites are drawing them more and more into the American pecuniary economic system. It is possible that as succeeding generations grow up, away from the close touch of the extended household and clan relatives, the importance of the nuclear family will increase. New generations may find satisfactions with a new pattern of relationships and value systems. On the other hand, native customs are strong and complex and apparently will long continue despite modern pressures. The Hopi and Tewa have thus far adjusted to modern conditions, and there is no reason why they cannot continue to make such adjustments while preserving most of their own traditional social and ceremonial organization.

Orthographic Note

Transcriptions of native terms are only phonetic approximations in so far as this is possible with the use of English sound symbols. Tewa speech sounds differ radically from English and other European languages. The glottal stop, tone, vowel length, glottalized consonants, and nasalized vowels all occur as contrastive features. Unfortunately it has not been possible to indicate these characteristics of Tewa phonology in this case study. For a more exact phonetic transcription of the native terms used in this study the reader is referred to the following publications of the author:

1. "The Hopi-Tewa of Arizona," *University of California Publications in American Archaeology and Ethnology,* Vol. 44, No. 3, 1954.

2. "Kinship and Linguistic Change among the Arizona Tewa," *International Journal of American Linguistics,* Vol. 21, No. 3, July 1955.

References

ADAMS, ELEANOR B., AND FRAY ANGELICO CHAVEZ, eds., 1956, *The Missions of New Mexico, 1776.* Albuquerque, N.M.: University of New Mexico Press.

AITKEN, BARBARA, 1930, "Temperament in Native American Indian Religion," *Journal of the Royal Anthropological Institute,* No. 60.

ASCH, S. E., in manuscript, *Personality Development of Hopi Children.* Reported in Thompson, Laura, 1950, *Culture in Crisis, A Study of the Hopi Indians.* New York: Harper & Row, pp. 94–95.

BEADLE, J. H., 1878, *Western Wilds, and the Men Who Redeem Them; An Authentic Narrative.* Cincinnati.

BLOOM, L. B., 1931, "A Campaign Against the Moqui Pueblos," *New Mexico Historical Review,* Vol. 6, No. 2, pp. 158–226.

———, 1936, "Bourke on the Southwest," *New Mexico Historical Review,* Vol. 11, pp. 217–282.

BOLTON, H. E., 1916, "The Espejo Expedition, 1582–1583." In H. E. Bolton, *Spanish Explorations in the Southwest, 1542–1706.* New York: Charles Scribner's Sons, pp. 161–196.

BRYAN, K., 1929, "Flood-Water Farming," *Geographical Review,* Vol. 19, No. 3, pp. 444–456.

CALHOUN, JAMES S., 1915, *The Official Correspondence of James S. Calhoun.* Washington, D.C.: Bureau of Indian Affairs, Government Printing Office.

CRANE, LEO, 1925, *Indians of the Painted Desert.* Boston: Little, Brown & Company.

DOZIER, EDWARD P., 1954, "The Hopi-Tewa of Arizona," *University of California Publications in American Archaeology and Ethnology,* Vol. 44, No. 3.

———, 1955, "Kinship and Linguistic Change Among the Arizona Tewa," *International Journal of American Linguistics,* Vol. 21, pp. 242–257.

EGGAN, FRED, 1950, *Social Organization of the Western Pueblos.* Chicago: University of Chicago Press.

HACKETT, C. W., and C. C. SHELBY, 1942, *Revolt of the Pueblo Indians of New Mexico and Otermin's Attempted Reconquest, 1680–1682.* Coronado Historical Series, Vols. 8 and 9, Albuquerque, N.M.: University of New Mexico Press.

HARRINGTON, J. P., 1912, "Tewa Relationship Terms," *American Anthropologist,* n. s., Vol. 14, No. 3, pp 472–498.

HILL, W. W., in manuscript. "Santa Clara Pueblo." In the possession of its author, Department of Anthropology, University of New Mexico, Albuquerque, N.M.

HODGE, F. W., G. P. HAMMOND, and AGAPITO REY, 1945, *Revised Memorial of Alonzo de Beuavides, 1634.* Coronado Historical Series, Vol. IV. Albuquerque, N.M.: University of New Mexico Press.

LA FARGE, OLIVER, 1936, in manuscript. Personal notes on the organization of the Hopi tribe, 1936.

NARVAEZ VALVERDE, FRAY JOSÉ, 1937, "Notes upon Moqui and Other Recent Ones upon New Mexico." In C. W. Hackett, ed., *Historical Documents Relating to New Mexico, Vizcarja, and Approaches Thereto, to 1773,* Vol. 3. Washington, D.C.: Carnegie Institute of Washington, pp. 385–387.

PARSONS, E. C., 1921, "Hopi Mothers and Children," *Man,* Vol. 21, No. 58, pp. 98–104.

———, 1925, *A Pueblo Indian Journal, 1902–21,* Memoirs of the American Anthropological Association, No. 32. Menasha, Wis.

———, 1926, "The Ceremonial Calendar of the Tewa of Arizona," *American Anthropologist,* n. s., Vol. 28, No. 1, pp. 209–229.

———, 1936, "Introduction." In E. C. Parson's, ed., *Hopi Journal.* Columbia University, Contributions to Anthropology, Vol. 23, Part 1, pp. xxv–lii.

SCHOLES, F. V., 1935, "The First Decade of the Inquisition in New Mexico," *New Mexico Historical Review,* Vol. 10, No. 3, pp. 195–241.

———, 1942, *Troublous Times in New Mexico, 1659–1670.* Albuquerque, N.M.: Historical Society of New Mexico, Publications in History, Vol. 11.

STEPHEN, A. M., 1936, *Hopi Journal,* edited by E. C. Parsons. Columbia University, Contributions to Anthropology, Vol 23, Parts 1 and 2.

STEWART, G. R., 1940, "Conservation in Pueblo Agriculture," *Scientific Monthly,* Vol. 51, No. 4.

THOMAS, A. B., 1932, *Forgotten Frontiers, A Study of the Spanish Indian Policy of Don Juan Bautista de Anza, Governor of New Mexico, 1777–1787.* Norman, Okla.: University of Oklahoma Press.

TITIEV, MISCHA, 1944, *Old Oraibi, A Study of the Hopi Indians of Third Mesa.* Cambridge, Mass.: Papers of Peabody Museum of American Archaeology and Ethnology, Vol. 22, No. 1.

THOMPSON, LAURA, 1950, *Culture in Crisis, A Study of the Hopi Indians.* New York: Harper & Row.

THOMPSON, LAURA, and ALICE JOSEPH, 1944, *The Hopi Way.* Lawrence, Kans.: United States Indian Service.

U.S. DEPARTMENT OF THE INTERIOR, 1894, "Moqui Pueblos of Arizona and Pueblos of New Mexico." In *Report on Indians Taxed and Indians Not Taxed in the United States at the Eleventh Census, 1890.* Washington, D.C.

———, 1937, *Constitution and By-Laws of the Hopi Tribe, Arizona.* Washington, D.C.: U.S. Office of Indian Affairs.

———, 1940, Code of Federal Regulations, Title 25—Indians, Chapter 1. Washington, D.C.: U.S. Office of Indian Affairs.

THE KWAKIUTL: INDIANS OF BRITISH COLUMBIA

Ronald P. Rohner
Catholic University of Washington
and Evelyn C. Rohner

Ronald P. Rohner received his B.S. in psychology and the Ph.D. in anthropology, the latter at Stanford University in 1964. He taught at the University of Connecticut until 1975, then at the Catholic University of Washington. He is author of *The People of Gilford: A Contemporary Kwakiutl Village*, the *Ethnography of Franz Boas*, and a recent book, *They Love Me, They Love Me Not*, a worldwide study of the effects of parental acceptance and rejection.

Evelyn C. Rohner was born in Vienna, Austria, and graduated from the University of Oregon with a B.A. in English. She received her M.A. in anthropology at the University of Connecticut in 1967. She is currently finishing work toward a doctorate in physiology. At the time of the study reported in this volume she was the teacher in the elementary school at Gilford Island.

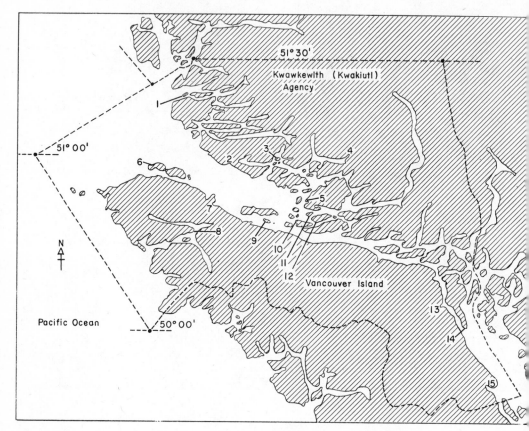

Location of Kwakiutl Reserves (see *Table 1*)

Contents

Part One   CONTEMPORARY KWAKIUTL

1. Fieldwork in Kwakiutl Life Space   117

   Kwakiutl Life Space, 117
   Fieldwork in Kwakiutl Life Space, 123

2. The Kwakiutl at Work   131

   Two Days in December, 131
   Commercial Salmon Fishing, 144

3. Being a Kwakiutl   151

   Social Control and Normative Standards, 153
   Drinking and Social Interaction, 160
   Death and Religion, 166
   Authority, Power-Prestige and Friendship, 172

4. Growing Up Kwakiutl   179

Part Two   POTLATCH PERIOD

5. Traditional Social Organization   189

   The Potlatch, 207
   Winter Ceremonials, 217

References   223

Fieldwork in Kwakiutl Life Space

Kwakiutl Life Space

LIFE FOR MOST KWAKIUTL INDIANS is confined to a slender strip of coastal water, fjordlike inlets, sounds, and hundreds of densely forested, almost impenetrable islands and outcroppings of rock between the western coast of British Columbia and Vancouver Island in Canada. Fifteen southern Kwakiutl Bands representing about twenty indigenous tribal groups occupy this territory between Smith Sound and Campbell River. One of these groups is the Gilford Island Band which is formally comprised of two closely related Kwakiutl tribal groups, the Koeksotenok and Hahuamis.[1] (See Table 1.) The residents of Gilford are the people described in this case study.

The Kwakiutl are today as they have always been—even in their mythology—a fishing people. Their self-identity is bound to the sea and to the life-forms within the sea. The great forests are exploited by white men, but only gradually and reluctantly are the Kwakiutl involving themselves in the logging industry. Agricultural enterprises are virtually unknown among the Indians. Some of the younger men take advantage of vocational training courses offered by the Indian Affairs Branch, and a very few go on for higher education. But ultimately many of them return to the sea, reaffirming a style of life that is as old as memory and tradition combined. Thus, even though the Kwakiutl are hardly the same people today as described years ago by the American anthropologist Franz Boas, important elements of cultural continuity with the past are nonetheless maintained.

---

[1] The Band legally consists of the Koeksotenok tribe, who traditionally occupied the village site, and the Hahuamis tribe. The Tsawatenok, a third Kwakiutl tribe, however, outnumbers either of the other two groups in the village. These three groups along with the Guauaenok form the Four Tribes of Gilford, an informally knit collectivity or confederacy who historically had exceptionally close contacts. Ninety percent of the residents at Gilford are members of the Tsawatenok, Koeksotenok or Hahuamis tribes. The Guauaenok are unrepresented in the community today. Most Tsawatenok, however, live on their own Reserve at Kingcome Inlet. Table 1 and the frontispiece map show the location of the various Kwakiutl tribes and bands.

TABLE 1.

TRIBES, BANDS, AND THEIR LOCATIONS IN THE KWAWKEWLTH (KWAKIUTL) AGENCY
(see frontispiece map)

No.	Band	Tribe(s)[a]	Location
1.	Quawshelah	Goasila	Smith Inlet
2.	Nakwato	Nakoaktok	Blunden Harbor
3.	Kwawwawaineuk	Guauaenok	Hopetown (Watson Island)
4.	Tsawataineuk	Tsawatenok	Kingcome Inlet
5.	Gilford Island	Koeksotenok and Hahuamis	Gilford Island
6.	Nuwitti	Nawiti (including Nakomgilisala and Tlatlasikoala)	Hope Island
7.	Kwawkewlth	Kwakiutl	Fort Rupert
8.	Quatsino	Quatsino	Quatsino Sound
9.	Nimpkish	Nimkish	Alert Bay
10.	Tanakteuk	Tenaktak	New Vancouver (Harbledown Island)
11.	Mamalillikulla	Mamalelekala	Village Island
12.	Turnour Island	Tlauitsis and Matilpe	Turnour Island
13.1	Campbell River	Wiweakam	Campbell River
13.2	Kwiakah	Kueha	Campbell River
14.	Cape Mudge	Wiwekae	Cape Mudge
15.	Comox	Qomox	Comox

[a] Spelling of tribal names follows Curtis (1915) with the exception of Qomox which is not included in Curtis. The Qomox are Coast Salish, not Kwakiutl.

Gilford Island itself is a mountainous land mass about 20 miles long and 13 miles wide. Nine mountains on the island rise over 2000 feet each, the highest stretching to almost 5000 feet. Steep slopes, sediment filled valleys and deltas separate the mountains. Rich needleleaf evergreen trees, bushes, fern, berry vines, and a wide range of wildlife cover the island. Different types of lush vegetation choke the often rugged and precipitous shore in their competition for sunlight. In many places the rising tide sweeps the stony walls of the island with the branches of the lower trees. This flora is sustained by a humid mesothermal forest climate, including about 54 inches of rain a year.

Marine life in the Gilford area is bountiful in its variety if not always in its yield. The waters are filled with clams, crabs, mussels, barnacles, varieties of cod, some octopuses and sharks, blackfish (killer whales), herring, halibut, oulachon, and five species of salmon.

The Indian village at Gilford snuggles against the base of one of the larger mountains that extends its slope to the shore. The community is about three times the length of a football field and about 100 yards wide. It is settled on an ancient clam-shell midden and is effectively bounded on three sides by dense forest and by water on the fourth. About twenty of the village houses are occupied continuously throughout the year. The others are usually locked or boarded by their absentee owners and comprise fair game for the vandalistic antics of village children.

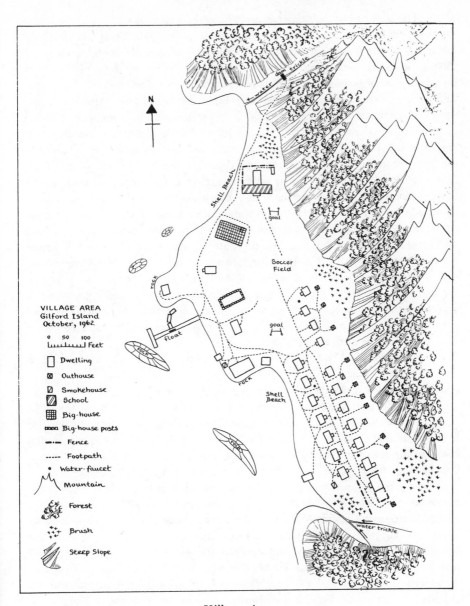

Village Area

The majority of the houses in the village, as well as the school and teacherage, were acquired from a Canadian Air Force base in 1950. These identical pre-
fabricated houses were transported to Gilford and arrayed on posts two feet off
the ground in two neat, parallel rows on a newly bulldozed end of the village. Thus
the disposition of houses at Gilford is exceptional among Kwakiutl villages in that
their style and arrangement look like the suburb of a Canadian or American town.

The interior of village homes is thinly partitioned into a number of rooms
of varying size. The kitchen and living room, for example, are unenclosed in
Ambrose and Louisa Cedar's house, and their two bedrooms are separated from
the living room by curtains that offer visual privacy but hardly mask sound. Their
living room is sparsely furnished with a sagging overstuffed easy chair and a
covered single bed that is used both as a couch and as a bed. Louisa has placed
handmade crochet doilies over the arm and back of the easy chair, hiding some
frayed edges. Plastic curtains are tied back from the windows; several windows
are cracked and two are boarded. A wood-burning heater stands at one side of the
room near a wall, and a Coleman lamp hangs from a hooked coat-hanger wire
that is nailed to the ceiling. A worn linoleum rug covers part of the splintered,
wooden floor. Louisa has several religious plaques and posters, family photographs,
snapshots and a calendar neatly arranged on the wall near the couch. She also
enjoys an arrangement of artificial flowers and several knickknacks on a shelf near
the entrance to the kitchen.

The Cedar family eats around a Formica-topped table next to the kitchen
windows overlooking the channel that bounds the village on one side. A short
bench, a wooden chair and three soda-pop boxes surround the table, and a
transistor radio that is rarely turned off rests on the windowsill next to the table.
A large wood-burning range stands against the partition separating the kitchen
from the living room. A rack used for both drying fish and for drying clothes
hangs over the stove. Nearby a second gas lamp is suspended from the ceiling.
One of the outside walls is lined with a counter in which a porcelain sink is
embedded. Cold water that is gravity fed into the kitchen from a tiny dam on the
mountain runs from the faucet, and the refuse from the sink drains onto the
ground beneath the house. Not all houses in the village, however, have running
water. Several families carry pails of water into their homes from one of the
faucets protruding from several paths around the settlement. The nine outhouses
in the village are shared by various families who normally lock them to keep un-
authorized people out and to keep them from being damaged by mischievous
children. A number of families use chamber pots for convenience at night.

The population at Gilford (about 100 people), as well as most of the
other small, isolated Indian villages throughout the region, changes constantly.
Individuals and sometimes whole families migrate easily from place to place among
the local Reserves throughout the area, although an individual's strongest attach-
ments are usually maintained with his home Reserve. Fluctuation of village size
and composition are also influenced by marked seasonal variation. The village
is practically deserted during the commercial salmon fishing season in the summer,
but it fills again briefly after the summer fishing season ends. The size of the
settlement is only moderately reduced in September after the residential school

Aerial and panoramic views of the village

children leave in the fall, but the age composition of the community is radically affected.[2] Population ranks swell again in the winter when members of other Kwakiutl Bands come to dig clams. Most of these visitors leave in early spring when the clam season is over. Finally, the village burgeons for a short time before summer fishing begins and after the residential school children return home.

Even within the village internal household shifts are commonplace. If one family leaves a house, a second often moves in, vacating its own home or leaving a host family to itself once again. Not infrequently this leads to conflict because the owners of the abandoned house may be unhappy about this intrusion. Moreover, young people often move or are moved within the village from one household to another where they live for indefinite periods of time.

Despite the residential instability of the villagers, the people spend most of their lives within the perimeter of an easily definable and circumscribed region. The psychologically real options for movement are restricted. The most extensive network of social relations for Gilford Islanders is localized among five other adjacent Indian villages—Kingcome, New Van, Village, Turnour, and the Bay.[3] When a Gilford Islander moves he usually goes to one of these villages.

The only way a person can travel in the region is by boat or pontoon plane;

[2] The Indian population of British Columbia was almost wiped out after European contact because of the introduction of diseases such as tuberculosis, measles and syphilis. Since 1939, however, the population has been burgeoning at an accelerating rate. Consequently 50 percent of the Indian population in British Columbia in 1963 was under sixteen and 75 percent was under thirty-two. The same trend holds true of the Gilford Island Kwakiutl: 50 percent are fifteen or younger and 75 percent are thirty or younger. Thus any alteration of the school-age population within the village seriously affects the character of the entire village.

[3] The full name of each village is Kingcome Inlet, New Vancouver, Village Island, Turnour Island and Alert Bay respectively, but we use these shorthand terms because they conform with the standardized usage of the Gilford Islanders.

A portion of the village as it looked in 1927 (Courtesy of the Provincial Museum, British Columbia)

consequently distance is typically reckoned in terms of the length of time required to get from one place to another by gill-net fishing boat, and not in terms of statute or nautical miles. Thus, Kingcome is about five hours away from Gilford. Village is about an hour away and New Van is approximately an hour and fifteen minutes from the village. Echo Bay, the closest inhabited place to the Indian village at Gilford, is forty-five minutes away and is on the same island. Simoom Sound is ten minutes further away on the other side of the cove from Echo Bay. Both Echo Bay and Simoom Sound are small, White settlements appended to Gilford Island on floats. Echo Bay has a general store anchored to the island as well as a provincial school and beer parlor on land. Other residents include forestry men and loggers who work for small, independent logging outfits. The settlement at Simoom Sound consists of a post office and general store built over the water where, along with the store at Echo Bay, the Indians buy many of their supplies.

Alert Bay with its paved roads and automobiles is the major commercial and social center of the entire region and is two hours from Gilford. The population of 1200 people there is evenly divided into about 600 Indians and 600 non-Indians. The Indian Agent's office is at the Bay along with two hotels, shops, beer parlors, fish canning companies, government offices, and the Royal Canadian Mounted Police (RCMP).

Indians and Whites in the Bay sometimes refer to the people of the more remote, isolated villages—such as Gilford—as "the islanders," and think of the island villages as being collectively depressed and conservative, whereas they view themselves as being progressive. Many Indians feel that living in Alert Bay gives them social and economic advantages not common to the remote villages. The islands are also thought of as being "tough places." Some individuals and families in these island villages share this negative evaluation of their village held by others. This, in part, accounts for the migration of families from the island Reserves to, most typically, Alert Bay. As a result, the isolated villages throughout most of the area are losing their population as families move to larger, more commercial areas. Quite frequently adults explain that they want to give their children a better education than is provided in the day schools situated on the island Reserves. This is often a legitimate reason; rarely, however, is it the only one. Not infrequently certain families complain about their home village, and state emphatically that they are going to leave as soon as possible. Some of these families have been threatening to leave for several years without acting on the decision or desire. Despite their disadvantages these traditional village sites still symbolize fundamental security and identity for many of the villagers. The village also provides for some of the older Indians a firm articulation with the fading image of a passing tradition. This is the life space of the Gilford Island Kwakiutl where our account unfolds.

Fieldwork in Kwakiutl Life Space

We did not specifically choose Gilford as our field station. We simply wanted a Kwakiutl village where my wife could teach while I conducted fieldwork; consequently the choice of community was made for us largely by the provincial

Superintendent of Indian schools. After we became settled and learned how to contextualize the village within the broader perspective of the surrounding Kwakiutl villages, however, we realized how serendipitous fortune had been. The village at Gilford is ideally suited in most respects for ethnographic fieldwork. It is small and compact, so we were able to have frequent and close contact with all of the villagers during the thirteen months of our residence. The size of the population made it possible for us to know everyone personally. Social life tends to focus within narrow boundaries because the community is isolated from other villages, and no one enters or leaves without others knowing about it. These are some of the structural characteristics of the village that make intensive fieldwork easier there than it might be elsewhere.

Before coming to Gilford we had expected a school enrollment of about twenty-five children in grades one to five, but on our first day Evelyn learned from one of the children that in fact she would be responsible for thirty-nine children ranging in age from six to nineteen and that she would be teaching every level from beginners through the eighth grade. The teacherage and classroom were in shambles when we arrived at Gilford because they were being renovated by carpenters hired by the Indian Affairs Branch. We cleared the sawdust and scrap lumber from one finished bedroom and part of the unfinished kitchen to set up living quarters. School was to begin in three days, but the classroom, books and supplies were in the same disheveled condition as the teacherage. Some of the supplies had not yet even arrived.

Evelyn was thrown completely off guard because she had not known that she was to be responsible for such a large class covering all grades. Moreover, she was dismayed by the fact that our quarters and the classroom were utterly disorganized and by the fact that many classroom supplies had not yet arrived. How was she to cope with all this in the three days remaining before school began? I helplessly watched as she became increasingly despondent over the teaching situation. Within two days she was almost completely withdrawn and apathetic. Her mood and attitude toward teaching changed several times every day, but remained essentially a feeling of futility and hopelessness.

Her unhappiness affected my own mood. I made no attempt to do systematic research during our first week at Gilford. I devoted most of my time to helping the carpenters complete their renovations, helping Evelyn prepare for class and making myself known within the community. I spent several hours each day probing around the village attempting to orient myself to it and to its inhabitants. I followed paths behind houses—which usually turned out to lead to outhouses—explored the beaches, and examined deteriorating totem poles, carved house poles and the big-house (traditional Kwakiutl multi-family dwelling), and I introduced myself to everyone I met. I felt I was being watched, so I attempted to make my actions as open as possible. I frequently engaged villagers in conversations and took notes on everything I saw and heard.

I was received with a mixture of curiosity and uneasiness which later turned to suspicion among a few villagers. My motives for being in the village were not clear. Evelyn was clearly the teacher, therefore her status was understood. She had legitimate work to do in the village, but what was I doing? Why was I there? Why was my wife working and not I? I attempted to establish myself as an anthropologist interested in the history, language and way of life of the people. My explanation satisfied no one because being an anthropologist is outside their existing lexicon of meaning. I felt threatened and insecure by this reaction, and I was disturbed because I could not explain my presence in the village in any way that made sense to the villagers. Within two weeks the resident Pentecostal deaconess confided to me that some of the villagers, especially the young men, had concluded I was a spy. My worst offense was public notetaking. "He's writing down all our secrets." Belatedly I stopped my open explorations and public note-taking.

Even though the school provided my wife—and later me—a secure identity within the village and allowed us to make progress in ways we would not have been able to do otherwise, the classroom posed the most immediate problem for both of us during the early part of the year. The children who had been shy and subdued at first became uncontrollably boisterous and inattentive in the classroom by the end of the first week. Evelyn discovered that the children were unresponsive to her attempts for eliciting group participation. She could not plan any activity involving the entire class. This aggravated the discipline problem created by the age differences among the students. The young ones became boisterous while she talked with the older ones, and the older students were bored and restless while she talked with the younger ones. The children tended to complete their assigned work perfunctorily, as quickly as possible, and they were not able to continue unguided to a subsequent task. A job which she expected the children to complete in fifteen minutes was indifferently completed by some in five. When a given assignment was finished, the children filled their time by talking, yelling, throwing things, scuffling, bickering and fighting. Evelyn found it impossible, for example, to coordinate the activities of each grade so that every child was busy while she taught reading to her beginners. She was unable to give her attention to one group without having children in another grade yell across the room, "Mrs. Rohner, I'm through! What can I do now?" If she did not respond immediately they began teasing each other or they pulled out their rulers and started a sword fight. When she did respond, the group with whom she had been working became restless and began to act up. By the end of the first week she was desperate, utterly dis-couraged and prepared to resign.

The following week she instituted a split shift system whereby children in grades one through four attended school in the morning and students in grades five through eight attended school in the afternoon. This resolved most of the problems created by a large class, but few of the classroom-control problems were ameliorated. Discipline and classroom control became increasingly difficult as the children became less inhibited in her presence. This was particularly true of the younger children.

By the third week the problem of classroom control approached such un-manageable proportions that we called a meeting of the parents in order to solicit their cooperation. Evelyn spoke to the parents about how important it was to her that the children learn; but, she argued, she could not be a policeman and a teacher at the same time. She described the problems of classroom management at some length, and then she explained the split shift and why it had been instituted. Most of the parents were in favor of the new system. We also explained to the adults that I had come to learn as much as I could about their history and about their way of life today.

During our coffee break several parents commented that this was the first time in the history of the school that the members of the community had been invited into the teacher's home for a meeting. Tears welled up in the eyes of one of the men when he told us this, and others concurred. Most of the teachers in the past had been distrustful of the Indians; several had been positively fearful or hostile toward them. Already, even before the meeting with the parents, we had unwittingly reduced some of the suspicion that the villagers had learned to hold toward new teachers by allowing the children and teenagers to visit us after school. But the fact that we invited the adults to our quarters was said to be novel in the recent history of Gilford. Certainly we had no way of suspecting beforehand that the parents-teacher meeting would be a major factor in our acceptance within the community.

The story was told the day after the meeting that I had been especially hired to write about the people of Gilford. Few villagers understood exactly what this meant, but they were proud that Gilford had been chosen. The role of anthropologist contained too many ambiguities for my behavior to be clearly understood or predictable, however, so I was cast into the status of *the teacher* even though everyone realized that Evelyn was actually in the classroom. My status as the teacher meant that I was in charge of the school and that, presumably, my wife was working for me.

Several people during the parents' meeting mentioned that a movie projector and screen belonging to the village had been in the Indian Agent's office for ten years. They complained that the Agency Superintendent refused to return the equipment. I said that I would talk to him and see if I could reclaim it. The idea was warmly received but, based on their past experience with Whites, several people believed I would not really try. Two days later I accompanied four men to the Bay and retrieved the projector and screen. Several young men from the village who had been very suspicious of me earlier travelled back to Gilford with us the same day. They accepted me into their conversation for the first time, and when we arrived at Gilford they invited me to join a beer drinking party with other villagers. Throughout the evening I was asked to recount how I reclaimed the apparatus. Our period of probation in the village ended. We were no longer required to prove ourselves in the same way. Other problems of adjustment and rapport arose throughout the year, but the one of general acceptance was largely settled.

We barely escaped the network of mutual grievances which is a normal part of village social interaction, however, because of our attempts to actively participate in community life. The most serious event occurred during our third month at Gilford. The tribal chief accepted me into his trust and confidence and loaned me his gill-net fishing boat, the *Dorothy Rose*, for the winter, thereby giving me priority over some of his kinsmen who had no boat. The chief had earlier admitted to me that he was reluctant to have the village men use the *Dorothy Rose* because they often damaged it. He had difficulty collecting the repair bills. "Sometimes I think they expect me to pay them for using my boat." Within two weeks a few villagers began resentfully complaining that the chief had loaned me the boat rather than some of his relatives who needed it for clam digging. The women were most voluble in their complaints, primarily to my wife. Fortunately the antagonism shown to us was limited to only a few villagers.

Chief Stanley Philip gave me explicit instructions not to loan the *Dorothy Rose* to anyone. I was to be responsible for it. The evening after the chief left the village with a load of clams for Vancouver, however, one of the village men told me that Stanley had instructed him to take the *Dorothy Rose* to a nearby trap line and pick up another villager. I was disturbed that the chief had not told me about this before he left, and I was not certain that Stanley had really instructed him to take the gill-netter. I wanted to keep my promise about not loaning the boat if Stanley had not made the request, but I did not want to offend the villager if he had. Stanley later admitted that he had instructed his son, Herbert, to take the boat. Herbert did not want to go, so he asked another villager. Stanley said that he would not ask anyone to use the boat again as long as it was in my charge. The next time he left the village Herbert asked for the keys, saying that he needed to take a load of iced fish to Alert Bay. Again, I did not know if this were true, but I hesitantly gave the keys to him anyway because I did not want to offend him by refusing his request. This was particularly true because he and his wife appeared to resent the close working relationship I had with his father. Repeatedly on other occasions Herbert said that he needed the *Dorothy Rose* for apparently legitimate purposes when his father was away.

We were in a position where we were constantly forced to make decisions about the use of the *Dorothy Rose* without having adequate knowledge of the proper normative standards by which such decisions should be made. The standards used by the villagers for evaluating appropriate use and control of property were not the same as the ones we were using, and it became apparent that neither Stanley nor the villagers perceived our use of the boat in the same way as we did. In effect it was free for us to use whenever it was not needed for other purposes; but who, I wondered, was to be responsible for maintenance, repairs, equipment, gas and oil? I believed that I was fully responsible for these when I accepted the boat, but I had no way of controlling them when it was used by others. I raised the question of responsibility with Stanley but he did not give me a satisfactory explanation. I later realized that the question was meaningless, based as it was on my implicit assumptions about the meaning of responsibility rather than on those held by the Gilford Island Kwakiutl.

During this time I reached a plateau in my fieldwork. The amount of information I was getting in relation to the amount of time I was spending to obtain it was decidedly dropping, and I felt I was drifting aimlessly. I had become habituated to the routine of village life and I was developing few insights and hypotheses for testing. Problems regarding the *Dorothy Rose* bothered me. And I was troubled by my relationship with Herbert, who had begun calling me

"Riley" and "Riley Rohner." I asked him what he meant the first time he said it and he explained, "You're leading the life of Riley." He saw me talking to, watching and working with the villagers, but he had no clear idea of what I was doing, so he perceived my activities as loafing. His joking caught me at a time when I was feeling particularly vulnerable in my relations with some of the men.

At about this time we began to feel the need for a vacation from the island—a chance to get away and take a look at ourselves and the village. Both of us were getting too caught up in village affairs and this was creating a great deal of strain and tension in us. When we left the village for two weeks at the end of December, with Stanley's approval we gave the boat keys to Herbert, who reluctantly returned them when we came back. He intermittently used the boat during the next few weeks. Tension regarding the *Dorothy Rose* increased when Herbert came by one day asking for the keys to the boat to go to Simoom Sound and pick up some crab pots. He had told me previously that he wanted the keys to put out Stanley's crab pots, but Stanley knew nothing of it when Evelyn mentioned it to him. I mentioned this to Evelyn who got angry because Stanley had told her that "There's no reason for Herbert to be using the *Dorothy Rose* now that the clam tide is over." The problem reached a climax a few days later when I asked Stanley why only one oar was on board the gill-netter. Two pairs had been locked inside the cabin when we left the village at the end of December. He gave me a penetrating stare and informed me that Herbert had said three oars were missing when we left. It was my word against his son's. All three of us were in an awkward position, but Stanley faced the greatest dilemma. Somehow he had to reconcile his feelings toward me, whom he liked and respected, with his paternal feelings and obligations toward his son. Shortly thereafter I relinquished responsibility for the *Dorothy Rose* in order to avoid further conflict.

We saw less of Stanley for a month. Herbert and his wife became much friendlier after the problem with the *Dorothy Rose* was settled and when they no longer had to compete with us for Stanley's favor. Herbert and his wife, Gertie, invited us to their home many times in the remaining months and we reciprocated. Eventually we became good friends. Herbert's wife wept when we left the village after a year of fieldwork, and a few weeks later she wrote to Evelyn, "Well I can't tell you how much I miss having you pop in any time of the day to visit me. I think I won't become friendly with anyone again as I hate good-bys, you know everyone here hated to see you all go. Well, I'd like to just say that you are *the* very best friend I've ever known, so there."

Anthropologists often pose a threat to people who feel their vested interests in a community are being disturbed by the work of the ethnographer. We posed such a threat to the resident Pentecostal deaconess because of our extensive participation in village life. The deaconess, Hilda, is a knowledgeable woman who helped us a great deal in getting oriented to the village and the surrounding area. She eased many of Evelyn's early problems of adjustment, and she supplied me with invaluable data, the absence of which would have made the initial months of research more difficult. Later, however, she felt insecure because of our involvement in community affairs. One afternoon she talked to two villagers, Henry and Norma, and chided Henry for drinking too much. Henry retorted that we, "the teachers," do not "talk bad" about the Indians' drinking and that in fact we drink with them ourselves. Hilda was angered by this comment and replied that she had nothing in common with us and that the only reason I drank with the villagers was to get information for my book. During parties throughout the remainder of the year, and during our revisit the following summer, I was confronted with the question, "Is it true that the only reason you drink with us is to get information for your book?"

A more hostile incident occurred when we were drinking beer on Herb's boat one evening and then moved to Patrick's place. Henry and Norma were in bed drinking. Norma was in a foul mood. She told us to get out of her house— "This isn't the Ritz, you fucking bastards." At one point she commented to the effect, "You'll have something else to put in your book, you spy." She was looking at one of the other men when she said it, but the comment was obviously directed toward me. She was equally as unpleasant to her brother, Pat. Most people, however, admitted that they did not really believe we drank with them merely to get information.

Throughout the year we voiced our approval of the perpetuation of customary Kwakiutl traditions and technology such as barbecuing salmon and clams, carving, painting and Indian dancing. The people of Gilford were pleased when we displayed with pride the contemporary artifacts we purchased from them, and they were flattered by our interest in their history and customs. Chief Philip spoke at length during several ceremonial dances about the work I was doing, and how my constant probing had renewed in him and others a fading interest in Indian customs. During one occasion, for example, he said, "I would like to publicly acknowledge my debt of gratitude to my esteemed anthropologist friend, Mr. Ron Rohner, for rejuvenating my long-lost interest in old Indian customs."

By mid-school year we received a letter from the Superintendent of Indian schools in which he wrote:

> What scares me is the vacuum that you will leave when you go South. The sympathetic involvement that has taken place since you arrived will be missed greatly. My grapevine has been most complimentary to you, but I do not think that complimentary is too accurate. The Indians are a bit overwhelmed but like what is going on. All the reports that have come to me have been good and this was to be expected. Too few try to understand; too few listen; too few care.

One of the young men who had been most distrustful of my activities during the year paid us the highest compliment, however. On our last day at Gilford he said to us, "I never was proud of being from Gilford until you came." We received many letters from the villagers after leaving Gilford. In one of them Stanley wrote, "We the Gilford Islanders will always remember you folks. You have left quite an impression on the Peoples."

Our feelings about the village are expressed in a letter that Evelyn wrote two months before we returned home:

> I have to laugh in a way. Last September I wanted nothing more than to go home. If there had been a convenient way of leaving this remote village, I probably would have done it. Now look at me. I love it and I am really sad that we will not return

next September. Of course there have been bad moments, moments of extreme homesickness on my part, times of extreme frustration on Ron's part. But what a wonderful ending to a year, a village in which feeling is good, a community that is functioning together.

As you can see, the Rohners have become extremely involved in their new home. I am thankful that we will be able to spend the summer here. Many of the people have expressed regret that we will not be back next year; Ron and I also feel that way.

2

The Kwakiutl at Work

Two Days in December

THE VILLAGERS GO TO BED between ten and eleven on school nights and they get up between eight and nine in the morning. The sharply defined time segments so important to White teachers, however, are ignored by villagers on weekends and during school vacation. This led us to believe that the Kwakiutl prefer to guide their lives according to events such as when they *feel* tired or *feel* some other pressure rather than to be locked into an arbitrary set of habits imposed by alien and intrusive institutions. Prescheduled events, except school, rarely begin at the designated time because few families start getting ready until it is time for the activity to begin. Both Indians and Whites sometimes refer to this orientation as "Indian time."

The day usually begins with breakfast of tea and toast, or occasionally hot chocolate or cereal. Children are sent off to school at nine and the workday begins, although schedules are so diversified depending on the week, month or season that an accurate, composite description of daily life is difficult. Men may go to the village float to work on their gill-netters—repairing the engine, pumping out the bilge, or drawing the boat onto the high tide beach to be scraped or caulked. Some men stand around idly talking to their neighbors or work on their torn nets.

Willis Drake, the chief councillor in the village, goes at least once a week to Simoom Sound and Echo Bay for supplies for his store in the village. He also picks up the village mail as well as supplies and mail for the school. People often hop a ride with him to get some of their own groceries and mail, including Unemployment Insurance Checks (UIC) and relief checks, or they send a note with Willis asking for supplies, generally on credit. Credit for subsistence needs is basic to the livelihood of the Indians. Since they rarely have ready cash available, a great strain would be put on them if merchants refused credit. The storekeepers know members of the community well enough to make decisions about the extension of credit; moreover, the store owners at Simoom Sound have an effective technique of forcing payment from negligent villagers. They run the area post office in which checks are received; sometimes, if a family is too far behind in its payment, the storekeepers do not forward the money. Rather, they send a note saying that the check is being held for them. With the money in his hand the debtor finds it hard not to pay at least part of his bill. A comparable technique is used by Chief Philip when he functions as the clam buyer on the clam scow. He automatically deducts debts before he pays his clam diggers. Credit is categorically refused at the beer parlor in Echo Bay.

I asked the store owner at Echo Bay about the relationship between Indians and Whites regarding the payment of bills. He explained, "Whites are either black or white as far as their credit is concerned. Either they pay their bills well or don't pay them at all. Indians, on the other hand, may pay well for awhile and then stop paying anything at all; later they may pay again." Overall, however, he feels that Indians are a better credit risk than Whites: "Many Whites take off when they owe me too much and never return. Indians almost always return to the area where their kinsmen live. In the long run it's often easier to force payment from Indians than Whites."

After Willis leaves the house in the morning, Lucy, his wife (as well as the other wives) straightens her house, washes the dishes and perhaps begins heating water for laundry. A few hours are usually required to get enough hot water to fill the large galvanized tubs. Several of the women have access to gas-powered washing machines, but others use scrub boards. While they are waiting for the water to heat they may relax at the kitchen table overlooking the channel and listen to their transistor radios, or begin preparing salmon or clams to be barbecued for a later meal. The villagers at Gilford do not have refrigerators so the preservation of perishable food is sometimes a problem. They have learned that barbecuing, smoking and drying are moderately efficient means of keeping marine life from rapidly spoiling. At one time they immersed foods such as wild berries in closed containers of oulachon oil, thus sealing out the air and preserving the fruit, but few people do this today. Barbecued clams, as the term is used at Gilford, are clams that have been removed from their shells, laced onto skewers and placed in front of an open fire to cook and smoke for an hour or two. The same method is used to barbecue salmon: a fish is filleted, secured within a stake frame and placed around a fire. Fish and clams for smoking are either placed on racks in a smokehouse and left for a day or two with a continuous smoky fire inside, or they are dried on racks over a small open fire and left in the sun or on a rack over the kitchen stove to dry further.

By the time the women have gotten well into these chores children and men are home for dinner. The midday meal is generally the largest of the day and may consist of stew, macaroni, wieners, sandwiches, clams or fish, and canned corn or some other cold, canned vegetable. The Kwakiutl almost inevitably include tea and bread with their meals. Potatoes too, are very common; they eat rice less frequently. Fish, barbecued clams and boiled potatoes are dipped into a bowl of oulachon grease which is in the middle of the table. Serving dishes are placed on the table and each person reaches for what he wants. Villagers eat few fresh vegetables and little fruit. They almost never drink milk, although they use canned milk in coffee. One woman calls fresh produce "White man's food." Occasionally, especially after a night of heavy drinking, they eat eggs and bacon. At least one meal a day typically requires the use of a spoon as the basic implement, but those meals consisting of fish and potatoes are eaten with the fingers. If anyone is hungry after a meal or between meals, he eats bread.

Meals are typically eaten quickly and almost in silence. Noisy or talkative children are admonished to be quiet. Whatever conversation occurs follows the meal over a cup of tea. Many of the families supplement their regular diet by trading food items. One family may give venison to another, and later, the second reciprocates with some other food such as fish. Leftovers are thrown to the village dogs, but when excess food is scarce the dogs forage for themselves. After dinner, the men go back out or take a nap and the children return to school.

Malnutrition, according to local medical personnel, is one of the most prevalent health problems among the Indians. Gertie, daughter-in-law of Chief Philip, was amazed when a doctor told her that she could eat three meals a day, feel satisfied and still not receive the nutrients she needs for good health. Because of malnutrition the Kwakiutl are susceptible to infectious disease of all kinds, including tuberculosis. Dental problems are also attributable to diet. Chronic anemia is yet another common health problem, and obesity in middle age is one of the most notable physical characteristics of the people.

Each family is responsible for securing its firewood. The Drakes, for example, are low on wood so Willis takes his gill-netter to get a log he saw drifting in the channel last night while he was jigging for cod and other bottomfish. After Willis relocates the log he lashes it to his boat, tows it back to the village, floats it onto the beach at high tide, and then sections it with a chain saw. Some of the other men cut logs by hand unless they can borrow a chain saw. The round sections are carried to a woodpile beside the house and split into four large pieces. All this is man's work. Either men or women chop one of the large pieces into kindling or into a size appropriate for the stoves.

The division of labor among the Kwakiutl is neither sharp nor crystallized, although certain jobs are customarily assigned to men and others are allotted to women. Men are responsible for most commercial and subsistence activities; women tend to the majority of the domestic chores. With notable exceptions men do not cook in the home, nor do they wash the dishes, but they do both when they are fishing. Women wash clothes and complete the little ironing that is done. Both men and women clean the house, but this is viewed as largely women's responsibility. Fishing of all types tends to be largely man's work even though men, women and children dig clams. Many women cannot read a tide table; consequently most of them are dependent on men for making decisions about when and where to dig. Women with the help of children usually dig clams for family use. More men dig clams for cash than women.

School is over at three in the afternoon. Willie Moon's parents are in bad credit-standing at Lucy and Willis Drake's store because they have been derelict in paying their bills. Edna Moon, Willie's mother, forgot to order bread, margarine and canned lunch meat when Willis went to Simoom Sound this morning, so after school she sends Willie with a note to the Drakes' store asking for these groceries rather than face Lucy herself. The Drakes stock only fast moving items in their back room such as candy, eggs, bread, canned milk, margarine, soda pop, canned lunch meat and occasionally fresh fruit. They also handle the village dispensary which contains ointments, aspirin, bandages and other first aid and medical supplies, for which they receive ten dollars a month from the Indian Health Services. The Drakes keep no written records of their income from the store, but they maintain a clear mental record of the debts and credits involving most people in the village. Lucy refuses Edna's request for supplies and makes several pointed remarks to Willie about people not paying their bills. She is confident Willie will repeat these remarks to his mother. Lucy has sent five notes to the Moons' home in the past two days saying, "I know you have the money. Please pay." Dunning through the use of notes carried by children is common among Gilford villagers. The adults who are dunned avoid going to the store because, as commonly expressed, "they are ashamed."

Forcing payment of debts is a frequent problem in a wide variey of situations. David Crow, a young shipwright in the settlement, for example, built a rowboat for another fisherman who delayed payment for many months. "Finally I flipped my cork," David scowled, "and gave him until the twentieth to pay or I'd take the boat away." Moreover, David feels that he is losing friends in the village by extending credit for work and then trying to collect. His father has admonished him on numerous occasions never to work on credit, "but only now am I learning the truth of what he said." Not uncommonly several years lapse before payment is made, and then it is made only after energetic insistence on the part of the creditor.

After Willie returned home with his verbal message and another dunning note from Lucy, he and three village adolescents forage around the village for beer bottles which they collect in preparation for shipment to Vancouver. Each case contains twelve bottles and is worth fifteen cents in the Bay or twenty-five cents if it is sent directly to Vancouver. On one occasion the village youths collected two hundred seventy cases of bottles; six months later several adults crated two hundred cases. This gives a rough but minimal approximation of the amount of beer consumed in the village during that time.

By the time Willie and his friends return home supper is ready. Supper, a lighter meal than dinner, consists essentially of the same foods. After supper Edna and her three kids put on their gum boots, hats, sweaters and caps, grab their clam forks, a couple of pails, one of their gas lamps and a pronged stake on which to hang it. They go to the low tide beach off to one side of the village to dig clams for tomorrow's dinner. Many village residents dig on the beaches adjacent to the village for family food but they do not often select these beaches for commercial digging because too many people have exploited them for too long. Paul, Edna's husband, joins half a dozen other men and a scattering of women who are congregating on the scow and on their boats. They plan to dig commercially. Two boats left for distant clam grounds over an hour ago to get there before the tide reached its ebb, but Paul and his companions do not plan to go as far. They are going to the west side of Mars Island, about twenty-five minutes from Gilford.

Before they leave, Paul and two other men go aboard the scow to pick up their gunnysacks. Paul needs a new clam fork because the handle of his old one cracked the last time he was out, and one of the other men needs some naphtha (white gas) for his Coleman lamp. The cost of the fork will be deducted later from Paul's clam sales. The radiophone behind the counter crackles and occasionally erupts with a noisy message between two seiners in the area. The radiophone on the scow provided the people's only immediate link with the outside world during our year at Gilford, but since then a permanent one has been installed within the village.

The official clam season typically opens on November first and at this time Chief Philip tows a scow to Gilford from a fish company in the Bay. The scow is tied alongside the float, and from the first day it becomes the business and social center in the village. It is possible to find men congregated on it or on the float beside it almost every day. Stanley Philip is the official clam buyer but Herbert or one of Chief Philip's other sons operates the scow while Stanley makes his daily rounds of neighboring villages and clam sites to buy clams from those people who cannot get to the scow. Gilford is commonly thought of as the clam center of the region and, for this reason, many Indians migrate to the settlement for varying lengths of time during the winter. The villagers and the visitors at Gilford dig most of the clams that are purchased on the scow.

The groups of diggers who typically travel together to clam sites remain fairly constant. The person who owns or has access to a gill-netter decides where to go and as many as seven people accompany him. The people assembling on the float with Paul, however, represent a potpourri of diggers who do not belong to any such semi-stable group. Paul is not happy about the prospect of digging this evening because the tide is poor—villagers usually begin digging at a 5-foot tide even though this is not considered a good one—and the temperature is dropping noticeably. Digging continues each day through the low point of the tidal period, or simply "the tide" as the Kwakiutl call it, and digging stops when the low tides have risen back to 4 feet.

By the time tides are at 4 feet it is late at night because corresponding low tides are approximately fifty minutes later each day. Low tide on the first digging day of the 1962–1963 season, for example, was at 5:37 P.M. Six days later at the end of the tidal period (most tidal periods are about ten days with an average of eight intervening days between periods), it was 10:00 P.M. The Indians rarely dig if low tide is after 11:30 or 12:00 P.M. because the yield in a 5-foot tide is characteristically much lower than in a 1-or 2-foot tide, and because the time during which they can dig is greatly reduced. For these reasons fewer Indians dig during 4- and 5-foot tides than during lower ones. Furthermore, most of the appropriate clam tides before February occur after dark, but by March and April some midday tides occur, and sometimes the tide goes low enough to dig twice each day in February and March—once in the morning and then again twelve hours later in the evening.

Paul's enthusiasm for this evening's work is diminished further as the clam crew approaches its destination because the wind is beginning to spring up. The Kwakiutl dig at night, in the rain and not infrequently in near-freezing weather; but they do not, as a rule, dig during periods of high wind. Gill-netters are usually anchored in a cove near the clam beds and the clam crew rows to shore in a dinghy that has been towed behind the gill-netter. High winds may cause the gill-netter to be swept onto shore or into the open water of the channel, or the row boat used to go between boat and shore may be swept away when the tide begins to rise. In either case diggers can be left stranded and their boats may be lost or destroyed. Paul is also concerned that the breeze will push the water too far onto shore, thereby keeping the tide—as poor as it is—from reaching its predicted low. Pat Cedar wrote about this regarding the 1963–1964 clam season, "Well. sure bad this year for clam digging. not so hot to much wind or two small of a tide. but I guess it will pick up soon."

After they arrive on Mars Island the men go their individual ways several yards apart and search for the best place to begin digging. Experienced diggers believe that digging is most productive when the tide begins to flow. The reasons given for this vary. Some say that the clams come closer to the surface as the tide rises; others say that it takes them most of the tide to find a good clam bed. Willis Drake, Gideon Amber and Jacob Abel are recognized as being outstanding diggers. These men are said to know exactly where to dig at each site, whereas most people have to search for a productive clam bed.

The clams are placed in a pail; when the pail is filled it is poured into a gunnysack which, when full, weighs approximately 60 pounds—equivalent to "a box." The box is the standard unit of measurement for clams. Clams are supposed to be poured from the sacks into clam boxes and then back into bags. A good digger can produce six boxes in an evening, but the average person digs only three or four.

Clams very often are not measured when the diggers sell them. But the men working on the scow informally assess the weight of each sack as it is thrown from the gill-netter onto the scow and into a corner. The clams are measured in clam boxes, however, some time before they are shipped to Vancouver. Chief Philip has one of his sons perform this task while they make the buying rounds of the various villages and clam sites. He measures clams not to check the weight of each sack, which experienced handlers can tell quite accurately by lifting the bag, but to check the contents. Some diggers put rocks, sand or other heavy objects in the sacks to increase the weight, or they deliberately do not fill the sack to an estimated sixty pounds. Stanley was incensed when the chief from a neighboring village did not quite fill his sack. As a precautionary measure some clam buyers weigh every sack, but this is very time-consuming. A second reason for transferring clams from one container to another is to examine and sort the clams themselves. Badly damaged clams and horse clams are thrown overboard. Moreover, government regulations specify that certain kinds of clams must be a specific size before they can be sold. For example, butter clams may not be less than 2½ inches across, whereas razor clams may not be less than 3½ inches across, and littleneck clams must be at least 1½ inches across.

After enough clams have been collected on the scow, Stanley hauls them in his seine boat to Vancouver, about a day and a half from Gilford. He usually needs to make two trips each tidal period because clams spoil quickly. Rarely do clams remain on the scow for more than four or five days. By the end of the 1962–1963 season Stanley had taken nearly 11,000 boxes (well over half a million pounds) of clams to Vancouver. This only accounts for the clams that Stanley personally picked up from nearby sites or that had been delivered to the scow at Gilford. The fishermen were paid $1.80 a box (three cents a pound) for clams during the 1962–1963 season, but the price varies from time to time. The following season, for example, the Indians refused to dig for Chief Philip until his company matched the $2.50 price offered by an independent buyer. When the fishermen began digging for the independent buyer, Stanley's company reconsidered and paid the $2.50 a box.

After Paul and the other diggers leave for their clam site, Pat Cedar and Charlie Bean row almost a mile to Bonwick Island in a borrowed, hand-hewn canoe. They have a .22 caliber rifle, a shotgun and a high-powered flashlight with them. They row quietly along the shore of the island beaming their light on the bank and into the brush, searching for deer. Deer are attracted to the light, and the reflection from the deer's eyes is easily visible and provides a fair target at close range. Pit lamping—the use of a spotlight at night—is illegal, but it is the most effective, and thus popular, means of hunting. Occasionally men also hunt in logged-out areas during the day. The official deer season runs from the middle of September to the end of November, but in practice the official season makes no difference to the Indians. The men hunt throughout the year, especially for deer, but also for other animals such as ducks when they are available. The Kwakiutl are allowed to get a permit to hunt for food outside the formal season, but they rarely bother to obtain one. In fact many of them are not aware that they are eligible for permits. A deer is dressed where it is shot to make it more easily transportable. It is skinned, quartered and butchered in the village and the meat, known simply as deer meat, is used for stew. We once invited Gertie and Herb Philip for a venison steak dinner, but they were unable to eat the meat because they have so many missing teeth.

By the time Pat, Charles, Paul and the other clam diggers return to the village it is nearly midnight. About half the diggers pause on the scow after selling their clams to buy a piece of pie, a hot dog, a cup of coffee or a pack of cigarettes from Gertie Philip, who has set up a small business there. The others go home to have a snack before retiring—coffee as a treat, but more often tea, plus bread or crackers, margarine, jam and sometimes other foods such as dried fish.

Henry Rochelle, a white man allied to one of the village women in common-law marriage, is a logger. He and Daniel Drake, Willis Drake's half brother, are the only men in the village who regularly log rather than fish. They leave the village at seven each morning in Danny's speed boat. Although some of the other men also log for brief periods of time, especially during the low income months of April and May when they have less to do than during any other time of the year, logging is not popular. In fact a few Kwakiutl express fear of working in the woods. Frank Bean, for example, described his work in one of the local camps and concluded that he is afraid of logging but that he needs the job. "I have to pull my share in the work or be a coward," he confided.

Logging in the "gyppo" or "gyp" outfits, as the small logging companies

Artistic representation of two ceremonial dance figures (Allen James)

are locally known, is sometimes dangerous, but it is probably no more so than some of the other jobs the Indians regularly perform. Danger is hardly a sufficient reason to explain the reluctance of the men to work in the woods—except that the Kwakiutl more readily perceive the risks there because they are not at ease in the forest. A more important reason for their reserve about working in the

Salmon hunter dance (Allen James)

lumber industry is that logging often requires them to be away from the village and from their families except on weekends. They are willing to do this for a few months, but seldom for longer. Moreover, the logging camp nearest Gilford is said to be understaffed, thus each man must perform jobs that normally require two or three men in the larger operations. Indians have the reputation among logging employers of being valuable and hard workers, except that they very often do not get to work on time. If they have been drinking or if some important social event is taking place, they frequently do not show up for work at all. A few of the men have a long history of being fired from jobs because of this.

Other men are just getting out of bed as Henry and Danny leave for work. Ambrose Cedar is in his early fifties, overweight and has a bad heart so he cannot fish or log anymore. Over the years he has become an extraordinary artist and craftsman. He makes his living largely through carving, but this modest income is supplemented by family allowance and an occasional relief check. Pat, his nephew, has a badly curved spine which Pat attributes to being pushed down a cliff; but it is the opinion of a local doctor that his hunched back is more likely due to tuberculosis as a child. Pat can do no heavy physical labor, and relies largely on art for his small income. He has watched his uncle carve and paint all his life and under this tutelage has become a capable and rapidly maturing painter. Jeffrey Hardy, also a brilliant craftsman, is the third village resident who gains most of his livelihood from a commercial craft. A few of the other men in the village also carve during their free time. The work of each of these men follows traditional themes. Ambrose and Jeffrey produce such artifacts as stylized ceremonial masks and hamatsa (cannibal society) whistles belonging to the traditional winter ceremonial dance societies. Pat often depicts dancing figures in their ceremonial costumes and scenes from these winter dances.

Craftsmen usually sell their products to the store owner at Echo Bay, but they sometimes ship them directly to dealers in Vancouver. The price paid for masks carved by different men varies greatly, reflecting not only the difference in quality but also the minimum price that some of the novices will accept. Jeffrey complained to me with annoyance that the "beginners are selling their masks cheap and bringing the price down on good ones."

Some basic changes have taken place in Kwakiutl crafts over time, mainly through the influence of Whites. Carving and painting are being transformed to suit the demands of the commercial market, or at least to match the Indians' perception of such demands. Traditionally, but essentially true today too, men worked with rigid materials such as wood, not excluding cedar bark. Women worked with pliable material, making cedar bark cloth, for example. Today women crochet, knit, embroider and make "shiny paper" pillow covers from the foil in cigarette packages. None of these have much commercial value but are used to decorate homes and are given away at potlatches.

The people are losing a large part of their traditional technology as they become increasingly dependent on industrially produced goods. At one time they manufactured fishing nets from the fiber of nettles; now they buy nylon nets. They once produced adhesives from the translucent tissue between the skin and flesh of the salmon; they now use glue and tape. They used to utilize natural elements in the environment to produce colored pigments for their oil base paints, but today they buy commercial enamels. Furthermore, relatively few younger people are able to cut and strip fish into thick pieces as they once did. Gertie Philip was annoyed and embarrassed when a group of older women found her experimenting with the technique of barbecuing salmon. The older women know the technique but she did not, and she admitted that she was "ashamed to ask them."

Ambrose is disgruntled this morning. He has had few requests for masks recently and he is almost broke. Louisa, his common-law wife, is sick; and yesterday his request for relief from the Indian Agent was denied. Ambrose's reproachful reaction to being turned down for relief is a typical one. Through the paternalistic policy of the Indian Affairs Branch, especially until recently, many Indians have come to expect assistance from the Agency as part of their natural right. Ambrose is doubly discontent, however, because some of the other villagers have recently received relief, and he feels that his need is at least equally as great as theirs. He went on to cite several people who have extra sources of income—for example, Harold Dick who has a trap line—and who nonetheless receives relief, whereas he—who is without such a supplementary source—has been refused. Villagers often become resentful when someone else receives welfare assistance, regardless of the need, and they do not.

Not infrequently Indians ask the Agency Superintendent for relief when they have been drinking or when they are inebriated. The Superintendent turns

Village woman making a clam basket

down all such requests, except under exceptional circumstances, asking, "Where did they get the money for liquor if they need relief?" Some Indians are almost automatically granted relief assistance when they apply for it because the Agent believes they never ask unless the need is real. He believes he has to use caution in filling other requests. Many Indians are reported to regularly give misinformation about their income when they apply. Similarly, the Indian Agent believes that he cannot necessarily trust the recommendations of the village band council because of the strong kinship bonds within the community and the resultant bias. On rare occasions a band councillor argues with a kinsman and refuses to recommend him for relief when it is genuinely needed; sometimes councillors recommend relief even though there is no real need.

Before sunup this morning, David Crow left the village in his gill-netter to try his hand at salmon fishing with his new trolling poles attached to the boat. He spent the past day and a half on the float, assembling equipment and stripping bark from long, straight, tapered saplings to be used as trolling poles. This is the first year that trolled salmon have been purchased on the scow. This is also the first time that most of the men are using trolling poles; in the past they trolled by hand. David and the other men who are attempting to master this new technique have had to learn from Whites and other commercial trollers about the type of equipment to use, how to assemble it and how to use it. A man sometimes leaves the settlement for two or three days between clam tides when he trolls with poles, but he rarely needs to stay away for more than a day when he trolls by hand. David is not sure how long he will stay out—perhaps a couple of days if he is successful but, if not, he plans to return home this evening. A number of men in the winter of 1963 viewed trolling with poles as more of a novel pastime than a serious occupational enterprise. Even though the price for trolled fish is fairly high, the small catch and the expense of running the gill-netter reduce the profit and often result in a loss.

Several hours after Dave left, Harold Dick and his common-law wife, Jennie Drake, set out separately from the scow, Jennie in Harold's canoe and Harold in a borrowed row boat. Jennie is going to jig for family food and Harold intends to check his trap line. Jennie is an obese woman in her fifties who speaks very little English. She knows more than any woman in the village about traditional technology and she is the only woman we observed going out alone in a boat to fish. Moreover, she is the person to whom others turn for information about basket weaving, making button-blankets (ceremonial dance blankets) and dance aprons, barbecuing clams or smoking halibut; she is also the reluctant village midwife. Jennie has been legally married twice. Her first husband, who is the father of Willis by another wife, died. She left her second husband and lived with another man until he died. Then Harold moved in with her. She has had fourteen children by these men, and the majority of the Gilford Island Kwakiutl with the surname of Abel (her maiden name), Drake, Bean, Crow or Dick can trace very close kinship affiliation with her. Furthermore, she is related to well over half the villagers if kinship calculations are extended to include bonds through marriage. But then, from this perspective almost all of the Gilford Islanders are related in some way to one another.

Harold's trap line lies along the northern perimeter of Bonwick Island across from Gilford. About 500 feet from Bonwick he spots a hair seal coming up for air. He raises his shotgun, fires, and swiftly rows to the spot where the seal is flailing in the water. He drags the dying animal onto his boat, kills it, expertly cuts off its nose, and then tosses the carcass back into the sea. The Game Commission has established a bounty of $5 per nose for hair seals because they attack salmon trapped in gill nets.

Hal continues on to check his line for mink and otter. He spent three days last month setting out his line; it takes him half a day to check it. Hal has his shotgun with him because if he spots a free animal he intends to shoot it—regardless of where he sees it or on whose line he happens to be. Pelts of animals that have been shot are often badly damaged and therefore less valuable than the pelt of trapped animals, but even a damaged pelt is worth more than none at all. Harold has a widespread reputation for poaching, that is, for shooting or stealing animals on the trap lines belonging to other men. Joe Abel, Jennie's brother, has had a lot of trouble with Hal poaching on his line. He describes Hal as a "real haywire guy, a real orang-utan." Although he has never pressed charges against Hal, poaching is in fact punishable by a heavy fine and/or jail sentence. Indians rarely lay charges against each other, even if one actually catches someone poaching on his territory. This attitude is characteristic of the Kwakiutl in most situations and is described more fully later.

Jennie has been home for a couple of hours by the time Hal returns. She caught so many fish that the light chop caused by the afternoon breeze combined with her own weight caused water to wash over the gunwales of her canoe. Her canoe was barely afloat by the time she reached Gilford. On the float she filleted half a gunnysack full of fish and left the remainder in the canoe. On the way to her house at the far end of the village she told people to take as many fish as they wanted. Most people took two or three, but one woman took a gunnysackful. Fishermen take what they need, share the excess and tighten their belts when the fishing is poor, since on many occasions fishermen return home with no fish at all.

These events illustrate two days in December. They do not begin to exhaust the complete range of activities in which the Kwakiutl involve themselves during other seasons. As revealed in Table 2, for example, winter gill netting opens before the trapping season closes at the end of February. The price of netted spring salmon during this time is considerably reduced from the trolled price of the same fish earlier, because the fish tend to be bruised or damaged as they are drawn back onto the boat.

Between these two seasons is the period of oulachon fishing for domestic household use. The people of Gilford fish for oulachon during March and April in the Kingcome River. Oulachon are also plentiful at the head of the Knight Inlet, about a day's travel from the village, but few Gilford Islanders go there. Traditionally certain tribes had fishery rights at specific locations, but not at others. Such rights on the Kingcome River were shared by the Four Tribes of Gilford (Koeksotenok, Tsawatenok, Guauaenok and Hahuamis), as well as the Nimkish and the Komkyutis. Other tribes shared Knight Inlet. Today these rights are not carefully

TABLE 2.
SEASONAL ECONOMIC AND SUBSISTENCE ACTIVITIES[a]

Sources	Length of Activity by Month											
	Nov.	Dec.	Jan.	Feb.	Mar.	Apr.	May	June	July	Aug.	Sept.	Oct.
Summer Salmon Fishing							—	— —				
Clam Season					— —	— —	— —					
Halibut Fishing						— — —				— —	— — —	—
Winter Trolling	————————											
Winter Gill Netting				—								
Trapping	—————————————											
Oulachon Processing					———							
Deer Season		— — —	— —	—	— —	— —	— — —	— — —	— — —	— — —	— — —	— —
Duck Season		—	— — —	—	— —	— —	— —					
UIC		—————————————————————										
Seaweed Collecting							——					
Family Allowance												

[a] The broken lines in the table indicate, for example, that the summer commercial salmon season opens in May, but the Kwakiutl at Gilford do not begin intensive fishing operations until the latter part of June. The clam season formally opens in November and closes in May but the villagers usually quit digging commercially in the middle of March.

guarded and members of different tribes may go to different places; nonetheless, a strong tendency persists to fish at traditional sites.

Oulachon, which are related to smelt, are netted, placed in earth pits, and allowed to partially decompose. The oil content of the fish is so high that the fish may be used as candles by simply drying them and inserting wicks in the dried carcass. After rotting for ten days they are placed in a large vat of boiling water which causes the oil to rise to the surface. The oil is scooped from the top of the water and is bottled in gallon jugs. Skill and experience are important in making oulachon oil, or "grease" as the oil is customarily called. Those people who do not have the expertise to manufacture it usually buy it from someone at the currently standardized price of $5 a gallon, although at times it is given away, primarily to close relatives or friends.[1] Grease is a staple in the diet of many families and is usually eaten with fish and boiled potatoes. It is also used as a

[1] The 1968 price was reported to be ten dollars a gallon.

medicine (rubbed on the body to reduce fever), and it figures prominently in feasts and potlatches (public display and distribution of property in the context of one individual or group claiming certain hereditary rights or privileges vis-a-vis another group).[2]

The months of March through May are among the most economically diversified as well as socially active. They are also the months when the people of Gilford have the most free time. Clam digging closes, winter gill netting opens and closes, the oulachon run passes, halibut fishing opens, and by the time it closes the commercial salmon fishing season opens. In addition, the Kwakiutl take advantage of special seasonal products such as berries, seaweed, crabs, and sometimes barnacles. Crabs are collected in spring on the low tide beaches or in shallow water. A few men put out crab pots. People occasionally eat barnacles after they are collected and steamed free from large chunks of rock. This is rather rare, however, since many people now are unaware that barnacles are edible. Berries are collected primarily by children during the late spring and early summer. In May adults travel a day's journey to sites where seaweed grows. It is picked, dried for several days on top of the big-house or sometimes on specially constructed platforms, and each night it is re-collected and stored in a warm, dry place. Fresh water such as dew or rain is said to spoil it. After the seaweed is dry it is finely ground and stored in containers. Seaweed is considered as something special to be eaten as it is or put into clam chowder or on cold canned corn.

The majority of the village men define fishing—especially salmon fishing— as their most important economic activity. Clam digging is less important for most Indians than fishing, both in their over-all life process and in their self-definition. This is true even though they spend almost an equal number of days throughout the year doing both. Many men could earn a great deal more money through logging, but they choose not to. None of the men during our year at Gilford could remember exactly how much money he had earned the preceding year in logging, clam digging, crafts or trapping; but many of them could recall quite closely how much money he earned from fishing (mean $1700; range $400–$3200). We interpret this as an indication of their close identity with fishing. Furthermore, there were ninety days in which people could dig clams during the 1962–1963 season. Given the fact that the diggers produce an average of at least three boxes of clams per tide per person, one could expect their mean personal income from clams that year to approach $500. In fact, however, the average (mean) income from clam digging during the 1962–1963 season was $200 or 60 percent less than expected. This too reflects the people's more casual attitude toward clamming. With these facts in mind we turn now to the commercial salmon fishing season.

Commercial Salmon Fishing

The Native Celebration in Alert Bay, or June Sports as the occasion is more popularly known, takes place during the last week of June each year. It informally marks the beginning of commercial salmon fishing even though the season

---

[2] We discuss the potlatch at greater length in the last chapter.

officially opens earlier. Although some men fish before the close of June Sports, the major event marking the season is the annual salmon run north in the area of Rivers Inlet, about a day's voyage. The opening of the fishing season at Rivers Inlet coincides with the celebration of June Sports.

The Kwakiutl Indians fish on two types of boats—gill-netters and purse seiners. The mechanics of gill-net fishing are quite different from purse seining. In the first place, gill netting is a one- or two-man operation, whereas seining requires a crew of four to seven men. More importantly the style of fishing is totally different on the two types of boats. Different kinds of nets and other equipment are used. Seiners fish during daylight hours (in the early summer from 4:00 A.M. to 10:00 P.M.) whereas gill-netters can fish equally well during the day or night. The process of netting the fish on seiners bears no relation to netting fish on gill-netters. In the latter, the gill net (from which this type of fishing takes its name) is managed from a drum anchored toward the stern of the boat. When a fisherman arrives at his chosen fishing grounds he drops his net out into the water through rollers secured off the stern. The boat is positioned down wind from the net so that the craft does not drift back into the net.[3] Once the net is out both the boat and the net are allowed to drift. Fish swim into the net and try to pass through but they cannot because the mesh is too small. Then they try to withdraw and in the process their gill covers become entangled in the net. Periodically the fisherman rolls his net back onto the drum, disentangling the salmon and other fish that have become caught as the net passes over the rollers. The task of bringing in the net takes about ten minutes if it is empty but it takes considerably longer if fish and debris are caught in it.

Gill-net fishermen at Rivers Inlet are extremely competitive with each other. Benny Otter described fishing at Rivers as "a panic." Potential conflict between seiners and gill-netters is reduced in the Rivers area because only gill-netters are allowed in the inlet itself. Gill-netters fish at night in areas where both may work, thus avoiding mutual interference. Nonetheless, violence or the threat of violence is reported to sometimes erupt.

During intervals between net checks, the gill-net fisherman sleeps, reads or listens to his radio; if fishing has been very poor he may make one set and leave it until morning. But the men usually sleep very little during the night at Rivers Inlet because of the large number of fish that swim into the net and because of the dangers of drifting into one another's net. Men who damage the net of another fisherman are responsible for making reparation. Moreover, a sleeping gill-net fisherman runs the risk of having his net or boat drift into a restricted area. Fisheries Department boats and planes carefully patrol the areas and levy a fine against anyone who has allowed his net to cross a restricted boundary.

A packer boat from one of the three fish-packing companies based in Alert Bay usually collects fish from the Gilford fishermen at least once a day. Each boat flies his company flag as identification for the packer. Occasionally,

---

[3] Gill nets, which vary in size and color, are suspended vertically in the water by a cork-line attached to the top of the net causing it to float, and by a lead-line at the bottom weighing it down. They vary in length from about 200 to 300 fathoms (1200–1800 feet) and they are usually 2 fathoms deep.

Village fisherman disentangling a salmon. The net in the water is supported by the cork-line behind the gill-netter.

however, depending on the area, the fishermen take their fish to a buyer stationed on a scow near land. The men are expected to sell their fish only to the company for which they work. No money actually passes hands except when a fisherman sells his fish to an independent buyer for cash; independent buyers often pay more than the fish companies. The men recognize that selling to independents is a risky practice, however, because they are dependent on their fish companies for credit, for financing boats, for nets and other equipment, and for a steady market. The companies extend credit at the beginning of the season for food and for supplies, and they perform other services as well. Part of a man's commercial success depends on his reputation with one of the fish-packing companies. A fisherman who is caught selling his fish to an independent buyer may lose favor with his company, and this can create a major hardship.

Purse seiners are much larger than gill-netters, and seining is done during daylight hours. Seiners carry large nets which are designed to be manipulated by two boats—the seiner itself and a skiff. The nets are typically 125–200 fathoms long and 9–10 fathoms deep. And as is true of gill nets, the top of the seine net is supported by a cork-line and the bottom is weighted by a lead-line; a purse-line is connected by rings to the lead line. The seiner crew may attempt to set the net to surround a school of fish; or the men may simply make set after set in an advantageous position, sometimes waiting several hours to take a turn at a good tie-up spot on the shore. The salmon are trapped when the bottom of the net closes and forms the purse. This is why this form of fishing is called purse-seining. Seine boats hold a set open for twenty minutes, the period of time authorized and enforced by the Fisheries Department.

A seiner crew is usually composed of four to seven men. Shares are computed on the basis of seven-man crews, but when seiners go out with a short crew each man receives a greater part of the profit. A full crew typically consists of the skipper, one cook, three men on the deck of the seiner, and two skiff men. Profits are divided into eleven shares, seven to the crew, and the remaining four go to the boat, the net and the skipper. The net and boat shares are taken by the owner of each, very often a fish company. The cost of food, fuel and some equipment is deducted from the gross earnings before shares are apportioned. If the seiner damages someone else's or its own net, this too is deducted from the gross earnings. Many skippers do not allow their crew to inspect the books. In this way the skipper can sometimes include deductible items that his crew would find objectionable, but the crew seldom shows any concern for what is deducted from the gross earnings before their shares are allotted. Some crews suspect their skippers of cheating, and for this and a variety of other interpersonal reasons the crews on most seine boats continue to change throughout the fishing season.

Most men at Gilford prefer to own or at least operate their own gill-netters rather than sign on as crew members of a seiner. One of the village men, Victor Philip, expressed the sentiment of many others when he explained why he prefers having his own gill-netter: "I'm my own boss. Some guys on seiners are real haywire and others get stuck doing all the work." Most of the village men, including older adolescents, have worked at one time or another on a seiner, but most of them agree that they can make more money by operating their own gill-netter—if they can get one. They catch fewer fish but they also have fewer expenses. Only one person receives the earnings—but he must meet the costs, too. None of the men at Gilford skippers his own seiner during the commercial salmon season.

Several of the village fishermen have had their own gill-netters in the past, but they had them taken away by the fish companies and now they work on seiners. A couple of the villagers, for example, mortgaged their boats to a fish company for nets costing about $1000 each. The men neglected to make payments on the nets and, as a consequence, they lost both their nets and their boats. The Indians understand why the nets were taken from them but they do not understand why they lost their boats. They do not realize the implications of a mortgage. The transaction was both honest and legal from the fish company's viewpoint, but the villagers see the Whites as cheating them. Chief Philip summarized this kind of problem with the observation, "Indians today don't have the business sense they used to have. They used to be good."

Fishing is a risky venture and it is becoming increasingly uncertain each year as more people enter the industry with more efficient equipment and as the provincial government enforces stricter limitations on the times and places where men can fish. One of the complicating factors in the fishing economy of the Indians, for example, and one which is creating a great strain on the economy, is the restricted fishing week. In the past, the fishing week extended from 6:00 P.M. Sunday to 6:00 P.M. Thursday. Toward the end of the 1963 fishing season the week was reduced to a two-day period beginning 6:00 P.M. Sunday and closing at 6:00 P.M. Tuesday. Occasionally the fishing week is extended a day or two, but far more often it is not. Although commercial salmon fishing is open from May to October, the most productive fishing tends to occur from the end of June through early August. Thus, the effective fishing season for the people of Gilford is about three months. Fishing closures are determined by the Fisheries Department as part of their conservation program. Fairly tight controls must be maintained at the northern end of Vancouver Island where the Kwakiutl live in order to protect the fishing interest of men further south, as well as to assure that enough salmon reach their spawning grounds.

The Fish Commission notifies fishermen of impending closures by radio broadcast. Seiners have a radiotelephone on board, but most gill-netters do not. Those people who do not have a radiophone are notified through the informal communication network of other fishermen and fish packers. Many people keep their transistor radios or radiophones tuned to the marine frequencies for fishing information. Listening to marine bands on transistor radios and use of radiotelephones to intercept messages have major implications for communication throughout the area. Few bands on the radiophones are restricted; consequently anyone who is interested may listen to conversations between boats or between ship and shore. This explains, in part, the celebrated "Indian grapevine" by which many people know about events as soon as, or even before in some cases, the people who are involved. Radiotelephones are used extensively by the fishermen to exchange information about fishing. Fishermen are often secretive about their location if they are discussing good fish catches because they know that others are listening. In fact Indians often speak Kwakwala, the native language of the Kwakiutl, in order to exclude at least non-Indians from this information. The radiotelephones are also vital to notify others of an accident or of a breakdown.

Boats travel from place to place searching for fish or move from an area which has been closed to one type of fishing, for example, net fishing, to another zone that is not restricted to net fishing. Although experienced fishermen usually know where fish are likely to be found, they also travel on the basis of personal and overheard conversation. Certain localized areas, such as the entrance to streams, are permanently closed to fishing. Other areas may be temporarily closed to gill netting or seining but may be left open to trollers.

A man's catch in certain places and at certain times is heavily dependent on the kind of fishing he is doing. Trollers may do well at one location, but not seiners or gill-netters. At another time in the same place seiners may do best. The type of equipment a troller or gill-netter uses also makes a difference. Troll fishermen experiment with different types of lures in a single location, searching for the most effective one. Since they are dependent on the fish seeing and being attracted to the lure, they must fish during daylight hours. Gill-netters try to use a net that is virtually invisible to the fish. Weather conditions such as intense sunlight, fog or wind influence the visibility of nets. As a result, the gill-netter with a light green net may be more successful at one particular time than a boat with a darker colored net, and so forth. Many of these variables are unpredictable, although certain rules generally hold true. These and many other factors combine to make commercial fishing an uncertain occupation.

Unanticipated events such as strikes called by the fishermen's union can impose even greater hardships on fishermen. The 1963 season, for example, was one of the worst that many of the Indians could remember because of a strike lasting from July 13 to August 3. The strike took the heart out of the fishing season, and it was compounded by additional closures and a scarcity of fish after the initial salmon run at Rivers Inlet.

Even though the brief Rivers Inlet run is usually the most productive part of the season, many of the men feel no sense of urgency to leave right after June Sports. Only a minority of the Gilford Islanders left immediately for Rivers in 1963. Most of them returned to Gilford for several days to make their final preparations. Those men who left right after June Sports were able to sell their fish before the strike began, but those who returned to Gilford were hurt the most. The former made from $200–$500; the latter made nothing.

Most of the gill-net boats from Gilford remained at Rivers after the strike began on the assumption that it would end in a few days. By the time it was finally settled, the majority of the villagers had returned home. Even at that time many families were beginning to feel a strong financial pinch. The men complained that they would rather fish at a reduced price than not fish at all. Some of them were resentful that the channel by Alert Bay was teeming with salmon and they were not able to go after them except for family food. Almost all the fishermen left Gilford the day the strike ended; seiners arrived to pick up their crews and the gill-netters traveled independently to the fishing grounds, but fishing was relatively poor throughout the remainder of the season.

Most families immediately felt the impact of the strike, because few maintain capital resources on which they can draw in an emergency. Moreover, almost half of the families at Gilford habitually rely on such administrative sources of income as relief, unemployment insurance and family allowance to supplement their income. Except in extreme cases, however, villagers were not eligible for relief from the Agency during the strike because the government could not be in a position to support the strike. Furthermore, the strike created a long-range hardship in that few of the fishermen were eligible for unemployment benefits during the winter because they had not been able to meet the requirement of a minimum of fifteen weeks of fishing.

We received several letters from villagers in the fall of 1963 expressing their feelings and attitudes toward the season. "the fishing is very poor the last few weeks," wrote Patrick Cedar. "O. well thats part of life I guess. you got take what you get and give what you got. Well its not that bad. good old winter will soon be here. go clam digging and so." The attitude of passive acceptance expressed in his letter is familiar among the Kwakiutl. The same theme was reiterated in a letter several weeks before the fishing season ended by Willis Drake, who wrote, "Fishing hasn't been good at all with all this fog were having. and the ten day closure we had. were going out to-day for four days and we heard there'll be another closure after this. Oh well I guess it can't be helped." Gertie Philip concisely revealed the economic hardship imposed by the poor fishing during the season with the statement, "Fishing was worse than poor, some gilnet fishermen even had to have welfare help."

The effects of the strike were minimally ameliorated because the clam season opened a month earlier during the 1963–1964 season than it normally does.

Pat Cedar wrote to us about this at the first of October. "Well the fishermen have it real bad. no fish at all. they having two week tie up. But do you know [Stanley] buying clams now. he doesnt [usually] come until Nov. But he's here. the digers just coming in so clam diging mite be better than fishing yet." However the consequences of the fish strike were not as severe as they could have been—at least from a basic subsistence point of view—because during the strike the Indians could fish for family food. On one occasion during the fishing season a seiner from a neighboring village came to Gilford with 1900 salmon. They left 400 on the float and distributed the remainder among three other villages in the immediate Gilford area. Each family took as many fish as they could carry. Some people even filled a row boat, but shy or unassertive people were left with few fish. Those villagers who took more than their share were sharply criticized. Large quantities of salmon such as this are usually home-canned as well as smoked and barbecued.

3

Being a Kwakiutl

EVEN THOUGH MOST OF THE VILLAGERS at Gilford are physically identifiable as Indians, they look and dress very much like the other fishermen and loggers throughout the area. Herbert Philip, for example, is twenty-eight, 5 feet 10 inches tall with black hair which he wears in a long crew cut. He wears colorless plastic rimmed glasses and although he still has all his front teeth, a canine is missing along with a few molars. Herb usually wears working trousers, a sport shirt, work jacket and cap. He is not noticeably overweight yet, but in a few more years he will be. His wife, Gertie, typically wears slacks and a well-washed blouse or short sleeved Orlon sweater. Occasionally she wears a house dress. Her flat shoes are badly worn and they are beginning to break down at the sides.

Both Herb and Gertie are reticent, emotionally reserved, soft-spoken, shy in front of strangers, and passively oriented toward life. Of the two, Gertie has a quicker temper and becomes very angry when she is irritated—for example, when she feels that Herb is not getting a fair deal. Shortly before the end of our year of fieldwork, for example, a chartered yacht tied up at the float. The teenage son of one of the yachtsmen invited Gertie and Evelyn, who had been strolling around the village, aboard for a brief visit. Early the next morning the skipper banged on the Philips' door and superciliously requested Herb to accompany him in a row boat to some spots where the skipper could catch crabs. Herb, in his agreeable fashion, went with the skipper. A few hours later he returned home carrying a can of Dinty Moore beef stew, four brass nuts and some bolts as payment. Gertie was outraged. She was annoyed with Herb for accepting the junk, as she called it, and she was infuriated with the skipper for insulting her husband. As she said to us that evening, "Who does the fucking bastard think us Indians are anyway? Herb went with him because he's a nice guy, not because he expected to be paid. And that crap isn't pay anyway."

Herb, as is typical of most of the villagers, has a fair sense of humor about himself and his own weaknesses, and he enjoys telling jokes about Indians and

Whites. One of his favorites is a story concerning the difference between Indians and White men: Indians scalp their enemies but White men skin their friends. A second anecdote relates to the interaction between an Indian and a White man in the city. A White man approached a bus stop where an Indian was standing and smugly said, "I'll give you a dollar for every question you can ask me that I can't answer, and you pay me fifty cents for every question I ask you that you can't answer." The Indian thought it over for a moment and agreed. "And to show you how fair I am," the White man continued, "I'll let you ask the first question." The Indian meditated for a moment and asked, "What has two heads, the body of a wolf, two tails and eight legs?" The White man was startled by the question and finally grudgingly pulled a dollar bill from his wallet, giving it to the Indian. At that moment the bus arrived and the White man hurriedly asked, "Well, what is it?" The Indian handed the White man fifty cents and stepped onto the bus.

The Kwakiutl are no longer exceptional because of their economic activities, their religious practices and beliefs, their social or ceremonial life, their house style or the food they eat. In most ways, in fact, they live in a style very similar to the White fishermen and loggers who also reside in the area. Therefore the Indians can be viewed as a rural, working-class, subcultural variant of the North American class structure, rather than being a distinctive cultural group.

What then makes the Kwakiutl unique today as a culture-bearing population? To be a regularly participating member within the social system at Gilford, in a very broad sense, implies a status with its associated role(s)—as demonstrated by the fact that the villagers maintain a definite set of norms that guide their behavior and by which they evaluate the behavior of each other and outsiders.[1] It is these norms and valued behavior standards that give life within the village at Gilford a large part of its distinctive flavor. Individual decision-making processes are guided by these norms as are interpersonal relations, and aspects of the Indians' world view. These norms and values also give a fair amount of stability and continuity to village life over time. That is, social systems survive only insofar as the constituent roles (which imply the maintenance of socially legitimated and recognized normative standards) are performed, and they are performed largely because they satisfy personality needs. Thus, the individual's motivation to continue performing the roles is provided. In this way the requirements of the social system are met in that the social roles continue to be performed, giving appreciable stability and continuity to the system, and simultaneously many personality needs are also satisfied. From this point of view, the subcultural system at Gilford has a double-edged quality about it insofar as individuals must adjust to the valued behavior standards if they are to live comfortably within the village, but at the same time, these standards supply the

---

[1] In our usage a status is a social position that is defined independently of its occupant. The test condition of a status is the question, "Are norms attached?" If the social position is not defined by a set of norms then it is not a status, and every social position that is defined by a set of norms is a status.

conditions for villagers to make a personal adjustment. A sense of security, a reference group for personal identity, and social approval are provided for those who adhere reasonably well to the normative standards. On the other hand, the villagers impose compelling and often subtle negative sanctions on the person who violates norms too extremely or too often. These sanctions are effective, of course, only for those Indians who are motivated to remain within the system.

Social Control and Normative Standards

Through at least minimal contact with Whites for over one hundred years, two general acculturative classes have developed among the Kwakiutl. The most prevalent is the *subsisting oriented* class and the second is the *future oriented* class. Subsisting orientation implies a focus on the present—on continued existence or the condition of subsisting at a day-to-day level. A central characteristic of this class is the need to cope with life in its immediacy, as it actually presents itself, rather than to strive to create some new form for an indefinite future. Villagers in the subsisting oriented acculturative category prepare for the predictable, anticipated or known future, but they generally do not plan for the remote or unknown future. Villagers tend to cope with the way things are now rather than attempt to change them. Men gather logs and cut them for firewood; they catch fish which are sometimes canned or dried for use in the winter. These activities are forms of preparation for a predictable future. Rarely do villagers plan, however, if planning is understood as thought and effort given to some long range goals which are considered to be at least potentially realizable. Consequently families rarely save money or other goods for some unknown exigency. Thrift and saving are not included in the value system of people in the subsisting oriented class. Individuals who conform to the same set of characteristics as the subsisting oriented, except that they tend to look to past traditions as being as good as, if not better than, contemporary living, are *past oriented*. This acculturative class is a special case of the subsisting oriented category. Almost invariably these people are fifty years old or more. This attitude is rarely shared by the younger Kwakiutl. With a major exception noted below, the Islanders tend to be characterized as subsisting oriented.

No individual who remains in the subsisting oriented web of interaction within the community can sink too low or rise too high, either economically or socially, because of the patterns of borrowing and sharing. Borrowing and sharing have sharp leveling effects and occur from an interaction between personal choice and social obligation. Items are borrowed (often permanently), given, exchanged and freely taken among members of the community. An individual or family in need may borrow from another who has a surplus. Requests are sometimes refused, but consistent refusal sets an individual apart from the remainder of the community and disrupts normal social relationships. It also directs criticism against the person who refused. An individual who accumulates material wealth and is interested in maintaining close social ties in the community must be prepared to share his wealth. But since they know that they may have to redistribute their wealth—and therefore not be able to enjoy it—the motivation to accumulate more than enough to satisfy short-term desires is weak.[2] It is in this sense that the pattern of borrowing and sharing has its leveling effect: a family experiences an unexpected need; they do not have enough surplus to meet the need and, therefore, they borrow from or share with other families who do have some excess, thus improving their own condition and reducing the minimal surplus of others. At the same time the recipient family establishes an obligation to reciprocate when their condition improves and when their benefactors are in need. This pattern is so well established that an Indian in the Agency office laughed to the Superintendent about government support of Indians. He said it would be impossible for an Indian to starve because of a minimum below which others will not allow him to go.

Within each of the Island villages one family or household sometimes tends to emerge that is conspicuously more acculturated than the others. This household tends to be *future oriented*. Of necessity, to reach this position they restrict important social relations with other families in the community. They do not involve themselves in the borrowing and sharing pattern to the same extent as others, although even they cannot go below a minimum of sharing without severing all relations. Not infrequently these families are in a position of formal authority, such as chief councillor. They have the most material wealth and they tend to plan for the future which often includes plans for leaving the village. Subsisting oriented villagers control the behavior of others by rewarding, among other things, conformity to their norm of not-rising-too-high (not becoming over-acculturated to White middle-class standards). Reward comes in the form of continued, close social interaction with other members of the village. Individuals who attempt to rise too high suffer deprivation of positive reinforcements in varying degrees. In some cases this deprivation is not too punishing because alternative villages are available to which they can migrate; but of course by moving they sever themselves from important social and kinship bonds. Many of these Indian families, who are classed as "progressive" by local Whites, are gradually migrating from their home Reserve to larger social and economic centers.

Stanley Philip is significantly acculturated (future oriented). He lives in Alert Bay and admits that he is "neither fish nor fowl in the Indian world." He knows that a large element of hostility and suspicion is directed toward him by other Indians, and to a certain extent by Whites. Stanley is often tempted to cut off all relations with Indians so he can improve his own position, but he is held back because of his desire to help them—even if in ways they do not want to be helped. On the other hand, members of the village sometimes make disparaging remarks about him for not doing anything for them. One reason for their criticism of him, however, is not so much that he has not done anything for them, but that in being more future oriented and in attaining a certain amount of material success he has had to violate many of the behavior standards held by the subsisting oriented members of the village.

Reciprocity and "non-stinginess" are two important norms guiding inter-

---

[2] This is, of course, only one of the reasons why an acquisitive tendency among the subsisting oriented class is low.

personal relations among the members of the subsisting oriented class. Both are related to the people's expectations of sharing and borrowing. Individuals who want to maintain their position within the network of social relations must reciprocate and be generous. A person who drinks someone else's beer on one occasion must furnish the beer on another, and an individual who buys beer but is stingy with it, that is, closely controls its consumption or removes the supply, is open to criticism. John Patch, for example, bought beer at Echo Bay and returned to the village with six of us. He drank the beer that was offered to him on the way back and then took his own beer to Paul Moon's house. He is reputed to have taken one case which did not belong to him. Frank Bean criticized John saying, "He drinks other people's beer, but won't share his own!" At another time Simon Cedar drank with a group in Alert Bay. At closing time he bought beer along with several others and took it away to drink by himself or with another group. Later he returned to the original party and was forcibly asked to leave. It was explained to me that, "It's not fair to drink all your own beer and then try to get in on the other party."

Sometimes norms of generosity and reciprocity come into conflict with other norms such as the generalized dislike of party crashers. Throughout the evening of a party to which I was invited, different people came to the door and asked to be let in. All of them were refused. The doors and windows were locked. A persistent couple, Daniel and Vera Drake, were alternately ignored in their attempts to come in and told to go away. Vera did most of the talking through the locked door, calling for both Patrick Cedar and Norma Rochelle to let them in. Finally Vera got mad and gave up when she and Daniel had been ignored or told to go away half a dozen times. She called to Pat, "All right, you just remember this the next time you come to my house for food." Pat is a bachelor who frequently eats with them and is dependent upon them for many favors. With the above comment the Drakes stalked away. Pat and his sister Norma jumped up and called for them to come back. They did not. Norma closed the door and said, for lack of anything better, "There's nobody there." Both Pat and Norma were disturbed for a few minutes. As the party progressed and those attending became more inebriated, the comments made to potential party crashers became ruder.

Noninterference, that is, the norm of not becoming involved in troublesome events unless they specifically concern the individual, is one of the strongest standards regulating interpersonal behavior within the village. We realized the power of non-interference on our return to Gilford from the Christmas holidays. Ordinarily, whenever we left the village, our return was heralded by children and adults who came down to the float when they saw our boat or plane come in. When we returned after Christmas, there was no one on the float. As we trudged up the path to the school, Edna, one of the village councillors, met us. She asked if we had stopped in Alert Bay. When we said no, she said, "Then you don't know what's happened," and explained how sorry she was that someone had broken into the school. "This never happened here before," Edna said, adding that she had no idea who had done it. We entered the teacherage to find a broken living room window boarded up by one of the villagers. There were blotches of dried blood here and there among the pieces of broken glass and it was evident from the location of bloody thumb prints that the thief had unsuccessfully searched for liquor. He had taken many of my wife's clothes, pieces of underwear and toiletries, all of which suggested that the thief was Benny, a villager with transvestite tendencies.

I approached Benny and invited him to our quarters to have a talk and to have tea. He knew he had stolen articles from the teacherage, but because he had been drunk at the time he said he could not remember where the things were now. We told him we would not press charges or give his name to the Indian Agent if he returned the things he stole. Benny went from house to house pleading for knowledge of the stolen garments. Each person he asked referred him to someone else who *might* know. He finally talked to a man who admitted he *might* know where they were, and the two men went together to look. The objects were lying in a loose bundle at the bottom of a bluff on the beach. A few days earlier a man had seen them and commented on their location to others, among whom was the man who admitted tentative knowledge of their presence. Probably most people in the village knew where they were, but they were unwilling to admit to any knowledge. They were unwilling to interfere in a problem which did not specifically concern them. A number of people later said to me that they had been afraid of becoming involved.

At times, in every society, people must make a choice between conflicting norms. For example, the norm of noninterference is often overridden when a close kin such as a child, sibling or spouse is being beaten by someone of more distant kin affiliation or by a non-kinsman. Joe Abel, for example, started to rough up his sister. Charles Bean took his mother's side against Joe, his uncle; Joe's son, Andy, sided with his father by throwing beer on Charles. Joe tried to break up the resulting fight between Andy and Charles, and another man jumped onto Joe's neck. Ultimately Joe's arm and several other parts of his body were burned when Charles pushed him against the stove. One eye was badly blackened, and he broke an ankle. On other occasions interpersonal alliances involving some of the same people take quite different forms, although certain people typically ally themselves with one another unless they themselves are fighting. Although alliances tend to be based on both kinship ties and bonds of friendship, individuals must at times also choose between loyalties of friendship and kinship.

Conflict is a prominent feature of interpersonal relations within individual households and within the village at large. In fact, conflict may be viewed as part of normal social interaction within the community, but it is rarely of such magnitude that it seriously disrupts the order and stability of the system. Indian families at Gilford and throughout the area are characterized both by their flexibility and by their extensibility. Friends and relatives move in with a family for greater or lesser periods of time, sometimes permanently. Patrick's household provides an illustration. Pat lives with his sister, Norma, his sister's common-law husband, and their three children. Open conflict exists between Patrick and his sister. Even though the house formally belongs to Pat, he complains that Norma tries to dominate the household. She sometimes attacks him verbally as well as physically, and once she slashed him with a broken beer bottle. The relationship between Patrick and his brother-in-law, Henry, is frequently discordant as well. At one time

Patrick borrowed Henry's speedboat and Henry later accused him of damaging it and threatened to take him to court unless he made reparations. Patrick retaliated, "Oh yeah, how about the rent you've never paid me?"

Rarely are outsiders such as the Royal Canadian Mounted Police brought into family conflicts because each disputant has an expansible set of complaints against the other. For every complaint made by one person, the second may retaliate with another on which the former may, in turn, draw up new ones. Because of this mutual set of grievances, a sense of justice is violated to have one person press charges against the second. Threats of such action are frequent, but such threats are rarely acted upon. Mutual complaints tend to reinforce conflict and future complaints, thus perpetuating them.

Whereas public displays of affection between spouses are unusual among the members of the village and among the Indians in the Gilford area generally, public displays of marital discord are not infrequent. The discrepancy between the two sometimes leads casual observers to the conclusion that Indian marriages are strife-ridden, but this is not generally true. An incident of obvious affection between spouses, for example, occurred when Ambrose Cedar fell asleep on one of the bunks in his boat. Louisa, his common-law wife, was very concerned about him because of his bad heart, and she insisted that he not be awakened. At one point while he was sleeping she moved across the boat to his side and put her face very gently against his, ran her hands through his hair and kissed his cheeks and forehead. She held him for several minutes. Later in the evening after we moved to Ambrose's place, he fondly patted her a few times.

Physical and verbal aggression between husband and wife is common, but most typically occurs during or following periods of drinking. Wife beatings occur periodically along with other forms of physical aggression. One husband has beaten his wife several times including while she was pregnant and, as a consequence, she aborted and has not been able to have any children. Beaten wives sometimes move out of their homes and live for a period of time with another family within the village, but more often they move away from the village altogether. Some wives say that they wait for their husbands "to get drunk and pass out" and then take revenge. Verbal conflict is more typical among some of the villagers than physical aggression, especially during periods of sobriety. To illustrate, Herbert took one of his young sons to the store at Simoom Sound and stopped at the beer parlor on the way back. While we were there the boy slipped off a log and fell partially into the water. A second man who was leaving the beer parlor saw the incident and commented on it to Herb's wife when he returned to the village. When we returned home late in the evening, Gertie met us at the float. She angrily called Herb a bastard and asked, "What kind of a fucking father are you anyway, keeping your son out this late?" She refused to speak to him except angrily for several days.

Jealousy is the most common cause of aggression between spouses. If an individual learns that his spouse has been involved in an illicit affair he may severely chastise his partner, physically and verbally. Marital jealousy is very common, and on one occasion Harold Dick sat outside his house most of the day because his common-law wife was angry with him. "She's jealous because she saw me with a woman in the Bay." Herbert also confided that he used to be very jealous of Gertie, but "I started thinking about it last summer and decided that if a woman loves me, fine; and if she doesn't there's nothing I can do about it anyway."

The preference or ideal among members of the community calls for sexual fidelity in marriage, but extramarital relations are not at all uncommon. Quite often in the past—but sometimes today too—an intermediary was used to make arrangements for an amour. As described to me by an elderly villager, a man or woman who was attracted to another sent a third person with a note saying, in effect, "I have liked you for a long time and would like to know if you would be interested in sharing my bed with me." If the second person was interested, he might respond, "I have liked you very much from the first time I saw you, and my thoughts have been constantly about you. I would be pleased to accept your invitation." The next step was to make more specific arrangements regarding time and place. In order to avoid shaming the uninvolved spouses, attempts were made by the lovers, as well as by members of the community, to keep the news from them. Husbands often beat their wives when they discovered what was happening. According to the same man, divorce was not formalized; one simply left his spouse and publicly, informally disclaimed her.[3] Either person might then remarry. Today marriages are still elastic and do not break up because of occasional infidelity, although repetitive unfaithfulness creates a great strain in the marriage relation and is instrumental in fracturing some. Some people say it is unusual for women to remain sexually faithful to their husbands if they are absent for a long period of time. Women who are obvious about their sexual activities, however, are sometimes contemptuously called pigs. Villagers almost always use discretion in the act of sexual intercourse, whether it be between husband and wife or illicitly. Spouses usually wait until other members of the household are asleep, but during times of drinking discretionary bars are somewhat lowered. The morning following a party or during the party itself a man and a woman— married or not—may be found, as the villagers say, on a bed "passed out together."

Conflict within the village sometimes gives the impression of being rampant, but effective social controls are nonetheless operating. Serious damage to the body or to property is rarely committed even during periods of the most unrestrained parties and fighting. Windows or furniture may be broken, but houses are not burned; a person may have his nose broken or his face cut with glass, but he is not mortally stabbed. In fact, according to the RCMP, major crimes of all types are infrequent among Indians. Most problems among Whites and Indians are minor offenses against body or property and are associated with drinking; when serious offenses occur, however, they are usually committed by Whites. Crimes committed by Indians are usually not premeditated. One RCMP officer reported, for example, that an Indian may see a power saw lying unattended outside and will pick it up. When challenged, the individual who committed the theft often readily admits having taken it and hiding it under his bed.

[3] This was probably not true, at least for ranking members of the community, during the famous Potlatch period, aspects of which are described in Chapter 5.

We are inclined to think that this last statement, however, is something of an overstatement.

The valued behavior standards on which the members of the community operate are not always clear to us, but the major forms of social control that are applied when norms are violated are more easily recognized. Among the Kwakiutl the process of interpersonal interaction itself is one of the most powerful mechanisms of social control. As we said above, a sense of security and, not insignificantly, identity among the subsisting oriented group is firmly anchored within the community. Because of it, special or coercive control devices are not usually needed. In the first place through a long socialization period individuals have internalized most of the normative standards in such a way that they are able to evaluate the behavior of others and to agree that a norm has been violated, and the offender is aware of the legitimacy of the evaluation against him. For most members of the village the community has become the primary reference group, that is, the group with which they identify themselves and in relation to which they think about themselves. Through this reference group an individual establishes his frames of reference through which perceptions, experiences and ideas about himself are ordered. To this extent members of the village are in a position to give positive social rewards and punitive sanctions. Any threat to one's position within this system—such as the withdrawal of acceptance, favorable recognition or approval—poses a personal threat to the individual. Thus, the withdrawal of favorable recognition and approval, in threat or in fact, is a powerful social control mechanism. It is often communicated to the individual through such media as gossip, indirect criticism and constrained social relations. This interpretation receives strong support from Pat Cedar, who had been drinking and felt free to discuss his feelings about members of the community and his relationship to them. He expressed his feelings of dependency on the affection and positive support he receives from some close kinsmen in the village. Throughout the conversation he cited specific situations where love was given to and withheld from him by these people.

Control is also effected through the pattern of ignoring someone. If invitations are being made for a party and the host does not want one person in the group to attend, he ignores that person, behaving as if he were not there; he neither looks at nor talks to the shunned person. The other invited guests behave in the same way. This technique is also used on other occasions to avoid trouble with an individual who is trying to incite a quarrel or fight. These social control techniques are not as effective, of course, among individuals who do not normally live in the village and who have little emotional or social investment within it. Higher authority is sometimes invoked when outsiders create or threaten to create trouble. Threats may be made to call the RCMP, or the authority of the Band council may be used in forcing the person out of the village. This type of control has a double edge. On the one hand it controls the behavior of outsiders, but on the other hand it generates an attitude of limited involvement on the part of visitors so that they never reach the point of being effectively controlled by the more subtle methods of social control normally employed.

Drinking and Social Interaction

The use and sharing of intoxicants have important relevance to subsisting and future oriented groups, and through the use of alcohol many of the community's normative standards and social control mechanisms are projected into bold relief. Some future oriented Indians do not drink, and those who do, seldom drink with other members of the village at parties. Several reasons for this are apparent. Individuals in the future oriented class would soon be depleted of their accumulated material goods if they drank with and shared their liquor with others in the normal manner, since the typical drinking pattern among the subsisting oriented group is one of drinking until one's money is exhausted. By not participating in drinking parties, members of the future oriented group are exposed to sharp criticisms by subsisting oriented Indians. One member of the future oriented category (Victor Philip, the previous chief councillor) occasionally drinks with his family and accepts a bottle or two of beer from others, but he does not join any major drinking parties. Victor claims not to drink for his children's sake, saying it is foolish for parents to talk against drinking and then to drink in front of their children. A further indication of the difference in attitude between the two groups is demonstrated by Benny Otter's comment to me. Acting on his authority as chief councillor, Victor refused to recommend Benny for relief. Victor lectured Benny about drinking away all his money. He pointed out how he had saved enough money in the fishing season to support his family during the winter, and told Benny that he should have done the same rather than squander it on liquor. Benny replied, "You're privileged that you don't drink"; he continued his story to me with an explanation of the enjoyment he receives from drinking parties. During the summer of 1962, Benny made about $3100, spent $200 on beer, paid a fish company for a new net, net repairs and other expenses, and ended the season with a gain of $37. This is not unusual.

Chief Philip, also a non-drinking member of the future oriented category, has strong feelings about drinking. Although he was one of the people who fought for the privilege of Indians to drink in the same manner as other Canadian citizens, Stanley now wonders if he were wise in doing so. He contends that Indians learned to drink heavily and rapidly by imitating local White loggers and fishermen. He would like to see Indians drink in moderation, but he doubts that they ever will because they have never been exposed to this style of drinking.

Drinking is the most popular and frequent pastime activity in the village. An informal, minimal count that I maintained of the incidence of drinking in the village while we were at Gilford yields an average of six days per month. This figure relates to periods during which a few families or most of the village were drinking, and they include periods from one day to six days of more or less continuous drinking. Sequential days of drinking do not necessarily imply that the same people are involved throughout, but indicate, as one villager insightfully pointed out, that when one group begins drinking others want to as well. The more who drink the more who want to drink until most of the village is involved and a plateau is reached. The people who begin drinking when the episode begins are often not the ones who are drinking when it is completed, unless enough time has elapsed for them to quit, become somewhat rested, and begin again. Typically, however, drinking episodes last for only one or two days.

The personal goal of drinking is to get drunk or to drink until one "passes out" or falls asleep. Once a person begins to drink we noted a sense of urgency on his part to continue until he is totally inebriated. While part of this style of drinking may be related to imitative behavior, it also seems related to the fact that drinking on other than licensed premises was illegal before 1962. Despite the fact that it was unlawful, Indians drank within the village and on their boats when they had access to liquor from bootlegging Whites. They tended to drink as much as they could as quickly as they could, thereby minimizing the risk of being caught because they threw the empty bottles overboard—or discarded the full bottles if it became necessary.

Drinking is now fully legal for the Indians. One of the village men remarked on the role played by bootleggers in the past. The conversation dealt with the time when Indians were dependent on Whites for acquiring intoxicants, and the village man quipped, "Back in the days when Whites were *useful* . . ." The gibe elicited a mirthful response from everyone on the boat, including the two Whites who had earlier been sources of liquor for most of the men at the party.

No one leaves a gathering until all the alcohol has been consumed, and the amount of available liquor contributes to the definition of a successful party. Men often spend everything they have, including money that was intended for food or other necessities. If one wants more beer he might crash somebody else's party or steal beer from an ongoing party. Jeffrey and Alice Hardy, for example, were having a party in their house along with two other people. Earlier that day the four of them had picked up six bottles of whiskey and eleven cases of beer. A group from one of the other parties within the village knew about this store of liquor and unsuccessfully attempted to crash Jeffrey's party. Benny, one of the members of this group, returned later and knocked out one of Jeffrey's windows in his attempt to get in. Jeffrey told Benny to go home; he had his own house and bed. "I don't bother you when you're drinking. Don't bother me!" He nailed his windows closed, but Benny made a second abortive attempt to get in by shattering a window in Jeffrey's door. Later that night, sometime after Jeffrey and Alice had gone to bed, Benny did manage to get into the house and was caught rifling through the suitcase under the bed where Alice hides her belongings. Jeffrey sent him home again, but he believes Benny was somehow able to steal four bottles of his whiskey because it was reported the next day that an empty whiskey bottle was seen in Benny's house; Jeffrey was the only person in the village who had hard liquor. On another occasion Norma Rochelle reports that she had six cases of beer in her house during a party, but the following morning only two cases of empties were left—four full cases had disappeared during the party.

Liquor may be obtained through ready cash, through stealing from a party, through crashing a party or through pawning one's personal or stolen possessions. Men who carve or paint sell their work at a great reduction in price, and some Whites in the area are pleased to do business under these circumstances. Many old and valuable ceremonial masks and other artifacts are sold for a fraction of their real worth to Whites because the latter know they can name their price with a minimum of bargaining when Indians are drinking and want money. Indians later accuse Whites of cheating them of their heritage because of these and related types of transactions. Methods used to obtain alcohol, however, are controlled and channeled within strict limits. Physical violence, for example, is almost never directed, in threat or in fact, against a licensed vendor who refuses to serve an individual when his supply of cash is gone.

Gilford Islanders are noted for their heavy drinking. This is due in part to the fact that few villages among the Islanders have such easy access to a source of beer. Despite the relative intensification of drinking at Gilford and the consequent fights and other disruptive incidents, the RCMP say they have less trouble with this village than most of the others. The reasons why Gilford people create less police trouble than many of the other villages are not entirely clear except that they appear to have fewer feuds than other outlying villages and their social control mechanisms are fairly effective.

Gilford Island Kwakiutl are not only thought of by others as heavy drinkers, but they think of themselves as hardy drinkers. This was expressed to us by Vera Drake in the following way: "Us Indians are tough! We can stay up all night and drink, and sleep the next day." Occasionally some of the villagers become concerned about drinking too much, however. Cecelia Cedar confided in my wife that she is beginning to like the taste of beer—really like it—and finds it hard to stay away from it. She and her husband do not fight except when they are drinking, or at least not much, and Cecelia feels she is bordering on or may become a drunkard, although she did not use these words.[4] Evelyn asked if she likes the beer itself or the effect it has on her, and she answered that she likes the beer.

One of the positive functions of drinking for the Gilford Islanders is to help relax normally constricted interpersonal communication, thus allowing dissatisfactions to be freely and openly expressed in ways they would not be if the person were entirely sober. Expressions of discontent tend to be circuitous and masked in normal, day-to-day interaction. It is an exceptional encounter for one person to be directly confronted by a second on some unpleasant matter. More typically, a disaffected person talks about someone else with the hope that the information will get back to the second person. Edgar Drake, manager of the village soccer team, for example, wanted to resign. Rather than tell the team about his decision, he simply did not show up for any of the scheduled meetings and, as a result, they were cancelled. Even though Edgar and Joe Abel, president of the club, saw each other daily, Edgar never told Joe he wanted to quit. He told a friend who told Joe, and then Joe told the others, "I *hear* Edgar's going to quit."

On another occasion, four white men from Echo Bay approached us with the idea of joining together the parent-teacher groups from Gilford and from Echo Bay. We brought up their proposal at the next village meeting. None of the villagers said anything until Herbert, who had been drinking, suggested that the

---

[4] The incidence of alcoholism among the Kwakiutl is reported to be very low. We know of no Kwakiutl, in fact, who can be correctly diagnosed as an alcoholic.

Echo Bay parent-teacher group vote first about the amalgamation—before the villagers commit themselves. "They might say no and make us go hang-dog around those White men." His suggestion was well received, and several people remarked after the meeting how happy they were that Herb had been drinking; otherwise the suggestion would not have been made. The two groups were not amalgamated.

Drinking not only improves the effectiveness of interpersonal communication, but it also lowers inhibitions regarding sex. Sweet, red wine, which is consumed as rapidly as beer, is considered to be an aphrodisiac for women. Frank Bean told me that women should not drink wine because it excites them; "it makes them feel loving and want to go to bed with a man." One night Willis Drake had been drinking wine when he knocked on Henry Rochelle's door and asked to be let in. Henry wanted his wife to ignore it, but she got up and let him in. Willis, who had the wives of two other men with him, asked for some whiskey to go with their wine. Norma poured them each a glass and went back to bed. One wife left soon after that. The next morning Willis and Mary Bean, the other wife, were in bed together, "passed out." Harold Dick is particularly noted for his sexual activities when he drinks. As the Kwakiutl express it, "he tries to fool around" with the daughters of his common-law wife. Once he placed a gas-soaked rag over the nose of one girl to "make her sleep more soundly, and tried to play with her." She woke up and scared him away. On another occasion Harold was caught "playing" with a two and one-half year old girl. The mother was outraged and said that she was going to report him to the RCMP the following week, which she did not do. Daniel Drake dislikes his stepfather for these sexual advances on his sisters and other girls; and when he is drinking, Dan often attacks Harold.

Villagers are physically modest on most occasions, but through the reduction of inhibitory mechanisms while drinking they become less so. On one occasion Larry's wife, Cecilia, came on deck from the gill-net cabin to urinate. She whispered to Patrick, who was on deck with me, and Patrick explained that I should go below for a moment. Cecilia said, "I'm not shy in front of Larry and Patrick, but you're. . . ." The sentence trailed off, probably to be completed as "a White man. You're different from us and might not understand." On the trip back from Echo Bay, everyone was sitting below deck drinking beer. Cecilia sat next to Frank Bean. Frank excused himself to go on deck and, as he got up, Larry yelled at Cecilia, "Get your hand off his prick." If he had not been drinking, he would not have been so outspoken.

Latent hostility is directly expressed (often through fights) during periods of drinking, and tensions that might otherwise fester and lead to less manageable strains are not infrequently resolved. As expressed by one of our informants, people usually realize that it is through the influence of alcohol that they fight in the first place. Fights may occur among a number of people, among all ages and across sexes. A man in his fifties can fight with a teenager on an equal basis. Fights are almost always contextualized in periods of drinking, but grudges are usually not carried on into sober periods. A middle-aged man at Village Island, for example, kicked his elderly mother and broke her hip. She was taken to the hospital and was later shocked to learn that the RCMP had sentenced her son to prison because he beat her. News of the affair spread rapidly throughout the area and public reaction to it gives an indication of the normative structure involved; many people were indignant at the man for his actions, but their ill feelings shifted to the RCMP for interfering.

Even though women drink almost as much as men, they are less physically combative. They too, however, occasionally become involved in fights, and they are certainly as knowledgeable as men in verbal aggression. Two of my journal-note entries reflect these facts.

> Emily was injured on New Year's Eve at Victor's place where they are now living. According to Norman, the place was fairly well torn up: a large mirror was smashed, a new radio ruined, and so forth. Emily somehow got on the bottom of four men in a fight and she was kicked in the stomach and in the back, damaging one of her kidneys. Several other women joined the fight too. Archie and Norm took Edna to the hospital in Alert Bay. The doctors doubt that the kidney will totally heal. After being released from the hospital she had one and one-half bottles of beer and passed out, apparently because of her stomach or kidney injury.

> The most serious trouble occurred at Jeffrey's. For some reason, Edna was in there and Darlene [her daughter] wanted her to come out. Jeffrey told Darlene to leave and she started breaking his windows. Finally he threw Darlene out of the house, violently shoving her against the post on the porch. Ralph [her brother] picked up an empty bucket and threw it at Jeff, striking him in the back.

Fights frequently result in black eyes and swollen lips, but when serious injury occurs, relatively little attention is given to it. Joe, a two-hundred-fifty pounder, walked on his broken foot for a month before he had the doctor place it in a cast. Because of his great weight he found crutches uncomfortable and abandoned them as soon as possible, and he took his cast off before the scheduled time. At another time Brian Abel broke his hand when he and Lawrence Cedar got into a fight on Lawrence's gill-netter. Larry ducked and Brian hit his fist against the engine of the craft. Brian did not seek medical attention for his hand even though it was broken, badly swollen and discolored. Most of the villagers agreed, however, that his behavior was extreme when, the next day, he tried to help the other men scythe down some of the grass and weeds in the village.

A few Kwakiutl tend to "go haywire" when they drink. Going haywire is defined by the villagers as unusual and the term implies an unrestrained, uncontrolled lashing out at other people and things. Lauren went haywire, according to Lawrence, and started shooting off Lawrence's 30–30 at the latter's gill-netter. The next day Lawrence made the comment, "My brother-in-law is really a haywire guy! I won't drink with him again. I didn't enjoy the party last night!" Another incident occurred between Joe and me. One day, after dinner I went to see Joe in order to get my clam fork which he had borrowed. He was eating clam chowder and was almost in a daze from drinking when I entered. He was in a foul mood and had been, I learned later, talking most of the day about fighting and not being afraid of anyone. He glowered silently, not greeting me when I came in.

After finishing his bowl of chowder and ladling out another, he finally asked what I wanted. I explained that I wanted my clam fork. He did not acknowledge my request, but began talking about not liking to be pushed around and "standing up for my own rights, fighting anybody any time." Up to this point his comments were simply a generalized verbal aggression directed at nothing in particular. After a few minutes he began working himself up and slammed the table with his fist. He intended to fight and I was his only accessible target. He menacingly removed his coat, but I told him I had not come to fight with him, that I did not have anything against him and that, in fact, I liked him. This pacified him for only a moment. He started working up to another rage, pounding the table more vehemently and stripped to his tee shirt. It was clear that I could not get up from my place without being attacked, and within a few moments I realized that he was not going to be pacified. I sat there motionlessly because each movement of my hands or head incited him to further rage. During the hour that I was with him, he mumbled in a semi-articulate rage about being councillor in the village but "not giving a God damned hell about any fucking cocksucker in the whole fucking village." Several times he apparently misunderstood what I was saying since he is very hard of hearing, and thought I was insulting him. More than once he picked up the table and acted as if he were going to throw it over me; once he tipped it so forcefully that most of the dishes shattered on the floor and on the bench where I was sitting. Joe's sister and her two daughters were frightened and ran out of the house. Later he picked up a beer bottle which he started to break to use as a weapon against me. Eventually I was able to retreat uninjured. The next day Joe remembered nothing about the incident until his sister and others reminded him of what had happened.

In no sense do drinking episodes always involve aggression, but when fights do occur, they are almost always within the context of drinking. The following description of a party, drawn from my journal notes, suggests the common tenor of village parties, although it contains more disparate elements than many parties. The description reveals obvious as well as subtle forms of aggression, tenderness, rancor, compassion, conflict and cooperation.

> The party was in a state of transition as I walked in. New people were arriving from Edna's and some of those who had been there began to leave. During the evening 15 people came in and stayed, or remained only for a few minutes. Charles was annoyed that people were coming to drink his beer even though they had beer at their own parties. As the party progressed some attempts were made at Indian-singing, but these attempts did not last very long. Alex tried singing some popular songs in English but was soon silenced by Edward. An attempt was made at playing *lahel* (Indian "dice"), but this too was abortive. I was buttonholed by Cecil who talked about mining and prospecting up Kingcome. Later I was buttonholed by Charles and by Norman who talked about soccer. Eventually I was able to free myself from these corners and mix and listen to the general tone of the evening. Charles at one point made the comment that he likes to fight. Clarence and Joe were having a running battle-conversation throughout the evening about fighting each other. Clarence made the comment that all he can remember about his childhood is Joe, his father, coming home after drinking and throwing him around like a wet towel. "I learned to fight the hard way." Joe only smiled at this. Early in the evening Joe had asked Clarence to wrestle with him, but the latter declined saying

that the house was not the proper place. Later Clarence tried to pick a fight with his father. He said, "You've had your day, now let me have mine." Each of them said that he could beat the other in a fight if it came to it. Charles had skinned knuckles from a wrestling match outside with Cecil. Charles praised Cecil's strength but said that he, Charles, was faster. It is common for one man to praise the ability or strength of another.

Alex and Darlene sat on the couch for part of the evening talking. Someone started to tease them and they protested that they were only "best friends." The women tended to talk among themselves as did the men, but there was no major separation by sex; each intermingled with the other. Peter and Greg sat on the floor not saying anything. Both were quite drunk, especially Peter who sat quietly with an owlish expression on his face. There was no consistency of seating among the people; they moved around at will, depending on interest and availability of seating. A number of people came in and out of the house on different occasions. Probably no one sat there for the entire evening without going out at least once.

Ralph came in once and said that Fred was stabbing himself in the stomach. Fred and Ruby had had a fight at Edna's. Ed went out as did one or two others. Charles suggested that Greg go too, but the latter declined as did some others (exemplifying the pattern of noninterference and noninvolvement). They returned in about half an hour saying that Fred was all right, and sleeping now. I did not discover whether he really did stab himself. Edna was sitting there at the time but did not go out to see what the problem was. She left it up to the men, even though Fred and Ruby (her daughter) were living at her place. Because Fred and Ruby have been living together for about one year their (common-law) union tends to be accepted by most people.

During part of the evening Alex and Ed sat on the couch side by side. Edward had his arm around Alex's shoulders and Alex was holding that hand, playing with the fingers. I have been struck several times by the importance of physical aggression among the men and the natural warmth of physical contact on certain occasions which contrasts with or is the obverse of such aggression. There is no shame or embarrassment in such an expression of friendship.

Some of the kids, for example, Ralph (age 13) and Willie (age 10) were up most of the night. Ralph had a bottle of whiskey in his pocket which was apparently given to him to hold in trust for someone. I later heard that someone was giving Ralph beer. A great deal of drinking is going on in the village tonight. Lawrence went to the Bay this morning and returned this evening with some beer. Cecilia (his wife) called a plane to pick her up, but by the time it got here she decided not to go because she was afraid that Larry would be on his way back to the village. This is the end of a clam tide and most people have some extra money to spend. More drinking is going on now than since before Christmas.

Death and Religion

Accidents are the principal cause of death among the Kwakiutl and drowning is the greatest single form of accidental death. Drowning often occurs in contexts of drinking when, for example, a man gets drunk in the Bay, buys more beer and attempts to travel back to his home village. We suspect that some reputedly accidental drownings are not accidents at all. They are probably suicides. The true incidence of suicide among the Kwakiutl is unknown, but threats and attempts are not unusual and often appear in association with drinking. James Jack, a visitor from another village, was drinking and began talking about death. He recounted an episode when Jennie Drake fell overboard and because of her great weight he could not drag her back onto the gill-netter. She pleaded with him, "If you can't get me up, let me go! Let me go!" With the help of seven men she was brought safely on board, but she wanted to jump back in once rescued. James concluded, "I guess she thought she should have died." He then summarized what may be a common Kwakiutl acceptance of death. "We never know when or where. Each minute we live is just one more of life. We never know what tomorrow will bring." He talked about natural death in the hospital and accidental death from such causes as drowning. I asked him which was a better way of dying and he responded indirectly by say that his father had been drowned as had his father's father and so would he, probably. Continuing, he said that his half-brother probably wanted to die at the time of his drowning. The latter had "fallen" overboard five times shortly prior to the final incident.

Funeral services follow procedures legislated by the various religious denominations. Church services, however, are often supplemented by more traditional practices to help kinsmen "forget their tears." An important chief of the Tsawatenok tribe died in March, 1963. The services for him were longer and more elaborate than most, but the range of events is similar for individuals of lesser importance. As I recorded in my field notes:

Monday Night

A church service was called by some of the W.A. [Anglican Women's Auxiliary] women in the evening. The Anglican Lay Reader did not know about it until it was over. About eighty people attended the service which was held in the community hall at Kingcome. It lasted from 8:30 to 10:30 and was conducted in Kwakwala. Refreshments of coffee, cakes, cookies and graham crackers were served at the end of the service. The service progressed in the following order: one song was sung from the Kwakwala hymnal and then someone by arrangement was asked to come to the front of the hall and talk. Most of the people talked about the deceased man and the impact of his death on his family. They thanked everyone for attending the service. Chiefs from other villages were the major spokesmen, but the service was officiated by the chief councillor from Kingcome. Songs were led by an elderly woman and the laywoman from Gilford was asked to give the concluding prayer.

Tuesday Afternoon

The official Anglican service began at 2:00 P.M. in the church. There were about 130 people in attendance. The service followed the standard Anglican form for a funeral service and lasted about half an hour. Six pallbearers carried the grey, commercial coffin to the graveyard half a mile from the village where the service was continued. About 50 people were at the grave which had been dug previously by some of the younger members of the deceased's family—sons and close relatives. The Lay Reader made a graveside reading and left; two other people stepped to the head of the grave and spoke briefly in Kwakwala. Much of the time at the grave was silent and very somber; some of the members of the deceased's family cried, especially his wife, daughter and son. The older son said in a loud, clear voice, nodding his head in finality, "*Hala kesla, ump; hala kesla,*" "good-bye, father; good-bye." During this time the pallbearers had been taking turns filling the grave. Two songs initiated in Kwakwala from the hymnal began weakly but picked up force as more mourners joined in. People began returning to the village, and about fifteen remained when the grave was completely covered and the artificial flower wreaths were placed on the mound. An old, ragged piece of lumber was stuck in the grave to mark the head.

Funeral Service: Indian

Following the graveyard service people went to the big-house, *gyux*, and continued the funeral service in Kwakwala and in Indian style. The big-house has an earthen floor, carved poles at either end and a cedar-shake roof. A huge opening in the roof allows the fire and smoke to escape. About 100 people attended in the *gyux*. A large, blazing fire about five feet across and three feet high was placed in the middle of the earthen floor. Twelve men were seated at the end of the hall on either side of the log drum. One of the men had a snare drum on which an Indian design was painted. Four Indian funeral songs were sung at the beginning, and a speech was delivered about the potlatches which the deceased had given during his lifetime. Other speakers mentioned similar topics. The deceased's oldest son, dressed as a hamatsa [cannibal dancer], entered the dance area through a curtained entrance; he passed completely through the building and out the main entrance. He will dance again tonight at the potlatch at which time his mother will give him some Indian names which belonged to his father.

Four women sitting at the head of the *gyux* near the rhythm section were dressed in button blankets. They had been especially asked to honor the deceased. A man from Gilford passed by, placing eagle-down on their heads. He circled the room making a ring of down on the floor behind him. This portion of the funeral ceremony lasted until 5:00 P.M., at which time it was adjourned until 7:00 P.M. the same evening.

Commemorative Potlatch and Indian Dances

The ceremony reconvened at 7:00 P.M. in the *gyux*. About 200–250 people attended; no empty seats or spaces were available, consequently many people had to stand around the door and outside. The building was filled with smoke much of the evening except when dry logs were placed on the fire, which created a good draft through the ceiling. At one time during the evening the roof caught fire but was quickly extinguished with several buckets of water from above. This potlatch followed the same general format as the one at Turnour earlier this year [see Chapter 5]. The same class of dances was performed at Turnour, but the specific dances varied in form and content because people at Kingcome have the legitimate right to perform certain dances and not others. Six masked dances were performed during the evening, including one *qolus*, "Thunderbird," and one Mountain Goat Hunter which differed from that at Turnour. A man costumed as a dog participated with the Hunter. Other features varied as well. There were also several Ermine dancers with their ermine cloaks and masks. Most of the dances, however, were *hamatsa*, the dancers wearing cedar rings around the shoulders and one on the head. Many button blankets are worn during the dances, especially by the women.

The dances lasted until approximately 10:30 P.M. and were followed by the distribution of goods and money. About $250 were distributed by members of the deceased's family. Goods consisted of such things as hand towels, embroidered dish towels, and embroidered pillow cases. Each person appeared to receive two items. About sixty loaves of bread were used for making sandwiches, some of which were made from oulachon. One of the women told me later that the plot had been made to give oulachon sandwiches to Whites to see how they would react. The general consensus among Indians is that Whites do not like oulachon grease or the fish. Coffee, tea, cakes, cookies and cupcakes were also served.

A man from Turnour continued the potlatch for his own purposes after the family of the deceased gave theirs. I could not tell when one ended and the other began except for a verbal comment made in Kwakwala. The same is true of the dances. Each man putting on dances asks different people to dance for him. The latter are then given gifts for performing. During the dances different men occasionally stood up and talked as they did at Turnour. The potlatches and dances today are greatly abbreviated forms of what they once were. Some dances which traditionally took several hours or longer to perform are now performed in a few minutes. Most dances now last only two to four minutes—enough time to circle the fire at least twice in most cases.

Religious beliefs among the villagers range from a firm commitment to the doctrine of a particular church, to a nondoctrinal belief in God and the divinity of Christ, to skepticism or questioning of both and finally to outright disbelief. According to Hilda, the Pentecostal laywoman in the village, most Kwakiutl have religious feelings, but one would have trouble in getting them to express these feelings. At another time she admitted, "Just because they come to church is no sign they profess religion." Not uncommonly someone may say he rarely prays and that, in fact, he does not really think about religion very often. Norman Philip expressed his feelings to me in the following way: "I never get on my hands and knees and pray. Sure, I go sometimes to Hilda's services, but I don't pay much attention to that." Cecil Abel observed, "I'm a materialist, I believe what my hands can touch." Religious feelings vary in intensity at different times. This is reflected in a letter written to us by Hilda in 1964. "Benjamin [Otter] really desires to follow the Lord and reads his Bible and comes to services more, etc. Others have requested special prayer, as they know they are away from the Lord." Benjamin attended services only infrequently while we lived in the village, and at that time he claimed not to be concerned with religion. Most of the members of the community attend the regularly scheduled Pentecostal services in the village at least occasionally. In addition, they often attend the special Anglican and other services that are held within the village from time to time, regardless of the denomination. To this extent villagers may be characterized as being eclectic in religious beliefs. Some frankly admit that they attend church services because others go and because they do not have anything else to do. Church services for some are simply social occasions, but for others they have deeper religious meaning.

Pentecostals do not believe in drinking, smoking, dancing, attending commercial movies, playing cards or the use of facial cosmetics. Because of these restrictions, especially on drinking, it is doubtful that many Indians will become true converts to the church, even though many find it attractive for other reasons.

Hilda supports several church-related activities within the village. She identifies herself as a children's worker and holds Bible Club, Young People's Meetings, and Sunday school once each week. The Bible Club meets after school for about an hour and is designed largely for children from three to twelve years of age. The Young People's Meetings are held during the evening and are restricted to children ten years old and over. They have Bible drills, quizzes, usually a Bible story and sometimes refreshments. Sunday school is held Sunday mornings for all the children. She also holds Sunday evening church services in her house or other village homes for the adults. Special services are held on such occasions as the birth of a baby, a birthday celebration, or a death. Refreshments consisting of sandwiches, cake, cupcakes, Freshie (a flavored powder like Kool-Aid which is mixed with water) and coffee are served following these special services. Food is supplied by the family for whom the special service is being held and is passed around by several adults or teenagers, male or female, while the others remain seated. As in potlatches, one does not customarily refuse food that is offered—even if it is far more than he can eat. The excess is taken home in a paper bag that is often distributed just for that purpose.

Occasionally Pentecostal visitors come to the village and hold services. A White preacher who lives at Turnour plans weekly visits by boat to New Van, Village and Gilford, but because of weather conditions he cannot always make it. Typically church services within the village conform to a standard format: several songs are sung from the hymnal which has been translated into Kwakwala; a prayer is led, usually by one of the villagers in Kwakwala, but sometimes by the deaconess in English; more songs are sung in Kwakwala; a second prayer is made; another song is sung from the hymnal and a collection is made; a passage from the Bible is read or a sermon is delivered if there is a guest speaker; a final song is sung and the service is concluded. The sequence of events is not always as given, but the specific elements are generally included. The villagers, who actively participate in most services, lead prayers, read from the Bible and call requests for hymns to be sung while Hilda plays her accordion. Even though they look at the hymnals as if reading them, most people know the hymns well enough not to be dependent on the translations.

Religious activities continue during the summer months through the Marine Medical Mission Vacation Bible School, which is basically a fundamentalist organization drawing from several denominations. Young adults, usually two young women, live in the village for about three weeks each summer, conducting Bible classes and other church-related activities. They concentrate primarily on children, but they also hold services for adults. The program is designed to be non-denominational in doctrine and is guided by a schedule printed at mission headquarters. The girls work about five hours each day, three hours in the morning with children from age three to twelve, and two hours in the afternoon or evening with the older children.

The daily program begins about 9:30 A.M. when all the children salute the Canadian and church flags, recite the accompanying verse, sing and read from the Bible. Children from age eight to twelve recite their memory verses and listen to a Bible story. The children play organized games outside during their recess. Following this, they work assignments in their workbooks and work on handicrafts such as coloring or cutting figures for flannel board stories. Before leaving, the children are told a story that has a moral and sing some hymns. The activities of the older group are similar to those of the younger, but their schedule is geared to their age level. Occasionally older children play softball or some other organized game in the evening and they may have refreshments following this.

Anglican church services are held infrequently among the Islanders, except at Kingcome where a church has been established for many years and where a lay reader resides. Anglican clergymen are scheduled to visit the Island villages about once a month, but while we were at Gilford services were held once every two to four months. Visits are made on the *Columbia*, which acquired a full-time minister after we left the village. Consequently, services are now reported to be held more frequently.

Competitiveness and mild conflict characterize the relationship between the Pentecostal deaconess and the Anglican lay reader and clergy. According to a minister in the United Church in Alert Bay, Anglicans dislike Pentecostals because the latter encroach on formally allocated Anglican territory. Anglicans and the United Church work fairly well together because each restricts its activities to territories which overlap very little; as a result they do not interfere with and antagonize one another. Hilda was once told by a former Anglican minister at Kingcome, "You're in my territory and therefore under my jurisdiction." She paid no attention to this pronouncement, although she admits that, "This is Anglican territory as far as [church] allotment goes." She says that she attends Anglican services when they are held in the village and sometimes tries to elaborate on a theme which is initiated during an Anglican service, but she attended no Anglican services while we were living at Gilford. She once admitted being annoyed when villagers come to her house to borrow benches, tables or dishes to be used in Anglican services. One representative occasion irritated her, for example, when a village man asked to borrow benches. She asked why he wanted them and he was embarrassed to tell her about the Anglican baptismal ceremony which was about to take place. She had not known that the *Columbia* had called in the village and was at that moment tied to the float.

A useful but rough index of the relative influence of and differential attitudes toward each denomination is found in the unique situation where the two groups held services simultaneously within the village. The Pentacostal service was attended by fifteen people, including eight children; twelve people attended the Anglican service, including four children. The majority of the village attended neither service. Some of the men who were fishing did not attend, as is true of a small group who were drinking. I asked Victor Philip which service he would attend, and he responded, "Well, since I have my choice I guess I won't go to either." A further indicator of religious orientation is found in the composition of the three major church groups in Alert Bay—the United Church, Anglican and Pentecostal. The United Church draws almost exclusively from the White population in Alert Bay, the Anglican from both White and Indian, and the Pentecostal largely from the Indian population. None of the churches has a large or consistent attendance from Indians or Whites. Members of the subsisting oriented class appear to attend Pentecostal services more frequently than Anglican, and members of the future oriented class appear to prefer Anglican more often than Pentecostal

Several reasons exist why relatively more villagers attend Pentecostal services than Anglican. An Anglican communion service furnishes an example of the difference between the two. It was attended by sixteen villagers, ten of whom took communion. The service, which lasted thirty minutes, was read from the Book of Common Prayer, and two hymns were sung in English which were notably lacking in spontaneity and volume. Members of the village were somewhat uncomfortable during the service because it was highly formalized and replete with symbolism in dress and paraphernalia. Both of the clergymen who officiated were in their clerical frocks. The members of the village are more accustomed to Pentecostal services with their spontaneity and casualness. The fact that a considerable part of the Pentacostal services are in Kwakwala and that audience participation is encouraged make these meetings much more comfortable. The

Anglican service, by contrast, is formal, mechanical, subdued and ritualistic, with a minimum of participation by members of the congregation.

The indigenous religious practices and beliefs of the Kwakiutl revolved around the acquisition of and right to supernatural or spirit power. Winter ceremonials were the occasion at which individuals publicly demonstrated their prerogatives in the religious dance "societies," especially in the $ts^{\varepsilon}eiqa$, "red cedar bark dance." The Kwakiutl had no belief in a single supreme being, but rather in many spirit forms, some of which inhabited the body of different animals, and others of which were purely spiritual. They also believed that humans have a spirit which leaves the body at death and goes to the spirit world. Spirits were believed to live in villages similar to those on earth.

The first Western religious influence came through Catholic traders, explorers and missionaries. Later the Anglicans became the dominant religious force in the Gilford region, and more recently Pentecostals and others have had a strong impact. The first missionary activities at Gilford were Anglican, and a mission school was in operation there from about 1889 to 1912. Reverend Herbert Pearson, one of the first missionaries at Gilford, gave us the following account about religious education among the villagers during the years he served both Gilford and Kingcome:

> Most evenings I went into different houses and read from the four Gospels, sang Hymns which had also been translated by Mr. Hall, and said Prayers from the English Church Prayer Book. Sometimes quite a number would gather around the fire and sing. Another difficulty was the Winter dances and Potlatch, held during the winter. For three weeks in January they would have their red bark dances, so called because every single individual would wear a strip of red bark around the forehead. These would last three weeks almost day and night. I have known them to continue for 36 hours on end. During that time the children would not attend school.
>
> On Sunday mornings I held service using of course the translated Prayer Book, there would be a fair number present, adults and children. Sometimes the whole tribe would leave for another village (Alert Bay or Fort Rupert, Village Island) or other for Potlatch and stay weeks. Thus it was almost impossible to have any real continuance in anything.

Authority, Power-Prestige, and Friendship

Formal authority within the village at Gilford is vested in the Band council, which is equivalent to a local government body in a rural municipality.[5] Even though the Gilford Island Band came under the provisions of the elective-system in 1957, as specified by the *Indian Act*, a Band council was not established at Gilford until 1961. Councils are concerned with all matters that affect the well-being of Band members, and they are accorded authoritative rights and obligations over the Band by the Department of Citizenship and Immigration. The intent of the Canadian government in instituting this system was to encourage the Indians

---

[5] The term Band refers to a group of Indians who share a common interest in specified tracts of land called Reserves and/or given monetary assets known as Band funds.

to become more involved in their own well-being. But many decisions such as who may join the Band, leasing Reserve land to lumber companies, the expenditure of Band funds, and the introduction of new Band council by-laws are subject to final approval by the Minister of Citizenship and Immigration.

The council system at Gilford is ineffective. One of the principal reasons for this is that the council is an intrusive institution with rules, obligations, responsibilities, rights and expectations that have no counterpart in the customary life of the Kwakiutl. This, in part, contributes to the apathy many villagers feel toward the Band council at Gilford. Moreover, as we describe more fully below, authority vested in the council is inconsistent with village normative standards, including the norm of non-interference. When a villager assumes office he is likely, if he acts in accordance with the norms associated with that status, to violate certain behavior-standards in a community marked by a preexisting network of mutual grievances. Thus, the councillor is apt to lose friends and, to a lesser extent, interpersonal power and prestige. This point, in fact, appears to be one of the most forceful reasons for the ineffectiveness of the Band council at Gilford. That is, in every enduring, face-to-face group, power, prestige and friendship structures emerge. An individual's location within these rank structures is dependent in part on his acceptable performance of social roles—including, of course, his reasonable adherence to normative standards. In general, a person who violates these standards loses power, prestige and friendship. This is what happens to the councillors who act on the authority vested in their position; the council itself thereby becomes less effectual because the members of the community collect additional grievances against those who hold office.

The implications of these facts become clearer after we elucidate the concepts of power, prestige and authority. We define power as the ability to influence the opinions or behavior of others; the more an individual is able to do this, the more power he has. Social power emerges only through the interaction of two or more individuals. To the extent that an individual acquires power within a group, he acquires certain rights over group action which are important in determining the outcome of group activity. Authority includes one type of power; it is the institutionalized right over group or individual action and includes the legitimate right to apply coercive sanctions in threat or fact. Authority is associated with a status or an institutionally defined social position that is identified independently of its occupant. Whereas an individual acquires authority solely by occupying a particular position or status in the social system, power is acquired only through an individual's ability to reward others in specified ways. It is not necessarily associated with any formal status. In every group individuals control differential access to rare and valuable resources which they may distribute among the members of the group, thereby rewarding them. The value of the resources is defined by the normative system of the group.

Prestige is defined here as social rewards—signs of social approval, esteem, respect, admiration or being highly regarded by one's associates. Power and prestige tend to be linked with each other. Thus individuals of high power tend to be individuals of high prestige, and vice versa. Power and prestige also tend to be distributed unevenly throughout the group; that is, no two individuals share the same amount of either. Consequently members of groups may be ranked in both a power structure and a prestige structure, and the two structures tend to be equilibrated or congruent, leading to the concept of power-prestige as distinguished from power *and* prestige.

I designed a sociometric questionnaire to measure power, prestige and friendship within the village just prior to the council election in 1963. I predicted that councillor choices would be made on the basis of both power-prestige and friendship. Since the balloting was to be secret, I asked each person who he thought the three people were who were most capable of acting as councillor, and I asked each person for whom he thought most people in the village would vote. The questionnaire predicted perfectly the new chief councillor and it accurately identified a small pool of villagers from which the other two councillors would be selected. Power-prestige and friendship choices were strongly correlated with councillor choices.[6] We conclude, therefore, that power-prestige and friendship are two crucial bases on which a member of the community is elected to office. In addition, as I expected, one person in the village received far more power-prestige choices than anyone else. He received over 19 percent more power-prestige choices than his nearest competitors—two people tied for second rank—who in turn received almost 2 percent more choices than the person in the third rank. Almost 60 percent of the villagers received only one or no power-prestige choices; they fell in the bottom two ranks of a structure ranging from positions one to thirty-four.

After the election it was clear that both the present and former councillors were high in the power-prestige structure—except for Victor Philip, the former chief councillor, who was in position number eleven in the ranking. Apparently the former councillors were able to maintain their position in the power-prestige structure. The new councillors, Willis Drake (chief councillor), Herbert Philip and Simon Cedar, were in positions one, five and eight respectively. The most noteworthy consequence of having been in a position of authority, however, is found in each man's position within the best-friend rank structure (which ranges from positions one to thirty-nine). Whereas the new councillors, Willis, Herbert and Simon, were in positions one, three and four respectively, the former councillors, Victor and Joseph Abel, were at the bottom of the friendship structure. Edna Moon, the third councillor, was in position number twenty-six. She was able to preserve part of her popularity because, as a woman, she acted least often on the rights and obligations of her status. The great incongruity between the power-prestige and friendship structures of the former councillors has massive implications for the ineffectiveness of the council system at Gilford. And, as we argue below, the former councillors seem to have lost a great deal of their friendship by being councillors.

We must point out, however, that the first chief councillor, Victor, almost certainly did not rank at the top of the best friend structure at the time he was

---

[6] High power-prestige choices are associated with high councillor choices and lower power-prestige choices are associated with low councillor choices. Best friend choices are also associated with the choices given for councillor. Individuals who receive many best friend choices do not necessarily receive many Band councillor choices, but individuals who receive few best friend choices rarely receive any councillor choices.

elected. Possibly he did not rank at the top of the power-prestige structure either because, as we noted earlier, he is a member of the future oriented class and operates on a somewhat different value-standard. Friendship and power-prestige are normally not achieved in situations where an individual violates or is marginal to the norms of the group. The other two councillors are members of the subsisting oriented class and should have ranked at approximately the same level in the two structures. Victor appears to have been elected to office for different reasons than the other two councillors. He was probably selected on the basis of his ability to read, write and speak English fluently, and to a lesser extent because of his acquired power-prestige and friendship within the village. These factors were also taken into consideration by members of the village at the second election. Some villagers expressed concern about Willis' deficiencies in these respects, especially his lack of fluency in English, but he was nevertheless overwhelmingly elected to office.

Authority as manifested in the council system was realigned with the power-prestige and best-friend structures of the village as a result of the election in 1963. Formerly only the power-prestige structure was aligned with the authority system. Presumably friendship was lost, as we said, in the enactment of the rights and obligations contained within the council. In order to operate as councillors, individuals occasionally violated those standards which had led to their original acquisition of friendship. This occurs because the rights and obligations of the council system are inconsistent with many village norms. Again, as we said, an individual in a position of authority has the opportunity to reward or deny rewards to others. He controls access to rare and valuable resources which may be distributed among the members of the group, thereby perpetuating power-prestige; but he may also distribute these in such a way that friendship expectations are violated. Demands are made on councillors which place friendship in jeopardy regardless of the decision made. Members of the village, for example, ask councillors to recommend them for relief. If the request is refused because of insufficient need or because the councillor is angry at the applicant for personal reasons, the latter becomes angry with the councillor. If the request is granted other members of the community become annoyed because they too were not recommended. They expect the councillor to recommend them for relief because they feel that their need is as great as or greater than the first applicant's or because they have as many or more rights based on friendship or kin ties.

Because of these facts we developed the hypothesis that the less an individual of high power-prestige controls and acts on authority, the better he is liked. For example, as we observed earlier, Edna ranked higher in the best-friend structure than the other two councillors. And, as noted, she acted least often on the formal authority granted her by the fact of her office. Because she infrequently acted on the power of authority she was able to maintain friendship ties more easily than the other two councillors. Stanley Philip, tribal chief of the Koeksotenok, provides a second illustration bearing on this hypothesis. He, along with the former councillors, ranked fairly high in the power-prestige structure in 1963, but all four were lowest in the best-friend structure. Stanley controls a great deal of authority in the village and he often acts as the official representative to the Canadian government for Kwakiutl Bands throughout the area. But he is a member of the future oriented class and operates on a different value-standard base from the members of the subsisting oriented group. Thus by violating village norms, he has lost friendship within the community.

The three new councillors had no authority at the time the questionnaire was administered. They all stood high in the power-prestige structure and because they had not yet been elected, they stood highest in the best-friend structure along with three other villagers who had never held office. Ambrose Cedar is the only exception in the village to the rule that the less an individual of high power-prestige controls and acts on authority the better he is liked. Ambrose is one of the highest power-prestige individuals in the village (ranking eighth along with Chief Philip and Simon), but he is at the bottom of the best-friend structure— even though he has never been in a position of authority. We have no explanation for this exception.

Before leaving Gilford in 1963, I made the prediction that the present councillors would lose best-friend choices during their tenure of office, and that by the next election in 1965 they would have fallen toward the bottom of the best-friend structure while maintaining their basic positions in the power-prestige ranking. Field research during the summer of 1964, however, suggested that this prediction needed modification to account for the impact of the chief councillor's wife, Lucy. Most people in the village recognize her as the driving force behind Willis, the chief councillor. In 1963 Lucy ranked among the highest power-prestige individuals in the village; she was also among the highest receivers of best-friend choices. On certain occasions Willis has antagonized members of the community by acting on his authority. Many people blame Lucy for "making him do it." In this way Willis maintained both power-prestige and friendship, but Lucy probably lost friendship. Willis was reelected in the May, 1965, Band council election, thus indicating that he had indeed been able to sustain his position in the power-prestige structure. He also appears to have been able to maintain most of his ties of friendship. Unfortunately we have no information regarding Lucy. As we predicted, however, the other two councillors were replaced by new ones.

An example of the ineffectual nature of the council is found in their inability to sustain a policing system in the village for the enforcement of a 9:00 P.M. curfew on school children and younger children. Different men in the village, including councillors, were assigned the task of sending children home who were found outside after 9:00 P.M., but all of them resigned after a short period, each complaining that he could not control the children of other people. Joe Abel resigned because he could not control the children of Willis Drake, who later accepted the position, then in turn resigned a short time later because he could not control Joe's children. Some men such as Harold Dick, however, are fairly efficient as "policemen" because the children are afraid of them, but parents become antagonistic toward individuals who interfere with their children. Here too the norm of noninterference is in effect.

Councillors are often placed in a situation of structural conflict. By conforming to the rights and obligations of the council system, they violate some of the normative expectations of the villagers. By conforming to the normative expectations of the villagers, they have difficulty performing their duties as councillors. A related set of factors contributing to the ineffectiveness of the council is the fact that the performance expectations of councillors are not crystallized; consequently performance evaluations are inconsistent. Neither the villagers nor the councillors themselves have a clear image of the range of behavior that is appropriate and legitimate for councillors. Certainly there is no consensual validation regarding such behavior. Councillors are inadequately trained or instructed by the Indian Affairs Branch regarding the range of rights and obligations connected with the council system. Councillors are given a manual which assists them but they are not given any practical training. A great deal of mutual misunderstanding exists between councillors and the Indian Affairs Branch, especially the office of the Agency Superintendent.

The effective authority of the councillors is further attenuated and bounded by the normative system in the village which has historical precedence and a great influence on those individuals who are motivated to remain within the network of social relations which characterizes the members of the subsisting oriented class. Villagers recognize the authority of councillors in general, but the normative behavior-expectations are unclear. No standards have developed which coordinate or clearly define the relationship between the authority of the council system and the preexisting normative system.

The effectiveness of the council system is further attenuated because many people in the village criticize the Band council, and councillors are often critical of each other and the village. The former chief councillor, Victor, made the indicative comment that when something goes wrong the council is blamed. "People never put the blame on themselves." The same man was disgruntled because village members did not support him or the other councillors. He insisted that apathy regarding the council and village activities is widespread among the villagers, and cited a number of examples to reinforce his contention; for example, refusal to clean and "modernize" the village, make home repairs, and discipline children. Victor feels that the use of intoxicants is one of the major reasons why none of these tasks was carried out. "They spend their money on beer instead of house repairs and for a boat," and "They think they're doing it behind my back, but I know what's going on." He continued, "People don't even try to cooperate. I've been kidding myself for a long time." From a social interaction point of view, Victor was at a double disadvantage because, first, as a member of the future oriented class he operates on a somewhat different value standard from the other villagers. Second, as a councillor he is in a position of formal authority and the authority of the council system is incongruent with the normative standards of the village. Consequently the fact that he is criticized by other villagers is not surprising. Joe, one of the other councillors, criticized him for not doing his job and stated, "He just doesn't have it up here." Yet when Joe learned that Victor was planning to leave the village he complained, "If you have a good man, who'll do that?" Edna, the third councillor, is volubly antagonistic toward Joe because she feels he carries his authority too far, and she criticizes him for fighting when he drinks. Joe recognizes that the people in the village have grievances against him and admits, "People say I've got a big mouth. That's what they call me." Villagers criticize Joe for looking after the interests of his own family and of himself, but not those of other villagers. Most people recognize his good qualities but talk most often about his bad ones.

Gertie Philip commented that the only time people in the village cooperate with each other is during a school activity. Presumably this is because such activities are generally organized by the teacher. She continued, "The thing about this village is that it's every man for himself." Another person said that villagers expect councillors to do things for them rather than for themselves, and Joe made a similar observation from his point of view. "They're waiting until they're told to do something."

The ineffectiveness of the Band council system at Gilford is duplicated in the apathy toward and ineffectiveness of other task oriented groups. Even though over half the adult males in the village express a moderate to strong interest in village activities, only one-third of them have actually held or presently hold office in any task oriented group. Such groups include the Water (Dam) Committee which is responsible for cleaning and repairing the dam and pipe lines leading into the village. The Dam Committeemen should drain and scrub the dam every six months or more, but in fact it may be cleaned once a year. Water in the dam collects a great deal of debris, including a dead cat several years ago. The Dam Committee is more active than many of the others, however, perhaps because of the importance of fresh water to the village. A Health Committee was established before the Band council was organized. This committee has responsibility for health and sanitation problems within the village. Committeemen are supposed to assure that beaches in front of the village are kept clean and that garbage and other waste material is thrown into the water from the wharf below the low tide mark. The beach in front of the village, however, is strewn with trash of all types. Important changes were made when the committee was first formed in 1960, but little has been done since then. Before that time outhouses and smokehouses were stationed along the edge of the beach. Since then outhouses have been moved behind the houses against the sharp rise of the mountain. One villager observed that the Health Committee is completely inactive because members "are afraid to try to make people do things." The Sports Club and Breakers Committee are fairly active during the soccer season because of the high level interest and involvement in sports among most of the men. An Anglican Women's Auxilliary (W.A.) was formed several years ago but it became almost defunct after a period of time because the president resigned at the birth of her child and the second president mismanaged the records, including the embezzlement of funds. The W.A. was reorganized by the new minister on the *Columbia* after we left the village in 1963. A Movie Committee was established while we were at Gilford for the purpose of selecting and showing commercial films. Members of the committee operated effectively during that time, and have continued since then.

4

Growing Up Kwakiutl

GERTIE AND MY WIFE were drinking coffee in Gertie's kitchen when they heard a fight outside. Gertie opened the door and yelled at two preschool youngsters tussling over a tricycle. She told the neighbor girl to leave the trike alone and to go home if she did not want to get hit by her son; the trike did not belong to the girl anyway. Gertie grumbled to Evelyn about the behavior of village children. A little while later there were more sounds of children fighting. Gertie got up and yelled at the two children. This time they were both her own and the older boy was beating on his younger brother while the latter feebly tried to take the tricycle. Gertie told the younger boy to leave the trike alone, it was not his and if he did not want to get beaten up by his older brother he should leave things alone that did not belong to him.

The children involved in the dispute over the tricycle that afternoon were two brothers age three and four, and a four-year-old neighbor girl. No attempt was made to control their aggression; in fact Gertie rewarded the actions of the aggressor-owner. As far as Gertie is concerned, the owner of the tricycle has the right to play with it and he is not expected to share his toys. If a child spoils his sibling's possession, villagers consider it to be the owner's fault for leaving the toy unprotected. The owner is expected to protect his property; if he neglects his possessions and they are spoiled, it is his fault.

A second incident which reveals villagers' feelings about rights of owner-ship occurred in the school during the early part of the year. Since the school has two classrooms but only one teacher, the second classroom is used for storage of extra desks and supplies. Evelyn told the school children that they were not to go there without permission, and we left the door to the storeroom-classroom closed but unlocked. After a few weeks Evelyn went into the storeroom to get some art supplies and noticed most of the pencils, erasers and crayons were gone. She was furious and expressed her anger to the students. I padlocked the second classroom. Evelyn was distressed by the incident because by locking the spare room she had taught the pupils that with locks on doors they could not enter; she wanted them to learn that they should not enter because they were told not to. Later she discovered that the thief had been twelve-year-old Leslie Drake, who, after obtaining the majority of very limited and valued supplies had simply thrown them on the beach. While the villagers clucked sympathetically at the loss, there was an undercurrent of feeling that we were foolish for not attempting to protect school property with a lock rather than with words.

Because the older children were sent to residential school in mid-October, the age range of children at Gilford during our year (except for holidays) extended from infancy to preadolescence and to the age group above sixteen. Major pranks and property destruction were at a minimum; there was no gas sniffing, rarely was beer stolen from drinking parties by youngsters—yet gas sniffing, beer stealing and property destruction were rampant at other villages (cf. Wolcott 1967). We explain this difference as being due to the absence of young adolescents, who are usually the "troublemakers" elsewhere.

Although one frequently hears complaints about destructive children, perhaps accompanied by the recounting of a specific incident, rarely is anything done about it because of the prevailing attitude of noninterference. Ambrose Cedar, for example, observed a gang of kids playing in the big-house and yelled at them to cut it out. The youngsters did not listen and he made no further attempt to stop them. On another occasion two children were breaking Coke and beer bottles against a water faucet. Harold Dick yelled at them to stop, but they did not pay any attention. He turned to me and said, "Those kids don't have ears, I guess." Later the same three-year-olds were doing something else and Norman Philip yelled at them once or twice to quit. He commented to me that, "It's no use yelling at them or getting after them. They don't listen. Beside, if their parents hear me yelling at their kids, they'll just come out and give me a good bawling out. They'll think I've been picking on their kids. Let the kids hurt themselves, I don't care. It's no use!"

That same day Herbert Philip, Harold and I watched several children playing on the porch of an abandoned house. They knocked out one of the windows and after a short time climbed through the window and began playing inside. I made the suggestion that, as councillor, Herb might want to correct the children; he responded that it was none of his business. "It's up to their parents to take care of the kids." All of the known tree burials and grave huts in the nearby cemetery have been demolished by the children. Adults and parents click their tongues, shake their heads and say that children should not do that. "I don't know what's the matter with those kids. They're just haywire, I guess."

Noninterference has its limits, however. Preschool children who wander onto the float are usually told to go home by anyone there and if they do not respond they may be carried off the float. A village rule states that no children are to be on the wharf, but little attention is given to this except in the case of the very young. Occasionally an older child is told to leave, but the issue is seldom pressed.

Women want children; consequently even children who are born as a result of casual sexual affairs are generally accepted. Four youths within the village who resulted from such unions are accepted by other villagers as well as their parents, although comments are occasionally made about their origin if someone becomes angry.

Infants are loved, petted, fondled and held by everyone who is old enough to do so. Teenagers stroll around the village holding or wheeling someone's infant, and children of any age go to the home of an infant and ask if they might take him out. Ten-year-old May Otter proudly recounted to Evelyn each new accomplishment of her infant brother. May and her eight-year-old sister, Betty, spent a great deal of time with their baby brother, and during their parents' drinking parties the two girls took care of him. One day Betty told Evelyn that she wished she could sleep in the classroom. Evelyn asked her why and Betty said she had stayed up late the night before to take care of her brother. Older siblings, both male and female, quite often take care of infants, especially when their parents drink.

A few parents partially abandon their children for periods of time, leaving them in the village to be cared for by someone else while they live away. Viola Abel, for example, locked the doors of her house and left the village without telling anyone. Louisa Cedar, the children's grandmother, cared for them during the two weeks of their mother's absence. Rita Bean has had two children placed in foster homes by court action because a health nurse found one of them alone and sick while her mother was away drinking. But this behavior is very unusual.

The most common form of admonishment applied to children is to hear a parent monotonously repeat, "Don't fool around. Don't fool around." Children generally continue until the tone of "don't fool around" changes, at which time they stop, at least briefly. Some mothers, when they become particularly impatient, yell at their children, "You fucking little bastards! You ass holes!" A mother becomes angry, however, when others do the same to her children. Youngsters quickly become familiar with such language: three girls were on the beach. The oldest, nine, became incensed at the seven-year-old and screamed, "You fucking bastard! You God damned son of a bitch. . . ." The latter retaliated in like manner, but less vociferously. The six-year-old who was with them listened but did not respond.

Around mid-year Leonard Drake, a ten-year-old first grade pupil, came into the teacherage after school to visit. He wandered freely about while Evelyn performed housewifely chores. He left after a while and I reached for our last package of cigarettes; they were gone. Leonard had been the only visitor in our quarters that day, so I went to the village and confronted the youngster who said he had given the cigarettes to his cousin. He went and got them. Willis, the boy's father, is usually extremely mild and soft-spoken, but he overheard the whole conversation and as I left he slapped his son across the face. This is the only incident of which we are aware of a father laying hands on his child when completely sober, and it was so extraordinary that the children talked of it in awed whispers the following days at school. It was still a topic of conversation among adults ten months later.

Another common but more subtle form of discipline is the use of ghost stories. We were unaware of the effectiveness of these stories until the days began to shorten in December. We noticed that as the daylight hours grew short our young visitors disappeared. Once a visiting group of school girls noticed it was getting dark, commented on it and rushed home. We began to realize they were reluctant to be out after dark. Incidents are recounted of ghosts visiting empty houses or peering through windows, sometimes doing minor damage. Many adults, too, are afraid of ghosts, or at least they are willing to impute unexplained events to the mythical person *bukwəs* "wild man of the woods." *Bukwəs* is generally considered to be harmless and has the peculiar ability of moving himself instantly from one location to another a great distance away. The *bukwəs* dance also figures importantly in some of the traditional winter ceremonials.

By age nine or ten, young people begin to identify with sex roles. Girls help around the house; boys are given more freedom to hang around the beach or on the float and occasionally they accompany their fathers fishing. If a man or a group of men go to the store and beer parlor they might take a boy along, but almost never a girl.

Sex role identity is revealed in children's drawings. Girls typically draw pictures of houses and people and sometimes such things as laundry, flowers, and tables with dishes, but they do not draw pictures of traditional Indian designs or boats. Boys at Gilford, on the other hand, most frequently draw pictures of boats and people (men and boys), usually a wharf, sometimes a canoe, fish net or fish and occasionally Indian designs. When the children tell stories about pictures they have created in school each child is able to specify who the people are in the drawings and whose house or boat is represented. None of the stories which accompany the drawings are purely imaginary, and only a few pictures contain fictitious elements, for example, a fence where there is none. The closest children come to making up stories is in the area of humor, where their stories sometimes take the form of *klikwala*, translated very loosely as "just fooling" (or a "white lie"). A child told Evelyn, "Oh, your husband's *really* drunk!" I entered the house at that moment without having had anything to drink. The children were delighted with their joke but were disappointed that I appeared when I did, thus limiting the impact of their *klikwala*. Some Whites misunderstand this form of behavior and decry its usage. The mother of a past teacher in the village, for example, was convinced that the children were inveterate and malicious liars.

Play also reflects sex role identification among children. A favorite activity among boys is to play fisherman. They run along the water's edge with a stick to which a model boat is attached on a line. Occasionally boys drag a piece of net along the ground and pretend to be fishing; on inquiry they will tell whether they are gill netting or purse seining. They sometimes use long reeds or straight sticks to "troll" the soccer field. Other games, except soccer, run in fads and cycles. Sometimes boys play cowboys and Indians using reeds as spears. We were never able to determine the differential attitude toward each, or to determine who usually plays cowboy and who Indian. Judging from the use of spears, however, most of them play Indians. The cowboy role seems to be fairly ignored. Large heavy darts intermittently come into style as do firecrackers and bows and arrows (which Kwakiutl adults do not use). During warm weather boys and girls swim either from the beach or off the float. When they have access to one, older boys enjoy using row boats or canoes and they handle them with proficiency. Children frequently scull the boats with planks or broken oars because they rarely have legitimate access to oarlocks or unbroken oars. Older boys from ten to thirteen often roam around the village, especially when parties are in session.

School represents a discontinuity in the lives of many children since teacher expectations are not reinforced in the home, in the village generally, or by other life experiences. As a result formal education tends to become compartmentalized and disassociated from other life experiences. To the individual it appears to have no basic, immediate relevance for his life at the moment, or for the perceivable future. This has an important bearing on the educational progress of the children and is one set of factors contributing to the high incidence of school drop-outs. School experiences tend to controvert some of the basic learning which takes place in preschool years and in nonschool activities. For example, independence and mild aggression are rewarded in nonschool activities but are negatively sanctioned in the school. The child must learn a form of compliance behavior in the classroom which is not expected out of school; competition with peers rather than aid and cooperation are expected. Concern about delimitable time units leading to the concept of punctuality is important in the educational system and becomes a moral issue for many teachers.

The most important difference between formal education and the cultural system of the villagers lies in the method of learning. This difference creates an important discontinuity in the enculturation process of the children. A Kwakiutl child learns, fundamentally, by observing, performing and then having his behavior rewarded, punished or ignored. Unlike middle-class children, however, the Kwakiutl child initiates most of his own action. He neither expects nor waits for verbal or formal didactic instruction. A child learns to operate a boat and set a net largely through observation of others and subsequently by trying it himself, either in play or by helping his father; he learns to ride a bicycle or to Indian-dance in the same way. For example, Ernest, a young adult, made the indicative comment that no one tells them of their errors when they Indian-dance. Adults or expert dancers do not attempt to make corrections or give instructions. Adults dance and expect the observer to learn the rules from their performance. I noticed the same thing. When I objected about dancing the first time without some indication of the proper way of doing it, Jeffrey Hardy said emphatically, "You'll never learn to dance unless you do it." When I protested further, saying, "Yes, but I need to know what I am *supposed* to be doing," he simply stared at me for a moment and turned away without any further comment. I danced as best I could from watching others. Later when I asked for comments and criticisms regarding my dancing I was told briefly by Frank Bean that I was "too stiff." No elaboration or other correction was offered. Verbal instructions are not totally lacking, however. Once Jeff briefly explained some fine points of dancing to Ernie Amber; Frank observed, "You should have been a teacher. You explained that well."

In the classroom, on the other hand, Kwakiutl children must *learn* to learn through verbal instruction, reading and writing. These methods of learning require language skills in English. Language skills are not as important in the native context; a very small part of becoming a fisherman, for example, is learned through verbal or written instruction.

The fact that the life of the children is structured to a very limited extent within the village constitutes another basic discontinuity between the social and cultural background of the children and the expectations of the school. Whereas parents are permissive toward the behavior of their children, school life is authoritarian and formal. This conflicting situation often imposes as much hardship on the teacher as on the pupils. The lack of structure and the degree of permissiveness by parents may explain, in part, why children bicker, swear, throw things, hit each other and generally pay no attention in the classroom.

Moreover, the children's experience with formal education has been highly inconsistent. Little continuity has existed in the procedures, demands and expectations of past teachers beyond the formal requirements of the Indian Affairs Branch, and the quality of teaching at Gilford has been inconsistent. Children have not had to meet and conform to a uniform set of demands by past teachers which might have allowed them to standardize their behavior and expectations for future ones. To this extent older pupils are not in a position to furnish models for the younger ones regarding appropriate classroom behavior. The inconsistency and discontinuity of educational experiences influence the performance of children. They experience many failures and little pleasure in school activities; as a result some develop a psychological set which predisposes them to anticipate and react to failure in characteristic ways. These include anger, giving up and, in the extreme, not trying in the first place. Many children have a low frustration tolerance for difficult school assignments. They react with anger, or sometimes, they cry if they cannot complete their work with relative ease and they often give up and refuse to try. Evelyn found beginning students were better able to grasp new concepts, commensurate with their age level, than older students. Part of the reason for this lies in the fact that the former have not experienced as many failures and have not developed a negative set toward trying.

One day Leslie Drake pushed Evelyn's patience too far by whistling while she was trying to teach a geography lesson. She told him to stop; he continued to whistle, and the other students became nervously silent. Evelyn walked to Leslie's desk and again told him to stop whistling. He looked her directly in the eye, puckered up and whistled. She slapped him across the face in total frustration and rushed out of the noiseless classroom into the teacherage. After a few moments she wiped her tears and returned to the still quiet classroom. From then on whenever a child went too far the closest part of his anatomy received the back of her hand. Here was a form of punishment expected from teachers and understood both by parents and students. Yet at the end of the year a six-year-old boy who had been spanked fairly often said, "Gee Mrs. Rohner, you nicest teacher we ever had; you never hit us once!"

School routine is further disrupted during periods of heavy drinking. If the children attend school at all they are often too tired to work and sometimes too tense. An increase of the noise level in class is often a good indicator of extensive drinking in the village, and periods of drinking in conjunction with conflict among members of the village are major contributors to the disruption of class-room routine. Willie Moon, who managed to come to school one morning, told Evelyn that he had three hours of sleep the night before. He had five the night before that. His brother Ralph did not come at all. The boys' father, Paul, apparently becomes abusive toward Ralph when the former drinks and, for the past couple of days Ralph had been trying to find a place to sleep where he would be out of Paul's reach.

Classroom control is further complicated by the fact that children reflect and react to tensions within the village. Evelyn often knew from the way the children behaved that a fight or other dispute had erupted in the village. Children carry parental gossip and feelings of animosity into the classroom and they tease or fight with the children of the people toward whom their parents are antagonistic. After Christmas vacation the pupils shunned May and Betty Otter, the children of the man who had broken into the school during our absence. Only by Evelyn's persistent attention to the problem and by forcing the students to talk about it were the two girls reaccepted into the group. For a few days comments had been overt and disruptive as, "Gee I don't want to sit next to you; your father's no good!" At another time the Hardys, grandparents of three school children ages six, nine and ten, excluded Willis Drake from a drinking party. Willis' oldest daughter in school is sharp-tongued and a school leader. She made sure that Jeffrey Hardy's three grandchildren were alternately tormented, picked on and ignored for a few days.

Only under extreme provocation, however, is Leonard Drake, the ten-year-old first grader mentioned earlier, ever picked on by the other students—although he would be fair game because he cries easily. Actually the whole village feels protective of Leonard, and their greatest wrath at a previous teacher was because he had dragged Leonard home from school by the ear. Evelyn too had to be careful in her handling of Leonard if she wanted to avoid student hostility.

Frequently we heard from city dwellers that, whereas the Indians may not know about "Dick and Jane," they certainly know all about their village environ-ment. This is untrue. The younger pupils express amazement that animals once lived in the shells found on the beach. They were surprised to discover they could make pots from the clay deposit we found near a stream at one end of the village. And none of them had ever looked closely at a snake. One day, for example, I came into the classroom with a small garter snake; the children screamed in fright. Eventually they calmed down and the snake was placed among the slugs and moss in a terrarium. The pupils spent the rest of the day lying on the floor, noses pressed to the glass, while Evelyn read to them anything she could find on snakes. Even at the level of the most elementary readers children are exposed to things which they have never seen or about which they have never heard. A few of the children have never seen an automobile, and most of them have never seen a horse or the other farm animals which are included in the vocabulary of early readers. At a more sophisticated level most of the children have never heard of an elevator, and the idea of an escalator—steps which can continuously ascend or descend—is strange indeed!

Prior to our arrival in the village many of the younger children had never been to a movie. One mother reported that when she first took her two sons to a movie in Alert Bay they continually asked, "What's that? What's that?" A second child, Adam Bean, was enthralled with colored slides which I had taken of the village, the surrounding area, and Vancouver. Evelyn reported that he was so excited, "He almost climbed into the screen." Adam, an eight-year-old boy, had never seen Alert Bay, but he was the only child of his age who had not.

Commercial movies were shown in the village during our year of research. Those who had the money or could borrow it often went to both showings. Two movies drew particularly favorable attention from the villagers, both adults and children. One of them involved a White man who became a Teton-Sioux after surviving the run of the arrow, and the second movie related to a White adolescent who had been captured as a child by a group of Indians on the Delaware. All commercial movies were selected from an annotated list by several men in the village. Even though we could not determine the educational impact of movies among the children, it should not be underestimated because the boundaries of their social universe were extended. The boundaries were further expanded through occasional slide shows given by such people as the doctor on the *Columbia*, the ship belonging to the Columbia Coast Mission. The children were impressed, for example, with a piece of human hair when they saw it under the doctor's microscope.

Many adults and adolescents remember school with distaste because of repetitive failures in conjunction with other negative experiences. Children typically approach school with substantial ambivalence and many Indian students leave school at the minimum age of sixteen because of these feelings. An adolescent girl who had dropped out of school could remember only one incident which she described as fun in all her years at school. She probably is not atypical. According to the Indians these observations are as true of experience in residential schools as in the village day schools.

A child learns about the major roles in the social system at a fairly young age. He knows what his parents do and how they do it; he knows about kinsmen and non-kin residents of the village; he has attended and sometimes participated at least marginally in all the recurrent activities of the village; he is aware at least vaguely of all the important relationships and events encountered by those around him; he believes that when he grows older he too will be a fisherman. A girl believes she will be a wife and mother. The child is prepared to activate these roles at the appropriate time. In short, adulthood holds no mystery for Kwakiutl children. To this extent formal education received in the classroom does little to realistically or importantly prepare most of the children, from their point of view, for the future.

Changes in status are not clearly marked among the Kwakiutl; although starting school, quitting school and marriage are incidents which mark changes in role behavior. When a male reaches sixteen and is no longer required to attend school he generally drops out. Girls attend school beyond sixteen if facilities are open to them.

Adolescent girls, unless married, are accorded adult status at a later age than males. They usually live with a family, frequently but not always their parents, and their activities are closely watched since the role of adult woman revolves around the home and child rearing. If a girl is unmarried there are insufficient indicators of her adult status. Males, on the other hand, are mobile and independent at an earlier age and are in a position to act out adult roles independent of marriage ties, hence they are accorded adult status at an earlier age. According to one of our informants, girls are thought of as "ladies" after their first menstruation, but being a woman in this sense does not imply full status as an adult female. Gertie described to Evelyn her feelings about the first time she menstruated. She was at a residential school and said that one of the staff members there made the girls feel dirty and bad about it. Few girls know about menstruation before it happens, apparently, and mothers and daughters or unmarried peers do not talk about such subjects very often. Another of our informants said that women know very little about personal matters before they are married.

Free time and its management create minor problems for adolescents as well as for some young married people. Problems typically take the form of restlessness and occur most notably during the slack economic season, the period between clam digging and summer fishing. Teen-age girls agree that winter is the best time in the village because everyone is there and they have more to do. A portion of each day is unoccupied by household chores or other tasks, especially during the evening, but during the slack season the villagers also have quite a lot of free time during the day. This free time is filled in various ways. Women spend a large part of it within their homes often doing nothing more than listening to the radio and gazing out a window. Several teen-age girls frequently stroll around the paths of the village together. Young men occasionally do the same, but men and women do not mix publicly unless they are married or courting. During the 1962–1963 school year some of the adolescent girls who had dropped out of school visited my wife several evenings each week, strolled around, helped their parents and relatives with household chores and talked of and sometimes did visit relatives in other villages. In the spring these girls organized their own soccer team.

During our year at Gilford there were a number of unmarried males in their late teens and early twenties. These men fished as crew members on commercial seine boats in the summer; during the fall they were generally idle, strolling around the village, attending dances at the school and visiting the missionary to play checkers. In the winter they dug clams, drank, danced, and frequently spent their time "walking around." In the spring, however, they trained for soccer. Each soccer team is a recognized group with its own uniforms, name and equipment, and competition among teams is strong. The members of the Gilford team— the Breakers—often practice from one to two hours a day. Other teams come to Gilford on weekends for a practice game or the Breakers may go elsewhere. Kingcome and Gilford play in serious competition each year during the month of May at Kingcome. A second major soccer event is the May Sports competition in Alert Bay. The largest and most serious sports event of the year, however, is the Native Celebration or June Sports in Alert Bay. June Sports typically lasts three days and involves many activities such as a parade, special Indian programs, athletic events of which soccer is the highlight, and various contests. June Sports is important because, as we said earlier, it also marks the beginning of the new salmon fishing season. Other free time activities, except drinking, are of significantly less importance in terms of their impact on village life. Young men sometimes play cards in the evening if several interested people can be found, and many people take naps during the day.

The transition from adolescence to adulthood is often dramatized by marriage. Courtship is an important activity during adolescence. Unmarried couples stroll around the village after dark, pausing now and then in the shadows. Dances in the school furnish another occasion when men and women may be together, but little overt romantic behavior is manifested in such a public setting. Romances are often short lived, but when they become serious the individuals involved may begin sleeping together fairly regularly. As we noted above, however, a girl who sleeps with too many men soon acquires a bad reputation and she becomes the butt of a considerable amount of criticism and gossip. The teen-age daughters of Edna Moon, for example, were accused of leading Jennie Drake's daughter astray. Edna was disturbed and angry about the accusations. An elderly informant told me that at one time it was shameful for a girl not to be a virgin at the time of marriage. He confesses that he does not know what the dominant attitude is now.

Albert Philip, a nineteen-year-old youth, lived with a twenty-one-year-old woman, Darlene Moon, in Darlene's parents' home during part of the winter and spring of 1963. They later decided to get married and, as expressed to us in a letter from Gertie Philip, "[They are] I think getting married as Darlene says its Albert's baby she is carring. they are both scared to tell Albert's parents. yet [the parents] know already about it." Albert's father later wrote, "I have conceded to have him married, so we would have a chance to have both, with us to try to adjust them to a more stable way of living." After the wedding Gertie wrote, "the wedding really was nice. Albert and Darlene are living with [Albert's parents], I think they aren't sorry about Albert finely marring Darlene as I sort of talked them into consenting because Albert was just living with Darlene."

The attitude of acceptance toward common-law alliances is further illustrated by Fred Drake, a twenty-two-year-old man who began living with a girl, Ruby, who was separated from her husband. The couple lived with Ruby's parents. Fred became a marginal member of both the young men's group and the adult males'. After they had lived together for a year, one of Ruby's younger brothers commented, "They should get their own house. They're married now." And as their year of common-law alliance progressed, Fred was identified more and more with the adult married men.

5

Traditional Social Organization

DURING THE POTLATCH PERIOD from about 1849 until almost 1930 the Kwakiutl were, in principle, totally rank stratified: each tribe was ranked in relation to each other tribe; each major tribal subdivision, the numima, was ordered in relation to each other numima, and each individual within each numima was ranked in relation to every other individual.[1] In addition, persons in different numimas were ranked relative to each other. Within this idealized serial ordering, however, there was sometimes equivocation and uncertainty regarding the proper rank-placement of any given unit: a tribe, a numima or, particularly, an individual. This was most notably true of the correct ranking of different persons vis-à-vis each other in different numimas. There was nonetheless a strain toward this ideal rank-structure model.

Table 3 reveals something about the nature of these facts. The Kwakiutl proper, the *KwaigyuL*, were the highest ranking tribe among all the southern Kwakiutl tribes. The Mamalelekala were ranked second and the Four Tribes of Gilford—the Tsawatenok, Koeksotenok, Guauaenok and Hahuamis—were in positions seven through ten respectively. The Mamalelekala were comprised of five serially ordered numimas, and in the late nineteenth century each numima had from six to forty-two ranked, hereditary, positions signaled by a discrete name for each position. The men holding these names formed the "nobility" among the Mamalelekala. This ranking was done largely for potlatch purposes where no two people could have their names called simultaneously to receive gifts, or where no two persons could sit in the same rank ordered seat at a potlatch, feast, or winter ceremonial.

Not only were the Kwakiutl rank stratified, but they were also segregated into semi-equilibrated social strata. Whether these strata should be called classes

---

[1] Elsewhere (1967:27) I wrote that the correct term designating the tribal subdivisions of the Kwakiutl is numimot (*nEᵋmī'mot*). The term actually refers to the members of the tribal subdivision, not to the subdivision itself. The term numima (*nEᵋmī'ma*) correctly identifies the subdivisions, although in practice some Kwakiutl do not distinguish between these terms anymore.

189

TABLE 3.
PARTIAL RANK ORDER OF KWAKIUTL TRIBES, NUMIMAS AND HEREDITARY NAMES
(SOCIAL POSITIONS): 1895[a]

Partial Rank Ordering of Tribes	Ranked Numimas (Mamalelekala)	Partial Ordering of Ranked Names in Numimas
1. Kwakiutl (*KwaigyuL*)		
2. Mamalelekala	1. *Kuek*[u] (Eagle)	1. 2. Creating Trouble All Around . 4. The Great One Always Alone in World . 6.
	2. *TEmɫtEmɫEls* (Ground Shakers)	1. Four-Fathom Face . 5. From Whom Property Comes . 15. Whose Body Is All Wealth . 32.
	3. *WiwomasgEm* (The Noble Ones?)	1. To Whom People Paddle . 15. Whose Property Is Eaten in Feasts . 21.
	4. *ᵉWⱥlas* (The Great Ones)	1. . 4. Always Giving Potlatch . 7. From Whom Coppers Are Obtained . 42. Around Whom People Assemble

TABLE 3. (*continued*)

5. *Mämalelaqăm* (The Real Maleleqala)	1. Catching Salmon . . . 13. Always Giving Blankets Away While Walking . . . 30. Getting Too Great

3. Nimkish
.
.
.

7. Tsawatenok
8. Koeksotenok
9. Guauaenok
10. Hahuamis
.
.
.

ª After Boas 1897:339–340, 1996:39; Rohner 1967:73

or status groups is, in part, a matter of definition. For ease of presentation, how-ever, we prefer to call them classes.[2] The Kwakiutl use two terms to designate these social and ceremonial classes. The first is *naqsala*, "nobility," and the second is *xamala*, "commoner."[3] At one time the Kwakiutl also had slaves who were usually war captives from other tribes. Slaves contributed little to the traditional social system except to give prestige to their owners; we give them no further attention.

Rank and class were determined primarily by inheritance—the inheritance of socially validated names and "privileges" such as the right to sing certain songs, use certain carvings or designs, wear certain ceremonial masks and perform certain dances. Associated privileges included the right to sit at a particular place during a potlatch, to have one's name called at a certain point in a sequence, and to receive greater or lesser amounts of property dependent on one's overall position in the rank structure. Those who had no or few (or unimportant) of these attributes were the commoners and those who had many or important ones were the nobility. Both noblemen and to a lesser extent commoners were differentiated into fine gradations of rank. At a certain point the distinction between low ranking noble-men and high ranking commoners sometimes became blurred. Commoners, how-ever, were excluded from important participation in the winter ceremonial dance

[2] The Kwakiutl are neither rank nor class stratified today in any important manner. Most of the data presented here relate to the Gilford Island Kwakiutl and cognate Bands around the turn of the century.

[3] The term nobility is not a good gloss of the Kwakiutl term *naqsala*, but it has been fairly well standardized in the anthropological literature so we continue to use it. Perhaps a better translation would be aristocracy, upper class or simply, chiefly class.

societies. And as expressed to us by one of our informants, "You're *xamala* if you don't have anything behind you for the potlatch."

The Kwakiutl also recognized class distinctions in other ways, for example in their social and kinship terminology. Several years ago two noblemen argued over a log for firewood. One accused the other of acting just like a *xəxis*, that is, as a *xamala* or commoner. The term *xamala* means, literally, an orphan. Neither an orphan nor an illegitimate child could be a nobleman because neither had anyone from whom he could claim the requisite names and privileges. The term *xamala* itself was sometimes used as a term of abuse or derogation by the nobility. Kinship terminology supplies a further illustration. A nobleman's daughter, *qidiL*, was referred to differently from a commoner's daughter, *tsedak*; moreover, a noblewoman who married a nobleman was called *modziL*. Out of respect to her huband, however, a commoner woman was referred to as *modziL* if she married a nobleman. Members of the Kwakiutl nobility married most often among themselves, thus perpetuating many of the important names and privileges in the chiefly class. According to one of our informants, noblemen also interacted socially more often among themselves than with commoners. In fact as a child one of the highest ranking men in Fort Rupert is reported to have been allowed to play only with other high ranking children. His parents would not let him play with commoner children.

Kwakiutl social organization has changed radically in the last half century. Today there is no significant tendency to associate only with members of the same class. In fact the rank and class system has broken down. Older adults in the village remember the social stratum to which they traditionally belonged, but many of the younger do not know where they would be placed. Spontaneous remarks sometimes made by members of the community, however, suggest that past traditions are not totally ignored; for example, Flora Abel, her son Andy, and several others were drinking. Andy became abusive toward his mother and she ran out of the house into a second house where another party was in progress. She asked some of the men to help her, but they ignored her request. She cried at a table, repeating over and over, "He can't do that to me. I'm *naqsala*! He can't do that. . . ."

We do not know of any children at Gilford today who have validated privileges. This further attests to the major changes in the Kwakiutl social system over the past decades. Over 70 percent of the men in the twenty to thirty-nine age group do not have any validated privileges, whereas almost 90 percent of the men who are forty and over do. A comparable trend exists regarding validated names: only 35 percent of the men from twenty to thirty-nine remember having any, and they have only one each, whereas more than 90 percent of the men who are forty or older have from one to four names, or more.

As we said, rank was acquired largely through inheritance, either through the father or the mother. But it could also be acquired through adoption. For example, if a grandfather wanted to make sure that certain of his important rights and privileges remained in his numima, he could adopt one of his grandchildren and transmit the names and privileges to him in a potlatch, or if a family line was threatened with extinction a child could be adopted and bequeathed names and privileges. The Kwakiutl also had other means of acquiring rank or, obversely, of transmitting names and privileges. One of the most unusual of these was through fictitious marriages. Boas (1966:55) describes such a situation:

> Difficulties arise when no daughter is available through whose marriage a name may be transmitted to her offspring. It cannot be done directly through the marriage of a son. For instance, a certain chief had two wives and only one son. The son married two wives but had no issue. Then the chief "turned the left side of his son's body" into a woman and gave him the name belonging to the eldest daughter of his line. Soon another chief, who wished to get the names belonging to the father of the man whose one side had been turned into a woman, wooed her, and the whole marriage ceremony was performed. The young man stayed in his father's house, but when the time for the transfer of names occurred, the appropriate ceremony was performed just as though a real marriage had been performed. Sham marriages of this type are the device resorted to in such cases.
>
> If there is no son, the father may call his foot, or one side of his body his daughter. The marriage ceremony is performed as though these were the women married, and the names are transferred in the usual manner.

At a marriage potlatch the father-in-law gave names and other wealth to his son-in-law to hold in trust for the former's grandchildren. Sons-in-law, however, often used these names for their own purposes—such as acquiring a position in a second numima—before transmitting them to their children. Still another, but unusual, means of acquiring rank and privileges during part of the last century was by murdering the man whose possessions one wanted. The murderer then claimed the names and other prerogatives of the vanquished. The evidence for this method of obtaining rank is uncertain, however, except in the case of acquisition of ceremonial privileges, such as the right to certain songs and dances in the winter ceremonial complex.

As we have seen, most rights and privileges were ordered in a prestige hierarchy. The overall social stature of a person was dependent on the number and importance of the privileges he could legitimately claim and these rights functioned to mark one person off from another. The value of these prerogatives was defined by the frequency and extravagance of the potlatches at which they were used. The most eminent person within the numima—as defined by his rights and privileges—was the chief, and the highest ranking person in the leading numima was sometimes designated tribal chief, at least by Whites. There was little difference between the numima chief and the second ranking man, or between the second and third ranking men, but an enormous social distance separated the highest ranking person from a person with no or only unimportant prerogatives.

The anthropological literature is inconsistent in its description of chiefs. Sometimes the term designates the numima head—the ranking person in the numima power-prestige structure—and sometimes it refers to all members of the nobility. Unless otherwise noted, we use the term in the former sense. Ideally the numima chief was the oldest son in a line of oldest sons traced back to a real or mythical ancestor, but if the oldest child were a girl she would be considered the ranking person, following the rule of primogeniture. The Kwakiutl, however, preferred males in the ranking positions because women were excluded from hereditary office in some of the ceremonial societies, regardless of their rank. The woman who succeeded to the office of chieftainess was given a man's name and even though she became a man socially, she was expected to transmit the names and other prerogatives which qualified her for the position to her son when he was an adult. If the oldest son died without heirs of his own, his younger siblings ranked in order of their birth, or if the oldest brother was not considered to be competent his younger brother might be able to claim his name and position.

Younger children of a chief received fewer and less important privileges than the oldest child. They were, therefore, somewhat lower in rank. Nonetheless they commanded respect, in part because they were potential heirs of the eldest brother even though they did not usually claim any formal status themselves. Over the generations children of younger siblings often slipped in the overall rank structure because at each successive generation they had less symbolic wealth to distribute. From this point of view many commoners were simply less fortunate kinsmen of the nobility. The highest chief's younger brother was usually not chief of the second ranking numima. This position was inherited by the person who claimed descent by primogeniture from his predecessor—sometimes, as in the case of two related Koeksotenok numimas, the man who could most legitimately claim descent through the senior genealogical line back to the second brother of the mythological founder of the tribe. The same principle of primogeniture held true for all other titled, chiefly positions.

The political status of chief implies little more than preeminent social status. But even though chiefs had little coercive authority, their position as numima administrator was a responsible one. Chiefs, along with other important members of the numima who acted as advisors, were responsible for making decisions regarding the timing and utilization of numima fishing grounds, clover beds, berry fields and hunting territory; it was also their responsibility to insure that the correct rituals were performed before this property was exploited. In addition they were the trustees of numima ceremonial prerogatives such as songs, carvings, names and dances. And it was chiefs who had the major responsibility for giving potlatches.

The chief's power and prestige were not his to be enjoyed effortlessly. In fact his stature could fluctuate and it was dependent on the support of others. This support in turn was contingent on three factors: his potlatching record, his generosity, and the importance of his kin group (Barnett 1968:46ff). A chief inherited the right to his position, but he had to assume it publicly and he was expected to maintain if not improve the prestige of that position through lavish potlatching. His numimot—members of his numima—were concerned about his success because his public performances reflected on them; they had a personal interest as well as a substantial financial investment in him. Thus, a chief was dependent on others for at least part of his potlatch resources because, often, he could not personally marshal together the material wealth needed to put on a munificent potlatch. For the most part a chief's numimot willingly contributed, not because they had to but because they wanted to. Moreover, the men in his numima regularly contributed a portion of the fish, seals, or other animals they caught, and women gave tribute to his wife by relinquishing a portion of the berries and roots they collected.

High ranking Kwakiutl were involved in a complex debt and credit obligation system. Single or double woolen Hudson's Bay blankets, valued at fifty cents
and one dollar and fifty cents respectively, constituted the currency-standard among
the Kwakiutl. The value of other items was measured in terms of them. Interest
was charged on all but very short-term loans. After less than six months six
blankets had to be returned for every five borrowed; seven blankets had to be
repaid for every five borrowed at the end of six months. The Kwakiutl collected
100 percent interest on loans of one year or more; the debtor was obligated to
return ten blankets for every five that he borrowed (Boas 1966:78). Moreover,
a person who had poor credit might pawn his name for a year during which time
the name could not be used. The debtor paid back one hundred blankets for the
thirty he received for his name, over 300 percent interest. A man could, however,
receive a short-term loan without interest, depending on his credit rating and the
feelings of his creditor. Successful Kwakiutl were involved in borrowing as both
creditors and debtors. A prospective potlatcher, for example, called his own and
other groups together for a feast at which time he loaned blankets to selected,
responsible participants. To be chosen to receive such a loan meant the recipient
was respected by the donor and recipients were obligated to repay the debt with
interest when the host was ready to give his potlatch.

The system of debts and loans worked well because the Kwakiutl did not
acquire wealth for its own sake. To hoard was shameful, almost unthinkable.
Wealth was important only insofar as it could be publicly displayed and redis-
tributed in feasts and potlatches—thereby raising the esteem of the donor.

Generosity was the second source of a chief's power and prestige. As we
said earlier, a chief's numimot supported many of his activities, but he in turn
was generous to them. Whenever he called his numinot together to announce or
discuss some important issue he feasted them. He frequently did the same before
and after potlatches as well, and he fed his supporters when they completed some
valuable service for him. As Barnett (1968:49) writes, "a chief flourishes—gains
adherents at home and acquires esteem abroad—through his reputation for
liberality."

The third source of a chief's power lay in the strength and importance
of his kin group which included affinal kinsmen (relatives by marriage). The
preeminent social and kinship unit among the Kwakiutl was the numima, an
ambilineal corporate descent group, membership being acquired through either
or both parents and traced back ambilaterally through successive generations to
the mythical or real ancestor of the numima. Noblemen within a numima believed
they were descended from the same founding ancestor. According to one of our
older informants, however, a man could "ask a stranger to be his numimot, if he
wanted to." This normally involved the acquisition of a name and other privileges
belonging to the numima. A child was assigned to the highest ranking position
available to either of his parents. Generally if both parents were of the same overall
rank, the first child was assigned to the numima in which his father had his
highest rank, reflecting a preference for the patriline. Subsequent children were
given successively lesser positions depending on those available to their parents.

Numimas were corporate groups because each had a name, held rights over fishing locations and other sites of economic importance and maintained certain ceremonial privileges. The members of these groups shared a set of oral traditions regarding its place of origin and adventures of the numima ancestors which usually explained why the numimot had the right to claim specified privileges. In addition each numima shared a set of factual or quasi-factual tales of recently acquired privileges. And each numima claimed ownership of one or more multi-family dwellings in its winter village.

In an important sense the structure of numimas is best described not in terms of people but in terms of a series of ranked positions forming the nobility. According to Boas (1966:50) the thirteen Kwakiutl tribes in the Gilford region shared 658 "seats," "standing places," or ranked positions. The Indian population in British Columbia barely escaped being obliterated from the time of the first European contact until 1890; gradual population attrition continued until about 1929 when the Kwakiutl began to increase slowly in numbers. Whites brought with them measles, smallpox, tuberculosis, influenza and venereal diseases, thus accounting for this gross decimation. Codere (1950:50) estimates that only 637 of the 1597 people surviving in 1898 were sixteen years old or more—not enough to fill the 658 seats in the Kwakiutl social system. As a result men were able to claim more than one standing place within a numima, and they could have positions in more than one numima—even though they tended to maintain primary affiliation with one numima. This created the anomalous situation where a nobleman, as potlatch host in one numima, could call out in rank order the names of his guests in the second numima. In the process he would call one of his own names as a member of the second numima.

Each numima consisted of one or several extended family household groups living within its own localized section of the village. The Kwakiutl lived in massive, beamed, multi-family dwellings, usually lined side-by-side facing the water. The one remaining multi-family dwelling (called big-house or *gyux*) at Gilford is no longer employed as a residence but is now used as a place for Indian dancing and other community activities. It is 70 feet long, 45 feet wide and about 20 feet high. The shake roof is supported by massive, hand-hewn beams about 3 feet in diameter, and the entire roof section is supported by four finely carved posts about 3 feet across. The frame of a smaller big-house stands next to it. The vertical poles supporting the four beams are carved; the figures on two of them represent the mythological origin and later incidents in the history of the Koeksotenok.

Big-houses were inhabited by several related families, a man—the "house chief"—his wife and children along with his younger brothers, their wives and children; other kinsmen and visitors sometimes lived with them. Each nuclear family (a man, his wife and their children) had a fireplace of its own within the big-house and a central fireplace was usually placed in the middle of the earthen-floored building. The smoke dissipated through moveable planks in the roof. Each nuclear family had its own bedroom-cubicle appended along the wall on a platform circumscribing the interior of the house. A house could contain ten or more of these compartments, but more often it contained only four. The entire assemblage was removed to seat participants for feasts and potlatches.

Many numimas in different tribes were unrelated except by later inter-

Frame of a big-house

marriage. A few of them, however, as with two Koeksotenok numimas, counted the separate family lines descended from two mythological brothers as separate numimas. Boas (1966:43), for example, gives one abbreviated version of the tale connecting these numimas: "Head-Winter-Dancer [Tseikami] came from the sky as a thunderbird. His four sons settled in four villages. The youngest one, a warrior, stayed with his father. Two of the others became ancestors of two [numimas] of the [Koeksotenok] . . ." In other cases mythological brothers could be the progenitors of different tribes. The Hahuamis, the second tribe formally constituting the Gilford Island Band, and the Tsawatenok, one of the Four Tribes of Gilford, illustrate this point. This tale was given to me by an elderly Tsawatenok

Interior of the big-house

Kwakiutl sailing canoes (E.C. Curtis)

man; it clearly contains several recent Biblical intrusions such as a reference to God and to the time before there was light on earth.

> *Qawadeilakala* with his four children and his younger brother *Koleili* lived before there was light on the earth. They heard the voice of God who said that they were to go and find a place which they could claim as their own. The voice promised them the cloak of a wolf for ease of transportation [i.e., transformed them into wolves]. The two brothers and four children came first to Kingcome. The older brother claimed *lalaq*, a site up Kingcome River as his own. *Koleili* did not want to share the same site with his brother, so he moved on to look for his own place. He travelled to *lax·oh* "clear-water" and then to Wakeman River. He stayed there for three or four years and then he returned to the Kingcome River to meet his brother. *Koleili* asked *Qawadeilakala* what the sound of the bird was like that the latter heard at his location. *Qawadeilakala* said that it sounded like *dzawadasli* (?), so the younger brother said that from this time on *Qawadeilakala* would be known as *dzawadEeinox*[u] [Tsawatenok]. *Qawadeilakala* then asked *Koleili* what the sound of the bird was like that the latter heard in his valley, and *Koleili* answered *ha*[ε]*wala* so *Qawadeilakala* said that from this time on you will be known as [Hahuamis]. The two brothers then separated again, each to his respective location.
>
> Later the two brothers met again and each wanted to try out his magical powers on the other to see which was greater. They had a magic rock called *x·welk* which they threw back and forth to each other. The two brothers, who wore hemlock cloaks, stood at quite a distance from each other while they threw and caught the rock. The older brother missed it on the third throw, and it landed on the right hand side of the river at *x·wellek*, a little above *tsœtsala*. The mountain where the older brother missed the rock is now called *x·welLeix*. Because the older brother lost the game, he took one of his children and pulled him apart into many pieces and turned the pieces into feathers which became birds to fly all over the earth. The younger brother went back to Wakeman. *Qawadeilakala* returned to his place and then started moving down the river to the present Kingcome village site. When he arrived there he saw what looked like worms but were really oulachon fish. He saw

another man there who claimed to have come from the moon. The latter gave him instructions what to call the oulachons, *mənmənLilaga. Qawadeilakala* had a dog which caught and ate an oulachon. The dog died. The man from the moon told *Qawadeilakala* to fear not; "The fish will mean a great deal when the time comes. They will do a great wealth." And then the man from the moon left. *Qawadeilakala*, who still had his wolf powers, wondered if he were alone on the earth with his brother, so he howled like a wolf. After the third howl he heard an answer from *x•oyalas* [Hoyalas, extinct group at Quatsino] so he found that someone else was on earth besides himself and his brother. The Hoyalas howled too and *hausit*, a people• on the West Coast, answered him.

Numimas were not always stable. Dissatisfied nuclei of closely related kinsmen sometimes spalled off from larger numimas to form their own. Of course they had to publicly validate the new numima by giving a potlatch. On other occasions internal dissensions were generated when a chief failed in generosity, became overbearing or was faulted on other counts. Here too a numima could disintegrate into two or more numimas. Moreover, ambitious noblemen, secondary chiefs or house chiefs could create a disaffected faction and break away. These new numimas, however, remained within the larger structure of the tribe—although each maintained a large element of its sovereignty, conceding little economic or political autonomy to the tribe.

Originally numimas appear to have been independent village-communities which eventually congregated at a single village site along with other numimas to form a tribe. Tribal structure, then, represents little more than an aggregation of several numimas within a common winter village.[4] Tribes did, however, function as a collectivity for ceremonial purposes—feasts, potlatches and winter ceremonials —and they did act, on rare occasions, as units of defensive action against other tribes, especially non-Kwakiutl. The Bella Coola raid is one of the most famous illustrations of this in the history of the Kwakiutl.

Around the fall of 1857 a ranking Bella Coola (another Northwest Coast tribal group) man, his wife and probably several other families were at Bond Sound near Gilford, perhaps to catch herring but more probably to collect roots and to trade. Several Koeksotenok families were also at the site. One of the Koeksotenok women stole a very valuable hamatsa whistle belonging to the ranking Bella Coola couple, but no retaliation was taken then, even though the theft was a capital offense. The following autumn the Bella Coola attacked Gilford in revenge. Boas (1897:427) gives the following account of the raid:

[The Bella Coola] landed above the village . . . and hauled their canoes ashore. Late in the evening they sent spies out to examine the village. About midnight, when all the [Koeksotenok] were asleep, the [Bella Coola] launched their canoes and divided. One-half went to the east end of the village, and one-half to the west end. They stayed in their canoes not far from the beach until it was almost daylight. It was foggy. As soon as it grew daylight they landed and many men went to the rear of the houses. As soon as they were ready the most courageous warriors broke into the doors of the houses and speared men, women and children. Whoever tried to escape through the rear door was speared by the men stationed there. Others

---

[4] Tribes split up into constituent numimas during the summer and migrated to their fishing sites.

of the [Bella Coola] looked after the valuable property and put it into their canoes. Now the [Koeksotenok] were all killed. Only seven men and five women were left. Then the [Bella Coola] set fire to the houses. Their canoes were deeply loaded with men's heads. They went home. At that time people of different tribes had stayed at [Gilford]; [Mamalelekala, Tlauitsis, Nimkish, and Nakoaktok], all guests of the [Koeksotenok]. They were all slain by the [Bella Coola] and also some who belonged to the [KwaigyuL].''

(Brief archeological excavations that I undertook in the village suggest that the Bella Coola probably also dismembered the bodies of their victims.)

A few days later the Fort Rupert Kwakiutl (*KwaigyuL*) organized a retaliatory war party, including four Mamalelekala war canoes, six Nimkish, two Tlauitsis, and eight Tsawatenok. In addition the subtribes of the *KwaigyuL* contributed sixteen canoes. The war party sailed to Rivers Inlet and was becoming discouraged because they could not find the enemy. But on their way two forward scout canoes encountered a group of Heiltsuk (Bella Bella, another Northwest Coast tribal group) who told them that the Bella Coola had barricaded their houses. The Mamalelekala canoes had been behind the others and when they arrived one of the Mamalelekala men killed the steersman of the Bella Bella canoes. The Kwakiutl then attacked and killed all the Heiltsuk. The Bella Bella men had been chiefs and hamatsas, and they had their ceremonial red cedar bark and hamatsa whistles with them. It was from this encounter (murder) that the Kwakiutl acquired what became the most important of the winter ceremonial dance societies —the hamatsa society—which we describe later. The Kwakiutl canoes returned home, satisfied that they had accomplished a great deed.

The village at Gilford was abandoned for many years after the raid. Some of the surviving Koeksotenok moved to Kingcome with the Tsawatenok. Most survivors moved to Village Island with the Mamalelekala because a large number of Koeksotenok had already been living at Village before the raid and the marriage ties between the two tribes were strong.

Beyond defensive maneuvers and ceremonial functions, tribes had only minimal corporate reality. They were, however, bonded together by a common mythological tale of origin. The Koeksotenok, for example, shared the following tale of origin:

> The first Koeksotenok man came from a cedar tree. His name was *Hawilqwolas* "one who comes from the cedar." He changed his name later to *Tsᵉeiqami* (Tseikami), "Supreme" or "Head-Winter-Dancer."
>
> *Q'aniqilaqᵘ* "Transformer" arrived at Islet Point by canoe where Tseikami was residing. Tseikami's son, *Tisamgit*, invited Transformer for food. Transformer was going to roast his salmon, and saw that Tseikami's children were roasting the same kind of salmon, Sisiutl [double headed sea serpent]. He was amazed that they could catch and eat the drippings of the Sisiutl without harm.
>
> Transformer put Tseikami through many trials. He put a rock around Tseikami's neck and attempted to drown him. Tseikami went under and Transformer started to walk away, satisfied that Tseikami was dead. He reached a certain distance, and heard singing behind him. When he turned around he was amazed to see that Tseikami was alive and singing. Later Transformer put Tseikami in the fire and when there was nothing but ashes remaining he departed, satisfied that Tseikami was

dead. He reached the same distance as before and again heard singing. When he turned around he saw Tseikami was alive and singing. Transformer changed Tseikami into a Saw-bill duck, but the latter was able to turn back into human form. After many such trials Tseikami and Transformer became friends as equals because Transformer could not vanquish Tseikami.

After his trials with Transformer, Tseikami returned to Viner Sound with his daughters. *Qolus* "Thunderbird" was up on the mountain and, looking down, saw Tseikami's fair daughters. He liked their looks and descended from the mountain. After making his face human by removing the Thunderbird headpiece, he sang a song before Tseikami. He asked and received permission to marry one of Tseikami's daughters. *Qolus* removed his Thunderbird cloak and commanded it back to the mountain. He then became fully human. It is from the union of Thunderbird and one of Tseikami's daughters that the Koeksotenok descended.

The Kwakiutl recognized one social unit larger than the tribe—the confederacy. This was nothing more than a cluster of loosely knit, informally related neighboring tribes who interacted among themselves more often than with other tribes. The Four Tribes of Gilford constituted such a confederacy; they came to Gilford during the winter, each living in a special residential area within the village, and they tended to potlatch and intermarry among themselves. Confederacies today, however, have little meaning beyond the fact that members of the Four Tribes still tend to intermarry among themselves.

Other significant changes have also occurred in Kwakiutl social organization. The rank-class system has broken down and numimas are no longer important to the Kwakiutl. Concomitantly, descent is no longer traced ambilaterally; the Kwakiutl have adopted the Canadian-American bilateral system where a child is equally affiliated with the kinsmen of both parents. This shift in the descent system is related to changes in their kinship system. As revealed in Table 4, for example, the Kwakiutl traditionally referred to their sisters and all female cross- and parallel-cousins by the same term, *waqwa*. They referred to their brothers and all male cross- and parellel-cousins by the term *nimwiyut*.[5] This form of nomenclature is known as Hawaiian cousin terminology. Today, for the most part only the older Kwakiutl know or care about the traditional kinship system. The terms currently used are a rough approximation of those used by Canadians and Americans. Now members of the village often label other people as a cousin or as a distant cousin without being able to trace precise kin linkages in such a way as to demonstrate the relationship. Anyone who is in approximately the same generation as oneself and who is thought to be related in some way is designated as a cousin; anyone at approximately the parent generation who is considered to be a kinsman is called an aunt or uncle.

Kwakiutl social organization has undergone other notable transformations as well. Traditionally, after marriage the bride and groom moved to the groom's father's community (patrilocal village residence), and indeed, they usually lived in the father's big-house (patrilocal household residence) as part of an extended family. Technically the bride and groom could move to the village of either set of parents (ambilocal village residence), or, for that matter, they could settle

---

[5] A cross-cousin is either mother's brother's child or father's sister's child; a parallel-cousin is either mother's sister's child or father's brother's child.

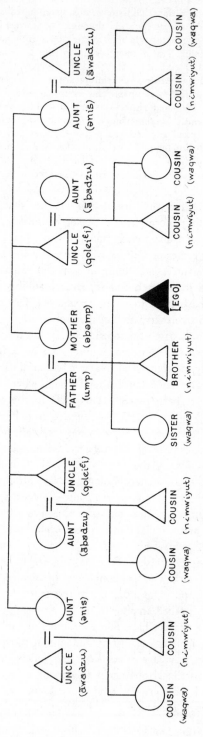

American-English and Kwakiutl Kinship Terminological Systems

in the groom's mother's village of birth. The decision was generally made on the basis of primary numima affiliation. That is, if a man had the right to claim a position in the numima of either his father or his mother, he and his bride typically moved to the community where he claimed the highest rank. If the bride outranked the groom, they could live with her parents; as the system worked, however, the Kwakiutl preferred to, and more often did live with the groom's parents. Today the Kwakiutl do not necessarily move to the village of either parent, and they prefer setting up their own independent household (neolocal village and household residence)—although in fact many of them do live with one or another set of parents for a least a brief time after marriage.

Even though the Kwakiutl had no obligatory marriage prescriptions, they tended to marry outside their own numima and often outside their own tribe in order to bring new and important names and privileges into one's own numima. Occasionally, however, a nobleman was encouraged to marry within his numima in order to perpetuate symbols of rank within his own line. He might, for example, marry his younger brother's daughter, or a half-brother could marry his half-sister if they had different mothers. Sexual relations between a man and his brother's wife were regarded as offensive, but through the custom of the levirate he could marry her if his brother died. It was considered bad form for the children of siblings (first cousins) to marry. Even today there is some feeling against this. Ernest Amber, for example, remarked to Roberta Drake, "Gee, I wish you weren't my first cousin. I could really go for you." Roberta was noticeably disturbed by the suggestion. Nevertheless, first cousin marriages do occur today.

The ideal marriage among the Kwakiutl was between a man and a woman of equal rank, especially if both were noblemen in the line of primogeniture in different numimas. Marriage among the nobility was arranged by the parents of a young couple; the boy and girl might never have seen each other before. Marriage arrangements were cloaked in the strictest secrecy—even excluding the young couple until the final details had been worked out—because rival families might try to break it up. Rivals could, for example, pay a young man to make love to the girl and persuade her not to marry her betrothed, or they could pay her to say that she had fallen in love with another man.

Boas (1966:53–55) summarizes the principal elements of traditional Kwakiutl marriage among the nobility.

Aside from this fiction [that a wife is obtained in war from a foreign tribe], marriage is conducted on the basis of the potlatch. Setting aside minor details, an agreement is first reached between the parents or, after their death, by those who assumed the parents' responsibility. The payment to be made to the girl's parents having been agreed upon, a binder is paid by the groom's representatives. When the number of blankets settled upon has been accumulated by loans from the groom's [numima], the bride price is delivered to the house of the bride's father. In addition to the stipulated price, blankets are paid to call the princess and to still others to "lift the princess from the floor of the house." Then the bride is handed over to her future husband's party and her father gives her husband blankets to represent her mat (*le'we*$^\epsilon$), food, and household goods, such as boxes, baskets, dishes, and spoons needed by the young couple. The value of these is often almost, if not quite, equal to the price paid. In some cases, the bride's father gives at the same time a copper (*sayabalaᵉyo*), names and privileges to his son-in-law, but ordinarily this payment is deferred until a later time, generally after the birth of a child, when "the repayment of the marriage debt" takes place. This does not consist of blankets, but of "bad things, trifles," which include food, household goods of all kinds and particularly a copper, names and privileges which are handed over in the "privilege box." The value of the goods paid at this time is far in excess of what the bride's father has received. It is important to note that the only payment in the recognized standards of value is made by the groom. All the return payments are in objects.

The fiction that the marriage is one between two tribes or villages is maintained throughout. The groom's party is said to arrive by canoe, and when repaying the marriage debt, the father-in-law is supposed to arrive on a catamaran—two canoes tied together and covered with a platform of planks. The mast of the catamaran is the copper (*Lak·Eᵉye*) given to the son-in-law.

After the repayment of the marriage debt, the obligations of the contracting parties have been fulfilled, and the marriage is ended. If the young wife continues to stay with her husband, she stays "for nothing," which is not dignified. A new contract has to be made in the same way as the first one, but the payments are generally much less. The whole matter seems to be a little more of a formality, although proud and rich people may make the same extravagant payments as they did in the first marriage. In the records of marriages in which many children are born, there are no references to this attitude, although the principle of the end of the marriage after the repayment of the marriage debt is clearly in the minds of the Indians. The repayment of the marriage debt may be delayed for several years and the children born during this period receive names and privileges from their maternal grandfather. Undue delay of the repayment of the marriage debt is liable to cause trouble. When a certain man seemed to evade this duty, his son-in-law had an image representing his wife carved. At a feast to which he had invited the people, he put a stone around the neck of the image and sank it in the sea. Thus he blemished the rank of his father-in-law.

Often, after the annulment of a marriage through repayment of the marriage debt, the woman is married to another man. After four marriages, her high rank is established, and it seems to be assumed that after this she should stay with her last husband.

The advance in social rank arising from the potlatch features of the marriage often overshadows entirely the primary object of a marriage, namely, the establishment of a family. Instead of this, the transfer of names and privileges becomes the primary consideration, and fictitious marriages are performed, the sole object of which is the transfer of names, privileges and property previously described.

The marriage system described by Boas no longer exists in its traditional form. The last arranged marriage at Gilford was in the 1940s; no one in the village today between twenty-one and thirty-five had his marriage arranged but more than 60 percent of those who are thirty-six or older, excluding common-law alliances, did have. Several villagers in recent years have rebelled at the attempt of their parents to arrange their marriage. Benjamin Otter, for example, recounted his behavior in 1945 when he discovered that his father was trying to make such an arrangement with the family of a girl whom he did not know. Benny ran away from his home at Turnour and started working in a logging camp. His father attempted to stop him by pulling back on the stern rope of the gill-netter as Benny left the float. But when he saw that he could not do it, his father shouted to Benny, "Don't come back, you dog!" (Calling a man a dog in Kwakwala

A chief's daughter with her abalone ear pendant and incised silver bracelets—both symbols of wealth (E. C. Curtis)

Chief holding speaker's staff and ceremonial rattle (E. C. Curtis)

is one of the worst invectives in the language.) A few days later Benny's brother-in-law, a chief from a neighboring tribe, came to the camp where Benny was working and told him that he should go to Gilford on Saturday, but he would not tell him why. Later that week Benny returned to Turnour Island to pick up some things he had forgotten. He had another argument with his father and returned to the camp. Again, Benny was told to go to Gilford. This time, on Friday, he complied. That evening his father instructed him to have dinner with a certain family, along with some other guests. Agnes Abel was cooking, but neither Agnes nor Benny knew they were betrothed and were to be married the following day. Only Benny's father, his mother having died at childbirth, and Agnes' parents knew of the arrangements. That night Benny conceded to get married as his father wished. But he did not discover that Agnes was to be his bride until the following day.

Church weddings and civil ceremonies in the Indian Agent's office are now the most popular form of marriage, although unformalized common-law unions are also frequent. Even those people at Gilford whose marriages were arranged and who went through the traditional Indian ceremonies—"Indian marriages," as some Kwakiutl call them—later had their union formalized by either a church or Agency wedding. Benny and Agnes, for example, were later married by the Agency Superintendent. The transition from Indian to White marriage ceremonies was not abrupt. At first, of course, the Kwakiutl followed their own customs. Later the Indian ceremony was followed by some form of White man's service. Now, however, the sequence is reversed. Indians are first legally married according to Canadian law and then they may have a potlatch.

A wedding took place at Kingcome during our year of fieldwork. The bride and groom were first married by an Anglican minister. Following this service the newlyweds, their families and guests went to the community hall for the wedding reception which was actually a modified potlatch. In order to facilitate the bookkeeping of the 200 visitors, Kingcome residents were directed to the right side of the hall, visitors to the left. The chief whose funeral service was described in Chapter 3 spoke in Kwakwala giving the history and rank of both the bride's and the groom's family. As part of the marriage debt, the groom's father gave a wallet of money to the bride's father which was to be distributed at another potlatch the following day. Following this, the chief spoke at length, giving marital advice to both the bride and groom. Then another ranking kinsman of the groom spoke about the history of both families. He too gave advice to the newlyweds and thanked the guests for coming. Few people appeared to listen to these speeches; children ran around and adults talked among themselves.

Several Tsawatenok danced in button blankets while the speakers beat rhythm on the floor with lengths of wood. Following this a Tsawatenok woman gave advice to the bride and groom. Immediately afterward a small group of people began assembling gifts to be distributed among the guests, and shortly thereafter food was prepared. Thirty cakes were lined side-by-side on a table along with a one-hundred-pound wedding fruitcake. The newlyweds sat quietly behind the table with some friends and relatives. One of the officials passed out paper cups for drinks and others distributed sandwiches. Kinsmen of the newlyweds reportedly bought 100 loaves of bread to make the three or more sandwiches each person received. Three or more apples and oranges were passed around next to each person. By the end of the evening Jeffrey Hardy had a pasteboard box full of cake, sandwiches, apples and oranges. Most guests, however, put their food in the paper bags that were circulated for this purpose.

After the food had been distributed several women passed out crocheted doilies made by the bride's family. All women present received waterproof nylon scarves. Immediately following the distribution of gifts the first speaker—the ranking Tsawatenok chief—spoke about the exchange of a copper between the two families. By 10:15 P.M. guests began to leave and an Indian dance band was set up. Children were taken home and the adults danced and celebrated until 3:00 A.M.

The following afternoon the potlatch was continued by another family as a part of the commemorative ceremony for someone who had died. Villagers, especially women, danced in their button blankets to the rhythm provided by four men sitting at the far end of the building behind a four-foot plank. The ranking chief in yesterday's ceremony gave a brief oration in potlatch-Kwakwala and then, on two separate occasions, relatives of the deceased distributed towels and pillow cases to the approximately one hundred fifty assembled people. Later the same chief called the names of men to receive money in rank order according to their potlatch position, and he publicly announced the amount each was to receive from the wallet in yesterday's wedding ceremony. The wallet contained approximately $350. Representatives of the Mamalelekala received first; Gilford received second and the Nimkish of Alert Bay received third. Some of the men were given $10, and at least one was given $20. Others were given $2 in addition to, in some cases, a handmade quilt. After the money had been distributed the chief of the Village Island Band gave a lengthy speech thanking the host and acclaiming his background and generosity.

Contemporary spouse choices tend to come from within the village at Gilford (village endogamy), and also from within the Band, but numima and tribal affiliation of one's spouse is now essentially irrelevant to mate selection. As we observed earlier, however, most spouses are still drawn from among the Four Tribes, reflecting the continued close contact among, especially, the Tsawatenok, Koeksotenok and Hahuamis. Two wives at Gilford came from Bands other than those represented by the Four Tribes. Consequently they have no preestablished social or kinship ties within the village, and as a result, they tend to be peripheral to the major social relations there. Alien people intermittently express a desire to leave the village, and shortly after our period of research, both of these wives and their families moved away.

The Potlatch

In Chapter 2 we described the potlatch as a public display and distribution of property in the context of one individual or group claiming certain hereditary rights or privileges vis-à-vis another group. While this statement suggests the general nature of the potlatch, the actual mechanics of the potlatch are more complicated than that description intimates. Potlatches may be described from an alternative point of view as a congregation of people who are invited to publicly witness and later validate a host's claims to or transmission of hereditary privileges, and to receive in return, each according to his rank, differential amounts of wealth.

Potlatches were given at critical life events: birth, adoption, puberty, marriage, death. They were given as penalties for "breaches of ceremonial taboo such as laughing, stumbling or coughing at winter dances" (Barnett 1968:36). Face-saving potlatches were closely related to penalty potlatches. They were, in Barnett's (1968:36) words, "prompted by some accident or misfortune to one's self or a member of the family. The capsizing of a canoe, a bodily injury and the birth of a deformed child" were all appropriate occasions for a face-saving potlatch. A third category of potlatch was the competitive, rivalry or vengeance potlach. These were extravagant, ostentatious contests with property, each claimant trying to give away or destroy more property than his rival and thus establishing his right to a contested privilege or position.

An essential feature of all types of potlatches was its public nature. The host, with the support of his family, numima or tribe, invited other families, numimas or tribes to act as formal witnesses to his claims.[6] The potlatcher traced

---

[6] Usually a family invited a family; a numima invited a numima, or a tribe invited a tribe. The host group did not receive gifts at a potlatch.

his line of descent and his right to the claim. No name, dance, song or other privilege could be used without having it publicly acknowledged and legitimated by the attendants of a potlatch. Since only people of substantial wealth could afford to potlatch lavishly or often, rank and wealth were but counterparts of each other—one implied the other. Under no circumstances did a host invite his guests as witnesses to an announcement or a claim without feasting them or distributing some form of property. In general the more grandiose the display of wealth, the higher was the prestige of the donor. Boas (1966:51), in fact, took the position that the principal motivation of Kwakiutl behavior was the desire to acquire prestige and respect. From the guests' point of view, a potlatch was a festive occasion, a time for entertainment and feasting.

As we observed above, potlatch guests received different amounts of property according to their rank. The same serial ordering held true at feasts where guests were called to be seated at special places of honor. Drucker and Heizer (1967:45–46) describe what they call the invariable distribution-sequence at potlatches.

> Gifts were given first to the chiefs of the highest ranked guest tribe, beginning with the first chief of the highest ranked numima of that tribe, then proceeding in order with the other chiefs of his numima. The second chief in rank of this tribe, that is, the first chief of the second ranking numima, was the next to receive his gift, and his numima brother chiefs were given gifts in sequence, before beginning with the third ranking chief and his numima, and so on through all the numima of the tribe. Then the highest ranking chief of the second tribe in precedence was given his gift (following the lowest ranked position in the first tribe), and the same order was followed, numima by numima, before beginning with the third tribe.[7]

Drucker and Heizer (1967:46–47) continue to describe quite a different principle of ordering at feasts.

> In a seal feast given to the Kwagyuł confederacy, for example, the first chief of the kwagyuł (gwetᵉla) was served a seal breast. Then the first chief of the kwᵉxa, the second tribe in rank, was served a seal breast, and a like portion was served to the first chief in rank of the walas kwagyuł. (The extinct q'omkutis were supposed to have preceded the walas kwagyuł.) Next, the second ranking chief of each tribe, in the same tribal sequence, was served a seal flipper, the third ranking chiefs, likewise in sequence, were each served a similar portion, followed by the fourth chiefs in rank. The remainder of the seals were distributed generally to the lower ranking chiefs. If the main dish of the feast consisted of some other food, the chiefs were called forth to be seated at the named decorated feast dishes in the same sequential order. If the guests were of a single tribe, as, for example, the nimqic or the mamalele-qala, the first chiefs of the numima were served in order, then the second chiefs, following the numima sequence, and so on. The same sequence was followed on certain other occasions, such as that of speech-making at the sale of a copper. Logically this feast sequence seems to conform better [to] the Southern Kwakiutl concept of relative rank in the expanded guest group than does the potlatch gift order.

---

[7] Not all Northwest Coast scholars agree with their description of serial giving at potlatches. Some would argue that gift giving conforms more with Drucker and Heizer's description of the ordering principle at feasts given in the following paragraph.

As suggested in the preceding passage, guests not only received in rank order, but there were marked inequalities in what they received. High ranking chiefs received more valuable property at a potlatch than lesser ranking men, thus providing each participant with a comparative standard against which he could measure himself vis-à-vis other recipients. The value and quantity of gifts distributed at a potlatch reflected not on the guests but on the donor. It reflected his wealth, rank, generosity, and the esteem in which he held himself. It also reflected, over time, the power and prestige that he would be able to maintain over other high status men. In addition, each man tried to return as much or, preferably, more than he received on a prior occasion.

Potlatch materials included a wide range of goods, including Hudson's Bay blankets, money, canoes, coppers, flour, kettles, dishes, sewing machines, tables and, in former times, slaves. A ranking Nimkish chief gave an extravagant potlatch at Village Island in 1921. The following excerpt tabulates the range and quantity of goods that were distributed.

The second day a xwe'xwe dance with shells was given to me by the chief of Cape Mudge. I gave him a gas boat and $50 cash. Altogether that was worth $500. I paid him back double. He also gave some names. The same day I gave Hudson's Bay blankets. I started giving out the property. First the canoes. Two pool tables were given to two chiefs. It hurt them. They said it was the same as breaking a copper. The pool tables were worth $350 apiece. Then bracelets, gas lights, violins, guitars were given to the more important people. Then 24 canoes, some of them big ones, and four gas boats.

I gave a whole pile to my own people. Return for favours. Dresses to the women, bracelets and shawls. Sweaters and shirts to the young people. To all those who had helped. Boats brought the stuff over from Alert Bay to Village Island by night. (This was to evade the Agent [because potlatching was illegal at the time].) This included 300 oak trunks, the pool tables and the sewing machines.

Then I gave button blankets, shawls and common blankets. There were 400 of the real old Hudson's Bay blankets. I gave these away with the xwe'xwe dances. I also gave lots of small change with the Hudson's Bay blankets. I threw it away for the kids to get. There were also basins, maybe a thousand of them, glasses, washtubs, teapots and cups given to the women in the order of their positions.

The third day I don't remember what happened.

The fourth day I gave furniture: boxes, trunks, sewing machines, gramophones, bedsteads and bureaus.

The fifth day I gave away cash.

The sixth day I gave away about 1000 sacks of flour worth $3 a sack. I also gave sugar.

Everyone admits that was the biggest yet. I am proud to say our people (Nimpkish) are ahead, although we are the third [in the Kwakiutl rank structure], Kwag·ut, Mamalelqala, Nəmgəs [Nimkish]. So I am a big man in those days. Nothing now. In the old days this was my weapon and I could call down anyone. All the chiefs say now in a gathering, "You cannot expect that we can ever get up to you. You are a great mountain." (Codere 1961:470–71)

Coppers were among the most prominent and important of treasure items at traditional potlatches, especially in the transfer of privileges at the time of marriage. Coppers are large pieces of beaten sheet copper cut into the form of a shield with a T-shaped ridge running down the middle of the bottom half.

They were painted with black lead, and a design was incised through the paint. Coppers were associated with wealth and have been loosely compared with thousand dollar bills in Canadian-American currency. Each copper had a name, and its potlatch history determined its value. For one copper which was named, "All other coppers are ashamed to look at it" 7500 blankets were paid. Another copper called, "Making the house empty of wealth" was worth 5000 blankets; and, "Steel-head salmon, i.e., it glides out of one's hand like a salmon" was purchased for 6000 blankets. Each copper was valued at the cost required to buy it, and it increased in worth at each transaction.

Potlatches were associated with every important change in social status—birth, marriage, death, among others—and they were the medium through which one's status could be changed. The acquisition of a new name in a potlatch, for example, signalled a change in status. Newborn infants were given a name, often the name of the place where they were born. A naming ceremony for low ranking people was modest, but it was often of substantial magnitude for ranking members of the tribe. The infant was given a second name at ten months. According to Barnett (1968:28), in recent times kerchiefs were distributed to men and children who witnessed this bestowal. The child received a "young man's name" a short time after his ten-month name. Only young men received the kerchiefs this time. When he was about sixteen or seventeen the youth received still another name in a "paint-giving-away name" ceremony. Only unmarried men participated and each received a shirt. Finally, blankets were distributed when the young man

Chief holding copper, "takes every-thing out of the house." The copper was valued at five thousand blankets (E. C. Curtis)

assumed adult status. Only men who themselves had gone through the ceremony and assumed a "spread-out name" could participate. It was at this point that a man began to acquire important potlatch names and privileges from his father.

We have already noted that death inaugurated an important series of potlatches. These occurred not just at the time of death, but could be given intermittently over several years in commemoration of the deceased. Such a potlatch was given at Turnour Island in March of our year in the area. Approximately 400 people from Gilford, New Van, Village and Alert Bay congregated at Turnour to attend the potlatch given by Brian Seaweed of Turnour Island and William King of Alert Bay. Brian gave the ceremony for his mother who died a year earlier; William gave his part because his son and daughter-in-law had come back together again. Kingcome villagers were not invited to this potlatch because William intended to go there and continue the potlatch later.

Fifty people from Gilford arrived shortly before noon, in time for dinner. The meal was served in a recently built, modern styled community hall. It consisted of beef stew, bread, butter, coffee and tea. After dinner the tables were folded up against the wall to make room for the performances which began at 3:10 P.M. when Gilbert Johnny of Fort Rupert took the speaker's staff. All the speeches that day were made in formal or potlatch Kwakwala. Gilbert thanked the people for coming and he told why the potlatch was being given. Chief Cesaer Walas of Turnour introduced the next event: men singing and drumming, and women wearing button blankets in mourning for the deceased. After a brief delay four songs were played, one with the women dancing.

Someone gave Brian Seaweed a small copper "to wipe away the tears." Brian received the copper and "mourned." A chief from Fort Rupert took the copper from Brian and gave a speech. The copper was then passed to a woman who spoke and handed it to Chief Walas. Brian's sons appeared from behind the screen at the far end of the building and stood by Cesaer while the latter spoke. After his talk Cesaer disappeared behind the screen. A man from Blunden Harbor spoke about the history of the copper which had once belonged to Brian's great-grandfather. The story associated with the copper dealt with its being used for bathing people and curing their injuries. While the man from Blunden talked, another man brought out a covered box which was also to help remove sorrow. The box was ceremoniously taken away by one of the Seaweeds: he approached the box, reached out his hands to receive it and then withdrew them. He turned in a circle a couple of times and then repeated his reaching gesture. This sequence was repeated three times before he took the box, walked around the false fire in the middle of the room and exited through a door.

Chief Walas spoke again with the speaker's staff in his hand. He said the old ways such as songs, dances and potlatches must continue. "We must hang on to the old ways."

Brian Seaweed and Cesaer Walas went on stage where Cesaer applied eagle down to the heads of the nine men on the stage behind the long "drum" and the one bass drummer. Cesaer passed out red bands to be worn on the heads of all special men at that end of the hall, including a White couple from Seattle who are professionally interested in Kwakiutl dances and who had been especially invited to perform at the potlatch. Brian gave head bands to selected individuals sitting on the main floor. Then Brian, one of his sons, Cesaer and two other men danced. They passed completely through the hall, out the door by the wood stove and shortly reappeared without Brian's son. The drums on stage beat time to their dance.

At 4:30 P.M. sandwiches and coffee were passed out to everyone present and the potlatch was adjourned until 6:00 P.M. The first performance after supper was the Raven dance. Brian's son came around the fire in hamatsa dress which consisted of red cedar bark rings crossing his shoulders and a red head band around his forehead. Cesaer spoke briefly. Since this was only a practice session for the main events of the evening, the audience had dwindled to about twenty-five.

The potlatch reconvened at 7:00 P.M. with nearly 200 people in the hall. Holding the speaker's staff, Chief Walas in hamatsa attire spoke behind a microphone which had just been set up. The chiefs of the attending tribes beat the rhythm. Cesaer called out names, and Brian distributed money to the chiefs on the platform. The White man also received money as a special guest and performer. About ten minutes later Brian distributed packages of Players cigarettes to the same people to whom he had given money. Whistles were blown off in a distance, and by 7:20 all the seats were taken; children were sitting on the floor. There was a continual undertone of conversation throughout the rest of the evening.

At 7:30 a hamatsa initiate danced around the fire and then exited. A man from Kingcome emerged wearing a button blanket. He danced with Brian and others. Several women in the audience stood beside their seats swaying their bodies to the rhythm. The Raven appeared next, danced briefly and a second Raven appeared. They danced, one at each side of the fire. In certain poses (for example,

An episode in the Turnour Island potlatch

A village man dancing in his thunderbird mask (Courtesy of National Defense, Canada)

when kneeling) one called to the other and the second answered, both vocally and with a clapping of the beak of the mask. Each Raven had a second person watching and following him around the hall. The dance itself involved a continuous fast rhythm and a constant change of head and body movement. Their feet followed the rhythm but their hands and head did not perform the same

Hamatsa (Cannibal dancers) inside the big-house at Gilford (Courtesy of National Defense, Canada)

movements. The hamatsa initiate reappeared and was immediately taken away by two men. Brian Seaweed began shaking his rattle and a hamatsa whistle sounded in the back room. Brian sang his own accompaniment. Then various people gave speeches and some women danced.

After a pause the Mountain Goat Hunter dance was performed. The Mountain Goat Hunter is supposed to capture the goat with a snare. He went off stage, returned and exited again. Cesaer Walas spoke and then Jeffrey Hardy from Gilford danced his hamatsa dance. His dance roused everyone in the room off their seats and as Jeffrey exited everyone shouted "whooo." The audience is asked to rise and be seated twice during his dance. Gilbert Johnny spoke. A man and a nine-year-old boy danced a hamatsa dance followed by the entrance of a Raven. The nine-year-old boy and the two men reappeared; the boy followed one of the men around the room, danced and copied his movements.

There was a brief intermission while apples were passed to the audience. The drums began again and six children ranging in age from two to six came out, some wearing button blankets, some wearing towels as blankets and some in plain clothes. A group of women in button blankets appeared, exited and reappeared. A man stood and mimicked the women, causing a great deal of laughter. An old man was called from the audience. He asked the audience for a knife. One person said he had one, but the old man ignored it and danced to me, speaking in Kwakwala and gesticulating toward me. I did not know how to respond because I did not know what he wanted. The crowd roared with laughter and after a few moments he went away. I asked my neighbor what it was that the old man wanted. He explained that the man had wanted a knife to cut the women open in order to see what was inside of them.

Cesaer explained in Kwakwala that the next dance was to be performed by the White couple who had been especially invited to dance the hamatsa. He then broke into English for the first time in the evening and said that "for you people who speak English the next dance is a surprise." After the couple danced there was a general round of applause for their performance.

After a pause the Ermine dance followed; Cesaer spoke again; then the Ermine mask reappeared, this time on a woman. At 9:30 Brian appeared wearing the same Ermine cape and mask and danced. Cesaer Walas took the cape and mask from Brian and performed. A man appeared in a blanket and performed a parody of the Ermine dancers. This finished Turnour Island's part of the potlatch.

Fort Rupert dancers performed next. There were many repetitions of the same dance—especially the hamatsa—by the same and different people. The men on the platform continued singing and beating rhythm. There were three hundred people in the hall. Those in the back of the room milled around restlessly and the crowd began to disperse. The children became very restless, wrestling among themselves, throwing things and making noise. At 10:20 P.M. three women did the Moon dance, two in masks and one without. Finally at 10:55 P.M. Cesaer Walas said that the midnight snack would be served. Mugs were distributed to the men, cups and saucers to the women and glasses to the children. Sandwiches, deviled ham on commercial white bread, were passed around. Sheet cake was passed out twice, cupcakes once and coffee twice. Cesaer announced that the cups, mugs and glasses were to be kept as part of the potlatch. Sixty gallons of oulachon grease were arranged on the floor for distribution. Each gallon jug of grease was valued at $5.00. Pieces of fabric, hand towels, dish towels, crochet doilies and anti-macassars, "shiny paper" pillows, commercial pillows, several stacks of dishes, plastic pails and dishpans were also distributed. A Sisiutl (the fabled double-headed sea serpent) with a raven carving was given to one of the men in the rhythm section on the platform. Apples were distributed among the children. Most gifts were distributed to women. Evelyn and I received a glass fruit bowl, a frosted white cereal bowl, two crochet doilies, fresh fruit, a mug, and cup and saucer. The grease was given to special male guests. Money was given only to men. I received $1.00; many men received anywhere from $1.00 to $7.00.

According to later reports Brian Seaweed gave $400 away in cash plus an unknown quantity of goods. William King gave away $300 and continued the potlatch at Kingcome with another $100. It was also reported that someone from Fort Rupert distributed $400 in cash and about $300 in goods.

Traditionally, all ceremonial occasions were marked by exacting standards of etiquette and proper behavior. Impropriety, whether accidental or intentional, required an immediate response. Such breaches of correct behavior as a mistake in ceremonial procedure, public quarreling or an accident witnessed by others, brought on a sense of shame and indignity. Payment was not always lavish but, as the Kwakiutl say, the offender must "cover (or wipe off) the shame" and re-establish his self esteem. Very often blankets were torn into strips and each witness was given a piece.

The Kwakiutl responded in a comparable way to insults. Occasionally pot-latchers deliberately insulted a guest by calling his name out of order, by spilling oulachon oil on him at a feast, by throwing him his gift or by presenting him with an inappropriate portion of food. The offended guest retaliated immediately. He distributed property or very frequently he destroyed it as he made a negative reference to the potlatcher. Violence, however, is reported to have sometimes erupted. On some occasions the offending host chose not to recognize the face-saving efforts of his guest. This often precipitated a rivalry potlatch between the two men. Usually, however, mistakes were unintentional. Even though the Kwakiutl relied heavily on "potlatch secretaries"—men who knew the correct rank placement of each participant and who maintained a record of the property distribution—errors were made. A host or his speaker would unintentionally call out of order the name of a guest, or misseat a guest or serve him incorrectly. If the host did not catch his error right away, the offended guest restored his own pride by giving the host a reprimand gift. The host was embarrassed by his carelessness and made a restitution in double the amount of the reprimand gift.

Rivalries developed when two men competed for the same name, song or other privilege. Each contestant tried to demonstrate his right to the claim by reciting his closer genealogical connection with it and, of fundamental importance, by outdoing his rival in the amount of property that he could distribute. When one of the competitors reached the point where he had no more property to give away he had to admit defeat. It is in the context of rivalry potlatches where the Kwakiutl reached their greatest destruction of wealth. One competitor would "break" his copper, that is cut off a piece, thereby destroying its value, and give the piece to his rival. The rival then had to bring out a copper of at least equal value and break it, perhaps giving both pieces back to his opponent. The greatest merit came to the man who threw his whole copper into the sea, "drowning it." Such ostentatious destruction of property showed a man's utter contempt for property—the implication being that the small amount he destroyed was of little concern to him. Canoes, house planks, blankets and, at one time, slaves could be destroyed. On other occasions oulachon oil could be poured onto the fire until the flames scorched the roof planks and the clothing of the rival who was forced to sit impassively or admit that his competitor had wealth enough to make him uncomfortable.

The witnesses to these dramas acted as the judges. Ultimately it was they who decided who the victor was. One man of high power and prestige could sway public opinion by recognizing the claim of one contestant over the other at a subsequent potlatch. Indeed this fact points out one of the basic principles of Kwakiutl potlatching: a successful potlatch in itself could not legitimize a man's claim. Rather, it was the behavior of other hosts who recognized his claim at later potlatches that validated his claim. The individual who demonstrated the strongest hereditary right to the claim, however, was usually the winner of the contest.

Drucker and Heizer (1967:104–106) give an excellent illustration of competition between two ranking Kwakiutl.

Ed's [Whonnuck] mother's father . . . was the direct descendant of the original Kwagyul eagle, since one of his forebears was the man responsible for the shooting of the kwexa [eagle] speaker in the kotink$^{\underline{w}}$ episode.[8] Ed's grandfather had only one heir, the daughter (Ed's mother); and according to the informant Whonnuck, his grandfather made it understood in his later years that he intended that she should inherit his eagle name and place, although he did not formally present her as his heir in a potlatch. He gave various names and other privileges to Ed's father in repaying the bride price, including some of the ceremonial privileges from his Awikeno grandmother, but the eagle place he did not transfer. When he died his daughter gave a mortuary potlatch at which she announced that she was the heir of her father's eagle place and took the name of doqwa'is. For a time she was not active in the place. Her intent was to give a major potlatch to place her son (the informant) in it.

Her father had a kinsman among his paternal relatives who was a "younger brother," who through other relationships had inherited a minor or low ranking place, although still reckoned as a chief's place, in the tribal potlatch order. This individual was actually the closest surviving male relative of the deceased eagle doqwa'is. He therefore gave a potlatch to the kwagyuł, the kw$^{\varepsilon}$xa, the nimqic, and the mamaleleqala in which he announced that he and only he was the proper heir to the late doqwa'is, his "elder brother." Henceforth, he said, he would respond when the honorific name "doqwa'is" was called in the potlatches to the chiefs of the kwagyuł tribes and would gratefully accept the gifts given to him in his proper position as second in rank of the Kwagyuł eagles.

---

[8] Traditionally the Kwakiutl recognized one rank higher than a chief. Men occupying this position were known as Eagles, and they had the privilege of receiving before chiefs at potlatches. It was for this Eagle position that Ed Whonnuck's mother and his grandfather's "younger brother" were competing.

Now this was a rivalry potlatch, in the sense that the giver was announcing a claim to rights that he knew perfectly well were contentious. In realistic terms, the "uncle's" legal rights were weakened somewhat at Kwakiutl law because he was not a real "younger brother" of the dead eagle but only a terminological one. Thus his rights as an heir were inferior to those of a direct descendant. His hole card was the generally recognized fact that, as Mr. Nowell put it, "the chiefs did not like to have women [take important roles] in the potlatch." He had given various potlatches in his lower ranking place, demonstrating his solvency and his knowledge of the duties of a chief. He therefore hoped the chiefs would decide the matter in his favor.

Ed's mother, however, had been well indoctrinated in the customs of the potlatch. She in turn gave a potlatch to the several tribes, repeating the assertions of her rights. She demonstrated her knowledge of the traditions by recounting them in detail. Then she ordered one of her father's expensive coppers to be brought out. She paid an important chief of the kw$^\varepsilon$xa to bend the copper over just above the "T" and paid other prominent chiefs to mark cuts symbolically with chisels, without actually cutting pieces from the copper. Then she ordered one of her kinsmen to tow it to the sea behind a canoe and to cut it adrift in deep water and let it sink. "This is my gift to you, O chief," she said to her rival.

The "uncle" immediately sent for a very valuable copper that he possessed. When his kinsmen brought it from his house, he had the copper cut into pieces in the traditional way, giving fragments to the guest chiefs, except for the "T" or crosspiece, which he nominally presented to his "niece" in unflattering terms, and then went down to the beach to hurl the object into the sea.

Technically the uncle at this stage was ahead on points, so to speak, for the copper he had broken was more valuable than that sunk in the sea by doqwa'is. But then something else happened. "We had a lot of good friends," Mr. Whonnuck said. "Dan Cranmer's people, Charley Nowell's [elder] brother, and a lot of other important chiefs all said they would give my grandfather's real daughter all their coppers and all their blankets, until she made her "uncle" go broke. Her nimkish uncle [mother's brother] sent for a very valuable copper he had, saying that he would give it to her if she needed it.

"These things among the Indians," Mr. Whonnuck went on, "are just like White people in politics. It is just like a [White] politician running for election—he has to have a lot of friends so he can get a lot of votes."

While Whonnuck's appraisal may be a bit *simpliste* as far as modern Canadian politics goes, we still like it because it casts light on a crucial point in the resolution of conflicting claims. The announced intent of several important and wealthy chiefs to back Ed's mother resolved the case in her favor. Their avowed reason for supporting the woman was one based on the prior right of a direct descendant over a remote kinsman, even though the former was a female. The informant's statement makes the real reason clear: his mother played a better game of politics. The so-called uncle was beaten at that point; he could not possibly hope to muster enough wealth to compete with the combined resources of the several chiefs, so he simply dropped out of the picture as far as the eagle place was concerned.

Winter Ceremonials

Summertime among the Kwakiutl was the Bakoos season, the nonceremonial, profane, or secular part of the year.[9] This period usually lasted from March to November when individual families and numimas were at their summer

---

[9] The orthography of Kwakiutl terms in this section follows, for the most part, that of Hawthorn (1967).

fishing stations or in some other way occupied with economic pursuits. The Tsetseka or ceremonial, supernatural season extended from November to March. The Kwakiutl returned to their winter villages then, and members of the secret ceremonial societies devoted themselves exclusively to the winter dances, feasts, potlatches and other ceremonial activities. No work was done that was not necessary for survival itself or for the ceremonials. The transition from the Bakoos to the Tsetseka season was marked by a four-day interval of festivities during which time the deaths of those who had passed away since the last ceremonial season were commemorated.

The entire social organization of the Kwakiutl changed during the sacred season. New ceremonial names were used and new songs were sung; the use of Bakoos names was forbidden, and serious penalties were imposed on those who neglected or forgot this prohibition. Tsetseka was the season when supernatural spirits came to initiate the young into different grades of dance societies. The whole social system was altered to conform to the individual's relationship with the spirits. Drucker (1955:163) describes the winter dances as "cycles of dramas revolving around a single theme: the protagonist's encounter with a spirit who kidnaps him, bestows supernatural powers upon him, then returns him to his village, repeating the experience of the ancestor from whom the performer inherited the right to the performance." And according to Boas (1897:431), the object of the winter ceremonial was to "bring back the youth who is supposed to stay with the supernatural being who is the protector of his society, and then, when he has returned in a state of ecstacy, to exorcise the spirit which possesses him and to restore him from his holy madness."

The right to membership in the prestige graded dance societies—the totality of which comprise the winter ceremonial—was inherited in the same way as other rights and privileges, that is, through one's parents or as part of a dowry from one's father-in-law at marriage. As we described with the Bella Coola raid, the right to membership could also be acquired by killing a man in another tribe who possessed it. The prerogative of claiming a particular place in one of the dance societies was as personal and individualistic as a potlatch name. Dance society membership corresponded closely with the composition of the nobility, but even a nobleman had to assume his right to a position by going through formal initiation. Commoners were excluded from important participation in the ceremonials because they could not be initiated into any of the dance societies. They were, in effect, an impressionable audience to the ritual and theatrics of the initiated.

During the Tsetseka season, the tribe was bisected into two groups, the initiated and the uninitiated. The initiated, in turn, were divided into two societies, the Seals and the Sparrows. Sparrows, who were the managers of the ceremonial, provided comic relief by mocking and teasing the Seals who were under the influence of the spirits. Women could not officiate in the Sparrow society even if they were in the line of primogeniture (Boas 1966:179).

Members of the winter ceremonial dance societies were rank ordered. The Seal society maintained the highest position. They were seated in the place of honor at the rear of the big-house. Among them, the highest ranking hamatsa claimed the ranking seat in the middle rear of the big-house. Other members of the Seal society such as the Bear dancers, sat on either side of him. The Nutlamatl (Fool dancers and messengers of the hamatsa) sat at the far end of the Seal society; the Killer Whale and Rock Cod societies, the singers, sat in front of the Seal society. In addition the song leader, drummer, and herald, among other hereditary personnel, each had his seating place. Each society followed its own format and ritual, but all of them used certain ceremonial symbols such as red cedar bark head bands and neck rings, eagle down on their heads to symbolize peace, and red or black facial paint.

Kwakiutl dance societies comprised four major groups, the most complex and important of which was the hamatsa society. As described by Hawthorn (1967:46),

> [Hamatsa were] under the supernatural inspiration of Bakbakwalanooksiwae, a powerful man-eating spirit, represented in the dance by the cannibal dancer or Hamatsa in human form. The second group was under the inspiration of Winalagilis, the war spirit initiator. The third group, the Atlakim dance series, could be used either for the Klasila [the four-day period preceding the Tsetseka season] or for Tsetseka display by changing the symbolic decorations. The fourth group was made up of the Dluwalakha dancers (meaning "Once more from Heaven")—those who had been given supernatural treasures or dloogwi, which were passed on to the novice, but who were not, as a group, involved in the convincing and terrifying displays of supernatural seizure.

According to Hawthorn (1967:39), the whole winter ceremonial was in a sense staged as a dramatic theatrical production. The intention of the initiates was to convince the uninitiated that the spirits and supernatural really were present within the village. Hawthorn (1967:39–42) continues with an excellent synopsis of the winter dances:

> The house itself was a stage, with seating arranged so that the wall next to the curtain was shielded, and the dancers could come and go unseen. The central fireplace was the focus of attention. Dancing took place around the fireplace—the dancers moved four times around, counterclockwise, pivoting at the front and the back of the house, then disappeared. The performers entered suddenly through the front door, while others left unnoticed.
>
> Illusion was managed in many ways. "Prop" men hidden above the beams of the house manipulated the strings that helped the dancers to control their magic tricks. Supernatural birds or other creatures, announced by thunderous noise on the roof, flew down through the air, appeared to pick up a person, and then flew up again. Underground passages increased the repertoire of magical tricks; such illusion gave credence to the presence of spirits. Curtis noted that some people even stayed home in the deserted village during the summer berrying and fishing times in order to prepare the tunnels under the floor of the Ghost Dancers' House.
>
> Staging was always deliberate. Even the apparently spontaneous destructive frenzy of the Hamatsa was subject to planning (Curtis 1915:179): "He advances on lines which have been secretly marked out on the floor, and those who have been previously warned by the initiator that hamatsa will bite them sit where these lines touch the edge of the open space, so that hamatsa can easily reach them."
>
> During the winter dance season the whole village, not only within the houses but also outside, become the scene of the pageant. A novice was sought after and

"Wild man of the woods" emerging from the forest (E. C. Curtis)

captured on the edge of the woods. Another novice—balanced on boards over a low-slung canoe—arrived apparently dancing on the water. The use of illusion was an important element: one novice was seen arriving by canoe with his sponsor when there was a sudden accident, the canoe overturned, and the novice was drowned. He was later revived and danced amid general rejoicing. Actually the drowning figure was a cedar carving which was weighted down and sunk. In another example of illusion the Hamatsa novice, fleeing to the woods, apparently disappeared in mid-

Ceremonial dancers in mythological bird masks (E. C. Curtis)

flight. The Hamatsas, wearing red cedar bark head and neck rings, went into the woods to capture the novice. On the way they were handed hemlock boughs, which they donned. They advanced toward the Hamatsa novice, who, in order to mystify the village spectators, quickly substituted red cedar bark ornaments for his green hemlock rings. When the crowd opened, he had apparently disappeared, quickly to reappear at a considerable distance in the person of a second substitute dressed exactly like him. This one was then surrounded and "lost" in the same manner (Curtis 1915:174).

In one part of the drama, the Hamatsa novice rushed out from the house with everyone else in pursuit. The Killer Whales, who had been teasing him, ran to take refuge in the water, where they were cornered by the novice. He was afraid to go into salt water, and they were afraid to come close to him for fear of being bitten. Several novices of the sea-creature spirits appeared for initiation at the edge of the ocean as though they had just come up from its depths.

Terror, drama, and comedy were balanced to produce good theater:

During the feast the grizzly bear may become aroused, growl and roar, and try to get out of the room.

The people scramble back to their seats along the walls, while attendants rush over to restrain the beast. After a terrific struggle, despite their efforts, a board will be torn loose, and they will all be sent sprawling, but instead of a grizzly bear the figure of a decrepit old man will totter forth (Drucker 1940:207).

Some dancers acted as buffoons and created a disturbance. Some were clumsy; some were mimics who staggered around imitating the actions of others:

While the real dancers are making their secret preparations behind the screen, the jesters amuse the audience. They dodge behind the screen, parody the coming performance. Or one may accuse the other of lying, then peek behind the screen and come out to report "the real truth" to a convulsed audience (Olson 1940:A:5, 175)."

Meticulous attention to the details of theatrical illusion and dramatic impact characterized the productions of the ceremonies.

Within the large plank house, the central fire cast lights and shadows. At the far end opposite the entrance door was a theatrical curtain made of wooden planks or muslin with the crest of the initiating spirit of the dancing house painted on. Behind the curtain, awaiting their cues, were the dancers in costumes. At one side was a small hidden cubicle to which the novice retreated. There were several such small rooms for the various dancers.

The dancing house in which the Tokwit dancers were going to perform was vacated and carefully guarded several days before the initiation. Underground passageways were dug, down which the dancer could disappear. A system of kelp speaking tubes was installed. Elaborate gear was brought to the house, such as false-bottomed chests in which the dancer would be concealed while apparently being consumed by fire.

Every opportunity to create drama was exploited. Here is an example cited by Drucker in a description of a Dluwalakha dance (1940:207):

"The novice . . . flies away for four days, descends again, is caught and dances four nights like the rest. On the fourth night, the master of ceremonies . . . is bade to call the dancer's spirit down from the sky. He stands under the smoke hole, shouting his request that the "honored one from heaven" descend to show himself to the people. He tries very hard. Suddenly there is a tremendous thud on the roof, a blare of spirit horns, and a commotion at the door. The master of ceremonies sends the attendants to see if the spirit he has been calling has arrived. They report that there is something strange and terrifying without. They assemble at the door, holding their blankets out to form a screen, then back in. All at once they break away, revealing the spirit—a naked dancer, painted black, wearing a hominoid mask. The spirit dances, enters the cubicle, and is sent away when the novice is purified."

During the dances various tricks were employed to create convincing illusions. An apparent beheading used portrait carvings and bladders filled with seal blood. The fire thrower handled burning embers in leather gloves with wooden palms skillfully put on by his attendants. He walked on the fire over wooden boulders wearing protective footgear. The Tokwit dancer climbed into a wooden box, was consumed by fire, and in due course was reconstituted.

Curtis (1915:212–13) described two other examples of illusion, summarized as follows:

"*Kinkalatlala walks about the house, making her cries. A noise is heard, and a wooden kingfisher appears. The bird descends to the dancer and follows him, darts at him and spears him with its long beak. It then flies up to the roof. The dancer has strings which raise and lower the bird, and there is a man above on the roof who also controls the strings.*

"*The female Mitla spirit produces salmonberries out of season. Four masked female attendants dance around her. Salmonberry shoots are let down from the roof. The berries are pebbles covered with resin gum dyed with iron oxide. The people eat them and pretend to fall dead, but are then revived.*"

A simple device was the use of the dancer's blanket to aid in concealment. A gesture of a blanket-covered arm would make a screen behind which one mask could be changed for another, or a whistle held under the blanket could be blown secretly.

These dramatic winter ceremonials are no longer produced, but the Kwakiutl still sing the same songs and perform the same types of dances, wearing finely carved, painted masks, button blankets and red cedar bark neck and head rings. The performances, however, are not embedded in the ritual context of a rank stratified system where only certain people have the exclusive right to use particular names, sing specific songs, perform certain dances. The dances today are severely abbreviated versions of what they once were; dramas that originally took an hour or more to complete are now typically performed in a matter of minutes. The use of tricks and illusions, and almost all theatrical props such as false bottom chests, kelp speaking tubes and underground passages have disappeared. Currently anyone who has the skill and knowledge can perform any dance. In addition, the Indians execute their dramas in novel contexts. That is, dancing is still an important component of potlatches (and here people who have the legitimate prerogative to claim specific dances tend to perform them), but the Indians are also beginning to popularize their art during, for example, the summer tourist season in Alert Bay and when a dignitary such as the Lieutenant Governor of British Columbia visits the villages.

Many Kwakiutl are developing a renewed interest in their traditional art forms and other indigenous customs such as carving, painting, dancing and perhaps noncompetitive potlatching. Some of this revitalization is due to the enthusiastic response of White consumers. Different aspects of traditional Kwakiutl culture are well enough preserved so that they may be revived and maintained, but with reformulated meaning. The Kwakiutl are unlikely to reproduce their former heritage, but essential elements from the past along with syncretisms from the present may be perpetuated in the future as a distinctively *Kwakiutl* life style.

References

*BARNETT, HOMER G., 1968, *The nature and function of the potlatch*. Eugene: Department of Anthropology, University of Oregon.

BOAS, FRANZ, 1897, The social organization and secret societies of the Kwakiutl Indians. *Report of the U.S. National Museum for 1895*, Washington.

*———, 1966, *Kwakiutl ethnography*. Chicago: University of Chicago Press. Helen Codere, (ed.).

*CODERE, HELEN, 1950, Fighting with property. *American Ethnological Society*, Monograph No. 18.

*———, 1961, Kwakiutl. In E. H. Spicer (ed.), *Perspectives in American Indian culture change*. Chicago: University of Chicago Press.

*CURTIS, EDWARD S., 1915, The Kwakiutl. *The North American Indian*, Vol. 10, Norwood, Conn.

DRUCKER, PHILIP, 1940, Kwakiutl dancing societies. *Anthropological Records*, Vol. II, pp. 201–230, Berkeley: University of California Press.

———, 1955, *Indians of the Northwest Coast*. New York: The Natural History Press.

*———, 1965, *Cultures of the North Pacific Coast*. San Francisco: Chandler Publishing Company.

*DRUCKER, PHILIP, AND ROBERT F. HEIZER, 1967, *To make my name good: a reexamination of the Southern Kwakiutl potlatch*. Berkeley: University of California Press.

*HAWTHORN, AUDREY, 1967, *Art of the Kwakiutl Indians and other Northwest Coast tribes*. Seattle: University of Washington Press.

*McFEAT, TOM, 1966, *Indians of the North Pacific Coast*. Toronto: McClelland and Steward Ltd.

OLSON, RONALD L., 1940, The social organization of the Haisla. *Anthropological Records*, Vol. II, pp. 169–200. Berkeley: University of California Press.

*ROHNER, RONALD P., 1967, *The people of Gilford: a contemporary Kwakiutl village*. Bulletin 225, Ottawa: National Museum of Canada.

*SPRADLEY, JAMES P. (ed.), 1969, *Guests never leave hungry: the autobiography of James Sewid, a Kwakiutl Indian*. New Haven, Conn.: Yale University Press.

*WOLCOTT, HARRY F., 1967, *A Kwakiutl village and school*. New York: Holt, Rinehart and Winston, Inc.

---

* The starred items in the bibliography are particularly recommended.

MODERN BLACKFEET: MONTANANS ON A RESERVATION

Malcolm McFee

University of Oregon

Malcolm McFee is a professor of anthropology at the University of Oregon where he has taught since 1965. He began his studies of the Blackfeet in 1959 as a graduate student at Stanford University and has made periodic summer field trips to the reservation over the intervening years to improve his understanding of reservation life and to record the changes that have occurred through time. He received his Ph.D. from Stanford in 1962, and subsequently taught at the University of Arizona before moving on to Oregon. He has also done fieldwork in Oceania.

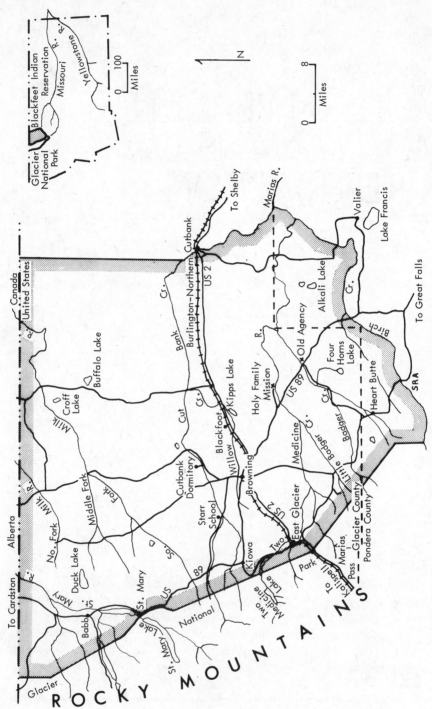

Figure 1. The Blackfeet Indian Reservation.

Contents

1. Introduction to the Blackfeet   229

Blackfeet Means Many kinds of People, 229
Fieldwork, 246
In Prospect, 247

2. The Blackfeet Reservation and Its People   248

Introduction, 248
The Regional Habitat, 249
Regional Population and Economy, 251
Reservation Population and Economy, 253
Summary, 260

3. Horse and Buffalo Days: 1850–1880   262

Introduction, 262
History before 1850, 263
Economy, 265
Social Organization, 269
Religion, 272
Values and Status, 273
Summary, 275

4. Dependency and Readaptation: 1884–1970   276

Introduction, 276
United States Indian Policies, 276
The Period of Dependency, 1884–1935, 278
The Period of Self-Government, 1935–1970, 284
Summary, 292

5. Intratribal Diversity   294

Introduction, 294
Socialization to White-Orientation, 295
Socialization to Indian-Orientation, 298
Analysis, 301

6. Social Interaction   303

   Introduction, 303
   Social Occasions Where Everybody Came, 303
   Indian-Oriented Social Occasions, 306
   White-Oriented Social Occasions, 314
   Other Social Expressions of Orientation, 316
   Summary, 318

7. Values   320

   Introduction, 320
   Values of the White-Oriented Group, 321
   Values of the Indian-Oriented Group, 324
   Summary, 330

8. Status   331

   Introduction, 331
   Status among the White-Oriented, 332
   Status among the Indian-Oriented, 339

9. The Future   347

   Summation, 347
   White-Oriented Society, 347
   Indian-Oriented Society, 348
   What Lies Ahead for the Blackfeet? 349
   Epilogue, 356

References   358

Introduction to the Blackfeet

Blackfeet Means Many Kinds of People

THE CENTRAL THEME of this book is diversity. In some ways American Indians are different from other segments of the United States population, yet it is an oversimplification to speak of "the Indian" and "Indian problems." There are Indian problems only in the sense that it is Indians who are involved with them in Indian communities. Then, too, all Indians are not alike. Not only do tribes differ one from the other, but there is often great variation within a single tribe. The Blackfeet are not like the Hopi, neither of these is like the Kwakiutl, and all differ from the Menomini: similarly it is impossible to describe the "typical" Blackfeet Indian. Many kinds of people and diverse ways of coping with reservation life are to be found among the Blackfeet, as I will try to show.

Albert Buffalo Heart, 1878–1964, was a respected elder and honorary chief of the Piegan tribe of the Blackfeet Indians, who lived in Browning, Montana, the economic and political hub of the Blackfeet Indian Reservation. He was a tall, heavy-set, distinguished-looking man, who dressed in worn, well-laundered wool trousers and shirt, moccasins, a neckerchief, and a hat with a tall undented crown. Buffalo Heart was a poor man by the white man's standards, but to the more Indian members of the tribe he was rich in the things that counted. He had lived a long life, had learned and practiced Indian ways, and was helpful and generous to his many kinsmen and friends.

During North American Indian Days, the annual Indian encampment that is one of Browning's main summer tourist attractions, he would be one of a group of advisers who tried to insure that the ceremonies were properly Indian. If the Sun Dance ceremony was to be conducted, he would be given a principal role, as he knew some of the ritual necessary for its success. He donned his ceremonial regalia—a beaded suit of white deerskin, a Plains Indian headdress, and an air of dignity—to greet distinguished visitors and to officiate in the adoption ceremonies in which visiting dignitaries were given an Indian name and adopted, symbolically, into the Blackfeet tribe. If any family conducted a memorial service for a deceased relative, or staged a give-away to honor visitors, he was called upon to be the crier. As crier he announced the import of the ceremony, led in chanting the proper song, or cried out the occasion for the give-away and called out the names of those to be honored with a gift.

In years past he had been employed by the Great Northern Railway as an official greeter of tourists arriving by train at Glacier Park, and as an entertainer at the inns within the Park where he and his friends staged Indian dances for the tourists.

Buffalo Heart, with others of his peers, had a place on the Honorary Tribal Council, and was given a small per diem for attendance at tribal council meetings. He was often chosen to accompany council members on trips to Washington, D.C. for the purpose of lobbying for or against proposed legislation which would affect Indians. In his regalia he furnished a bit of Indian color, as well as advice, to the proceedings.

Buffalo Heart and his fellow members of the Honorary Council felt that they represented the voice of the full-blood portion of the tribe and took every occasion to make long speeches in Blackfeet, urging harmony and trust, and asking for more attention to the needs of the people. But people paid little attention to the speeches; instead they talked, moved about, and impatiently filled in time until the Honorary Councilmen had had their say. On several occasions councilmen told the interpreter: "Tell him to make it short." The people in general felt some pride in their old-timers, but mixed this with a feeling of impatience and bare tolerance when the chiefs seemed to be taking themselves too seriously.

Buffalo Heart, and the others like him, usually lived among clusters of full-bloods in the more run-down areas of town, in small outlying communities, or, in a few cases, in more remote areas of the reservation. Buffalo Heart lived in a small two-room shack on Moccasin Flat, an area of shacks and cabins without sewer or water service, on the edge of Browning. The houses immediately surrounding his were occupied by some of his kin—a married son and his family, two married daughters and their families, and the family group of his brother.

The old man's home was the center for Indian gatherings. Here he and his friends conducted the religious rituals, bundle openings, and other ceremonies they wished to celebrate. Those who were singers would gather here occasionally for a song service—a meeting where they would drum and sing old and new songs. Buffalo Heart served as a tie to the old days, a source of information on lore and ritual, and an available medicine man for those who wished an Indian cure. The younger members of his family might participate in these functions, but usually just watched with a respectful air. As one family member said: "You join in even if you don't believe—it's part of the old Indian ways."

Buffalo Heart, however, was more than a man of the past. He was a medicine man and conducted curing ceremonies, yet he and those whom he had cured more often availed themselves of the services of the local doctors and hospital. Buffalo Heart was known as a Catholic and attended church occasionally, yet he was also considered to be a repository for, and a leader in, the present-day

Browning, Montana: The administrative seat of the Blackfeet Tribe.

*The drummers and part of the crowd at the North American Indian Days Cele-
bration.*

practice of the Indian religion. How did he combine or compartmentalize these
two beliefs? Did he perceive the Catholic ritual as a modern means for expressing
Indian beliefs? The priest, it was said, was perplexed by these questions.

There were varying perceptions of Buffalo Heart among the tribal members. Some would speak respectfully of him: "He is one of the chiefs, one of *our*
people and looks after us." Others chose to praise another and saw Buffalo Heart
as an old codger who had no right to the name of chief. The other chiefs might
also dismiss his tales of the past and his religious knowledge as "lies." "He doesn't
know anything. The truth is. . . ." So Buffalo Heart was a prophet and honored
person to some, the butt of jokes to others, and, it must be noted, the judgments
varied according to the situation and the person to whom the remarks were addressed. Nonetheless, this man was given a role to play, a role with limits im-

posed by the occasion, the time available, and by the particular people with whom he interacted.

His tie with the past was real. His father, in his youth, had hunted buffalo, fought the Cree and the Flathead, and raided the Crow camps for horses. His father had been fully conversant with Indian lore and religion, and even though a baptized Christian had remained a participant in the old culture. Buffalo Heart, himself, had lived through three-quarters of a century of radical change, a period during which new subsistence patterns were required and the problems a man was called upon to solve were concerned less and less with game and other Indians and more and more with dealing with the white man and his technology and beliefs. Buffalo Heart had tried subsistence farming, then ranching, and finally he had turned to day labor. He had seen a few Indians succeed in these endeavors,

Painted tepees: These designs are the personal property of the man who owns the tepee.

while he and the majority, due to what he believed were misfortunes beyond their control, failed. In his old age, no longer able to work, he accepted old age assistance, leased his lands to white ranchers through the local office of the Bureau of Indian Affairs, which manages lands held in trust for Indian owners, and reverted to being more fully "Indian." He admittedly did not know the old ways thoroughly. He and his friends tried to pool their knowledge, to revive the old ways and to teach these to their relatively uninterested children. He spoke of the better days of the past, which to him were the days of his father's youth. These were the buffalo days of which he had learned from the stories his father and his father's friends had told during the evenings around the fire. These days were real to him not just legend. As he saw it, Indian life in those days was not a patched up thing of half forgotten bits of knowledge which he sometimes felt life to be today.

Albert Buffalo Heart represents a small number of Blackfeet tribal members I have known and heard about, one segment of the reservation population that shares a particular status, a belief system, a mode of action, a way of life that is not limited to, nor necessarily characteristic of, old age. There are younger men and women who approximate Buffalo Heart's knowledge, beliefs, and aspirations; there are other men and women of equal relative age who share memories with the old man but who think, believe and act in another world. I will introduce a few more "representative types" to show some of the varied adaptations and adjustments made to the environment of the Blackfeet reservation. The incidents described in this section have been altered in place and detail to maintain the anonymity of the people involved, but they are based on and retain the spirit of actual events. The quoted remarks and conversations are verbatim statements made to me in situations that were similar to the contexts that have been constructed here.

I met John Arrowhead in Browning where he was waiting for the mail—a lease check was due, he said. He had just finished a fence building job and said that he hoped to find another job soon, perhaps herding sheep or "rock picking"—removing rocks and boulders that had weathered to the surface in wheat or hay fields. John is a short, wiry man, dressed in denim pants, a cowbody shirt and boots. He seldom wears a hat and nothing about his dress appears to be symbolic of the traditional Indian. Arrowhead is fifty-seven years old, had completed seven years of school, and said that he had traveled widely. His travels, usually to work in the harvesting of crops or with cattle or sheep, had taken him over a great part of the country.

During the years that I knew him, the jobs were infrequent. He is known to be a good worker, is still strong and capable, but prefers to spend more time in town, visiting and drinking with his friends. Sooner or later during our visits he would ask: "How about helping me out until my check comes? I need 50¢ to buy some gas for my friend so he can take me out home to get my clothes." I frequently gave him money and then drove around a corner to watch what happened. John would stall around for a bit, then head for the bar. Many summer days are spent standing in the shade of a building, watching the passers-by, talking with friends, and trying to get a little money for wine. He is available if a job is offered, but that seems to be a secondary consideration.

John knows much about the old religion, the societies and the Indian social activities, but he does not have the experience, status and authority to use this knowledge. He too talks of "his people," the full-blood group that once lived near each other on one part of the reservation and who still called that region home. He called the elderly man from that area "chief" and told of the important things the old man knew. Arrowhead speaks both Blackfeet and English and during conversation with me would break off in midsentence to greet a passer-by in the Blackfeet language, then resume our discussion in English. His English is adequate, but spoken with an accent and with occasional grammatical errors, usually in tense and gender, that indicate that English has been learned as a second language. He said that this was the case—he and his family spoke Blackfeet when he was growing up and his English had been learned in school.

John claims to have been a "great dancer" and a "champion" singer, but was always on the fringe of the crowd at the Indian dances and ceremonies that I witnessed. He was present, watching, often helping in some necessary but menial task, but was never in costume, never participating in dances or rituals. He knew what was going on and would describe and explain the proceedings to me. John would tell stories about the power and importance of the old ways. He believes these powers, one sensed, but he does not participate in the rituals concerning them. He does not play a significant part either in Indian social activities or in non-Indian community life. His social role remains unclear to me; he is, it seems, a bystander, one of the crowd, a man for an occasional job, but more often categorized by his acquaintances as a "good worker but a wino," a man of whom they have limited expectations.

Conversation with Arrowhead seems to confirm this view. He can not place himself. His talk is mostly of the past, of travel, work, or *past* participation in Indian dancing, singing or ceremony. He *had* been a "champion dancer . . . a good bronc rider." The highlights of his past may have become embellished by imagination. He took me on a tour of "his land" to show with pride "his cattle, his horses, his house." I knew, and he knew that I knew, that the land was his, but the house and stock belonged to another man who leased the land. In the situation of relating to a white man, at least, the need for status is more impelling than sticking to the facts.

Questions about the future draw a blank. The future lies just beyond to-morrow: "I've got a job coming up herding cattle." He evidently expects tomorrow to be like today. "I'll look for you if you come back next summer," he said, "I'll be around." He gives no clues as to further concern for what might lie ahead.

In contemplation of the past he rarely goes beyond his own experience. On occasion he vaulted back to a "Golden Age," a legendary past he and his friends accept of the trouble-free days of the Indian before the white man came. Then everybody lived well and had plenty to eat. They never became sick and lived long lives. "They didn't fight all the time either." Buffalo Heart, with all his belief in the traditional culture never went back that far. He tried to retain Indian ways of a life that his father had known; he found the better days to be those that began to disappear with the buffalo. Arrowhead holds no hope for a miraculous return of his Golden Age; Buffalo Heart, on the other hand, clung to the hope, it

Sound and a variety of sub-standard housing can be found together in some sections of Browning.

seemed, of retaining, if not regaining, some aspects of his better life. To Arrowhead, those better days are gone, part of what was lost when the white man "took everything from the Indian." The white man has become the scapegoat for all John's ills; he can do nothing about this and evidently expects no changes for the better.

John rents a small three room shack on Moccasin Flat where he lives with his wife and the younger two of their four children. His wife has made this place quite comfortable in spite of its run-down condition. John said that he also has a house on his land, where he used to live, and to which they sometimes go for a few months during the summer. Some of his friends are unmarried and live with members of their family, some have separated from their wives and have no fixed residence. Most of his close friends are equally improvident, with a life style similar to that of Arrowhead.

Why does Arrowhead not participate in the Indian ceremonies about which he knows so much? He is, he said, a Catholic, but seldom goes to church. How much does he understand of Christianity? How much does he believe in the old religion? Along with these questions, yet to be answered, are others. What factors contribute to the apparent differences between Arrowhead and Buffalo Heart? In what ways are they similar? Are the differences and similarities to be explained by age, skills, experience, education, or what? These same questions arise again and again as these men are compared with other tribal members.

I met several other older men, in ranch dress, who came to town once a week or so. One, Roy Conrad, age sixty-eight, is a farmer from the east side of the reservation who comes to town to shop, get his mail, and conduct business with the council or the agency. He and his sons farm on a small scale but he feels that they are economically independent. Roy takes an active interest in the tribal affairs, and while he has some knowledge of the past Indian culture—much of which he had learned from others in the past few years—Roy is more concerned with the recent past of the Indian, the relationships among the tribe, the agency and the tribal council. He told about the successes and failures of the various government programs and assessed the strengths and shortcomings of the various agents and superintendents who had ·represented the Bureau of Indian Affairs over the past forty years. He felt that the best days were those before 1934, before the Wheeler-Howard Act gave many political and economic powers to the tribe. His "Golden Age" falls in the early 1920s when a "good" agent acted as a "father" to the people and set the full-bloods to farming. "Everybody had a small ranch or farm, lived on it, and were doing all right." Since then, the council has taken over, the farm program died out, liquor has been admitted to the reservation and "ruined the young people." The full-blood has "lost out; the white man has taken over the best lands, and the whole tribe has gone down hill."

Roy is an occasional observer at the Indian Days festivities but takes no active part. He thinks that these affairs and the money spent for them are time consuming and wasteful. The people would be better off if the time and money were spent for getting themselves established on farms or ranches. Farming requires steady work with little time left over for hanging around town, dancing, drinking, and visiting.

Like Buffalo Heart and Arrowhead, Roy is a full-blood Blackfeet, and I met others who share his attitudes. Some of these are less successful economically than Roy, and are in town less frequently. Bob Sorrel Horse is one of these. He lacks the drive and, as he lamented, the capital with which to realize the "dream" he has of building a small ranch. "I think a lot when I'm alone. I have this dream to get some money and fix this place up right—a nice house and a good place. First I'd get electricity in to pump the water. I had planned to remodel the house— my father built this a long time ago—to have a place I'm not ashamed of." The dream has not been realized, but I was impressed by the order he maintains around his log cabin and by the effort that has gone into the utilization of the little Bob has.

Because these men are seldom in town, I did not get to know them well enough to assess their cultural backgrounds, but did gather that they had had the opportunity, in their families and during their childhood and youth, to learn aspects of the traditional Blackfeet culture. They speak Blackfeet as well as good English. The Indian accent, which I can only describe as a rather musical variation in pitch and a fairly explosive phrasing, neither of which conforms to general English speech patterns, but which are more familiar to the speaker of Blackfeet, is slightly noticeable. These men appear to have lived within this more traditional cultural context without having absorbed much of it, and at the same time have striven toward goals of economic success more related to those of western culture. They feel no need to reaffirm, exaggerate, or separate an Indian part of their lives as opposed to a white part. They are Indians. They can be antiwhite in matters concerning the tribe and the reservation, but see their future in terms of work, money, and building capital—the ranch, the farm, the herd. Some people represented by Roy and Bob achieve more success than others in this endeavor.

I also met some younger men, in appearance and dress youthful counterparts of John Arrowhead. They, however, spend less time standing around, seem to be more animated in their conversation, and move more often at a somewhat quicker pace. Like Roy and Bob, these men are not in town regularly. Joseph Renault, for example, is seen for a few days and then is gone for weeks at a time. He appears to differ in a number of ways from the others I have talked about.

Upon acquaintance, I found that this man is an active seeker of work, is known to be a good worker who is called whenever jobs are available. He also leaves the reservation to look for work in the harvests, to fight forest fires, or to take construction jobs. His employment is irregular and seasonal, yet he takes advantage of all such work available.

Joe is thirty-two years old, ⅝ Blackfeet, married but separated from his wife. When home, on Badger Creek near Old Agency, he lives with his mother, a sister, her two children, and two of his children that his mother is raising. These seven people live in a two room frame house that is badly in need of repair.

Joe knows something of Indian practices and has participated occasionally in social dancing. He speaks English quite fluently and claims to know very little of the Blackfeet language. He talked of both work conditions and old Indian ways during our discussions, but as a participant in the work realm and as one who was marginal to the Indian ways. He is a Catholic by faith, but here, too, is seldom a participant. I met him in town, where he frequently comes "between jobs" to meet his friends, have a few drinks and then, when his cash is gone, leave to find more work.

Because the opportunities to get better acquainted with Joe were few, I have but a shallow impression of his way of life. He impressed me as a man who, if trained, could become a steady worker, or who might just as readily fall into a pattern of life like that of Arrowhead as jobs become harder to find as he grows older. I learned little of his values or the beliefs to which he is committed; his goals, at least as he expressed them, seem to be limited to the next job and the spending of the money he earns. He talked occasionally of going on relocation, or of signing up for on-the-job training, but hinted that these thoughts have been with him for several years and have never gone beyond the inquiry stage. He had been in the Army for two years where he had learned welding, but found no demand for that trade on the reservation. "I may go to Denver and get a welding job," he said once, but he never went and I felt that in all probability he never would. If, in later years, he should go, and is successful in finding a trade and sticking to it, he might avoid the Arrowhead pattern. Yet he gives the impression that he would expect to fail and would return to the reservation. What creates these impressions of a man who at first seems so open and self-assured? The assurance is there when he talks of the present, but when he is led into thinking about the future he give the impression that this is unexplored territory. He has only vague ideas to work with. Also, he seems to have but shallow ties with the past, limited to his own experience plus what little he knows of his parents' life. Perhaps he is yet too young to be concerned with the past; but why no thought of the future? Again a question for further reflection.

I met some younger men, visibly Indian, who also were raised in the more traditional full-blood homes, but who are better educated than others from a similar background. They speak both languages fluently and are able interpreters. Raymond Black Plume expressed a primary goal of these men. "I want to make a life by combining what is best of the Indian way with the best from the white way." These men see themselves as representatives of the full-blood group within the council, and actively seek office. Raymond has served several terms.

He participates in Indian ceremonies and knows much of the old religion and rituals, although he himself is a Christian and an active church member. His commitment to the old beliefs is difficult to assess. Although he is more than tolerant of the old practices, and gives the impression of being a respectful non-believer, occasional statements lead me to believe that there is much in the old religion that appeals to him, and he may have assimilated some of this into his Christian practice. Raymond's father, recently dead, had been one of the "chiefs," so Raymond's knowledge of Blackfeet lore and life came directly to him in his childhood home. Beyond this, he has traveled widely and has studied and accepted much white culture from his schooling.

I met a few others like him, all of whom are interested in tribal affairs, and work regularly in council or agency jobs, or as clerks, teachers or tradesmen. These people, while differing as individuals, represent another kind of full-blood Indian.

Raymond, age forty-one, is married and has four children. His frame house has four rooms and, differing from those mentioned earlier, has more furnishings, including a refrigerator and a television set. He has a recent model automobile that is kept in good condition, but shows little attention to minor details of upkeep.

The house is located near those of other members of his family along a small creek, several miles from Browning, where the family members pooled their labor to develop a stock ranch. When Raymond is serving on the council, or employed at a council or agency job, he can count on his brothers, uncles, and nephews to look after the place, while his income, which is large in terms of the reservation average, will be used to keep all the family going when they need money.

These activities also indicated that Raymond is keenly interested in the present, ongoing activities of tribe and ranch. He also likes to talk of the past—a past in which he is interested and of which he has heard much from his father. However, he has no desire to return to those days, only a wish to use what good the old culture has to offer for today. He also thinks much about the future. He has goals for the people and for himself. He intends to build up the ranch until it can support the family. "I'll be ready if termination[1] comes," he said; "I'll be able to take care of myself and family." His progress toward this end appears to be slow, but he is making headway.

Raymond said that his greatest problems arise from the jealousy of his

---

[1] Termination of the Bureau of Indian Affairs and the special relationships between Indians and the federal government.

friends and neighbors. The people like to see one of their boys get ahead but at the same time are jealous of his success. Consequently he is often the subject of gossip. People like Arrowhead praise him at one time, while at other times they lump him with the "crooks" on the council who see to it that all the benefits go to members of their own families but do nothing for the other people. He is criticized by Sorrel Horse for the conveniences to be found in his home. "Just go call on one of those councilmen. He'll have everything in his house, a radio, TV, a refrigerator, and probably will even have beer in it. He'll tell you that he's worked hard for it. But he hasn't. He tries to live like a white man while we have nothing." Such criticism and gossip soon led me to believe that even the full-blood Blackfeet do not see eye to eye on many things. They differ as to what they want in life, how to get these things, and in their ability to achieve them. Raymond said that there is conflict also between the full-bloods and the mixed-bloods. The latter, who make up roughly three-fourths of the tribal population, are more progressive, according to Raymond. "They try to push things the old folks don't understand. It isn't a caste division, just a mistrust of method and plan."

Many other people I met varied in family backgrounds, in jobs, or in personal appearance from those already discussed, but there were certain basic similarities in attitudes toward themselves and others, similarities of comprehension of, and interest in, Indian ways versus white ways. These characteristics make one person more like Arrowhead, another more like Raymond Black Plume, and yet another more like Joe Renault. There are many others, however, who seem to represent variations of a contrasting way of life.

Carl Hunter, thirty-seven years of age, is ⅝ Blackfeet and the son of mixed-blood parents. He had completed the eighth grade and served two years in the army, eight months of which was in active combat in Korea. His wife is ½ Blackfeet, and they have five children.

Carl owns no land or home of his own. He and his family live with his father, a widower who owns a two-room log cabin built in 1939 under one of the reservation housing programs. This is one of several houses clustered along Blacktail Creek from which the daily water supply is drawn. The home is sparsely furnished. The wood range serves for both cooking and heating. A wooden table and kitchen chairs provide dining and seating facilities. A cot, two double beds, and a crib complete the furnishings. The limited space and the sleeping requirements for eight people allow for little more.

Carl is employed regularly during the time of year (seven months) when work is available. He has worked on the railroad section crew and as a ranch hand, but considers construction labor to be his main occupation. His income is not high, but is steady and sufficient to qualify him for unemployment benefits. His father has land which is leased for grazing and receives a small pension for his years of service as a janitor and caretaker for the Bureau of Indian Affairs. This money, pooled with Carl's income, usually carries the family through the winter. Only occasionally is it necessary for the family to apply for welfare assistance.

According to Carl, neither he nor his father have any knowledge of the traditional Blackfeet culture. All of the family have been raised as Catholics. Both his father and mother had attended the Catholic boarding school and stayed to work there for several years—his father as a caretaker and his mother as a cook.

Carl attended the small public school near his childhood home followed by a few months at Browning High School. He dropped out because there was no bus service from his home to town at that time and it was hard to find a place to live in Browning. No one in his family can speak Blackfeet. He takes no interest in the more Indian social events, such as dancing, encampments, and stick games; his recreational activities center around card games and visiting with his family and neighbors along the creek during the winter. During the rest of the year he spends most of his spare time hunting. A few evenings are spent with his brother and a few friends in town, where they get a bottle and drive around in a car, stopping now and then for a few drinks. They usually end up at a friend's house where they play cards and "hang one on."

Carl, like some of the others, also seems to live in the present and think little about the future. He talks easily of the past, but with an air of detachment that puzzles me. He can relate a series of troubles and tragedies almost as if these things had happened to someone else. Is he a stoic, or is he carefully guarding his emotions from a stranger? His life conditions are extremely barren and harsh compared with mine. How can he appear so happy and satisfied with things as they are? Is it because he has neither known nor expects to know any other way? Yet he has had opportunities both on and off the reservation and in the army to meet others who live differently.

To probe into these questions, I asked about job opportunities on and off the reservation. What do the tribe and the bureau do to help people find work? "They are trying to attract industry to the reservation," he replied, "and are building programs for relocation and on-the-job training. None of these has produced much yet." His reply when asked whether or not he has considered relocation was that he had thought about it but never applied. "I don't have much trouble getting a job. Some of the fellows have gone on relocation and done all right. Others didn't like it and came home." The answers imply that he is doing well enough at seasonal work. There was no expression of dissatisfaction with his own subsistence pattern.

By my standards, eight people in two rooms is overcrowded, so I asked if there was any provision by either the tribe or the bureau to help a man if he wants to add onto or repair his home. "Yes, they have a setup for that," was the answer. "I guess we could get a loan like that if we needed it." This again seems an expression of satisfaction with the way things are. He recognizes no need for either more room or for repairs.

Carl has nothing to offer when asked about his future plans. I inferred that he would continue as he is. What culture pattern does he reflect—Indian or white? Or is his outlook a clue to a new subculture that has developed under reservation conditions? Is this a way of life related not so much to the reservation as to a more general American subcultural pattern that develops under conditions of deprivation, a way displayed here by a man who happens to be part Indian and who lives on an Indian reservation? This question will require further examination.

Robert Thompson was in town to get parts for a mower. His ranch is north of town and the prairie grass was about ready to be cut for hay. Robert appears to be about twenty-six years old, said he is married and has two children. He is 1/8

Blackfeet and his wife is $\frac{1}{16}$. He was dressed in the familiar blue denim pants, cowboy shirt, boots, and hat.

The ranch Robert operates belonged to his father who had established the home and herd in 1940. Robert had been given a few cows while he was in school as payment for his work on the ranch. As his father grew older, more and more of the work had been turned over to Robert and his brother, until they have assumed complete charge. His father is dead; his mother lives with him.

What is Indian about Robert? He said he does not speak the language, although his father could. He knows nothing about the old Indian religion, lore, or medicine. He and his parents before him were raised as Catholics and attended church regularly. His great-grandmother was a full-blood Blackfeet, but his father and grandfather had both married white women, so he felt that his home background and training had been no different than it would have been if he had had no Indian ancestors, and had been born and raised on a similar ranch across the reservation line. Because they have lived on the reservation, he and members of his family have picked up, by observation and hearsay, a superficial knowledge of Indians and Indian ways, but he evinced little interest in these things. A few of his relatives have taken an interest in the more formal aspects of pan-Indianism; they participate, for example, in the major Indian Pow Wows such as the annual Indian Encampment at Sheridan, Wyoming. Their participation is limited to marching or riding in the parade, entering a daughter in the Miss American Indian contest, or acting as a judge for this and other contests. They neither camp in the tepee circle nor participate in the dances.

Robert has gone to school with people who are more Indian than he, so he knows many kinds of people. His social activities, however, have been limited to his family and their close friends—people much like himself. He casts Indian problems into one or the other of two contexts. His immediate response to a question about Indians is to talk about reservation problems, of land, leasing, cattle, employment, and of the conflicts between "Indians" (the reservation population) and the "whites" (government officials, white farmers who bought or leased Indian land, and the local merchants). Within this context he is aligned with the tribe and the Indians. When the discussion turns to matters of Indian culture, his focus changes. At times he felt that people should let the Indians live the way they want to. At other times he commented that these beliefs and practices are doomed to extinction and should be helped on their way. The impressive thing was that this does not concern him. He suggested that I call upon some of the "Indians." "They can tell you about this." Within this context, Robert did not see himself as an Indian. What is an Indian? When and under what circumstances do people of mixed-blood see themselves as Indians and when not? Does the full-blood Indian think of people like Robert as Indian or white? Are they considered to be Indian or non-Indian by the white people who live around them?

Robert's recreational activities center around the ranch life. He rarely attends the local Indian Days festivities. He is, however, among the audience at all local rodeos, fairs, and school meetings, and takes part in a few community service projects—those concerned with community development, schools, youth programs, cattle and range management programs.

An urban home, Browning.

It is difficult to find anything Indian about Robert Thompson. He neither looks nor acts like an Indian. He knows nothing of Indian ways, and does not consider himself to be an Indian except in the limited context already mentioned. He is, nonetheless, a member of the tribe and a resident of the reservation.

There are other people who are noticeable because they dress more like city people than like country people and tend to live in the larger and more expensive homes on the reservation. One of these is Henry Rogers.

Henry is forty-five years of age, his wife is white and they have two children of junior high school age. He shares many of the traits of people like Robert Thompson, but has a distinctive life style that sets him apart. Except when hunting or fishing he dresses in sports clothes or business suits. He is urbane and sophisticated. Henry knows more than most of the people about history, literature, and the world of business and politics. He has kept abreast of world-wide current events. After two years of college, Henry served in the Air Force as a master sergeant, and he has traveled extensively around the United States. Unlike John Arrowhead, Henry's travel was not as an itinerant laborer, but as a tourist and sight-seer, a visitor of historical sites, museums, night clubs, and other tourist attractions. He lacks Robert Thompson's interest in rodeos and the first hand contacts with ranch life. His interests are in business and politics at both the tribal and national levels.

He and his brother had inherited land, and rather than lease it for grazing as so many others do, they have contracted pasturage to outside cattlemen, that is, they "run cattle." This means providing range and care for outside herds during the grazing season at a set price per head "run" on their land. This is a method of land exploitation, according to Henry, that for a little management and expense yields up to ten times the income that can be gained from the usual grazing lease contracts. Henry lives more by brains than brawn. Such an operation leaves him free for other ventures—to serve on the council, to hold an agency job, to promote a new venture for the tribe, or to work on a new business deal of his own. Henry is an administrator, a promoter, an entrepreneur.

Henry owns one of the better homes in Browning. The house is well maintained, the large lawn is mowed regularly. Shade trees, shrubs and flowers are numerous. The house is well furnished with overstuffed furniture, a coffee table, bookcases, television, radio, a hi-fi set, refrigerator, freezer, electric stove, and central heat—all the comforts of middle-class city dweller's home. Each of these things, by itself, would not set Henry apart from his fellow tribal members. Other people have well-maintained houses; other have lawns, trees and flowers. Many have new cars like Henry's. It is the total combination of these things, coupled with his sophistication and more widely ranging interests and economic operations, that differentiates Henry from the others.

As I got to know Henry better, I became aware of certain values, drives, and attitudes that were unlike those of the other people I have described. Henry is interested in the old Indian culture, but his knowledge of this has been acquired intellectually, through books and studied observation. He is $\frac{1}{4}$ Indian but has had nothing of Indian life transmitted to him through his home environment, childhood training, or other experience. He remained apart from the Indian behavior expressed by friends and schoolmates during the years he had attended a small country school. In the Browning High School he mixed with people more like himself. He was then among the "more Indian" of the pupils but does not appear to have recognized the things that made them different from him and his friends. The segregation between his friends and others had not been a conscious act. It just "came about." He went away to college and found work in Great Falls after dropping out. Following this came World War II and his years in the service, after which he settled in San Francisco for a year.

Henry returned home to help his brother set up a program for the use of the family lands and while doing this became involved in the problems of Indian land management. At this time he became aware of the plight of the large majority of the reservation residents. He had found a new goal for himself. He bought his house and stayed in Browning to pursue his interest in Indian affairs and to try to better the conditions of the Indian people. Neither he nor I could separate the motives that spurred this interest. He is genuinely involved in this cause and at the same time the cause offers an opportunity for personal achievement—in politics, in tribal affairs, and in economic ventures. It suffices that Henry has found a goal toward which he can apply his particular interests, abilities, and drives.

In this work he often finds himself teamed with Raymond Black Plume, and it was by contrasting these two men and their approach to and understanding of the problems of the Indian that I became aware of other characteristics of Henry Rogers. Both men have a genetic tie back into the traditional Blackfeet culture. Raymond, however, has learned what he knows of it by growing up with it; Henry has learned of it by study in later life. Raymond grew up under conditions that exposed him to two sets of traditions, ideals, goals, attitudes, and beliefs. He has had to select and adjust, to reconcile and accommodate, to give and take from what he encounters as he formulates his goals and adopts means to achieve them. Henry, on the other hand, has been socialized to the white pattern. His new dedication to the solution of Indian problems has awakened an interest in Indian traditions. He learns what he can of Indian ways, but has no need to internalize these, or to accommodate to them in his everyday life. Raymond's goal is to make a life by combining what he finds to be the best of both the white and Indian traditions. Henry, whether he realizes it or not, works toward changing the Indian to greater acceptance of white ways. He would retain the symbols and ritual of "being an Indian," but spoke of providing steady work and better education as the bases of change. If these could be gained, he believes, the people would correct other deficiencies. Raymond, on the other hand, emphasizes better housing and improving sanitation first, then jobs and education. To Henry, better homes and sanitation would follow from more jobs and education. Raymond supports the preservation of Indian ways because they have a meaning for him—they are a part of his identity. Henry supports these same things because he feels that the Indian children need the knowledge of their cultural heritage as a psychological support for their feelings of self-worth as they learn to live in the modern world—they need to know that they are not just the "descendants of heathen savages." He wants to set up formal elective courses in the schools to teach Blackfeet history and culture. Raymond, in the meantime, teaches these things to his children and their friends as a part of their childhood training, by story and example. One man is involved objectively and rationally; the other, more subjectively and emotionally.

Henry, because of his experience, has different values and attitudes that have not been changed by intellectual understanding of Indian problems. Two incidents I observed seem to support this. Once during a discussion of housing conditions on Moccasin Flat, Henry expressed the wish that he could get the council to make an appropriation to buy grass and flower seed to give to all the householders in that area. If the council would do this and encourage the people to plant the seeds, he thought, it would make quite a difference in the appearance of the neighborhood and should help get the people interested in the improvement of their homes and yards. I do not think that Raymond would support such a plan. He has neither lawn nor garden; other problems are more pressing in his eyes, other needs more important.

The second incident occurred at a public gathering that I attended with Henry and some of his relatives. A small full-blood boy came up to play with Henry's six-year-old niece. The two children chattered away together, but their play was halted when it began to involve physical contact. A slightly older niece broke up the play remarking: "You can't let those full-blood children touch you. They are dirty and have germs." This reveals a difference in attitudes toward cleanliness and health that reflects a social distance between some members of the reservation population. These are differences in attitudes based on dissimilar backgrounds and experience and in no way raise a question about the sincerity of Henry's concern about Indian welfare. He sees things from one perspective, a viewpoint that might be shared with some of the men I have described, but undoubtedly at odds with the point of view of Buffalo Heart, Arrowhead and Black Plume.

I have shown some of the kinds of people I met on the Blackfeet reservation. Even when allowance is made for individual differences, these people vary considerably in experience and life styles. Several questions were posed above about these men and their modes of adaptation and adjustment to reservation life. These and similar questions guided my fieldwork. The things I learned, the data I gathered, analyzed and reported in detail elsewhere (McFee 1962), provided the foundation and support for what follows.

Fieldwork

The fieldwork for this study was done during the summers of 1959 and 1960 and as I returned to the reservation in 1963, 1967, and 1970 to increase my understanding of these people and to observe the developments in their lives over time. I began my study with the assumption that there were many kinds of people on the Blackfeet Reservation and my fieldwork procedures and data gathering methods were aimed at uncovering and demonstrating the greatest variety possible.

Field techniques included observation, sometimes as a participant in some activity, and both formal and informal interviewing. I was known to be an anthropologist interested in studying the way of life of the people on the reservation, and in this role was accepted as an observer at all public functions. It was a pleasure to accept all invitations into homes, to private parties or other gatherings. In some situations notes could be taken freely—the notebook was recognized as part of my anthropological equipment. In other situations where note taking did not seem proper, or where my role was unknown to most of the people present, no notes were taken. In such cases the conversations and activities were written up as soon as possible after the event.

During the spring and summer of 1960 I tried a sampling procedure to help insure that I was meeting a random collection of people and to further my aim of finding variety. Observation and informal methods were continued, but a major effort was put into collecting data by formal interviews, using a questionnaire with the members of a random sample of adult men in order to get comparable data from a wide range of people. Less formal methods were continued during the subsequent visits.

Guides, interpreters, or other helpers were seldom used because often the man selected for this purpose was disliked by an informant and became more of a hindrance than a help. In most cases where I was working with men in the sample, I asked for directions to where the man lived, went there, introduced myself, explained my purpose as clearly as I could and then asked the man to work through the questionnaire with me. Each was assured that his anonymity would be protected, and names were not appended to the interview notes.[2] No one refused to be interviewed. Some gave less information than others and some were more willing than others to answer questions, but all men contacted gave some answers to my questions. I encouraged people to talk at length about the questions and this, as well as the great distances I had to travel to find a specific individual

---

[2] Fictitious names are used throughout the book, except in quotations from public sources.

and the frequent necessity of making more than one trip, limited the number of interviews achieved.

The result was a set of minimum basic answers to the questionnaire from the carefully controlled sample of thirty-three men, plus a large body of additional information from most of them, usually about their experiences, family backgrounds, attitudes, goals, and values. A generally similar body of data was recorded by the less formal methods from forty-five other people, men and women. These data were expanded by observation of daily life—the context within which people did or did not do the things they said they did, agreed or disagreed vocally or visibly with each other's statements.

Other sources of information were used. Permission was obtained to examine the minutes of the tribal council meetings. Records and documents held by the tribe and agency were made available on request, and the archives of the Museum of the Plains Indian, at Browning, was a valuable source of information. In addition, tribal and Bureau of Indian Affairs officials, museum personnel, school administrators, clergymen, businessmen, and citizens gave willingly of their time to answer questions. I am still amazed and pleased at how many people were willing to put themselves out to help my study, to talk with me, and to explain their point of view, when there was no reason beyond civility for them to do so.

All these sources of information served as cross checks on the reliability of the data. The information received from one person was checked for accuracy by questions put to other people, and by comparing answers from other sources, one against the other. Lack of agreement among respondents need not be interpreted always that one was right and the other wrong—they simply disagreed. Also, much of the information could be checked out by observation. I was there and could often compare reported events with actual events, reported behavior with actual behavior. Such cross checking uncovered two cases where the answers to my questionnaire were shown to be so questionable that the data could not be used.

In Prospect

In the rest of the book I shall examine further the variations in the lives of the Blackfeet people, the social groupings that appear to be present, and the cultural characteristics of these groupings, and I shall try to explain how these came about. Toward these ends the reservation and its people are described in relation to the state and nation. The purpose of the next chapter is to note the many things the Blackfeet share with the rest of the nation, and to identify the ways in which they, as a whole, are distinguished from their non-Indian neighbors. The roots of these differences lie in the Indian heritage, described in Chapter 3, and in the history of culture change since the beginning of their white man problems, reviewed in Chapter 4. In following chapters I shall examine in more detail the social and cultural variation within the tribe that I introduced in this chapter, and shall review in the Epilogue the kinds of things that might have happened to Albert Buffalo Heart and the others between 1959 and 1970.

2

The Blackfeet Reservation
and Its People

Introduction

THE BLACKFEET INDIAN RESERVATION, as a geographical region with definable borders, can be described by the usual environmental concepts. The people who live there, however, cannot be treated so simply, because the population is greater than the membership of the Blackfeet tribe for whom the reservation was established. Both whites (about 3,500) and Indians (about 6,400) live here, and among the latter are found both members of the tribe (about 6,200 of the 10,000 plus tribal enrollment) and nonmembers (about 200).[3] Yet all share many political economic and sociocultural activities that make up the general way of life of this region, the counties within which the reservation lies, the state of Montana, and the United States of America.

This is an American community and it exhibits many of the social and cultural dimensions of such a community. But it differs because it is located on an Indian reservation and the bulk of the population is Indian. These people are Indians in addition to being citizens of the United States, Montana, county and town.

For this reason the discussion is presented in two parts: (1) a description of the geographic, economic, political and social dimensions that are shared by the greatest number of the people of the region; and (2) an examination of the unique and particular cast given to these dimensions because this is a reservation

---

[3] These and other population figures to follow are estimates based on figures from a variety of sources. Each source, the Census Bureau, the Bureau of Indian Affairs, and the Blackfeet tribe define the population differently. The tribe is concerned with tribal members; the B.I.A. with all Indians on the reservation of ¼ or more Indian descent for some purposes, or with only those Indians who hold trust lands in other cases, which means only Blackfeet but not all Blackfeet Indians. The U.S. Census figures probably include all persons who claim to be Indians, Blackfeet or other, yet may not include, by this definition, some persons who are on the tribal rolls. Land use and other economic figures, too, often differ because the information is reported in common categories, but these categories are given differing definitions.

Reservation grazing lands.

for Indians. This provides a summary of the environmental, social and cultural characteristics shared by *all tribal members* who reside on the reservation which will serve as a context for an examination of intratribal differences.

The Regional Habitat

The Blackfeet Indian Reservation, approximately 2,400 square miles in area, is located along the eastern slopes of the Rocky Mountains in northwestern Montana. It is bounded on the north by the United States-Canadian international boundary, on the west by the foothills of the Rockies, on the south by Birch Creek, and on the east by a line commencing at the junction of Cut Bank Creek and the Marias River, extended northward following the center of Cut Bank Creek for twenty miles, and then directly north to the Canadian border (see Fig. 1, frontispiece map).[4]

The land within these boundaries consists mainly of high, rolling prairies which are interrupted by numerous rivers and creeks, and occasional ponds, lakes, buttes, and hills. A narrow strip, three to ten miles wide and about sixty miles in length, along the western border includes a few barren peaks of the Rocky Mountains and the forested hills and valleys of the foothill region. The mountains reach heights of eight to ten thousand feet, but the greater portion of the reservation ranges in altitude between forty-five hundred feet in the west to thirty-five hundred feet above sea level in the east.

---

[4] The northern boundary was established by the Treaty of 1855 (U.S. Statutes XI, 1859:657), the western by the sale of the mountain portion east of the Continental Divide by an agreement ratified by Congress in 1896 (U.S. Statutes XXIX, 1897:353). The southern boundary was established by an act of Congress in 1874 (U.S. Statutes XVIII, 1875:28), and the present eastern border was set by an agreement of sale between the Blackfeet and the United States, ratified by Congress in 1888 (U.S. Statutes XXV, 1889:113).

This is predominantly short-grass prairie country. The hills are covered in late spring and summer by highly nutritious native grasses which can be mowed for hay in early fall. The uncut grasses and the stubble become dry by fall, yet they retain their nutrients and provide good grazing throughout the better part of the winter (Burlingame 1942:268, *Montana Almanac* 1957:74).

Trees are confined mostly to the immediate foothills of the Rockies where both evergreen and deciduous growth is quite dense, and to the river beds and valleys where cottonwoods and willows predominate.

The reservation and the nearby mountains support an abundant wildlife population, including birds, fish, game animals—for example, bear, deer, antelope, elk, mountain goat, and sheep—and fur bearers, such as beaver, mink, badger, muskrat, and skunk.

Hunting and fishing of game varieties is controlled on public, federal, and tribal lands by state, federal, and tribal authorities. The Indians are not subject to these regulations on the reservation and hunting and fishing provide an important supplement to the diet of many families. Some men trap for furs as either a regular or supplementary source of income, but the game population, while numerous, is not sufficient to provide subsistence for more than a few.

The climate varies with the relative distance from the mountains, but the plains part of the reservation can be characterized as a region of low precipitation and low humidity. Most of the moisture falls during the months from May to September, with lesser amounts, in the form of snow, sleet and rain, falling during the winter for an average annual total of about fourteen inches.

Lower Two Medicine Lake at dusk.

Winters are long and cold, summers short and hot. Extreme temperature changes, up to 40 degrees, occur frequently during any season and within any twenty-four hour period. Winter temperatures, from November through March, average 24 degrees Fahrenheit but may go as low as 50 degrees below zero, while frequent chinook winds often raise the temperature to 50 degrees above and rapidly melt any accumulated snow. Summer temperatures range into the 100's but again, rapid fluctuations accompany sudden storms. The earliest frosts are apt to occur in September and the latest in May, giving an average of 100 to 102 frost free days annually. The area is subject to persistent westerly winds, which can attain velocities to seventy-five miles per hour.

All in all this is a region of definite and intense weather, be it hot, cold, wet, dry, calm, or windy. A man can either lean into the wind or go with it, either seek protection from the cold and heat or endure these when necessary. The climate is an environmental phenomenon that requires active accommodation.

Regional Population and Economy

The reservation includes portions of two counties. Approximately 70 percent of Glacier county's 2,974 square mile area and perhaps 40 to 45 percent of its about 12,000 population are included within reservation boundaries. The southern portion of the reservation incorporates approximately 17 percent of Pondera county's 1,643 square mile area and about 7 percent of its estimated 7,800 population. Major concentrations of people in the area are in its small towns, the largest of which is Cut Bank, the Glacier county seat, with a population nearing 5,000 persons, followed by Browning with an estimated 2,400, East Glacier near the western reservation line with perhaps 350, and Valier, the county seat of Pondera, with about 750 persons. Other towns and hamlets will be introduced later.

The main line of the Burlington-Northern Railroad (formerly the Great Northern Railway) from Chicago to the Pacific coast transverses the Blackfeet reservation, and major east-west U.S. Route 2, parallels the railroad. Both connect Browning, the major trade center on the reservation, with cities to the east and west. U.S. Route 89 runs through the reservation from north to south, connecting Browning with Canadian highways to Banff and Calgary to the north and providing rapid access to Great Falls, Montana, 125 miles to the southeast.

An airport at Cut Bank, 36 miles east of Browning and just across the reservation border, and landing strips on the reservation, at Starr School and Babb, are available to private and nonscheduled aircraft, and an additional air strip is planned for East Glacier. Scheduled airline service is available at Kalispel, 100 miles to the west, and at Great Falls.

Telephone, telegraph, radio and television provide ties into the network of national communication. Television comes in from Great Falls and from a Canadian station at Lethbridge, Alberta. Radio stations in both nearby towns and distant cities provide a variety of programs. *The Great Falls Tribune,* a daily, and weekly publications of *The Cut Bank Pioneer Press* and Browning's *Glacier Reporter,* provide newspaper coverage for reservation readers.

Ranching and farming are the major economic pursuits of the people of these counties. The northern and western portions contain excellent natural grazing areas and are extensively used by both residents and outsiders for grazing of beef cattle, sheep, and horses. The eastern third of Glacier county and the greater portion of Pondera are subject to lesser amounts of rainfall than the more westerly portions but have more frost free days, and have been utilized to a greater extent for both dry and irrigation farming. Principal crops are wheat, barley, and hay.

Oil and natural gas production and refining are important industries, with the principal producing fields lying just to the east of the reservation limits. Producing wells on the reservation in both the northeast and southeast corners may be tapping these same fields. Oil is also being pumped in the northwest part of the reservation and there has been revived interest recently in exploring the potential of the western foothill strip. Oil lease money and bonus payments for leasing rights have provided a fluctuating but important prop to the local economy. There has been little manufacturing or lumbering, although the foothill strip, adjoining national forests and Glacier Park, has a lumber potential that is slowly being realized as the tribal mill in Browning increases its lumber output and new wood products industries are being attracted to the reservation.

The population, with an economic base of beef, wool, grain, and hay, also supports businesses, services, schools, churches, and government. Banking and financing institutions are available in Cut Bank, Browning, Conrad and Valier. Dependent children, and also those who are needy, aged, blind, or disabled are provided for by the county public welfare system established by state law and financed by tribal, county, state, and federal funds.

Like the other people of Glacier and Pondera counties the tribal members are citizens of the United States and of the state of Montana. They participate in national and state politics and in the county, precinct, school district, and town governments according to their places of residence. Reservation boundaries, it will be seen, create an added dimension. They overlie the county system but do not obliterate, change, or directly affect it. Democrats, Republicans, independents, and disinterested voters play their respective parts at all levels of politics.

The reservation region is served by the Montana State Public Schools system. County school districts, with one or two exceptions, cross reservation lines. The public schools that have Indian pupils receive federal support under the Federal Impact Area Act (PL 874) (U.S. Statutes LXIV, 1, 1950:1100) and the Johnson-O'Malley Act of 1934 (U.S. Statutes XLVIII, 1934:596) which in differing ways provide for payments to public schools in lieu of the taxes not received from Indian lands held in trust. Elementary schools, varying greatly in size, plant, and staff, are found in all settled and rural areas, and high schools are located at Browning, Cut Bank, Valier and Conrad.

Religious and other organizations here are similar to those found elsewhere in rural regions of the United States. Many denominations of Christian churches have followers here and each town has one or several churches. Similarly, one or several religious and secular lodges, service clubs, veterans' organizations, youth clubs, ranch, business, trade, and labor organizations are found in the communities of the area.

From this brief description it can be seen that the reservation shares a physical environment greatly similar to that of adjoining regions in Montana, and that its population participates in the life of county, state, and nation in much the same way as its surrounding neighbors. The people share in the United States economy; they work for wages, farm, ranch, and engage in the businesses, services, and government familiar to that economy. They send their children to the public schools, attend similar churches, and have in their midst the usual church, social and civic organizations. With few exceptions they wear the same kind of clothing, live in houses, drive automobiles, and enjoy the same radio and television programs. As I will show later, the expected rural American class structure appears to be present.

There are, however, some characteristics that make this area and its people different from the surrounding regions and populations. The major factors contributing to this separation appear to be:

1. A homeland has been reserved within the country for tribal members and the use and disposal of this land is restricted by governmental regulations.

2. The tribal members are defined *legally* as Indians. Like other ethnic groups, Indians are usually recognized by themselves and others as a separate social category. This is the *social* definition of an ethnic. In addition the Indian has been given a legal status which further sets him apart from the general citizenry.

3. The Indian is a conquered indigen, not an immigrant. This factor has social implications that require another study.

Reservation Population and Economy

The present Blackfeet reservation includes over 1½ million acres of land of which 936,848 acres are owned in trust status by individual Indians or by the Blackfeet tribe. Other than some reserve areas to be mentioned later, the balance of the land has been removed from trust as the Indian owners have been legally declared competent to handle their own financial affairs, and fee patent titles to their allotments have have been issued. In Indian bureau idiom, the land has become "alienated" from B.I.A. management. Some persons have retained their land in fee patent, while others have sold the land either to other tribal members, the tribe, or to whites. Approximately ⅓ of the land within the reservation is no longer owned by tribal members.[5]

The reservation also includes 4,982 acres which have been reserved by the United States for agency and reclamation purposes, and about 11,000 acres of submarginal government land leased to the tribe and re-leased by it to ranchers for grazing use. The lands have been given a use classification according to soil, vegetation, and availability of water, and the leasing of land to an ultimate user is governed by these classifications.

---

[5] These land use figures are approximate, compiled from Fagg and Associates (1970:47) and unpublished B.I.A. Budget projections. Such figures change from year to year as individuals remove their lands from trust and, perhaps, offer it for sale.

The ownership of mineral rights on reservation lands is complex. The original allotment under the Act of 1907, to be discussed later, vested both surface and mineral rights in the allottee. The 1919 allotment reserved the mineral rights of the newly allotted land in the name of the tribe. Subsequent issuance of fee patents and the sales of fee patent lands have included or excluded mineral rights according to the terms of each transaction so that no exact figure for Indian ownership of mineral rights is available.

Reservation, then, means land, "a part of the public domain, set aside for use and occupation by a group of Indians" (Federal Indian Law 1958:20). The inhabitants are not restricted to the reservation; they can come and go at will, but on the reservation they are subject to controls that have developed around use of the reservation lands. Certain legal privileges and restrictions have developed from both the interpretations of federal trust obligations and the past history of federal-Indian relations.

The Blackfeet reservation differs from the surrounding region, then, because approximately ⅔ of the land is held in trust either for individual allottees or the tribe, and its use is governed by federal laws and directives that do not apply outside the reservation. Alienated lands are not affected directly by such regulations, but a person owning such land finds that problems arising over such things as boundaries, trespass, water rights and rights-of-way involve him with trust regulations. Other ramifications of reservation land and related restrictions will be examined in what follows.

An Indian is a person defined as such by law. But the law has been built over time from decisions made in individual cases, so that it is difficult to write an all-inclusive definition. In general a person can be defined as an Indian if he qualifies on two counts: "(a) that some of his ancestors lived in America before its discovery by the Europeans, and (b) that the individual is considered an 'Indian' by the community in which he lives" (Federal Indian Law 1958:6).

A Blackfeet Indian and a member of the Blackfeet tribe is defined more specifically. Present-day tribal membership is restricted by the Blackfeet Indian Tribal Constitution to persons "of Indian blood whose names appear on the official census roll of the tribe as of January 1, 1935, . . . [and] all children born to any blood member . . . maintaining a legal residence within the territory of the reservation at the time of such birth" (Blackfeet Constitution 1936:1). No limitation was imposed by a necessary degree of Blackfeet descent or "blood" until 1962 when the tribal constitution was amended to require ¼ or more blood quantum for membership thereafter.

An Indian reservation, by its being, introduces legal qualifications that further set apart the area and the people. This is "Indian country," a concept that has been given legal currency. The definitions are diverse and complex, but in essence, Indian country is land owned by, or reserved for, Indians and subject to the jurisdiction of the United States. The reservation is one form of Indian country, and the federal government has jurisdiction over trust land and over any problems arising from its occupancy, use, or conveyance. It has reserved jurisdiction over ten "major crimes" (murder, manslaughter, rape, assault with intent to kill, arson, burglary, larceny, robbery, incest, and assault with a dangerous weapon) committed

Flood house: A typical house provided under the Rehabilitation program to replace housing destroyed in the flood of 1964.

by Indians against Indians in Indian country (Federal Indian Law 1958:320). Yet Indian country remains a part of the state in which it is located and non-Indians are subject to all state laws. Indians are subject to state laws only in matters not legally reserved to the federal government or, by its regulations, to the tribe. Indians also are subject to state law when not in Indian country. The complications arising from such overlapping jurisdictions are considered later in this chapter. (See Brophy and Aberle 1966:Chapter 2 for further discussion of these complications.)

The reservation population is quite dispersed. Many families live on their ranches, farms, or allotments along the stream valleys or scattered on the broad flats; others live in houses clustered together in towns and hamlets. Many details of both topography and settlement patterns were altered drastically in June of 1964. Heavy rains and rapidly melting snowpacks in the mountains caused major floods throughout western Montana. All creeks and rivers on the reservation overflowed their banks and two irrigation dams broke, releasing torrents of water into Two Medicine River and Birch Creek. Lives were lost and homes and ranches of many years standing were destroyed. This resulted in population shifts and changes in residential patterns the full effects of which are still evolving. One noticeable shift has been the movement of people from some of the rural districts into new homes in Browning, and similar shifts from the river and stream valleys into clusters of new houses at Starr School and Babb.

The regions of scattered dwellings are named after the rivers or creeks along which they are located—for example, Two Medicine, Badger Creek, Little

Badger, Birch Creek, Milk River—or for rail stations, schools, and historical characteristics—for example, Durham, Meriwether, Seville, Pontrasina, Badger-Fisher, and Old Agency. Browning, the agency town, and East Glacier, at the southeastern entrance to Glacier National Park, have been mentioned already. Other towns are Babb, Starr School, Blackfoot, and Heart Butte.

Babb, near the northwestern corner of the reservation, consists of scattered homes, a post office, churches, elementary school, motel, grocery store, and several cafes and bars. It serves as a tourist stop and as a community center for the approximately five hundred people who live in the surrounding countryside.

Starr School is a hamlet located seven miles northeast of Browning on Cut Bank Creek. Several houses are grouped around a school, a Catholic church, a Baptist church, and a community hall, and others are scattered up and down the creek. Since the 1964 flood the hamlet has been enlarged by the addition of flood rehabilitation homes and houses built under other tribal programs arranged in city block fashion with paved street, curbs, fire hydrants and common water and sewer service. This is a center of a largely full-blood population of about two hundred people.

Blackfoot is a rail point eight miles east of Browning consisting of a post office, stock loading pens and a few houses.

Heart Butte, in the southern tip of the reservation is another center of full-blood population. An elementary school, Catholic church, combination post office and store, a community hall, and scattered houses form the community center for the three to four hundred people living in this part of the reservation. The people go either to Browning, thirty-six miles north, or to Conrad or Valier for business and shopping requirements.

The old Cut Bank Indian Boarding School, on Cut Bank Creek seven miles north of Browning, is now a dormitory for boys and girls of elementary school age who for reasons of isolation, broken homes, or other problems cannot live at home during the time schools are in session. These children are taken by bus to the public schools in Browning.

School and community hall at Starr School.

The tribe is both a political entity with legislative, judicial, and executive powers, and a business corporation. The Corporate Charter of the Blackfeet Tribe establishes the tribe's sphere of authority over the handling of funds and the use of tribal assets for the benefit of its members. All tribal members are shareholders in the corporation and have a vote in its affairs. The nine members of the tribal council direct both the political and business affairs of the tribe and the corporation (U.S., Blackfeet Corporate Charter 1936).

Councilmen are elected by the secret ballot of eligible tribal members and serve for a period of two years. Each council supervises the voting and defines the boundaries of the election districts for the election of its successor body. Four districts are regularly recognized and each is served by an established number of councilmen. Since an amendment to the tribal constitution in 1964 reducing the Council from thirteen to nine members, Browning district is represented by three councilmen, and Seville, Heart Butte and Old Agency by two each (*Glacier Reporter,* July 2, 1964). Candidates file for election in the district in which they reside, but each voter votes for candidates from all districts. Residents of one district, therefore, may have a strong voice in deciding who will represent the voters of another district.

The tribal council elects its own officers, appoints its own court officers and police, and hires its secretarial and administrative staff. This body has been given broad powers for political and economic action within limits reserved by law to the Bureau of Indian Affairs and the Department of the Interior. Tribal actions concerning disposal of trust lands, and involving tribal credit or expenditures above an established amount are subject to review or approval by the Commissioner of Indian Affairs or his representatives.

Tribal membership legally defines a person as a Blackfeet Indian, and such membership provides a set of privileges and liabilities not shared by nonmembers. The income derived by a tribal member from crops raised on trust land, or the proceeds from the sale of stock grazed on trust land, are not subject to federal income taxes (Federal Indian Law 1958:883). All lands held in trust by the federal government are exempt from local and state property taxes. Qualified tribal members are given preference over nonmembers in the awarding of grazing or farming leases of trust land, and tribal members, like other Indians of ¼ or more degree Indian descent, are given a preference credit in applications for employment by the Bureau of Indian Affairs. These are a few of the privileges that go with tribal membership. As members of the corporation, the people also share in the earnings of the corporation. Occasionally, more frequently in the past when oil exploration was more active, the council votes a per capita payment as a distribution of tribal income in excess of that required for the operational expenses.

Such privileges are offset by some liabilities—particularly for men who feel competent to handle their own affairs. Trust lands must be leased through the agency land office and all use, leasing, procurement of fee patent titles, and sale of land come under government supervision. The man who has his land held in trust must request and receive permission to make certain uses of his land, have his plans reviewed and approved more often, go through more red tape, than the man who has a fee patent title to his land.

The allotment acts provided that the inheritance laws of the state should govern the distribution of allotted lands upon the death of an allottee. The laws of Montana recognize disposal of property by will, and the federal government recognizes the transfer of trust title, in whole or in part, by will. In the absence of a will, state laws define the succession and the share of an estate each heir shall receive. The result of fifty years or more of practice has been an increased fragmentation of original allotments to the point where an allotment may have as many as fifty owners, or have been portioned out into a series of plots too small to serve economic ends. The B.I.A. recently estimated that about 475,000 acres of reservation trust land had multiple owners (Blackfeet Agency FY 1972 Budget and Program Memorandum). The agency is charged with the duty of keeping records of such changes in ownership, and with leasing such lands for the benefit of the owners. A lease requires acquiescence of many owners and the monies received must be credited to the accounts of all heirs. Until more people make wills, and more frequently pass undivided ownership to fewer people, the land fragmentation will continue to snowball and the work load of the agency will increase in proportion. This is the "heirship land" problem that plagues the economies of most Indian reservations where tribal lands were alloted to individual owners.

The trust status of the land makes it poor security for mortgages so it is difficult for the owner of such land to borrow money for short or long-term operating expenses and capital improvements. The inability to secure ready financing, the multiple ownership situation, plus other factors that will be introduced later, have contributed to the present economic condition of the tribal members.

In 1962 I wrote:

On February 1960 in an area in which the predominant industries are agriculture and stock raising, it was reported [in unpublished tribal documents] that only 40 tribal members are farm operators, and of this number it is estimated that perhaps only 10 are farming sufficient acreage to be considered an economic unit. The farming family's income must be supplemented by wage work. One hundred and fifty families of tribal members are listed as ranchers, with an average of 85 head of beef cattle, or equivalent in sheep. A conservative estimate of the stock required for an economic unit is 100 head, so many of these people may also need supplemental income. It was estimated that another 27 families are self-supporting, or have received the financing which should make them self-supporting, in business, other non-agricultural enterprises, or as regularly employed wage earners.

In a credit appraisal of an estimated 1,200 Blackfeet families, 700 families were listed as having poor security risks. These latter had neither the experience nor the aptitude, neither the training nor the inclination, to operate a going enterprise or meet the standards of financial responsibility set by the council for prospective clients of a Revolving Loan Fund. These figures indicate that approximately 983 families of the tribe are unable to be self-supporting and depend upon casual labor, income from the leasing of lands if they have land, tribal per-capita payments and welfare for minimum subsistence.

Figures on non-Indian use of reservation land reveal the gap between Indian use and the potential of the region. Seventy-five non-Indian operators lease grazing land for stock enterprises, with an average of 5,067 acres each as compared to an average of 2,666 among the 150 Indian operators. One hundred seventy-five non-Indian farmers cultivate farms that average 560 acres each as compared to an average farm size of 200 acres for the 40 Indian farmers. The non-Indians are operating economic units on land leased from Indian owners. Many more Indian families could be self-supporting on their own land if problems of land ownership, financing, and training are ever solved, yet it is obvious that this land base is insufficient to support the population by ranching and farming alone (McFee 1962:40–41).

Comparable current figures are not available, but it is my impression that little has changed. Fagg & Associates (1970:71) report on 713 families of which 392 have incomes of less than $3,000 (median $2,716). This differs from another 1968 report showing about 62 percent of 1,830 families earning under $3,000 and a median annual income of $1,700 (Blackfeet Indian Reservation—City of Browning "Model City" Application 1968:41).

This does not mean that nothing has changed; it has. The population has increased, some people have improved their lot, and others have fallen on hard times. New ranches and farms have been started, others are in the process of breaking up. The sum of all this, however, is a rather bleak economic picture for the reservation as a whole for which there is no simple explanation. It reflects legal, social, cultural, and historical factors that I will discuss in Chapters 3 and 4.

The reservation and tribal organization bring a member into a further regional political alignment, in many respects akin to a municipal political division. The Indian Reorganization Act of 1934 and subsequent legislation have given to the tribe a broader range of powers than is usually enjoyed by a local jurisdiction. But for a few limitations and some federal review, the tribe is autonomous.

Tribal courts are given jurisdiction over civil and criminal actions brought by an Indian against another Indian. The right of jurisdiction in the case of the "ten major crimes" committed by Indians on Indians reservations has been reserved by the federal courts, but the balance of law and order matters are under tribal control. These are not subject to state or county regulation unless specifically turned over to such authorities, or shared concurrently with them, by an act of the tribal council and by an acceptance of these obligations by the county or state (Federal Indian Law 1958:319).

Non-Indians living on the reservation are subject to county and state laws and enforcement. They are affected, in addition, by tribal regulations. The tribe can regulate land use and impose taxes on nonmembers in the form of business licenses, camping fees, and hunting and fishing fees.

This overlapping jurisdiction in the area of law and order makes for a complex problem of law enforcement and requires guarded cooperation between tribal, county, state, and federal enforcement agencies. A breach of peace or a crime must be analyzed according to where it happened and who was involved in order to determine what level of enforcement has jurisdiction. Do you call the tribal police, the sheriff, the state highway patrol, or perhaps the F.B.I. agent? Actions by other than the correct officers must be sanctioned by immediate or previous agreement among the various governing bodies.

The tribal and federal regulations also affect nonmembers whenever these latter become involved in leases or other financial dealings with Indians, or where nonmembers become a party, injured or the injurer, in legal disputes, crime, or misdemeanors with members of the tribe.

Tribal members vary greatly in the degree to which they are affected by being both "Indians" and residents of the reservation. These differences are of major importance to this study and are given careful examination in later chapters. There are, however, some general results that are common to all.

There are a few times when all members recognize themselves as Indians. This unity of identification is most often expressed at tribal election time, when the rallying cry is for "Indians" to support the candidate who will protect the tribal land base from exploitation by the "white man." Indian identification comes to the fore in any discussion of land leasing and use where the tribal member may be in competition with a nonmember. Men who otherwise seldom identify as Indians remark that they have trouble in leasing land. "We Indians are supposed to have priority, but it's hard to get a lease away from a white man." Another informant complained: "I have to pay 45¢ an acre for grazing land, while the white man gets it for 31¢." I found no evidence to support this charge; the important point here is that it is "We Indians" who believe this. Members are Indians according to their interests when reservation policies and programs are considered detrimental to those interests. The government and the "white" man become the field against which common Indian identification stands out.

The tribal members are also affected when identified as Indians" by their white neighbors. A member runs the risk of meeting discrimination in social, political, and economic spheres because people categorize him, and act toward him, in terms of stereotype. He is an "Indian" regardless of the degree of discrepancy between the individual and the stereotype. Differences in physical appearance, education, speech, dress, manners, and wealth may temper the stereotyping of individuals, but the white man tends to act first according to the popular idea of what is an "Indian," and then add his qualifications: "He's a white Indian." "He's a good Indian." "Of course he is just a little bit Indian." "They are good neighbors even if they are Indians." Men of minimal Indian descent, who neither know nor express any Blackfeet cultural characteristics, are still remembered as Indians if they retain tribal membership and live on the reservation. One of these men told of a remark that came back to him after he had been given a well-earned political appointment in a town adjoining the reservation. A leading citizen was said to have remarked: "It's getting to be a fine state of affairs when we have to go down on the reservation and bring back an Indian to run that office." Differences in the discrimination encountered by tribal members will be examined in later chapters.

Summary

The Blackfeet share much of the way of life of their white rural neighbors, but differ from them by being Indians and residents of an Indian reservation. The general ecological and social characteristics shared by all tribal members have been described and some intratribal differences have been indicated. The present conditions have developed during the course of prolonged contact between the members of two societies with differing cultures—the Blackfeet Tribe and the United States.

Before examining the variation to be found among the reservation population and what this means, I will explore its historical antecedents; the Blackfeet culture of mid-nineteenth century, before the destruction of its buffalo hunting subsistence base, and the years of attempts at readaptation to the changing economy and the increased engulfment, direction and control by the white men who were the major agents for change.

3

Horse and Buffalo Days:
1850-1880

Introduction

"PEOPLE LIVED LONG LIVES in the old days before the white man came," said Arrowhead. "They didn't get sick in those days." Earlier I said that he and his friends were recalling a legendary past, but it was more than that. Arrowhead was voicing an old ideal. In both myth and ethnography such phrases are repeated. People prayed for protection in times of trouble, for good health and a long life. Names were given to assure these blessings. Yet people knew that in reality life was often harsh; men faced dangers in the hunt and in war; disease did strike; people became weak and infirm with advancing age. They prayed that they might escape these misfortunes. They knew too that a man would be judged to be less than a man if he failed to avenge the death of a kinsman or comrade, if he were unwilling to risk the dangers of a horse raid to acquire wealth and fame. Hunting too had its dangers, but a man must be a good provider. So children were taught to honor, emulate and support those who faced such dangers, to face up to the real world but to hope and pray for the ideal. This led to a counter view that expressed the recognition of the reality that went hand in hand with the ideal. Young men were told that it was better to die young in prestigious battle than to live on into the tribulations of old age (Grinnell 1907:189–190; Ewers 1958:103, 324). This expression of an old ideal by Arrowhead revealed a bit of the past that lives on in slightly altered form among some members of the Black-feet tribe today. These inconsistencies were part of the reality of prereservation days, long after Indian life had been affected by European influence, yet before the Blackfeet had fully recognized the immensity of their white man problem.

The Blackfeet Indians probably saw their first white man during the mid-eighteenth century, and the earliest unqualified extensive record of contact was that of David Thompson, an explorer for the Hudson's Bay Company, who at the age of seventeen, spent the winter of 1787–1788 with a Piegan Blackfeet band along the Bow River in what is now southwestern Alberta (Glover 1962:48). Thomp-

262

son found that horses, guns, metal, smallpox, and a few other elements of European culture had preceded him by at least fifty years as a result of contact and trade with neighboring Indian tribes (Glover 1962:240–251). The earlier indirect influence, and the later increasing association with the European immigrants led to extensive changes in Blackfeet culture, but on the whole the Indians made an orderly adaptation to the changing ecological and cultural conditions for another seventy years or so after Thompson's visit (Ewers 1955, Lewis 1942, Wilson 1963). The Blackfeet experienced a period of cultural elaboration rather than of disruption and decline, so that the Piegan and the other Blackfeet divisions—the Blood and the Northern Blackfoot, who later came under Canadian jurisdiction—were at the height of their power at mid-nineteenth century.

The closing decades of that century, however, were times of radical change. The buffalo, the keystone of the Blackfeet economy, were decimated and by 1884 the Indians had become dependent upon the United States government for subsistence. The Piegan were confined to a reservation, and both ecological conditions and the policies of the dominant society forced further changes upon them.

Seventy-five years later, when I began my fieldwork among them, the Blackfeet tribe remained in a small portion of its original territory, but the intervening events had markedly changed its composition, social organization and cultural characteristics. The tribe was no longer the homogeneous group described by the early writers. Its members reflected the years of changes brought about as people of two societies, each organized and guided by differing cultural directives, adjusted to each other and to changing conditions. Even a casual observer of the reservation scene could note a wide range of differences in appearance, speech, dress, and economic adjustment among the tribal population; could recognize some of the kinds of people described in Chapter 1.

History before 1850

The Blackfeet spoke a language of the Algonkian stock, a linguistic affiliation that has been the basis for inferring that they had migrated into the plains from the northeastern woodlands in precontact times. Early migration problems are still unsolved, but Thompson's host during his winter visit, Saukamappee, an elderly Cree living with the Piegan, recalled how in his youth he had accompanied his father and other Cree warriors on a journey to join the Piegan and other allies in an attack on an encampment of "the Snake Indians on the Plains of the Eagle Hill. . . ." The Piegan were found camped along the north bank of the North Saskatchewan River, across from the Eagle Hills (Glover 1962:241), which would place them somewhat north and west of present-day Saskatoon. Both Ewers (1955:300) and Lewis (1942:10) use this evidence to infer that this region was Piegan hunting territory early in the eighteenth century, and noting that the usual relative positions of the Blackfeet divisions put the Piegan in the van of a subsequent movement west and south to the Rocky Mountains and into what is now Montana. It was here that they were studied by Grinnell, McClintock, Curtis, Uhlenbeck, DeJong, and Wissler who visited the reservation during the two decades

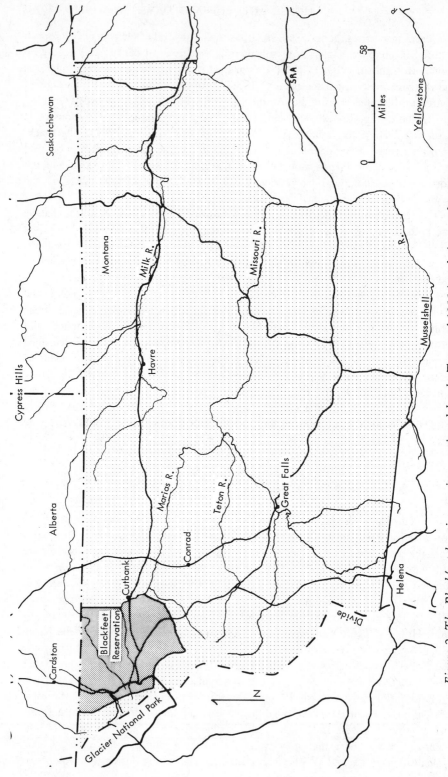

Figure 2. *The Blackfeet hunting territory assigned by the Treaty of 1855 in relation to the present reservation.*

following the destruction of the buffalo to study and record aspects of the classic Blackfeet culture. The following description is based upon their published works and upon the writings of Ewers who has extended and synthesized much of the earlier work (these sources are included among the Recommended Readings).[6]

By 1850, then, the Piegan ranged within a portion of the territory, roughly 27,500 square miles in extent, assigned to them a few years later by the treaty of 1855 (Fig. 2)—a hunting territory bounded on the west by the Rocky Mountains, on the north by the U.S.-Canadian border, on the south by the Musselshell River and on the east by an undetermined line at about 109.5 longitude which included the Sweetgrass Hills and the Bearpaw Mountains (Ewers 1958:122–123; Kappler 1903:553). The topography and climate was generally similar to that of the present reservation.

Economy

For the Blackfeet of prereservation days the buffalo was the major source of food, shelter, clothing, tools, and ornamentation. Ewers (1955:149–152) has given the most complete review of the many uses of the animal indicating that most all fleshy parts were eaten, sometimes raw, most frequently cooked, during the times of the year that buffalo could be hunted. Meat was dried and stored, sometimes mixed and pounded with fat and dried berries to make pemmican, both effective ways of preservation for use during the winter months when hunting was difficult. In addition, Ewers lists eighty-seven nonfood uses of the buffalo including the manufacture of tepee covers, bedding, shields, some articles of clothing, containers, straps and thongs from the hides, cups, ladles and spoons from the horns, tools of bone, fuel from dung, ornaments from hair, hide and horn and so on down to using the tail attached to a stick for a fly brush. In the trading days, too, the meat and hides of the buffalo could be used to gain guns, ammunition, utensils, knives, axes, blankets, coffee, tea, tobacco, whiskey, and clothing from the white traders. Roots, berries, elk, deer, rabbits, fish, eggs of ducks and geese and occasionally the birds themselves were used as food, and their hides, horn, antlers, bone, feathers, along with grasses, willows, and so forth, supplemented these nonfood products of the buffalo. It seems fair to say that the buffalo was the bulwark of the Blackfeet economy and, as will be shown later, much if not most of the culture—other practices, beliefs, even the values by which people were measured—were expressions of a way of life built on hunting buffalo.

The horse had assumed great importance in Blackfeet life since its intro-

---

[6] Grinnell studied the Blackfeet during the years between 1885 and 1907. McClintock first visited the reservation in 1896 and subsequently spent many summers living and studying among the Indians until 1910. Curtis was a frequent visitor between 1898 and 1910, while Uhlenbeck and DeJong conducted linguistic and folklore research in the Heart Butte and Two Medicine regions in 1911 and 1912. Wissler, with the help of D. C. Duvall, did fieldwork during the decade from 1903 to 1913. As curator of the Museum of the Plains Indian, Ewers lived in Browning from 1941 to 1944 and returned for fieldwork again during 1947. Through his own fieldwork and extensive study of ethnological and ethnohistorical sources, he has been able to extend, synthesize and reinterpret what is known of this culture.

duction to these Indians sometime between 1725 and 1750. From one perspective the horse, its ownership and use, was another hallmark of Blackfeet culture, but horses too were of value largely because of the buffalo and its place in the economy. Horses were a major tool of production.

Possession of horses increased the range and the effectiveness of hunting activities. Horses could carry more provisions than could dogs and people, allowing a man to accumulate more posessions, both material items of Indian manufacture and others gained by the more frequent and efficient trading horses made possible. At least one limitation on seasonal migrations was imposed by horse ownership. The movements of people, influenced by the migrations of the buffalo, the requirements for water, protection from the weather and enemies also had to be guided by the requirements of feed, shelter and protection for the horses.

The gun was another productive tool but did not equal the importance of horses in the subsistence pattern of the Indians, largely because the smooth-bore flintlock guns they owned, prior to the introduction of the repeating rifle in about 1870, were inferior to the bow for hunting buffalo.

In general the decisions about how many people should camp together and the techniques to be used in hunting were based on the seasons of the year and the migration patterns of the buffalo. The sequence of development of the animal from winter leanness to summer prime, the seasonal condition of hides for differing uses, the range and weather conditions and the seasonal migrations of the herds all played important parts in determining the hunting techniques to be employed.

Ewers (1955:124–129) divided the yearly round into four general divisions:

1. A winter period of five to seven months during which the small bands of Indians camped in sheltered valleys, subsisting on stored dried provisions and whatever game could be killed by small groups of men hunting on foot or on horseback, depending on the weather conditions. This was a period during which the Blackfeet were relatively sedentary, and camps were moved only as pasture, game, and fuel supplies were depleted in their valley.

2. A hunting and gathering season of approximately two months in duration started with the advent of spring. At this time of the year the buffalo began their migrations away from the sheltering river valleys toward the pastures to the east and north. The grasses and root plants began to germinate, and the Blackfeet, too, left their winter camps to hunt and collect in their separate bands.

3. During the summer the buffalo were out on the plains in great numbers, and the scattered bands of Indians came together as a tribe for a cooperative summer hunt. Buffalo bulls were at their prime during this two to three month summer season and were killed for fresh meat; hides were collected for use as robes, tepee covers, clothing and for trade. This was also the season for gathering berries and other plant products. This coming together of the bands provided for important social and ceremonial activities that I will discuss later.

4. A fall period of two to three months in length followed the breakup of the summer camp and continued until the arrival of winter storms forced the people again into winter camps. This was a season of active buffalo hunting by

individuals and small groups. The cows were in prime condition and the Blackfeet concentrated on gathering the meat and berries to be dried and stored for winter use.

The most common technique for hunting buffalo during the late nineteenth century was the chase in which mounted hunters followed the herd and each man selected an animal, rode it down and killed it. By this time the Piegan had abandoned the earlier method of driving the herds into confining canyons, compounds or over a cliff to be killed and butchered below. Men hunted on foot only when they lacked a buffalo hunting horse, or when heavy snowfall made horse travel impossible. Although other animals might be hunted on foot, the horse was of major importance in hunting buffalo—the Blackfeet "staff of life."

Horses, then, were a form of production capital, and their importance led to another form of economic pursuit, the horse raid. A man could build a horse herd by buying animals from his neighbors, by having them given to him, by natural increase among his already acquired stock, or by raiding and taking horses from enemy camps. This was a dangerous but quick way to build capital, and success in such dangerous pursuits added to a person's prestige, so horse raiding became ". . . an established industry among the Blackfeet" (Grinnell 1907:244).

Labor was quite sharply divided by sex. Men were the hunters and defenders, women the collectors and manual laborers. In addition to hunting and fighting, men butchered the animals while on the hunt, made their weapons, shields, and drums, and painted designs on these. They also made pipes, horn utensils and often their own ornaments, leggings, and coats.

Women's work makes a longer list. They occasionally helped with light butchering when they accompanied a hunt, but did all butchering, preparing and preserving of meat once it had been brought to camp. Women gathered plant foods, prepared meals, made the clothing, packed, moved, and unpacked provisions and possessions, carried wood and water, cut tepee poles, put up and dismantled the tepees, made and decorated leather carrying bags (parfleches) and other containers, manufactured utensils, dressed and tanned skins and hides, made saddles and horse gear, made travois, and reared the children.

It would appear that the women did the most "work," which may be overlooking the fact that hunting, an avocation for us, was often an arduous occupation. Nonetheless, it was true that men had more time for socializing. Young men often dressed up in their paint and finest clothing, to stroll around the camp in order to be admired by the girls; and the older men spent much of their leisure time in feasting one another.

A similar division of labor and male advantage was a part of childhood. Young boys were free to play, until as they grew older they were given the task of caring for the horses. The games they played were preparation for hunting and raiding. At a much earlier age girls began to carry wood and water, do light gathering and collecting, and take lessons in the preparation of foods, clothing and in dressing hides—learning the women's work.

The Blackfeet were much concerned with personal property and had their own definition of what it entailed. Resources were unowned, food and materials were open equally to all according to one's energy and ability. Tribes, bands, and even families might have their favorite and usual area within which to hunt, but these ties to a territory were unrelated to ideas of ownership of land, game or plants. Once labor had been expended, however—an animal killed, a horse stolen, a plant gathered, a stick or stone picked up, or a dream dreamed—the product was imbued with value and became personal property.

It is possible to separate food from other types of property because it was not owned by individuals in the same way as were other goods. Food "belonged" to the collector but was put in charge of the women of the collector's own or adopted family upon return to camp. Food then belonged to the family, yet even this title was clouded by a series of social obligations. A hunter was obliged to share with anyone who had helped him in the kill, with the man whose horse he had borrowed, or with the man from whom he had obtained hunting power. He was expected to provide some part of the meat for the sick or disabled, and he also might have had obligations to some of his in-laws. The family used what remained. In times of famine these rules were set aside and food became band property to be shared by all. Food had additional uses, both ceremonial and social—feasts were an important part of many rituals, to be described later, and as part of the everyday social life of the men, as noted above.

Horses and other goods were individually owned by men, women or children. Personal dreams, experiences, exploits, and the symbols of these were also personal property and all could be transferred—sold, exchanged, given, or loaned, in whole or in part—by one person to another. These other goods appear to have been free of forced sharing in times of scarcity. The rule appears to have been that none should starve, but other needs of the poor had to be met by appeals to the generosity of those who had more. The unfortunate were cared for but usually given worn or castoff clothing, tepee covers, tools, robes, and so on, rarely things of much value.

Goods other than food were used by their owners or were used as exchange goods. Exchange might be for economic reasons, as when a man gave a horse to a medicine man for a cure, or to get a charm to insure success in horse stealing, war, or other endeavor. Goods might be given in exchange for the supernatural power of another. One kind of property could be used to purchase another, for example, furs and guns for horses, or horses for tepee covers. Another type of transfer was for ritual reasons, as when goods were offered to the sun in the Sun Dance, to ghosts or other spirit forces in propitiation, petition, or thanksgiving. Here too could be classified the practice of placing some of the property of a deceased with his body in order that he might have the use of such things in the next world.

A third use, more difficult to classify, would be the exchange of property in gambling. The Blackfeet were avid gamblers and some on occasion were known to have gambled away all their possessions.

The fourth use of property was its transfer, by gift or exchange, in order to gain increased prestige and status. Among the Blackfeet property was accumulated and wealth created, to be used for the demonstration of generosity. A man secured horses and other goods in order to give them away. He loaned a horse to another hunter, in part to share in the meat, in part to create an obligation for a repayment, but this act was also a display of generosity toward one of less wealth and thus established a moral obligation that could be converted later into support for one's opinions in council. A man of property gained position within his band by sharing generously with those less fortunate than himself, and gained stature within the tribe by feasting members of other bands and the giving of gifts to the leaders of other bands. *Generosity was a major requisite for prestige and status.*

In summary, resources were unowned, food and materials were open equally to all according to his energy and ability. Food became the property of the one who took it, to be shared first with his family, then with others to whom he might be obligated and with the unfortunate. In times of famine, food became band property to be shared by all.

Horses and other material goods were individually owned and were bought and sold, borrowed and given. Personal dreams, experiences, exploits and the symbols of these were also personal property and could be transferred by one person to another in exchange for other goods.

The distribution system fostered individual gain and accumulation. The consumption system countered this by imposing social sanctions that rewarded charity and generosity with prestige and status. This force will be examined further.

Social Organization

A child born to Blackfeet parents began early to learn the patterns of social interaction. He was first of all a member of a household—the occupants of a single tepee—which included the parents, unmarried brothers and sisters, and perhaps one or two other relatives as well, such as a grandparent, a maiden aunt, or other wives of the household head.

As the child grew older it learned that its family was the minimal economic unit of the Blackfeet society. The father was the decision maker, the one responsible for the protection and good behavior of its members; the first wife was the owner of the tepee, responsible for the other wives if any, for the care of the children, maintenance of the tepee and other duties within the women's realm. The child learned too about other kinsmen, that he had important relatives on both sides of the family—in other words, kin were recognized bilaterally.

As acquaintances were made beyond the household, he or she learned that there were other families that regularly lived near and traveled with one's own. These were members of the band, the day in and day out hunting and gathering group that was the basic economic and political unit of the Blackfeet. It was the band that moved according to the requirements of the yearly round, camped alone through the winter, joined with other bands in the summer for the tribal hunt. The child learned the band name and identified with it: he was a child of his parents and one of the Small Robes, Skunks, Lone Eaters or whatever his band might be (see Grinnell 1907:208–210 for one listing of band names). Over the years he learned too that the people who gathered during the summer hunt were fellow Piegan, and that among other people encountered on occasion were some who spoke his language, did things his way, were Blackfeet of the other divisions—the

Siksika and the Kainah—who often came to the aid of the Piegan in times of conflict.

While kin ties were basic to band formation, friendship and self-interest played a part as well, and people changed bands when they felt it advantageous to do so. Ewers believes that this shifting band allegiance had developed with the inequal distribution of wealth that followed the acquisition of the horse. Poor people became more dependent upon the generosity of the wealthy few and attached themselves to the bands of those men who could best provide for them.

Band membership then was based first of all upon kin ties, but with no absolute rule of descent. Wives usually joined the band of their husbands and children belonged to that of their father, but it was not unusual for a man to join his wife's group. A widow could choose to remain in her husband's band or to return to that of her parents. A man could change band affiliation "even in middle life . . ." (Wissler 1911:19). Other persons attached themselves to the band for various reasons, and long residence with a band, and acceptance by its members, was tantamount to band membership.

The tribe was a larger association of individual bands whose members recognized common ties of language, kinship and culture. It was an organized unit only during the few weeks of the summer hunt, and tribal discipline operated only at this time. Even here the bands retained their spatial and functional autonomy; each band had it habitual place in the camp circle and continued to operate as an economic and political unit with only a part of its powers surrendered to the tribal organization.

Like other Plains Indians, the Piegan had a series of men's organizations, or societies, of which there were three basic types: age-graded warrior societies, religious societies and cults, and the less formal dance association.

The named warrior societies (Mosquitoes, Pigeons, Braves, All-Crazy Dogs, etc.) were corporate groups, that is, they continued over time, surviving the individual members. Groups of young men of a similar age sometimes started a new society, or, more usually, got together and bought memberships in an ongoing society. Similarly the old members would in turn buy into the next age-rank. The transfer was between individuals and such purchases could occur at any time. It was customary, however, for several men to transfer at the same time. Periodic transfers of this kind made possible a progressive movement of membership from a lower to a higher ranking society as men grew older. The oldest society might continue as its ranks were renewed from below, or eventually die out as its members passed away.

These were the groups granted policing powers at the summer encampment. In addition they served to promote the military spirit of the members through war games and intersociety competition in races, dancing and games.

The medicine men's societies and related cults were less formally organized gatherings of men who owned important medicine bundles and powers. These men conferred together to aid in the organization and presentation of the Sun Dance and to promote the spiritual and material welfare of the tribe. The dance organizations were social clubs made up of young men who organized for the purpose of staging social dances during the time of the summer encampment.

Membership in one or more of these organizations created loyalties that cut across the ties of kinship and band affiliation, and helped to contribute to tribal solidarity. In other words, a person identified first with his kinsmen and with his band, but later established additional and potentially conflicting ties of loyalty by marrying someone from another band and by membership in a society that drew its members from many bands.

Band and tribal leadership was not inherited but open to all who could command a following. A band headman gained a position of influence by displaying the qualities (see below) valued in his society and by his continued exercise of these attributes. His influence depended upon his power to persuade others, and the support of many followers increased this ability. He conferred with family heads and all decisions were reached by mutual agreement.

Band leaders formed a council during the tribal encampment and one of them, by election or selection, came to be considered the chief of the tribe. The chief had no institutionalized authority and little disciplining power. His chiefly functions were to guide the council to agreement and to mediate in cases of conflict and uncertainty.

There were no formalized institutions for social control except for the policing duties of the associations under special regulations put into effect at the summer encampment. Conflict was first of all a matter between individuals, then a concern of the families and finally of the bands. The delinquent person was cautioned, ridiculed, gossiped about, and shamed into conformity. Ostracism and violence were the ultimate penalties within the band, but usually gossip and shame served to restore order. Boys and girls growing up in Piegan society were urged to achieve the ideals of that society. Boys were told to be brave, to be good fighters, able to defend themselves against their peers and to protect younger children. They were praised for skills and daring, even for sexual exploits. Girls were urged to be quiet, dutiful, sober, hard-working, and to protect their virginity.[7] Both were rewarded with praise when they achieved, and punished with sarcasm and gossiped about when they misbehaved or failed. These sanctions contributed to a developing concern with their own identity and to a strong sense of shame, and such concerns in turn gave added force to these mechanisms of social control. Gossip and shame were also used to curb intratribal conflicts among adults. A cluster of tepees made an ideal setting for effective ridicule. Wissler (1911:24) describes a process of "formal ridicule" that was used to curb "mild persistent misconduct." When the people were quietly settled in of an evening, a headman would call out to a neighbor asking him if he had heard about that silly fellow two tepees down who had been mistreating his wife? Men in other tepees would join in telling what they thought of the man and his behavior, all to the discomfort of the victim and the enjoyment of everyone else. Sarcasm, ridicule, and the accompanying laughter, added up to an evening of entertainment for all but the victim, who was soon highly motivated to mend his ways.

---

[7] The double standard in ideal sexual relations set up some strains; in order for one sex to achieve the other had to fall short of the ideal. I gather from the literature that there was a mix of failure and success in the attainment of these ideals on the part of both boys and girls (Ewers 1958:98).

In the more serious cases of adult disputes, force and physical punishment were employed if gossip failed. In cases of murder, a revenge killing might take place if a high payment was not offered in retribution and accepted. A person who disrupted the summer hunt might be beaten and have his clothing and weapons destroyed. An adulterous woman might have her nose cut off, or be put to death by the members of her husband's warrior society (Grinnell 1907:220, Ewers 1958:97–98; Wissler 1911:24–26 discuss specific punishments).

These forces contributed to the development of some general personality characteristics of the Blackfeet. Grinnell found them, like other Plains Indians, to be "talkative, merry, and lighthearted," and fond of joking, even though they appeared reserved and quiet when with strangers (Grinnell 1907:181). Wissler commented on their fondness for jest and practical jokes (Wissler 1911:52–53). In addition, I get a picture of a brave, resourceful people, industrious and aggressive, yet much concerned with self, jealous, and easily shamed. These characteristics and their expression were further reinforced by the Blackfeet beliefs.

Religion

While learning all these skills and rules, the young people were learning as well the beliefs that gave the practices validity, supported the rights and privileges of age, gave meaning to the Blackfeet world, and added supernatural reinforcement to the moral code.

All of the Blackfeet universe was invested with a pervasive supernatural power that could be met with in the natural environment. A man could seek and avail himself of this power through proper behavior and ritual. He went alone to a remote place to fast and pray, and to await the dream or vision that would transfer power to him. If he was successful the supernatural appeared to him, usually in animate form, and promised aid and success in all or specific endeavors, if the man in return would observe faithfully a series of taboos and periodically re-enact in ritual the experience by which he had received the power. The spirit-being instructed the petitioner to make a medicine bundle containing the symbols of his power and taught him the appropriate songs and rituals. The spirit was now his guardian and could be called upon for protection in times of trouble.

The powers, paraphernalia, and rituals became the personal property of the owner. He and the spirit dealt with each other as individuals, and any group benefits to be expected from this relationship were dependent on the inclinations of the individual owner. The complete power, bundle, songs, and ritual could be sold, or transferred, by one individual to another for a price. The owners of some bundles could sell short-term benefits of their power, as well, usually by going through the ceremony of the bundle for the benefit of an individual, the family, band, or tribe, or through the preparation of a charm to be used by the purchaser. Ewers relates how Wolf Calf acquired horse medicine power and how he used it, how he transferred parts of the power and how these parts and the bundle itself were transferred to a series of men from those days in the early nineteenth century on up into the time of Ewer's informants of the 1940s (Ewers 1955:258–261). The point here is that these powers and their symbols were subject to the same controls as any other property. A man, therefore, incurred both rights and obligations with the attainment of power. He was expected to be generous with it, but at the same time he expected to be paid in goods or prestige for the help he gave.

The Blackfeet believed that the possession of a guardian spirit and power were important for success, so such powers and the bundles that represented them were highly valued. Not all men were successful in their vision quest, but this was not held against them. They were just unlucky. Neither they nor anyone else expected much of them, however, and they could hardly advance in prestige without some successes. Such men might be motivated to gain property to enable them to purchase power from someone who had had the experience, and men with power often sought to transfer it because it was a restricted and often burdensome property. As with other kinds of property, the bundle owner was expected to be generous with his power. Bundles had to be opened periodically, and the owner had to provide a feast for invited guests as a part of the ritual. In addition, the bundle owner had to observe a number of taboos associated with each bundle—it had to be displayed properly, no one should walk between the bundle and its owner, and numerous restrictions were put on the owner's behavior. Some men owned several bundles, but whether one or many, some owners found the responsibilities, expenses and taboos too burdensome and sought buyers for their power.

Values and Status

Perhaps, as already indicated, one of the most persistent themes of Blackfeet life was the high value put on individual prestige, a value that operated through and maintained a status structure. This was not a true class society with easily recognized social divisions, but a structure of status positions, each shading into a higher one. The high status people were distinguished readily from those of low status, but the separations along the line might be imperceptible.[8] The whole system was an expression of Blackfeet values, and the highest status was achieved by the man who best represented these ideals.

The major characteristics valued by the Blackfeet and by which men were judged appear to have been bravery, generosity, wisdom, and skill; these were displayed in warfare, horse raiding, hunting, religious knowledge and the acquisition of property for use in the service of others.

It is difficult to establish a hierarchy of the importance of these different attributes. Bravery and generosity appear to have been essential. The ethnographers differ in their ordering of exploits by which a reputation for bravery was established, but all agree that war honors were ranked, and that the killing and scalping of an enemy ranked below the more dangerous feats of successfully wresting the weapons from an enemy and escaping without injury, or stealing into the center

---

[8] Ewers believes that social classes were forming in the late 1880s under the influence of horse ownership. A small rich class, a numerous middle class, and a number of poor were recognized, grounded in respect for individual rights and property rights (Ewers 1955:240–244).

of an enemy encampment and making off with a fine horse that had been tethered to its owner's tepee. Bravery was measured, then, according to the relative danger of the exploit and the most dangerous deeds were those related to war and raiding. But brave deeds alone were not enough. Unless a man were generous with his goods and helpful to his neighbors, he would be branded as selfish and stingy and his supporters might abandon him. This emphasis put stress on acquiring property with which to be generous which in turn made skill important. But all these traits were enhanced if a man had supernatural support. Power increased a man's self-confidence and the expectancy of success on the part of himself and others. Ewers remarked that the horse raider ". . . was a courageous, alert, resourceful fighting man. Nevertheless, he did not attribute his success in war to these qualities. Rather he attributed it to the power of his war medicine" (Ewers 1958:127).

A man of ability, achievement, and with supernatural support was able to attract followers in his ventures of war and raiding, or in his political maneuvers. Influence began to build as he used these qualities and property to rally members of his family and band. He drew first upon the ties of kinship and then attracted followers from other groups to gain leadership within the band. The maintenance of this position, and the advance to higher status depended upon his ability to exercise all of his personal attributes in correct ways.

The ideals were a standard, of course, and probably few attained the ideal. But those who did stood as examples to the children, as noted earlier. People measured each other and themselves by the ideals, and in a society where gossip was an important control over behavior, verbal praise was eagerly sought. What people said about you was important, and the amount of praise a person received could be increased if he spoke well of himself. This seemed to be a response among the Blackfeet. People talked about their good deeds as well as the good and bad deeds of others, and were much concerned about their own good name. Men who aspired to leadership tested each other's claims; while rising on their own claims they could climb faster, in a relative sense, if by gossip they could cut down the man above them.

In a sense then, property was the measure of a man's achievement, and the use of property became the means of validating a particular status and rising to a higher one. Property was accumulated to use in the gaining of further goods and, above all, as a means of expressing generosity. Highest status went to the generous man; a stingy man was the butt of gossip, and lost status among the Blackfeet.

Claims of power, bravery, skill and generosity were subject to public judgment. Opportunities were given, particularly at the Sun Dance, for the recital of coup claims, and public acceptance of these served to validate them. Men called upon to fill the roles in the Sun Dance ritual, society initiations, and naming ceremonies were selected from among those of accomplishment, and before performing the required act the man recounted the achievements that qualified him for the honor being bestowed upon him. Similarly, the woman who sponsored the Sun Dance, and the women who cut the buffalo tongues as a part of the ritual, publicly proclaimed their virtue. In ordinary conversation and in the give and take of daily life people might boast and overelaborate their exploits, but in these formal situations they tended to curb such over-enthusiastic self-appraisal. On these occasions anyone who knew such claims to be false or exaggerated was expected to challenge the claim. A woman who came to cut the tongues, for instance, would not only have claimed to have been a good hard working wife, free from the charge of adultery, but would also have related, naming names, the occasions on which she had resisted seduction. "You, Brave Eagle," she might have said, "You remember how you surprised me last fall when I was picking berries, and tried to get me to commit adultery. I told you off, didn't I." If she had told the truth, Brave Eagle would have had to confirm her statement; if she had lied, he would have had to contradict her. After all, his manliness was being attacked—if she was right he lost status as a great lover even as she gained or retained her prestige as a virtuous woman. Concern with self, public proclamation, and public validation kept people from making false claims. They advanced by validating deeds and virtues and by exposing the false claims of another.

Summary

The Blackfeet culture was based upon and integrated with a hunting and gathering economy in which the buffalo was most important. The hunting band was the major economic and political unit. While the band was essentially a kinship group, people did change bands when it was to their advantage to do so. A band leader held his position by popular support, and gained power in tribal councils according to the number of followers he had. Power and leadership were exercised through persuasion and influence. No one could dictate and important decisions were reached by unanimity.

Both private ownership of property, other than land and resources, and the rights of the individual were held in high esteem. People strove to accumulate property, but material wealth was not the goal. Rather, property was given away to exhibit generosity.

Generosity, bravery, wisdom, and skill were highly valued personal qualities. War, horse raiding, hunting, and religious practice provided the major avenues for the achievement and display of these values. Men used bravery and skill to acquire fame and property, and they sought, or bought, supernatural power to aid in these endeavors. They used their gains to exhibit wisdom and generosity in order to attract a personal following that would lead to increased influence and higher social position.

The loss of the buffalo seriously undermined the whole culture. The Blackfeet faced radically altered conditions of life and were called upon to make unprecedented changes. New subsistence techniques were necessary. New skills had to be learned and old ones became obsolete. Economic dependency led to the loss of much political, religious and social autonomy. The following chapter is used to trace the readaptations that accompanied the events subsequent to this catastrophe.

4

Dependency and Readaptation:
1884-1970

Introduction

THE UNSUCCESSFUL HUNTS of 1883–1884 marked the end of the subsistence pattern on which the Blackfeet had built their culture. The Indians scoured the region for food, and moved in around the agency to ask for help from the agent. In Blackfeet culture those who had food shared it during times of want; the agent supposedly had food and as a leader he was now expected to validate his status by caring for those who had none. The United States government had acknowledged responsibility for the Blackfeet in the 1855 and subsequent treaties, but agency supplies were inadequate to meet famine conditions. Up to ¼ of the Piegan perished during the winter of 1883–1884 (Ewers 1958:293–294).

The Indians had to find a new and meaningful subsistence base as well as new ways in which to express old values and to maintain prestige and status. At the same time, the government, upon which they were dependent, pressed them to accept new value and prestige systems, quite different from their traditional ones.

The following historical review of the Blackfeet adaptation and adjustment since 1884 includes a statement of the general objectives and attendant values expressed in United States Indian policies of the period, a presentation of the means used to further these aims, and the Blackfeet reactions to them during (a) the period of dependency to 1935, and (b) the period of self-rule under the Indian Reorganization Act from 1935 to the 1960s.

United States Indian Policies

The prevalent policy of the period emphasized the eventual "civilization" and assimilation of the Indians, although the means to these ends were often diverse and inconsistent. There appeared to be general agreement by this time that the Indian could be civilized most effectively through education and agriculture. The Indian Commissioner, in his report for 1885, made an impassioned plea:

> It requires no seer to foretell or foresee the civilization of the Indian race as a result naturally deducible from a knowledge and practice upon their part of the art of agriculture; . . . those races who are in ignorance of agriculture are also ignorant of almost everything else.

> It should be industriously and gravely impressed upon them that they must abandon their tribal relations and take lands in severalty, as the cornerstone of their complete success in agriculture, which means self-support, personal independence, and material thrift.

The Indian, he continued, must be taught to work, to send his children to school, and to seek "material independence" (U.S. Comm. Ind. Affairs 1885:III–V).

Two major themes alternated in ascendancy throughout eighty to ninety years of attempts to achieve this goal for the American Indian:

1. The end could best be accomplished by drastic pragmatic programs intended to produce a quick cure regardless of the expense in individual maladaptation.

2. Progress could only be made slowly through humanitarian programs that would allow for gradual, individual readaptation and assimilation.

The goals, and the two approaches to their implementation are expressed well in the following statements selected from Senate debates over the question of allotting land to individual Indians.

The goal was restated eloquently by Senator George H. Pendleton of Ohio in 1881:

> . . . we must encourage them to industry and self-dependence . . . and we must stimulate within them . . . the idea of home, of family, and of property. These are the very anchorages of civilization; . . . (U.S. Congressional Record XI 1881: 906).

The short term approach was advocated by Senator Henry M. Teller of Colorado in 1886:

> I suggested on a former bill the opening of the country, putting side by side with the Indian farmer of a white farmer; . . . Give to our people, . . . the right to go upon the Indian lands and make, side by side of the Indian farm, a farm tilled by the aggressive and enterprising Anglo-Saxon, and in a little while contact alone will compel these people to accept the civilization that surrounds them on every side (U.S. Congressional Record XVII 1886:1762–1763).

Senator John T. Morgan of Alabama advanced the humanitarian viewpoint:

> The measure which the Senator proposes here must be one of growth. Of course we know that all this western country at some future day must be populated jointly by Indians and white people; but until the Indians get into condition where they can be protected against the white men who would sell them whiskey,

. . . powder and shot, and out-deal them in all their transactions, it is the duty of the Government of the United States to preserve them in some form or other until they have matured sufficiently to become able to control their own domestic affairs, and manage their own property (U.S. Congressional Record XVII 1886: 1764).

These two themes will be seen to alternate in ascendancy in governmental policies from that time to the present. The goal of eventual assimilation has been questioned seriously only in the last forty years. The debate culminated in the passage of the General Allotment Act of 1887 that authorized the President to permit the allotment in severalty of reservation lands to Indians (U.S. Statutes XXIV 1887:388).

The values stressed in that policy are work (industry), self-dependence (self-support), individualism (independence of the tribe), and acquisitiveness (implied in home-building, material thrift, and private ownership). These are some of the qualities valued by the culture-bearing agents of American society who came into long and continuous contact with the members of the Blackfeet tribe. The Americans apparently gave little thought to either the preservation of the Indian value and status systems or to ways in which these might be used to implement governmental policies. The Blackfeet probably thought of the whites as a minority group who had promised to help them and turned to the white man for help with little thought that Indian values were in serious jeopardy.

The following review of the history of United States-Blackfeet relations from 1884 to 1970 attempts to trace the interplay between the American and Blackfeet value systems during the course of economic readaptation. The events of history tend to be those seen and recorded by whites, and for many years even the thoughts of the Blackfeet had to find expression through the white man's pen.

The Period of Dependency, 1884–1935

1884–1891   Following the winter of 1883–1884 the first efforts of the agents were directed toward relieving the famine and providing for the future sustenance of the people. A new agent made his first report in the fall of 1884 in which he wrote that he found few results of past efforts to make the Blackfeet sedentary and self-supporting farmers (U.S. Comm. Ind. Affairs 1884:106–108). During the next six years the agents attempted to build up the agency farm and herd, to encourage the Indians to raise grain and produce, and to forward other programs of "civilization."

From this time on, the dependent Blackfeet were subjected increasingly to the American concepts of law and order. The Indian police, under the agent's direction, were instrumental in eliminating warfare and horse raiding. In 1888 the agent reported that Indian "depredations" had ceased and there had been no horse "stealing" during the preceding year (U.S. Comm. Ind. Affairs 1888:152). American pressure against war and horse raiding had eliminated two more traditional avenues to the acquisition of property and prestige; hunting, as a major expression of skill, had already lost its place in Blackfeet life.

In his report of 1888, Agent Baldwin was less optimistic about the agricultural possibilities on the reservation than he had been in previous years (U.S. Comm. Ind. Affairs 1888:150–152). The crops failed in 1889 and 1890, and in 1891 the agent reported that no crops had been planted in the past year either by Indians or by the agency because of fear of further drought (U.S. Comm. Ind. Affairs 1891:265).

In 1888 the agreement whereby the Blackfeet relinquished claim to the lands to the east of the present reservation boundary was ratified by Congress. In return the United States promised annuities, in the amount of $150,000 for a period of ten years, to be paid in the form of goods and services necessary for Indian progress toward civilization (U.S. Comm. Ind. Affairs 1888:303).

The first ration of cattle and horses under the agreement was issued in 1890. Agent John Catlin summed up the preceding five years of agricultural endeavor as "commendable," but wrote that the Indians had experienced failure "through no fault of their own." The Indian interest in stock raising led to his recommendation that grazing be given precedence over agriculture in future programs (U.S. Comm. Ind. Affairs 1890:114). Efforts to establish farming as an economic base had met with little success.

1892–1905   By 1892 the Piegan herd had been built up to 6,827 head of cattle and 4,616 head of horses. The Indians were moving out over more of the reservation and claiming land in anticipation of eventual allotment. They were beginning to establish herds, build houses and corrals, and to shift the emphasis of cultivation to raising hay for the stock (U.S. Comm. Ind. Affairs 1892:280–281, 807). Each subsequent report emphasized the suitability of the area for stock raising and reported a substantial increase in the Indian herds.

In 1898 a severe winter and a shortage of feed caused a 40 percent loss among the Indian cattle, and the irrigation engineer for the agency recommended extension of the irrigation canals in order to increase hay production (U.S. Comm. Ind. Affairs 1898:187–188). Indian ranchers, however, had a chance to recover from this setback. Additional cattle were included in the annual issues and stock raising continued.

An agreement for the sale of the Rocky Mountain portion of the reservation was approved by the United States government in 1896 (U.S. Statutes XXIX 1897:353). The conditions of the sale assured another ten years of annuities after the obligations under the 1887 treaty had been met.

By 1904 the agent reported a total of 20,509 head of cattle and 12,000 head of horses owned by the Blackfeet, and claimed that only 10 percent of Indian subsistence had been dependent upon government issues for that fiscal year (U.S. Comm. Ind. Affairs 1904:610–611, 600). Thus in the first two decades of dependency Blackfeet had tried farming and experienced failure. They were then encouraged to try stock raising and had begun to make some economic adaptation as herdsmen.

Their *cultural* readaptation, up to this time, had been less successful than the economic development. The increasing settlement of the lands around the reservation and the efforts of the police, as noted earlier, had ended horse raiding. Christian missions, particularly from the Roman Catholic church, had been intermittently active among the Piegan for several decades, but Father Imoda had discounted their success at conversion prior to 1870 (Bradley 1923:316). In 1890 the Holy Family Mission school was opened in the Two Medicine valley (U.S. Comm. Ind. Affairs 1890:115) and in the following years Christianity gradually gained predominance over the Blackfeet religion. In the meantime, agents, missionaries, and teachers actively combatted any expression of many elements of Indian culture.

> Sun dances, Indian mourning, Indian medicine, beating of the tom-tom, gambling, wearing of Indian costumes . . . selling, trading, exchanging or giving away anything issued to them have been prohibited, while other less pernicious practices, such as horse-racing, face-painting, etc., are discouraged (U.S. Comm. Ind. Affairs 1894:159).

In addition, the children were forbidden to speak the Blackfeet language in the schools (U.S. Comm. Ind. Affairs 1893:174). Several informants, who attended either agency or mission schools during the first decades of the twentieth century, recall being punished for "speaking Indian" in the schools or dormitories.

The suppression of elements of culture that the white men thought were inconsistent with civilization did not eliminate the practices, but did hamper and limit their expression and transmission. The readaptation process was slow, but the agents usually found some grounds for optimism.

1905–1920   Progress in stock raising continued through 1905 and 1906. The agent persistently attempted to keep encroaching herds off Indian pastures, and continued a practice begun in 1904 of issuing leases and permits to both white and Indian stockmen for grazing privileges on tribal lands.[9]

The economic growth was again reversed by a severe winter in 1906 and 1907. The losses among the stock were heavy and "impoverished some of the industrious and worthy members of the tribe" (U.S. Comm. Ind. Affairs 1907:13–14). An investigation into conditions on the reservation was ordered, and the investigating officer's report sheds some light on the progress of economic adaptation to that time:

> He reported that the mixed bloods—about three eighths of the tribe—were able generally to take care of themselves, but the full bloods as a rule had little knowledge of ranch or farm work, were unwilling to stay a reasonable length of time in one place or to work where they could not be in parties, were very apt to quit on little or no provocation and regardless of the interests of the employer, . . . (U.S. Comm. Ind. Affairs 1907:13–14).

A federal act of March 1907 provided for the allotment in severalty of the Blackfeet reservation. Each tribal member would receive 280 acres of grazing land and 40 acres of irrigable land, or 320 acres of grazing land only. Surplus lands would be opened for public settlement. An appropriation was included for the construction of an irrigation system for the lands to be allotted; the money

---

[9] The first such permit recorded was for a five-year lease of 2,400 acres to the Conrad Investment Company (U.S. Comm. Ind. Affairs 1904:77). An increasing number of leases are reported for most of the following years.

appropriated to be reimbursed from proceeds of the sale of the surplus reservation lands (U.S. Statutes XXXIV 1907:1015, 1035). Allotment surveys and work on the irrigation projects were carried on during the two years following the enactment of the legislation (U.S. Comm. Ind. Affairs 1908:61; 1909:4–5). Irrigation construction provided an additional source of labor and income for many Indians.

The last annuities under the agreement of 1896 were paid in 1908. Henceforth Indian rations and aid were dependent upon tribal income, reimbursable government appropriations, and occasional relief measures. The statistics from the agents' reports for the next few years give a picture of continuing economic progress for the tribe as a whole.

The First World War relieved some of the pressure on reservation resources —good weather and abundant crops prevailed generally until 1917; livestock and produce found a ready market at high prices; and many Blackfeet were drawn into the armed forces, thereby reducing the local labor force. But all of this does not reflect accurately the condition of individuals. A process was going on that was slowly segmenting the population.

First, the population was growing—from 2,063 in 1905 (U.S. Board Ind. Comm. 1905:facing 16) to 2,957 in 1920—and becoming increasingly hybridized. White men were marrying the Indians' daughters. The full-blood Blackfeet loved the grandchildren these marriages produced, but they were "half-breeds," and hard to accept as "real Indians." Of the total, in 1920, less than half, or 1,141 persons, were full-bloods, while the balance were mixed. Among the mixed-blood population, 956 were ½ or less Indian (U.S. Comm. Ind. Affairs 1920:67). Secondly, the individually owned herds were growing and the returns from this business were high, but as the superintendent wrote in 1918, 3 percent of the tribe owned 95 percent of the stock when he reported for duty in 1915 (U.S. Congress Sen. Report 451 1918:3). An investigator for the Board of Indian Commissioners, in November of 1918, found that the full-bloods were divided as to their capabilities as stockmen. He reported that "about one-third of the 300 and more full-blood families is incapable of handling cattle." Another third probably could become cattlemen if properly instructed and supervised, and the balance of the full-bloods were doing well at the industry. A number of mixed-bloods had built prosperous looking ranches and had had "marked success at this business" (U.S. Board Ind. Comm. 1918:352–353).

Other forces were already at work that were to alter the uneven progress of the Blackfeet. Beginning in 1917, the Indian Bureau began pressing for the rapid reduction of Indian dependency by the removal of "competent" Indians from trust status (U.S. Comm. Ind. Affairs 1917:3–5). By 1920, 1,011 Blackfeet had been awarded fee patent title to 312,250 acres (U.S. Comm. Ind. Affairs 1920:171) under a policy that was to result in the alienation of reservation lands and the creation of a large number of landless Indians.

A drought cycle began in 1917 and continued for four years (U.S. Board Ind. Comm. 1921:55; Whetstone 1956:145–146). The end of the war, in 1917, resulted in the loss of markets. The drought and falling prices brought bankruptcy to both cattlemen and farmers in this part of Montana by 1919 and 1920. Veterans returned to swell the labor force. The Blackfeet shared in this change. The white homesteaders and cattlemen could abandon their places and go elsewhere; the Indian could not and had to rely again upon the government (U.S. Board Ind. Comm. 1921:56). The Indian, however, did have the agency to turn to, an advantage not shared by the white man. During the winter of 1920–1921 rations were issued to "over 2,000, or about two-thirds of the entire population" (U.S. Comm. Ind. Affairs 1922:12). Several informants reported that their families and friends were ruined at this time. A few were able to make a comeback, but many abandoned their ranches and did not try again.

In 1919, a second allotment of reservation lands was authorized in the annual appropriation bill for the Bureau of Indian Affairs (U.S. Statutes XLI 1919:16–17). After this no further allotments in severalty were made to the Blackfeet Indians.

The Blackfeet generally were dependent again. Thirty-five years of attempted economic readaptation were behind them. They had tried farming and found it unrewarding. They had found satisfaction in stock raising, but only a few were able to succeed at this in the face of cold winters, periods of drought, and the fluctuating markets regulated by national and international conditions. Large numbers of younger men had been employed in seasonal labor, railway and irrigation construction work, harvesting and ranch labor and had served in the armed forces. These jobs provided some cash income but little training for long-range adjustment. Unused allotments were leased to others to provide another small cash return to the Indian owner. Many people depended entirely upon the rations issued and the cash that could be earned by wage work or leasing of land.

Periodic crop failures and price fluctuations made it difficult for the Indian to understand or to develop faith in long-range plans. Each government program offered future rewards and security, but the promised rewards never materialized; the only tangible things were cash, rations, and relief. The white man's values of thrift and hard work had been developed and maintained by a better than average experience of success; few Blackfeet, by 1920, had experienced enough consistent reward to become imbued with these values. Every ten years or so their best efforts had resulted in failure.

1920–1935   The next fifteen years were in many ways a repetition of the the past, and reinforced more than they changed the expectation patterns. Montana farmers, generally, experienced a severe depression during this time (Montana Almanac 1957:122) and this was capped by the national depression and the droughts of the Dust Bowl years that began in 1929 and 1930 (Toole 1959:240).

In 1921 a new and dedicated agent, Frank C. Campbell, began a "Five Year Program" of subsistence farming and economic development financed by reimbursable Indian bureau funds. He visited each Indian home and by consultation won support for his program. The Blackfeet were given a sense of participating in the planning of their own economy. The agent consulted with them and made a place for indigenous leaders with whom the people could discuss and resolve their problems (U.S. Board Ind. Comm. 1923:47; 1925:22–23).

Campbell remained with them until 1929. His program benefited many people, but others wanted more independence. They wanted to restock and operate their ranches, to continue their own operations with a minimum of governmental interference (Ewers 1958:322–323). Nevertheless, the Five Year Programs gave many persons a sense of accomplishment and helped carry the Indians through a period of widespread hard times.

The wholesale granting of competency and fee patents was halted in 1926 when it was recognized that "the lands of a vast majority of Indians who had been given absolute control of their allotments [had] passed from Indian ownership in various ways . . ." (U.S. Comm. Ind. Affairs 1926:10–11).

The cycle of success and failure was not broken by the Five Year Plans, however. The enthusiasm of both the Indians and the agents died down during the years between 1929 and 1935 and the greater number of the Blackfeet returned to economic dependency (Ewers 1958:323).

In 1933 the Works Progress Administration (W.P.A.) and the Civilian Conservation Corps (C.C.C.) programs were established to meet national unemployment and the benefits were extended to Indian reservations (U.S. Sec't. Interior 1937:218). Like the irrigation construction of earlier years, these programs provided a source of seasonal cash labor, an important prop to the economy, but one that provided little training for permanent employment on the reservation.

At this point in Blackfeet adaptation, new national Indian policies were being formulated. The Meriam Report, a monumental study of the Indian problems published in 1928, questioned the whole doctrine of assimilation of the Indians.

> He who wishes to merge into the social and economic life of the prevailing civilization of this country should be given all practicable aid and advice in making the necessary adjustments. He who wants to remain an Indian and live according to his old culture should be aided in doing so (Meriam 1928:28).

This, and many other of the recommendations, became official policy with the passage of the Indian Reorganization Act in 1934 (U.S. Statutes XLVIII 1934:984). The act provided, among other things, for the cessation of allotment of Indian land, a limitation on the sale of restricted Indian land to other than tribal members, and the establishment of a revolving loan fund from which Indian corporations could borrow to further either tribal or individual enterprises. Tribes were authorized to organize and to adopt a constitution, and those who organized were given broad powers of self-government previously denied to them. Organized tribes were also empowered to incorporate and manage tribal properties and income. Actions of both the political and business organizations were subject to approval and review by the Bureau of Indian Affairs.

In addition, the traditional cultures were given recognition for the first time. A circular sent to all agencies in 1934 illustrates the sharp reversal from previous communications about Indian cultural practices:

No interference with Indian religious life or expression will hereafter be tolerated . . . and it is desirable that Indians be bilingual. . . . The Indian arts are to be prized, nourished, and honored (U.S. Sec't. Interior 1934:90).

The Indians were to have a choice, and to be allowed to play some part in decisions about their future development.

The Period of Self-Government, 1935–1970

The Blackfeet Constitution and the Blackfeet Corporate Charter were accepted and approved in 1935. The population continued to grow: the report for 1935 lists the membership of the Blackfeet Tribe as 3,962, of which 561 were living outside the reservation jurisdiction (U.S. Sec't. Interior 1935:163). The economy improved slowly after the bad years of the early thirties. The stockmen, in particular, were aided by a provision for a repayment cattle pool authorized in 1934 (see U.S. Sec't. Interior 1937:212–213 for repayment in kind program, and 1944:241 for a review of the program). A man could build a herd by borrowing cattle from the pool and repaying in kind from the increase.

The Johnson-O'Malley Act (U.S. Statutes XLVIII 1934:956) passed in 1934 and amended in 1936 (U.S. Statutes XLIX 1936:1498) authorized the Secretary of the Interior to contract with a state or other political units, and with schools, colleges, and private corporations for educational and medical services, agricultural assistance, social welfare, and relief for Indians. The Annual Report for 1934 stated that the Browning schools were assuming the task of educating the Blackfeet children from that district (U.S. Sec't. Interior 1934:85).

The majority of the Blackfeet still were attempting to readapt to the immediate present, to find success in a new economic endeavor. They were pressed to close a wide cultural gap in a short period of time, and to make things more difficult, the national economy would not stand still. Ranching and farming were changing in both production and marketing practices. A writer for the *Montana Almanac* noted a trend away from subsistence farming in the 1920s as homestead holdings proved to be too small for efficient farm and ranch operations, especially with the increasing use of power machinery in subsequent years (1957:202).

The Indian's future on small subsistence farms of 80 acres, or on a ranch using a 360 to 420 acre grazing allotment, was not promising. A successful operation required the use of leased land and adequate capital. The heirship status of individual trust lands made leasing difficult, and trust restrictions inhibited the mortgaging of such lands. The day of slowly building a ranch or farm from a cow, some seed, and hard work was disappearing. Few Blackfeet were established sufficiently in the 1930s to build and maintain a remunerative enterprise.

From 1936 through 1940 general drought conditions continued in the region (U.S., Indians at Work IV, 7 1936:37, 8 1936:37–39; Toole 1959:240—for Montana from 1929 to 1939). A few men held onto their farms and ranches, but most were forced to rely on wages from occasional labor and welfare payments. One report stated that general poverty was the lot of ¾ of the Blackfeet people in 1936 (U.S., Indians at Work IV, 4, 1936:38).

An additional source of unearned income was provided when the Indians were declared eligible for Social Security benefits by an act of 1936 (U.S. Statutes XLIX 1936:620). This provided categorical aid to the needy, blind, aged, and the dependent children. In 1939, 91 old persons, 186 children, and 3 blind persons on the Blackfeet reservation received this help (U.S. Statistical Report 1939:15).

From about 1936 on, the impact of modern medicine began to be felt by the Blackfeet. The agency physician reported an increased desire for obstetric service, "an increase from an average of ten a year to 127 in the fiscal year for 1936" (U.S., Indians at Work IV, 4, 1936:39). A new hospital was opened in 1937,[10] and during the fiscal year 1940 a staff of twelve served 1,181 patients in addition to providing dispensary treatment to 5,204 cases. Five field employees administered to an additional 4,945 (U.S. Ind. Affairs Stat. Supplement 1940:82). C.C.C. nurses and Red Cross workers were also tending to the health of the Blackfeet (U.S. Sec't. Interior 1937:218). The medicine men were losing their hold. By 1959 informants reported that all the Indians used the Public Health Service hospital and medicines. Only a few medicine men were left and while they did some curing, they too went to the white doctor on occasion.

The tribal council attempted to further self-help improvement projects using revolving loan funds appropriated by Congress. The Office of Indian Affairs encouraged other enterprises by providing farm and home extension workers to advise the farmers and ranchers, and to organize women's community clubs for instruction in homemaking. The extension agents encouraged the growth of 4-H clubs to teach agriculture, stock raising and homemaking to the boys and girls (see reports in U.S., Indians at Work III, 12, 1936:43; and in U.S. Comm. Ind. Affairs 1936:179–184; 1937:211–217).

By 1941, the eve of World War II, the Blackfeet had made but slow recovery. The long-range economic problems had not been solved. They, like other Indians, were still leasing the land to others rather than using it themselves (U.S. Sec't. Interior 1941:451–452). The C.C.C. remained an important economic prop.

The war years, 1942–1945, had far-reaching effects on the Blackfeet. The C.C.C. program was suspended in 1942 (U.S. Sec't. Interior 1943:317), but several hundred young men and women served in the armed forces and worked in defense plants around the country (Ewers 1958:324). The "greatest exodus of Indians from reservations that has ever taken place" occurred during the war years (U.S. Sec't. Interior 1944:237). Indians were meeting other Americans, learning new skills, and seeing more of the outside world. Ready markets and higher prices for farm products coincided with increased rainfall to bring general prosperity to the Montana farmers and ranchers (Toole 1959:241), and the Blackfeet shared in this.

Like all past periods of activity and increased economic advance, this one met reversals after the war. The greater number of the Indians returned to the

---

[10] Reported under construction (U.S. Sec't. Interior 1936:175); all hospitals under construction in 1936 were reported completed in 1937 (U.S. Sec't. Interior 1937:234).

reservation when the military forces were demobilized and the war industries were closed (U.S. Sec't. Interior 1946:353). Wage work fell off and a "downward trend in family incomes set in" (U.S. Sec't. Interior 1946:351).

The young people returned with money to spend, but the opportunities for investment were scarce. Few of them owned land with which to start a ranch or farm. They had the money to build new homes, but again no land of their own upon which to build. Not many had the experience and motivation to overcome these handicaps.

While the Indians were readjusting to peace time reservation life, the general U.S. population was expanding, both in numbers and in movement of population. The demands for new land revived pressures for the removal of trust restrictions on Indian land (U.S. Sec't. Interior 1951:368–369). Once again there was an increase of fee patent awards and the sale and alienation of more land.

The council and the agency persevered in endeavors to resolve the reservation economic problems. Stock raising and agricultural programs were initiated, and national programs for relocation and on-the-job training for Indians were pushed. By 1949 the cattle holdings of the Blackfeet had increased to 14,678 (U.S. Sec't. Interior 1950:356), but the figures, as usual, do not tell the whole story. As in the past, only a few were able to keep a ranch going over time to remain as one of the 150 families engaged in stock raising in 1959. Accounts of informants' experiences during this period show some of the personal and tribal problems of adaptation during the postwar years.

> I started years ago to build a herd with repayment cattle. At that time they accepted repayment as a man was able to make it. I took ten years to pay back fifty head. Then they made changes and required that repayment be made within two years. One bad year made this impossible. 1947 was a bad year. The people needed hay to get their cattle through the winter. The government wouldn't finance feeding. Then, because the Indian wasn't able to feed, they came in and hauled away the cattle. I managed to borrow $700 from a friend in town and made it through the winter.
> —a presently successful rancher, mixed-blood, leasing 2,400 acres.

> My father had a ranch and I helped him from the time I left school until the war. After the war I got a job in California and stayed there until my father asked me to come back and help with the ranch. I worked on the ranch for two years, then my father, who was getting old, sold off his stock in 1948 and I went to work for another rancher.
> —a steadily employed farmhand, ¼ Blackfeet.

> I had a good herd and then got sick and couldn't take care of them. Nobody would. Some were stolen so I sold them all.
> —a full-blood pensioner.

> My father bought this land and is leasing more to farm. I dropped out of school to help and now I'm running the farm. My father got a F.H.A. loan to improve the house and we're doing good.
> —a young farmer, ⁵⁄₁₆ Blackfeet.

> I was farming, had 80 acres of grain but that wasn't enough to make a living. Then I ranched on the 580 acres. I had sixty-five head, including calves—loan cattle. The loan requirements insist that you stay with the cattle, but I took wage

jobs to make enough to live on, so they took my cattle. Just didn't have enough land for farming or ranching.

—a seasonally employed construction worker, 1/16 Blackfeet.

I have about thirty-five head I'm running with family stock on other people's land. These are loan cattle. I've been taking five to ten head a year and haven't been pressed for payment. Just pay them back when I can. The family helps take care of them. I want to lease some land but I find it hard to do. The Indian gets priority but somehow it seems hard to get land away from the white lease-holders.

—a regularly employed carpenter, 1/4 Blackfeet.

I was raised on a ranch. Before the war I was living and working for my uncle who had cattle. I had some loan cattle and was just getting started. Then I was called into the Army. They only kept me six months, but no one would take care of my cattle while I was gone so I turned back the loan cattle and sold the rest. After the war I came to town and worked for wages.

—an irregularly employed laborer, full-blood.

This is the way these men see the problems, and whether or not they are correct in their appraisal is beside the point. The important thing is that, for various reasons, many men failed to make a go of ranching and farming while a few others did. The successful ones appear to have had family support. Only by cooperation, in which some of the family took wage earning jobs while others tended the ranch, were most enterprises kept going.

The pressure for ending trust status of Indian land culminated in the adoption of House Concurrent Resolution 108 in 1953 calling for the "earliest possible" termination of federal responsibilities over specified Indian tribes (U.S. Congr. Record XCIX, 8, 1953:9968). The Blackfeet were not included among the Indians to be "freed," but the resolution was interpreted as a statement of intent to end rapidly the trust status of all Indians. In response to this resolution, the

issuance of patents in fee nearly doubled as compared with the previous year . . . while the disposition of allotted holdings through advertised sale more than tripled . . . (U.S. Sec't. Interior 1953:24).

A brief moratorium in effect during 1958 was lifted the following year "in compliance with a congressional request. . . ." (U.S. Sec't. Interior 1959:253). The Blackfeet continued to lose reservation land to nonmembers.

While federal and tribal authorities were attempting to increase the industrial capacity of the reservation, other forces were working against them. The population was growing—from the 3,921 resident members in 1941 to 4,850 in 1960 to more than 6,000 by 1970. The increasing number of Blackfeet who had left the reservation often included the most educated.[11] The land sales and continued fractionization of allotments through inheritance procedures made land consolidation and utilization increasingly difficult. The trend toward larger farms

---

[11] This out-migration continues, largely because there are few opportunities on the reservation for turning learning into income. Weber tried to find a correlation between schooling and income among his Babb sample and concluded that for making money ". . . in a community with very few jobs other than those demanding physical labor, comparative youth and vigor are more important than variations in schooling" (1969:16).

and ranches increased the need for additional capital, but funds were not available to meet the demand. Periods of declining employment, that is the recession of 1957–1959, cut into individual earnings from wage labor. No new proven oil fields had been tapped, and interest in oil exploration decreased. When individual and tribal earnings fell off, the demand for welfare funds increased. The council contributed the greatest share to the county welfare program, so the relief the people received was yet another drain upon tribal income.

Tribal self-government suffered under these pressures. It was difficult to get a majority of the tribe to support any political or economic measure. The council, itself split on issues, despaired of tribal unity:

> Members of the Blackfeet Tribe are generally very poor. Their income is meager and consists mostly of income from leased trust land, casual labor, and participation in Tribal programs operated with Tribal income.
> It is very difficult to convince these people that Tribal income should be assigned for any purpose. Most of our people see only the spectre of having their income, and consequently Tribal programs and their direct benefits, diverted into programs designed for only more progressive members of the Tribe. To these people, it is a matter of personal survival. Any possible reduction in Tribal income to them automatically means a reduction in personal income.
> . . . until at least thirty per cent of the adult population of the Tribe becomes self-supporting and thus able to plan and to think in terms of the future, it appears that programs requiring popular approval for use of locally supervised Tribal funds will certainly be limited to those programs which meet the daily emergency needs of members of the Blackfeet Tribe. (Letter from the Secretary of the Blackfeet Tribal Business Council to the Commissioner of Indian Affairs, March 3, 1960, Blackfeet Tribal Council Documents.)

Consequently, long-range programs were often deferred, per capita payments were made, and in most cases, the recipients spent the money for immediate needs.

The pessimism reflected above should be tempered, however. Even as he wrote the letter, the tribal secretary and other councilmen were working on plans for improving the housing on the reservation. Following councils, in face of continuing criticism by many tribal members, invested money in programs to develop tribal resources and provide more opportunities for employment on the reservation: one of the first fruits of this effort was the establishment of the Blackfeet Forest Products Enterprises in 1963. This group was funded by the tribe in the amount of $10,000 and given the authority to lease a mill site and to award a franchise for the erection and operation of a sawmill to a private operator. The mill was to hire local help and to use logs cut by Blackfeet labor from the tribal timber holdings. Mill operations have suffered from breakdowns because of the age of the equipment acquired; several operators have taken the concession and given it up in the face of difficulties; but the mill continues to operate, troubles are being ironed out, and the hours of work available to local men has gradually increased to the point that the sawmill and attendant timber cutting operations appear to be a small but important prop to the local economy.

With a tribal investment of both land and money, and a loan from the U.S. Economic Development Administration, the Business Council has developed an industrial park adjacent to the railroad just south of Browning. The council, with the help of the Browning Industrial Development Corporation formed by private citizens both members and nonmembers of the tribe, has actively sought to attract small industries to the industrial park with some success. One industry, a wood products prefabrication plant, is presently in operation, constructing houses for tribal housing programs, and negotiations continue with other potential occupants.

The tragic flood of 1964 had left 129 families homeless. An emergency appropriation to the B.I.A. provided 5.5 million dollars for relief and reconstruction of homes, roads, dams, and canals on the reservation (*Glacier Reporter*, August 20, 1964). By late October 1964 the first units were being fabricated and hauled to the home sites in the old communities (*Glacier Reporter*, October 24, 1964). Some families chose not to move back to the old location and had their homes erected in city block patterns in Browning, Babb, and Starr School. In many, but not all, instances the new homes were roomier and provided more modern cooking and sanitary facilities than had been the case with the houses they replaced.

Good homes have been scarce on the reservation for many years, with only 32 percent of Indian families living in sound housing in 1969 according to a B.I.A. estimate (FY 1972 Budget and Program Memorandum). Housing programs developed by the Blackfeet Indian Housing Authority have been making

Several generations of housing: One log house has been renovated and expanded under a B.I.A. Home Improvement program.

New home constructed by the owner under the Mutual Aid Housing program.

an impact, however. Low-rent home consruction programs have been funded by the U.S. Department of Housing and Urban Development; fifty such units were completed and accepted in 1966 and another fifty-five were nearing completion during the summer of 1970. Construction had started during that summer of fifty middle income rental homes financed by a tribal investment of land and F.H.A. supported loans. In another program, the Housing Authority, supported by the U.S. Federal Housing Assistance Administration began Mutual Help Housing construction. The first units under this program were occupied in 1965 and additional units have been completed and occupied in each succeeding year in Browning, Babb, and Starr School. This is a cooperative endeavor drawing on the resources of many agencies. The F.H.A.A. made a loan for the purchase of material and wages for supervisory labor, the B.I.A. provided general supervisory help, the tribe through the Housing Authority selected the candidates for home ownership. The purchasers contributed their labor to build their own house and to help their neighbors, and agreed to pay off the loan with small monthly payments geared to the family income. No one buyer could occupy his house until all houses of any one segment of the program were finished. These projects take time; the faster builder awaits the slower, but with cooperation the job gets done.

Other tribal investments of land combined with federal loan programs have resulted in the completion of a new tribal office and community center and a new modern jail.

The attention of both the tribe and the B.I.A. has recently turned to the development of the tourist potential of the reservation. For many years the Blackfeet have been aware of the tourists. Many have earned money as entertainers at the lodges of Glacier National Park, others have profited from the sale of Indian crafts to tourists passing through the reservation to and from the park. The Museum of the Plains Indian has attracted an ever increasing number of visitors since its opening in 1941, and the Blackfeet Arts and Crafts Association has supplied and sold local Indian work through the museum gift shop and through its own shop at St. Mary. Duck Lake in the northern part of the reservation has long been famous as a fishing spot and attracted its share of travelers. But it is becoming apparent that the tourist potential has hardly been tapped. Plans are well along for a major tourist complex, with a lodge, campground, dining facilities, bar, marina, Indian tepee village and other facilities on Lower St. Mary Lake. Some camping facilities are already available and others are being planned. Such enterprises will surely produce revenues for the tribe; how many jobs will result for tribal members is another question. Concessionaires often bring their own employees in spite of efforts by the tribe to guarantee these jobs to local people.

Head Start, Community Action Planning and other ventures supported by grants from the U.S. Office of Economic Opportunity continue to relieve some of the problems of the tribe; yet much needs to be done. I feel a sense of optimism about the future, but find this feeling difficult to support except for certain material signs of an improved economy—new buildings, homes, roads and services. For many people, however, the basic problem of a meaningful job and a reliable income seem as far away as ever. New industries help, but still do not provide jobs for all who need them among a growing population. Employment reports still show high unemployment and a primary dependence on firefighting and other seasonal and sporadic kinds of wage labor for jobs. Robbins's study of the Heart Butte region does little to allay these fears. He reported that only 50 percent of the cash income reported by the members of his sample came from employment, another 20 percent derived from land leased to others and 30 percent of the income for these households came from welfare funds (Robbins 1968:198). Heart Butte is not representative of the whole reservation, but may well indicate the economic conditions in the underdeveloped rural areas.

A similarly gloomy view is expressed by local people in an application for the support of a Model Cities Program:

> The lack of Employment Opportunities is basic. Year round jobs are scarce. Available opportunities in this area are mostly seasonal, thus throwing many workers into a low income bracket. This is true of Indian and non-Indian alike. Jobs that do become available are oftentimes accompanied with unrealistic requirements, i.e., setting educational levels too high, years of experience for the job too extreme, or emphasis on racial preferences.
>
> There are not enough diverse fields of interest—no technical challenges. Work categories are numbered and few. Economic resources are undeveloped to a great extent. . . . Training is limited particularly in specialized fields. . . . Poor work habits must be overcome as job and training opportunities come forth. . . . A careless attitude has built up along with the feeling of uselessness. . . .
>
> The role of the male is decaying in the home due to this feeling of uselessness. The woman has taken on an increasing role in family providing and management. The male role must be revitalized if there is to be job success. Learning skills would be an encouragement. . . .
>
> Low income is prevalent on the Reservation, particularly among Indian families. Approximately 62% of the resident Indian families have annual incomes below $3,000.00, and the mean income is $1,700.00. It has been estimated that approximately 3,000 persons receive some form of welfare financial assistance during part of each year. In the case of large families, the assistance standards are sometimes actually competitive with available earned income, since many local jobs, cowpunching for example, pay far below minimum standard wages. . . .

The overall picture is one of widespread economic impoverishment which in the case of many families is shared with emotional impoverishment. As is true among most people who live in chronic poverty, the poor people of the Reservation have a feeling of hopelessness and helplessness in controlling their own destiny (Blackfeet Indian Reservation—City of Browning "Model City" Application 1968: 39–41).

This must be read as a portion of a document requesting economic assistance; nevertheless, the problems are there and the solutions will not appear immediately. The much-maligned councils are working on long-range programs that appear to offer promise of improvement, but they do this in the face of continuous opposition from those tribal members, both on and off the reservation, who want tribal spending cut and income distributed in per capita payments instead of being invested in industrial developments. The tribal council is severely criticized by its constituents and accused of everything from mismanagement to out-and-out graft. Some of these charges might be true, but I think it is important to note that this is a tribal body, elected by the tribal members, attempting to deal with local problems under the surveillance of local people. In this respect it is much like local governing bodies anywhere else in the United States. I think it is better for the Blackfeet to be at work solving their own problems through their elected representatives than to have these tasks turned over to either private or federal "experts" and all of the accompanying elaborate bureaucracy.

Overshadowing these economic and political problems and pervading all decision and debate is the concern about "termination." Termination is sometimes defined as the withdrawal of federal responsibilities for Indians, at other times as terminating the special relationship between the federal government and Indians. Its proponents usually talk about giving the Indians the full rights, privileges, and responsibilities of their citizenship. Usually these words are pronounced with less stress on "responsibilities" than on "rights" and "privileges," because the main responsibility to be gained is that of paying land and income taxes, a responsibility that has been denied the man who kept his land in trust. To most Indians termination signals the abrogation of long-standing treaties and the removal of federal protection from unfriendly and rapacious whites who "really only want to take our land away from us." Land is, perhaps, the one remaining tangible tie to the past, as well as an emotionally loaded symbol of Indian identity. Indians criticize the B.I.A. but resist its abolishment. It is the only remaining defense between them and termination, and when someone says "termination" the Indians hear "extermination."

Summary

The emphasis, in this chapter, has been upon the economic problems of Blackfeet readaptation following the depletion of the buffalo. The pressures put upon the people, both directly and indirectly to change other parts of their culture can be summarized now and related to the problem of the maintenance or replacement of the traditional value and prestige systems.

The end of the hunting economy made hunting skills obsolete. Migratory seasonal dwelling patterns lost their function. Dependency undermined band and tribal leadership. Warfare and horse raiding were stopped. A man no longer was able to exhibit bravery in the hunt, in war, or on the raid. He no longer could use these means to acquire property with which to display generosity.

Other cultural characteristics were seen to have been under strong pressure. Indian beliefs, religion, ritual, curing practices, and some aspects of social life had been discouraged or outlawed for many years. The acceptance of hospitalization and modern medicine reduced the importance of Indian curing as a channel to prestige. The conversion of many people to Christianity, and the suppression of religious expression and ritual undermined these beliefs and practices. The religious avenues to status were slowly blocked.

Many people remained committed to the old values but were hard pressed to make economic adaptation and at the same time express the traditional values. Generosity could still be practiced, but even this was made difficult under the new conditions. The practice of generosity often blocked the economic success the Indians were asked to achieve. A good and generous man could not hoard his cattle when his family and friends were in need, yet if he was generous with his stock the herd was depleted and his enterprise failed. The qualities that bolstered prestige among the Indian-oriented militated against gaining prestige among the white-oriented, and vice versa.

There is, to be sure, another side to the coin that must be recognized. Reciprocity was important to the survival of the poor. This tended to support and even generate generous behavior, making it difficult for me to decide whether the present stress on generosity is a carry-over from the old days or a response to modern conditions. Probably both factors are present in the patterns of daily reciprocity; cultural persistence seems evident in the rhetoric of generosity and surely most apparent in the give-away ceremonies.

The increased hybridization of the population was noted. This contributed to quite divergent home environments and socialization practices among the tribe.

All of these factors resulted in differing economic, social, and cultural accommodations among the tribal members. A few succeeded and many failed in subsistence endeavors. In varying degrees, some people retained Indian beliefs, practices, and values, while others turned to new ways. Still other members of the tribe, mainly mixed-bloods, learned little or nothing of Blackfeet culture but were socialized in white ways.

Some of the results of these processes were described in Chapter 2. In the following chapters I examine the present community in more detail, to show the type of social organization that has evolved in order to accommodate the varied sociocultural combinations that have developed during eighty-six years of change.

5

Intratribal Diversity

Introduction

TWO SOCIETIES EACH ORGANIZED AND GUIDED by different and often conflicting cultural directives came into contact, and it was this that set in motion the processes of change reviewed in the previous chapter. The Blackfeet were dependent and subordinate. The institutions involved with Indian affairs were charged to assimilate the Indians, and in this they have been partially successful. The Blackfeet tribe of today is recognizably different from the tribe of the past. Houses have replaced tepees, automobiles and farm machinery have made the horse relatively obsolete. Subsistence is gained within a money economy at ranching, farming, business, services or wage labor. Schools, churchs, and other institutions of the general white society are supported. Most people speak English, all dress like their non-Indian neighbors. Perhaps most surprising is that anything of the traditional Blackfeet culture remains in light of the concerted effort that was made to stamp out these traditions, yet much persists.

It is my thesis that the present Blackfeet tribe represents a bicultural and bisocial community. Albert Buffalo Heart and Henry Rogers represent life styles too divergent to be fitted into one social network, or even into one cultural tradition. Two societies and two cultures remain, localized on the reservation, all embedded in the wider state and national milieu. The larger theme of two societies in contact, interacting and changing, is reproduced on a smaller scale within the tribal membership.

This division appears to be recognized by the people themselves. In the local idiom, people are either "full-bloods" or "mixed-bloods"; or at other times are classed as "real Indians" or "assimilated Indians," but these labels do not cut the tribal membership domain in the same ways. By descent an "assimilated Indian" frequently turns out to be a full-blood, or the "real Indian" is found to be a mixed-blood. Essentially both sets of stereotypes recognize two differing life styles, which at first seem easy to explain as two different responses to change. One group, it

294

might be said, is made up of the "progressive" members of the tribe who have accepted more change than the "conservative" or "traditional" segment, which has resisted change. Anthropologists have sometimes used these labels to describe social divisions within Indian reservation communities. This process of differential acceptance and rejection of change has played a part in the evolution of the Blackfeet community, but other factors have also been at work to further complicate the matter.

One complicating factor is the presence of numerous tribal members of ¼ or less Indian "blood," who cannot be considered as Indians, or as members of families that have become assimilated. In one sense they are Indian only by the grace of one Indian grandparent or great-grandparent. Yet they live on the reservation and play an important part in tribal affairs. At one point I thought I could distinguish three categories: "real Indians," "assimilated Indians," and "Indians by technicality," but the last named do not form a distinct social group. They interact with the "assimilated" people and share a common culture. I gradually came to recognize that there were really two relatively distinct social divisions within the reservation community and named these the *Indian-oriented* and *white-oriented* societies. These cumbersome but appropriate labels recognize the cultural "directions" toward which the people in each group are oriented.

Many interrelated processes have led to this condition. In the preceding chapter culture change was described in terms of the development of the tribe as a whole in response to historical events. Another view of the same events could be taken from the perspective of the individuals who made their own adaptation and accommodation to the changing conditions of daily life. From this position the differential experience of persons with the two cultural systems, in home, school, church, work experience, and travel, seems most important. Of these the socialization experience in the childhood homes looms large when seen in the continuity from child to parent to grandparent back through time to the buffalo days. A few sketches from representative family histories should serve to indicate the complexity of the transmission processes that maintain and perpetuate the two social divisions in the reservation community.

Socialization to White-Orientation

A middle-aged full-blood man, who I shall call Ray Hawkins, told me about his childhood home and training. His parents saw the end of the buffalo days and concluded that the old life was ended. He remembers his father telling him, "The Indian days are gone. In a few years he will be only a thing in a museum that people will pay to see. You must live like our white brothers." His parents took up ranching and brought in a white tutor to teach the children English and other things they needed to prepare them for the new life ahead. Ray recalled that the tutor brought "books, a blackboard, chalk, paper, and pencils and set up a real school with recess and all." The children seldom left the ranch and were not allowed to play with other Indian children. "We were scared of the Indians," this full-blood told me, "If they came near the house we would hide under the bed." Later they were sent to school in Canada. Both his parents and the school stressed the values of hard work, honesty, thrift, and education, and this man and his wife have been guided by these principles in the raising of their own children.

This case represents an abrupt break in the continuity of socialization and is an example of one way by which a full-blood family can move from Indian to white orientation. Missionary and governmental attempts to gain the same result by removing Indian children from their parental homes and into boarding schools failed more often than not. Perhaps the change occurred in this case because the parents had made the choice; they changed their own living style, and withdrew from contact with many of their past kin and social ties. They further insured the change by providing the tutor and the schooling that gave the children the experiences the parents were unable to supply, that prepared them for a way of life so different from what the parents had known.

Other paths to white-orientation are discernible in the life stories of some mixed-bloods. Oscar Swanson is $\frac{1}{16}$ Blackfeet and his paternal grandfather was an immigrant from Sweden who came into Montana in the late 1890s as an employee of the railroad. He married a mixed-blood woman and they built a successful cattle ranch. Oscar's father was raised on the ranch and evidently learned very little of the Blackfeet culture from his mother. This seems to have been a common pattern in such marriages, even where the mother was a full-blood. The man was boss, he set the goals for the family and the Indian wife supported these. In some cases the wives were the driving force that made their white husbands successful. Oscar's mother was the daughter of a white family that had come from the midwest to homestead just east of the reservation. She and Oscar's father had gone to school together and were married soon after their eighth grade graduation. These two continued the ranch operation and raised their children in the way of life they both knew. Consequently, Indian traditions, language, and beliefs are strange to Oscar. He is one of the "Indians by technicality" who qualifies for tribal membership because his great-grandmother was a Blackfeet, and he resides on the reservation. Like Robert Thompson, described earlier, he feels that being part Indian has had little effect on him; life would have been much the same if he had been born and raised just off the reservation by white parents. His children, now $\frac{1}{32}$ Blackfeet, continue in the patterns of socialization established by their parents and grandparents, yet remain as members of the tribe because they were born prior to the restrictive amendment to the tribal constitution.

Many of the white-oriented members of the tribe are from similar background, but the variations are interesting and show the international influences that have affected reservation life. Anthony Garceau, an elderly cattleman, was the son of mixed-blood parents. His paternal grandfather was a French fur trapper who married a Canadian Cree girl. Their only son, Anthony's father, was raised in a trading post. He went to school for a few years, worked for the trader for a time and then started ranching in southern Saskatchewan. Anthony's mother was born at Fort Benton, the daughter of a Piegan girl who had married another French immigrant fur trader. Her mother died when she was a child, so her father sent her to a convent in Winnipeg where she was raised and educated. At about the age of eighteen she visited friends in Saskatchewan where she met and married

Mr. Garceau. Shortly after Anthony was born, his father died and his mother brought the children to the reservation where she worked in the schools to support them. Neither parent had learned to speak their native Indian languages, so French was the language used in the home. The Garceau children, along with their Blackfeet-speaking friends, learned English in school.

Anthony left school while still in his teens and began ranching on his own. He experienced all the ups and downs of that industry, but rebuilt after each loss and gradually established a successful cattle ranch which he managed until old age and infirmities made it necessary for him to turn the operation over to his sons. His children were raised in a home and educated in schools that provided no influences from traditional Blackfeet culture.

Several other genealogies show a similar history indicating that people from many parts of Europe and the United States have contributed to the genetic and cultural mix that makes up the present Blackfeet tribe.

Another successful white-oriented rancher, Harry Wilson, recalled that

> My grandfather, old man Wilson, originally came from England. He was in the army sent out to Alberta to pacify the Indians. He married a daughter of one of the chiefs he had fought against. Later he moved the family to Fort Benton where he set up a trading post. My father was raised there and came to the reservation just after the turn of the century, where he married my mother, a white woman.

This man, again, was one of a second generation of mixed-marriages where the white parent stayed to direct the training of the children to ranch life. But Harry had an experience not shared by others of his family. His paternal grandfather died, after which his grandmother married a Blood Indian and went to live with him in Alberta. Harry went to visit them when he was still a young boy and stayed for three years, where he became a favorite of his stepgrandfather who set out to make him a medicine man. He learned much of the lore, customs and ritual from the old man and was allowed to participate in many of the ceremonies. He remembers that by the time he came home he could speak Blackfeet fluently and had almost forgotten how to speak English. He inherited many of the old man's things and remembers much of what he learned during that visit. Harry learned to appreciate the Indian traditions and he retains an empathy with and understanding of the Indian-oriented that allows him to participate legitimately in some of the rituals.

After his return home, he entered again into white-oriented life, became a successful rancher both on and off the reservation, has held political offices and been a 4-H leader. He married a white woman and they have had five children all of whom have been raised in white ways. This family too is listed on the tribal roll and those who have remained on the reservation play a part in reservation life.

Harry's experience in two traditions has not been unique among the white-oriented of his generation. Two cases come to mind where the mothers of children in their teens were remarried to full-blood men following the death of their white husbands. In these cases the children had an opportunity, which some of them took, to participate in Indian-oriented activities and to learn from their stepfather and his friends of Indian traditions. The two people I knew had learned the language and established recognized positions within the Indian-oriented society. They work with the Indians, dance with them, and often play a part in the rituals, yet, in balance, remain white-oriented in belief, values, and life-style. Such people are effective mediators between the two divisions and able interpreters of the Indian to the whites.

The experiences of many other mixed-blood families parallel in general those that I have described. They begin with the marriage of one white and one Indian parent who train their children to white ways. There are numerous varia-tions in the details of subsequent marriages and experiences: children in the sec-ond generation frequently married mixed-blood spouses whose background was similar to their own instead of continuing a series of marriages to whites, as was done in the cases cited. The occupations chosen and the relative success or failure at these differed widely too. They share one basic element, however, over several generations the socialization patterns have been those of the dominant society and this has produced white-oriented tribal members.

Socialization to Indian-Orientation

The main avenue to present-day Indian-orientation has been the continuity of socialization to traditional ways modified by the attempts of the parents in each generation to cope with changing conditions and by each person's experiences with school, church, agency, and neighbors. Typical family histories are hard to find. Indian-oriented people were faced with many more options than the white-oriented. White-oriented families knew and were committed to the goals of financial inde-pendence; they were familiar with and supported what was taught in the schools and churches and knew what farming, ranching and business were all about. Most of the Indian-oriented, on the other hand, were from families where the things the parents and grandparents knew and understood did not fit the times. People in each generation learned bits and pieces of two traditions and had to learn which behavior, old or new, was appropriate depending on the circumstances. They were involved in the experiments with new subsistence techniques, in experiments that more often than not failed to produce a reliable and meaningful economic base for family and personal development. The following cases can only suggest some themes common to the backgrounds of the Indian-oriented people.

James Red Robe was born to full-blood parents in 1920. His childhood memories are of living in a cabin on Little Badger Creek, where his parents were raising potatoes, vegetables, chicken, and sheep under Agent Campbell's "Five Year Plan." He and his brothers and sisters were raised here and completed the eighth grade in the neighborhood school where they learned to speak and read English.

James' father, Harry Red Robe, and his mother were both born in 1890, and had lived through the trials of readaptation after the end of the buffalo days. Both parents became Catholics and had a few years of sporadic schooling, but gained most of their knowledge from what their own parents knew and taught them, plus what they learned by living through the years of change. Harry got his name when he was registered on the agency ration rolls. Here Red Robe found that the name he had paid an old medicine man to give his son was not important. The encounter with the agency roll clerk is not hard to imagine: Clerk to interpreter—"He is his son and a Christian. We have to give him a Christian surname. No one can pronounce the old man's name; what does it mean in English? Red Robe? All right tell him that his name is now Red Robe and his son will be called Harry Red Robe. We'll have to name the rest of the family too."

Harry tried and failed at farming and ranching in turn as many others did, but managed to keep his family alive and together with what he raised, supplemented by wage work on ranches, irrigation canal construction and by drawing rations when all else failed. The best days, according to James, were those that came after his father had quit ranching and devoted his time to raising horses, visiting, taking part in Indian social and ritual activities, interrupting these every now and then to work for the ranchers who were leasing his land. James remembers all the meetings, dances and ritual occasions. Both he and his father belonged to the Slick Feet, a society to which most of the men in the neighborhood, even a couple of white men, belonged. The "real" members, according to James, were the Indian men who had "paid" to get in. People came from all around when the society sponsored a dance. They camped along the creek, feasted, danced and had give-aways. "Everything was horses in those days, only a few people had cars. I can remember times when men brought unbroken horses right into the hall and gave them away."

James worked on his uncle's ranch and began to build a herd of his own using loan cattle. He was just getting a good start, he said, when he was called into the service during World War II. No one would care for his stock so he returned the loan cattle and sold the surplus. Since the war he has worked for wages at whatever he can find to do. He married a girl from a similar background. She works hard to raise their children and to maintain a home on what James brings in supplemented with what the older children can earn, help from kinsmen, and welfare payments during the winter.

James is Indian-oriented—he remembers and values what he learned about Indian ways from his parents and friends. He has been cured several times by an old man and has seen others cured as well. He has been present at bundle openings and participated in the Slick Feet rituals. "I didn't used to believe all that stuff, but after the cures I changed my mind." He insisted, however, that his children were good Catholics, and that he is the only one in his own family that still believes in some of the old Indian religion. I am unable to predict the orientation that will be taken by his children. He says that they do not speak Blackfeet and know nothing about the traditions. They do not take part in Indian social activities. On the other hand the people the children see most frequently are Indian-oriented and their own friends are the children of Indian-oriented families. James could give me no idea about what goals he had in mind for them.

Edward Chief's Son told a generally similar story except that his forebears had been among the leading families of Blackfeet society. His grandfather and father had managed to accumulate a little more, and build a larger following of kin and friends than Harry Red Robe had been able to do. Both of his grandfathers had been medicine men, bundle owners, and ritualists. None of them had been band chiefs, but had gained names as men of note within their bands.

Edward said that both of his parents were raised as Catholics and both had gone to about the fourth grade in school. They spoke some English but the Blackfeet language was used in the home while Edward and his brother and sisters were growing up. Edward told me little of his father's work experience. He was one of the "ranchers" who had ended up leasing his trust lands to other ranchers. The father, while nominally a Catholic, was also a bundle owner, curer, and ritualist who had sponsored a Sun Dance in which Edward and his brother had taken part. The children heard old stories, tales, and legends from their father and his friends during many an evening; they went with their parents to visit friends and relatives, to bundle openings, song services, and society dances. He learned to dance and sing and was taught much of the ritual. The father taught his children through story, example, and experience to appreciate Indian ways.

Edward has had more experience with the outside world than James. He served longer in the army and was sent overseas during World War II. He married soon after the war and has maintained his family on the lease money from his own and inherited trust lands, irregular wage labor on the reservation and, in past years, by traveling out of state with his family to work in the hop, apple, and potato harvests. In school he participated in sports and 4-H work, and he is presently an active member of the American Legion. He is a member and a leader in one of the Indian societies and frequently sings with one of the song groups.

This man is not much more secure financially than James, but he has more self-assurance and an established role among the Indian-oriented segment of the community. Some of the difference may stem from the relative social standing of their respective parents and the expectations that followed from this. Edward said, "I know I'm a full-blood and like to keep the old things alive." Unlike James, he teaches these things to his children and encourages them to learn to dance and to take part in Indian social activities. I would predict that they will be Indian-oriented when they grow up.

Raymond Black Plume's background was similar to that of Edward. He too is descended from leading men on both sides of the family, but he and others like him often appear to be younger children of large families who are singled out, for reasons not clear to me, for more education. It may be that they showed greater interest and could be allowed more time away from subsistence chores. Raymond did well in school, and completed high school where he was active in sports and Boy Scout work. One of his teachers took an interest in him and saw to it that he was included in several trips to West Coast cities. The teacher encouraged him to continue his education and helped him win a scholarship that supported him through one year of college. Raymond did not continue with college work, but he had acquired a proficiency in English and the social experience with white people than enables him to be an effective spokesman for the Indian-oriented group in the council and in national Indian organizations. Raymond, too, values his Indian heritage and, with the support of his wife, teaches his children the "best of the old and the best of the new."

The Indian-oriented group includes mixed-bloods too. Several people registered as ⅛, ¾, and ⅝ Blackfeet include an English or French trader or trapper in their genealogies. In these cases, however, whether married or not, the white grand- or great-grandparent either died or left his family when the children were very young. The mother returned to her family where she and her kinsmen raised the children in traditional ways. These children usually married full-bloods and socialized their children to be Indian-oriented. People with these backgrounds are essentially Indians who happen to have had a white grandfather or great-grand-father. The white man did not remain as a guide or model to teach his descendants anything about white culture.

Not all men and women from such backgrounds end up as Indian-oriented. At each generation there have been those who turned to the new and tended to forget or failed to learn much of Indian culture. Some left the reservation and became assimilated, some remained on the reservation as white-oriented, but many others who made such a break, often as they approached middle age, have either rejected the white world or felt rejected by it and returned to resume or relearn the old and now more highly valued Indian cultural patterns.

Analysis

These few examples of socialization experience leading to one or the other cultural orientation seem to show some common features. Parents teach their children what they know and believe. Where a parent was white-oriented and remained to direct the training of his children, or provided a teacher and model to the same end, the children tended to become white-oriented. Bruner (1956: 608–609) considered the presence of a "white model" to have been an important factor in the assimilation of the Mandan Indians. Where the experience of the parents, what they knew and believed, was from the Indian culture, this was transmitted to the children. Where the parents seem uncertain about what their children should be, as James now is, the next generation may be ill-prepared for a place in either group unless their peers, a teacher, or some elder provides a model or guidance that will give the children goals they now appear to lack.

These examples show, too, the complexity of the processes that underlie the present social diversity. The assimilation model held in the minds of administrators, priests, ministers, and teachers appears to have been one in which an Indian couple raised their children as Indians, the school and church changed or altered these children toward assimilation goals, and these upon becoming parents, moved their children even further toward that assimilation. Such a progression has occurred and some present tribal members are white-oriented because their family histories have followed such a course, but many other paths have been followed. Some tribal members are white-oriented because they were raised in families where there had been few or no traits of Indian culture to transmit, others had moved in one or two generations from Indian cultural backgrounds to a white-oriented life style and commitment. Other tribal members are Indian-oriented because members of their families have resisted assimilation, have sought to retain some things from the past even as they accepted some aspects of white culture. There are other

Indian-oriented people who had apparently rejected their cultural heritage but later in life came to value things that they had been exposed to during childhood and either learned or re-learned to be Indians again. There are those, too, among the Indian-oriented who have maintained the values and attitudes and a few of the practices learned in their childhood homes while at the same time learning to adapt to and even to use much from the white man's culture.

In this chapter I have suggested that there are two contrasting social groups living on the Blackfeet Indian reservation that differ significantly in their cultural orientations, and I have stressed that differing socialization patterns have been at work throughout the history of Blackfeet and white contact that maintained and perpetuated this division. One segment of the tribe has blocked or delayed assimilation forming an Indian-oriented society even as other tribal members moved toward assimilation and joined those who were born assimilated to form the white-oriented group. More of the content and direction of these differences in cultural transmission will become clear in the following discussion of the interaction patterns, values and status structures of the two divisions.

6

Social Interaction

Introduction

THE FOLLOWING ASSESSMENT of social interaction is based on observations made during the course of interviews, during attendance at group and community social gatherings, while visiting people in varying situations, and by observing people in stores and on the street. In addition, much information was gleaned from comments of informants and from the local weekly newspaper.

The original orientation categories used reported interest or participation in some social activities as defining criteria; the concern now is to show that these people actually did attend and participate in these affairs but did not take part in others. Then other forms of social gathering for which I have data are discussed to further support the contention that people of each orientation interact more frequently among themselves than they do with people of the other orientation.

As my fieldwork progressed, the impression grew that in some situations people of both orientations participated in relatively equal numbers; in other contexts the Indian-oriented people formed the majority in attendance, while other social gatherings attracted mainly white-oriented persons. The three types of social gatherings are discussed separately and in that order.

Social Occasions Where Everybody Came

Both Indian- and white-oriented people were noted at political rallies, tribal council meetings, church, sports events, and rodeos. Other situations where relatively equal participation between people of both orientations was noticeable were in business and work contexts where the relationships were those of buyer-seller, service-client, and employee-employer.

Council meetings draw people from all segments of the tribe, as it is at these meetings that issues of interest to all are discussed. The largest crowds turn out when meetings are held to vote on per capita payments, or decisions about the use of Indian land are being considered. At such meetings people of both orientations are present and are equally vocal in support of or in opposition to proposals made. Both orientation groups are represented in the council. At meetings I attended, one or two old timers used the time prior to the opening of the meeting to make speeches, loudly haranguing the usually inattentive audience about the problems of the full-bloods. Council minutes frequently record the speeches of the Honorary Councilmen, who contribute to the debate, such as the translation of a speech recorded several years back in which an honored elder spoke about procedures in preparing a land claim case against the U.S. government:

> I am speaking to all of you my people. We have the time and we have the chance to discuss the true evidence that we have and we should use them for our discussions. Don't use things that will puzzle up our claims. Use the facts to determine your progress. In my memory there was a time when a claim matter came up and several members of the tribe tried to use evidence that was not right. I told them to bring out only the true facts and if they were presented with our faith in them we would be sure to win our case. I believe that if we proceed according to treaties and agreements made with the government we will make some progress on our claims. Let's work with the chosen leaders of our tribe. I'm sure they are doing the best they can for us . . . (Unpublished documents of the Blackfeet Tribal Council).

Campaign meetings are held in Browning and the outlying communities preceding each biennial election of tribal councilmen. As many as sixty-five to seventy candidates run for office, and most of them attend these meetings to explain their stands on political issues, and to solicit voter support at the polls. Most of the meetings I attended in Browning took place in a centrally located building where the attendance was mixed. The orientation differences were recognized, however, by arranging other meetings at the homes of some of the "full-bloods" where Indian-oriented people were most numerous of those attending. Attendance at meetings in the outlying communities is proportionate to the composition of the community population; that is, Starr School and Heart Butte have a larger proportion of Indian-oriented present than at similar meetings at Babb or East Glacier where the population is more balanced or even largely white-oriented.

The political meetings draw interested people from both segments of the reservation population because the issues discussed affect the affairs of all. All candidates at meetings I attended made some allusion to their own Indian identification, that is, "we Indians," "the white man is after our land and we Indians must prevent this." Speeches emphasized the need to stop white encroachment, the imminence and dangers of termination, the need to preserve the land base. Calls were made for better education, more jobs, more per capita payments and better management of tribal funds. Some candidates spoke in English, others in Blackfeet, and the speeches of both were translated into the other language by an interpreter. I was impressed by the fairness of the interpretation. Often the translator was a candidate himself, yet he translated objectively the remarks of the other speakers, occasionally turned a haltingly given speech into a forceful and dynamic one, and included remarks that were critical of his own candidacy or performance in office. On one occasion the interpreter gave introductory recognition to candidates who were unable to attend and commented that "your support at the polls would be most appreciated" by those candidates. People running for office draw upon ties of kinship that might have been overlooked or ignored in the recent past. It is often said that if you can get the support of a few key people you can be assured of the "full-blood vote," indicating the belief that kinsmen will vote with their family leaders.

People of both orientations attend church services according to individual interests and needs. Leaders of the different denominations actively proselyte among both unaffiliated people and the membership of the other churches. Interest in church attendance appears to follow the patterns indicated in the responses to my questionnaire where only three of the Indian-oriented and four of the white-oriented reported regular church attendance.

Rodeos and sports events are occasions for the largest gatherings which include relatively equal attendance and participation by people of both orientations. The rodeo attracts the largest crowds. These are public events open to all who buy a ticket and are given wide publicity; the participants are largely local people and drawn from both orientation groups.

People from both groups were seen in attendance at rodeos held in Browning and at Birch Creek during each summer of fieldwork. The informal grouping in the stands and around the grounds appear to be based on family and friendship ties. Families—parents, children and grandchildren—sit together. People apart from their families sit with their friends. In the rural areas, the spectators sit in cars and trucks, or stand around the arena. They cheer for their kinsmen and friends and jeer at the opposition; it is a lively and often moving crowd. Cultural orientations appear to operate in the smaller groupings that make up the larger crowds.

The sports events draw smaller numbers of people than do the rodeos, but the nature of participation and attendance is similar. One such event, an elementary school track meet I attended, appeared particularly noteworthy because it is comparable in many respects to the Easter Egg Hunt described later in this section.

This track and field meet between the Browning and neighborhood elementary schools was an activity in which children took part without regard to the orientation of their families. It was held at the Browning High School track on a cold, blustery spring day and people of both orientations attended—parents, teachers, and track fans. Informal groupings by family and friends were noted here too, but it was a moving crowd and interaction patterns were hard to identify.

Various other public ceremonies attract participants and on-lookers from all segments of the population, usually on the basis of who has an interest in the particular event scheduled. I recall two such occasions: a ceremony honoring an Air Force contingent from Malmstrom Air Force Base near Great Falls in 1959 and the dedication of a War Veterans memorial by the War Mothers on the grounds of the Museum of the Plains Indian in 1967. Both ceremonies were held on the Museum grounds and drew participants from both orientations—Tribal Councilmen, Honorary Councilmen, the American Legion Color Guard, and in the latter ceremony, the War Mothers and families of veterans who had died in action.

The Air Force ceremony struck several of us as a test of the time sense of two cultures. Two Air Force generals were to be honored by being given a Blackfeet name and honorary membership in the Blackfeet tribe. The ritual called for a speech by an elderly chief at the conclusion of which he would pronounce the name he was giving the general, and place a war bonnet on the head of the newly adopted tribesman. A second chief would then make the bestowal to the other general. Air Force plans called for a jet plane fly-over as the war bonnet was put on the head of the senior officer. Four members of the Honorary Council, the master of ceremonies and an interpreter, dressed in Indian regalia, stood in an informal group at one side awaiting the beginning of the ceremonies, while to the other an Air Force contingent consisting of the two generals, fifteen full colonels and a captain, and a color guard of a sergeant and five enlisted men, were drawn up in formation. There was much synchronizing of watches on the military side, a relaxed unconcerned waiting on the part of the Blackfeet. The jets were evidently airborne somewhere over the horizon; if there was radio communication between the planes and the group on the ground, I did not see it.

The ceremony began. Air Force participation could be and was done according to a planned time sequence, but no one could predict how long one of the chiefs might choose to speak. Yet even as I was figuring the odds on outcome, the old chief concluded his speech and pronounced the name, the interpreter translated it, the war bonnet went up and the jets came over the horizon, over the group on the ground and out of sight in the direction of Great Falls. Someone, I will never know who, had good medicine.

The War Memorial dedication was a concern of local people and brought together an audience of families of veterans and tribal dignitaries. It marked the success of a drive begun many years earlier by the War Mothers (mothers of war veterans) to raise money for such a memorial, so commemorated too their persistence and hard work. A procession of tribal leaders, some in Indian regalia, the American Legion Color Guard, the Boy Scouts, and the War Mothers was followed by speeches from the Gold Star Mothers and the unveiling of the pylon shaped monument upon which was mounted a bronze plaque inscribed with the names of tribal members who had been killed in action in U.S. wars. Later in the day the War Mothers staged a give-away ceremony in memory of these war dead.

Indian-Oriented Social Occasions

The social occasions where most of the participants and spectators are people of Indian orientation include several public, semiprivate and private gatherings. Some are formal occasions while others are informal in their organization. Formal public occasions include the North American Indian Days celebrations at Browning, a Sun Dance held in conjunction with one of these, and periodically scheduled Indian dances. Horse races and stick game gatherings in the outlying communities are frequent forms of public entertainment organized on a less formal basis. The private and semiprivate gatherings are those to which attendance

is invited, tacitly or directly, and some of the formal occasions for such congregation are medicine bundle openings, curing ceremonies, song services, and private
parties. House to house visiting, gatherings of families and friends, the visiting
grouping at the formal public activities, in office buildings and stores, and street
corner visiting are kinds of informal private interaction.

The Indian Days celebrations are annual affairs sponsored by the reservation community. The tribal council makes an appropriation to underwrite the
celebration, and local businessmen make cash contributions or put up prizes for
competitive events. The four day celebration, held in late June or early July, is a
reenactment of the traditional Blackfeet summer encampment and advertised
widely as a tourist attraction. Families who own tepees are encouraged to pitch
them on the encampment grounds and to camp there with their families. Indians
from other reservations are invited, resulting in a camp circle of fifty or more
tepees formed by local people, visitors from the Canadian Reserves—Blood, North
Piegan, Blackfoot and Cree—and from surrounding United States Indian communities—Warm Springs, Yakima, Umatilla, Crow, Gros Ventre, Cheyenne, Assini-
boine, Flathead, and Cree, among others. Sleeping and cooking tents are erected
behind the tepee circle and upwards of seven hundred people live on the grounds
during the encampment. Each family camping on the grounds is paid a cash allowance toward their maintenance and shares in a daily meat or food ration.

The formal program opens with a parade through the main street of
Browning and out to the encampment grounds near the Museum of the Plains
Indian, a half mile west of town. A regular program of Indian dancing to the
accompaniment of singing and drumming by local and visiting singing groups is
scheduled each afternoon, and continues long into the evening if the weather
permits.

The dancing sessions are interrupted frequently by both planned and un-
planned intermission activities—special dance contests, games, and "give-aways."
Some of the last mentioned gift giving ceremonies are sponsored by the Indian
Days Committee to honor and give gifts to invited guests from other tribes.
Others are put on by individuals and families who wish—and are expected—to
give gifts in remembrance of a deceased relative, to give a new and significant
Indian name to a child in a public naming ceremony, or to honor some other
person by a display of generosity in his name. The person to be honored and his
family form a procession and pass four times around the dance arena as the singers
drum and sing a favored song. A similar procession is formed for the memorial
give-away, and a close relative carries a photograph of the deceased relative. Increasingly distant relatives join the procession with each turn. Quantities of gifts
are brought in and at the conclusion of the processional, a crier acting for the
family calls out the names of those to be given gifts. Occasionally a tepee with
furnishings is given, sometimes horses, more usually blankets, cigarettes, and cash
make up the gifts.

Another almost regularly occurring part of the program is a ceremony in
which distinguished visitors are adopted into the Blackfeet Tribe. These people
are given an Indian name and a war bonnet, or other tokens of their new status,
by an honored elder. In 1960, Indian Days coincided with the U.S. Governors

Conference at Many Glaciers Lodge in Glacier National Park. Six of the governors who visited the encampment were honored by adoption and given names, and the Governor of Virginia was selected to respond for the others. He began by remarking that the people of Virginia felt a special and warm regard for the Indians. "If it had not been for the help of the Indians the Jamestown settlement would not have survived that first winter." A Blackfeet standing beside me gave me a dig in the ribs with his elbow and said, "that's the day we lost the war."

The encampment also provides the opportunity for other forms of social expression. Medicine bundles are opened with attendant prayers, dances, and face-painting. Men may be "captured" to become members of the Dog society, an honor that must be paid for in goods or cash. People visit from tepee to tepee, drink coffee, eat, and talk. Sometimes one or more of the elderly Indian-oriented leaders will provide a lunch of boiled beef, bread, salad, doughnuts, cookies, cake, and coffee to all who wish to come.

By midafternoon a stick game or two gets under way near one of the concesion booths behind the tent area and usually continues until dawn. Sometimes known as the "hand game," this is a popular and widely known Indian gambling game. All that is required is space, two poles, planks, or timbers placed about three feet apart parallel to each other, two "bones," or short wooden cylinders about ½ inch in diameter and two inches long, one banded and the other plain, and some plain sticks about ten to twelve inches long, usually ten to a side to use as markers. Two teams line up facing each other behind each pole. One person starts the game by intently shuffling, showing, and after many flourishes hiding the bones, one in each hand. His team chants and drums with sticks on the pole in front of them to give him support and to confuse the opposition during the hiding. Finally he extends his hands so that one of the players on the other side can choose by one of several signs which hand holds the unmarked bone. If the "guesser" fails to choose correctly, his side forfeits one of their marker sticks and the "hider" tries again; if he guesses correctly, the bones and roles change sides. The game is over when one side wins all of the marker sticks. Bets between individuals, both participants and onlookers, are placed before the game begins and other bets are made frequently on the results of individual guesses. There are many variations in the procedure that I have not mastered. A bettor gets a lot of action for his money whether he fully understands what is happening or not. The drumming, chanting, joking, as well as the strain of waiting for the outcome of a game in which large sums of money are at stake, contribute to an exciting time.

People spend the rest of the time during the encampment doing the necessary chores of camp living and enjoying the pastimes appropriate to sex and age— the children play games, older people work on costumes, play blackjack, visit, loaf, or go into town.

In spite of this being a community enterprise with fairly large crowds that are attracted to it, the people in relatively continuous attendance are the Indian-oriented. The people who camp on the grounds and participate in the festivities include and appear to be like the men I interviewed and classed as Indian-oriented. In retrospect, I would sort the onlookers into four categories: (a) Indian-oriented spectators from many parts of the reservation who spend much time on the grounds and can be seen in attendance day after day, (b) a number of people recognized as of white-orientation who make a brief appearance, spend an hour or two watching the proceedings and then leave, (c) a few white-oriented people, who because of special community roles and interests have reason to be in attendance more frequently, and (d) a changing tourist attendance of twenty-five to one hundred persons who spend varying amounts of time enjoying the spectacle. The patterns of attendance and participation appear to be changing. During the past ten years, many older people have died and fewer expert ritualists are left, but younger people are getting involved in the dancing. In 1959, I noted that few teenagers were dancing; the dancers tended to be either over thirty or under twelve years old. In 1970, these youngsters had become teenagers and were still turning out. More children were dancing. All age ranges seemed to be represented. In addition, several children from white-oriented families were seen to be buying costumes and learning to dance.[12]

The most recent Sun Dances were performed in 1959 and 1964 and the ceremony I observed (1959) was held in conjunction with that year's Indian Days. The religious ceremonies were held on the encampment grounds preceding the secular festivities. A "Medicine Lodge" was constructed with appropriate ritual by setting up a circle of ten poles around a center post: rafters were strung between these poles and from each pole to the center post and lashed into place with strips of hide. An opening was left to the east, and the wall and "roof" at the west end were covered with leafy cottonwood branches to make a sun and wind shelter for the ritualists who worked inside. The participants were largely people of Indian-orientation as were most of the spectators. Modern Indian-orientation does not require full knowledge and belief in the old religion. While the key roles were filled by older men who knew the ritual, other people were chosen more because they came close to the model of "good Indian people" than for their knowledge of the ritual. Some others were selected because they were kin of the more traditional participants or were among the social and political leaders from both segments of the community. One woman told me that she had been "captured" and had paid for the privilege of "owning" the knife and the right to cut the hide into strips for the lashings on the Medicine Lodge. This was traditionally a male prerogative, and in this case a male relative acted for her. In 1964 a young man conducted the ritual, thus assuming a role usually reserved for an older man. He had been trained from childhood by his grandfather and other elders, so perhaps was better qualified in this respect than most living elders, but his action appeared to have made some of the older people uneasy. Such changes aside, the ceremonies are solemn, the key participants are involved in rituals that have deep meaning for them; the other participants pay respect to the beliefs expressed, and the families and friends of the people involved watch the proceedings with mixed emotions of interest, understanding, tolerance and respect.

Social dancing at the Indian Days Celebration functions as both entertainment for the tourists and recreation for the participants. The dancers do not

---

[12] Participation by these young people might introduce some confusion into my orientation schemes, but for reasons I will discuss in the final chapter, I think that their participation does not signal a turn toward Indian-orientation on their part.

await an audience but start dancing when they feel like it, often whenever a singing group begins to drum. The entertainment rarely follows the schedule, but starts and stops according to the mood of the individual dancers. Some arrive on time, others an hour or two late. Evening dances are or are not held depending upon the weather and the inclination of the dancers, rather than upon the presence of an audience. In fact many dancers show signs of impatience with the tourist onlookers who often invade the dance circle to take pictures. Tourists appear to be a tolerated nuisance rather than spectators to be entertained. The Indian visitors, who understand the dancing and participate at least vicariously, are the more orderly, appreciative and appreciated audience. The point is that the dancing at the encampment is a social and recreational outlet, and for the people involved it is an experience that plays a very important and meaningful part in their lives. During these days they are "Indians," doing things that symbolized this identity. They stress social positions of importance among "Indians" that may have little relation to the world at large. People have a special competence here that is recognized by their peers.

People who own dancing costumes leave the reservation frequently during the summer and fall to participate in similar Indian gatherings held throughout the plains area. Indian-oriented families may be gone for most of the summer, and the anthropologist who stays behind knows that he is missing out on events that are an important part of the lives of these people.

In the late fall, winter, and early spring a series of social dances, often coinciding with national holidays, are held at the community halls in surrounding neighborhoods. People from other parts of the reservation are invited or are free to attend. Often people came from neighboring reservations as well.

These dances, at the Heart Butte, Starr School, or other community houses, are usually sponsored by one of the men's societies. Those I attended in the spring of 1960 were scheduled for an early evening start, yet it was usually around nine o'clock before the dancing began. The Grass and Fancy dancers were in costume and Grass, War, and other dances by those in costume were mixed with Owl dances—round dances for men and women partners—in which all could participate whether in costume or not. Here, as in the Indian Days program, time was taken for give-aways—at least one was put on by the sponsoring society to honor guests and others were put on by individuals for varying reasons. At midnight the wives, sisters, and daughters of the sponsoring society members served a lunch to all in attendance, then dancing was resumed to continue until dawn. Newspaper and informants' reports indicated that the dances I attended were typical and that they continue to be held.

The attendance and participation at these dances confirmed the reports from my sample; those I identified as Indian-oriented were present, while few of the white-oriented people turned out. The crowds (usually estimated from three to four hundred in number) were made up of the same people who had been seen in most constant attendance at the Indian Days programs.

The more Indian-oriented communities of Starr School and Heart Butte alternately sponsor horse racing in their neighborhoods almost weekly during the

A round dance for couples—everybody is invited to dance whether in costume or not.

A give-away ceremony.

summer and fall. Horse owners and racing fans from many parts of the reservation turn out to visit and watch the horses run. Interregional rivalry is often intense. The fastest horses become well-known so the outcome of the races often turns on the weight and ability of the jockey and the possibility of gaining an advantage at the start. Much time is spent in getting the betting arranged, so that two or three races are about all that can be run in an afternoon.

Stick games are often played after the races, and at Heart Butte the games are a regular part of the year-around weekend activities. A public room arranged for playing the stick game as well as pool and cards was a regular gathering place for the people of Heart Butte until it burned down a few years ago. The weekly stick games have moved to a new location on Badger Creek.

The horse races attract some white-oriented horse fans, but the majority of the crowd is Indian-oriented. Races are occasions for Indian rivalry and above all to enjoy each other's company. The stick games have a regular but more limited following and with few exceptions, players and observers are Indian-oriented.

Song services are meetings of the singing groups and serve both as practice sessions and as forms of social gathering for the people involved. The sessions are uually held in the home of one of the singers, a relative, or a friend. A few kinsmen and friends—young and old, men and women—attend and the evening is spent in singing and drumming old and new songs. The sessions break up at the discretion of the singers and may be followed by a late supper.

Bundle openings and curing ceremonies (according to informant and newspaper reports) are religious rituals to which guests are invited. The reports indicate that those in attendance are always people of Indian-orientation. Some are believers and others are sympathetic but noncommitted members of the participants' families. The activities on these occasions are determined by the ritual of the particular bundle or cure, but involve singing, drumming, prayers and some dancing by selected participants. The owner of the bundle regularly paints the faces of those in attendance as a mark of prayer for their well being. Bundle opening ceremonies are followed by a feast. One such ceremony held at Starr School was described by one of the neighbors:

> The beaver dance given by Jim White Calf was held at the home of Jim and Amy Whitegrass despite the terrific storm and sudden cold. There were many people from Browning out to see this rare dance, that has long been forgotten. Among those attending were Mr. and Mrs. Fish Wolf Robe, Mr. and Mrs. Charlie Horn, Mr. and Mrs. Tom Many Guns and Mary Ground besides the many people of our community. The dance began with the rythmic [sic] beating on hides to certain songs. The bundle was opened by Jim White Calf and Maggie Many Hides. The bundle consists of many skins of useful animals and small birds that are of help to the owner. The beaver for "energy," the otter for "speed," the ermine for "beauty," the swan for "grace" and the little birds for their endurance of the cold in the winter. The people were then painted and eight danced in a most graceful manner. Maggie Many Hides, Mary Ground, Isabelle, Cecile Horn, Mrs. Fish, Annie Old Person, Mrs. Tom Many Guns all danced like beavers with sticks in their mouths and hands. The usual meal was served after a monstrous amount of energy was put into the dancing and singing. A delicious berry soup, boiled meat, fried bread and a dessert were consumed by everyone. At the end of the dance one certain lady gets up and dances with little small deer hooves and punches a man in the crowd and it goes on until everyone is dancing. It was a most enjoyable occasion for a grand time was had by all (*Glacier Reporter*, October 12, 1961:6).

This "dance" was "long forgotten" by the reporter and others in the community but not by the bundle-owner and the named participants, several of whom owned or had owned bundles themselves. Here was a gathering of Indian-oriented people conducting an Indian ceremony. Some undoubtedly experienced the deep religious experience of a beaver bundle opening, others had a "grand time" at a "most enjoyable occasion," a social gathering of people who shared interests in aspects of Indian culture.

The social grouping of Indian-oriented people gains further support from observations of informal clustering. At the Indian Days encampment, and at the social dances in particular, it was relatively easy to watch for the Indian-oriented people and to notice with whom they spent their time in informal groupings— visiting, chatting, watching, and relaxing. Most of such visiting was with people of similar orientation with only occasional mixing among men of differing orienta-

The forming of the tepee circle for North American Indian Days.

tions. Other observations and reports further support these conclusions. Visits to homes, reported visiting among families and friends, and observations of grouping on other occasions reinforced the pattern.

In 1962 I wrote:

> Perhaps the most visible visiting pattern for the Indian-oriented people is the very regular daily congregation in sidewalk groups. From late spring to mid-autumn as many as eighty people can be seen standing or sitting at fairly predictable locations around the town. The location is determined by people's inclinations and by the requirements of sun, shade, or shelter from the wind. People pass many hours a day, visiting and watching the passers-by. White-oriented men are on the street but stop for only short periods of time and then move on, but the Indian-oriented man and his friends make this a major avocation.
>
> If the weather is bad the visitors form smaller groups and move into the nearby

buildings for shorter periods of time. Most of the men, if asked or if they happen to volunteer the information, have a reason for being there. They are available if someone should be looking for a hired hand; they are waiting for the mail, or keeping an appointment. Sometimes this is true but a comparison of the time spent with the chores accomplished strongly indicates that visiting with friends and watching the town activities with them, are the important objectives (McFee 1962:141).

There have been changes in these patterns since that time. Some businesses have moved to other parts of town diluting the concentration of occupied buildings in the central section, and the people have shifted too. Groups are smaller and scattered. The two grocery stores still serve as gathering places, the new Community Center and Tribal Office Building, located south of town and near much of the new low rent and mutual aid housing development, will undoubtedly provide a new focus for informal visiting groups and draw them further from the center of town. These patterns too will change but this form of visiting will continue. There is little else to do between infrequent jobs, and money is scarce. Some people will move into the bars when they have money, but there is a limit on how much time and money can be spent there. Others have no interest in the bars anyway. So men and women pass the time with the street corner groups or wander off to continue visiting in cars or at one another's homes.

Indian-oriented people appear to spend more time in social interaction with people of similar orientation than with others. It was to be expected from the way Indian orientation was defined, that people of this category would participate in the social activities that have been described. An examination of the limited participation by these people in other reservation social activities makes the social unity of this group more apparent.

White-Oriented Social Occasions

The areas of predominantly white-oriented interaction are again both public and private. The public social gatherings that I observed were most frequently centered around school and civic service themes and included P.T.A. meetings, school programs, commencement exercises, Youth Club activities, children's Fishing Derbies, and an annual Easter Egg Hunt. Other activities, such as bowling tournaments and civic club meetings, are of a semiprivate nature in that there is selective membership. The private occasions, as with the Indian-oriented group, would include parties, picnics, and visiting.

There appear to be no large community enterprises that draw crowds of white-oriented people together comparable to the Indian Days Encampment and the Indian dances around which so much Indian-oriented sociability is focused. Perhaps the unbalanced attendance at school and civic meetings—activities involving the children of the community—is most striking and comparable. The limited adult attendance at these events indicates a real social division within the community that can be explained, in part, by the cultural orientations.

School plays, commencement exercises, and the other child and youth activities in Browning invite public support.[13] Children from families of both orientations attend and participate; yet very few of the parents who turn out to watch their children perform are Indian-oriented.

The P.T.A. meetings and school commencement exercises I went to were not attended by many Indian-oriented people. No Indian-oriented were seen at two P.T.A. meetings, each attended by from fifty to sixty people. In 1960, twenty-one (over a third) of an eighth grade graduating class of sixty-seven were from identifiable Indian families, yet few Indian-oriented adults were in the audience.

The high school commencement held on the evening of the same day, differed considerably in the nature of attendance. In this instance a class of thirty-three graduating seniors included twenty-five tribal members. Eight of this number (approximately a fourth) could be identified as children from Indian-oriented families. The proportion of Indian-oriented among the seniors was smaller than for the eighth grade class, but more Indian-oriented adults were at the high school commencement, making up an estimated fifth of the audience. Even so, the largest part of those in attendance were white-oriented. Even smaller Indian-oriented attendance was reported for the preceding and following graduations.

The larger Indian attendance in 1960 may have been because the valedictorian was a full-blood boy. I had seen him dancing at the Indian social dances and at the Indian Days Celebrations, and on these occasions he wore a beaded buckskin suit that he had made and decorated himself. He was one of a very few young men who wore their hair in braids. Perhaps some of the Indian-oriented came to the commencement to see an Indian-oriented boy graduate with honors.

Attendance at the annual Easter Egg Hunts and the Fishing Derbies is more indicative. While these affairs are not comparable to an Indian Days Celebration, they are community sponsored, scheduled, recurrent and locally advertised. Children participate regardless of the orientation of their families. Perhaps these events and the previously described track meet are most comparable and the differences in attendance at each most revealing. In short, Indian-oriented parents attended the track meet but did not respond in the same way to the Egg Hunt and Fishing Derbies.

I observed the Easter Egg Hunt of 1960 and arrived too late for this event in following years. As usual it was held in an open field behind the Museum of the Plains Indian on the afternoon of Easter Sunday. The weather was much the same as it was for the track meet held one month later—cold and windy. Approximately five hundred children, from Indian, white, and white-oriented families took part. Children from the Cut Bank Boarding Dormitory were brought

---

[13] The description of these particular events is restricted to those held in Browning because it is the largest and most heterogeneous of the reservation communities. People of both orientations, local people and residents from the other communities, come to Browning to attend events that interest them. Attendance at similar affairs in outlying communities reflects the orientation balance of the community. Children's activities at Starr School and Heart Butte, for instance, are attended by more Indian-oriented people; similar events at Babb or East Glacier are attended almost wholly by white-oriented persons. Browning differs in that it has quite large populations of people from both orientations; selective turnout here is more significant.

in by bus; children from Starr School and other nearby neighborhoods came in cars driven by a teacher or parent to join in the search with the youngsters of Browning.

Members of the Browning Youth Club and the American Legion had distributed quantities of eggs, which had been boiled and colored by school children, in the furrows and stubble of the forty acre field. Some of the eggs were marked and cash awards were given to the finders of the special eggs. Prizes, donated by service clubs and local merchants, were given also for the most eggs collected by one child and to the runners-up.

This was a large area and people arrived at irregular intervals. Many watched from their cars, others moved about the periphery of the field, making an accurate count of the adults difficult, but it was apparent that the majority of those present were white and white-oriented people. Indian-oriented parents were few and even the Indian-oriented political leaders were absent.

The Fishing Derbies I witnessed drew a much smaller crowd, approximately two hundred children and sixty adults. The contests are held at a small lake adjacent to U.S. Route 2 a few miles southwest of Browning. The children fish along the shore, while the parents help with putting on bait and removing the fish that are caught. They cheer the children on, visit with each other, set up picnics, and eat. Everybody has a good time when a Fishing Derby is sponsored. An estimated third of the children taking part in these contests were from Indian-oriented families, yet only four or five Indian-oriented adults were in attendance.

In the realm of semiprivate interaction are included civic club meetings and bowling tournaments. The informants and the newspaper reports indicate an almost completely white-oriented participation in these activities.

Civic club membership is selective and based upon business, school, or political leadership. The selection factors are many and complex but it is clear that very few Indian-oriented people belong to these organizations—these are areas of predominantly white-oriented interaction.

Newspaper reports indicate that selective factors operate to maintain a predominantly white and white-oriented participation, particularly in team and tournament play, at the bowling alley. Factors of social selection also work in private gatherings and visiting patterns between families and friends. The bonds of kinship draw some of the Indian-oriented into the visiting patterns of white-oriented people, but these occasions are infrequent. Economic and status factors also appear to be important determinants of Indian-oriented participation in private activities.

Other Social Expressions of Orientation

The social division of the community that I am describing is given overt, but inexact, recognition by the use of the labels—"mixed-blood" and "full-blood." These "racial" stereotypes are used in many contexts but in most cases point up a division in culture that is only partially related to the number of Indian ancestors of any individual.

Ewers remarked on the rapid hybridization of the tribe and the decreasing

numbers of full-bloods, and he noted the tendency for the latter to consider themselves to be "the real Blackfoot Indians—the true descendants of the great warriors
and wise leaders of old and the preservers of all that is left of Blackfoot Indian
culture" (Ewers 1958:328). According to the stereotype, the full-blood is conservative and the mixed-blood progressive. The surnames of the people still further
label the difference—an English, French, or American name implies mixed genetic
heritage, while the Indian name (in its agency recorded translation) is a badge
of Indian heritage.

There are some grounds to support a popular notion of spatial separation
of the two groups. Generally the lands north of Browning are thought to be
mixed-blood territory and the full-bloods claim the southern part of the reservation. Recent migrations of people have upset this balance but the idea lingers on
as an element in social separation. An increasing community feeling among concentrations of full-bloods at Starr School and Heart Butte, and some spatial clustering in Browning, is tending to replace the old regional division. Mixed marriages
and shifting populations, however, are breaking down even these full-blood strong-
holds.

The full-blood-mixed-blood distinction is not equivalent to my categories
of Indian and white orientations. Of the eight Indian-oriented men in my sample,
only four are full-bloods, while one full-blood is categorized among the twenty
white-oriented people. But the popular full-blood and mixed-blood labels gain
some validity when it is noted that the Indian-oriented of the sample are all ¾ or
more Indian, while the white-oriented men are, with the one exception, ⅝ or less.

Such stereotypes produce conflicts. A series of statements by informants
illustrate the mechanisms of social distance that appear to be important in limiting close social interaction between people of the two orientation groups.

For example, "Full-bloods hate mixed-bloods. They are tainted with the
blood of those who robbed and ruined the Indian."

An informant overheard a mixed-blood girl complain, "They [full-bloods]
are to blame. In the old days when things were bad they sold their daughters to
the white men. Now they hate us."

A mixed-blood man said, "Full-bloods hate the mixed-bloods and would
like to run them off the reservation. They get confused when I ask them, How
about that white son-in-law of yours and your grandchildren? They finally decided
that those were all right."

One man observed that little social distinction is felt by the children until
they reach the upper grades. Then the more Indian children develop feelings of
inferiority and inadequacy and drop out of school. "Much of the school problem
is social," he said, "You see a bunch of grade school kids playing, mixed white
and Indian, and you stop and ask them who is white and who is Indian? They
just stare at you. The question doesn't make sense. At high school things begin
to show up. Mostly social. The kids begin to want to invite each other to affairs
at home. They begin to notice that they haven't the kind of clothes others do.
They begin to feel they can't participate and drop out."

A recent high school graduate (mixed-blood, white-oriented) could offer
no explanation of full-blood problems in the schools, either scholastic or social.

He neither knew what the "Indian" boys in his class did or thought, nor could he say what had caused others he had known in the lower grades to drop out. His father (mixed-blood, businessman and active in community service) explained this: "He doesn't go around with those fellows."

"The full-bloods are forgotten. The half-breeds up north are running things for their own benefit."—a full-blood.

"Full-bloods probably expect to be discriminated against. They realize that they are in a different class, so act that way and so are discriminated against. They tend to stay by themselves."—a mixed-blood.

"There is conflict between the full-bloods and the 'breeds.' The latter are more progressive. They try to push things the old folks don't understand. It's not a caste division, just a mistrust of methods and plans."—a full-blood.

Numerous factors are at work here—historical, economic, political and cultural. The elements of status and values that underlie these attitudes will be examined further in the following chapters. The accounts are offered here to indicate that a bicultural division is recognized by the people themselves, that the two groups have been stereotyped and labeled, and that both spatial and social separation have been attributed to these groups. One consequence has been a curtailment of social interaction between members of the two societies.

The concepts of cultural orientation cannot be confused with the stereotypes. The real division is cultural. Orientational differences however tend to produce behaviors frequently attributed to the stereotype. "Full-blood" behavior in many dimensions is the behavior of an Indian-oriented person. People who are Indian-oriented, regardless of genetic heritage or degree of acculturation toward American life, will adopt practices that others attribute to "Indians." Then too it must be remembered that orientations are not indelible labels to apply to individuals, but rather are indicative of social structure. They stand for social categories for which there are predictable behavioral expectations, norms, and underlying values. Individuals can move from one category to another by conforming to the proper set of norms and expressing the values common to that category. The degree of Indian "blood" does not "tell."

Summary

I have tried to show that the Indian-oriented and white-oriented people engage in social interaction most frequently with members of their own group. A series of public, formal and informal, social situations was reviewed, some of which were attended predominantly by Indian-oriented people, others by white. Another list of public gatherings was given in which attendance from the two groups was relatively equal. It was shown further that informal grouping at these affairs tended to be with people of like orientation. An additional tendency for limitations upon intergroup sociality was observed in informal and private entertaining and visiting, and the overt recognition of this social separation was commented upon.

The key to these attendance patterns seems to lie in the kinds of social affairs that attract the Indian audience. Where the social activity contains some symbol of Indian-ness, the Indian-oriented turn out. The Indian Days Celebration, the Indian social dances, bundle openings, stick games, and song services are highly symbolic to the Indian. Consequently, the attendance at these is mainly Indian-oriented. Conversely, white-oriented interest is minimal.

Where the occasions lack continuity with Indian interests, or lack some symbolic aspect for Indian identification, the Indian-oriented fail to participate. In the areas of sociality where mixed audiences were reported, some Indian identification symbols can be recognized. The rodeo, for instance, is directly related to past Indian experience with horses and with cattle raising—a form of white economic activity at which the Indian has achieved some success.

Sports events, too, carry some of the flavor of racing, physical activity and prowess from the past, and again, and probably of more significance, these are areas in which the Indian has been able to achieve a success recognized as such by the members of the dominant society. When viewed in this light, the Easter Egg Hunt stands in sharp contrast to the children's track meet. Sports are given Indian recognition while an Egg Hunt symbolizes nothing Indian. Indian-oriented people turn out to watch their children compete in the track meet but not at the Egg Hunt.

The high school commencement appeared to attract more Indian-oriented persons than did the eighth grade graduation program, but this may be because the high school valedictorian was an Indian. He was a symbol of Indian success in a white man's game, and it was success by an Indian who practiced Indian ways.

The observed interaction patterns indicate that there are separate social groups. Examination of the values and status systems will further substantiate this relationship and give additional insight into the reasons behind the kinds of participation in community and private social affairs.

7

Values

Introduction

TWO AGGREGATES OF PEOPLE each of which shares distinctive patterns of sociocultural characteristics have been identified as Indian-oriented and white-oriented, and evidence has been offered to show that the people within each category associate more frequently with each other than with people of the other orientation. If these are more than just aggregates of people with similar interests, however, it is necessary to show that each has the *esprit de corps* that Linton called the motivating power of a society (Linton 1936:107). This power can be found in the goals and related value judgments of each group, and these are examined in this chapter to see if contrast can be found in the value patterns of the categories.

People judge and evaluate the behavior of others on the basis of shared goals or purposes that follow from the premises they hold about the nature of man and the world and these premises influence how they raise their children. Values then relate to desired ends, decisions about the proper means to these ends are ethical judgments. These matters are intricately interwoven and do not separate easily for discussion. In one sense members of both divisions share common goals—to live the good life and be well thought of by their fellows. But these seemingly common goals are based on and defined by differing premises, emphasize different standards. I will try to show how these groups differ in their interpretation of the good life and the good person, and what characteristics each uses in judging and evaluating their fellow man. Values, purposes, means, ends may not unravel well, but the basic idea should be clear—prestige accrues to those who best fit the model of the ideal person held by the members of the group that "counts" for the individual. If there are two contrasting social groups on the reservation, the ideals and attendant evaluations should differ accordingly.

Values of the White-Oriented Group

The category "white-oriented" and the characteristics by which it is defined in the context of the study, intimates that this group, in most respects, approximates the social structuring and culture of the American community of which the reservation is a part. The values of this segment of the reservation population are assumed to be similar to those found in a neighboring non-Indian community. The present purpose is not to analyze thoroughly either white-oriented or American values, but to establish that there is a similarity between the two, and to sketch the background against which a contrasting Indian-oriented value pattern stands out. The values can be abstracted from statements occurring repeatedly among the interview data, and they can be compared with some American value orientation about which there is agreement.

The values expressed in the field-interview data that appear to be most useful in separating the white-oriented from the Indian-oriented are closely related to those that were abstracted, in Chapter 4, from the speeches of governmental officials of the 1880s: work, self-dependence, individualism, and acquisitiveness. These are highly interrelated concepts. Work is a means by which to achieve valued ends, in this case independence from others, the accumulation of property for self-security and the security of one's immediate family. It is also an end in itself. It is good to work. A man who is known as a good worker gains some prestige in the community. A white-oriented man uses these values as a measure of others whether or not he appears to practice them himself.

Some of these valued characteristics were indicated in the economic data gathered from my sample (McFee 1962:114–124) and some of those findings are reviewed to show that the values are reflected in actual behavior. Only three of the twenty white-oriented men were irregularly employed. Two were regularly employed at seasonal labor, but all others had year around employment. Again, the relative dependence upon family support and welfare aid appeared to be significant. Twelve of the twenty received no family support, three others did, but they were active participants in a successful family ranch or farm enterprise. Only one white-oriented man reported use of welfare.[14]

These figures, of course, reflect the influence of other factors, such as economic potential, relative age, education, health, and opportunity. But they are related also to motivation and to the degree of commitment to the white-oriented value system. The following excerpts, paraphrased from interviews with white-oriented subjects, illustrate some of the ways these values are expressed.

> I've been ranching all my life, and had to get a fee patent—they held me down. The reservation rules tied you all up. I'm independent and have trained the kids to be the same. I wanted to build up the ranch for the boys. Two of them

---

[14] These and the following figures, based on the answers given by members of the sample to my questionnaire are used to indicate some trends apparent in the limited data. Because of the small and incomplete sample it would not be safe to treat these trends as well supported generalizations about the whole population.

are running it now. The youngest . . . isn't set up. He's working for the railroad, but there's no future in that. You work for them for forty years and all you have is a pension, and then you only work six months a year if you're lucky.
—mixed-blood rancher

I worked with a fellow about my age whose mother always complained. "My poor boy, always having to work." It made me sore. Why shouldn't he? I've always worked. I tried taking some time off work once and about went crazy.
The people [Indians] just don't understand what they're up against. They're looking for someone to take care of them.
—mixed-blood business man

No wonder the Indians are a happy-go-lucky bunch. They don't have to work. Lease money, per capita, and relief keep them going. They need to be put on their own and made to work their way out of it.
After I graduated from high school the old man talked to me and asked me what I was going to do. He said I couldn't just run around in the car, I had to do something. I've always had a job and haven't had to ask the people for anything.
—mixed-blood business employee

My parents emphasized hard work, honesty, thrift, and education. The Indians are clannish, but I'm more of a lone wolf. I'd rather take care of myself than to get help from the family.
I have fee patent title to my land so I can make my own deals without all the red tape and delay that you get at the agency.
The best days were under Stone and Campbell when everybody had a farm and was working.
—full-blood, self-employed contractor

Indians drop out of college because they haven't learned the value of an education. They can't manage their own affairs. In college it's all up to you. I have a tribal scholarship and work during vacations. I have an interest in the family ranch and help there and work for other ranchers too.
—mixed-blood college student

Many more clues appeared scattered through the interview data, and gained additional support from observation. White-oriented people prefer to be busy. They do not spend much time with the street corner groups. In fact a good indicator of orientation may be the time a person spends in such gatherings. Only the more elderly white-oriented men can stand or sit quietly and comfortably in conversation for any length of time. Most seem to have to be actively talking or listening. They jiggle their change or their keys. They look about more often and with quicker head movements than the Indians. In a comparatively short time the white-oriented person moves off down the street or into a building, off about their "business" or giving that impression, at least. The Indian-oriented on the other hand, can stand or sit quietly for an hour, two hours, or most of the day and do not feel compelled to talk all the time if nothing need be said. "Busyness" is not so important for them as it is for the white-oriented.

Often in white-oriented families both husband and wife hold steady jobs, and in some cases both are working and saving to develop a ranch or business for future economic independence. Compared to the Indian-oriented, the white-oriented persons are more concerned about the education and future of their children; they encourage them to go on to college, or to get other training beyond high school. They give more attention to improving their homes, and feel the need to buy and maintain furniture, appliances, equipment, and automobiles. They early encourage their children to take on responsibility for chores, to work and to plan for their future. They cannot understand how anyone could think and act otherwise, unless they are "lazy and immoral."

The values expressed in the interviews and observations are similar, in kind, to those commonly attributed to middle-class Americans. The emphasis upon and appreciation of work, self-dependence, individualism, and acquisitiveness noted in the above quotations, and the additional characteristics of concern for education and for the future, are all recognized, under one name or another, in the social science studies of American values.

In one such study, Williams, a sociologist, recognizes the difficulty of isolating a common set of values for a large, complex, and heterogeneous society (Williams 1970:450), but finds support for fourteen major "value orientations," which are "certain dominant themes [abstracted] from the many important regional, class, and other intracultural variations" (Williams 1970:452–453).

Work is mentioned both as a valued means to other ends, and as an end in itself, and is subsumed as one aspect of the "Activity and Work" orientation. Activity is stressed and, according to Williams, ". . . it is no accident that business so characteristic of the culture can also be spelled 'busy-ness.'" (Williams 1970:458–461). Self-dependence and individualism are included as constituents of an orientation called "Individual Personality": "to be a person is to be independent, responsible, and self respecting, and thereby to be worthy of concern and respect in one's own right" (Williams 1970:495). The emphasis upon acquisitiveness is included in the "Material Comfort" orientation; a condition that "is highly approved and sought after." The material comfort orientation, according to Williams, does not reveal the "specific values . . . involved," which appear to be complexly interwoven in the idea of the "American Standard of Living" with its

> undertones and overtones of meanings—from nationalistic identification, to symbols of success, competence, and power and from a token of moral excellence to something very close to a terminal goal at the level of hedonistic gratification (Williams 1970:469–470).

At this level of analysis it would appear safe to assume that the value orientations of the white-oriented sub-culture are broadly similar to the values of the general American public. They are consistent with the economic, social and cultural life of the nation. The individual ideals of success, prestige, and higher status, achievable through the expression of these valued characteristics are considered contributory to the progress of the country. These values are a part of the complex American culture, and are linked with expectations that success will follow upon their practice. The white-oriented Blackfeet have learned these expectations through experience and example.

Values of the Indian-Oriented Group

The characteristics valued by the traditional Blackfeet, mentioned in Chapter 3, still persist in attenuated form. The changing conditions of life have required, however, that new avenues for their expression be found. At first glance such things as bravery, skill, wisdom, and generosity appear to be characteristics that would be valued by the average American. In order to understand how Indian-oriented and white-oriented definitions of these differ, it is necessary to recognize that since the life goals of the two groups are not the same, the premises from which value judgments are made are not the same.

The white-oriented values were seen to be consistent with the national economy and culture, and sufficiently integrated with these to be both vehicles to individual prestige and expressions of national goals. White Americans and white-oriented Blackfeet work toward their own and the nation's security, and to build a better future for their children.

As was shown in Chapter 4, the Indians had little choice but to accept the economic system of the dominant society and were pressed to accept the white values that went with it. To date the Indian-oriented, in general, have experienced little economic success and, perhaps because of this, have not adopted the values. In turn, the persistence of traditional values has contributed, in part, to this lack of economic success. This will be examined later. It is assumed that the present values of the Indian-oriented are the result of both persistence of traditional traits and new interpretations of these developed during the attempts at economic readaptation.

Because the Indian-oriented have developed no expectancy of success in the white man's economy, they have become neither imbued with the associated values nor committed fully to white goals. Instead they appear to have made more explicit what was once an implicit life goal of Indian society—to retain their ethnic identity. I make this inference from statements about "keeping the old ways alive," "showing the young people the things from the past," and from the attachment people show to bundles, regalia, doing Indian craft and art work, and other "Indian" symbols. The major common goal, hence a prime value, of the Indian-oriented society is to be *Indian*, and the present value judgments can be understood best as they relate to this goal. To illustrate this relationship, values are isolated that in reality are intricately interdependent.

Individualism, a valued characteristic in the old culture, is highly valued today. The Indian is concerned with individual achievement, social acceptance, increased prestige, and higher status, interests he shares with the white-oriented, but the expression of these values by individuals of the two orientations differs in light of their separate goals.

The differences show up clearly in the way that Indian-oriented parents tend to treat their children. Ideally, children are seen as little individuals whose rights and wishes should be respected. They should be guided and directed, but not forced into doing things. Indian parents think that white people are being cruel when they spank their children; teasing and ridicule are acceptable correctives. Children are wanted, loved but not coddled; no elaborate concern is expressed when they get bumps. Injuries are cared for, assurances given, and then everybody's attention turns to other things.

Babies and young children go wherever their parents go, with little concern shown about feeding and sleeping schedules. Children are at most public gatherings and play about quite freely regardless of the occasion. At one political rally I was sitting behind a young couple who were letting their son play with his father's keys. The rattling of the keys often made it hard to hear what was said, but nobody objected. Several times the keys fell to the floor with a loud clatter. I thought, hopefully, that that would end the game, but each time the father picked up the keys and gave them back to his son. I interpreted this to mean that the child's interests were as important as anyone else's.

A mother might suggest several times that her child share a toy with another, but the matter is dropped if the child is persistent in refusing. Children make many such decisions for themselves, because it is their right to do so. If they get too far out of line they will be ridiculed. This attitude continues throughout their lives. A school official told me about his frustration when a bright young student decided, against his urging, not to go to college. The boy's father was easily convinced and offered to push the case with his son, but returned several days later to report that he had tried. His son had said no, he did not want to go. That ended the matter. White-oriented men reported that their fathers rarely took no for an answer.

Present-day Indian-oriented people still have the strong emotional commitment to their name and self-image that was an attribute of the Blackfeet in the horse and buffalo days. Indian and white informants alike mention jealousy as a strong Indian personality trait and blame this for the inability of the Indian-oriented group to unite in support of any specific program. This self-concern perpetuates shame and gossip as powerful agents of social control. Other contrasting interpretations of individualism become apparent in later descriptions of the requisites for status within the Indian-oriented group.

Bravery, once manifest in war, hunting, and horse raiding, remains a valued characteristic. Ewers noted this in Blackfeet patriotism and their response to World Wars I and II. Many young men enlisted, the relatives of many honored them at a feast, and old men sang war songs and prayed for their success (Ewers 1955:322; 1958:324). Blackfeet continue to serve in our overseas conflicts. But in modern life the opportunities for achieving distinction by the regular exhibition of bravery are limited. This quality contributes to success in occasional fights, sports, and rodeos, and in some kinds of employment—the ranch hand and the fire fighter often have their bravery tested. But it is no longer a chief requisite for economic and social achievement. Other attributes are given greater recognition.

Skill is important today. Because Indian identification is the goal, abilities that contribute to this end are valued by the Indian-oriented; dancing, singing, art, crafts, and oratorical skills are recognized as important to the expression of ethnic identity. Several women are well known for their leather and beading work; the Blackfeet Art Association furthers the work of many tutored and untutored wood carvers and painters.

It was suggested that Indians participate in sports and rodeos because these were related to traditional Indian activities, and because Indian success in these activities had been given recognition by white people. Skills in these events are highly regarded by the Indian-oriented, perhaps for these same reasons.

The people of this group gain subsistence within the white economic system so that work skills become important. For the most part the Indians must work to get money to buy the necessities of life and the other things they want. Work is the principal means by which to acquire goods and property, and competence at work increases the chances both of finding work and making more money. In addition, work skills are valued as indices of personal achievement. Indian acquaintances identify themselves and others with some comment about what a man is, does, or has done, and past or present economic abilities are included in this appraisal. Unemployed men, talking to a white observer, usually point out past accomplishments, jobs at which they excel, or catalog the land, stock, and other possessions they own that might impress the investigator with their personal worth. Remember that John Arrowhead recalled that he had been a "champion dancer" and "a good bronc rider." He had traveled and worked in many parts of the country, he said, and told many stories of his adventures during those times. He took me on a tour of his "land" to show the house, ranch, and stock he owned. The land was his undoubtedly, but all else belonged to the leaseholder.

This suggests another reason why economic skills, like excellence at sports, are valued by the Indian-oriented. They are aware that these skills and abilities are given recognition by their white and white-oriented neighbors. Not only do these accomplishments contribute toward earning a living and a sense of personal achievement, but they also enhance the image of "the Indian" among the white men.

The Indian-oriented value work skills but have not adopted the American appreciation of work as an end in itself. Some of this is reflected in the responses to my questionnaire. None of the eight men from the sample who were classified as Indian-oriented were regularly employed. Four of these owned land and earned some lease income from that; five received some financial support from other family members, while three had been dependent on welfare to get them through the year. Neither these nor the figures given above for the white-oriented are exactly representative of their respective groups, that is, not all white-oriented people are well off, nor are all Indian-oriented poor, but a comparison of these indicators does show the generally lower economic position of the Indian-oriented. The Indian works hard and well but feels no compulsion to work beyond the time necessary to satisfy short-term needs. Several factors contribute to this attitude, such as the irregular and seasonal jobs the Indian-oriented people are accustomed to getting, the apparent lack of interest in many things the white man considers essential, and the social restrictions on accumulation of property which will be discussed under the heading of generosity. Local, state and bureau school officials met to discuss problems of Indian education during one of my visits. Several speakers claimed that the Indian children were low on motivation and high on the scale of dropouts. One official recognized the value discrepancy when he stated,

"You won't achieve your educational goals until you teach the Indians to want what you want." The Indian-oriented value social participation, visiting, attending Pow Wows on this and other reservations, horse races, and stick games more than long and steady labor. You do not have to work endlessly if you prefer social participation to extra furniture, appliances, a lawn, and a savings account. It is difficult for persons with this attitude to win acceptance and high status within the white-oriented structure.

Wisdom, too, is valued to the degree that it contributes to the maintenance of Indian-ness. Thus knowledge of the old religion, lore, and rituals is highly regarded, even by the Indian-oriented who no longer believe in them. One inform-ant commented, "I know I'm full-blooded and like to keep the old things alive." A woman was disappointed to hear that there would be no Sun Dance at the 1960 Indian Days Encampment:

> Indian Days aren't any good if they don't hold the Medicine Lodge. The dances don't have any meaning unless they have the Lodge. I'd take part if they had one. Even if you don't believe in it it's part of old Indian ways. You make prom-ises to people. You have to help them, so you give things and help.

Modern knowledge is also good. But the Indian-oriented, in general, display an ambivalence in their attitudes toward education and it is difficult to isolate the many factors that inhibit Blackfeet progress in school. Among these would be, the gap between home and school environments and the language problem. Chil-dren raised in homes where English is a second language do not have the rein-forcing context of constant use to increase their language ability. Books and magazines, too, would not be available to be used to further develop language and reading skills. The effects of failure and fear of failure in relation to the Indians concern with self-image are also undoubtedly important. Motivation is limited by these and is not overridden by parental authority. The Indian-oriented may urge their children to attend school but, like the men the school official told about, do not order them to do so. As individuals, children have the right to make their own decisions—after they get beyond the age where the truant officer makes it for them.

The Indian-oriented leaders value the knowledge that comes from school and in general support the idea of education. The knowledge gained is valuable and necessary if the Indians are to deal successfully with the white man. Indians can combat white ways by learning from them,[15] but this goal is hard to translate into meaningful immediate objectives for the children. They accept the idea of schooling but find the subjects they study uninteresting and unrelated to any personal goals they might formulate. Many of the jobs available on the reserva-tion do not require much schooling, so many Indian families do not provide an example of the economic returns that counsellors say follow a good education. A well-educated Indian-oriented leader expressed his thoughts on this problem as it related to college attendance:

---

[15] A form of antagonistic acculturation. See Devereaux and Loeb 1943:133–147.

Many of our smart children have disappointed us. They didn't go ahead as they planned. Money problems was one reason, but many had no vital interest. They really didn't know what they wanted to take when they went to school. Because of this they found the courses uninteresting and discouraging.

Wisdom and knowledge, of both old and new ways, serve other ends but appear to be most highly valued when they contribute to the major goal of being Indian. Both Indian- and white-oriented people value wisdom, but the contrasting goals lead to the accenting of different realms of knowledge and the uses to which it is put.

Generosity is a key value of Indian-oriented persons that has survived with the least amount of reinterpretation. It is considered an important requisite to being an Indian and, as such, appears to provide the major motivation for acquiring skill and wisdom. People are expected to share with others and to help those less forutnate than themselves.

Generosity takes both private and public forms. Indian-oriented persons are hospitable and feel a responsibility to care for others that insures that the improvident, aged, disabled or sick will be provided with the minimum requirements of existence. This relatively private form of generosity is relieved somewhat by welfare and charitable sources, but often these are not enough and some people need the help of family and neighbors to make it through the winter. In some cases those on welfare may be considered to be better off than others, and their grown children turn to them for help that is seldom refused.

Public generosity covers the various "give-away" ceremonies mentioned in earlier chapters. This giving is largely a reciprocal gift exchange among peers. No strict accounting is kept of gifts and repayments, but the reciprocity is recognized and people joke about giving blankets to a visiting friend so they can get them back next year when they visit the other reservation. Private generosity by all and public display by a few are forms of generosity that are expected and are controlled ultimately by expressions of public opinion. Many people act generously and spontaneously because it is the right thing to do; others give more begrudgingly because of fear of social disapproval. A person who fails to provide what is expected is called "stingy," and undisputed stinginess causes a person to lose standing within the Indian-oriented group. People do not take chances that might start such talk. Thus the discussion completes the circle back to self-concern and the controlled expression of individualism. A white official told of an incident that sounded probable even though its authenticity could not be checked.

A woman asked him to order a young man out of her house. He had moved in with the family and was just hanging around, eating their food, and making no effort to help out. When the official suggested that she was the one to tell him to leave, she replied that she could not do that. But it would be all right if he would come and do it for her: "Only don't tell that I said for you to do it." Another man had returned to take up residence on the reservation after being away for several years. But the pressures for generosity and the compulsion to follow the rules made him think he had better leave again. "This town breaks you; too many friends that want money and rides here and there."

Candidates for council offices often make gifts of a dollar or two to prospective voters as evidence of their generosity, an act that is criticized if the man has not been helpful in the past. "At election time they're always willing to lend you a dollar, but after they're in they won't give you a nickel." Past generosity, however, can pay off. "They told me not to vote for him, that he wouldn't do a good job. I think that's right, but I voted for him anyway because he always helps people that need it." The feasting at Indian Days, bundle openings, song services, and the political rallies appears to be another form of generosity display.

Generosity can block successful economic adaptation. Ewers wrote that sharing and generosity survived in the 1940s and that the "drain of the 'have-nots' upon the 'haves' has the effect of limiting the economic progress of ambitious individuals" and possibly was "inhibiting the desire of fullbloods of extensive family connections to achieve material success" (Ewers 1955:321–322). In 1959 and 1960 three cases were known, and others reported, where land was sold for large sums of money. Relatives and friends moved in with the recipients and spent several days celebrating the sale. Some stayed to live with the now 'rich' friend or relative. This is reported to be a common practice that has caused the rapid depletion of such income and returned numerous, now landless, Indians to poverty and the welfare rolls.

Often this is more than economic reciprocity. It is a necessary adaptive arrangement for the poor. The economic flow may be one way with the returns, if any, very difficult to assess. In 1959 I visited the home of an elderly woman who had received a large oil bonus payment several years earlier. The money was held in trust by the B.I.A. and she was given regular payments from this account to cover her living expenses. She lived in a good house in town and had living with her at the time two adult sons and several grandchildren. Several other people seemed to come and go, including an elderly couple—a son-in-law by a previous marriage and his present wife. This wife told me that she came by occasionally to help with the housework, and that every week the old lady received her money from the superintendent. "She gives me $5.00, my husband $5.00 and $15.00 to her eldest son." It appeared that quite a few people were partially dependent upon her largess. When the old woman died it was discovered that her account was depleted and she was in debt. The household broke up, the people scattered to fend for themselves, and the now vacant house is falling apart. The reciprocity seemed to be mainly in chores and social support provided by a circle of dependent kin and friends.

The emphasis on generosity has still another face. Too much success, too much accumulation of unshared property, brings the quick reaction of gossip. "He's stingy." "He's trying to live like a white man." "They get all the cattle and won't let us have any." Only a very few who wish to be accepted by the Indian-oriented have been able to walk the fine line between stinginess and generosity. These few have become economically self-sufficient and yet retained a name for generosity among their following by judicious and controlled giving.

Summary

The Indian- and white-oriented groups share some values that appear to be congruent but are seen to have differing definitions. Members of both groups, for instance, would acknowledge that it is good to be generous, but the white-oriented man qualifies his generosity by a prior emphasis upon self-support. It is not good to carry generosity to a fault by impoverishing one's self and family as Indian-oriented men are wont to do. The Indian values work and acquisition of property as a means to an end, but does not agree with the white-oriented persons who see these qualities as ends in themselves.

The values are defined differently according to the different assumptions about the good man and the good life of the two groups. White-oriented activities are directed toward future progress, an end the Indian-oriented find unrealistic. Past experiences have provided no basis for optimism about the future. The major goal of the latter group appears to be the maintenance of Indian identity, and the value judgments are influenced by this end.   .

The feeling of circularity that wells up in this and other discussions of values, goals, means, ends, purposes, and so on, reflects, I believe, the very circularity of the social scene. People learn to value the things valued by their group, to behave in ways that are acceptable to the group to which they do or aspire to belong. Self-concern may be both the motive for general conformity as well as the root of control; self-concern and concern for status make one responsive to gossip and criticism as well as contributing to one's being a follower and supporter of valued ideals and practices. Membership in one group requires approximation of standards that differ from and may militate against membership in the other. Adding this dimension to the contrasting patterns of association further supports the view that these are separate societies. The value patterns of each group are used by the group members as bases from which to judge the social worth of their neighbors, and the values are reflected in the assignment of the status positions that are considered next.

8

Status

Introduction

THE NATURE AND SEPARATENESS of the two orientation systems are illustrated in this chapter by a review of the status patterns within each group. People conform to a particular set of norms and adopt the related values of the group with which they wish to identify, and acquire a higher or lower status within the group according to how well they exhibit valued characteristics. The status systems of the two orientation groups are examined here to identify areas of contrast and to suggest the nature of intragroup leadership and social organization.

Economic achievement plays a more important role in defining status among the white-oriented people that it does among the Indian-oriented, and a man's house is one important symbol of how well he is doing economically. I use housing, therefore, in my discussion of status among the white-oriented group, but do not give similar treatment to Indian-oriented housing because they do not give this much weight in judging their peers. In the proper place I will describe some Indian-oriented homes and then take the opportunity to point out some characteristics of home furnishing and maintenance that seem to follow from the differing values of the two groups. The general economic and housing conditions on the reservation must be remembered, however, to avoid making hasty inferences.

The visitor to the reservation sees much substandard housing which he is apt to register in his head as "Indian housing." He is right in one sense; most of the houses are occupied by tribal members, but he is in error if he thinks that this is the kind of housing the Blackfeet prefer. The descriptions in Chapter 4 should have made it clear that poverty and poor housing are both prevalent, and while these two tend to go hand in hand, home construction on the reservation has been hindered greatly because trust lands could not be mortgaged, as well as for lack of money. The present housing programs have taken a decade or more of planning, land purchase, condemnations, and financial maneuvering to get under way and are just beginning to allow the abandonment of some hundreds of shanties, shacks, and cabins that have accumulated over the past half-century.

My analysis of the economic data gathered from my sample clearly demonstrated widespread poverty, but not everybody is poor—there are relatively affluent people both among the Indian- and white-oriented groups. The differences within each group are probably greater than those between them, but the average standing of Indian-oriented people, as a whole, is lower than that of the white-oriented (McFee 1962:120–124). To the extent that there is a positive correlation between income and housing, then, it is to be expected that a higher percentage of the Indian-oriented live in substandard housing than do the white-oriented. In what follows, then, I assume that adequate housing is desired by all and difficult to come by regardless of cultural orientation: the maintenance and furnishing of what-- ever kind of house people live in, however, does seem to me to be a fair indicator of some of the value differences described in the preceding chapter. This is what I will be talking about when I mention housing.

It should also be remembered that my sample was male so that much of what follows may reflect a male emphasis. Women play an integral part in establishing the status of the family. They maintain the homes, raise the children, and often contribute to the family income as well. All in all their influence often may be more important than that of the men in status achievement. A study of women and their role in reservation life is sorely needed.

Status among the White-Oriented

The white-oriented society can be divided roughly into three status classes: low, middle, and high. Class boundaries are indistinct, but high status can be distinguished from low, while the middle class shades imperceptibly into the two extremes forming what Stern, in his Klamath study so aptly called a "status gradient" (Stern 1966:214ff).

WHITE-ORIENTED LOW STATUS   Low status people generally, are the least educated and least trained in the skills essential to regular employment. Consequently they are often irregularly employed, live in poor houses, dress poorly, and have few possessions. Poverty is a condition shared by low status people of both groups.

White and white-oriented people tend to lump low status people together regardless of orientation. While this is reasonable by many criteria, such judgments overlook cultural factors that make a white-oriented man different than his Indian-oriented counterpart. These distinguishing characteristics will be seen more clearly in the later discussion of the low status Indian-oriented.

The low status stratum encompasses a range from hard working, but irregularly employed men at the top, to a few improvident individuals at the bottom of the scale. The more ambitious of this class actively seek work and are considered to be good workers by those who know them. However, the jobs they find are seasonal and provide insufficient income for economic stability.

In general, low status men express little commitment to success and prog-

Sub-standard housing. Note the evidence of attention to interior housekeeping and the definition of a yard.

ress. One of the men interviewed had gone to Denver under a federal relocation program, but found the work too difficult so returned to his family. Another remarked that the relocation program was intended to help the Indian find work. He, with an average annual income of $2,250, had thought about going on relocation, but never applied. "I don't have much trouble getting a job," he said.

None of the low status men I interviewed own their own homes. Two talked about fixing things up around the houses they occupied but have not made improvements that would be expected if they were concerned about material comfort. Housing appears to be poor and inadequate when eight to eleven people live in a two room shack. In 1960 I visited a man who had lived with his wife and eight children in a house owned by one of his relatives. This was an old, two-room, unpainted structure with shiplap outer walls that had been patched here and there with plyboard. Some of the original asphalt roof remained visible among the many patches that had been applied over the years. The ceiling and some of the interior walls were covered with wallboard, others with cardboard. A single light bulb suspended from the ceiling by its cord hung in each room. Well worn linoleum covered the floors. The rooms were simply furnished: a wooden table, wooden chairs, an old overstuffed chair, a kitchen storage cabinet, two fiberboard wardrobes, a chest of drawers, three double beds, and a crib. A wall-hung kitchen sink with a cold water tap was the extent of interior plumbing; a wood range served for both cooking and heating. Family photographs, two Charles Russell prints, dishes, family keepsakes, a radio, a throw rug, and a few other possessions were on display. The interior of the house was crowded, but neat, orderly, and well-scrubbed; the exterior was stained, cracked, and in disrepair. A sagging fence partially marked off a yard area between the house and an outdoor toilet. Two shrubs grew as evidence of an early attempt to garden and there was considerable debris scattered about the dirt and weeds that made up the yard. To me there appeared to be much that needed to be done to make the place livable, yet when I asked this man, seasonally employed with an income of about $2,500, about the availability of federal or tribal home improvement loans, I was told: "Yes they have a setup for that. I guess we could get a loan like that if we needed it." I do not know if this family still lives in this house, but it is there today. The only visible changes through the years have been further deterioration and the addition of a television antenna.

When asked about future plans, these men have little to offer. They express little expectation beyond returning to the old job, or finding a similar one, each spring. The inference is that they are not dissatisfied with present conditions. Family responsibilities, lack of credit, uncertain employment, the weather and the seasons are the factors that govern the economic condition of the low status men. It is unlikely that these men can be "successful" but they try; the idlers are those who have given up.

The improvident ones, at the bottom of the scale have lost any initiative they once might have had. Most of these, like their Indian-oriented counterparts, are called "winos" and "bums" by their fellow townsmen. Some are alcoholics in fact, others in name only. These men are community problem cases—the concern of the police and welfare authorities.

Yet these men are white-oriented in spite of the apparent lack of commitment to the values of their group. First of all, they are not Indian-oriented. They know little or nothing of Indian language or customs and do not take part in Indian social activities, nor do they seek Indian identity. Secondly, the low status white-oriented persons have the knowledge and habits of their group. They are peripheral participants in the economic, political, and social life of their community. Those who work are rewarded with the accolade, "a good worker," which puts them on a rung above the improvident on the status ladder. But they have little influence or social standing. Low status people do not run for political offices; they are neither members of service clubs or other organizations, nor do they take part in the P.T.A., Youth Club, Boy or Girl Scout, or 4-H Club work. Low status persons spend their spare time with members of their families or with others of similar status. Reported recreational activities include hunting and fishing, card games with neighbors or family, an occasional movie, driving around in a car with friends, and drinking.

Low income, irregular labor, and limited participation are the interrelated characteristics that most clearly separate the low from the middle status. Lack of training contributes to a low income; poverty, in turn, limits both self-improvement and social participation.

WHITE-ORIENTED MIDDLE STATUS   The middle status white-oriented class includes the majority of the white-oriented group and, in reality, is more a convenient collection of a series of gradually changing ranks than it is a single status position. The people who occupy these status positions, however, share a few general characteristics: they are (1) regularly employed, (2) committed to individual progress, (3) active participants in community affairs, and (4) they clearly support and exemplify the white-oriented values.

Individuals in this classification represent a wide range of economic and social achievement. Occupations of middle status people range from regularly employed craftsmen through clerical workers in business, agency, and council to businessmen, politicians, small farmers, and ranchers. Not all are financially independent, but all are building toward that goal. This is a characteristic that stands out in the interview materials. These people think about their future and the future of their children—they have plans for tomorrow. It shows in "Bob Sorrel Horse's dream" reported by a poor white-oriented full-blood rancher, who, by his industry may just qualify for middle status even though his annual cash income seldom exceeds $2,000:

> I have this dream to get some money and fix this place up right—a nice house and a good place. First, I'd get electricity in to pump the water. I had planned to remodel the house . . . to have a place I'm not ashamed of.

Yet while he dreams, this man acts. He cared for his small herd of thirteen head of cattle and a few horses, had a sound shelter and well-maintained corrals for the stock. The grounds around the house were uncluttered, all garbage and debris was in one pile some distance from the house. A good supply of firewood was cut and stacked near the house. A clothesline, outhouse, and small utility shed were all in good order.

The house in which six people lived was an old log structure with two rooms on the ground floor and one loft room above. It was well chinked and the old hand split shake roof was in good repair. Water was carried from a pitcher pump mounted at the well a few feet from the cabin door; there was no electricity, and gas lanterns provided the light. A wood range provided the heat. The interior walls were painted, cotton curtains hung at the windows and a worn rug covered part of the linoleum floor. The home furnishings consisted of a painted washstand, wooden table, wooden chairs, a kitchen cupboard, one double and two single beds, homemade closets, a nightstand, and a high chair. Family photos, a calendar, a radio, two rifles, fishing gear, and other family possessions were to be seen. The children's bicycle, tricycles, wagon, and a stroller were stored in the shed out back. A zinc washtub hanging outside on the front wall of the cabin provided the clue to the laundry facilities. Everything was worn, clean, orderly and in good repair. This man was poor, yet he maintained what he had and dreamed of something better in the future.

At the upper end of the scale, this same concern for the future is expressed by the well-to-do rancher, quoted in the earlier chapter, who built up his ranch for the boys and was concerned that the youngest son had no future with the railroad.

Middle status people join the service clubs, farm and cattle associations, and support and participate in community improvement projects. The leaders of F.F.A., 4-H, Boy and Girl Scouts, and the Youth Club are either whites or tribal members of this class. These people sponsor the Easter Egg Hunts, the Fishing Derbies, local sports events, and often the rodeos. They are not always the leaders, but are the active supporters of community, church, and school enterprises.

Middle status people are active politically. Tribal council positions and a few county elective offices are sought and often won by people of this classification, and they are actively supported or opposed, advised or criticized, by their peers.

People of middle status tend to live in well-constructed, well-maintained

Two kinds of rural housing.

homes. For example, Ray Hawkins, whose annual income was about $3,500, lived with his wife and four children in a four room frame house. It was freshly painted inside and out and the composition roof was in good condition at the time of my visit. There was a fenced yard, with lawn and flower beds, an outdoor fireplace and a picnic table. This house had electricity, inside plumbing with both hot and cold water supplied to the bathroom and kitchen. The interior walls were all lined and painted; the floors were wooden, covered with cotton rugs in the living room and bedrooms and with linoleum in the kitchen and bath. The comparatively large kitchen had built-in cabinets around and over the sink, an electric range and refrigerator, a heavy dining table, and solid wood chairs. There were cotton curtains at the windows. The bedrooms had built-in closets, beds and chests of drawers. The living room was well furnished with a fairly new davenport and living room chairs, each with its antimacassar. There was a coffee table, an ottoman, a piano, table lamps, a record player, and a radio. The windows were draped and family photographs, some of the children's art work, music, and numerous books were on display.

Not all middle status persons have good homes, but evidence of improvement is apparent in the houses they do have. This may amount to anything from a fresh coat of paint on interior walls to a new roof, a new entryway, or the addition of one or more rooms. When I reviewed the data from my sample, I noted that two of the fourteen homes of white-oriented middle status sample members were scored excellent and nine good. The middle status people do not all plant lawns and gardens, but with rare exceptions, all lawns and gardens on the reservation are planted by middle or high status white or white-oriented people.

Home improvement, and a tendency toward the acquisition of more appliances and other possessions with increased income, demonstrate the underlying values of acquisitiveness and material comfort. White-oriented people, above the low status category, buy, use, and care for more home furnishings and appliances. A middle-class American would recognize an air of material comfort that goes beyond utility, memorabilia, and decoration, and differs in this respect from the average Indian-oriented home regardless of financial condition. This elusive and hard to define impression may become clearer by contrast with Indian-oriented homes described later.

The white-oriented tend to identify home and possessions with family status. One white community leader, acquainted with sociological literature, assessed the class positions of the town, and used home improvement as a key to attempted upward mobility. Even Indian-oriented people are aware of this "have things" aspect of white living. An Indian who acquires too many appliances and other home furnishings is accused of "trying to live like a white man."

WHITE-ORIENTED HIGH STATUS Highest status among the white-oriented persons is held by a few men or families who own large farms or ranches, or operate successful businesses. In most respects they resemble the middle status people in that they are industrious, ambitious, acquisitive, and active in community affairs. These people, however, stand out for their greater success. They are financially independent, have larger, well-maintained, and better furnished homes like that of Henry Rogers described in Chapter 1. They are leaders in community enterprises and politics and, further, they meet on more equal terms with the white business leaders of the community and region.

In addition to the economic and social attributes just mentioned, these men share a broad knowledge of men and events beyond the local scene. Their interests lead them into contact with men of like interests beyond the reservation and county boundaries. They have traveled widely and have a lively interest in American history, politics, and business affairs.

The economic independence attained by these men has left them freer to pursue other affairs. They can afford to spend more time in public service work. All have become interested in improving the conditions of the reservation population. I mentioned earlier the two who had learned about Blackfeet culture in later life, and display a great interest in the Indians. They know this culture intellectually but have not internalized an Indian point of view. These people have white values and goals and, whether they realize it or not, are working to change

the Indians toward a greater acceptance of white ways. Like the government officials, they feel that the opportunity for steady work and a good education will
solve most of the problems faced by the Indian. Remember, too, Henry Rogers'
idea that the council should buy some grass and flower seed to give to all the
householders in town. He and other high status people are pleased that the low
rent and mutual aid housing programs include lawns in the plans. His suggestion
and these plans are realistic from the point of view of those who subscribe to
white-oriented values, but overlook the fact that the Indians do not share these
same values. It will be interesting to watch the results of the planting programs
to see whether or not the Indian-oriented occupants care to maintain these lawns.

The man I called Harry Wilson has a different view of the Indian because
of what he learned about Blackfeet culture as a child during the few years he
spent with his Indian stepgrandfather on a Canadian reserve. Before and after
this visit, he was raised in a completely white-oriented home, but as a consequence of this training and the considerable participation in Indian society that
it allowed, he has a deeper understanding of the Indian-oriented people. His idea
of service is to help them maintain their own culture. He is able to take part in
their ritual and social activities, but serves primarily at a managerial level with
the local and national committees that promote pan-Indian celebrations, arts and
crafts. This man is white-oriented, but has had experience that enables him to
empathize with the Indian. He helps the Indian-oriented to affirm their traditions, while others of his class can only affirm their own and try to help the
Indians by changing them.

Perhaps because of their greater association with white people, the high
status white-oriented, and a few in the class below who approach this status, are
the ones most conscious of social discrimination or at least most vocal about it.
I asked everybody I interviewed about this and people at this social level had the
strongest feelings about it. The complaints were less about discrimination in the
economic sphere than about social slights. One man stated that everyone gets on
well until some white businessman's daughter becomes too interested in a mixed-
blood boy. The white parents soon step in and break it up. A woman complained
that she was never invited to local women's meetings, teas, or other parties, and
a study of membership and attendance lists for social groups sponsored by the
white business people and agency employees appears to support her contention.
The high status white-oriented person is economically and culturally the same as
many of his white neighbors. He aspires, and is qualified, to be fully accepted.
Away from home he meets little discrimination but, like the man mentioned earlier
who became the liquor store manager, his Indian heritage is often held against
him in the local and neighboring towns. This discrimination, felt strongly by the
persons most nearly integrated into the American society, emphasizes again that
the major difference between the white-oriented segment of the tribe and other
American people around them is due to their being legally defined Indians, members of an Indian tribe, who live on a reservation. Their white neighbors too easily
stereotype all Indians and discriminate against them accordingly without understanding any of them or noting individual differences among them.

It must be noted that the Blackfeet too are caught up in the racist beliefs that are so prevalent in our society. In general, they dislike blacks, foreigners, and, of course, whites. Some Indians expressed dismay when they found that fair housing laws meant that whites could not be excluded from the tribally sponsored but federally funded low rent housing. This observation is made as a part of the description and is in no way intended to excuse discrimination against the Indians.

The status levels of the white-oriented community reflect the scale by which white or white-oriented people assess themselves and their neighbors, and these are congruent with the status patterns of the region, as I explained in a footnote to my earlier report (McFee 1962:178). The white-oriented people are socially, politically, economically and culturally, a part of the mainstream of American life.

As the white-oriented share status and value systems with the white people, they tend to assess the Indians by these same standards. The white-oriented person will tend to place an Indian-oriented person in a class just below his own even when they are equal in most other respects. The improvident Indian is ranked lower than the improvident white. White-oriented people measure all others by their own standards, in relation to themselves and their kind.

The Indian-oriented person, however, sees the relative status of the tribal members from quite a different perspective. Social worth is measured by different standards in Indian-oriented society, and the standards reflect commitment to other values.

Status among the Indian-Oriented

The people of one segment of the Blackfeet Tribe consider themselves the real Blackfeet Indians and dedicate themselves to being Indian. Toward this end they share elements of culture that differ from that of the surrounding population and associate most frequently with people of like orientation. The group has its own measures of status based upon expressions of the values supported by its members, and because of differing goals and values, the status system of the Indian-oriented is incongruent with that of the white-oriented society. The Indian judges his group and the whole tribal population by another standard that results in a dissimilar ranking.

For present purposes the same threefold classification of status—low, middle, and high—is used, but the positions are discussed in another order. In Indian-oriented society, high status is achieved by the attainment of prestige and influence through behaviors that express the values of the group. This is the same general principle that operates among the white-oriented society, but the bicultural situation, in which the Indian-oriented are an economically and politically dependent minority, has opened two avenues to higher status for Indian-oriented people. Low status people are relatively homogeneous, middle status less so, and the high status category can be split into the two types based upon knowledge of and proficiency in the white man's world. Because of this the high status classes are described first, then the low status, followed by a brief description of the large middle class that, by its judgments and support, make or breaks people's status claims. The discussion of the characteristics that make for the achievement of high status will describe best the ideals of the society against which the lower rankings are also measured.

INDIAN-ORIENTED HIGH STATUS   The joint requirements of maintaining Indian identity and achieving this within the political and economic framework of white culture have opened two channels to prestige and leadership within the Indian-oriented group. The ideal leader in this situation would be a man wise in the ways of both traditional Blackfeet and modern American cultures. He would be an authority on how best to be an Indian, yet well educated, skilled, and able to meet the white man on common ground. He would be experienced sufficiently to gain acceptance and influence in white society and to act as an able interpreter of each group to the other. The history of Blackfeet and American relations is too short to have produced such an ideal in one man. Instead, as more and more tribal members become white-oriented, some men gain high status by their greater knowledge of Blackfeet culture as it is known today. These leaders form a least acculturated high status stratum that for the sake of simplicity, will be called the *chiefs*. Others, better educated and more experienced with white culture, find high status by playing the roles of intercultural interpreters and mediators. They are accomplished spokesmen for the Indian-oriented point of view, and as a more acculturated high status class are labeled *interpreters*. There are more than generational differences between these two status types.

Chiefs are usually older men who know and support the currently known traditions and beliefs. They vary in their knowledge, belief and dedication, but all, together, form a repository of what is remembered of the old ways. One of these men recognized that much of the old culture had been lost, "things beyond the memory of even the old timers," but he and others of his status are "trying to show the young people the things from the past," with special emphasis on keeping the language alive. Their qualities and characteristics are those given in the description of Albert Buffalo Heart, so will be only summarily reviewed here.

Through their age, knowledge, and practice of Blackfeet ideals each of these men has gained the respect of a numerous following of kinsmen, friends and people from a particular region who recognize him as their chief, or respected elder. So these men are given respect and loyalty but little political power. It appears that the old leadership structure persists among the Indian-oriented group. People tend to shift their loyalties according to kinship, friendship, and self-interest. The leadership that develops carries responsibilities and influence, but rarely true authority. The chiefs are recognized as links to the past, authorities on tradition, and symbols of the Indian, but as the roles given them will show, these things are peripheral to the present political and economic sphere.

Chiefs perform a variety of public duties that center around their position as authorities on tradition. They serve on the Indian Days committee; they help in planning the program and in the regulation of the camp; they don ceremonial regalia to take part in the dancing and exhibitions that make up the program. If a Sun Dance is held, it should be sponsored by people of this class and the principal roles will be filled by chiefs and their families. They are called upon to greet distinguished visitors and to officiate in adoption ceremonies and giveaways.

Several of these men own medicine bundles that they open on the proper occasions, and they help conduct the ceremonies at the bundle openings of other people. A few know curing practices and rituals and conduct curing ceremonies even though they and their patients also go to white doctors.

Some of the chiefs serve on the Honorary Tribal Council and receive a small per diem for attendance at council meetings. Members of this honorary council are chosen frequently to accompany delegations to the state and national capitals to lobby for or against proposed legislation that might affect the tribe. Both in the council and on such trips, the chiefs see themselves as spokesmen for the full-bloods and take every occasion to speak out, usually in Blackfeet, urging harmony and trust, and requesting more help for "the People"—the full-bloods.

The people, in general, take pride in their old timers but want them to exercise their influence outside of the council. They are handicapped, too, as political leaders because they speak little English and so fail to communicate directly with many of the people they seek to influence. They wish to arrive at decisions by the traditional council method that requires lengthy discussion and unanimity. The dominant culture and society within which they must act, the white and white-oriented leaders that must be influenced, do not allow time for this method of resolving issues. The men are extended the courtesy of free speech, but this does not include giving much attention to what they say.

These men have attained this status by the routes of wisdom, skill, and generosity. Wisdom and skill have developed through their experience. Their fathers, as youths, saw the last of the buffalo days and told their sons about that life, so their tie with the past is real. The chiefs have lived through ¾ of a century of the changes described in Chapter 4, so the wisdom they profess has a basis in experience with the white man. They were active participants in the trials of change, having tried many of the programs for economic readaptation with varying degrees of success. In the course of these economic ups and downs these men accepted some change, but also tried to maintain the traditions as they knew them, a difficult and dangerous job in face of the strenuous efforts of the government to stamp out these traditions. Their ability to do this has made them both the advisers and symbols they now are for numbers of people.

The high status position of these men is fairly stable but still depends on the numbers and support of their followers. Their claims to status must be validated by continued service and acts of generosity. They are not wealthy, but they have shared what they had in better times and perform services presently that validate their positions.

The chiefs do not present a united front, and are still rivals for additional prestige. They criticize one another and are gossiped about by other people. One old man will dismiss the tales of another as "lies." Another will be criticized for telling war stories. "He once put a story in the paper about how he scalped a Crow [Indian]. People laugh at him. He shouldn't tell those stories, they don't belong to him. My daddy told me not to tell these war stories, they're the property of the people who did the things."

The chiefs, then, are honored for their ability to symbolize tradition and to advise about and maintain these traditions. The knowledge and experience that has gained them this status, however, cannot be translated into effective, practical political and economic leadership, so that another type of Indian-oriented leader must fill this gap.

Interpreters,[16] like Raymond Black Plume, form a high status class made up of relatively younger men who are better educated, were raised in Indian-oriented homes, speak both languages fluently, and have assumed, or gained, leadership roles in the community. They express the ambition to "make a life by combining what is best of the Indian way with the best of the white way." They are capable of fitting into a role made necessary by the reservation complex wherein two contrasting societies attempt to function under a common political system. They can talk to and better understand both sides. At the same time, these leaders *are Indian-oriented*. They want to be accepted by the Indian society and want to maintain Indian identity, but both the bicultural milieu and their personal qualities lead to an understanding and participation that differs from that of the chiefs.

The interpreters know much of the old religion and lore. Quite often their fathers had been of the chief class and these men had been taught some of the traditions in their homes. But they are not committed, openly at least, to the old religion. They are members, and often leaders, of Christian churches. Those who are Catholics look for elements in Catholicism that support Indian values and they are adept at finding Christian analogues for Blackfeet beliefs. Others have joined minor Protestant churches and stress that the predominant Indian attendance at these makes them Indian churches. There is some evidence that many Indian-oriented persons are changing church affiliation frequently and that this is caused possibly by a search for a white church that is most congruent with the Blackfeet religion.[17]

The interpreters participate in Indian ceremonies and are given parts to play in the Sun Dance. They do not have the traditional wisdom required for the roles, but they are Indian leaders who are sympathetic and "good." They tend to express Indian values, and subscribe to Indian symbols. Interpreters frequently put up a tepee for Indian Days, wear a chiefly costume on appropriate occasions, stress their Indian names, and belong to a men's society.

In addition to their Indian training, these men have had the opportunity to get a good education in American schools, to travel and otherwise become experienced with much of white culture. They are capable of competing with the white-oriented, and through ability, hard work, and some economic success are well accepted by the white-oriented community. They could succeed on their own in any rural off-reservation community. The interpreters are not wealthy. They usually earn good salaries in agency or council positions but they use this income to help support a family ranch. Their less acculturated kinsmen work the ranch in return for some financial support. All share in the profits and losses from the enterprise.

---

[16] In an earlier paper I included the interpreters among what I called the 150% Men—people who knew two cultures well (McFee 1968).

[17] The Blackfeet have not accepted the peyote cults common to so many Indian reservations even though these are active in reservations in the surrounding region.

Because of their Indian-orientation, however, they must curb their economic ambitions in order to maintain their status. The very capabilities that make them valuable leaders within their group subject them to constant surveillance and criticism. In addition, their youth is held against them. In the past, status through wisdom came with age and in the eyes of many of their people they are wise too soon. So these men cannot acquire too much; they must be generous and helpful, and build a following that will attest to their wisdom, skill, and generosity in future years.

It is possible that in later life these men might take over the positions of custodians of tradition as these become vacated by the present chiefs, but this is doubtful, even though some people occasionally refer to them as "young chiefs." The tentative prediction would be that high status positions of both types will be filled from below where the factors of relative education and experience tend to produce differential experience within the Indian-oriented society. People of lower status already give indications as to how these positions will be filled.

The interpreters also differ from the chiefs, and many other Indian-oriented people as well, in the furnishing and maintenance of their homes. Most of the chiefs live in small frame or log houses with minimal services and simple furniture. They rarely have appliances—a wood range serves for both cooking and heating. The structures are unpainted inside and out and no attempt has been made to fence or otherwise mark the house lot or "territory." The interpreters, on the other hand, seem to have accepted more of the white-oriented interest in things. As a class, they live in larger three- or five-room houses which are painted on the inside at least. They build closets, have more furniture, own refrigerators, radios, and television sets. Often there is a fenced area around the house or some other border defining feature. The interpreters' homes look like those of many middle status white-oriented families—larger and better furnished than that of Bob Sorrel Horse, but not as freshly painted and filled with things as was Ray Hawkins' home. Here again is a sign that the interpreters aim for the best of two worlds.

INDIAN-ORIENTED LOW STATUS   Low status Indian-oriented people can be described by characteristics quite similar to those of the same status in white-oriented society. These people are poor. Some are hard workers and others improvident, but lack of training limits these men to irregular wage labor. They do not find regular seasonal jobs but must take work where and when they can find it. Several of the improvident ones, like their white-oriented counterparts, are called "bums" and "winos" and are problem cases for the authorities. But there is a difference between men of the differing orientations even at the lowest status level. They face in different cultural directions, and the analysis of the data from my sample showed that the Indian-oriented low status man is more a part of his society than the lower-class white man is in his.

In contrast with the white-oriented group, economic factors fail to separate the low from many of the middle status people in Indian-oriented society. Irregular work, low income, poorly maintained and crowded houses are characteristics shared by people variously ranked on the status scale. The ultimate criterion for status assignment is social participation.

Low status people do not take part in as many social activities as do the people of higher positions; they are often present but usually as onlookers. It is significant, however, that they are not isolated from their group as is often the case with the improvident white-oriented person. The low status Indian-oriented man is welcome to attend Indian activities if he behaves. If he misbehaves he is eased out, perhaps locked up in the jail, but people do not disown him for this. They joke about it as if his actions were to be expected, and welcome him back when he settles down. If he behaves he may be given a job to do, such as ushering, police duty, or helping with the serving of the food. He is one of them, perhaps a kinsman, at least a familiar person in the community and he is given some community support.

These men have much spare time and spend a great deal of it in the street corner groups. If they, or one of their friends, have a little cash or can beg some from a tourist, they will buy a bottle of wine and get drunk. Such loafing and drinking groups are made up of Indian-oriented people.

These men fill a traditional and expected status. The Blackfeet had, in the past, a few improvident and unfortunate people who lacked the "power" to succeed. This was not held against them and it was a social duty to see that they did not starve. The low status people of today are treated in much the same way; they are thought of as unlucky and not entirely responsible for their condition. They may stir up trouble but the tendency is to keep the quarrels within the group; they are criticized and admonished but not ostracized. White and white-oriented persons let the more impersonal authorities deal with the low status trouble makers and expect public agencies to take care of the shiftless ones. The Indian-oriented group feels a responsibility for their own low status people. They are "our people" and "we'" take care of them. Family and group responsibility does not end when authorities step in, and the improvident are cared for regardless of welfare. The aid may be given grudgingly but it is forthcoming.

INDIAN-ORIENTED MIDDLE STATUS   The majority of the Indian-oriented group are assigned to a middle status that encompasses a broad range of individual differences. The same qualities requisite for high status count here, and conformity to Indian values is more important than economic condition.

These are the people who live the Indian-oriented life described in the previous chapters, who affirm the Indian-oriented values and both support and take part in the Indian-oriented society. The middle class actively supports the leaders of their choice in both the traditional and the modern spheres and differs from the lower status people because of their more complete involvement in the life of the community. It is the attitudes, opinions, acts, and wants of these people that assign and validate social status; they are the Indian-oriented public that awards some people with loyalty and influence and penalize others with gossip, criticism, and shame.

This class includes people with a wide range of knowledge of and skills in the traditional culture, and in education and experience with the white. These differences in their knowledge and skills establish both limitations on and possibilities for upward mobility for these people. The poorly educated person cannot expect to gain high status of the interpreter type, and as a consequence they are most apt to follow the pattern established by the chiefs. There is evidence in the behavior of several men that they have such ambitions. They have quit drinking and "chasing around," and have become active in a men's society, a dancing or singing group, and are learning more of the old culture from association with the chiefs. They serve on committees that plan and stage the Indian Days celebration and holiday dances, and attempt to live up to the highest values of the group. Their families are supporting them in this move. The brother of one such man spoke of him proudly: "My brother quit drinking twenty years ago and learned Indian singing. He won a singing contest and now he's a champion singer. He's the boss." Others support the similar ambitions of one of their relatives; they say that this man "isn't so much of a singer" and that he really "doesn't know much" about Blackfeet ways. His ambitions are being challenged as a part of the validation process he must go through.

Several younger men appear to be grooming for the interpreter high status positions. They are learning Blackfeet traditions in their homes or from the elders, and at the same time are doing well in school. One man appears to be a likely candidate for a position as an interpreter. He went on to college and gained additional experience in American society; he is fluent in both languages and was raised and trained in aspects of the old culture. His Indian-oriented accomplishments and success in school already have gained him the respect of the Indian-oriented, and his early success in school earned the respect of many in the white and white-oriented community. He is now going through another testing, having dropped out of college and returned to the reservation to pick up irregular labor and drinking patterns that are not appreciated by the higher status people of either orientation. Nonetheless he is forgiven by the Indian-oriented and will be by the white-oriented if he "straightens out" later and picks up his previous goals of assuming the interpreter role. Other interpreters have traveled this road.

I visited many kinds of Indian-oriented homes and with the exception of those of the interpreters found one characteristic common to all—regardless of the size of the house or financial standing of the owner, they gave little evidence of concern for the material possessions prized by middle-class whites. For instance, one middle status Indian-oriented family, the Chief Sons, lived in a four room frame house in Browning. The siding of the thirty year old structure had been covered during the past ten years with asphalt shingles; the shingle roof was in good repair, but the outside trim had not been painted since the original application. The floors were covered with linoleum, the plastered interior walls retained the original paint. The plumbing fixtures had been installed or replaced in 1958 and were in good repair. Heat was provided by the wood range. Each bedroom had a bed, a wooden chair, and a small table. Clothes were hung on wall hooks and on a cord stretched across one corner of the room. The living room was furnished with a worn davenport, a table and some wooden chairs, and an old cabinet phonograph and radio combination that was inoperative. Floral print paper curtains hung at the windows, several Russell prints and a religious calendar were on the walls, and a plaster religious figurine stood on the radio cabinet. Family photographs, including many of the children, and elders too, in Indian costumes were displayed in the bedrooms. It appeared that meals were eaten at a small table in the kitchen. Inside everything was worn, orderly, and clean; outside there was less order. There was no fence, no lawn, and several shrubs grew unattended. There was little to indicate any concern about how the place looked to a passerby.

Another Indian-oriented middle status home was an old log cabin to which an entryway and bedroom had been added. The structure was sound but unpainted. The old cabin part served as a combination kitchen, living room, and bedroom. There was no water service. Water had to be carried daily from a community hydrant a block away in three water buckets that were placed on a bench beside the wood range and a washstand. The range did double duty for cooking and heating. The furniture consisted of a plain wooden table and wooden kitchen chairs and the beds—two in the bedroom and one in the main room. As in the first house, clothes were hung on wall hooks. There were cotton print curtains at the windows and colorful patchwork quilts covered the beds. The walls were covered with family photographs, a religious calendar, and some articles of Indian beadwork. Paper flowers were on the table, and several plants were growing in tin cans that had been covered with colored paper and placed along the window sill in the entryway. Again, everything inside was neat and clean contrasting with the unfenced yard which was bare of plantings and cluttered with debris.

These examples support but do not prove my impression that there is a difference between the two orientation groups in the way they furnish and maintain their homes. I was in several middle status homes that, like the first one I described, had a refrigerator and overstuffed furniture and that, with the exception of the interpreters' homes, came closest to "having everything," as one of the Chief Sons family said of their house. Cleanliness and decoration with things that interested the family were important, but no one seemed to feel that paint was required. Exteriors received only the most necessary repairs, and the Indian-oriented more often than not showed little concern about marking off or maintaining a private space around the house. Thus there was attention to comfort, but it did not seem to be the same kind of material comfort sought by the middle-class whites.

White and white-oriented people seemed to want to define their yards and order them, which may be in part an expression of concern about what others might think: lawns, fences, flowers, and paint are status symbols in white middle-class society, but have little part to play in establishing a social position among the Indian-oriented. The latter are interested in doing other things with their time and money.

These differences remain impressionistic and need further and careful study. The new housing, freshly painted, that has indoor plumbing, hot and cold running water, electric or gas ranges, space heaters, and that encourages the building of fences and the planting of lawns will both encourage their use and maintenance and provide a test for my thesis that the two groups differ in their evaluation of such things. Time will tell how much the Indian-oriented people choose to invest in these, and whether or not they will differ from their white-oriented neighbors in this respect. For the present, at least, I find these differing concerns about work, money, home furnishings and maintenance, generosity and proper social relationships, and the values that underlie them, to be basic to the maintenance of the contrasting social structures of the two groups.

9

The Future

Summation

THIS STUDY OF THE MODERN BLACKFEET has provided evidence that the tribe is made up of two contrasting societies, each with its own culture, associational patterns and internal organization. These contrasting societies are held together because all tribal members are "Indians" by both legal and social definitions, and because they live together on an Indian reservation. The two societies also participate in economic and political systems at the tribal level that are held in common, and these systems, in turn, are intricately involved in the economic and political life of the State of Montana and therefore the nation. In addition, various kinds of kinship ties, coincident interests and associations form weaker bonds between the groups. Most of the arguments in support of this conclusion have been set forth, so only the salient characteristics of the two societies will be summarized as a basis for some reflections about the future of the Blackfeet tribe.

White-Oriented Society

The white-oriented society was found to be organized around basic values of work, self-dependence, individuality, and acquisitiveness. People of this orientation believe in these values and, in general, practice them. They keep busy, hold steady jobs, stress their ability to take care of themselves, and rarely turn to people outside their immediate family for help.

White-oriented persons work toward future goals. They want to build toward the social and economic betterment of themselves and their children and believe that this can be accomplished best by education, hard work, and acquisitiveness. To this end they build ranches, farms, or businesses, or hold a good steady job. Acquisitiveness is evidenced in the ownership and maintenance of property, homes, furnishings, and equipment that contribute to economic independence, material comfort, and serve also to symbolize, both to the individual and others, the degree of success achieved.

Persons of this orientation associate mainly with people of similar orientation and aspire toward full participation in white society. Such aspirations often are thwarted both because white people identify the white-oriented with an Indian stereotype, and they too see themselves as "Indians" in opposition to "white men" when the privileges of Indian status are under attack. The aspirations are realistic, however, because in most respects the white-oriented segment of the Blackfeet tribe differs little from the majority section of American society.

A brief investigation of the status system within this group revealed a pattern similar to the general American class structure. Like most other Americans, white-oriented people make their judgments of individual worth according to standards introduced and maintained by the dominant society. One can conclude that the white-oriented society among the Blackfeet is organized around a series of class norms. An individual who aspires to belong to this society will find social support to the extent that he approximates the behavior set by these norms and displays a commitment to the values of the group.

Indian-Oriented Society

The patterns of the Indian-oriented group stand out clearly despite the many features shared with both white and white-oriented society, and especially in the areas of contrasting premises and values. The major goal of this group is to retain its ethnic identity as shown by the attachment these people have to things and practices that symbolize Indian-ness. Traditional definitions of the good person, and particularly the value placed upon generosity, persist and serve as both symbols of being Indian, and a check against the achievement necessary for full economic integration with the dominant society.

This goal tends to make the Indian-oriented Blackfeet present rather than future oriented. They asserted tradition, a tradition made up of remembered Blackfeet culture, borrowed pan-Indian elements and incorporated elements from white culture, but this is not to be interpreted as living in the past. The future is uncertain for most Indian-oriented people; past experience has made them suspicious of long range plans. Consequently the tendency is to avoid risking present positions for unknown future benefits, to live each day as it comes and to remember real and legendary better days of the past.

The Blackfeet Indian-oriented society is organized in conformity to these norms and expectations. A man is judged by his display of Indian traits and particularly by how generous he is with the fruits of his achievement. Expressions of such judgments were recorded and used to construct a scale of status, from low to high, and the resulting class structure appeared little related to similar levels in both the general American society and the white-oriented Blackfeet group.

Of particular importance, as an indication of Indian-oriented accommodation to the bicultural milieu, is the duality apparent in the Indian system that led to the identification of two high status classes—the chiefs and the interpreters. The chiefs attain influence because of their knowledge of the past; they represent continuity with the Blackfeet forebears and the traditional culture. The interpreters, on the other hand, are supported because of their knowledge of and experience with both cultures which enables them to mediate between the subordinate and dominant groups.

The Indian-oriented society in these ways provides tribal members with an alternative route to influence and higher status—another set of class norms regulating the behavior of persons who wish to associate with people who aspire to be Indians. Approximation of these norms and evidence of commitment to the values of the group will help a man gain acceptance and social support from this society.

Two hundred and thirty years of adaptation and adjustment to change has resulted in a bicultural community held together by special bonds. The past events have not resulted in tribal disorganization, but in a reorganization that accommodates the simultaneous persistence of many traditional social and cultural characteristics from both interacting societies. A large part of the tribe has adopted the culture of the dominant society and aspires to assimilate. A smaller number, for reasons already mentioned, retains more from the Blackfeet past and resists further change. The reservation social structure has changed to accommodate these contrasting points of view. The structure of a nonreservation community tends to be unilinear, with one general set of values, and one status hierarchy. But the physical and social boundaries of the reservation and the tribe incorporate two societies, and make possible a bilinear structure that offers a choice of alternative limitations and possibilities for adaptation. An individual, consciously or otherwise, can choose, and possibly choose again, which pattern he wishes to follow. His choice, and his acceptance and class assignment, depend upon what he brings to the situation in the way of aspirations, experiences, and capabilities. Herein may lie the potential for the development of a true and viable cultural pluralism that can serve as a model for American society as a whole. That hope guides my reflections upon the future.

What Lies Ahead for the Blackfeet?

An oracle, whether a social scientist or anything else short of Delphian, takes risks. I put myself in double jeopardy: my reading of the present may be faulty, and, as is most usual, the future conditions may be very different from those I foresee.

No one in the present day should be unaware of the problems confronting American Indians, and what I have described should indicate that the Blackfeet too have troubles. There is heavy drinking, even alcoholism, among too many old and young alike. Crime, vandalism, and juvenile delinquency are too frequent. Several cases of suicide have been reported; alcohol-related and tragic deaths from violence, automobile accidents, and exposure too often occur. Underlying all this is the pervasive poverty and lack of economic opportunity that undermines self-esteem.

Too often, I think, these problems have been described as Indian problems, when they are mostly local expressions of national problems. Such an emphasis has tended to reinforce a negative stereotype of the Indian held by many neighboring whites and even by some of the white-oriented tribal members. The Indian aspect of these problems is that the Indian-oriented tend to be treated as second-class citizens on the reservation, and they, and the white-oriented as well, are treated as second-class citizens off the reservation. This creates resentment for all and identity problems for many of the young people. Some of the resulting frustrations are expressed in ways that create social problems. Beyond this, the causal factors and their antisocial expression are the same as those to be found in every community in the country, and like most other communities, the Blackfeet recognized the problems and are trying to do something about them. A Crisis Clinic, Alcoholics Anonymous, Community Action Programs, the town, the tribe, the B.I.A., church and civic organizations, and concerned citizens are at work. The solutions to these problems may be found elsewhere, they may be found here. Information, support and sympathy are needed: sensational publicity is rightfully resented.

These and other problems should not be glossed over or ignored, but at the same time they should not be stressed to the neglect of more positive aspects. The positive side to the problems described above is that they are recognized by local people and that local people are trying to do something about them. Prophets of gloom and doom are not hard to find, so in these final pages I am going to look more at the strengths than at the weaknesses to show some of the things that I think augur a better future for the Blackfeet.

The problems of an inadequate economic base and the attendant poverty are all pervasive, but these too have been recognized for a long time and the tribe, bureau, and town of Browning have been cooperating in attempts to create a viable economy. History militates against predictions of success in these endeavors. It is easy to see in retrospect how planners erred when they began so early and persisted so long in promoting small subsistence farming and ranching as the key to Indian economic security, at a time when the trend in these occupations was toward increased use of machinery and the utilization of increasingly larger land holdings. Present plans, too, may prove to be out of step with future trends. These trends, of course, are difficult to identify and action to improve the economy must be taken on the basis of the best predictions and the hope that some of the plans will be in tune with tomorrow.

The present plans for reservation economic development are predicated on (1) relocation of some of the population to industrial centers through federal support for on the job training, (2) attracting small industries and their payrolls to the reservation, and (3) increased exploitation of tourism. Success depends not only on how well these are implemented, but on where they lead.

Of these ventures, I am least optimistic about the relocation programs. These were not discussed in earlier chapters because my major concern was with events on the reservation and because accurate figures about the results of the past years efforts are not available. Bureau reports show upwards of sixty persons per year off the reservation engaged in on-the-job training or in vocational schools, but I do not know the actual rate of permanent relocation. I have talked to several men, and have heard of others, who tried relocation and for varying reasons failed and came back home. I have been told that many of those who are reported to have made a success of these ventures were already off reservation and employed prior to their entering the program. These men had availed themselves of the opportunity to better their job. These programs affect the reservation economy, however, by reducing the level of unemployment on the reservation and by contributing to the training of those who leave and return. There has been gain for individuals, but to my mind, the gain to the reservation has been slight. Too few have successfully relocated to have reduced significantly the number of unemployed, and the skills learned by those who have gone to the cities and returned more often than not have been of little use on the reservation.

I would question, too, the compatibility of this program with present trends in the cities. Relocation is being supported at a time when our cities are becoming increasingly untenable, fraught with the problems of underemployment, decaying housing, underfinanced services and overtaxed transportation facilities. It does not seem to be the proper time to encourage Indians to go to the city where they must learn and try to hold a job in a situation of possibly declining employment, and risk as well the possibility of having to move into the local poverty pockets of wretched housing. I would think that one would choose poverty among friends and in the country over poverty in the city among strangers. I feel that relocation programs are dead end streets that might be opened if they were redirected toward providing employment for Indians in small industries in small cities, at least until we can read with more certainty what the future holds for our major cities.

If it develops that the solution to city problems results in further decentralization of industry and population, then the present plans for local industrial development may turn out to be the plans of farsighted men. At present the reservation seems too far from population and commercial centers to attract industry, but it is on main transportation routes and has space, clean air, clean water and a good supply of capable, if untrained, workers. These features could be very attractive to management personnel who like the country, the scenery, hunting, fishing, and outdoor sports and are disenchanted with the city and its problems. But, if industry does come, the planning must be such that these advantages are preserved and some of the benefits of that industry accrue to the present residents. Industry will have to be more conservative and less exploitive of the natural and human resources of the region than it has been elsewhere.

The tribe and the townspeople have made a heavy investment and have incurred a considerable debt to build the Industrial Park, to make the sewer, water, and street improvements, to build homes in preparation for industrial expansion, and to make the community attractive to management personnel. If things work out, these debts will be self-liquidating and the reservation community will have made marked economic progress. If the industries do not come, things will be no worse than before. The physical improvements will remain, and better housing was sorely needed. True, everybody will be deeper in debt, but debts have been incurred for less important reasons. Capable administrators in many other U.S. towns have elected the same route to the revival of local economies.

An extension of the recent and steady upward trend in tourist activity supports a prediction of success for this venture. Again space, water, clean air, in addition to good hunting and fishing and the proximity to Glacier National Park, provide a strong base for tourist development. Tourist facilities appear to be a sound investment that would, in the long run, continue to bring in outside money regardless of the ups and downs of the national economy. The trends in this industry can be influenced by what developments take place in the cities. Will changes encourage city dwellers to spend more of their leisure time at home, or result in ever increasing search for open space and sport? Concerns for the environment will play a part in the planning and building of tourist facilities. What if studies show that tourist activities should be curtailed in the interest of preserving the very attractions the local people wish to exploit? What is the future for the automobile, motorboating, motorcycles, and ski-mobiles? Substitutes for the internal combustion engine will change the nature of motor service operations. Radical changes in recreational facilities might result, if automobile and related private, engine-powered personal transportation and sports equipment were curtailed and mass public transport was expanded. Highway construction, parking facilities, power boat and automobile servicing facilities, motels, campgrounds designed for auto traffic all would be affected. Different kinds of facilities would be needed depending on the forms of transportation that evolved. Curtailment of motor driven equipment might greatly increase the use of horses for recreation. The reservation is well suited for raising horses, and already has more than are needed for present purposes. A right guess here would make a big difference in the odds for success in tourist development. The positive aspect here is that the resources are on or near the reservation and at present these are relatively untouched. There is less of a vested interest to oppose change than would be the case if the region had already been highly developed. Little present or planned development would stand in the way of such a change.

Another trend that some predict for the U.S. economy that may affect the outcome of reservation programs is the prospect that computers and other forms of mechanization will put work as we know it out of style. If, in the next few decades, there will be fewer jobs as we know them one of two things will have to happen. The high value placed on work for its own sake will have to give way to other measures of personal worth, or other activities now called play or recreation will have to be brought into the definition of work. In either case such a change would seem to work against the success of the industrial development, but boost the prospects of success in the area of recreation. Many tribal members who have trouble finding jobs, but have developed the skills of crafts, art, and sociability may find themselves better prepared for the future than those who appear successful under present conditions. Projected plans for some form of minimum guaranteed income would have unforeseen results but could be only an improvement over present conditions.

Local and tribal participation in these attempts at solving the economic problems of the reservation have contributed along with many other experiences to the development of an increasingly viable and capable group of community leaders. This is my greatest source of optimism. The Blackfeet have never lacked for active and intelligent leaders and they have had years of experience in practical politics. The heartening factor has been the trend to a broader political base, increased autonomy of decision, and the greater participation by more of the community in political and social action. With each passing generation those who have taken leadership roles have had more education and more experience with the outside world than those who preceded them. Tribal members play leading roles in national Indian organizations. They have in the past and continue to serve in the state legislature and senate. There were Blackfeet at Alcatraz. More youth are going to college and some of these are talking of returning to the reservation to play a part in solving local problems. The tribal council and its committees has always provided a good training ground for leadership. To this has been added the Community Action Programs and other O.E.O. sponsored activities. The Browning Industrial Development Corporation and the Housing Authority, both provide opportunities for leadership training and participation for more people. Some of the O.E.O. programs are reminiscent of the old C.C.C. programs that provided short range income that was a help for people when they needed it, but had few long range economic benefits. The Community Action Programs, however, appeal to me most because they are involving young and old and most of them are centered in the community. The workers involved get to know their neighbors, learn of the community problems and what resources are available to help solve them. Even youngsters out cleaning up vacant lots are doing something with their neighbors for the community. They are learning about organization and practical politics—knowledge that should stand them in good stead whatever the future brings. The faults of these programs and organizations are the faults of all of us, as are the strengths. The Blackfeet are becoming increasingly able to run their own affairs with less governmental paternalism.

That last sentence raises the very sensitive issue of termination. This is a very sticky problem, too complicated to elaborate on here. I will side with those who oppose it for the following reasons. I agree with those tribal members who fear political domination by the county and state if the Bureau of Indian Affairs and the special relationships between tribe and the federal government were terminated. First, land would be lost rapidly if trust restrictions were removed. It is of course every citizen's right to buy and sell his property, but too many Indian owners still are too inexperienced in financial matters to protect their own interests in even the most honest land transactions or to benefit by converting land to cash. Secondly, much reservation land would be lost if it was removed from trust status and put on the tax rolls at a time when too few Indian owners make enough money from their land to meet taxes. Thirdly, the Indians feel that the present climate of discrimination in off-reservation communities would result in loss of services, poorer services, and unfair treatment in local and state courts is present federal and tribal programs were turned over to county and state. I think their fears are well founded.

The other side of the argument has some merit too. B.I.A. programs have often been overprotective, fostering overdependency and expectations of paternalistic care and these have created some problems. Some of the hamlets, particularly Heart Butte, are so dependent on tribal and governmental help that the people could not exist there without it. One result of termination would be that the people in Heart Butte would lose their remaining lands and be forced to move. This move would take them into slum areas of Browning or Great Falls, and fully on the welfare rolls of those communities. The new economic base must be secured before the trust protection can be removed.

The Blackfeet complain about the bureau but fear the alternatives more. Some of their leaders think the best move would be to let Indians assume administrative positions in the bureau where they could have more say about what should be done and how to do it. This, they say, "would hold the wolves at bay, while we work out our problems."

Termination is just one more product of the red man's burden—the white man problem. Not only have the white men taken over most of the land, the authority, and decision making powers about Blackfeet life, liberty, and pursuit of happiness, but they have married into the tribe as well. All these influences have produced, among other things, white-oriented tribal members. White people remain a problem on the reservation, some more of a problem than others. The white merchants, ranchers, and farmers, at least, are known; some are good friends. Their roles are familiar and for better or for worse predictable patterns of interaction have been established. White Bureau of Indian Affairs employees usually fit into known patterns too. Their roles are known and people recognize that some will visit with them, become friends and help out in community affairs, while others will remain aloof. Public Health Service employees are less well known. Most, with a few appreciated exceptions, come and go more frequently than do the bureau employees. They tend to remain isolated in their own residential area, and rarely enter into the economic and social life of the community.

It has been my experience that white people living around the reservation tend to be more hostile to the Blackfeet than those who live further away. The Blackfeet know, and often dislike, the established relationships in the neighboring off reservation towns. These feelings are unfortunate. People of very similar backgrounds and interests are prevented from establishing what could be very congenial friendships if these attitudes did not prevail. More Blackfeet would find off reservation jobs available if their white neighbors could exercise their biases more selectively. White-oriented tribal members, too, often lose touch with the Indian-oriented, stereotype them and, as a consequence, are branded in return with the white man stereotype.

Then there is the white tourist: a whole industry is being planned to attract greater numbers of them and their money to the reservation, yet all tourists are not loved. Too many American tourists do not know what to expect of Indians, or arrive with wrong expectations so firmly fixed that they cannot learn from experience. Too many look for the movie or comic strip Indian, the "noble red man" in buckskins or feathers who says "How" and talks about "bucks" and "squaws" and "papooses," and is considered to be either inordinately wise and taciturn or somewhat short on intelligence. Others seem to expect to find illiterate people living in squalor and filth. They may find some of what they expect. Some Indians dress up for them and play the movie Indian for the edification of the tourist and the benefit of their own pocketbooks. Visitors can see a drunken Indian, there is poverty, unkempt appearing housing, and not everything is neat and orderly in appearance. But they have excluded the large and significant middle: the educated and industrious who are all around them wherever they go. They have not entered the houses that appear as shacks on the outside, but are clean, orderly homes inside. They have excluded the many who are impoverished but not licked. All of these are hurt when people, who must think that none of them can understand English, make audible derogatory remarks about them, their homes, their town, and their children. The Blackfeet do not talk of "bucks, squaws, and papooses," and feel that these terms indicate that they are less than human. They are men and women, have husbands, wives, and children, like anybody else. They react with concealed resentment, and usually with extraordinary courtesy, when someone enters a restaurant and then leaves, saying loudly: "Let's go somewhere else. This is run by Indians and is apt to be dirty." The charitable ones chalk such behavior up to ignorance on the part of that tourist; it is that, but it is bad manners as well. Luckily not all white tourists, just too many of them, are like that. It is part of the Indian's white man problem.

Among other white visitors to the reservation is the anthropologist. I have a vested interest, a bias here, that must be recognized, so will not examine this problem in all its detail. I only offer a few defenses: anthropologists have recorded much of what Blackfeet elders told them of the past culture, and modern Indians do turn to these records to learn of their past and use these books as guides for the revival and perpetuation of tradition. For my part, I can only hope that I have repaid some of my debt to the Blackfeet by not acting like the worst of the tourists, and that by this book and my teaching I can educate future tourists not only to better behavior, but more importantly to a greater appreciation for and understanding of the Blackfeet in all their variety.

There is one more development that bolsters my optimism: That which I will call the third generation phenomenon. The children of white-oriented families who have achieved a measure of economic security are taking an increased interest in Indian traditions. They are buying or making costumes, learning to dance and participating in the Indian Days and community social events. As some say, "They are taking an interest in their Indian heritage." This is being furthered too, by the college youth who have been taken up in the red power and other student Indian movements. They and their peers on the reservation are not only asserting their Indian identity, but their tribal identity as well. Over the past decade I have noticed not only the more recent participation of the third generation white-oriented, but the earlier shift from costume, song, and dance that was Indian, to a greater emphasis on those things that are authentically Blackfeet Indian.

These young people can play an important part in the elimination of white-oriented misunderstanding of and unrecognized discrimination against the Indian-oriented. They can be interpreters from the white-oriented side who can work with the Indian-oriented interpreters toward better understanding and cooperation between the two social divisions of the Blackfeet community. In the best of all worlds such communication could lead to a unified but diverse community, a working cultural pluralism, a more viable society that could solve its own problems and deal with and eliminate most of its white man problems. Utopian? Perhaps. But I think that the seeds of such a development are present and that the maintenance of the reservation system for a while longer might allow it to work out.

Credit too must be given to the Indian-oriented and the full-bloods, past and present, who have endured, who have persisted in preserving what they cherished and believed in in the face of strong and often violent opposition. They have maintained traditions. These traditions have posed a dilemma for some who find it difficult to choose between the old and the new, but have given many others a source of identity and pride that has enriched the quality of reservation life.

Epilogue

Albert Buffalo Heart and most of his peers have died during the past decade. Some of their names, along with those of deceased white-oriented tribal leaders, can be read on a plaque at the entrance to the Museum of the Plains Indian. He and men like him have left a legacy of past tradition—knowledge and beliefs, modified by their personal interpretations and understandings. Some of their medicine bundles and other possessions symbolic of their power, experiences, and continuity with preceding generations have gone into museum and private collections. Others have been transferred to members of their families or other tribal members who may or may not perpetuate the beliefs and activities that went with the symbols.

A new generation of elders has taken their place and these will play the role in different ways and from slightly different backgrounds. Some of the new chiefs own bundles, know some rituals and parts of others. Some of them do not. They all share a knowledge of the language and a commitment to perpetuating the traditions as they know them. What they know and do will undoubtedly be reformulated by them into a fairly cohesive and organized Blackfeet "tradition," somewhat different from that which went before, but still capable of providing support for a continuing Indian-orientation. Young men are preparing to fill these roles in their own turn.

John Arrowhead is still there. His life goes on with little noticeable change from year to year. Roy Conrad is dead and his sons carry on the farm and too, perhaps, the memories of what their father told them of his life, his knowledge and experiences. Bob Sorrel Horse still works but falls short of his dream. In fact much changes and much remains the same.

Amid the ebb and flow, the change and the sameness, in spite of the continuing tragic waste of talent and potential, a younger generation is developing that should be better able to meld the old and the new. The future reservation citizens should be better able to mediate the social divisions and to work toward producing a viable cultural pluralism. Hopefully, the Raymond Black Plumes and the Henry Rogers will come closer together in understanding and in their aspirations, and teach their children to incorporate the legacy of their parents, the teachings of the school, and what they learn by participation in reservation life into their own tradition—a tradition that does include, or allow expression of, the best of the Indian way and the best of the white. If diversity is as important to the perpetuation of a people and a culture as it is for the survival of a biological species, then the future generations of the Blackfeet have been well served by the diversity bequeathed them by their ancestors.

References

BLACKFEET INDIAN RESERVATION, TOWN OF BROWNING, 1968, "Model City" Application. (Mimeographed) Browning, Montana.

BLACKFEET TRIBAL COUNCIL, n.d., Records and Documents. Browning, Montana.

BRADLEY, LT. JAMES H., 1900, "Affairs at Fort Benton," *Contributions to the Historical Society of Montana* 3:201–287.

————, 1923, "St. Peter's Mission," *Contributions to the Historical Society of Montana* 9:315–316.

BROPHY, WILLIAM A., and SOPHIE D. ABERLE, 1966, *The Indian: America's Unfinished Business*. Norman, Oklahoma: University of Oklahoma Press.

BRUNER, EDWARD M., 1956, "Primary Group Experience and the Processes of Acculturation," *American Anthropologist* 58:605–623.

BURLINGAME, MERRILL, G., 1942, *The Montana Frontier*. Helena, Montana: State Publishing Company.

EWERS, JOHN C., 1955, "The Horse in Blackfoot Indian Culture," Bureau of American Ethnology, *Bulletin 159*.

————, 1958, *The Blackfeet: Raiders on the Northwestern Plains*. Norman, Oklahoma: University of Oklahoma Press.

FAGG, HARRISON G., and ASSOCIATES, 1970, *Browning-Blackfeet Comprehensive Plan*. Billings, Montana.

The Glacier Reporter (Browning, Montana), 1959–1970.

GLOVER, RICHARD, 1962, *David Thompson's Narrative: 1784–1812*. Toronto: The Champlain Society.

GRINNELL, GEORGE BIRD, 1907, *Blackfoot Lodge Tales*. New York: Charles Scribner's Sons.

KAPPLER, CHARLES J., 1903, See U.S. Congress, Senate.

LEWIS, OSCAR, 1942, *The Effects of White Contact Upon Blackfoot Culture with Special Reference to the Role of the Fur Trade*. Monographs of the American Ethnological Society, No. 6. Seattle: University of Washington Press.

LINTON, RALPH, 1936, *The Study of Man*. New York: Appleton-Century-Crofts, Inc.

MCCLINTOCK, WALTER, 1910, *The Old North Trail*. London: Macmillan and Co., Ltd.

MCFEE, MALCOLM, 1962, *Modern Blackfeet: Contrasting Patterns of Differential Acculturation*. Unpublished Ph.D. dissertation, Department of Anthropology, Stanford University.

————, 1968, "The 150% Man, a Product of Blackfeet Acculturation," *American Anthropologist* 70:1096–1103.

MERIAM, LEWIS, *et al.*, 1928, *The Problem of Indian Administration*. Institute for Government Research, Studies in Administration. Baltimore: The Johns Hopkins Press.

The Montana Almanac, 1957. Missoula, Montana: Montana State University Press.

ROBBINS, LYNN A., 1968, "Economics, Household Composition and the Family Cycle: The Blackfeet Case," in *Spanish-Speaking People in the United States*. Proceedings of the 1968 Annual Spring Meeting of the American Ethnological Society. Seattle: University of Washington Press.

STERN, THEODORE, 1966, *The Klamath Tribe: A People and Their Reservation*. Seattle: University of Washington Press.

TOOLE, ROSS K., 1959, *Montana: An Uncommon Land*. Norman, Oklahoma: University of Oklahoma Press.

U.S. BOARD OF INDIAN COMMISSIONERS, 1905–1925, *Annual Reports*.

U.S. CONGRESS, 1881, *Congressional Record*. Vol. XI.

———, 1886, *Congressional Record*. Vol. XVII.

———, 1953, *Congressional Record*. Vol. XCIX.

U.S. CONGRESS, SENATE, 1903, *Indian Affairs, Laws and Treaties*. Charles J. Kappler, ed. Senate Document 452, 57th Congress, 1st Session.

———, 1918, *Blackfeet Indian Reservation*. Committee on Indian Affairs, Report No. 451, 65th Congress, 2nd Session.

U.S. DEPARTMENT OF THE INTERIOR, 1934–1959, *Annual Reports of the Secretary of the Interior*.

U.S. DEPARTMENT OF THE INTERIOR, Office of Indian Affairs, 1883–1926, *Annual Reports of the Commissioner of Indian Affairs*.

———, 1936, *Constitution and By-Laws for the Blackfeet Tribe of the Blackfeet Indian Reservation, Montana*.

———, 1936, *Corporate Charter of the Blackfeet Tribe of the Blackfeet Indian Reservation, Montana*.

———, 1936, *Indians at Work*. Vol. III, No. 12; Vol. IV, No. 4; Vol. IV, No. 7; Vol. IV, No. 8.

———, 1939, *Statistical Report of Public Assistance to Indians Under the Social Security Act as of October 1, 1939*.

———, 1940, *Statistical Supplement to the Annual Report of the Commissioner of Indian Affairs, 1940*.

———, 1970, *Blackfeet Agency FY 1972 Budget and Program Memorandum*.

U.S. DEPARTMENT OF THE INTERIOR, Office of the Solicitor, 1958, *Federal Indian Law*.

U.S. STATUTES, 1859, *Statutes at Large*. Vol. XI.

———, 1875, *Statutes at Large*. Vol. XVIII.

———, 1887, *Statutes at Large*. Vol. XXIV.

———, 1889, *Statutes at Large*, Vol. XXV.

———, 1897, *Statutes at Large*. Vol. XXIX.

———, 1907, *Statutes at Large*. Vol. XXXIV.

———, 1919, *Statutes at Large*. Vol. XLI.

———, 1934, *Statutes at Large*. Vol. XLVIII.

———, 1936, *Statutes at Large*. Vol. XLIX.

———, 1950, *Statutes at Large*. Vol. LXIV, Part 1.

WEBER, KENNETH R., 1968, *Economy, Occupation, Education and Family in a Tri-Ethnic Community*. Unpublished M.A. thesis, Department of Anthropology, University of Oregon.

WHETSTONE, DANIEL W., 1956, *Frontier Editor*. New York: Hastings House Publishers, Inc.

WILLIAMS, ROBIN M. JR., 1970, *American Society: A Sociological Interpretation*. 3rd ed. New York: Alfred A. Knopf, Inc.

WILSON, H. CLYDE, 1963, "An Inquiry into the Nature of Plains Indian Cultural Development," *American Anthropologist* 65:355–369.

WISSLER, CLARK, 1910, "Material Culture of the Blackfoot Indians," *Anthropological Papers of the American Museum of Natural History* Vol. V (1).

———, 1911, "The Social Life of the Blackfoot Indians," *Anthropological Papers of the American Museum of Natural History* Vol. VII (1).

————, 1912, "Ceremonial Bundles of the Blackfoot Indians," *Anthropological Papers of the American Museum of Natural History* Vol. VII (2).

————, 1913, "Societies and Dance Associations of the Blackfoot Indians," *Anthropological Papers of the American Museum of Natural History* Vol. XI (4).

————, 1918, "The Sun Dance of the Blackfoot Indians," *Anthropological Papers of the American Museum of Natural History* Vol. XVI (3).

THE MENOMINEE[*]

George and Louise Spindler

Stanford University

George and Louise Spindler began fieldwork with the Menominee as graduate students in anthropology at the University of Wisconsin in 1948. They have maintained contact with the Menominee to the present. George Spindler is professor of anthropology and education at Stanford University, where he has been since 1950. Louise Spindler is research associate and lecturer at Stanford. The former obtained his Ph.D. at University of California at Los Angeles in 1952, and the latter at Stanford in 1956, the first graduate of the department of anthropology there. The Spindlers have also done fieldwork with the Blood Indians of Alberta, Canada, and the Mistassini Cree, as well as in Germany. George Spindler has done fieldwork in school systems in the United States. They are joint editors of several series in anthropology and have published both jointly and independently.

[*]The original case study is called *Dreamers without Power: The Menomini Indians.*

SOUTH BRANCH

COUNTY TRUNK M

DIRT ROADS

LAKES

KESHENA

TO SHAWANO

HIGHWAY 55

WOLF RIVER

WEST BRANCH

KINEPOWAY

NEOPIT

DIRT ROADS

ZOAR

HIGHWAY 47

TO PHLOX

N

TOWNSHIPS CEDED TO
THE STOCKBRIDGE
AND MUNSEE

Menominee County

Menomini Phonemes[1]

Consonants

	Labial	Dental	Alveolo-palatal	Mid-palatal	Glottal
Voiceless stops	p	t	c	k	ʔ
Voiceless fricatives			s		h
Voiced nasals	m	n			
Semivowels	w		y		

Vowels

	Front			Back	
	Short	Long		Short	Long
High	i	i·		u	u·
Mid	e	e·		o	o·
Low	ε	ε·		a	a·

---

[1] From Slotkin 1957.

Contents

Menomini Phonemes   363

1. The Confrontation   367

   Adaptation, 367
   To What Did They Adapt?, 372
   The Confrontation, 373
   The Consequences of Confrontation, 374
   That Which Was Lost, 375

2. *Omɛ·ʔnomɛ·ne·w*   380

   What Are They Like?, 380
    Interpretation, 386
   How the System Works, 393
    The Economic Base, 393
    Social Organization as Related to the Economic Base, 397
    The World around Them: Menomini Cosmology, 402
    Power: Getting and Maintaining It, 408
     What Is Power—What Does It Look Like?, 408
     How Does a Person Gain Power?, 408
     How Does a Menomini Maintain and Protect His Power?, 412
    Ceremonial Organizations as Related to Power, 416
     The Metɛ·wen, *416*
     The Ni·mihɛ·twàn, *424*
     The Okeceta·wɛ·se·man, *430*
    Witchcraft and Social Control, 433
     Offending Elders, 436
     Aggressive Behaviors, 438
   Becoming a Menomini, 440
    Attitudes toward Children, 440
    Constraints upon Behavior and Sex, 442
    Social Participation, 445
    Storytelling and Preaching, 446
    Conclusions, 454

3. The Peyote Road   456

     The Ideology, 456
     The Peyote Ritual and Meeting, 462
     Symbolism, 468
     Inspiration and Instruction through the Medicine, 471
     Conversion, 473
     Visions, 477
       Visions and Curing, 478
       Prophecy in Visions, 479
       Heaven, 481
       Episodes, 481
       Heavenly Message, 482
       The King's Palace, 483
       In-group Symbolism, 484
       Peyote Power, 484
     Protection, 485
     Peyote Cures, 487
       Attempted Cure and Prophetic Notification, 489
       An Unsuccessful Attempt, 491
     Peyotism and Personality, 492
     The Peyote Women, 493
     Conclusion, 495

References   497

The sawmill from which, together with the associated lumber industry, most Menomini make their living.

One of the Dream Dance drums and the singers at an annual fall rite.

1

The Confrontation

In the beginning me·c-awe·tok, the Supreme God, created the world by put-
ting islands into the great waters. Then he took up some earth like wax and
moulded in his hand the image of a human being. Then he blew his breath four
times upon it and it came to life and it was his son, Jesus. He placed him across
the great waters on the other islands and old German country and gave them
to him to protect and rule. Then the Supreme God took up red clay, made
a tiny image and blew his breath upon it four times. The last time he blew
life into the clay and made meˀnapos, his servant, to protect this island and
his grandmother's people and he decreed that Jesus and meˀnapos should be
friends and brothers, each to remain on his separate island and to take care of
his people. All went well until Columbus crossed the ocean. . . . Then every-
thing began to conflict so that now no one in this world can ever understand it.[1]

Adaptation

THE MENOMINI were confined over a century ago to a reservation (see p. 362)
that was a fraction of the size of their original territory. They could no longer live
by fishing, gathering wild rice, hunting, and marginal horticulture, though some
continued to try to do so. The fur trade that they had come to depend upon
collapsed during the first half of the nineteenth century. The Whiteman's[2] religion
and education were presented as exclusive channels to self-improvement, and to
approval by the dominant society. The Whiteman's technological and occupational system was the only set of instrumentalities that was productive in the

---

[1] The beginning of a version of the birth of *Meˀnapos*, the Menomini culture hero, as
told to Alanson Skinner (Skinner and Satterlee 1915:241).

[2] The term "Whiteman" is frequently used in this book to denote the dominant American cultural system as Menomini perceived and experienced it. This is the term they have
used themselves.

Preparing a powwow for tourists, 1960.

Menomini leaving a general council meeting.

These traditional shelters were still in use near Zoar in 1953.

A new house (1969) in Neopit.

changed setting, and the Menomini, for complex reasons, of which prejudice was only one, were denied anything resembling full-scale participation. Paradoxically, however, the Menomini, with the help of some astute White politicians, preserved the forest cover on part of their nearly 400 square miles of reservation long after the original forest had been ravaged elsewhere in the northcentral states, and it is from this forest that most of the Menomini today gain their livelihood, though in a very different manner than did their ancestors who once roamed the same forest. To all of these radical changes in the conditions of their existence, the Menomini have made adaptations.

The next two chapters describe two of several adaptations the Menomini[3] made to the long-term confrontation between them and the Anglo-Americans. The first is represented by a small group of Menomini together with a few Chippewa and Potowatomi, who actively maintained the Dream Dance (sometimes called the "pow-wow" or Drum Religion), Medicine Lodge, and Chiefs' Dance, or War Dance. They lived together mostly around Zoar, well away from the population centers at Neopit, where Menominee Enterprises, the lumber industry, is located, and Keshena (see map, p. 362). We termed them the "native-oriented" group because these people were oriented toward the native cultural traditions, as they understood them, and tried to live according to them. A few members of the Dream Dance and other organizations lived in the two towns but attended ceremonial meetings and "song services" at Zoar frequently. The second adaptation is represented by the Peyotists, or Native American Church. This small group also lived mostly around Zoar but again some members lived in town. Some peyotists also participated in Dream Dance or Medicine Lodge meetings but the membership was more characteristically mutually exclusive. Most Menomini do not now, and did not in 1951–1961 (the decade represented in this writing) belong to either the native-oriented or peyote groups and many looked upon these groups with some suspicion or were derisive about them. After all, they clung to old ways, they were not Catholics, or they used a narcotic (peyote) that many regarded as dangerous or evil as a sacrament.

We studied with the Menomini every summer from 1948 through 1954, with the exception of one season (1951). We have visited the Menomini almost every year since then and did some intensive fieldwork in 1961 and again in 1969, and have maintained contact up to the present (1976). When we wrote the original case study (G. Spindler and L. Spindler 1971) we decided to confine our interpretations largely to the decade 1951–1961. The latter is the year of termination, when federal support and control was withdrawn and Menomini were "on their own." The reservation became a county in the state of Wisconsin, the poorest county, with inadequate health and other services. The years following termination were desperately hard. Economic survival became impossible in a one-industry county. Though the Menomini had been largely self-sufficient before termination, now costly state and federal programs that had little lasting effect, were mounted.

---

[3] The spelling "Menomini" is used throughout the text, as it was in the original case study.

Finally, in a desperate attempt to save the tottering economy, several thousand acres of land and a man-made chain of lakes, the "Legend Lake Project" were sold to outsiders. This aroused the Menomini people to action. A militant campaign to save the Menomini lakes, forest, and people was mounted at the state and federal capitols. After a long campaign, finally, in 1974, the Menomini were restored to reservation status. Termination was acknowledged as a disastrous and costly experiment. The people are now struggling with the consequences of the events set in motion in 1961.

Since 1961 much has changed among the Menomini and the groups we describe in the following two chapters, and other adaptations we described in the original case study (1971) for the decade under study, are no longer so distinguishable. Most Menomini speak little of their native language or act in ways that are obviously traditional Menomini. Some have good incomes and their life styles are indistinguishable from that of middle-class whites in the surrounding area, at least on the surface. Others have smaller incomes but are no more distinguished from whites of the same socioeconomic level. One would be rash, however, to predict that all "native-oriented" behavior patterns, beliefs, and values have disappeared or will disappear. Dream Dance meetings are still held. In fact there has been a recent increase in participation as men and women who are by no means traditional in other respects become interested. And many people dress in Indian costumes and dance Indian style at public and social affairs. The Medicine Lodge has not been held on Menomini land to our knowledge since 1954, but a few members still travel to other places, particularly among the Winnebago, when it is held. The Peyote church is not as active now as it was in the decade 1951–1961 but its core members still practice, and join other peyotists in meetings nearby.

We have selected the native-oriented and peyote groups' adaptations to the confrontation between Menomini and Anglo-American culture and power for special attention because, although the membership in these two groups is, and was very small compared to the whole tribal population, they constitute clear statements of the attempt to maintain identity, to remain distinctive, that is represented, in other usually less dramatic ways among other Menomini and certainly among nearly all other Native American communities.

It was indeed a privilege to do fieldwork with the native-oriented and peyote groups. We lived off the reservation but close to them in a tent, our preference for we enjoyed so living, where they could freely, and did often, visit us. We did all the usual things anthropologists do in the field and were able to interview, observe, and administer psychological tests to nearly every man and woman in the two groups. We attended dozens of Dream Dance and War Dance services and rites, were invited participants in the last Medicine Lodge ceremony held on Menomini land, and in another held away from the reserve, and participated in nearly all peyote meetings held on the reserve during our period of most intensive fieldwork. It is impossible to convey the vitality of the life styles in these two groups during the period we describe. During some seasons there were Dream and War Dance "song services" (in addition to major rites) two or more

times each week. We were literally exhausted trying to keep up with the ceremonial and social life. It was an intense period, for them, of revival and reaffirmation of their culture. Our presence, as well as that of Sidney Slotkin, another
anthropologist, during two seasons at the beginning of the period, may actually
have stimulated some of this activity, but whatever the causes, a tradition-oriented,
identity-maintaining activity was intense.

But this activity was not an attempt to manipulate identity to attain
political ends (see Bennett 1973). There was self-conscious purposefulness about
trying to keep traditions, to "keep the drum going," and to educate the children
in the Menomini way, but these groups were not seeking public attention and
expected no reward for their behavior other than their own satisfaction. There
were still old people who spoke almost no English and who knew the rituals and
their meaning in the framework of the complex Menomini cosmology. These
elders guided the young (some of whom were in their fifties!) as they always had.

It was possible, some nights when we were deep in the woods near Zoar,
listening to singing and drumming at a song service or rite, watching the dancing
(which was usually quite subdued) and sometimes dancing ourselves, hearing
almost no English (all prayers and ritual interaction was in Menomini), to feel
that the twentieth century had never happened. Of course this was an illusion and
there is always danger, in such circumstances, of romanticization, but the whole
experience made a deep and lasting impression on us that a new generation of
anthropologists who have studied other aspects of Menomini life cannot share.
These were not "just poor rural folk" at Zoar, to use recent phrasing that denies
the existence of a distinctive culture to people like the Menomini. These were
people with a distinctive, dramatically different culture, who knew it well and
knew that they knew it. They were struggling to maintain it against what seemed
to be overwhelming odds. After all, for two centuries, the whole weight of the
white establishment—the church, the schools, the economy, the government had
been directed at stamping out their culture and making them into whites—
though at the same time denying them full entrance and participation in Anglo-
dominated society.

To What Did They Adapt?

The Menomini are not to be seen as merely responding to the impact of
Anglo-American culture. They are and always have been adapting to the total environment, and they are a part of their own environment. They impute meanings,
make decisions, and produce rationalizations for their behavior that become self-
sustaining and constitute a part of the environment to which adaptation must
be made. Nor are the Menomini dealing with some fixed, static, and certain cultural entity. The "American" culture to which they were adapting in 1854, when
the reservation was created, is remarkably different from the American culture to
which they are adapting today. Even during the span of our fieldwork with
them, we have seen phenomenal changes in our own way of life.

Furthermore, the Menomini were never and are not now adapting to an abstract Western culture. They have adapted to the culture as represented by the people with whom they have come in direct contact—initially, missionaries, fur traders, and rum runners; later, priests, soldiers, and teachers, merchants and farmers, government agents, politicians and professionals, tourists land developers, and owners of vacation homes. They have also adapted to a local northeastern Wisconsin culture that is still regionally distinctive, and quite different from, for instance, that of the peninsula area of northern California. They have adapted to this culture variously; some to its laboring-class segments, some to the culture of its farmers, some to the way of life of the middle class of its towns, and others to its deviant elements. They had to adopt to Western culture in its various forms and also to political domination, loss of independence, and to economic deprivation.

The Confrontation

Underlying the diversity of contacts and adaptations, there appear to be some very pervasive differences between Menomini culture and Western culture. The orientations toward reality, the assumptions about what a person should be like, or even what a person is, are very divergent.

The critical discongruities between cultural systems appear to be something like the following. In Western culture, and in Anglo-American middle-class culture in particular, material power through use of technology is regarded as a means of accomplishing desired ends. In traditional Menomini culture material power cannot function by itself. Spiritual power is the basis for action and accomplishment. A man or woman without this spiritual power, or access to it, is powerless. In Anglo culture people must be aggressive in interpersonal relationships and social interaction to obtain personal recognition or business or professional success. In traditional Menomini culture aggressive people are suspected of being witches. In Anglo culture extraverted emotional expressiveness is valued as personal salesmanship. People should be friendly, evocative, lively. In Menomini culture emotions are rarely allowed to come to the surface. In Anglo culture the social interaction rate is fast, and matched by a torrent of words. In Menomini culture social interaction is slow and words are paced and few. In Anglo culture people are supposed to make decisions on the basis of rational and practical considerations. Among the traditional Menomini important decisions are made on the basis of dreams. There are other divergencies that will become apparent in this case study as the native-oriented group is described. We have cited these here in general terms in order to make one point clear—the differences between Western culture, particularly its Anglo-American version, and the traditional Menomini culture, could not easily be resolved. There are, of course, many regional, ethnic, and class differences in the non-Menomini population of the United States. The comparison is phrased in terms relevant to the Menomini-Whiteman confrontation as the Menomini appear to have experienced it.

The Consequences of Confrontation

When people are confronted with a politically and economically dominant cultural system[4] that is sharply divergent from their own and intolerant of divergence, they suffer severe disturbances in every sector of life. Their subsistence base may be destroyed, as was the case with most American Indian tribes. Their political status is radically altered. The roles and statuses within the established cultural system are obliterated or seriously threatened. These external conditions are matched or exceeded by internal processes. The self-image is damaged, and the sense of identity that all functioning cultures provide is made ambiguous or is lost. Emotional controls, reinforced as they are in all communities by social sanctions, break down. The very process of thinking may become disorganized, for the logical and instrumental linkages that once seemed self-evident and valid are no longer so (G. Spindler 1968). Wise old men become irrelevant. Tribal lore becomes ridiculous. Values and beliefs lose their credibility. A cultural system is a total way of thinking, perceiving, feeling, acting, and justifying one's actions.

When divergent cultural systems meet under conditions of dominance and subordination, the people in the subordinate system do not simply disappear. They adapt. They try to re-create the social and cultural bases for identity and for the maintenance of emotional and cognitive controls. Some move to an identification with the dominant system, irrespective of its divergence. In so doing, they must forget whatever they once were. The forgetting usually takes the form of active suppression of the past, and active identification with the confronting culture. A few people in this situation are able to handle the confrontation by segmentalizing action and thought. They live compartmentalized social and occupational lives, and think, when involved in different situations, in different frames of reference.

Other individuals, for a variety of reasons, including differences in experience, emotional stability, and social alignments, are unable to identify with either the new culture or the old, and mill about in a no-man's-land—socially, emotionally, and intellectually. Group alignments, opinions, and behavior patterns shift and turn, as people try desperately to make some sense out of their situation.

Yet others adapt by attempting to synthesize potentially divergent aspects of the confronting cultures in the form of religious or social movements. Among the Menomini the Peyotists seem to do this with some success. The ritual and belief of the Native American Church, as practiced by the Menomini, are an

---

[4] We will use the term "cultural system" to denote what is frequently encompassed by the terms "society" and "culture," following our usage, with Alan Beals, in *Culture in Process* (Beals, Spindler, and Spindler 1973). A cultural system is an organization of ideas, values, and norms for behavior, and of social interaction, statuses, roles, and authority. It includes ecological adaptation, technology, and actual groups. A cultural system has boundaries of some sort and the decision-making capacity. Although we think of "culture," in the strict definitional sense, as referring only to the ideational dimension of cultural systems, to avoid cumbersome usage and where meaning is apparent, we occasionally use "culture" to stand for cultural system.

interweaving of traditional Menomini, pan-Indian, and Christian elements. This synthesis provides a basis for a consistent world view and a recognizable identity.

There is still another style of adaptation. People may attempt to exclude certain of the most discongruent aspects of the divergent confronting culture and maintain as much as possible of the traditional culture. By reducing the amount of discongruent cultural demand and by reaffirming the validity of the traditional culture they provide for themselves a basis for identity, and for the maintenance of cognitive and emotional controls. This is the native-oriented group among the Menomini. (See G. Spindler, 1968 for further discussion of theory).

This framework puts into sharper focus the adaptive processes involved in the Menomini situation. The native-oriented group should not be understood simply as consisting of stubborn people who will not give up the past. Their way of life should be seen not as a sort of magical survival of disembodied traditional cultural elements but rather as the manner in which this group has tried to cope with the confrontation between the culture of their ancestors and Western culture, in the various forms in which it has been encountered by them.

Likewise, the Peyotists should not be seen as simply a group of deviants who are deviant for the sake of being deviant, or as a group of neurotics, or as a group of "natives" who have been "turned on" and who are stretching their minds with the bud of the cactus *Lophophera williamsii*. They are group of people who are trying desperately to get along in a semantic environment that is so deeply conflicted that there is no way to make sense out of it. Peyotism provides them with a kind of ready-made solution. It puts together what everyone else has left apart.

Neither Peyotism nor nativistic reaffirmation are transformative, revolutionary, or militant. They are accommodative. Transformative or alternative movements of a militant character have now become significant among the Menomini. The threat of personal deprivation in recent events connected with termination has spurred such movements on.

That Which Was Lost

The next chapter will deal with some aspects of the traditional Menomini culture as the present way of life of the native-oriented group is described but no single chapter, or single volume, however massive, could really do justice to this lost culture. Everyone who has done research with the Menomini, including such people as Leonard Bloomfield, Felix and Marie Keesing, J. S. Slotkin, Sister Inez Hilger, Francis Densmore, W. G. Hoffman, Samuel Barrett, and Alanson Skinner, has recognized explicitly the richness, subtlety, and complexity of traditional Menomini culture.[5] We have ourselves seen enough in the versions of this culture still operant in the native-oriented group (and among the Peyotists in a

---

[5] This list does not include people like David Ames, Gary Olfield, Rachael Sady, Robert Edgerton, William Hodge, and others, who have done significant, recent work with the Menomini but who did not study the traditional culture.

different context) to come to some understanding of this complexity. However, to gain more depth one has to go back to the writings (such as Hoffman 1896, Skinner 1913, 1915, and Skinner and Satterlee 1915) done before the flu epidemic of 1917–1918, which took many of the elders and thereby dealt the prospects of continuity in Menomini tradition a severe blow.

The Menomini had a complex cosmogony. They thought of the universe as divided into strata (including the earth as one), with deities and powers resident in each that had different power relationships with each other and with man. The underground strata, in opposition to those strata above the earth, were the evil underworld, where the White Bear, the Underground Panther, the White Deer, and the Horned Snake dwelt. These forces were inimical to man.[6] The residents of the upper strata, in contrast, were friendly to man, or at least could be placated by him. The Thunderers, in the level just below *Me·c-awe·tok*, the supreme force in the universe, were especially friendly to man, and waged unceasing war against the horned serpents, who were man's most consistent persecutors.

There were innumerable lesser gods, genii, and goblins, such as the Flying Skeleton, the Wanderer, the Little God Boys, the Cannibal Spirits, and the North Giant, and there was a system of complex sacred bundles. Each bundle contained "medicines," such as "thunder eggs" (rounded stones), miniature war and lacrosse clubs, roots, powders, and so forth, which were invested with powers evoked by ritual, song, and reverence, and which could do great good or harm. There were also pictographs, done on birchbark or hides (see Fig. 1). These were often used as wrappings for bundles, and functioned as memory joggers (mnemonic devices) for the owner of the bundle as the complex rituals necessary for their use were carried out. Others were used in the same way by storytellers. Figure 1 shows an unusually complex scroll, made of birchbark, exhibited by one old man as he told the tales. He inherited it from his father, and it could be traced to his father's grandfather, but no further back (Skinner 1913:74–78). Each strip can be "read" in some detail. The bottom strip, for example, shows, from right to left, the village of the Thunderers in the sky, then Wickano, the leader of the Thunderers, the powerful wind which he controls and his clouds, Wickano at his resting place, one of his associates, and the rain which belongs to them, Wickano again, a tornado, the clouds behind which Thunderers stalk their prey, and, last (far left), a Thunderer pouncing upon one of the evil serpents from the underworld. Certain songs go with different parts of the scroll and punctuate the storytelling.[7]

There were many dance and ritual associations, including the Tobacco, Braves, Harvest, Totem Animals, Rain, and South Wind Dances and the Bear, Buffalo, Thunder, and Witch associations. Each association or dance group had

---

[6] This statement must be modified in respect to certain deities and forces. The White Bear, for example, holds up the earth and is the sacred ancestor of the Menomini.

[7] Such scrolls were more common among the Chippewa, with whom they may have originated, but irrespective of origin, they were a significant part of Menomini culture when it was studied by Hoffman and by Skinner.

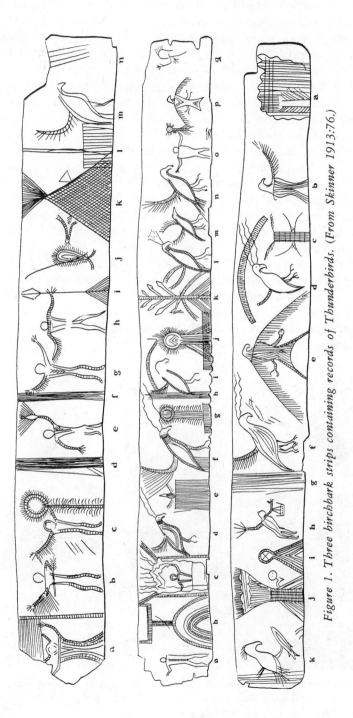

Figure 1. Three birchbark strips containing records of Thunderbirds. (From Skinner 1913:76.)

its own songs, employed certain medicines, and controlled certain powers. There were also several classes of shamans, some of whom combatted witches, others of whom witched (in many cases these two activities were combined), some of whom were clairvoyant, some of whom were concerned with all forms of curing disease, and some of whom had special skills, such as jugglery.

The folklore of the Menomini is complex. Skinner (Skinner and Satterlee 1915) collected 129 episodes, but he acknowledges the existence of many more that he or his associate, John Satterlee, did not record. There are sacred tales of the origin of the universe, tales of the culture hero *me?napos*, fairy tales, true stories, and tales of European origin modified to Menomini taste. There are themes of power loss and gain, soul loss, vengeance, love, consequences of bad behavior, dreaming, imposters, contests, and many others. There are props, such as the magic canoe that goes by itself, the inexhaustible kettle that never gets empty, the mummified dog kept in a box, ever ready to come to life when needed, the singing snowshoes that precede the hunter to the lodge and sing like birds, an animal (lynx) head ball that, when batted or thrown at any object, bites it and brings it back. These and many other props enliven the stories as they were told by old men and women nearly every evening during the winter.

The traditional culture mapped the universe for the Menomini individual. It provided a style of thinking and imaginative content. It also provided instrumentalities for survival, some of them material, such as weapons, tools, means of transportation; some of them intangible (from the Western point of view), such

The authors lived in a tent near the northeast edge of Menomini lands during most of their fieldwork. This brought them into close proximity to the native-oriented and Peyote groups, which lived not far away.

as "power" to be acquired through dream and vision and maintained by ritual. It provided a language that was subtle, complex, and radically different from any Western language in its organization of action and object, time and occurrence. It provided a social map within which all persons could be placed, with kin terms and associated appropriate behaviors, and totem and clan identifications. It explained origins, geography, marriage, conception, birth, life crises, and death. It provided a philosophy of education, rules for teachers, a theory of man in nature, a set of values to live and die by.

Menomini culture, in its total complexity and subtlety, has been lost. There was no place for it in the scheme of things that resulted from the White-man's occupation of the New World as the Whiteman defined this scheme. The Menomini culture as a way of thinking as well as a way of doing was discongruent with Western culture, and no form of real divergence was tolerated in the Anglo-American mania for assimilation and conformity. It is tragic that this was so. However, this book is not about this tragedy. It is about two of the ways in which the people called Menomini have coped with the conditions they encountered. The focus is upon those segments of the population that have adapted by exclusion, reaffirmation, and synthesis. The next chapter is about the native-oriented group, and Chapter 3 is about the Peyotists.

* * * *

About our father the God Above, whom all worship, and none have seen: this song is in his praise, this true one. This is the way the words were given to the old lady who dreamed our drum. The Creator promised to help the whole world through the drum. The gods below helped also. Never shall this earth be destroyed, upset, or turned wrong.[8]

The song:

> God himself has agreed to help this earth.
> The earth shall never be destroyed.
> The earth shall be protected by us.
> The world shall never be destroyed.

* * * *

The next chapter is about the native-oriented group and its culture in the light of its past. Though the present way of life of this group is an adaptation to contemporary conditions, it is also a product of the history of the Menomini, and of the traditional culture. To provide time depth for the picture of current adaptation we have, therefore, drawn from ethnohistoric sources, from the writings of observers who met the Menomini before the old way of life was reduced, as well as from our own observations and those of contemporary ethnographers.

---

[8] Thomas Hog, as told to Skinner (1915:201).

$$\boxed{2}$$

Omɛ·ʔnomɛ·ne·w[1]

What Are They Like?

THE FOLLOWING EXAMPLES of cultural and psychological characteristics are drawn from observations of the contemporary native-oriented group and from older sources describing the Menomini of the past. The latter are printed in italics so the reader can more easily compare the two kinds of statements.

Our friend did not seem quite as relaxed as we rembered her to be. Then the child on the bed began to cry restlessly. She got up slowly and walked hesitatingly to the bed to stroke her daughter's head. Then turned to us almost apologetically to say, "She's got some kind of illness. She's hot, and she hasn't kept anything down for two days." We did what we could—gave the child a little aspirin—and offered to take her in to the hospital to see the doctor. Then it dawned on us that last year there had been no baby and that the one swaddled in blankets looked virtually new-born. "Yes. She's new. She came three days ago." Then the story came out. . . .

Our friend's husband had gone on one of his long trips to a neighboring reservation many miles away. In the meantime our friend had borne her fourth child during his absence and while everyone else was gone. She was isolated. She had no car and could not walk to the highway to get help. Her five year old daughter had become ill. There was no food left in the house. She said all of this quietly, with none of the hysteria or blaming that would have been normal for a woman in similar circumstances in our world. She merely stated the facts. [Reported in G. Spindler 1963:359]

Whatever misfortune may befall them they never allow themselves to lose their calm composure of mind, in which they think that happiness especially

---

[1] We use the native term for wild-rice people, from which the word "Menomini" is derived, to indicate that this chapter is about the people who have tried to keep their culture, even though they only rarely now actually harvest the wild rice that was an important staple of their ancestors.

A member of the Medicine Lodge and Dream Dance standing before his house in 1952. Today he is the most active leader of this group, but he lives in town.

consists. . . . Even the pangs of childbirth, although most bitter, are so concealed or conquered by the women that they do not even groan. [Father Jouvency, 1710, in *Jesuit Relations* 1896 vol. 1:277]

After a year's absence, during which we thought often about our Menomini friends and with great anticipation about our return in the spring, we drove up to an area near the Zoar community hall where the Dream Dance rituals were held, where many members of the native-oriented group lived. There we saw a group standing and sitting about. Some of the men were playing poker on a blanket spread on the ground. Others were kibitzing. We parked our car, got out, and tried to walk casually, not run, into the circle of what we perceived as old friends who would greet us with the enthusiasm of long-lost members of the family. But we had forgotten what the native-oriented Menomini were like! Expressionless faces greeted us. Some even turned away, as though preoccupied with other matters more interesting. Only the children stared, but quietly. I walked over to the group of people clustered around the poker game and joined the kibitzers. Ranks opened so I had a place to stand and a clear view of the game, but otherwise no special notice was taken of my arrival. I stood across from a man about my age with whom I had, I felt, formed an especially close friendship, and who had been enormously helpful to me in my research in the past. He continued with his game, taking no notice of me whatsoever. I began to feel acutely uncomfortable. Perhaps there had been a long winter of gossip about the White strangers who had

Our friends are grouped around a blanket spread on the ground, playing poker. The shelters were built for and occupied during the annual fair and pageant.

invaded their privacy for too long. Perhaps we were suspect of witchcraft, or at least of bringing bad luck. Finally, after several minutes of paranoid fantasy on my part, my friend Nepenahkwat glanced up, smiled quietly, and said calmly, "Hello George, I see you made it." And then continued with his game.

We stayed for several hours that afternoon. During the first hours we gradually became aware of the fact that the people were glad to see us, that they had thought about us during our absence, and that they had looked forward to our return. We also reestablished our timing and role-taking in social interaction with native-oriented Menomini. We realized again that these were different people, with a different psychology, and a different set of norms for proper behavior. Overt emotionality is not displayed. The loud, overstated greeting normal for the situation in our own society would not only have been in very bad taste according to Menomini standards, but it would have been virtually impossible for a native-oriented Menomini adult, properly educated and formed in the traditional framework, to act that way even if he had, conceivably, wanted to. [G. Spindler 1963:357–358]

. . . they have a mild but independent expression of countenance. . . . [Major Pike, 1810, cited in Hoffman 1896:34]

. . . My grandfather remarked, that he regarded the Menomonees as the most peaceful, brave, and faithful of all the tribes who ever served under him [Mr. Grignon, 1856, cited in Hoffman 1896:34]

It is not because it is me. It is not because I know these things that I speak this way. I am not proud just because I know this little. It is because my father was important in this and I got it from him, not because of myself. But it is because my father was there when they brought the drum to my grandfather's place. [Menomini elder, addressing the Dream Dance group]

A few "true stories" are told for the purpose of inculcating the principles of honor, virtue, and bravery among the children. Many of these have a moral, either stated or implied, contrary to the popular idea of North American folklore. The four most common of these are chastity, bravery, reverence, and guarding against undue pride. [Skinner 1915:235].

Sit quiet like a stone, and let thoughts come to you. Think about a leaf in a pool. [Menomini elder, speaking to his grandson]

. . . They [witches] done that to my father. He used to be one of the leaders of the Medicine Drum. He owned a drum. The one P. has. Well, my father's eyes pretty near killed him in those days. One old fellow used to stay a lot here and knew the persons who done that to him. It made his eye white and he just had one eye after that. [Did he know who did this?] *Yes, he knew who did it, but didn't want the fellow to know that he knew it was him.* [Menomini woman, in L. Spindler, field notes]

Witches and wizards are persons supposed to possess the agency of familiar spirits, from whom they receive power to inflict diseases on their enemies, prevent the good luck of the hunter, and the success of the warrior. They are believed to fly invisibly at pleasure from place to place; to turn themselves into bears, wolves, foxes, owls, bats, and snakes. [Reverend Peter Jones 1843:145, cited in Hoffman 1896:152]

I feel that sometimes a baby being born, maybe one of our grandfathers might have his spirit in the little boy. There's one funny thing about the little boy I lost. Old men used to understand babies. Now, nobody understands their language. That baby used to talk all the time. We gave him an Indian name but he wasn't satisfied with it. He had some little power, maybe from his grandfather. My brother-in-law was married to a White girl and I never told her about eating when she was that way. She had a habit of feeding my baby and you know, you're not supposed to kiss a baby or anything then, and have to keep soiled things away from men's clothes and always keep clean. I never had any soiled things laying around. Nowadays it's easy with those pads. Now, my aunt says she wishes things had been like that when she was young. Well, she fed my baby and a few days after the baby had stomach trouble and diarrhea. *I wasn't really blaming her.* I was thinking the little boy had some power that was killed by her. And this boy [she points to her son] here seems to know ahead when I'm going to menstruate. He wets the bed each time. My aunt says I got to be careful of him, as someone must have ate with him when she was menstruating. [Menomini woman, in L. Spindler 1962:40–41]

There is no Nation among 'em which has not a sort of Juglers or Conjuerers, which some look upon to be Wizzards, but in my Opinion there is no Great reason to believe 'em such, or to think that their Practice favours any thing of a Communication with the Devil. These Impostors came them-

selves to be reverenced as Prophets which fore-tell Futurity. They will needs be look'd upon to have an unlimited Power. They boast of being able to make it Wet or Dry; to cause a Calm or a Storm; to render Land Fruitful or Barren; and, in a word, to make Hunters Fortunate or Unfortunate. They also pretend to Physick, and to apply Medicine, but which are such, for the most part as having little Virtue at all in 'em, especially to Cure that Distemper which they pretend to. [Hennepin 1689:50, cited in Hoffman 1896:141]

. . . The oldest leader of the Dream Dance group (and the most powerful) took liberties with a sacred drum left in the charge of a younger man and made a public apology for the action in a speech. He said:

My children, I am good to you. I care for you all the time. I pray for you to the Gentle Spirit. I cure you when you get sick, with good medicines. Somebody here does not feel good about things somehow. Now, all right . . . I did not take that drum away from anybody. I did not want to hurt anyone's feelings. . . . That is all I have to say. [G. Spindler, field notes]

The harmony which subsists among the savages is in truth displayed not only by their words, but in actual conduct. The chiefs who are the most influential and well-to-do are on equal footing with the poorest, and even the boys—with whom they converse as they do with persons of discretion. They warmly support and take in hand the cause of one another among friends; and when there are any disputes they proceed therein with great moderation. . . . Seldom are there quarrels among them. [From the memoirs of Nicholas Perrote, 1667, quoted in Keesing 1939:40]

Yes. Some go to both [the *metɛ·wen* or Dream Dance and the Peyote church]. But it isn't good. *But we don't like to tell them not to come to the meetings.* The old men all think it keeps our prayers from gettin' to our grandfather's spirits. Lots of times when something goes wrong with our prayers, they think those ones who go to both bring in evil and keep prayers from gettin' there. [Menomini woman, in L. Spindler, field notes]

I have had no trouble with the savages. None of them have been angry with me because I declared the false divinity of the sun, of the thunder, the bear, of the underground panther, of Manabus, of their dreams, nor because I spoke against superstitious feasts and against the Jugglers {Cese·ko}. They had no objection to cover themselves before me . . . there were some who fasted without blackening their faces. . . . [Father André, 1671–1689, in *Jesuit Relations 1896–1901*, vol. lvii:265–282]

No one has the right, on the basis of position or prestige, to exercise direct authority over another, not even a father over his son. Children are given their earnings from the dances put on for tourists to spend as they will. A child of five years may own and keep the money thus gained. There is love and honor in traditional Menomini marriage, but no "obeying." Strong men do not order weak ones about. [G. Spindler 1963:376]

The savage does not know what it is to obey. . . . The father does not venture to exercise authority over his son, nor does the chief dare to give commands to his soldier. . . . If the chiefs possess some influence over their men . . . it is only through the liberal presents and feasts which they give. [Nicholas Perrote, first French fur trader to visit the Menomini in 1667, in Blair 1911:144–145]

Among themselves, the rights of the individuals were paramount. A husband might not sell or dispose of his wife's or children's property, nor had any other person, except the owner, any right to them. If a member of the family chose to bargain off personal possessions, no other member ever interfered in any way. Even infants had the sole right to what was theirs. [Skinner 1913:6]

One dream I always think about. Just before this baby was born I used to have a garden where this building is. I dreamt I was out there picking corn. J. B. came over and wanted me to help him right away pick potatoes. I kind of laughed in the dream about J. B. because he never had a garden. I told him I'd help him. I had to get my corn in right away that evening. He told me if I helped him he'd give me half of his potatoes. I saw potatoes ready to be dug up late in the Fall. I saw J. B. startin' on one row with sacks here and there. Then he was gone and I was alone. While I was bending down it seemed like there was a light above me gettin' brighter and brighter. I was afraid to look up. I was alone. It looked like some kind of sun. I saw *Seꞏsos'* [Jesus'] face. I got scairt and couldn't look longer. I tried to find a place to hide. I was all alone and couldn't find a place to hide. He was all white. I told my aunt about that dream and she told me maybe I was goin' to be left alone. She said it was a good dream and the Lord was watchin' over me. I said I felt like I was alone. She almost guessed my dream. I was left alone September, October, December. W. left for awhile and lived with M.'s wife at Eagle River. After the baby was born, he came back Christmas. He asked if he could come home. While he was gone, J. B. used to come and cut wood and bring water for no pay—just meals. [Menomini woman, in L. Spindler, field notes]

For a girl to dream of things on high meant long life, happiness, virtue, and perhaps social elevation. In one instance a girl dreamt of a large fat man, who appeared and told her that she would have a long life, that she had power over the winds, and that she might hear what people said of her, no matter how far away they were when they spoke. She dreamt also of the sun, who said she would have a long life and promised protection. Should she desire anything and pray to the sun for it, it would be granted her. The sun commanded her always to wear a red waist as a sign of the eight virgins who lived in the east. They too would hear her prayers. All these things were a reward for her suffering, for she had fasted ten days. [Skinner 1913:43]

At a tribal council meeting held to discuss the budget for the following year, a great deal of criticism was directed at the large expenditure for installation of a heavy cable suspended across the mill pond, from which logs were snagged and pulled over to a lift. During the heat of the arguing, old Kime·wan rose and addressed the mixed group of conservative, transitional, and elite members in Menomini, saying:

There has been much talk about the money that has been spent. Many people seem unhappy. I do not know much about these things, but I see what is going on. Now let it be said that I do not understand the purpose that our brothers had in installing that cable. But I have noticed that it has some use. This fall, as the leaves began to drop from the trees, the birds were all lined up on it, wing to wing. For them it is a good thing, because it gives them all an even start on the way south. [G. Spindler, field notes]

We came to a cottage of an ancient witty man, that had a great familie and many children, his wife old, nevertheless handsome. They were of a nation called Malhonmines; that is the nation of Oats. [Radisson, 1654, cited in Kessing 1939:42]

One day a forest fire started here. I picked up W. in my truck to go out to it with me. On the way W. said, "It's too bad we didn't stop to get Fred [his brother-in-law] because he could tell us exactly where the fire was. [But he said that Fred was asleep.] It took about one-hundred men workin' hard to put that fire out." Then, on the way back, W. said it was really too bad that we didn't pick up Fred and take him with us, because, "He's got a nice extinguisher about this long [6 inches] and all he would have to do is wobble it about a little and the whole fire would have been put out without all that expense and trouble."
"There's a lot of kiddin' goin' around here about your brother-in-law. The one 'brags him up.' the other 'runs him down.'" [Menomini male, in G. Spindler field notes]

In 1911, while attending an outdoor ceremony of the dreamers, I stopped to talk with John Keshena, an Indian storekeeper, when chief Sabatis came up. Sabatis at once began to revile Keshena, warning me to purchase nothing of him. "Tobacco, anywhere else five cents, ten cents he charges! He lies, he steals, he cheats!"

During this tirade Keshena grinned pleasantly, and seemed not in the least offended. At the conclusion of his outburst chief Sabatis turned to me and said, smiling at my surprise, "Oh that is just our Indian way! I can joke with him, he is my brother-in-law!" [Skinner 1913:20]

INTERPRETATION

The Menomini in the native-oriented group think, say, and do all of these things. These samples of behaviors and attitudes furnish important clues for understanding what present-day Menomini are like. Except for the historical materials (indicated in italics), these are excerpts from conversations with and observations of Menomini in the present native-oriented group. This homogeneous group includes only about 3 percent of the Menomini population, yet it represents traditional Menomini culture as it exists today in its attenuated but most visible form.[2] The Medicine Lodge ceremony and the Dream Dance are still alive among the native-oriented group; members believe in the importance of power and the guardian spirit; menstrual taboos are observed by many of the women; belief in the power of witchcraft flourishes; the members still utilize hunting, fishing, and gathering subsistence techniques and use the Menomini language in ceremonies (some elders speak almost no English).

Members of the native-oriented group share a patterned set of values, attitudes, and perceptions about the natural world and the world of people around them. One part of this shared pattern, expressed in the examples of behaviors, includes emotional control. The Menomini woman who bore a child while alone and cared for another sick child at the same time seemed to exhibit control under the most trying of situations. Her control, however, is different from that of most White women in our society. The fear and hysteria were absent, as she had learned to live with isolation and had learned to "accept" misery when present. Isolation in the woods during menstruation was a familiar situation. She was not "controlling" the fear and anxiety. They were not there. She displayed a quality that might be called *equanimity under duress.* She also displayed a dependent, waiting attitude toward fate and what it might bring. She had made a sacrifice of food and tobacco to the Dream Dance drum for which she was the keeper, and that rested in its coverings on a special bench on the eastern side of her kitchen, where the light of the new day would touch it each morning through the nearby window. So she had reason to hope that the spirits might take notice of her predicament and take pity on her. Apparently, it worked, as it had many times in the past, from her point of view, since we arrived and took action.

This characteristic attitude or quality of waiting expectantly may be termed "latescent" (L. Spindler 1962). These attitudes are related to power. Although most of the members of the native-oriented group did not receive a guardian spirit through a vision while fasting, having power is all important today for survival; and, as is seen in the samples of behavior, dreams are still used to predict the future. Power is secured by displaying passivity while fasting and dreaming, quiescence (lack of excessive bodily motion, silence), receptivity, and expectancy. These attitudes can be subsumed under the term "latescent" (activity existing in possibility, depending upon an outside entity for realization). This term char-

---

[2] The language spoken (other than English) is most often Menomini. The Medicine Lodge and Dream Dance, shared with other woodland tribes, has certain characteristic Menomini features, and the cosmology and mythology is identifiably Menomini. However, a synthesis with southern Chippewa, Potowatomi, and Ottawa has been taking place for generations. These central Algonkian peoples were much alike, culturally, when contact first occurred. They probably became more alike as time went on, but particularly so after reservations were formed and the viability of the traditional cultures was seriously threatened. As a response to the overwhelming pressure of the White cultural system, the conservative elements of the tribes drew together. Cultural synthesis as well as genetic fusion occurred. This does not invalidate the description of this group as native oriented, since it is, or of labeling it "Menomini," since its members are on the tribal roll (with a few exceptions).

acterizes the affective tone of social interaction among and the shared personality characteristics of native-oriented Menomini.

This attitude of passive acceptance and receptivity is constantly evidenced in behaviors and beliefs. For example, in the quotation concerning the father who was witched and losing his eyesight (p. 21), the Menomini woman stated in a matter of fact tone, "Yes, he knew who done it, but didn't want the fellow to know that he knew it was him." When women retired to the menstrual house to be separated from men, as they were a threat to a man's power at this period, it was stressed that, as one informant said, "They had to be quiet." When parents selected a husband for their daughter, he was unquestioningly accepted by her. When a strange man came to marry her, a Menomini lady merely commented to the authors, in restrospect, "I was surprised." Her voice implied, however, that she was also frightened and did not want to marry the man. This seemingly passive approach to life does not mean despondency, as the native-oriented Menomini are resilient, vital, and flexible in their adjustment to daily problems—the air of expectancy and the potential for action are always present.

The quality of equanimity under duress is closely related to these latescent attitudes. The passive, quiescent, waiting expectancy is an important part of the Menomini ability to endure privation and hardship, but latescence is based on the expectancy that if the proper rituals are performed, the fates will provide—unless the fates decide otherwise—while equanimity under duress is part of a survival drive, which takes into account the realities of the situation and makes it possible to retain the necessary emotional balance even when the reality conditions are very threatening.

The marked control of expressive emotionality, apparent in the description of the reception of the authors by the native-oriented group after a long absence (p. 19), is congruent with the other qualities just described. It is more readily observable and of a somewhat different order, yet is another facet of the same behavioral pattern. We found that the members of the group were actually glad to see us, had thought about us during our absence, and had looked forward to our return. A loud, expressive greeting to anyone would be completely at odds with the native-oriented Menomini pattern for interaction, either with people or in their environment. The necessity for composure and equanimity when confronted with any strong emotion is an accepted part of their action system. Loud voices are threatening and disturbing. A group of twenty native-oriented Menomini can sit in a small room carrying on conversations without the noise level ever reaching the point at which one has difficulty hearing his friend, and there are long silences that no one attempts to fill with talk. Silence is not embarrassing. People, even children, are never ordered about. Even pointing a finger at someone is considered in poor taste—one points with one's lips. Asking direct questions of anyone is distasteful. The Menomini language itself contains a preponderance of goal-action, or passive-type, construction rather than the actor-action or command-type construction used extensively in English. Direct criticism of others is not expressed, either in their presence or behind their backs. One might say to another person about someone else, "There could be some people here that don't do just right. Sometimes they could have enough to get along on but they try to get it from someone else."

This reduction of overt emotional response, especially aggressive response, is related to the importance of possessing power and the fear of power loss through witchcraft. If a person controls expression of aggression of any form—by refraining from gossip, practicing generosity, hospitality, tolerance—he will not be a target for an act of witchcraft. Any old person may be a witch. A native-oriented Menomini cannot really blame another person for committing a "sin," even though he is himself directly involved. This is apparent from the description of behavior dealing with the White girl (p. 21) who had fed a baby while menstruating, causing its death, according to its mother, who merely said, "I wasn't really blaming her. I was thinking the little boy had some power that was killed by her." There can be no personalized guilt feelings about deviant behaviors since a person's strength or weaknesses are dependent upon the amount of power she or he has at the time.

Another shared value is autonomy. Each person is responsible for his own behavior, and no one has the right to exercise authority over another or his possessions. "Even infants had sole right to what was theirs," Skinner remarked (1913:6). No one is his neighbor's keeper. When a ceremonial gathering is to be announced, a *skape·wes* (messenger) is appointed. He travels about from house to house, passing tobacco to those who should be notified, and telling them the time and place. However, the tobacco is not given only to the "head" of the household or family. It is passed to every person who might be expected to come, to man and wife, brother and sister, and each older child. Collective notifications are never given; even when people from another tribe are to be notified, it is necessary to travel to the places where they live and pass tobacco to each individual. The same principle applies to transportation. People are expected to arrange their own. Even old people may not be taken care of in this regard, and an old man of eighty, who is important to the conduct of the ceremonial because he is the only one who knows the ritual, will have to stumble across the fields and through the dark woods to the gathering by himself, unless a member of his household happens to be coming to the gathering and the old man is standing by the car when it is started up. This is not individuality, as we conceive of it. Whites often call the Menomini "individualistic." Their latescent attitude and seeming reluctance to originate social interaction give support to this stereotype held by the Whites. Autonomy should not be interpreted as not conforming to the norms of the group, as members of the native-oriented group conform closely. In fact, part of the conformity is to be autonomous. However, no one is anyone else's "boss." No one is responsible for anyone else's welfare, except in those areas of reciprocation dictated by kinship obligations. No one can be discredited because of the actions of another, not even a father by his own son. The attitude of acceptance of others' behaviors is a part of this complex. Examples of acceptance of religious differences, given previously (p. 22), are to the point.

Another quality, more peripheral in nature yet a part of the shared pattern for behavior, is a keen sense of humor. This is constantly apparent in day-to-day interaction. The example given from the speech of the important elder, Kime·wan, is typical (p. 24). The comment about the controversial cable serving as a prop for the birds disrupted the council meeting and gave the budgeteers something to think about. Humor among the native-oriented Menomini may serve as a release of tensions built up by the constraints imposed upon expressiveness and particularly the expression of aggression. This is apparent in the relations between a man and his father-in-law and brother-in-law. The examples of behaviors presented previously include some of the ribald and grotesquely humorous remarks passed between brothers-in-law and by one about the other— "The one 'brags him up,' the other 'runs him down'" (p. 24).

Another related quality which belongs to the ideal of striving for harmony in interpersonal relations referred to by all students of Menomini culture is hospitality. In the past "it was considered a duty to look out for a guest's welfare and to treat him with the utmost respect" (Skinner 1913:6). All strangers, unless hostile, were to be considered as guests. The cautious regard for the wishes of others was revealed in the patterned treatment of the host. He addressed the guests in the set words: "N'hau! Come in if you so desire, but you need not if you do not wish to." When the food was brought by his wife, he would say, "Now eat, if you so desire, but refrain, if you do not care for this kind of food. It is what we eat every day; we have nothing better to offer you" (Skinner 1913:6).

The shared qualities of the native-oriented group form a pattern— equanimity under duress, latescence, control of overt emotionality and aggression, autonomy, keen sense of humor, and hospitality. The reader might well ask from what kinds of materials this pattern was derived. The authors observed and interacted with the members of this small group over a period of years. Observations of the kinds of behaviors that have been described were carefully recorded. The activities of individuals in the group as they acted in a wide variety of situations over a long period of time could be observed. This "participant-observer" technique is the hallmark of anthropological fieldwork, and there is no substitute for it. Other techniques were also used in collecting data (See G. Spindler and L. Spindler 1970, Chapter 11, for a detailed description of how fieldwork was done among the Menomini).

The Rorschach Projective Technique (the "inkblot" test) was given to seventeen adult males and eight adult females in the native-oriented group, and life histories were collected from two of the males and four of the females. There are many problems concerning the validity of interpretations for the Rorschach, even in our own society, and the problems are compounded by cross-cultural usage. In this particular application, however, the Rorschach seemed to produce results that were congruent with the other observations. Following is a brief interpretive summary of the Rorschach responses of the native-oriented Menomini (for details see G. Spindler 1955 and L. Spindler 1962).

Members of this group produce an adequate number of responses by usual standards, but there is a marked tendency for the range of content to be narrow and for various stimulus properties of the inkblots to be used very selectively. The perceptual field can therefore be described as narrow. The responses that are given within this narrow field cannot, however, be described as "rigid," as one would expect them to be if respondents from our own society were thus "constricted." That which is used is used flexibly. Overt emotionality is not displayed. (This is a very consistent feature.) Responses are careful, and obvious features of the blots, such as bright color, are rarely used. More subtle features, such as achromatic shading, are emphasized. The action quality of human figures in movement is passive. Human figures are rarely projected as doing anything but "sitting," "standing," or "facing that way." Motives for human action are not imputed. Animal figures are most frequently projected as being in action, such as "eating," or "climbing a tree," or "sneaking away through the brush," or "looking out from behind a tree." They are rarely perceived as engaged in aggressive action, such as attacking another animal. The concentration on animal figures is such that the perceptual structure could be described as zoomorphic. There is little content that we could describe as "morbid." The passivity and the quiescent quality of responses is not hopeless or depressive. The intellectual functions are adequate—there are virtually no distortions or breaks in reality. There is little drive to produce more than is necessary to complete the task as perceived. No native-oriented respondent asked, "How many responses do most people give?" as many acculturated respondents did. Once a response is given, it is regarded as a problem solved, and there is little point in solving it again for the sake of accumulating a "good score."

In summary, the typical native-oriented pattern of psychological characteristics revealed in Rorschach responses appears to be highly introverted, sensitive to the environment but able to maintain equilibrium despite its variations, not achievement oriented, lacking generally in overt emotional responsiveness and exhibiting a high degree of rational control over it when it does appear, motivated more by biologically oriented drives than by self-projective fantasy, intellectually uncomplicated but reality based and adequate in terms of its setting, lacking in rigidity, without evidence of high anxiety, tension, or internal conflict. This picture of the native-oriented Menomini suggests that the basic premises upon which the personality is predicated are radically different than the ones we understand in Western culture. It is limited without being constricted, sensitive without being imputative. It is a type that accepts fate, retains equanimity under duress, and achieves control under provocation. However, it is unsuited for the competitive struggle in a society that is structured around social and economic manipulation and requires focused interpersonal aggression for achievement within its framework.[3]

It is apparent that the patterns of psychological characteristics derived from analysis of Rorschach responses is congruent with the shared cultural patterns derived from analysis of behavior in the environment. The inward-oriented, cautious approach to the outside world revealed by the Rorschach seems related to the dependent type of value orientations, the deep fear of witchcraft, and the latescent type of pattern for social interaction. Further, the low aspiration level and realistic intellectual approach expressed in Rorschach responses is congruent with the fatalistic attitude toward the world, where achievement motives are

---

[3] In Chapter 5 there is further discussion of the native-oriented psychological structure, in comparison with that of the elite acculturated. The point is made there that the range of personality characteristics among the present native-oriented group is probably narrower and that the modal personality type is more withdrawn than for the Menomini in the prereservation period. The statements made here, however, hold good for the period for which we have direct evidence.

irrelevant and one's "success" depends solely upon the amount of power that one controls. The Rorschach, however, did not reveal other important features inferred from the analysis of ordinary behavior. For instance, autonomy, a very important feature, could not be shown directly by any of the Rorschach indicators. Materials from the Rorschach did, however, support the assumption of homogeneity existing in the native-oriented group—both cultural and psychological.

It is apparent that early explorers and missionaries and traders who were the first to contact the Menomini in the seventeenth century noticed many of the same kinds of behaviors and attitudes observed by fieldworkers from 1896 to the present. Descriptive phrases used by priests and early explorers—generous, soft-spoken, suppression of criticism in face-to-face relations, strong sense of humor, fear of sorcery—are applicable to the contemporary native-oriented Menomini. It is tempting to conclude that there has simply been a tenacious persistence of basic attitudes, values, beliefs, and psychological "set." However, this inference is subject to strong criticism by some anthropologists and ethno-historians. Some might call these apparent similarities between the Menomini of the past and the present convergences, emerging fortuitously over time. An explanation more compatible to the authors is that many of these patterned traits have continuity with the past and are kept alive because the people in the native-oriented group self-consciously choose to identify with their culture in every way possible, as a way of adapting to the impact of Western culture and the ensuing conflict and confusion. This is done by copying methods of child-rearing from grandparents, reinterpreting one's dreams to emphasize their importance in predicting the future, cautiously observing the implicit and explicit "rules" of one's grandparents for good living, and, in some cases, reviving old dances and customs such as the War Dance, which was relearned recently from the Chippewa. The psychological characteristics described do not occur in a cultural or social vacuum, or somehow magically outlast the cultural system in which they were functional. The native-oriented Menomini are as they are because an attenuated, though recognizable, native culture has been kept alive. Surely neither the culture nor the personality is an intact and complete version of the culture or personality of the past, but that there is continuity seems undeniable.

Members of the native-oriented group feel the discrepancies existing between the expectations of the more acculturated Menomini and Whites and those of their own group. The realization of these discrepancies tends to reinforce the culture patterns of the native-oriented group and gives them at times a somewhat exaggerated quality. One woman in this group, who was painfully aware of the situation, remarked:

> Sometimes I think a lot about a future when I'm alone. I'm a great one to think about the future. Seems like the young children are getting worse. We was all raised different. I warn my children and try to tell them things. I gotta wait a little until they are older. I try to tell 'em things my father told me. But, they learn things from different children. I try to break them of different habits. I wonder if I'm gonna be strong enough to get 'um on my side. [L. Spindler, field notes]

The way of life of the native-oriented group can be said to represent, at least in part, a resistance or a reaffirmative movement. Its members are not, however, trying to reform the outside world, or even transform the conditions of their own existence. They are attempting to exclude certain aspects of the outside world and turn in upon what they know of their own past. Many of the members have attempted to adjust to the outside world and, upon returning, have brought strengthened commitments to the "Menomini" way. This strategy can be effective so long as there is a group of some size to maintain the cultural boundaries with sufficient man- and woman-power to fill crucial roles, such as elder, learner, transmitter, and provider, as well as specific positions in the religious organizations that are the most visible manifestations of the reaffirmation of a native-oriented way of life.

The section to follow will deal with the interplay between the behavior patterns and psychological organization of the Menomini already described and the social system in which they operate. A given kind of social system tends to select and reinforce certain kinds of psychological structures and patterns of behavior in order to make the social system work.[4] The next section of the chapter will deal with religion, subsistence activities, the structure of authority and social control, witchcraft, and ceremonial organizations that provide the framework of meanings within which the native-oriented Menomini act.

How the System Works

The Economic Base

Although much has changed in the environment of the Menomini during recent decades, the subsistence activities of the native-oriented group exhibit some continuity with the past. The old way of life was always one of seasonal and intermittent activity to gain a living from the forests, streams, and lakes. The Menomini had small gardens before the Whiteman came in which they grew squash, beans, and corn, but they were basically hunters and gatherers. They also made extensive use of the resources of lakes and streams, particularly of sturgeon and wild rice.

> *The Malhominis {are adroit}* . . . *in spearing the Sturgeon in their river. For this purpose they use only small Canoes, very light, in which they stand upright, and in the middle of the current spear the Sturgeon.* . . . [La Potherie, 1665, in *Wisconsin Historical Collections*, Madison, Wisconsin, vol. xvi:9 cited in Keesing 1939:20]

---

[4] We are aware of the problems concerning shared motivations and the operation of social systems discussed by Anthony Wallace (1961) and others. For national systems and whole societies the problem is more significant than for this small group of native-oriented Menomini. There is variability in roles and personalities in even this group, however. In our analysis to follow we are stressing what people in this group have in common rather than the ways they are different.

Because of their horticultural and maritime habits, it was possible for them to live in villages for a part of the year, for their environment, as a rule, was quite productive during the summer months, and there was always the wild-rice harvest in the fall. During the harsh winters, however, the people probably usually resumed the nomadic hunting life that represents the basic subsistence pattern of the northern forest tribes. During this time it was not possible for large groups to live together in villages. Each extended family or small band went on its way, hunting over a territory defined by usage, and the threat of starvation was always present.

The fur trade, beginning almost immediately after the earliest contacts with the French in the latter half of the seventeenth century, caused substantial changes in the social and economic adaptation of the Menomini that will be discussed later. The small band became the basic unit, and this band was nomadic. The semisedentary seasonal village pattern declined, though the persistence of village sites into the nineteenth century suggests that the pattern was never entirely abandoned.

Today the people no longer gather in villages in the summer and fragment into nomadic bands in the winter, or roam about in fur-collecting and -trading groups, and yet their life retains a nomadic and intermittent character. Some of the men in the native-oriented group work with logging crews in the forest, but this work is dependent upon the season of the year, the depth of the snow, and the "cut" needed to keep the sawmill operating. All of the men and boys fish and hunt. Until recently most families went to pick cherries, potatoes, and strawberries, in season, for farmers and orchardists in Wisconsin and Michigan. A few baskets, paintings, bas-relief carvings, and, particularly, beadwork items are sold to tourists. Many individuals and families pick ferns and evergreen boughs. A fast worker can make $15 per day in season. A few people go to Minnesota to gather wild rice each year.

In addition to these activities, members of the group have organized themselves into a loosely defined "troupe" that performs weekly "play dances" for tourists, often traveling to various towns throughout the state.[5] In relation to the amount of time and energy expended in putting them on, they do not provide a very substantial addition to the income of this group. On three consecutive Sundays in 1958 the "take" ran between $12 and $30. This was divided so many ways that each participant received no more than $2, and usually less. This was "pay" for at least six hours of dancing in the dusty, hot arena. Obviously, the pleasure derived from the dances was more important than the money. Although a Whiteman or acculturated Menomini would have regarded the business as a failure, the members of this group seemed quite unconcerned with the amount of the gate proceeds and saw nothing foolish about going through with it week after week. One man even quit his wage job so that he could make a costume and paint some signs for the affair.

---

[5] This activity has grown in significance in recent years, and the troupe, consisting only of native-oriented individuals in 1958, now (1970) includes individuals from transitional and acculturated families.

Some members of the dance troupe from the native-oriented group in 1952. The beadwork designs, costumes, and, particularly, the roach headdress are all of the woodland type, distinctive from the Plains style, which has recently become popular.

Some of the ladies, ready for a powwow for tourists, in 1960.

Hunting is an occasional source of meat, and some men spend long hours in the woods. The dense forests of the Menomini area still shelter deer, bear, and partridge, and the many lakes float their share of ducks and occasional geese. Skill in hunting is highly valued. One man who is regarded as an excellent hunter shot thirteen bears in five years and averages about seven deer a year. The technique most used is to take position near a deer run or watering place, or sometimes by a salt lick set out to attract game. Once in position, a man may wait for his quarry for a whole day or night with hardly a movement. When food runs low, a man will go out to stay until he kills something. One man stayed out four days with only a half a loaf of bread and a pound of salt pork for provisions, but he came back with the hindquarters and hide of a bear. The man and his wife ate none of it, despite the fact that they were very hungry, and it was sold to the restaurant near Keshena, because eating bear meat would be dangerous without ritual precautions that the hunter did not have the power or knowledge to carry out. He did, however, pay his respects to the bear before he shot him. The hunter killed one bear from his platform and another appeared on the scene within a minute of the first—but the hunter did not kill this one. He coughed instead, and then shouted, "Hey, Chief, what are you doing around here?" If the bear had stayed, he would have shot him, he said, and he declared, "You know, bears aren't like deers. They are like human beings." This attitude is of long standing.

> . . . the animal or bird forms that may thus be adopted by an Indian are sometimes the same as the totem of which he is a member. Under such circumstances the animal representing the totem, and the "familiar" or ma'nido, is seldom hunted or shot; but should he be permitted to hunt such an animal the hunter will first address the animal and ask forgiveness for killing him, telling him that certain portions, which are tabu, shall be set up in the place of honor in the wikö'mik. For instance, should an Indian of the Bear totem, or one whose adopted guardian is represented by the bear, desire to go hunting and meet with that animal, due apology would be paid to it before destroying it. The carcass would then be dressed and served, but no member of the Bear totem would partake of the meat, though the members of all other totems could freely do so. The hunter could, however, eat of the paws and head, the bones of the latter being subsequently placed upon a shelf, probably over the door, or in some other conspicuous place. Due reverence is paid to such a relic of the totem, and so strictly observed is this custom that no greater insult could be offered to the host than for anyone to take down such bones and to cast them carelessly aside.
>
> Due reverence must be had by the Indian for his so-called guardian or ma'nido, neglect in this direction sometimes being considered as the direct cause of misfortune or sickness. [Hoffman 1896:64–65]

The method of hunting is in sharp contrast with that used by most White hunters, who select an area where there is good cover and a number of them "drive" the area. The frightened game moves ahead of them, to be shot by hunters posted at strategic points where they can cover a certain area. This method is foreign to the native-oriented Menomini. Each man hunts for himself. He settles down and waits for the game to appear rather than forcing it out. When he kills, the meat is not distributed piecemeal to all the members of the group, or even to his relatives. His in-laws, if nearby, will receive a sizeable chunk. If there is a seasonal rite for the Dream Dance or a meeting of the Medicine Lodge, he will contribute his meat to feed the participants, but otherwise, he and his immediate family consume it as rapidly as possible.

Life in this mode has its ups and downs. People still go hungry, though almost no one starves today.[6] From the Whiteman's point of view, however, there is little security. There is rarely food in the house for more than a very few days ahead. No one has freezers or food storage lockers, and work is intermittent. The typical pattern is to work hard at cherry picking or greens gathering for a few weeks. When that is finished, there is money for food and a few bottles of beer for awhile. Then there is no point in working. Work in itself has no value. There is nothing to "get ahead" toward, from their point of view. As long as there is enough to eat, things are fine, and when the food runs out, something "always comes along," if one can wait long enough to see what it will be.

The values and attitudes and psychological organization described here are functional in this setting. Equanimity under duress is a good quality to possess in an intermittent and seminomadic subsistence economy. Autonomy is apparent in the lack of organized cooperation in economic endeavor. Latescence makes it possible for one to wait for the game to come rather than drive it out, or to wait expectantly, rarely hopelessly, for the next thing to turn up that will put food in the pot. It is not necessary to live this way in present-day Wisconsin, but if they did not live this way, the native-oriented Menomini would cease being native oriented. It is their way of life and has continuity with the past.

SOCIAL ORGANIZATION AS RELATED TO THE ECONOMIC BASE

The social organization of the Menomini has undergone some rather drastic shifts over the centuries as shifts in the economic base have occurred. The transitions have been from a more sedentary village-type existence to a large-scale hunting (for furs) economy to the reservation-type economic patterns. And now (1970) the terminal phases of adaptation to non-ward status and to the problems of survival in a competitive economy are in process. (This is dealt with briefly in Chapter 6.)

Early records refer to the tribe, or a portion of it, as living in a "village" at Menominee River (Keesing 1939:34). This village type of life was based on a fishing and wild-rice economy. Early documents and origin myths of the Menomini point to the existence of a dual organization or moiety system defined

---

[6] "Almost" is correct, for in 1965 one man, living in an isolated cabin and ill, died of a combination of his ills and malnutrition.

as the Thunderers and Bears, with subdivisions into patrilineal totemic[7] descent groups[8] and some larger groupings in phratries[9] (Keesing 1939:38).

> *The Bear {came out of the ground and} ... was made an Indian. ... He found himself alone, and decided to call to himself Kine'u, the Eagle, and said, "Eagle, come to me and be my brother." Thereupon the eagle descended, and also took the form of a human being. While they were considering whom to call upon to join them, they perceived a beaver approaching. The Beaver ... was adopted as a younger brother of the Thunderer. ... {Then} the Sturgeon ... was adopted by the Bear as a younger brother and servant. ... The Elk was accepted by the Thunderer as a younger brother and watercarrier ... {and} the Crane and the Wolf became younger brothers of the Bear {also the Dog and Deer which were associated with the Wolf in a sub-group}. ... The Good Mystery made the Thunderers the laborers ... {and} also gave {them} corn ... {They} were also makers of fire. ...*
>
> *The Thunderers decided to visit the Bear village {at the Menominee river} ... and when they arrived at that place they asked the Bear to join them, promising to give corn and fire in return for {wild} rice, which was the property of the Bear and Sturgeon. ... The Bear family agreed to this, and since that time the two families have therefore lived together.* [From the sacred origin myth in Hoffman 1896:39–41]

Exogamy [marriage outside the clan (or the older term "gens")] was required and polygyny (one man married to two or more women) was accepted.

> *Marriage outside of the gens was imperative, and disregard of this rule would have been incest, because of the putative relationship of all those claiming descent from the same totem. Violations of the rule are said to have been unknown in old days.* [From a reconstruction by Skinner 1913:19]

Kinship terminology, and the behaviors associated with it, are apparently of long standing. The system of terminology is largely classificatory (lumping specified sets of relatives together under one term); in this case, for example, father and father's brother are given one term. Father's brother's children or mother's sister's children (parallel cousins)[10] are given the same terms as brothers and sisters. Some of the other outstanding features of the system are as follows: (1) Distinctions are made between parallel and cross-cousins (mother's brother's children or father's sister's children). (2) Nephews and nieces are important on either side.

---

[7] A descent relationship, in this case through the male line, to a presumed animal ancestor.

[8] These may be regarded as clans since descent from a remote and fictive ancestor is the basis for relationship.

[9] A union of two or more clans for social or ceremonial purposes.

[10] See E. Schusky, *Manual for Kinship Analysis* (revised edition, 1971) for a glossary of kinship terms and an explanation of the principles of kinship systems.

A person's nephews, nieces, and brothers- and sisters-in-law are his closest relations next to the parents, nearer even than an actual blood brother or sister. If a man goes to war his nephew, on either side, or his brother-in-law, must follow him regardless of any hindrance. This is a great point of honor, and most strictly observed. The nephew must act as a servant to him and protect him from danger at the risk of his own life. If the uncle is killed his nephew must get a scalp from the enemy in revenge, or never come home alive. In a like manner the nephew is his uncle's blood avenger, should the uncle be slain in an intertribal quarrel. Nephews and nieces are greatly indulged by their uncles and aunts, who refuse them nothing for which they ask, no matter how costly it may be, or how inconvenient. It would be a great disgrace to do so. [From Skinner's reconstructions from elderly informants, 1913:20]

(3) Restraints are observed in the parents-in-law relationships.

A man may never speak to his mother-in-law, and must be respectfully silent in her presence. Though there is no fixed rule to this effect, the same thing is usually observed in the case of his father-in-law. To the father-in-law belong certain privileges in dividing his son-in-law's game. In the case of a bear, he skins the animal and keeps the skin, one side, the head and neck, while his son-in-law gets the other side and all four quarters. This rule is not followed in regard to any other game. [From Skinner's reconstructions of the old culture, 1913:20]

(4) Prescribed joking relationships exist between certain classes of relatives.

The joking-relationship exists between a person and his uncles and aunts, nephews and nieces, sisters-in-law and brothers-in-law, on either side, but is strictly tabooed between cousins. Any joke, no matter how rough, is permissible, and so is sexual intercourse. [Skinner 1913:20]

Hereditary chiefs—heads of descent groups—with the chief of the Bear group as tribal chief, were included in the formal social structure of the precontact Menomini. The lineage chiefs probably constituted a village council and regulated civil affairs to a limited extent. Aside from this civil leadership there were said to be chiefs who won prestige through individual dreams or due to their special prowess. Those persons acted as keepers of the war medicines and as public spokesmen for hereditary leaders, and as masters of ceremonies during public celebrations (Keesing 1939:40). In spite of certain formal structures of control, it is probable that the Menomini and other tribes in the area had little secular authority exercised by any leader. The Menomini were described by the Jesuit Father Allouez as a people who "have neither laws, nor police, nor magistrates to check disorder" (quoted from Keesing 1939:40). The problem of social control will be dealt with later in the chapter.

Materials given here regarding the groupings and their organization and functions is inferential to a large degree. The system began to disintegrate in the seventeenth century, and there are contradictions in the materials of early students such as Hoffman and Skinner. There is agreement, however, as to the general outline of the totemic descent groups but disagreement as to the specific names and number of groupings.

After the French fur traders arrived (1667), readjustments in the social system were necessary. The Menomini became primarily hunters and trappers. The older village and clan system broke down and the "band" system emerged to meet the demands of the new fur-trading economy. By 1830 there were nine bands. All of the able-bodied Menomini set out by canoe along the inland rivers for the fall and winter hunt. Since large groupings would not be feasible under these conditions, families ranged in congenial groups. As the forest areas nearby became denuded of game, the groups had to go farther, and each then tended to claim customary rights over a given river path and hunting territory; because of the credit system, the fur traders sent agents along with the band. During the summer months the Menomini camped at places convenient for fishing and making gardens, and gathering maple syrup, berries, and wild rice. These groups tended to remain stable, with the summer sites located near the fall canoes routes. Bands were primarily friendship groups, but tended to follow clan lines. Later the distinctiveness broke down, but some of the bands retained strong clan marks up to the reservation period. The small family or household group fit into the band organization as well as it had the village type. Monogamy became more prevalent. There were more men, as there was less warrior mortality, and the monogamous family was a less unwieldy canoe-and-hunting-trip group. The individual family grew in importance in the loosely knit band system, and this trend toward individualism has continued to the present among the native oriented. Kinship behaviors and terms of address were little changed by this shift to band organization.

Modifications occurred, however, in the tribal leadership. Certain new standards for leaders included success in obtaining furs, directing hunting and trading operations, and obtaining credit, in ability to orate, and in getting along well with Whites and other Indian tribes. A new institution in the form of a tribal council came into being which was to grow in importance. Frequent tribal council and inter tribal councils were held. Ability to excel in formal oratory was a great asset for a leader at the council meetings, and continued to be so until contemporary times.

When the Menomini reservation was formed in 1852, a sedentary-type subsistence was required, and the band system of the fur-trading era began to distintegrate. The various band leaders, it is said, chose locations that appealed to them on the reserve, and the members of their bands either grouped themselves nearby or selected other areas where they and their families might live. However, the band type of organization did not entirely disappear. Peoples regrouped in congenial cooperative groups under different leaders and were still called bands. When these new bands became settled and less isolated from other groups, they in turn tended to lose their unity (Keesing 1939:150). The old totemic dualism seemed to persist in the division of the tribe into "Christians" and "pagans." Those following the traditional religion also divided into two groups more or less based on the old division of Bear and Thunderer. When some

families started to farm and others began to log, a variety of regroupings occurred to fit the environmental demands of the particular subsistence technique.
Members of the contemporary native-oriented group live in and around Zoar,
where they have resided since the early reservation period. They are often referred to as the pagan group by others. The area is surrounded by dense woods
and streams, which make it possible for some members of the group to continue
to hunt and fish in Menomini fashion. The social organization remains similar
today to that found in the early reservation period.

Many of the older members of the native-oriented group have a totem
or clan affiliation. It was common practice until very recently for each individual
to have his totem painted, usually upside down, on a grave stick at his place of
burial. Some marriages are still arranged by elders. The kinship terminology
described by Skinner in 1913 is still in use in the Menomini tongue (mixed
with Potawatomi and Chippewa terms) and is frequently projected indirectly
into the English kinship usage, as, for instance, when referring to a parallel
cousin, in such phrases as "He is like a brother to me." The same term is used
for father and father's brother, for mother's father and father's father, and distinctions are still made between cross-cousins and parallel cousins. All of the people
around Zoar are conscious of kin relationships to each other, and this has created
a powerful force pulling them together into a cohesive group. The exact relationships are not always clear in the minds of some of the younger people. They
will often declare that they know they are "close" to so-and-so but are not able
to explain just in what way. One man remarked, "We're all related here at Zoar
but we don't always know just how. Only the old people know."

Some of the old obligations and prerogatives between relatives have been
retained. The old joking relationships, particularly between a man and his brother-
in-law, are very much alive, as shown in the behavior examples given previously.
The outsider coming into the situation is shocked, at first, by the ribald attacks
on another man's character, origins, house, and family, committed under the sanctions of this system, that seem so out of place among an otherwise restrained
people. Other kinship obligations survive in the distribution of meat killed in
hunting and the understanding that certain relatives, when called upon, must
provide economic help in time of distress, or when a candidate is being "put up"
for the Medicine Lodge.

Elders are still the most respected persons in the group. Great powers
are attributed to elders, and all are potential witches. This is the group from
which the leadership is drawn. The elders know the ritual of the Medicine Lodge
and Dream Dance, are in direct contact with the supernatural powers, can
prophesy with their dreams, can name a child appropriately, and are the authorities
for questions on kin relationships. No man under sixty could pretend to much
knowledge or experience in these matters, but not all men over sixty are leaders.
Positions of prestige and leadership are a function of age, inheritance, and amount
of sacred power controlled by the person. During the decade under consideration,
the elder with greatest authority was in his seventies, but he was also the son
of one of the last of the true shamans, did curing with both charms and herbs,
and was known as the only man resident in the native-oriented community who
could honestly claim to have gone successfully through the major puberty fast

and achieved his power through a vision. His leadership was threatened only by an elderly woman, who is a lineal descendant of chiefs and is regarded as a powerful witch. This system of symbols and sanctions represents little fundamental change from that of the old culture but is in sharp contrast to that operating for the rest of the Menomini community.

The exercise of authority is much like that described by the Jesuits and fur traders two centuries ago. As mentioned earlier, Nicholas Perrote, the fur trader, wrote: "The father does not venture to exercise authority over his son, nor does the chief dare to give commands to his soldier. . . ." Social control for this group will be discussed in a later section in connection with witchcraft.

THE WORLD AROUND THEM: MENOMINI COSMOLOGY

All them [spirits above] what God created is good. And there is some *awe·toks* [spirits] that isn't good; belong someplace else . . . under the ground. [Menomini informant, in Slotkin 1957:26]

The earth is believed to be an island, floating in an illimitable ocean, separating the two halves of the universe into an upper and a lower portion, regarded as the above of the benevolent and the malevolent powers, respectively. Each portion is divided into four superimposed tiers, inhabited by supernatural beings, the power of whom increases in ratio to their remoteness from the earth. [Skinner 1921:29]

And this we call *awe·tok*, this sun, that brings the light every day. . . . They even put up tobacco [for the sun]; . . . This sun here, he's got lots of power. He watches over the Indians, too. Sometimes he gives them power [as a guardian spirit]. . . . Sometimes that *ke·so?* [sun] would give them power so they could see at night. [Menomini informant, in Slotkin 1957:28]

In the highest tier above the earth resides the deity to whom all others are subordinate. The testimony of the early writers is unanimous that this being was the sun. . . . [Skinner 1921:29]

. . . the Great Spirit saw the Indians, his people; he did not like what was happening; the Indian being killed; those spirits killing him; all kinds of animals killing him. That great spirit, the Great Spirit, thought it over. This is what he thought, one time: "Well, instead I will make some ones to watch over these, my children the Indians. I will make them." . . . Then he probably made the Thunderbirds. He put them over here; he put them everywhere. He put the Thunderbirds, large birds, to watch over these Indians; . . . They would speak to them, and feed them, in order that the Thunderbirds should look after them carefully, so that they might be allowed to live well. That everything would grow abundantly here, for them to eat; that the Thunderbirds would water [everything] with the water they carry—that it would rain

properly so that everything would be wet—that is what the old people probably would pray for. [Menomini informant, in Slotkin 1957:27]

*Beneath the supreme being, in descending order, . . . are three tiers of bird-
like deities. First . . . come the Thunderbirds, gods of war.* [Skinner 1921:30]

They [the stars] just watch over everything in the night. Just like that
[Indian] policeman; maybe that's why he got that star [shaped badge]. He's
taking care of people. If they do something wrong, well, he can go and put
them someplace [i.e., in jail] . . . *wa·pananah* [morning star] is some kind of
a chief of all stars, head one. When he comes out, it's getting daylight.
[Menomini informant, in Slotkin 1957:30]

*In the eastern sky dwells morning star, often personified as a man of large
stature, with an enormous mouth. Morningstar frequently appears to young
men in their dreams with promises of strength and success. He, too, has influence in martial affairs, and with the sun, was one of the joint donors of the
war bundle through the thunderbirds.* [Skinner 1913:81]

1st informant: The Bear is one who lived over here in the Underground
Place; that is the White Bear. White Bear is the one underground who holds
up the earth. He is also one whom the Great Spirit thought about, who himself holds up the [sky] above, over here. They speak to each other back and
forth, the Great Spirit and White Bear; they tell each other something. That
is the way those two work; they are alike.
2nd informant: . . . they say that he has got as much power as Great Spirit
got; he's got lots of power, too. And he's taking charge of everything here.
Them berries what's growing in the woods, all the berries, he owns that; he's
taking charge of that so they come up good. [Slotkin 1957:32–33]

*Beneath the earth, there is, in the lowest tier, the Great White Bear with
a long copper tail, who, in addition to being the chief and patron of all
earthly bears and the traditional ancestor of the Menomini tribe, is the principal power for evil.* [Skinner 1921:30–31]

1st informant: That Hairy Serpent is one who is not good. . . . That is
the one that sometimes swims by [like a water snake], too. . . . He would
swing his tail at him [i.e., an Indian in a boat] on the top of the water, so
that he would capsize; then he would capture him. Therefore he is not good,
that Hairy Serpent. [translation]
2nd informant: *Mi·ʔs-kenu·pik* is in every lake. It must be one [in the
lake] over here, down the hill there; there's a lake there. And [in] every
lake there's a *mi·ʔs-kenu·pik*; that's where he is. Even in the rivers; we see
them [in a] spring, little creeks, towards that river. He comes out that way.
[Slotkin 1957:32]

During the Spindlers' period of fieldwork Horned Hairy Serpent was reported seen in a lake near Keshena. Four men, returning from fishing, said they saw something big in the water and rowed near until they saw that it was a tremendous serpent. They shot at it, with no effect. They were so frightened that they jumped out of the boat and ran as soon as they came to shallow water. After a day or two a party of men went back to investigate. They saw nothing but found a track on the road where the huge serpent had apparently dragged himself across the dirt. Some nonbelievers said that the "only serpent those guys saw was in a bottle," and that "some jokers must have dragged a sack of sand around to make tracks." Rumors of *mi·ʔs-kenu·pik* still persist today (1970).

> *The horned snake is the best known of these evil animals because he is nearest to, and consequently most frequently seen on, the earth. The great horned serpents, or as they are more often called, Mīsikinūbikuk, "hairy snakes," are gigantic reptiles with bodies of the usual form, but covered with black or golden scales, while on their hairy heads grow stag-like horns. They seek to destroy man, and come above the ground to search for him whenever they dare, but in this effort they are rarely successful, owing to their relentless enemies, the thunderbirds. For a Menomini to see one of these snakes in his waking hours is a bad sign, perhaps foretelling death in his family; to see one in a dream is an evil omen and the dreamer, if he has been fasting for a vision, should at once break his fast and start it a second time. Should he accept the vision, he becomes possessed of the malign powers of sorcery and witchcraft.*
>
> *A sorcerer often claims to possess a scale or a portion of the flesh of one of these serpents which he keeps carefully hidden in one of his medicine bags to use in practising witchcraft. It is well known to the Menomini that isolated and lonely hills, ponds, swamps, or sloughs are apt to be the homes of these monsters.* [Skinner 1913:81–82]

The Giant is one who is not good; he is not good. That Giant wants the Indian; he kills him in order to eat him. He eats them, that Giant. [Menomini informant, in Slotkin 1957:34]

> *In the north, whence the cold winds blow, there dwells at the end of the earth a race of malevolent giants {mänupäwuk . . .} driven there by Mä'näbus {Menomini culture here} because of their desire to destroy mankind. That they may not return during his absence Mä'näbus has made an ocean separating their country from the rest of the earth and mankind. When the south winds blow, the odor of human flesh is borne to their nostrils and they attempt to wade the watery barrier. But it is too deep even for their magnificent size, and they soon give it up. That they may never swim to the other shore, Mä'näbus has thoughtfully created gigantic bloodsuckers or leeches which attack the giants and drive them back.* [Skinner 1913:83]

. . . *pe·hcekona·h* [sacred bundle] is the same one as *pe·hcekona·h ne·yo·htah* [the one who carries a sacred bundle on his back] . . . he is a spirit. That is why I say that I myself am afraid of everything. Well, this *pe·hcekona·h*, as he is called, is a great spirit; some time ago he was a person; that is what he was in the past. . . . When he tells someone that something is going to happen —he warns them . . . they feel his very presence. That is how much of a spirit he is, that *pe·hcekona·h*. That is why it is really hard to talk about him. Wait until tonight; I myself will offer tobacco to that *pe·hcekona·h*. [The informant is a sorcerer. Translation, in Slotkin 1957:34.]

The "wandering man" {Petcikunau naiota, "Bundle Carrier,"} is an individual bearing a burden ceaselessly over the face of the earth. He sometimes lingers in one locality for a long time, and then he may not be heard of again for years. He rarely appears to anyone save to foretell misfortune; but he is not infrequently heard by travelers as he rustles along through the leaves or bushes at night. A gift of tobacco or liquor will cause him to go way. If he is angered, he will pursue the person who has offended him, and even throw sticks at the fugitive. To be hit with a stick thrown by the "wandering man" means death. To defeat him in a wrestling match is most propitious and means long life and happiness. [Skinner 1913:83]

George Spindler reported to a group of Menomini a dream about some tiny Indians sitting on the crosspieces of the inner supports of the Spindlers' tent and poking holes in the roof with their spears. He shouted at them in his dream, but they kept right on poking holes. This was serious, because it was raining hard! As the episode was told, everyone nearby listening became silent and stayed so for a few minutes. After a while one of the men said, "George, you know who them little guys was?" "No, do you?" "Well, them's the Little God Boys. They stick around, pester you like that. But don't do nothin' to scare them off. They're good to have around. They look after you. Just cause you trouble in little ways."

The "little god boys" are pygmies who dwell particularly at "death's Door" on Lake Michigan. They are friendly to men. One of their most remarkable qualities is the power to pass through stone as though it did not exist. [Skinner 1913:83–84]

Well, that is why I exist. . . . It is because of my soul [*netɛ·ʔcyak*] that I live. If something should happen to me, then it leaves, and I die.
My soul is that which travels all night; that soul of mine walks [then]. Well, this one is always right here; it stay here in my body, that one, my soul. There are two souls of mine. One travels at night. This one right here maintains me; it is right here. That soul of mine is the one that is like a shadow [*kawe·hseh*]. [Translation, in Slotkin 1957:44–45]

While we were interviewing two ladies near their homes, some distance back in the woods, one old man, known to be irascible, approached George Spindler. "You smart Whiteman. How many souls does a man have?" George Spindler replied "Only one," thinking that the old man, quite drunk, would be only angered by an "Indian" reply from a Whiteman. But the old man shouted, "You God damned Whiteman! You think this Indian is dumb! He is smarter than you damn Whitemen. A man has two souls, one here [he struck his forehead], and one here [he struck his chest]." With that he stomped off to his house, shouting over his shoulder. George Spindler asked one of his sons, standing nearby, "What did he say?" "He says he is going to kill you!" George Spindler circled the house and looked in the window. There on the floor lay old Pe·sek, passed out. Under him lay his shotgun. The fieldworkers left shortly, taking the ladies with them to finish interviewing elsewhere.

> . . . *every human being is possessed of two souls. One, called usually agawétätciuk {"a shade across"} resides in the head. This is the intellect, and after death it wanders about aimlessly, lingering about the graveyard. It is for these spirits that sacrifices of food are offered. They are ghosts as differentiated from souls. . . .*
>
> *The soul, or tcebai, dwells in the heart and is the one which travels to the hereafter. It is the tcebai for which all funeral services are held.* [Skinner 1913:85]

First they go down this way [pointing west]. And that fellow over there [Na·hpaʔtɛh], he knows what kind of a person this is. Maybe he [had] been killing people by witchbag and stuff like that, suffered people [i.e., made people suffer], he [Na·hpaʔtɛh] tells him what road to follow. And he comes to kind of a swamp, like, you know, water and lots of mud. That's where he drives them kind of people, and they're going to suffer there a long time. And the good people, that fellow takes them there [to the Abode of the Dead], and fix them up good. But bad people, he don't take them [there]. [Slotkin 1957:46]

It appears that the cognitive world of the contemporary native-oriented Menomini remains similar to that of the Menomini when the traditional culture was yet intact during the time of Skinner's early work and even to early contact times. The beliefs concerning the ordering of the sky beings, those of the earth, and those of the underworld remain similar even in detail, and the fear of the evil spirits on all sides is still pervasive today. As a most-powerful shaman said of one of the spirits (*pe·hcekona·h,*" the bundle carrier"), "That is why I say that I myself am afraid of everything. . . . Wait until tonight; I myself will offer tobacco to that *pe·hcekona·h.*" Another inference that can be drawn is that the Menomini belief system is dualistic, with continuous cosmic conflict between the good spirits above the earth and the evil spirits below.[11] With the world and the heavens and the underworld peopled with such spectacular, often dangerous, beings, it is not surprising that most of the religious observances of the contemporary group and those reported by the early explorers and missionaries are

---

[11] The extent to which this dualism is a result of Christian influence remains a puzzle. Probably, the concept was reinforced by the Christian cosmology, but the dualism in Menomini thinking is different. Good and evil are not absolutes, and any one spiritual entity, person, or thing may have attributes of both.

those concerned with securing and maintaining supernatural power, partly as protection against evil forces. Another inference to be drawn is that there is no real separation between man and animal in the Menomini belief system. Figures in the puberty dream appear in either animal or human form. Witches can take the form of an animal. As the Rorschachs also showed, the concept of the peopled universe for the Menomini is zoomorphic rather than anthropomorphic.

Powerful men and women who control both good and evil powers have always been held in awe by the Menomini. In earlier times people were identified who were primarily "witches" performing evil acts and who had received one of the underworld spirits as a tutelary in a vision, but these were very few in number. Usually, a shaman was and is able to control both good and evil forces. Until rather recent times, shamans in special groups spent a large portion of their time combating evil powers exercised by witches or those possessing an "evil bag" made up of parts of animals representing underworld spirits (owl skins, bear claws, and so forth). The earlier religious groupings included the *Wa·beno* and the *Cese·ko* or Jugglers. These shamans worked more or less entirely as individuals (Keesing 1939:50). None of the authors' informants had direct knowledge of the *Wa·beno* cult, whose members claimed the Morning Star or the Sun as their tutelary spirit. They were said to be able to furnish hunting medicine, prescribe herbal remedies, and sell love powders and charms which would cause an indifferent person to fall in love with the owner. They claimed a special immunity to fire and boiling water.

The *Cese·ko*, or Jugglers as they were called by the early writers, persisted until the first quarter of the twentieth century. They were diviners and doctors of great powers who worked in a special lodge when they consulted the spirits to cure the sick. The small birch bark lodge swayed from side to side (thus the term "shaking-tent rite" is often applied); wind was heard, and voices spoke to the seer. The *Cese·ko* supposedly replied through the medium of the turtle, who acted as an interviewer. It was the role of the *Cese·ko* to find out the cause of the patient's illness, which was usually witchcraft since disease was unnatural. The *Cese·ko* would then attempt to coax the soul of the patient to return and enter a small wooden cylinder, where it was imprisoned and delivered to its relatives. The cylinder was then attached to the patient's breast for four days so that the soul could return to his body. If the patient had been wounded by a witch's arrow, the *Cese·ko* proceeded to extract the arrow by sucking through a bone tube. He then vomited forth the arrow, displayed it to the onlookers, and announced that the patient was cured. The witch's arrow was usually found to be a maggot, a fly, a quill, or some other small object. (See Skinner 1921:72.)

Several living Menomini in the native-oriented group have witnessed a shaking-tent rite:

> I seen him, J., shake a tepee by Dutchman's tower. It was just three poles stuck around and canvas around it. He was supposed to doctor someone. He had three tepees and got in one and called his spirits and wanted them to get this person who was witchin' this woman. They hears his voice—the witch—and he started shakin' each tepee as fast as he could. He went in one at a time; you

couldn't see him—and shook them as fast as he could. He asked the man if he was gonna quit hurtin' the woman and the man said if they left him alone, he would. I wasn't supposed to see it; I was too little about twenty-five years ago. They had one in Flambeau and Moe Lake lately. That woman was real sick. They brought her in on a stretcher. It was a scary outfit; you could hear that man's voice way up in the air—the one who was doin' the witchin'. [Menomini woman, in L. Spindler, field notes]

The values, attitudes, and psychological organization described earlier for the native-oriented Menomini are congruent with this belief system. Keeping in touch with the deities by gaining special powers is crucial in order to survive in this world peopled with spirits and monsters. The latescent, expectant attitude is appropriate for a person waiting for power to be bestowed. And each person must keep himself under control at all times lest he anger a malevolent spirit or an elder with special powers. In securing power or in using one's special powers, each person behaves autonomously. He or she has a special kind of power unique to him or her and gained in a unique fashion. As mentioned earlier, even the shamans in special cults such as the *Cese·ko* worked as individuals, with their own interpretations of the phenomena at hand and their own manner of performance in dealing with it.

POWER: GETTING AND MAINTAINING IT

What Is Power—What Does It Look Like?

Power is white, like when the sun is shining. Like that [pointing to a sunbeam], see; that's a power, see? . . . When God [translation of *Kese·maneto'w*] wants to do anything, it goes; he's got power in him. He's the only one that got power. And *tata·hkesewen*, that means power [too]. [Male informant, in Slotkin 1957:25]

According to Menomini elders, power is an immaterial and invisible force that gives off a bright light. "It produces characteristic effects in things which are subjected to it, and can be transformed from one thing to another. People who do not have power are ineffective and weak; once they obtain such power, they become effective and strong." The Menomini used three terms interchangeably for power: *tata·hkesewen* (that which has energy), *me·skowesan* (that which has strength), and *ahpe·htesewen* (that which is valuable) (Slotkin 1957:25).

How Does a Person Gain Power?

Until recently, every normally socialized Menomini went through the *mesa·hkatɛwɛ·w* (Great Fast) at puberty. Preparation for the Great Fast began during early childhood with short fasts of a day or two and instruction in the properly humble state of mind. When the individual felt ready for the ordeal and had received proper instructions from an elder, he or she went off, with a charcoal-blackened face, into the woods, to a tiny bark wigwam already constructed for this purpose.

They are taught from the age of four or five years to blacken their faces,
to fast, and to dream . . . being led to believe that thus they will be successful
in fishing, hunting, and war. [A seventeenth century Jesuit missionary in
Jesuit Relations 1896–1901, vol. lvii:265–287]

One stayed alone, quite cut off from all human contact, and with no food for
periods ranging up to ten days or even two weeks or longer. During this time
the initiate was supposed to banish all thoughts from the mind except those concerned with the purpose of the fast—to receive a vision and through this experience find the source of the power, in the form of a guardian spirit, that would
guide and keep him through his whole lifetime. His attitude must be humble,
supplicatory, so that the powers will take pity on him and notify him of their
interest. If he is successful, the Golden Eagle, the White Bear, the Buffalo, or
one of the many other spirit powers that reside in one of the layers above the
earth, usually but not always in animal form, would appear before him. The
Golden Eagle would take the supplicant on his back and fly over the forests and
lakes, pointing out natural features that are significant in Menomini mythology.
The Buffalo might chase him over rough terrain to the point of exhaustion, and
he would fall face down into a sacred pool from which he might drink the source
of life. If he was unsuccessful, he might either receive no notification from the
spirits or be visited by one of the creatures inhabiting the strata below the earth,
such as the Horned Hairy Serpent. If unsuccessful, he tried again after a lapse
of some time. If he was visited by one of the underworld creatures for the
fourth time, he was doomed to live a tragic life as a witch that used bad medicines
to harm others, or as one who some day would murder a loved one.

After I had fasted eight days a tall man with a big red mouth appeared
from the east. The solid earth bent under his steps as though it was a marsh.
He said, "I have pity on you. You shall live to see your own gray hairs, and
those of your children. You shall never be in danger if you make yourself
a war club, such as I have and always carry it with you wherever you go. When
you are in trouble, pray to me and offer me tobacco. Tobacco is what pleases
me." When he had said this he vanished. [This was Morning Star. Menomini
informant, in Skinner 1913:44.]

Visions often came to a girl in the form of the sun or the wind and
insured qualities such as long life and happiness, unless an evil spirit came as
a visitation, imbuing the girl with special evil power (L. Spindler 1970).

What happened during the Great Fast determined to a considerable degree
what the initiate would be in his or her present lifetime. Whether a man would
be a good hunter, a ceremonial leader, whether a woman would be a good
mother and wife, or a witch, was decided by the events at that time. The person's
access to the power pool through a guardian spirit—the all-permeating, universal
sacred power in living things and inanimate objects alike—was defined at this time.

Today there is only one person in the group who had the Great Fast and
received its benefits, though until very recently there were a number of old

people still living who had. One elderly medicine man remarked during an interview:

> Hardly nobody ever has that now [the Great Fast]. K., who is older than I, had the big fast. I went to school when I was about five years old. If anyone else says they had that, they are not speaking true. K. is all there is who had it, now living. That is all. *Naha·w!* [Translation, in G. Spindler, field notes]

A woman informant in her late thirties remarked:

> Both me and my brother were supposed to fast when punished. We couldn't fast the four days. We couldn't do it. [L. Spindler, field notes]

Sister M. Inez Hilger, Benedictine sister, who worked with the Menomini in 1936, had several informants who had fasted. One relates:

> My great-grandmother fasted for forty days to receive her power. She used to tell me how she had made a hammock of tanned deerhide and had fastened it between trees on a hill, deep in the woods. She lay in this hammock fasting from all food. Whatever physical strength she received, she imbibed from the sun. Whenever she would tell me of her fast, she would say that after the forty days there was nothing left to her body but her bones and the skin over them. It was at this time that the humming bird became her medicine [*equated with tutelary spirit*]. Whenever I saw her use her medicine bag, I looked for the stuffed humming bird in it. I fasted only ten days. [Italics mine] [Hilger 1960:55]

In spite of the present situation, the pattern of securing a guardian spirit remains an integral part of the culture both in spirit and in specific form. All adults in the group had fasted for short periods as children. Some received notifications from the spirits in these preparatory fasts and ritually observe the relationship thus formed. Others have inherited both the powers and obligations of ritual observance from departed relatives.

> Like the buffalo, not so many here have been given power by them. Or like longhorn steers. You fast, and sleep, and come to in the dream. You see a longhorn coming. This longhorn chases you all over. All over the country. Like one story, a fellow told me. This fellow he run all over the country trying to elude it. Finally he see a pool, he's thirsty, played out. So he think, "If I let him get me, he can get me right here." Well then the longhorn steer come right up to him when he's laying there drinking water. He sees his image, his hair is all white. The steer, instead of hurting him, tells him, "That's what I'm trying to tell you! You drink that."
> It tastes like whiskey. Then the pool turned into a wooden bowl. That fellow, he thinks about that. Now he has to use whiskey in the future. He takes a half-pint, pours it in the wooden bowl. Then he drinks it like cattle would, and offers tobacco. After he drinks it, he turns it over with his head

like a cattle would. Whoever succeeds, gets the tobacco. I got to do that too, from my father, it comes down. [He inherited the long-horned steer as a tutelary spirit] [G. Spindler, field notes]

For the Menomini dreaming is and was a very significant activity. No dream is casually dismissed. Aside from the dreaming done during the fast periods, night dreams quite frequently carry great import.

> *Among . . . Menomini . . . , regular "night-dreams" have much importance. For instance, a man may dream of drowning, or of being saved from drowning, in which case he makes and always carries about with him a small canoe as a talisman.* [Skinner 1913:47]

The individual usually tries to find the meaning in the dream, but if he is unsuccessful, he talks about it with an elder, who has great powers and who, by virtue of his nearness to the end of life, is close to what we would call the "supernatural." The interpretations placed on the dream experience can foretell a significant event, provide revelation concerning life, death, and sacred powers, or dictate a specific course of action ranging from how to make a special drumstick or beadwork design to how to prevent one's husband from running off with another woman. The following is a dream from a young woman whose close relatives possessed great power and who wished to keep the Dream Dance intact, observing their prescribed code of ethics which taboos excessive drinking. This prophetic dream tells of the recent deaths of men who had drunk too much:

> You know, I had a funny dream that told all about them people who died here. The children and I was looking for W. [husband] and we came to a place where we heard a lot of noise and looked in. There was a bunch of men playin' some kind of a game. They was all sittin' around a big table. In the middle was three jugs; one was marked "whiskey," one "wine," and one "beer." And each time someone would win, they would pour him a drink from one of the jugs. I saw W. sittin' there and I got scared and got him away from that table. At that table was all those people who died—W., S., N., and X., the only one who didn't die. He was drinkin' a lot at that time. All of them later died of drinkin' and I began to wonder. I wonder about X. now. [Menomini woman, in L. Spindler, field notes]

Even songs are acquired in dreams. In fact, most significant innovative behavior or important individual decision making among native-oriented Menomini is based on a dream experience and its interpretation.

> *They look upon their dreams as ordinances and irrevocable decrees, the execution of which it is not permitted without crime to delay. . . . A dream will take away from them sometimes their whole year's provisions. It prescribes their feasts, their dances, their songs, their games,—in a word, the dream does everything.* [A seventeenth century report, in *Jesuit Relations* 1896–1901, vol. x:169–171]

The dream experience is a dramatic example of the difference between the cognitive world of the native-oriented Menomini and that of the Whiteman, with his rationalistic-objective view of the universe. For the Menomini the separation between mind and body, man and animal, spiritual forces and material forces, natural and supernatural is absent in their framework of belief and rationality. If the fieldworker uses the term "vision" to describe what the Menomini sees and experiences when talking to a spirit, he is gently corrected. The Menomini would say, "A Whiteman might say that, but this was no 'vision,' this happened." The term "dream" is more acceptable, for they have had many dreams and know that one is directly involved with the events in a dream—that they seem real, so real that even Whites listening to the accounts wonder if they really happened.

To be a part of the native-oriented group one must literally be a "dreamer" (passive, receptive, quiescent), and the autonomous character of the relationship between individuals and "power" is apparent. Each has his or her own experiences and carries out his or her own rituals. It is also apparent that the ability to retain one's equanimity under duress is functional in the requirement to fast in isolation. While the Great Fast is no longer possible, the short fasts required of young children reinforce this ability.

How Does a Menomini Maintain and Protect His Power?

One must observe the power rituals connected with one's tutelary spirit or special powers. Drinking whiskey in a wooden bowl while crouched on one's knees on the floor is a good example, quoted earlier, of observing ritual for a long-horned steer or buffalo tutelary spirit.

After having fasted for an indefinite period, not longer than ten days, the supplicant is approached by a being who addresses him and promises its aid and patronage for life, exacting a pledge that the dreamer will remember to make certain sacrifices from time to time in its honor and keep about his person some token of the meeting. [Skinner 1913:44]

Women have special taboos to observe during menstruation and following childbirth, when they are considered a threat to the power of the male or small child. A woman is isolated during these periods, using her own utensils, refraining from touching herself or looking up, which might offend the gods above. If a man eats food prepared by her at these times, he is in danger of losing his guardian spirit, which lives inside him, in the form of a tiny turtle or fish. If he finds out about the woman's condition in time, he can take an emetic and vomit the food before it kills the little animal. Menstruating women are careful not to feed, touch, or even breathe upon a small child for fear of causing its death. A small child may be a powerful reincarnated elder, whose power must be protected. Although some women in the native-oriented group do not isolate themselves during menstruation today, they are extremely careful during this period to refrain from contaminating others. An example is given in the quotations at the beginning of the chapter, in which a White woman fed a baby while she was menstruating and the baby died. The informant said of her child: "He had some little power, maybe from his grandfather. . . . You're not supposed to kiss a baby or anything then [while menstruating] and have to keep soiled things away from men's clothes and always keep clean. I never had any soiled things laying around." While she believed that her baby's death was due to the contact with the White woman, there was no personal blame, as the woman was ignorant of the taboo. The Menomini woman said, "I wasn't really blaming her. I was thinking the little boy had some power that was killed by her."

> *If . . . a man, fitted by his supernatural guardian with a tiny turtle, fish, or other small animal living in his vitals should eat food in . . . a dish . . . that had been touched by a menstruating woman, the tiny animal upon whose presence his good fortune depends will surely die and he will vomit it forth. The man may live after this; but his power is forever destroyed.* [Skinner 1913:52]

In order to protect and maintain one's power, a person must at all times strive to be a proper Menomini. A good man respects the rights of others and does not arouse antagonism (particularly in older persons), lives quietly, observes the sacrifices required to maintain good relations with the sources of his powers, and is modest, even-tempered, and guards himself against undue pride. The necessary behaviors required of a good Menomini are incorporated into the Commandments of the Dream Dance Drum (*kakiʔhkotakan teʔweʔhekan*). One of the owners of a Dream Dance drum relates some of these requirements:

> They told us that when we talk about one person, you talk about God [*Keʔseʔmanetoʔw*]. . . . Another thing. Everything God owns; He puts everything here. Indian should ask Him first; like if he should pick them berries or hunting deer, or anything like that. That's the way it should be done.

> And the women, it's the same thing, should help one another. Like if one of them has a lot of work to do, the other women should make up their mind to help each other. Like sometimes a woman has got to scrub and clean up the house there, has too many kids, and couldn't do that.

> All the members should be one person and treat each other right, just like sisters and brothers.

> If someone owns something better than the other one, we should not be jealous just because he owns some good things. [Slotkin 1957:42–43]

One's power may also be strengthened by participating in a War Dance or by sponsoring ghost feasts for the deceased. During our period of study a ghost feast was held for a member of the group who was accidentally killed. The sister of the deceased was asked what the dead girl especially liked to eat, and these items were purchased—oranges, lemons for lemonade, peach halves, apples, sweet rolls. Her spirit was considered to be present.

If a person's power came from a spirit in the underworld, he or she is obligated to observe proper ritualistic behavior as those receiving other spirits do. Evil powers may also be inherited when an elder leaves a bag to a person. The bag must be "fed" by killing persons, often relatives. The witch takes the guise of an animal—dog, turkey, owl, bear, ball of fire, and the like—when he or she goes out to perform rituals. If the witch is killed while in animal form, it will return to its own form and then die in a few days. Sister Inez Hilger, in 1936, had an informant who inherited witch bags from a great grandmother and used one as she had seen her grandmother do:

I inherited her two "medicine bags"—the very powerful one, and another one. I no longer have them. Having them in my possession put me under an obligation to kill one person each year with each bag. This is our old belief. But I did not wish to kill persons. I knew I would regret such a thing on my deathbed. I gave the two bags to two old, distant relatives. I had kept the bags stored in a trunk for a long time. I did use one of them once in the manner in which I had seen my great-grandmother use it. And this is how I used it: I attached a strap to the bag, slipped the strap over my head so it rested on my right shoulder, slipped my left arm through, and let the bag rest on my abdomen just in front of the left hip bone. The body had to be nude when this "medicine bag" was being used, for the bag had to rest on the bare skin. I talked to the bag and then slipped into bed. When in bed I changed into an animal that I wanted to be changed into. I changed into a dog. That is, my spirit changed into a dog; my body stayed in bed. Then I went out of my body but I did not go far away. I only went out here into the woods, and up this hill and then I returned to my body. I did no harm to anyone. If anybody had touched me while in this spirit form, I would have been able to return to my body, but I would have died soon after that. [Hilger 1960:56]

Contemporary Menomini informants in the native-oriented group have the same patterned set of beliefs concerning witches as those described by Skinner in 1913. Concerning the bag, one informant remarked:

He [father] said that when a person gits that bag, he's supposed to use it on somebody and if he doesn't, one of his own dies. ["Feeding the Bag," in L. Spindler 1970]

Another informant describes the witch transformed into a ball of light:

You can see them [witches] coming in a big cloud of light, and you have to watch out. The person gets scairt like he was hypnotized. When this young woman's baby died [next door] they watched around the house and graveyard but couldn't see it [the witch]. It was slick work that time. [L. Spindler, field notes]

A different informant describes the witch transformed into a dog:

My dad started to get witched one time. Dr. White gave him up as dead. That night some boys was goin' to Neopit and met a dog. That dog looked at them and up to his whiskers it was all fire in there and they killed the dog and my dad started gettin' better the next day and we heard an old lady died in S. Branch and so we knew she did it. [L. Spindler, field notes]

The people quoted above are all women. It became obvious after several periods of field work that Menomini native-oriented males talked about witchcraft reluctantly, as it was too dangerous. Transitional males spoke somewhat more freely on the subject, but the acculturated and elite males didn't speak of it at all. A partial explanation for this discrepancy in response between males and females could be that the women in this male-oriented culture recognize their lesser involvement with the important male-dominated "instrumental" activities of the culture, related to the maintenance of the society's institutions. Therefore, their "expressive" roles of mother and wife (see Zelditch 1955 for instrumental-expressive differentiation) may free them somewhat from direct responsibility for the consequences of dealing with important areas such as those subsumed by the "supernatural." A reinforcing factor may have been the fact that the anthropologist collecting the responses is also a woman from a society where the men have played the important instrumental roles.

Witches and wizards are persons who, through self-mortification, such as fasting and sacrifices, have obtained the patronage of some one of the Evil Powers, in return for which they are obliged to slay members of their own tribe as votive offerings. They attack and destroy their victims by magically transforming themselves into balls of fire, owls, bears, foxes, turkeys, and other animals, and traveling from great distances at night with remarkable speed. Arrived at the lodge of his prey, the sorcerer discharges enchanted arrows at him, causing disease, and, if the attacks are repeated, death. Witches are known to have magic bundles, the most notorious of which contain the entire hide of a bear, or the skin of a horned owl, which are worn when assuming the shapes of these animals. With the skins is included a bandoleer, or shoulder pouch, covered with tiny bags holding bad medicines, the worst of which are portions of the body of the terrible Horned Hairy Snake.

The witches are said to be associated in a society having eight members, four using the bear and four the owl as mediums of murder. Their rites are said to include a disgusting form of cannibalism, for witches are supposed to haunt the graveyards where their victims are buried, and so magically to obtain the heart and lungs of the murdered persons, which they are credited with devouring. Witches also destroy their victims by shooting and stabbing rude effigies of them made on the ground or on birch-bark, or by torturing dolls of grass or wood. They also steal the luck away from hunters, sending their arrows or bullets astray; they cause children to drown; and practice other nefarious arts. [Skinner 1921:69–71]

One pervasive theme in Menomini tales and myths is that the hero is helpless without his particular dream-bestowed power, and that he may lose it by abuse, neglect, or lack of constraint. If his bundle is lost or stolen, he is easily overcome by his enemies, or he may starve because he can kill no game. However, the hero is particularly successful only because he has acquired a certain power. Similarly, in contests between individuals, such as those in a struggle between a great *mete·w* and a *wa·beno*, one of the central figures realizes and admits that his power is not strong enough to withstand that of the other, so gives in without further contest. The individual is dependent upon this power as something not of himself, but as something gained by him through the exercise of proper behavior, of which general constraint is an important aspect. (Skinner and Satterlee, part 3, 1915; Hoffman 1896; Bloomfield 1928.)

Whether it is power from good spirits of the upper world, or evil spirits of the underworld, the importance of gaining and maintaining power remains today at the core of the entire native-oriented Menomini value system. One's power—measured in terms of one's ability to conquer the environment—may fluctuate, but it is vital to one's existence. All persons in the group must continually attempt to appease the power-giving spirits.

CEREMONIAL ORGANIZATIONS AS RELATED TO POWER

The *Mete·wen*

The Menomini traditionally had a number of specialized rites. The most important was the *mete·wen* (Mystic Rite or Medicine Dance). Today the *ni·mihe·twan* (Dream Dance) is the important rite for the native-oriented Menomini and is held most often. As one Menomini remarked:

> I think the *mete·wen* is just going to go away gradually; that's what I think. There isn't enough people interested in it, the younger folks . . . they only had *mete·wen* once a year, and that isn't enough for anybody to learn anything from it. And that's what I think; maybe they [the elders] are not interested in it, they don't have it often enough. [Slotkin 1957:13]

This seems to be a rather accurate assessment of what is happening. The Medicine Dance is of less importance today than it was only a few years ago. The four-day ritual is so complicated that only a few of the elders know it in its entirety, and most of them are very aged. The authors were fortunate enough to witness three Medicine Dances during their period of fieldwork.

The Medicine Dance and the Dream Dance are both rituals directly related to the Menomini concept of power—power to combat evil, power to use evil at times, and power to control the environment. The stated intent of the Medicine Dance ritual is to prolong life and insure the good health of its members by assisting them in gaining access to power and protecting them against the machinations of witches and evil power.

The *mete·wen* is the older of the two ceremonies and has the most elaborate ritual. Most students agree that it is probably of early postcontact origin and, as Keesing (1939:47) suggests, possibly a phenomenon springing from the same source of insecurity created by the first impact of contact with Western civilization as in other "nativistic" movements. Many of the elements, however, are of great antiquity, and the ritual and beliefs of the Lodge have been a funda-

The mete·wen *shelter, 1954. The wall tents on the sides are occupied by onlookers and relatives who are not in the society.*

The initiates sit quietly and solemnly, waiting for the ritual to begin.

mental aspect of the religious systems of all central Algonkians. This organization still played a vital role in the lives of the native-oriented Menomini until as late as 1960 and remains an integral part of the belief system of the native oriented.

The *mete·wen* is an exclusive organization with membership by invitation or inheritance of a medicine bag. The candidate pays for his or her instructions in installments. An installment is made for each of the four parts of the ritual after the part has been repeated in instruction. It is believed that the teachings are of no use if the payments are not large. Each member becomes a possessor of a medicine bag (an otter, mink, or other whole small animal skin filled with small packets of herbal medicine), the power to shoot a small magically endowed cowrie shell (a *megi·s*), and a medicine for retrieving it.

The acknowledged intent of the society is to prolong human life, and to this end the lore of real herb, root, and magical medicines, as well as its special property, is zealously guarded. Every prescription is strictly proprietary. Even at the point of death a person may not have it without paying an exorbitant price, though he be a relative or a friend of the owner, and new discoveries and revelations are kept secret until purchased. The lodge also seeks, for a price, to see to the final settlement of the souls of the dead in their future abode, and the relatives pay well for ceremonies in behalf of the deceased. [Skinner 1920:22–23]

The Medicine Dance ritual, which was given to the Menomini by the culture hero *Mɛʔnapos*, is divided into four parts.

The ritual of the Menomini medicine lodge is divided into four parts, the first of which is the dramatization of the initiation of the hero-god Mä'näbus, the ceremonies representing the first mythical performance of the rites. The leaders impersonate the great Gods Below and Above the novice Mä'näbus. The second part is the Jebainoke {or Jebainoket}, the private funeral ceremony at which the soul of a deceased member is recalled from the hereafter, feasted, and dismissed forever, according to the command of Mä'näbus, the master. The third part is the Uswinauamikäsko, or Obliteration Ceremony, a public and more elaborate form of the Jebainoke held in a medicine lodge erected at or near the grave. [Skinner 1920:23–24]

One ceremony which we attended was an initiation ceremony for a young woman who was taking the place of her deceased father and a reinstatement or renewal ceremony for an old member. In conversation with the woman before the ceremony she said excitedly:

They're gonna have a dance here next week—Saturday night and all day Sunday and I'm gonna be put in to take over my dad's place. We're givin' a joint dance with J. His wife died about a year ago too. The old men are out cuttin' poles for the lodge now. My sister said to be sure and invite you folks. It's kinda easier givin' it together; all the food and presents ain't so much then.

[Do you know what the different motions and songs mean in the dance?]
I don't know much about it. I've watched it. [She feigns innocence, as the ceremony is secret.] They haven't told me. They're gonna sing evenings at L.'s and they'll tell me then what to do. F. is supposed to tell me all about it.

[Where will you get your medicine bag?]
They're havin' trouble about that. I don't know what become of it [father's medicine bag]. They're tryin' to get a bag from someone who has three or four. They'd have to clean the bag out. Each person would donate a little medicine for my bag. F. [medicine man] will tell me all about it.

[Who will take your father's place?]
There'll be some Winnebago, M., who is gonna take the place of my father

While the meteˑwen *drum is beaten and one of the elders sings, a ritual offering of water is made to the candidate.*

Saturday night and after that he's like my dad. They're gonna "dress him" and adopt him Saturday night and give him a new suit of clothes and a rug and feed him. There'll be people from Wabeno and Wisconsin Rapids there.

It can be inferred that the length of time spent in learning the ritual and the amount of payment is greatly reduced today.

The singing for these particular Medicine Lodge rites began three days before the opening of the formal ceremony. Three elders talked to the deceased man's "spirit" just "like he was here," to inform him that a *meteˑwen* was being held for him and to ask him if the gifts were sufficient, and if it was alright for M. to take his place as a stepfather for the two initiates, and other of the deceased relations.

The sponsor was a Catholic who said, "I wish I had followed that up, but I was baptized too soon." He owns an inherited medicine bag and feels that his wife died because the bag's "hunger" had not been satisfied by the giving of a ceremony. So he proposed that one be given so that "no more bad luck" would befall any members of his family.

No medicine bag for the initiate was available. "A week ago the hock shop [in Shawano] was full of them," said one of the women charged with responsibility by the sponsor for arrangements, "but everybody must of got theirs for the dance, so there's none left when we need one." George Spindler, commissioned as one of the four *skaˑpeˑwes* (ritual attendants and messengers) for the affair, was given two wool blankets and two packages of plug tobacco and asked to approach several elders who were thought to have bags, but who, for various reasons, were not coming to the ceremony. These attempts were unsuccessful, and the ceremony began without any bag for the initiate. The problem was solved when one of the Winnebago visitors gave up an "extra one" she had in exchange for the blankets and tobacco.

One of the high points of the ceremony was the "dressing" of the visitor taking the initiate's father's (recently deceased) place as ritual father. Behind a blanket held up by two of the *ska·pe·wes* he was washed and then dressed from the skin out, with necktie, tie clasp, socks, shoes, underwear, suit, and hat. After that, with the blanket down, he was fed a complete meal, with soup, fried chicken, potatoes, rice, blueberry pie, and coffee, which he ate on an oilcloth spread out before him, in his new clothing. Finished with his meal, which he ate slowly and thoroughly while everyone watched, he led each of four dancing rounds, carrying one of the blankets given to him, and a new aluminum pail.

The Medicine Lodge ceremony just referred to was held in a long, round-roofed structure with rounded ends made of bent saplings and covered with canvas instead of the bark that was used in earlier days. The lodge was approximately 50 feet long and 15 feet wide. Within it was an elongated circular path around which the members danced, with a hearth at one end and a mat for the candidate to kneel on (or fall on) at the other. On a cross-pole in the middle hung the blankets and calico that were to be given by the families "putting up" the ceremony to the four leaders after the ritual was finished. On another

The ritual father dances around the lodge with some of his gifts.

mat along one side the leaders sat, giving their chants, telling the legends, or beating the water drum. Along the horizontal poles of the framework of the sides hung the medicine bags of the members, when they were not being used. The ritual continued from sunset one day to sunset the next. The four *ose·ha·wuk* (*mete·wen* leaders), sometimes singly, sometimes together, exhorted the members to follow the *mete·wen* way carefully and told the story of the Lodge's origin, interspersing their telling with songs that can be sung correctly only by a throat long practiced in giving the right resonance and tremolo to what seem to be minor keys. At intervals some, or all, of the members danced around the circular path with a loose-jointed step that was at the same time graceful and bearlike, holding their medicine bags before them with both hands, and shaking them at the nondancers so that they might feel their power. Occasionally, the peculiar cry that is the earmark of the *mete·wen* ceremony, "Whe-ho-ho-ho-ho!" rang out above the reverberations of the water drum.

The most dramatic part of the ritual was the time when the candidate was "shot" with the medicine bags of the four *ose·ha·wuk*, and then received her own, to become a fullfledged *mete·w*. Before this important moment, the candidate had received instructions from one of the *ose·ha·wuk* concerning the use of the medicine bag and the powerful medicines it contained. She had to pay for these revelations. She passed through many hours of ritual leading up to this point, for the "shooting" does not take place until a few hours before the close of the ceremony.

The candidate dances slowly around the lodge with one of the elders behind her.

The candidate collapses when "shot"; the old man with her was reinitiated in this ceremony.

When the long-awaited moment arrived, the male members of the Lodge danced around the long circle of the lodge, chanting as they went, to the accompaniment of water drum and rattle. The four leaders passed the candidate, then proceeded to the end of the lodge opposite the candidate, who was standing before a blanket spread on the ground. At this point one of the leaders chanted, "I will now shoot the *megi·s* [the cowrie shell] at her, that she may feel its power and become our child." Then, one at a time, each of the *ose·ha·wuk* blew on his medicine bag, and danced rapidly toward the candidate, shouting, "Whe-ho-ho-ho-ho-ho!" When he neared the candidate, who was trembling in anticipation of receiving the full impact of the powerful medicines, he jerked his medicine bag up and forward, at the same moment crying "Ho!" and thrusting it directly at the initiate. The candidate shuddered with the force of the shot. She was not making believe, for she had been taught that the medicine bag has great power, and she felt it, as one man expressed it, "Just like lightning had struck you."

When the last of the four *ose·ha·wuk* had shot her with his medicine bag, the power-filled candidate collapsed, apparently knocked unconscious by the terrible force. She appeared to remain unconscious until she was revived. While one of the leaders chanted, "Here you have seen the power of the *mete·wen* and the *megi·s* given to Mɛʔnapos by Mɛ·c-awɛtok [the Supreme Being] that we have gotten from him. Our sister lying before us has had it put into her heart. She, and all of our children will feel its strength." The other *mete·wuk* then gathered around the prostrate form and covered her with their medicine bags. Then an *ose·ha·w* raised the initiate by her shoulders, shook her, and a *megi·s* fell from her mouth. As consciousness returned to the initiate, she slowly rose from the ground and began a dance, imitating the Great Bear, while showing her *megi·s* to all around her. Then she went before the *ose·ha·wuk*; one of whom lectured to her about the meaning of her initiation and presented her with his own medicine bag. The initiate has to try to see if she has the sacred power. She blew on the bag, then circled the lodge, dancing slowly and thrusting the bag at various of the members. As each *metɛ·w* was shot, he sank to the ground, but revived quickly, got up, and circled the lodge himself, using his own medicine bag in the same way.

This is a dangerous time for anyone not a member of the lodge to be too close, for he may get hit with a stray shot. If this does happen, everything stops, while the *ose·ha·wuk* seek out the careless *metɛ·w* who aimed so badly, and shoot him in turn. This, along with a number of other procedures, usually enables the leaders to extract the stray *megi·s*, and the victim survives.[12]

By this time it was noon of the last day of the ceremony. It continued until sundown, with more chants, drumming, shooting, and ritual. However, for the initiate the climax was over, for she had new life and power. She had become a *metɛ·w*.

> *Now comes the most spectacular, and one of the most important, parts of the ceremony—the shooting of the sacred power into the candidate by the four osehauwuk. Lining up in the eastern end of the lodge, each shaman in turn takes his animal skin medicine-bag, blows on its head, and holding it before his breast, trots down the lodge. In front of the candidate he points it, jerks its head forward, and the essence of its power passes into the candidate's body. The novice quivers, and, on the fourth shot, collapses, falling on his face. The fourth shaman leaves his medicine-bag lying on the candidate's back, for him to keep as his own thereafter. The shamans then shake the candidate to remove all the beads from his body.* [Skinner 1920:179–180]

The leaders of the *metɛ·wen* are all-important, for it is only from their memories that the secret songs, speeches, and steps of the ritual may issue. There were only four such men during the authors' fieldwork period who knew the ritual, which accounts in large measure for its dying out. Only one of these four men is still alive (1970). The Lodge is probably only about 300 years old, as suggested earlier, but many of the native-oriented Menomini today think of it as being the "real" Menomini religion.

The medicine bags have both good and evil power. Though they are all-important in the life-renewal aspects of the *metɛ·wen* and contains herbs and medications for curing, they are called "witch bags" in English by members and nonmembers alike. Everyone agrees that the bags can kill, and that a bag unsatiated by a ceremony becomes very dangerous, causing death or illness for the owner or his close kin.

---

[12] George Spindler was hit by a stray shot and spent a week in the hospital with a fever of "undiagnosed origin." This was interpreted as proof of the power of the "medicine." (See G. Spindler and L. Spindler 1970.)

Your grandfathers give you in addition all sorts of medicine-bags that shall be right and great for you and your people to use. The greatest one, to begin with, is the otter-skin; it is the leader. Next is the mink, especially a white one, if you can get it, after the fashion of your grandfathers' bags. Different kinds of animals you shall use in their likeness, and it shall continue in rotation along the north side {of the lodge}.

The serpent-skin, representing the horned, hairy snakes, shall be the bag of those who know and have that one and its medicines of both good and evil. [Skinner 1920:61–62]

The *Nĭ·mihɛ·twan*

The *nĭ·mihɛ·twan* or Dream Dance,[13] introduced about 1879, is today the major ceremonial organization still operating among the native-oriented Menomini. It too, like the *metɛ·wen*, originated as a "nativistic" movement—a reaction to the disorganizing and threatening impact of Western civilization. It is related to the "Ghost Dance" originating farther west but is more accomodative in orientation. The rite represents a combination of some Christian with many aboriginal elements, but is essentially native North American in pattern and has been invested with characteristic Menomini attitudes and values.

Unlike the *metɛ·wen*, membership in the Dream Dance group is relatively open, and the sacred knowledge is obtained at the cost of only a few ritual gifts. Further, the weekly meetings or seasonal rites are more intimate and more directly related to everyday life. Since the rite is definitely a product of acculturative pressures, it is flexible and has subsumed many of the functions of other rites. The dogma and cosmology of the organization resemble traditional Menomini beliefs. It is crucial that a man obtain the supernatural power necessary to enable him to carry out his activites, and, as was true before the Dream Dance came to the Menomini, this is done by petitioning the spirits, but through the sacred drum and the ritual related to it.

The doctrines of the Dream Dance group are based on revelations received by a young Sioux woman from the Great Spirit. He gave her the original Drum and taught her the rituals. One of the members related the contemporary version of the origin myth:

They who are White [White soldiers] killed almost all the Sioux [in a battle]. It was then that the woman—she is said to have hidden among reeds; in order to breathe there, she parted the leaves [of the reeds]. She probably lay in the water for four days. When four days had passed, it is said that the Spirit [*awɛ·tok*] then came to her. He probably told her, "Come, arise." At that time she thought it was only some person; she did not know that it was the Spirit who was speaking to her. And he told her this. A little while later she arose from the water. Oh, I pity you!" he told her. "Arise!" he told her. "You will go eat; it is I who will take you. Nothing is going to happen to

---

[13] *Nĭ·mihɛ·twan* means literally "dancing rite," but it has long been referred to as the Dream Dance.

you; it is I who pity you," that one probably told her, he who was standing there above the water. . . . Then he is said to have taken her where these White men [mo·hkoma·nak] were eating; he took her there. "No one will see you. It is I who intend to help you," he told her. "Do not be afraid; come with me." Then she went with that one; he took her there. A big table was there [in the White soldiers' camp]; one plate was not being used. It is said that he then pointed it out to her, so that she could eat as much as she desired [invisible to the White soldiers]. When she was full, he took her some place.

She went with him. When she opened her eyes, she saw that Drum there. "Well, then, this is what I give you," he told her. At that time the Drum probably made a noise, and she saw the drumsticks moving. She heard singing. She listened to them there; at first she heard them singing four songs there.

Well, after this was finished, the Spirit spoke to her. He told her everything; he told her how the Indian should perform it [the Dancing Rite]; he gave her to understand how to do everything that is good. [He told her] the way everyone should act: to help himself, to be good to one another. That they should not be the way they still are—people harming one another, killing one another—no! That was what the Spirit told her. "I give you only that which is good," he told her. [Translation, in Slotkin 1957:17–18.]

Many years ago, during a war between the Indians and the Whites, the natives were driven out of their country. A young girl became separated from the rest of her party and secreted herself in the bushes until dark, when she made her way to a river and hid under an overhanging bank. There she remained for eight days. All that time she had nothing to eat and saw no one.

As she fasted with a downcast heart, a spirit came to her in her hiding place, and called to her in her own language: "Poor little girl. Come out and eat. It is time for you to break your fast. Do not be afraid, I am going to give you happiness because your people have been expelled from their country, and because of your suffering you have won my pity. Now your troubles are at an end. Go and join the enemy, but say nothing. Go to their table, help yourself, and no one shall see that you are not one of them. Then come away and you shall find your friends. You shall travel through the thick forests and over open plains, even among the White people, but fear nothing. Look straight ahead and not backwards or downwards. Even though the White people pass so closely in front of you as almost to touch you, do not fear, for they shall not see you."

"When you arrive among your people once more, eat and be satisfied. Then you may all escape through the prairies and the woods, through the ranks of the enemy, and you shall never be seen, for I shall protect you. When they have all reached safety I want you to tell them that I sent you to give them power and strength. Instruct them to make a little drum {the drum has grown bigger since} to decorate it, and elevate it above the ground, for as it came from the heavens, so it must stay above the earth. Then your people are to beat upon it whenever you desire my aid; and, as your prayers arise to my ears with the sound of the drum, I shall grant your heart's desire."

The Dream Dance drum most frequently used in services. The beadwork around the top tells the story of the origin of the rite. Note also the ordinary drumsticks, sacred pipe, tobacco, and the "chief" drumstick (beaded, to the left of the drum).

"When you feel sad at heart, or sick, or fear war, or desire victory in battle, tell it to the drum, which you shall call your grandfather, and give it a present of tobacco, and your words shall be wafted to me. You shall receive help every time you use it, but you must not beat upon it without cause. You shall have joy and success in all your undertakings. Tobacco must be used to make the spirit of the drum, your grandfather, happy, and love and friendship shall rule among its users."

"No worthy man shall be prevented from taking part in these rites, and those who participate must live clean and honest lives, cease drinking, be sober, follow the rules I have laid down for you. . . . You must never neglect the drum, your grandfather, and you must use it at intervals in remembrance of me. Now, go where your people are, and tell them of my instructions, and cause them to spread the news throughout all the Indian nations, that they too may receive my help." [Skinner 1915:175–176]

The *ni·mihe·twan* ritual centers upon a large drum, about 30 inches in diameter, about 12 inches deep, constructed of rawhide stretched over a circular wooden frame. There are four such drums in the native-oriented group. The head of the drum is painted red, to symbolize the dangerous spirits, and blue, to symbolize the good spirits—corresponding to the dualistic concept of the universe held traditionally by the Menomini—with a yellow line bisecting these two colors to symbolize the course of the sun and the right path of life. The sides are decorated with beadwork in the form of symbols denoting the origin of the rite.

Each drum has a number of offices, which are related to each "leg" of the drum—one for each of the four directions of the compass. There is a drum owner, a man in the older age group, who retains major responsibility for the conduct of the ceremonies in which it is used. He is the authority on proper ritual, and he is supposed to look out "like a father" for the people occupying offices connected with his drum and their families. "He sits there just like God, and watches what we do. If we do anything wrong [in the ritual] he is supposed to tell us. He is supposed to look out for us too, and not be stingy with anything." There is also a "keeper" for each drum who maintains the drum in his home in its sacred wrappings, keeps a lighted lantern near it at night, and is responsible for its care.

When a "song service" (which may be held any time) or a seasonal rite is being conducted, from four to eight men sit around the drum, singing in chorus and hitting the drum in unison. The drum has a deep and resonant tone that is exhilarating, if deafening—especially in the confines of a small room. The floor, windows, and human bodies vibrate with every beat. The people claim that the service makes them "feel good," that they forget their worries and troubles. The ritual is, indeed, a means of renewing power. "The old man in the drum," *Kemɛ·hsomen,* is the intermediary between man and spirits, particularly *Kesɛ·maneto·w* (Great Spirit). When the drum is hit, its voice, symbolized by a

Children at the Zoar community hall, where most Dream Dance song services were held.

small bell suspended on a wire inside the drum and most apparent in the deep voice of the drum itself, notifies the spirits through *Kemε·hsomen* that the ceremony is being held and asks for their "blessings." "When that drum is hit, his [*Kemε·hsomen's*] voice is sent all over, in all four directions, to all those spirits. *Kesε·maneto·w* hears that and gives us what we ask for. That old man in the drum gets those messages out." It is believed that in order to keep group and individual access to sacred, life-giving power intact, it is necessary to hold the seasonal rites and frequent song services. Without this access to power, bad luck will ensue. Through the medium of the rites and proper ceremonial sacrifices (mostly of tobacco), the drums are a means of renewing power and therefore securing good luck, as well as revitalizing the spirits of the participants.

During the meetings, when drumming, singing, or praying is not going on, someone is speaking. One of the old men exhorts all present to do the right things, usually ending with a plea to observe more closely the old ways. The drum has a number of special commandments (*kaki·hkotakan tε·wε·hekan*) that are supposed to guide the conduct of the men and women who are members of the Dream Dance group. The requirements are congruent with those accepted for being a "good" Menomini (see specific requirements given in the section on maintaining power, p. 51). After the meetings anyone may speak. All these speeches are presented and received in a highly formal and very serious manner. Anyone who gets up to speak, including even the missionary, is heard with the greatest courtesy and respect. Sometimes during the meeting, usually at the beginning or end of any speech in which exhortation or explanation is involved, the speaker says something like this: "I am not proud just because I know this little. It is because my father was important in this and I got it from him, not because of myself" (see p. 20).

The drum (*tε·wε·hekan*) is the most sacred object in the Dream Dance or powwow for a variety of reasons. It is the most important material embodiment of power. It is believed that the Great Spirit, and all the good spirits he created, put some of their power into the original Drum given to the Sioux woman who is believed to have introduced the ritual to the Menomini (Slotkin 1957:35). When asked what the Drum's power can do, one informant replied:

> Well, if you ask him anything, if you want something, put your tobacco there. Say, "I want to go hunting; I want to go hunt deer. I want to go pick berries." Anything like that. Put your tobacco in there. Not all persons can do that successfully; just those that believes in the Drum, he can get help from the Drum. [Slotkin 1957:35]

It is believed that the power of the drum is so strong that the drum, like the Menomini elder performing an act of witchcraft, can cause some misfortune to come to a person who openly flouts the moral code of the group. An elderly informant relates an incident of this sort:

> Some way, this old lady got mad, and took an axe, a sharp axe, and hit the Drum. She was going to bust that Drum entirely. [She] hit that Drum once;

The elders watch over the Dream Dance services.

couldn't break it. And hit that Drum again twice; couldn't do nothing. So she hits that Drum again third time; no. But the fourth time, then that axe went through. [What does that show?] That shows that there's something in the Drum, pretty strong. When she bust that Drum [on] purpose—that old lady had a brother—and she lost this brother right away, because she done this wrong. [Slotkin 1957:36]

The drums are also a source of individual powers, particularly for the drum keeper who has the drum in his house, and cares for it. The relationship is virtually identical to that maintained with the guardian spirit gained through the Great Fast, usually through the medium of a sacred bundle representing that spirit, and with the relationship now maintained with individual, inherited guardians. One night a drum keeper had a dream. In the dream he was out hunting and two deer approached him. One of them said, "I thought I'd tell you, that fellow [the other deer], he just gave you his life." This dream prompted the man to go out hunting the next evening. In order to insure the prophecy and to take advantage of the offer of the deer to "give up his life," the Menomini man made a sacrifice to the drum in order to notify the powers of his and the deer's decision, and to secure the "luck" (the power) to perform the deed successfully. He said:

Well, I had some tobacco, and I cut it up and put it in the tobacco boxes [ceremonial wooden bowls associated with the drum] and lit some of it in two pipes. Anything you do, you got to have tobacco. Just the plug kind—it goes farther that way. If you're going out hunting, if you're keeping a drum, and you have some tobacco cut up in fine pieces, you put it by the drums, and you smoke some yourself. I smoked first one [pipe] then the other. And I talked to that drum, like if I was talking to you. I'd say. "I'm going out. I'm going to try to get some meat. Would you mind helping me out?"

He went out hunting after the sacrifice to the drum. He waited by a salt lick for several hours until it was almost too dark to see any more. Finally, two deer approach the lick. One of them threw up his head, startled, probably, by the scent of the man, and bounded off in the brush. The other started to run, then stopped and turned toward the man. The Menomini shot this one, the one that gave him his life in the dream the night before, through the heart. "That's happened many times. I'd ask for help. . . . I'd get it. I believe to this day that it's this way. I asked for that deer, and I got it."

The native-oriented system of belief is encapsulated in this sequence of events just described: the dependence of the individual upon revelation through dreams; the importance of keeping one's access to power intact; the dependence upon the power thus gained for success in all the ventures of life; the quiescent, waiting expectancy that if the proper rituals are observed, "fate" (as we might term it) will provide; the autonomous character of the relationship between these powers and the individual; all of this is clear. The Dream Dance reaffirms the validity of the traditional cultural system each time it is held, even though it began as a religious movement in recent times. Without such visible manifestations of a separate identity and belief, the native-oriented group is unlikely to exist for long.

Membership in the Dream Dance is dwindling today. One member sadly stated: ". . . we ain't much of us left. . . . And we are short handed today. We ain't got enough people to fill out the Drum the way it's supposed to be" (Slotkin 1957:16). An elderly woman member of the group, when asked about the fate of the group, passionately exclaimed:

> . . . they say, "It's going to be lost, after a while." The different Catholic people, they always say, "It's going to be lost, this Indian way." No! She [is] not going [to be] lost! There's lots of Indians all over, all kinds; the same religion what I got, he's got it! She's not going [to be] lost! If every tribe said that, she'd be lost; she'd be lost, I guess. But never! She's not going [to be] lost! I know it myself! Lots [of people] know it! [Slotkin 1957:15]

The *Okeceta·we·se·man*

The *Okeceta·we·se·man* (Chief's, or Warrior's, Dance) is the third rite held by the native-oriented group. The Menomini had it "long ago." As one of the leaders explained:

> It was a real War Dance then. They could take out the boys, and come back with the things they were after [scalps] before you [Whitemen] come over. It died out until just lately—it was lost. Then the Chippewa came over [about

1925] when I was a boy, and they told the Menomini, "We didn't come here to show you anything, but if you want to do it this way—you got some songs of your own, but maybe you'd like to do it the way we do it." So now this is a copy of the Chippewa, on the good side of it, not just for war. We use this now for a religion. Like if you were to go to church. Of course it's also used for the boys being drafted. We had a War Dance for the boys over there in Korea. We do it regularly for those boys.

The *okeceta·we·se·man* should be given with the seasonal rites of the *ni·mihe·twan*. "We always used to wind up the last day of the powwow with the War Dance. Now there's too many workin' so we let that last day go" (so the *ni·mihe·twan* can be held over the weekend). The War Dance, like the *ni·mihe·twan*, is often given more casually. The same leader continues:

> We go over there . . . put tobacco down and just sing most every evening. Pretty soon the whole family was there. Then the neighbors would come over. It made a pretty good habit. It's the same way like with the *ni·mihe·twan*. You don't have to do it any certain date. There's regular ceremonies come just certain times of the year [seasonal rites] but otherwise it's any time you feel like it.

There are actually more War Dance drums in the native-oriented group than *ni·mihe·twan* drums. During our earlier field work there were at least six active drums, owned by specific individuals who were responsible for their care and use. The drums are not as sacred as those in the *ni·mihe·twan*, but no ceremonial object can be treated lightly. The War Dance is also more light-hearted than the *ni·mihe·twan*. At every rite we attended there was a lot of whooping and dancing, and the songs and drumming have a beat that is irresistible. Old men and women who appear to be on their last legs will get up during a dance and join in like they had suddenly lost their years. Nevertheless, there is a strong sacred aspect to the ceremony. Each of the songs is connected to the spirits in one of the four cardinal directions. When these songs are sung, these spirits are propitiated. Before the singing begins, a prayer of notification is given by one of the older men present who informs *maʔmaw ko·hne·waw* (our Great Father), and the *awe·tokak* (spirits) of the purpose of the dance, and asks, for example, ". . . to help out each and every one in the hall at the time, and to watch out for those boys over in Korea."

When we recorded the songs at one rite, the leader asked, ". . . don't think anything of what this Whiteman is doing. It isn't as if we were doing anything wrong. Don't think hard about us, for what we are going to do." Near the end of the singing and dancing he named four songs, one for each cardinal direction, and said again to our Great Father:

> I just named these four songs. For my part, I'm glad we did just what we did [recording the songs]. It was the right thing to do, so our children and

The War Dance drums and singers at an informal "song service."

their children can hear these songs. We don't want to bother you [our Great Father] with this and that. Maybe you could watch out for us, and all the boys over there. Now we will quit for awhile, so I will name those four songs. [G. Spindler, field notes]

Like the *ni·mihe·twan*, the *okeceta·we·se·man* gains and maintains power. In this way it is a significant support for the continuing validity of the native-oriented group and its culture. Power maintenance is an underlying assumption in the conduct of the ceremony and the prayers. With power one can ward off sorcery, and even physical damage. The following version of the origin story makes this clear.

There was a great Menomini chief, the greatest of all, a long time ago, around Sturgeon Bay. They had guns by that time though. This chief was always leading war parties, with maybe thirty or forty Menomini. One time they went to fight the Sioux, two hundred of them. They was up a hill. There was a Potowatomi chief there too, but he was not as great. The Menomini told the Potowatomi chief to take the warriors back across the river. Then they, the Sioux, shoot at the Menomini chief alone. But they can't kill him. He run back and forth . . . they shoot, but they couldn't hurt him. So he come across the river and joined his [the Menomini war party]. Just then a last shot came across the river and hits him in the belly. Then he takes off his fur belt, strikes it, and bullets drop out, all flattened. That was how the *okeceta·we·se·man* started, and they got all them songs in there. That chief, he had that power.

He made that drum [the drum used in the rite] and he painted his totem on it. [G. Spindler, field notes]

WITCHCRAFT AND SOCIAL CONTROL

"No one has the right, on the basis of position or prestige, to exercise direct authority over another, not even a father over his son." This has been true of the Menomini since the time of the first contacts with Whites. In spite of certain formal structures of control during the pre-fur-trade period, it is probable that little direct secular authority was exercised by any leader among the Menomini. The Menomini were described by the Jesuit Father Allouez as a people who "have neither laws, nor police, nor magistrates to check disorder" (quoted in Keesing 1939:40). Even earlier Nicholas Perrote, the first French fur trader to visit the Menomini in 1667, remarked, "The savage does not know what it is to obey. . . . The father does not venture to exercise authority over his son. . . ." In 1913, Skinner, who worked closely with the Menomini for many years, remarked, "Among themselves, the rights of the individual were paramount. . . ." (Fuller versions of all these quotes are given in the introduction to this chapter.)

Among the present native-oriented group there is virtually no "leadership" in our sense of the word. One day a group was sitting about after an afternoon of dancing for tourists at a nearby "woodland bowl." It had been suggested that it would be helpful to have a battery-operated loudspeaker system for the master of ceremonies to use in his announcements to the assembled crowd. A Whiteman had offered to sell one to them for $50. The group was faced with the decision—should they or should they not buy it? Everyone sat quietly, saying nothing. A man of about forty years who was the intermediary between the group and the proprietors of the "bowl" and the owner of the loudspeaker system said, "What does the group think?" No one spoke for a long time. Someone finally said, "Well sometimes those people can't hardly hear." An indistinguishable murmur or two emitted from the assemblage—neither in agreement or dissent— or so it seemed, at least. Another period of quiet waiting. Another question by the intermediary. "Well, what does the group think?" Another murmur or two. So it went for some time. So long that the White man, who was waiting in his car for their decision, came over. "Well, what's the answer? Do you want to buy it or don't you? I can't wait all day." No response. In exasperation he stomped back to his car. "This man, he wants to know. What does the group think?" the query came again. No arguments, no open discussion, a few half-voiced murmurs. The people standing and sitting around left to attend to other business. Had a decision been reached? We thought not, but we were wrong. The intermediary went over to talk to the White man. He said, somewhat apologetically, "I guess the people don't want to spend the money." How did he know? Apparently, there had been no sentiments expressed in favor of the proposition other than the comment that "those people can't hardly hear." The absence of general consensus was enough. No "leader" would try to coerce or convince others that a given course of action was best, even though the intermediary thought, as we knew he did in this instance from other discussions with him, that a loudspeaker system was essential.

Elders are the "cynosure" of Menomini society—individuals who attract the bulk of attention and public prestige (see LaBarre 1946:173 for use of the term). Powers become stronger as one grows older. Thus the elders possess the greatest supernatural power because they have lived the longest, have knowledge of the esoteric rituals through which power is secured and maintained, and because, like children, they are closest to the supernatural. The Menomini regard life as a never-ending cycle through which one passes to be born again. This emphasis on age is patterned into the whole ceremonial and belief complex. It is the "old man" (grandfather) who is represented by the Dream Dance drum and who notifies the spirits related to the four directions of the needs and wants of the members. It is the old men who exhort the Medicine Lodge and Dream Dance groups to live right—not to be aggressive, not to boast, nor to gossip—to be generous and kindly to others, especially old people.

It is the elders who know the rituals, have the greatest access to the spirits and their powers, and, therefore, have potential for both beneficent and harmful behavior, can prophesy with their dreams, and are the authorities for questions on kin relationships. They are, therefore, all "leaders" in a sense. Their authority is sharply limited, however. Even the oldest man in the group referred to previously, the only member who went through the Great Fast, does not exert direct authority over others. For example, he once took some liberties with the Dream Dance drum of which he is "owner," kept by a younger man in his own home. To be a drum keeper is to be entirely responsible for the care and maintenance of the drum. Not even the owner is supposed to remove it to use in a ceremony without the direct knowledge and permission of the keeper. Under the pressure of unusual circumstances that arose in the absence of the drum keeper the old man removed the drum from the keeper's house to use in a cere-mony. Upon learning of this, the younger man was quite disturbed and made a few very indirectly critical statements to others concerning the old man's action. At a song service some time later the old man arose to make a short speech. "My children, I am good to you. I care for you all the time. I pray for you to the Great Spirit. . . . Now somebody here does not feel good about things somehow." (See p. 22 for the full quote). He then proceeded to apologize indirectly for his action and added, "I did not want to hurt anyone's feelings. . . ." Even with his high status as an authority on all things important in the traditional framework of the native-oriented group, and even with his great capacity for good or evil because of his access to great powers, he did not and could not exercise direct authority over another younger man charged with an inviolable responsibility. In his indirect apology, he exhibited his concern about possibly having given offense for seeming to have exercised an authority he did not have. Never during our fieldwork did we observe an exception to the mode of leadership described.

In a system of this kind social control must function in indirect and subtle ways. Some of the ways in which social controls are effected among the native-oriented Menomini are: by indirect gossip (the drum keeper said enough about the old man's "indiscretion" so that the old man was brought to make a virtual apology); by reward (the old man can cure the ill and intercede for the people with his powers); by dreams [many times people have dreams that are publicly interpreted as prophecies of dire results for drinking, desertion, and failing to keep up ritual observances (see p. 49)]; by witchcraft (the constant threat that socially deviant behavior will result in the use of sorcery by the injured party). This last means of social control—witchcraft—is the most dramatic and the most effective.

According to the Menomini belief system, all powerful elders are potential witches. Again, the emphasis is upon power, which is today, and was probably in precontact times, the most important force in the lives of the Menomini. From the earliest accounts one might conclude that powerful shamans existed who possessed both good and evil tutelary powers and that the same shaman who performed an act of witchcraft on his patient might also cure him of the effects of this act. The contemporary Menomini witch also plays a segmentalized role, utilizing good as well as evil powers obtained from specific tutelary spirits of the underworld or through the use of a witch bag inherited from relatives or friends. So the same person who adopted several orphaned boys and who is in general considered wise and generous could, upon occasion, use his evil powers. The Menomini belief system also equates the witch with the "protector," one who watches to see that members of the group do not get too far out of line, that they conform to the basic rules that represent the Menomini value system. As the informant already quoted said, "He [an elder observing a ritual] sits there just like God, and watches what we do. If we do anything wrong, he is supposed to tell us. He is supposed to look out for us too, and not be stingy with anything."

In contrast to the situation in the majority of cultures for which witchcraft is described in the literature, the Menomini witch is not the deviant, the antisocial person, or the one who neglects social obligations, or the agitator who is accused of witchcraft and scapegoated by the community. He or she belongs to the group with greatest power and prestige—the elders. Social control is achieved among the native-oriented group by the threat of witchcraft by power figures rather than through accusation of the witch by the community. These dynamics of social control are strikingly different from those found in many other cultural systems. In contrast to the Menomini belief, which defines the witch as a respected elder who controls the deviant, the majority of cultures described in the literature define the witch as the recipient of punishment, a symbol of evil—the deviant who represents all of the negative values of the culture (see Fitzgerald 1964). The Menomini system, which is lacking in superordinate controls in the ordinary political power sense, provides fertile ground for the development of witchcraft as a kind of control.[14]

---

[14] We do not intend our analysis of witchcraft and social control in the present native-oriented group as a model to be applied without modification to the traditional cultural system when it was intact. Though the general characterization of the Menomini, past and present, as lacking strong forms of direct secular authority holds good, it is also true that most of the secular machinery of political and social adjudication and control that did exist in aboriginal times has long since ceased to function. It is probable that, as a consequence, witchcraft is more important in the native-oriented group today than it was in the past, even though many of the specific patterns and the general style have remained in force for a long time.

Everyone knows that he or she must repress hostile emotions (control of overt aggression), practice self-control (equanimity under duress), show concern for others (generosity, hospitality), respect others' rights (autonomy), show respect for elders, and never behave in an aggressive manner (quarrel, be too successful at any endeavor, show off). Children are taught by the elders at a very early age what proper behavior is. The Dream Dance drum has its own set of commandments similar to the requisites mentioned here (see p. 51). The good man lives quietly (quiescently) and observes constantly the sacrifices required to maintain good relations with the sources of his powers (in a latescent manner).

The fear of witchcraft is more than a concern about a specific act or situation; it is converted into a state of generalized apprehension. The very young child has been taught to fear owls, representing an evil spirit of the underworld, and as he grows older, he has the feeling that he is being constantly watched. This fear is not operative at the explicit level only but has become internalized so that it is "conscience-like" in its effect, with guilt factors present (L. Spindler 1970).

What are the penalties for deviating? Following are some accounts of native-oriented persons who were witched or anticipated being witched for exceeding cultural norms or disregarding amenities.[15] The incidents deal with persons known and named by the informants. Most members of the group know and agree upon the reason why the victims were witched though no one person told of being witched himself or herself. Members of this group do not feel the need to elaborate about incidents that happened in the distant past or to unknown people, unlike informants from other acculturative groups (see L. Spindler 1970).[16] The accounts are abbreviated and are related in a simple, matter-of-fact manner. The power of the witch is accepted as a given factor.

Offending Elders

Account 1

Old Sh. was goin' to give away his bag. We took care of him when he was alone. My father used to tell us we were supposed to always help out old people and do all we can and never make a fuss, because some day you might come across some old person who might happen to have that bag. No person can ever get the best of you or hurt you if you have that bag. "Just tell that old person you don't want no pay—don't take it at first. Turn

---

[15] Accounts 4, 5, 8, 9, 10 and 11 were given by women who are transitional now but who were raised by native-oriented parents, and their stories conform to the native-oriented pattern.

[16] The number and types of witchcraft accounts vary sharply in the various acculturative groups. This became clear after a detailed motif analysis of the accounts was made by L. Walker (1966). Accounts of the native-oriented members involved only "basic Menomini" motifs (see L. Spindler 1970). The accounts of witchcraft at other levels include introduced elements foreign to the traditional pattern as well as elaborations of old elements.

it down so you won't hurt their feelings and make him think you did it just for pay."

Sh. thought a lot of me and said, to my husband, "Your wife will lead you right." One time Sh. said if we wanted it [the bag], no one could pick on us. He asked us and said that he was gonna leave it. He asked me one evenin', "What do you think? Would it be right for you to take that?"

Another thing they used to say if you hurt old men's feelings, your child might die and hurt your feelings. I talked to Sh. in a nice way and tried to find a way not to hurt his feelings.

Account 2

[Question: Did your mother or father do much preaching, telling you what you should do?]

Yes. My mother did a lot of preachin'. She always told me to be nice to people, especially older people. She said to always wait on older people and never ask them for anything or they might hurt you. When I married B. she said, "Always be good to that old lady [mother-in-law]. Beat her up in the morning and get breakfast and do what she says. Don't lie around and look at books or anything like that. Get up early and work real hard, then she won't get mad at you. If she does, she won't hurt you, but she'll get someone you like best like your brother or mother or sister."

Account 3

A long time ago they never took children to doin's. If they did, the child had to sit still, because if it would stare at one person, the person wouldn't like it. My mother never took us anyplace. It's different now. All those old people are gone. There was one old lady we was always afraid of. When they'd have a powwow down at the hall full of people, one old lady would just walk around and look at each person and size them up from head to foot. M. used to put her head down and she'd feel that old lady lookin' at her. When they had the Medicine Dance, that old lady used to shoot her bag [beaver skin] around. It's kinda dangerous you know. You still can't trust 'em [people shooting medicine bags during the metɛ·wen ceremony].

Account 4

[Did you hear much about witchcraft?]

Yes, one time when it happened to my sister's baby. N. [medicine man] helped me. My sister's girl was threatened by an old lady who said she would make her pay for not payin' more attention to her. The baby got scairt by a pine snake, like N. said it would. It was a big, fat, healthy baby too. The old lady that threatened her had a bag [a witch bag]. The baby got sick and we went to the hospital and they sent it back, as they couldn't find anythin' wrong. We gave her N.'s medicine but the baby died. Maybe that other person's medicine was more powerful. There are four [witches] in a clan. They all work together. There's a trail over here. My Grandmother hears them at night.

My baby was threatened and I went to N. for medicine. He knew who done it and gave me medicine so I could find out. With one dose I could hear when it went by. I'd hear it but I couldn't see. It was just somethin' that wasn't human. Usually they do that to you [witch you] because of jealousy. You never know the reason why they done it.

Account 5

Do you know a long time ago we didn't use to laugh in front of an old person? They was awful strict about that. They [the old person] might make your mouth turn [paralyzed].

Aggressive Behaviors

Account 6

If people used to dress better than the rest or think they were somebody, they had to watch out.

Account 7

I had a step brother who was killed like that. He used to be a *good cook*. He was a *good little hunter* too and just for that reason they witched him. There was one man that used to come and tell my mother she thought she was smart to have a boy like that, so she suspected him.

S. was witched because he was such a *good dancer*. He was only two or three years old. He had two good legs then and somebody didn't like it. His dad knew who did that. He couldn't do anythin'. [This same incident was related by other informants, see Account 9; the victim, now a grown man, was crippled.]

Account 8

[Question: Do you ever hear stories about witchcraft?]
I've heard lots.
Well, I'll tell you. My sister could speak English real good. She was a good piano player—graduated from Flandreau—a pretty girl about five feet three inches. When she came home she couldn't get no job in the office. Finally they put her on the advisory board but not much money. She was for the Zoar district. Some people at Zoar didn't like her—she was *too smart*. We were told someone witched her and she gradually failed and got sick and died. We knew who did it. My father said never to say anything. People will have to pay. One old man, C. D., said some kind of creature would howl around our house when my sister died. I went out in the evening to see. I would stand out under the pines. I could hear a strange sound. It was a

lonesome sound, circling around the house four times. When she died I
never heard that again.

Account 9

[Did someone witch your brother?]

Since he was three my brother got crippled. He used to *make money* dancin'
and some didn't like it. He was a real good dancer. They think they know
who done it to him [witched him] but they can't do nuthin' about it.

Account 10

[Informant brings out a yard of cord from inside a pillow in her house.]
I got this one time years and years ago when I was witched through jealousy.
A man came in my house one time and looked around and saw everythin'
all nice and was jealous. After that I used to see a bird watchin' me; it was
him. Then my throat and heart begun to hurt and my husband took me all
over to doctors but they couldn't help me. Then that Chippewa—the one
I told you about—called me up there. He took me in that tent [he was
a *Cese·ko*] and gave me this to put on. Then he made the tent shake and I
heard all sorts of shrieking voices and my throat got better. He said it was
that bird's beak goin' back and forth from my throat to my heart. He told
me to wear this whenever I travel and no harm can come to me when I have
that on. I can tell whenever a witch is near when I'm wearin' it.

Account 11

They can't find the body [of the boy who drowned]. His dad used to *show
off*. He wouldn't say "hello." But he talks different [now]. You should be good
to people. . . .

The fear of an involvement with witchcraft among members of the
native-oriented group is still very real. Very few witchcraft incidents were told
by the men in this group, who are more directly involved with power gaining
and power retention. A powerful male elder, who cautiously avoided speaking
of witchcraft, remarked, "There are many things that I can't talk about; if we
were to do so, it would take much time, a lot of tobacco, and a lot of money."
Fear is probably greater today than previously since none of the younger men
have undergone the Great Fast to receive a tutelary spirit (which protects one from
evil powers, as well as bestowing special good powers upon one). Further, there
are no powerful shamans left to combat the witch.

One is not personally responsible for the amount or kind of power that
is bestowed upon him according to Menomini belief. The witch, therefore, cannot
help that his tutelary spirit was evil or that he inherited evil powers. Many "good"
old men and women have witch bags, but no one expressed a desire for receiving
one. In fact, most informants expressed great fear of the bags and desired to
burn or destroy them. One informant said, "I told S. not to take the bag [witch

bag] if she wanted her family to grow up. Father said it wasn't right for people to have it. So she burned it. His bag harmed people. It was hidden." Another informant said, "My mother had one, but she didn't want it and put it in the swamp."

The attitude of the members of this group toward the witchcraft act itself is one of "passive acceptance," which also characterizes their attitude toward all supernatural powers. To a large extent, fate decrees whether or not a person will receive great powers. If he does not, there is little that he can do about it. Therefore, one accepts his lot. This "acceptant" attitude is illustrated in the remarks of a woman when she was asked why she had married a man whom she neither knew nor liked. She replied, in a matter-of-fact manner, that his (her husband's) old father would witch her if she did not.

Viewed in broad perspective, witchcraft might be thought of as a behavior pattern that contributes to the functioning of the group. It serves an "adaptive" function for the native-oriented group in that it insures social cooperation and preserves the status quo of the group by vesting the elders with special powers. In the absence of direct social controls exercised through positions of secular power, witchcraft and the threat of witchcraft serve as means of controlling or preventing behavior that is potentially disruptive in interpersonal relations. The structure of motivations and controls represented in the socially required values and psychological organization characteristic of individuals (equanimity under duress, latescence, control of emotionality and aggression, and autonomy) is congruent with this type of social control. Beliefs and participation in witchcraft, like beliefs and participation in religious patterns, both express basic processes in the native-oriented cultural system and serve to validate and maintain them.

Becoming a Menomini

ATTITUDES TOWARD CHILDREN

How are individuals with the values and psychological organization needed for the maintenance of the cultural system produced? In the native-oriented group of Menomini the influence of the culture on the child is apparent even before the child is born. The parents are expecting a reincarnated elder in the form of a baby and are prepared to treat the child as such. As one woman said, "I feel that sometimes a baby being born, maybe one of our grandfathers might have his spirit in the little boy." This means that the baby, like all elders, is a favored person to be shown special privileges. Children, like old people, are close to the supernatural, to the power that pervades all things and from which man receives life and energy. The autonomous attitude characteristic of native-oriented Menomini is expressed in the respect adults have for the possessions and rights of all children (see the quote on p. 22). As pointed out in an earlier section, children even receive equal shares of the earnings of the dance group, and the money is theirs to spend as they wish. Respect is also shown in the special observances for children. During the first year of life each child must be given

The young boys learn from the older men.

a name. An elder is requested to give the name, and it is bestowed at a feast given by the parents for as many people as they have food and place for. The elder gives the matter serious thought, sometimes mulling it over for several months. When he is ready, the feast is held. After the food is consumed he rises with the child in his arms and gives a talk, giving the name and explaining why it is selected and asking the spirits for a long life for the child. Sometimes the name is given in recognition of some special characteristic the elder believes he sees in the child. Other times the name of a deceased person is given in recognition of the possibility that his spirit has been born again in this child. This event is of great importance because if a child is not pleased with his name, he may depart to the spirit world from whence he came.

Children are carefully watched to see if they are at ease with their name. If one stands quietly in the midst of play, as though preoccupied with some inner distress, the parents will take the child to an elder, who will attempt to talk with it to see whether it has the right name. One family in the native-oriented group had a year-old daughter whose head shook. After several months a cousin said that she needed a different name. A feast was given and a powerful elder called in to rename her. The mother said, "That was all that was the matter. After she got her new name, her head stopped shaking."

If the child weeps ceaselessly, or is listless or sickly, obviously something is wrong and the worried parents send to the local doctor. Although the physician may try all his cures, they are in vain, the trouble is more deep seated, the doctor diagnoses the case as beyond his power and it is given to some old seer, preferably one of those gifted with the power to understand the languages of babies, which, while Menomini, is a peculiar dialect unintelligible except to the initiated. [Skinner 1913:37]

Respect and concern for children extends through all the years of growing up. When a boy kills his first game—no matter how small or large it is—a feast is held to celebrate this event and his praises are sung by all present. In the earlier days a formal rite was given at this time; most men in the native-oriented group remember this event as a less formal but still important occasion. One man related:

That old grandfather of mine tell me how to do . . . circle . . . if you see no tracks you know he isn't there. Circle around again. The deer knows you circle, he stay still. Sure enough, the second time I circle, I see the deer hiding, laying against a windfall, ears down. So I shot him in the head. First deer I ever killed. Gee! I was happy! First deer I killed. I start whooping, run home. My mother and grandmother was surprised. "Is it really so?" they kept asking. We took pack straps, knives, a little hatchet. I took them up there, sure enough, there he was. The old lady [grandmother] was pretty good. She cut it up and we packed it home. That was pretty good.

The women sliced it up good. They made sticks to roast the meat close to the fire. Then they cook what they eat. The ribs and chest they boil, the best part for them. Then the men folks come. We waiting for them. When they come in, the grandfather come first. He had nothing, just his gun and pack strap. He say, "Who that is?" The old lady, she laugh, "I guess your grandson beat you!" The grandfather say then, "Just for that we offer a prayer for to give thanks so this boy be a good hunter." So they all come; they was happy, for quite a while. We had a feast. We offer prayer . . . eat afterwards. I was fourteen when that happened. That I remember good.

This same attitude toward children extends to everyday matters. The little girl who fills her pail with wild blackberries is praised—but never in such a manner as to imply that she did better than someone else. When the boys and girls hop around the dance area in imitation of the adults, all the Menomini present whoop and clap as though the children had done something quite marvelous. Unlike the situation often existing in middle-class America, Menomini adults treat children supportively without "possessing" them.

Constraints upon Behavior and Sex

How are the constraints so necessary to the maintenance of Menomini culture imposed upon the child? The child's first direct experience with restraint is with the swaddling cloths and blankets in which it is wrapped. The cradle board is no longer used, but children are enfolded in several layers of cloth, and are usually placed in a blanket that is folded in such a way that it can be tied at both ends and suspended as a hammock. Even on hot days babies are enclosed in this manner, sometimes with only the head and face peeking out of the tightly folded blanket. When a male baby is born, his penis is pinched by an old woman in attendance, usually one of his grandmothers, so that it will not grow to abnormal size and so that he will be able to control his passions when he grows to maturity. Doubtless this act has little direct effect on the child, but it is symbolic of the value placed upon control.

In other aspects of child care than those just described, however, children in the native-oriented group are treated with tolerance and permissiveness. They are nursed whenever they are hungry or whenever they fret. Weaning is gradual, and even children in the walking stage may be given the breast if they are ill or uneasy, and if there is milk. Toilet training is carried out casually. Children are encouraged to "hold back" when they can understand the reasons for doing so, but no particular fuss is made if they do not succeed. Menomini mothers are puzzled by the concern displayed by Whites over such matters.

Until the child can run about by itself, the mother, a grandmother, or an older sibling is always nearby. Infants and young children are held a great deal. Fathers and older brothers as well as mothers walk about holding children in their arms, even when talking with strangers. Apparently, it is assumed that everyone likes to hold babies because during a conversation the holder of a baby will hand it over to the person with whom he or she is talking without asking if the recipient of the frequently rather damp bundle wants to hold it. Despite the supportive holding of babies by almost everyone there is little demonstrative fondling, hugging, or kissing. Babies are frequently held facing away from the holder. In general the interaction rate between adults and young children seems low to the White observer. The behavior of the mother is aimed primarily at avoiding catastrophe such as the death of a child by neglecting to observe particular taboos, invoking the wrath of an unappeased elder reincarnated in a newborn baby, or experiencing power loss by not treating the child as he wishes to be treated. She must continually watch the baby for evidence of strange behaviors of any kind—undue sadness, excessive crying which may indicate that a reincarnated elder wishes a special naming ceremony and a change of name. When unusual signs appear, a feast must be given and a new name tried. Sometimes, this occurs several times.

Discipline is very mild. No adult in the native-oriented group remembers being whipped as a child, and none of them whip their children now. "They used to be good to me, never scold me, and I used to be good that way too. I never went through anything like being hit on the face . . . like I saw one White man do to his kid. He hit him right on the mouth, like he was a man," as one fifty-year-old man in the native-oriented group said.

Children are never struck until they are eight years of age. . . . Pulling a child's ears makes it scrofulous and striking it about the head makes it deaf and foolish. "Only White men are capable of such barbarities." [Skinner 1913:41]

Another man in his thirties relates, "I don't remember ever getting a real switching. Oh maybe just a little bit on the legs, that's all. When I didn't mind, like maybe I cried for some little thing, or they can't make me be still, or maybe I didn't listen to my ma, then maybe I got a dipper full [of cold water] in the face. Then I had to listen!"

Small children are scolded or a little water is thrown in their faces to wash away their trouble. [Skinner 1913:41]

The attitude of adults toward children and the conception of proper treatment seem clear in the following comment by one middle-aged man:

I remember how nice and quiet my uncle used to talk to me, so I always listen to what he say, and try to do what he want. So one time we took a boy [adopted one]. He was mean, used to run around, his parents treated him bad, but we treat him like my uncle treated me. We keep him clean . . . get food what's good for him. If he like something to eat, we get that for him. We try to keep him around us all the time. We think he get better if we treat him like that. After a while he did. He minded good, listened, try to do like we say.

Children under the protection of the gods must not be scolded until they are well grown, for they may become offended and go back to their friends or relations. [Skinner 1913:40]

When a child is out of line and does not evidence sufficient control over his or her behavior, a most effective method for bringing him or her under control is to threaten him with the owl. The fear of the world of spirits and ghosts surrounding him is inculcated in the child at a very early age.

Children receive little instruction about sex—but they need little since its natural manifestations are apparent in the close quarters of a shack or hut. Masturbation is rather casually discouraged. Adults never expose their bodies in toto, but a woman will nurse a child in public with no concern. In the past the typical restrained attitude toward sex was manifested in the use of a *mɛʔnapos* blanket, a soft deerskin with a single hole in the middle, which covered the woman during intercourse and minimized direct contact. These blankets were used until very recent times by married couples, and the attitudes symbolized by their use are still a part of the value system of the native-oriented group.

. . . there was formerly a taboo against the contact of the skin of males and females. To obviate this difficulty Ma'nabus prepared a large buckskin, with a single perforation, to cover the woman. This robe was handed down to mankind and to comparatively recent times the custom was still in vogue among the Menomini.

Certain persons in every band were granted, through their dreams, the right to possess these robes. The skins were beautifully painted and ornamented and kept as sacred articles, to be rented out to those who wished to use them. Anyone who wished to hire a blanket first approached the owner with a present of tobacco as a preface to his request and on its return another present had to be made in payment. If the users soiled the robe, an indemnity was demanded by the owner. [Skinner 1913:30–31]

SOCIAL PARTICIPATION

One of the most rewarding aspects of growing up in Menomini culture is the fact that a child is a participant in the important happenings of the group. When a Dream Dance is being held, all of the children down to the smallest baby are in the room where the service is conducted. Adults are tolerant of potential disruptions that would disturb Whites in similar circumstances. A baby that starts to fret when a prayer is being offered or a tobacco sacrifice is being made is held gently, given the breast, or carried out of the room without any visible tension or anger on the part of the mother or other attendant who carries it out. Very young children are encouraged to take part in the affair. Toddlers dance, held at first by their upraised arms by older brothers or sisters.

One eleven-year-old boy was given a regular place around the drum. He used his drumstick to help the fast-moving and highly synchronized beat, and tried to join in the rather complex and very quick-tempo songs. His beat was a little ragged, and his singing was far from being a positive contribution to the chorus, but the men carrying out the service treated him like a full member of the ritual group. His careful and self-conscious attempt to replicate every move and posture of the men, even the facial expressions, was an impressive demonstration of how learning occurs in this group. His youngest brother, age three and one half, ran over to him one night shortly after he took his place at the drum. The eleven-year-old promptly found a stool for him and gently sat the child on it next to him. The little boy sat on the stool quietly, absorbed by the activity, while two choruses were sung. Then he became restive and started to run about the room. His older brother got up, took him by the arm, and rather firmly sat him down again upon the stool. The little boy, unaccustomed to such firm treatment by his brother, started to sob quietly—apparently fighting for control but not quite achieving it. Finally, his brother took him by the hand, and with a very solicitous look upon his face, led him out of the room. The next time a song service was held, the little boy sat again upon the stool by the side of his older brother, but this time he stayed there quietly for about an hour, then got up and walked carefully over to his mother's side and climbed upon the bench beside her. At later services he took the same position by his brother during the early part of the evening. He had learned something. Seven years later he sat with his brother, now a young man, at the same drum, but now he had his own drumstick, and tried to sing, like his brother had before at the age of eleven.

This is the way roles are learned in the native-oriented group and one reason why the way of life of this group has persisted for so long in the face of intensive pressures for change from the outside world. In a small homogeneous

Younger children learn from older siblings.

group of this sort, the child is able to assume and understand the roles of every member of the group and to learn what the expectations of each member of the group are for him or her. As Margaret Mead once wrote, growing up in a homogeneous group allows for "effective *prefiguring of future experience* and reinforcement and consolidation of past experience" (Mead 1949:550).

STORYTELLING AND PREACHING

Native-oriented Menomini believe strongly in the power of the spoken word. As soon as children can understand, adults are constantly "putting a bug in your ear," as one young man expressed it. There are several different ways of putting a bug in. In the old days there was a regular cycle of stories and myths told through certain times of the year. Usually, some elder who was both powerful and wise would establish a special reputation as a good storyteller. He would hold forth by his hearth on certain evenings, and parents would bring their children to hear him. Older people in the present group remember these storytelling times when as many as twenty children might be listening at the same moment.

The mass of popular folklore is comprised in the group known as "true stories." While these are, for the most part, not sacred, they range from simple narratives of daily life to supernatural experiences. The former are droll, exciting, or explanations of natural phenomena. . . . They are told in public at any time when apropos, but generally around the fire in the evening. The latter are often in the nature of confidences, and are imparted only in private....

Naturally inclined to the dramatic, the Menomini embellish every myth and fairy tale with a richness of gesture and vocal inflection that cannot be transcribed on paper. The sign language, now almost obsolete as such, is still used to render the tales more graphic. A number of signs otherwise lost may be resurrected by a careful study of gestures used in story telling.

Every character in the story has its peculiarity of speech by which it is known, a fact that is true of Indian mythology in general to a much larger extent than has been recognized. These idiosyncrasies are mimicked by the narrator. [Skinner and Satterlee 1915:235]

Still today some Menomini elders tell stories "with a richness of gesture and vocal inflection that cannot be transcribed on paper." The type of stories remembered by the older and middle-aged people today as most entertaining consist of stories about various wizards and heroes and their exploits; stories of war, hunting, love, ghosts, and magic; and stories about "how the skunk got his stripes" and "how the crane got the black ring around his neck." The other major type of story includes the cosmogonic myths—the origin of the Menomini; the nature of the stratified universe and the beings in it; and, particularly, the *Mεʔnapos* cycle, stories about the culture hero of the Menomini who was part hero and part buffoon. This latter category of stories were told in a more serious vein, usually to older children and during a period of weeks when the cycle would not be interrupted.

The most basic Menomini values, such as the relationship of power to the entire system of belief and action, are represented in these stories. In the myths the hero is helpless without his dream-bestowed and ritually maintained power, and he may lose it by abuse, neglect, or lack of constraint. However, the hero is particularly successful only because he has acquired a certain power. In contests between great shamans, one of the contestants may realize and admit that his power is not strong enough to withstand that of the other so he gives in without further struggle. The individual is dependent upon this power as something beyond himself—something gained by him through proper behavior. This attitude, as described earlier, persists today among the members of the native-oriented group. Many of the tales contain explicit or implicit rules for behavior which are accepted today: A good man is brave, respects the rights of others, and does not arouse antagonisms; he lives quietly and observes the sacrifices required to maintain good relations with the powers; and he is modest, even tempered, and guards himself against undue pride.

Today the children do not have the opportunity to hear these same stories and myths told in their fullness and richness, but all children in the native-oriented group have heard stories. The content is attenuated, but the themes are recognizable. For example, one night a man in his late thirties was telling his children about a great hunter. He always got his bag full of ducks. He went out to his favorite spot and waited for the ducks to fly in during the half-light moments of dawn. Suddenly, there was a rush of wings as a flight settled in before his hiding place. He rose to shoot, but slipped and fell, discharging his shotgun harmlessly in the air. The ducks all rose in a flurry of beating wings. One big black duck, however, stayed on the water. The great hunter reloaded his gun and shot the unfortunate laggard. To his consternation he saw that he had shot his own hat, which had flown off his head when he fell down, and it floated, crownless and tattered, on the surface of the water. The great hunter went home, disgusted. That evening, as though to remind him of his ineptness, a large crane flapped past his house by the river, wearing the brim of his hat around his neck. Now every time he sees the ring-necked crane, he is reminded of his clumsiness on that morning.

Grandparents still tell children "bedtime stories," and the adults in the group remember when their grandparents told them stories. "Grandmaw told us kids a story every night before we went to sleep. First thing next morning she would ask us what the story was about. If we couldn't tell her, she would tell the same story again the next night. She would do that until we could tell her what the story was about." What the grandmother was looking for was the moral point of the story, "that we shouldn't offend anybody's feelings," or "not to envy what someone else has got."

Adults seem to always be ready to point out a moral to children. One little boy stood by the window looking longingly out at the blizzardy landscape. "Gee, I wish it would get clear so I could go out and play tomorrow," he said. The next day dawned with a bright sun and he could go out. Before he did, however, his mother pointed out to him that he had asked for such weather the day before, and this showed that one should never wish for things unless one really wanted them to happen. Frequently, the moral point will be made with a proverb: "He who brags bites his own tail." "People who mind others' business get long noses." One who talks too much will get a big mouth." "He who spits at him gives him his life."

The constraint so necessary to the maintenance of the Menomini cultural system is sometimes taught directly. One young woman relates:

> He, my father, did right and treated all people the same. He was kind to everybody. Even the children today brag about my father. My father always made us sit every time we ate anything. He said the food wouldn't do no good otherwise. He said we would be just like horses, running around and eating, and our food wouldn't do us no good. We had to sit a while after we ate to let our food digest. We could never talk very much while we was at the table. He didn't even like us to stretch or things like that after we ate. I used to think my father was awful hard on us, but I can see now, that he was just tryin' to raise us right and teach us the right things to do. So I keep tellin' my children the same things as my father told us. [L. Spindler, field notes]

Children are taught to be quiet and not ask a lot of questions. "Sit quiet like a stone, and let thoughts come to you. Think about a leaf in a pool." Children are taught explicitly to be generous and respect old people: "Father said, 'Live in peace. Be good to every person. If you live somewhere . . . if you have something to eat . . . feed him . . . even though there is only one meal in your house, feed him anyway, especially if it's an old lady or an old man.'"

Much of the moral instruction given a child is formalized in the "preachings" that every Menomini child is supposed to receive from an older person, usually a grandparent, starting at about age eight. Grandparents have already played a very important role in the child's education before that time. Children spend almost as much time with their grandparents (particularly on the mother's side) as they do with their parents, and sometimes considerably more. Menomini mothers have always claimed a rather high degree of freedom. They dance, help collect greens and ferns, hunt and fish, and travel; to increase freedom of movement, children will sometimes be left with grandparents. The attachment to the older people on the part of the children is usually great, but it is given a special character by the respect toward and fear of old people as retainers of great supernatural power. Children are taught never to irritate old people, not to stare at them, or talk loudly around them. They are told to fill their pipes, run errands for them, and never hurt their feelings. In the words of some of the present-day native-oriented Menomini quoted previously:

Another thing they [parents] used to say if you hurt old men's feelings, your child might die and hurt your feelings.

My father used to tell us we were supposed to always help out old people and do all we can and never make a fuss, because some day you might come across some old person who might happen to have that bag [witch bag].

The child had to sit still [at meetings], because if it would stare at some person, the person wouldn't like it. My mother never took us anyplace.

It is never forgotten that all old people are potential witches. So children listen well to their grandparents. When the child reaches the eighth year, it is believed that he is no longer likely to want to go back to the spirit world. His own spirit is satisfied with the treatment it has received. So it is now time to lay out the virtues he is expected to acquire and live by in a more directive fashion than heretofore. This preaching continues, with content appropriate to age and role, until the youngsters are married.

Grandmothers tell young girls that they will be getting married someday. They should look after their husbands, keep their clothes well, put good food on the table, not be lazy around the house. They should avoid love potions to get or hold him because these potions are dangerous and may kill him, or cause him to become so jealous that he will kill her.

Father used to preach to us to understand things. He was always yelling and preachin'. But now today, I'm glad he done those thing. He never liked love medicine. He said "Whenever you get married and can't seem to hold your husband, don't start askin' for love powder. If you use it on him, he won't be in his right mind. I'll tell you one good thing on how to hold your man. Keep his table full and keep his clothes good."

My mother did a lot of preachin'.... When I married B., she said, "Always be good to that old lady [mother-in-law]. Beat her up in the morning and get breakfast and do what she says. Don't lie around and look at books or anything like that. Get up early and work real hard, then she won't get mad at you. If she does, she won't hurt you, but she'll get someone you like best like your brother or mother or sister."

He [father] told me to always treat my in-laws good and to be good to my husband. That's why J. and me get along so good. We been married twelve years now.

Young girls were told that a menstruating woman is dangerous, that when she menstruates the first time, she will be given utensils of her own to cook with, and that she should stay away from men and children during her menstrual period thereafter to avoid causing them to become ill or die.

... I am always careful about eatin'. I cooked by myself and used my own pots and pans. . . . Some have two stoves. They're all careful at that time not to eat among others or the old folks will get sick . . . it would kill them [their guardian spirit], or give them diarrhea or something. When a girl gets that way, we was all told that for one year not to touch a baby. Some old person's spirit is in a little baby and she might kill them.

[Did your mother have you go off by yourself when you began to menstruate?]
Every month I was home [from school] I did my own cookin' off by myself, away from the house with my own dishes. It wasn't bad. It was kinda fun. . . . We had to be real careful about where we stepped at that time and about feedin' babies.

Young Menomini girls are told about the penalties of loose sexual behavior and that when they are married, their husband can tell "if they have been good."

Well, you know, she [aunt] started telling me about married life first. She said, "Some day some man will come," and said, "If you want to get married, you should behave and not run around and have things to do with other fellows. If you do get married and have done bad things, your husband will find out and pick on you and you'll never get along after that. If you behave and wait until you're really married, your husband will have nothing against you and you'll get along. Your husband can tell if you was good or not."

My grandmother used to scare me half to death about goin' around boys. She used to say, "Your tits will get real long and heavy and hang down if you go around boys before you're married." Then they used to say a boy's tits would get big too if he hung around girls.

A man got the same preachin' to. He was supposed to do the same as the girls. It wouldn't matter as much, though. They would tell him that some fellows have children and don't marry the girls and that he would be having children with no one to take care of them.

Girls were instructed about medicines that can cause abortion if used during the first few weeks of pregnancy and about medicines for taking after the birth of a child.

There is Indian medicine. A bitter root, like a physic. It's better to take it the first month. If two or three pass, the woman doesn't know if she will die.

Some medicines we drink for one month after we have our babies. You have to add fruit trees (roots) to the medicine, wash roots, pound. Take apple tree, wash that, tie up with string, let dry until it's easy to pound, tie each up separate. When dry, take one root, pound up, sift, put aside, then take next [raspberry], keep on, then mix all fine stuff together, then put away in jar. This will be for after a baby.

Young people are given rather elaborate directions for making medicines when they are initiated into the Medicine Lodge:

We don't allow any kind of bad medicine [in the Lodge]. After my mother died, I took out her medicine. When they put me in [initiated me], each put a medicine in that bag . . . one for headaches—sneezing medicine. Another gave me something for diarrhea. Eight old men and two women gave me medicine. They pound all medicines together and mix them together. I got to keep track so I write down what they're for. There was one old fellow from Wabeno who gave me medicine in case someone ever dopes you with love powder. You put it in the middle of your head and you'll be back to normal. They give you just a little, like samples, then you go to them to find out how it's made. You sample it first, if it's good, then go to the person to learn.

A transitional woman who was raised by a native-oriented grandmother, known as a doctor with powerful medicines, learned about medicines from her. She then began to practice medicine herself.

I know lots of good medicines. If you got some cancer on your skin, you take the skin of a frog and put over it and it takes it all up when you pull it off. If there is some left, you just pick it off with tweezers. If it's inside you, you find some rotten log and boil it up into tea and keep drinkin' that.

Those medicines my grandmother told me about all came to me later in a dream and I did lots of doctorin' all around.

Young girls are told by the elders to always treat their husbands the same way whether he is drunk or sober. One woman describes how she continuously took her husband back after his sprees in a patient, acceptant manner.

He [husband] used to drink and leave me when I had my babies—a boy and then twins. He done a lot of drinkin' and ran around with women. He lived with a Oneida woman for two weeks. . . . When we came here he started that up again and left me and never came home. . . . I had to stay by myself because I wasn't divorced. I wanted to see what J. [husband] was going to do. [Why?]
I suppose I'd have to take him back if he wanted to.

Grandfathers also tell young boys to be generous, to feed old people. They tell them not to boast of their exploits or abilities and never to envy someone else's abilities. Boys are cautioned about looking for bad medicines and are told to keep away from menstruating women. They are told about their obligations to in-laws and their responsibilities to any guardian spirits they may have inherited. They are warned about sex and the diseases that can come as a result of dalliance. They are told to treat their wives well and cautioned about the danger that sorcery may be directed at them by the wife's parents if they do not. They are told to mind their own business and never to talk carelessly about important things like religion or the spirits.

In former times this period of being "preached to" would have been climaxed by the puberty fast, followed by an intensive period of instruction on the esoteric and sacred aspects of Menomini belief. Individuals who received unusual guardians or vision experiences would be given prolonged and specialized instruction, with all of the details of ritual and cosmogonic rationale, by an old man who was one or another kind of "medicine man." Today the puberty fast is no longer possible for the young people, and even though there is continuity in the way individuals maintain sacred power and the expectations people have concerning it, the loss of the puberty fast is a serious blow to the efficacy of the native-oriented educational system. Adolescent education is the weakest link in the process today, and it is during adolescence that young people frequently move away from the native-oriented group into the transitional and acculturation-oriented groups in the Menomini community. The native-oriented group is shrinking but shows surprising strength in view of the predictions made by every student of Menomini culture since 1890 that the Menomini culture would disappear completely during the next decade or so. This ability to survive is related to the effectiveness of the educational system just described.

Why do Menomini children grow up, within the native-oriented framework, exhibiting the socially required behaviors and psychological orientations —autonomy, equanimity under duress, latescence, and emotional control? One answer is that they grow up this way because there is no reason for them not to. These qualities are taught—directly and indirectly in the way young children are induced into more advanced roles, in the things children hear elders saying at ceremonials, in the moral points underscored again and again by parents and grandparents with a definite point of view, making observations and reinforcing behavior in different contexts as events occur that lend themselves to such interpretation. They are taught in myths and stories told now in attenuated but recognizable form. They are revitalized and encapsulated in highly explicit preaching by respected and feared mentors during the period of most intense development just before and into early adolescence.

Menomini children early in their experience encounter all of the statuses and roles constituting, in their arrangement, the social structure of their society. This minimizes anxiety-arousing and frustrating discontinuities in education and experience. Discontinuities do exist, however, since children must attend schools run by White men and women with very different ideas about proper behavior than the children's parents have. In spite of these potentially conflict-laden situations, the educational experience for children in the native-oriented group has been successfully refractive in many cases to the impact of the educational experience contrived by agents of the dominant society. Adults who have undergone a tradition-oriented socialization experience in childhood, including the learning of the Menomini language, rarely (possibly never) are psychologically reoriented in maturity, even though they may take on specialized occupational roles and acquire the accessory behaviors necessary to get along in today's world.

Perhaps the most important factor in the success of the educational system is the fact that children in this society do not grow up resisting what they are being taught or the cultural agents doing the teaching. The encounters they have had with cultural agents (parents, grandparents, aunts, elders) during the early years of experience have been more than favorable—they are designed to make children feel "at home," to make them want to stay. Children are treated with tolerance and supportiveness. It is true that these are qualities in varying degrees characteristic of many nonliterate groups, but Menomini children are treated with special respect. Respect, even for children, is probably characteristic of social systems exhibiting a high degree of individual autonomy. In the Menomini case this feature is emphasized and reinforced by the belief that children and old people possess the greatest power and are closest to the supernatural. This respect, however, does not result in complete permissiveness. There is gentle, constant, consistent discipline in the restraints with which children are surrounded. At the same time Menomini children are supported and rarely threatened by authoritarian demands or crude violations of their person in the form of physical punishment. Most encounters with cultural agents during the early years of life are favorable and, as a result, the child is open and receptive to learning and to becoming what the carriers of his culture want him to be.

The discontinuity between experience in Whiteman schools and that in the Menomini family and home was very great. Euro-American concepts of child training and education are radically divergent from those of the traditional Menomini. Strict discipline, abrupt interference with the child's activities, use of crticism rather than praise, and corporal punishment were foreign to the Menomini and were interpreted by them as lack of respect for the child, if not down-right cruelty. Our case histories contain instances of shocked parents who tried to protect their children, sometimes by removing them from school and from what they saw as harsh and unnecessary behavior on the part of teachers and school administrators. The culturally patterned tendencies of Whiteman school personnel were reinforced by prejudice on the part of Whites toward Indians. These conditions have surely ameliorated in recent years, and in any event by now many, if not most, Menomini have become callous to violations of this sort as they have become acculturated, so the discontinuity is not so great as it was a generation ago. However, the initial discongruity between Whiteman and Menomini concepts of a good education have played a determinant role in the long-term, fundamental educational failure of the Whiteman schools, for Menomini as well as other Indians (See B. Berry, 1969).

Conclusion

In this chapter we have described and interpreted the first of the adaptive strategies represented by the various acculturative groups of Menomini. In doing so we have moved back and forth between past and present to give depth and completeness to the cultural and psychological features that tie the Menomini to their own origins. However, this technique of presentation should not be al-lowed to obscure the fact that the native-oriented group is an adaptation to the prolonged confrontation of the Menomini and Whiteman cultural systems. We have tried to make this clear as we have proceeded, but we reemphasize it now, for it is a crucial point in our analysis. The native-oriented cultural system is an attempt to maintain a way of life that is dying. The majority of the men in it under fifty had a Whiteman school experience superimposed upon the tradi-tional education we have described, and fairly extensive experience in the outside world. They chose to identify with the native-oriented group, and to become members of the ceremonial organizations. This is less true of the women, for they have had, as a rule, less outside experience, but their self-consciousness about their identity is clear. The native-oriented group is literally a reaffirmative move-ment on a small scale. Its religions, dances and songs, witchcraft, and myths and stories are all affirmations of a cultural system that is highly discongruent with that of the Whiteman. The people in it, with the exception of the elders, who have known little else and are heuristically native oriented, are maintaining control and identity by reasserting one way of life and attempting to exclude the other, in its most disruptive moral and philosophical forms. They are, of course, only partially successful. In the long run the attempt seems doomed, but the attempt is interesting and significant, for it is one of the ways in which people in such a situation attempt to cope with the exigencies of cultural confrontation between discongruent cultural systems, either between separate, or formerly sep-arate, societies, or within one large society.

3

The Peyote Road

The Ideology

PEYOTISM is an intensely personal experience. This is so even though there is a high degree of patterning in ritual, symbolism, and belief that is both specific to the Menomini and shared widely with other Indians in North America. Each convert to Peyotism is searching for something. We see Peyotism as an adaptive strategy, as a way of reducing cognitive and emotional conflicts stemming from the confrontation between Menomini and Whiteman cultures. This is a conceptualization, an abstraction from specific events and individuals. To the individual the Peyote Road is a means to salvation, a resolution of personal conflict, a way of life, and a religion.

It is appropriate that the Peyotists should speak for themselves. Though we will interpret what they say in terms of our framework, much of this chapter has been "written" by the Peyotists themselves, as their statements were recorded by the Spindlers and by J. S. Slotkin.[1] This way the motivations and perceptions of the people may be understood. Our first concern is with the ideology of Menomini Peyotism.

1. We speak to Almighty God in our native tongue. God has given me His name in my language, *Kesɛ·manetoˑw*, it means God, you know. He has given it to me. And I can pray to Almighty God right here in my own tongue because He has given it to me that way. And he teaches me that, in Peyote meetings. He doesn't teach me that in other religions, you know. For instance, this Catholic church, it doesn't teach me that way. There those prayers are already printed by some smart man; all you got to do is repeat it, and learn

---

[1] J. S. Slotkin, aided by his wife, Elizabeth Slotkin, worked with the Peyotists in 1951, and subsequently became a member of the Native American Church and a delegate to the national meetings of the organization. His most important publications are *Menomini Peyotism* (1952) and *The Peyote Religion* (1956). We worked independently and our results complement rather than contradict each other.

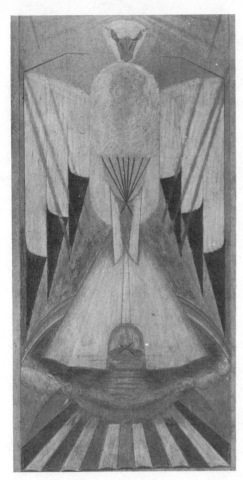

A crayon drawing by a Menomini Peyotist, Mr. Star Shoshey. The tepee is shown supported by the sun and its rays, leading as paths to the door, and protected by the Water-bird, with the head of the lamb of peace.

it, and memorize it. That ain't no prayer for me. If I'm going to talk to God, I must talk to Him right away from my heart; I must tell Him just what I think, and what's troubling me. And I think the Peyote does that for me. [Peyotist, in Slotkin 1952:617]

2. I'm going to tell you. Indians [are] awful poor; you know that yourself. It's pretty hard, it's pretty hard to understand. Some of the Indians, some of them, they don't believe God; they don't believe what these white people believe. But this stuff here [peyote], if you use it, you'll think, "I wish we get benefit from God." We pray. We know we're poor. But at the same time, I wish we save our souls when we die. That's all we want. The rest, we don't care; we can't get it. Even if the government, if we ask something—we have a council—we don't get it. . . . [Peyotist, in Slotkin 1952:607]

3. I went to a meeting to find out about Peyote. After I had taken a few herbs I saw a book open before me, with several verses in it. There was something above that, too, but I couldn't seem to look up. It said in the book: "Follow the path of Peyote, it is the only true path to me." Then a hand

came into my sight, and this hand pointed to the herb and a voice said, "Take of this, it is the true way." [Peyotist, in G. Spindler, field notes][2]

4. What I tell you ain't gonna be much. I know only just some. I've been in this a long time, but I still know just some, not much. Some of the old people been learning this for fifty to sixty years know more, but still, they not know it all. When they learn about it they ready to go. They're all finished here. Why you want this? You gonna do anything? This other fellow [J. S. Slotkin] wants to find out about Peyote too. I told him, "You come to meetings, you learn there! I can't tell much like this. If you and I sit there all night, eat peyote, we can talk the next morning. You learn for yourself what it means." [Peyotist, in G. Spindler, field notes]

5. There ain't no preaching in our ceremony. We get our knowledge from the Almighty direct. We don't need nobody telling us what the word is. That's what peyote is for. You take that, and the medicine will do the rest. God will talk to you himself. You don't need no bible. [Peyotist, in G. Spindler, field notes]

6. I used to run around, drink, act wrong lots of times. I didn't take this religion seriously. But then I changed. I used to go to the meetings, sit there, take one or two peyote, not really work into it like I should. Then I started thinking. I gave up all this drinking. I went to meetings, prayed right, thought, took lots of peyote. I got a boy in Waukeshaw [state prison]. If he had followed me he would have been alright, but he wouldn't listen. [Peyotist, in G. Spindler, field notes]

7. This here is the Indian religion—Peyote. It's good for you, cures you when you ain't well and it gives you knowledge. Things you never knew before you know when you eat that herb. The only way to know about peyote is to take it, it is the only way to learn. You eat the herb and sit there all night and sing and you learn things that you never knew before. There's an old man here who has taken it for a long time. He learned all that is in the Bible by taking the herb. He can't read or write and he never seen a Bible but he can tell you everything that's in it because of peyote. He even knows some things that's supposed to be in the Bible that ain't; things you White men forgot when you wrote the Bible; things you left out when you went from the Old Testament to the New Testament. He can tell what's going to happen too. It's our religion, we don't need no White man stuff. Them nuns ought to go away, we don't need them. We don't want White men around when we take peyote; we let Spindler in and he took some too, but I don't think he learned nothing. [From a Peyotist's responses to the values picture study technique administered by Robert Edgerton to respondents from the Spindler acculturation sample (Goldschmidt and Edgerton 1961)]

---

[2] The full texts for these and other Peyotists who gave accounts of their beliefs and experiences to the Spindlers are available in the *Microcard Publications of Primary Records in Culture and Personality*, B. Kaplan, ed., 1958.

8.   Almost reminds me of our fire place . . . that you seen last Sunday. The fire is right in here . . . or the ashes of it. You know . . . this fire here . . . it goes right up like that. If you do something wrong in everyday life it goes right through there. [Question] Here's the fireplace, and the trail that goes in there. We get rid of our sin in that fire, and the trail goes right through. [Question] These could be angels, watching the fire from each side. That's the way they're shaped. [Peyotist response to card I of the Rorschach, in G. Spindler, field notes]

9.   Jesus Christ, tell me what our all-in-all father, Great Spirit, wants of me. And as for this medicine here, that was found here where we live, these [rites] are according to the commandments of Great Spirit, our father, so that we should know what must be done. It is the commandment of our all-in-all father, Great Spirit.

And again, he really sent you here, Jesus Christ, when you walked around here where we live, in order to teach us the way we should live. Now then, I thank you for teaching us about this medicine.

Well then, pray to this medicine, so that we will know how to act as we should according to the commandments of our all-in-all father, Great Spirit. This [Peyote] led the way for us which we should follow; it is a good way, one on which there is light. You [Peyote] are helping us so that we can learn that which we should follow. That is what I am praying for, Peyote. And that you will teach us how to behave when something is tempting us. Also that when we are ill it [Peyote] will heal us properly, so we will stand up straight and awaken well. That is what I ask of you; that you will help us.

I thank Great Spirit, our father, for his commandments from which we have learned. [An excerpt from a much longer prayer by the leader of a Peyote ceremony blessing the peyote to be distributed and asking that the purpose of the meeting be fulfilled. It was given in Menomini, translated by Slotkin (1952:593). Slotkin notes that during this prayer the leader "breaks down and weeps three different times."]

10.   You [white people] want everything! He give us here, this earth; now white man take away from us—just where we got this little place here, what we live on now, to take away from us. [From a Peyotist's conversation with J. S. Slotkin (1952:608)]

11.   It seems like—speaking about this Native American Church—the white man—what he did years ago, years back, way back in the beginning —he was supposed to come here, in the first place, to help these Indians. But instead of that he kind of turned around and beat him [out of] his country; seemed like he take everything away from him. Now, today, we see this Menomini reservation—still some Menomini here—well in the first place, this is their country! Not only this reservation, but they own the whole of North America. Now today [they own] just this little piece of land here. And through this Native American Church, it seems like the foundation is coming out somewhere. Seem like you going to find that foundation, what belongs to the

Indian. In other words, it seems like you're going to come here, and you're going to take that away from them, and take it away to the old country. Kind of looks that way, too. [Peyotist, in Slotkin 1952:622]

12.   That night the medicine worked on me. Pretty soon I see what looks like a mountain shaped like that moon [the half-moon altar] . . . it looked like a great big mountain. Pretty soon it seemed like I was on top of it. Then I turned around and I could see something going, like the way it's supposed to in meetings. Pretty soon I see somebody, he had on dark pants and a white T-shirt and some kind of cap, like a police cap. He looks like he was standing on top of the world, in the East I could see that . . . the world and him standing on top of it. He must be real powerful, I thought, whoever he is. Then he was moving his arms, back and forth, stretching. Then, all of a sudden, I could feel him hitting me. "I got to pound that good stuff into you!" It was that Peyote. It was him. [Peyotist, in G. Spindler, field notes]

13.   . . . because I'm weak; and if I'm weak, well, I got to use that [peyote], because there's me·skowesan [power] in there, in that medicine. [Question] From the Almighty; they got it from there, me·skowesan; he put it down there in that Peyote. [Excerpted from a longer conversation about various forms of power and their relationship with peyote between a Peyotist and J. S. Slotkin (1952:641)]

14.   My old aunt was the one. My mother died when I was little and this aunt raised me. I lived with her. That was when I had my other wife, that's dead now. . . . I used to go to all this powwow doings. I never knew what it was all about. I never prayed or nothing. I just go to have a good time . . . never heard a word about God . . . same with mete·wen too. I just sang songs, danced, listened to the drum. I never thought about what any of it meant. Then one day (I was about twenty-nine at time) my old aunt called me over to a meeting. She handed me a big dipper full of tea. She said to me, "Drink that, it's something good. I want you to have this." Well, I couldn't hardly say no to her. So, "Alright," and I took it down. Then later I had some more, another big dipper full of tea. I sat there all night, and listened to them praying. Everything was good, *good*, just right. . . . So that's how I got started. I learned about God. I thought a lot about it. I prayed. After I got into that I pulled away from the powwow and mete·wen, and all that stuff. [Peyotist, in G. Spindler, field notes]

15.   We had a meeting up to Hayward, so I went up there. They had a tepee and everything, just like we do. I went in there, prayed, sang, like you seen. Then after midnight, that's a good time, suddenly I hear something . . . a sound . . . kind of a ring, like if when those telephone wires get hit by something. It got louder and louder. I was just sitting there, then a light from far off, way up, like a star . . . like as if I was outdoors like now, came towards me. It come fast, coming right towards me. Then it come real close, right up in front of me, and busted . . . just like one of them fireworks. It come up to

me and busted, all in little pieces of light. [Colored?] No, not colored, just bright light. I could see everything clear. That was good. That meant everything was going alright. It was a message from heaven. It showed me that I was doing good, doing the right thing, that I should keep on.

One other time I remember that was best. This was about ten years ago . . . in a meeting like the other one. I eat peyote all evening until midnight. I thought about my life, what I done . . . everything. Then midnight I went out for a little while . . . it's alright then . . . a intermission. I stand out there by myself, all alone. Then I heard that sound again, like I told you before . . . way up . . . loud and high. Then suddenly I hear another sound, like birds make when they fly . . . "swish, swish" . . . and somehow I could feel their wings on my face. I wondered what that was. I stood there and thought about it. Then, again, suddenly, I hear the same sound as before . . . that was something. I wondered. Then it came to me what it was; it was angels, come down from heaven. They come to show me our prayers was good, that God was listening. [Peyotist, in G. Spindler, field notes]

Certain themes appear in the statements above which occur in some form in most conversations with Menomini Peyotists. These recurrent themes do not appear to be specific to the Menomini, for Winnebago Peyotists whom we interviewed expressed them, and they are contained, in varying degrees of explicitness, in accounts from other tribes. This is not surprising, for Peyotism is today the most widely shared "Indian" religion in North America. It apparently diffused from the Kiowa-Comanche during the late nineteenth century. They in turn received it from the Apache, who got it from Mexico.[3] The Menomini received it in 1914 from a Potowatomi Peyote missionary, who lived for a time with a Menomini family who had become disaffected with the Dream Dance and Medicine Lodge and had moved away from the rest of the conservative group around Zoar. Use of peyote as a sacrament in a religious ceremony is pre-Columbian, but the present ideology and ceremony are a product of recent history, built upon a traditional cultural foundation. The present ritual in both the cross-fireplace and half-moon altar forms is composed of a medley of elements, many of apparent Plains Indian origin and some of Christian origin. The ritual and the supporting ideology are clearly a response to the defeat, deprivation, and confinement which Indians experienced nearly everywhere after the first half of the nineteenth century. We paraphrase and summarize this ideology as follows:

Peyote is God's (Great, or All-in-All Spirit *Kese·maneto·w*) gift to the Indian. The Whiteman has everything else. He has the Indian's land, his forests, and now he even wants to take away the land he gave the Indian by treaty. He is rich, he has fine clothes, money, cars, big houses, much furniture, much education. But the Indian has peyote, to give him the power of the Holy Spirit and cure him of sickness. (See statements 2, 7, 10, and 11.)

Peyote is a means to salvation after the ignorance of the days of the Medi-

---

[3] There are arguments about the exact origin of Peyotism which are well summarized by Weston LaBarre (1960).

cine Dance or after the sinfulness of one's previous life. It pulls men up from the dark pit. It shows them the light, the path to salvation and right living. (See statements 3, 6, 8, 9, and 14.)

By taking peyote at the meetings one can acquire some of the power put in the sacrament by the Great Spirit. (See statements 7, 12, and 13.)

Peyote gives one knowledge—of oneself as well as of heaven and earth and other things beyond ordinary knowledge. Peyote makes one think about oneself, all that one has done, all one's past life. (See statements 6, 7, and 15.)

One can learn only by taking peyote. It does no good to talk about it, or try to find out about it by reading books. Peyote is the teacher. (See statements 1, 3, 4, 5, 7, and 9.)

After years of going to meetings and partaking of peyote you will know only a little bit. No one knows very much. All the people are ignorant, but the ones who go to many meetings, pray, and take much peyote, and think about their past lives, are the only ones who know anything. (See statement 4.)

This ideology says much about the appeal and the functions of Peyotism as a response to the confrontation of Menomini and Whiteman culture. It appears to be a response to deprivation ("the Whiteman has everything else"), and it offers the security of knowledge and power and is a possession of the Indian. It offers salvation—the resolution of self-doubt and conflict about right and wrong, reflecting the discongruent demands issuing from native versus Whiteman culture, and reassurance that one is "doing right." We will observe the ramifications of this ideology in its functional context in the further explanations by Peyotists, and the observations of the ethnographers, to follow. The next section will deal with the Peyote ritual, its setting, paraphernalia, and ascribed meanings.

The Peyote Ritual and Meeting

Ceremonies are held in a large white tepee of the Plains type made of muslin sheeting or canvas in the yard of the person giving the meeting during warm weather, but during winter they are held in homes. The tepee is always oriented with the "door," frequently with a "caboose" (wall tent) entrance, to the east. The leader of the ceremony always sits directly across from the entrance. The tepee meeting begins with an opening prayer outside the tepee at sundown on Saturday and ends in the early hours of Sunday morning. It is usually called by one of the members for a declared purpose. The family giving the meeting furnishes a prepared tepee ground, and with the help of the officers appointed for the ceremony, puts up the tepee and arranges cedar boughs around the circular seating space inside and splits 4-foot lengths of ash firewood. The sponsoring family also provides most or all of the food consumed the next day by the participants who stay on.

After the opening prayer the leader ($meya \cdot we \cdot w$) or "chairman" requested by the sponsors enters first, then the rest of the assemblage enter. The men sit in the circle of the tepee on the cedar boughs and blankets. Their wives, if present, sit in back of them, half-crouched against the sloping tepee poles. The meeting

The tepee.

is then opened by the leader, who asks the person giving it to explain its purpose. When he is finished, the leader announces appointments to the places of drum chief, cedar man, fire tender, and sometimes waiter, gives the first prayer, and explains the procedure for the night. Then the peyote is passed, first (sometimes) in ground and moistened form, then in solid buttons. Each person may take as many as he wishes the second time, but usually only four the first. (The peyote is passed four times throughout the whole service.) With this, the singing and drumming begin, each man taking the staff and gourd rattle as he sings. He is accompanied by the rapid beat of the Peyote drum—a small copper kettle with a head of tautly drawn tanned buckskin and with an inch or two of water in the bottom—played either by a regular partner or by the man seated next to him. The drum, staff, and rattle are passed from man to man, clockwise, as each sings four songs. There is a recess (*nawa·c ape·w*, "he is there for awhile")[4] around midnight, and another pause about 3:00 A.M., which is marked by the prayer of the cedar chief. The ceremony ends at sunrise with consumption of blessed water and a communion breakfast (*mi·p me·cehsiya*ʔ, "we eat early in the morning"). Most participants and their families stay on the next day for a later, more substantial breakfast and dinner.

---

[4] For the accurate phonetic spelling and translation of this and many other Menomini terms we are indebted to J. S. Slotkin (1952).

In the center of the tepee ground is a carefully laid fire of clean split staves, the ashes of which are swept at dawn into the form of a dove or Waterbird. There is a half-moon altar of sand between the leader's place and the hearth, with a small pedestal for the "chief" peyote, and an indented line drawn along the top of the half-moon's ridge to symbolize the difficult and narrow path the Peyote member must follow through life. Material paraphernalia used during the meeting include the drum, a staff held by each singer in turn, and a gourd rattle to accompany his singing (together with the drum used by his "partner"), an eagle-feather fan, a bunch of sage, a small cloth bag for the cedar (dried, crumbled sprigs used as "incense"), a whistle made from the wing bone of an eagle, a larger cloth bag for the peyote that will be consumed during the evening, and the "master" or chief peyote (*oke·ma·w maski·hkiw*), an unusually large and perfectly formed peyote button kept in a buckskin bag. The leader usually has his own "kit" of "tools," kept in a small suitcase or (in one instance) a musical instrument case, and placed before him in careful order upon an "altar" cloth. Individual participants frequently bring some personal tools, such as fans.

Christian symbols are apparent in the material structure and paraphernalia, as well as in the prayers and speeches. The tepee's poles represent Jesus Christ and the disciples. The staff is carved with crosses. Sometimes ten carefully selected sticks used to start the fire are regarded as representing the Ten Commandments. Many prayers and songs are directed to Christ by name. The leader sometimes crosses his breast with his hand before lifting the blessed water to his lips in the sacred silver cup. The basic conception, premises, and procedures, however, are native North American, if not specifically Menomini, warped to fit the peculiar needs of the members and penetrated here and there with Christian ideas.

The ultimate declared purpose of taking peyote is to acquire the power with which it has been invested by the Creator (*Kese·maneto·w*). This power cannot be obtained by merely consuming peyote. It comes to one only when the person approaches it in a proper state of humility and after long preoccupation and concentration. If the person is "filled with sin," the medicine will only make him ill, but once Peyote power is acquired, it will enable him to do wondrous things and serves to protect him from evil, including sorcery.

The atmosphere during the first half of the meetings is serious, intense, and quiet. Toward midnight, however, the voices become more emotional and the drumming more rapid. The songs become a cry for help. The prayers become pleas for salvation, for aid and relief from manifest fears, doubts, and guilt feelings. Men pray aloud, give testimonials at certain periods in the ceremony, and frequently break into tears.

Each man seeks his revelations and salvation, and gains power individually. As stated in the ideology, there can be no instruction in the Peyote way; this must come to the individual through his own experience in meetings. Much of this instruction is gained in visions, and some in dreams. However, all members are aided in their striving for revelation, knowledge, and "cleansing of sins" by the efforts of the group in concert—through collective and individual prayers, singing, and drumming and the maintenance of a sacred atmosphere throughout the meeting.

Following are notes drawn from the observations of one of the meetings attended by George and Louise Spindler. Each meeting is different, even in details of ritual (individual leaders and officers introduce minor variations), but all conform to the same general pattern.

We arrived at 7:30 P.M. The members were standing about the yard talking quietly. At 8:45 P.M. the fire tender—a Winnebago from Wisconsin Dells, called us all in. The usual prayer was offered before the door of the tepee (in Menomini) by the chairman of the.night.

After arranging ourselves in the circle of the tepee on blankets laid on fresh cedar over straw, the leader got up to introduce the evening's ritual, state the procedure, and announce the appointment of officials: cedar man (T. B., a Winnebago from Wisconsin Rapids), staff and drum keeper (a Winnebago from Wittenberg), fire tender (a Winnebago from Wisconsin Dells).[5] He also called upon M. to explain the purpose of the meeting. M. arose to do so, saying that the purpose was to "bless the children going off to school."

After this the meeting procedure began with the first passing around of peyote, and the usual singing and drumming, with the drum, rattle, and staff being passed clockwise to each man—who sang four songs.

The meeting was recessed ritually when the drum, and so forth, arrived back at the leader's place about midnight. He preceded his songs by the piping of the eagle-bone whistle—four shrill notes. After his songs were ended water was brought in, cedar was sprinkled on the fire, and the water was blessed by wafting an eagle-feather fan over the incense of the burning cedar and then over the water four times. This blessing was also distributed to the assemblage by shaking the spread feather fan around the circle of participants (this was also done several other times by the fire tender). Then the members stretched out their hands to the fire and made as though to bathe their heads and bodies in its radiance and in the incense of the cedar. The water was then passed in a bucket and each member drank from the silver cup carried by the fire tender, who also served as waiter. The water is regarded as possessing a beneficent power, so one hand is held under the cup to catch any drops. Many of the members laved their faces in some of the water, poured into the palm of the hand.

The meeting was then open for talking. Several men spoke, explaining how they came and thanking M. for putting up the meeting.

Recess was then called and we all went to the yard for about fifteen minutes. We reentered then, and the meeting resumed with a prayer and an announcement by the leader as to procedure for the rest of the evening.

The drumming and singing then proceeded again—two times around the circle—ending at the leader's place with the blessing and cedar incense procedure as before. The "tools" (fans, staff, gourd rattle, drum, and so forth)

---

[5] There are Menomini who can and do fill these offices, but asking qualified visitors to do so is a way of honoring them.

were "smoked" at midnight and at dawn—whenever the cedar incense was burned in the fire and the rest of the blessing procedure had taken place. By then it was dawn (4:30 A.M.) and the water was brought in a second time and the same procedure was followed. Each time the water was brought in it was placed on a cross drawn in the ground before the fireplace and in front of the door of the tepee, and the fire tender, who brought in the water, prayed over it (in Winnebago). This was the only cross used—except for those carved in the staff or represented in the beadwork of the handles of the feather fans.

The meeting was concluded after a third round of singing, at 7:00 A.M., with the ceremonial consumption of fruit, meat, and grain (all wild), brought in by the leader's wife. This was preceded by the usual blessing procedure—"smoking the tools," and piping on the eagle-bone whistle.

The food, consisting of wild rice, venison, and blueberries, was brought in, in large bowls, and placed on a folded mat before the fire. Mrs. R. (the leader's wife) kneeled before it and prayed long—in Menomini. Then the food was passed clockwise, each person taking a spoonful or two. Several took some of the ground venison in their handkerchiefs, to be given in morsels to the members of their families later, as a way of distributing the blessings of the meeting through the blessing given specifically to the food.

When this was finished, the leader announced that the meeting was open to any talks, by any person present who might wish to speak. T. B., D. P., and G. Spindler responded.

After this the leader prayed again, then asked the assemblage to rise together, but pray individually, "each person in his own language," and each one did, conversing with the Creator in familiar terms and asking for blessings for themselves and others. Then the members filed out one by one.

The day following this night was occupied by informal talking, mostly about the meeting and individual experiences during it. A "lunch" of sandwiches and coffee was served in the tepee at 9:00 A.M., and a dinner at 12:40. The persons at the meeting all stayed for dinner and began to leave at 3:00 P.M.

The preceding was a summary of the procedure of one evening. A topical summary of some specific observations, with interpretive notes, follows. They are given in the form in which they were written up in G. Spindler's field notes immediately after a meeting that took place after we had attended several others.

1. Several men cried openly at the meeting. M. cried when he got up to announce the purpose of the meeting. He had just mentioned his father; that he missed him even now, and burst into tears. He continued crying as he spoke. T. B. got up at dawn to speak and cried all the way through his talk. He spoke in Winnebago. The others broke into tears here and there throughout the meeting as they prayed. This overt emotionalism is in striking contrast to anything we have seen in the *metewen* or *ni·mihetwan*. The people in these organizations on the whole exhibit a remarkable composure and constraint both in meetings and outside.

This crying, and the group acceptance of it—the tacit assumption that people will cry, and will unburden themselves—would seem a powerfully attractive factor to people who are seeking some outlet for their frustrations and anxiety, and some acceptance and sympathy.

2. The group support and in-group spirit is an impressive feature of the meetings. The sharing of this long and emotionally laden ceremony, the confessatory atmosphere, all combine to produce a sense of closeness between members that even we, as visiting Whites, felt. One feels loved and accepted.

3. However, despite this "groupness" of feeling, the degree of introversion exhibited is remarkable. Most of the time the men sit cross-legged and stare into the fire (women do not sit in the inner circle). Occasionally, one will get to his knees and bow over, almost touching the ground with his head, and remain in that position for as long as one hour. Men will break into prayer audibly at almost any time—but particularly as a song is being sung. Sometimes three or four people will be praying at once so that there is a low babble of voices. These prayers seem to be triggered by some process internal to the person, and not dependent on the place in the ritual or any specific procedure of the ritual or meeting, as it would be among Whites, or in the *metɛ·wen* or *ni·mihɛ·twan*.

4. The songs sound frequently like a "cry for help." They are sung in a high voice, almost falsetto, with sobs, and a great variation of volume. They sound sometimes as though someone were crying in a minor key and in rhythm with a drum. The singing, the prayers, and speeches all seem to be cries for help, in both content and procedure. This is accompanied by a clear narcissism or egoism in the content of the speeches. Men arise to explain at length just why *they* came to the meetings, what good it did them, and always what trouble *they* had at home, in *their* families, in *their* lives. M. W. spoke of his father, his childhood, his children, and O. P. said, "I don't get around to these meetings very often, but M. came to me while I was up at cherryland and said . . . so . . . I and I. . . ."T. B. gave a long speech about his difficult life and broke down in tears during it. Another Winnebago did much the same. This is in clear contrast to the *ni·mihɛ·twan*, where the prayers and speeches are quite impersonal—where one of the "old men" will usually preach, exhort the group as a whole to follow the standards or rules of the drum better, come to meetings more often and so forth, and the prayers are for the group as a whole, at a definite and foreknown place in the ritual, and involve spiritual cognizance of the procedure or sacrifice, or are for some individual who is going on a trip or going to war.

5. I consumed eight peyote buttons during the evening taking two at once and the rest at intervals until 3:00 A.M.[6] I felt slightly nauseated toward the end of this period. I am not sure what other effects I obtained. I did feel,

---

[6] Consumption of peyote varies individually, and the effects vary greatly from time to time and from one individual to another. We observed many people who only ate three or four buttons, a few who took fifteen to twenty, and some who claimed to have eaten fifty or more. Six to fifteen buttons would be, we believe, a modal range for regular members, despite claims to the contrary. Women members eat none at all or (usually) not more than four.

however, very stiff and sore, especially in my lower back, before midnight. This feeling left me after midnight, and I became completely absorbed in the drumming and singing. I tried to let myself "get in the mood," and I seemed to. I felt as though I could sit in any position without moving, for hours, and I did sit cross-legged and immobile for at least two hours in one stretch. I seemed unconscious of my body, though not numb, just detached. It did seem a little like a waking dream state, but I did not sleep, nor did I feel sleepy until about 5:30 A.M. I felt that it would have been easy to drop into a "vision." I did not, possibly because I was so conscious of my role as observer.

The impact of the hours of drumming and repetitious singing, the fire in the center of the tepee, the introverted behavior of the members, and the emotionalism in prayer and speech, all absorb one completely and make one forget discomfort, probably whether one consumes peyote or not.

The drumming seems to contribute to this state as much as the consumption of peyote. The drum is hit very rapidly and quite hard. Each man, as he gets it, shakes water up onto the buckskin cover, then picks up the drum in both hands, places his mouth over the lip of the kettle and onto the drumhead, and blows hard, thus expanding the drumhead by air pressure from inside, the purpose apparently being to make it as taut as possible.[7] Then the drummer begins, pushing his left thumb into the drumhead until he finds a spot where the drum is especially sonorous and at a pitch appropriate to the singing style and the particular voice of a given singer. This pitch may thus be varied as the songs are sung.

The beats are so rapid that there is an almost continuous roll of sound, itself in a minor key. It is literally hypnotic in its effect.

Most of the men who are not drumming will keep the beat with their right hands all night. They may do this by tapping their fans, if they have them, or by shaking gourd rattles, or by merely moving their right hands to the drum's beat. Many of the men seemed quite unaware of the movement of their hands.

Symbolism

The symbolism of the ritual is complex. Each move, each tool, the tepee itself and its structure, have specific meanings.[8] There is variation in these meanings, but there is a fund of common understandings as well. By interpreting the symbolism of the ritual we can see more clearly how Peyotism is the synthesis of Whiteman and Indian beliefs within a native-oriented framework. We have already mentioned the tepee poles, the Peyote Road on the ridge of the half-moon, and the pieces of wood used to start the fire, but there is much more. The

---

[7] The drum chief, it is said, is supposed to do this, but we saw others do it in each meeting we attended.

[8] Slotkin (1952: 580, 581, 586, 587, 643–657) has provided detailed information on symbolism, frequently in the words of informants, that has been essential, in combination with the authors' own observations, to the following analysis.

officers of the meeting themselves represent supernatural forces. The leader guides the members along the Peyote Road as *Keseᵐanetoᵂw* guides man along the path of life. He is closely linked with the chief peyote, also representing the Great Spirit, because the latter invested peyote with power. (Sometimes Peyote is thought of as another personified being, or force, but there is considerable variability on this point.) The drum chief sits to the right of the leader and symbolizes Jesus, the cedar man symbolizes the Holy Ghost (*Wayiaskaset aweᵗtok*, "the one who is a good spirit"), and the fire tender represents the angels (*aᵗseniᵗwak*, "spirits of the four directions").

These representations seem at first glance to be Christian in origin, but this impression is misleading. *Keseᵐanetoᵂw* is not equivalent to the Christian God, even though when Peyotists see him in visions he is often dressed in flowing white robes and has long brown hair and beard (explicitly a Whiteman), for he invests peyote with power which is all-pervasive and resembles much more closely traditional conceptions of power than the Christian conception of grace. *Keseᵐanetoᵂw* does not usually punish anyone. However, the Holy Ghost seems to be as much a puzzle to the Peyotists as it is to Christians, and apparently

An altar cloth prepared by one of the members of the Native American Church, with embroidered peyote buttons in the corners and the crown of thorns, the crown and cross and insignia, and the lamb of peace in the center. A staff is being used to hold the cloth straight.

represents good, bright spiritual force closely allied to *Kesɛ·maneto·w*, and in contrast to the Bad Spirit (*Mace·ʔawɛ·tok*). The latter is sometimes called the "Devil" in English, but is actually thought of more as standing for a number of bad spirits who are inimical to man—a conception close to the traditional. The Holy Ghost is also thought of by some as power—that which is invested in Peyote. There is, however, only one explicitly non-Christian spirit in the Peyote pantheon (other than Peyote, himself, a problematic figure in Menomini belief, and the *a·sɛni·wak*, who appear ambiguously here and there) and that is the Waterbird, *A·we·skeno·hsɛh nepe·w*, "little bird of the water" (some say it refers to the loon). The Waterbird is often represented in the form into which the ashes of the fire are shaped by dawn by the Fire Chief (though sometimes this figure is said to be a dove) in Peyote jewelry and in carvings of beadwork associated with Peyote tools. The notion of Waterbird is a part of the Peyote complex as it diffused from other tribes, but among the Menomini the idea is fused with that of Thunderbirds, which bring rain that is necessary to life and battle bad spirits.

Some say the half-moon is not necessarily a moon, but a ridge, along the top of which is the Peyote Road. Others say the moon is the light of the night. It guides man through the darkness. All agree that the Peyote Road is the way man must travel, falling neither into the fire on one side nor into the darkness on the other, and that the ritual takes one along the road. In any event, the half-moon altar and ritual is considered (by Menomini Peyotists) to be the "true Indian way" in contrast to the cross-fireplace altar and service used by the Winnebago and others, and at first by the Menomini.

The meanings ascribed to other tools are sometimes ambiguous. Both the eagle-bone whistle and the cedar "incense" (smoke from crumbled dried cedar leaves put in the fire) seem to be forms of notification or communication, linking man and supernatural forces together. The shrill sound of the whistle is heard, by both man and the angels, in the four directions (cardinal points of the compass), or by *Kesɛ·maneto·w*, at significant intervals during the service. The cedar smoke rises to the heavens and to *Kesɛ·maneto·w* and other powers and is simultaneously smelled by participants. Power is requested and is invested in the smoke, in which the tools, and one's body, may be laved, thus partaking of this power. Some say the smoke takes the prayers of the members with it as it rises to heaven. In any event it does not seem that either the cedar smoke or eagle-bone whistle are Christian in origin, though the ascribed meaning of both appears to include some Christian notions (for example, "angels," and "carrying prayers"). The meaning ascribed to the fan is quite literal. It represents the cooling relief of a fan when one is fevered and ill (or anxious?). The feathers used also represent the Waterbird, which is a beneficent power. The cane is interpreted as support to lean on, literally and figuratively, and to "get to the Almighty" with, or to heaven. The water drum is perceived as an appropriate accompaniment to singing, and possibly does not have other ascribed meanings, but the crisscrossing of the ropes used to tie the buckskin drumhead on forms a star shape which is interpreted by some as the Morning Star, an important deity in traditional belief.

Whatever the Christian elements, the underlying principle seems to be that the specific symbolism is less important than the representation and manipulation of power. All ritual objects and acts, whatever their origin or specific "meaning," participate in power. They both represent power and at the same time bring power to the meeting, to the participants, and into their lives. It is difficult to grasp this principle, for it is cloaked in so many guises. The cedar smoke is important because it carries power. Smoking one's ritual paraphernalia and one's self is a way of acquiring power. The fan is important because it fans, and the fan becomes a metaphor. It "cools," "refreshes," "cures." However, the fan is made of feathers representing the Waterbird, a being with great power, so the fan, used to waft the cedar smoke over other paraphernalia and one's self, participates in, reinforces, and distributes power. The chief peyote is a direct representation of power, and *Kesɛ·maneto·w* is important, not as a stern dispenser of justice, or even of love, but as the origin and bestower of power. Peyote as a medicine must also be understood as power. This medicine does cure the ill, but it is not medicine in the limited Western sense. It is medicine as in a medicine bundle in the old culture. It is the means through which power is concentrated, acquired, and directed. The Peyote Road is not just the path to heaven. Menomini Peyotists are as vague as anyone else about heaven (it is a "bright" place where "good souls" live well forever); it is the path of power that keeps one from disaster. Peyote power is the means to some degree of security and certainty, to survival, avoidance of disaster, curing of ills, to comfort, and to salvation.

With this interpretation it is clear that Menomini Peyotism is more nativistic than Whiteman-Christian in its orientation, however much it is a response to the impact of Whiteman culture. But given the specific expression (for example, Christ and the twelve disciples, angels, and prayers) of Christian elements, it must also be seen as syncretistic—synthesizing elements of both traditional Menomini and Christian belief. This synthesizing helps to make the incongruity between these two systems more manageable for Peyotists. The synthesizing is done within a native-oriented framework. The labels for some objects and events, and the quality of certain limited ideas, such as the images of God and Christ, are Christian. The underlying principle is native. The principle of power and the process of synthesis will be apparent in the personal accounts to follow. These personal statements will show, as no abstract discussion could, what Peyotism means to the participants, and how it functions in the situation created by the confrontation of Menomini and Whiteman culture.

Inspiration and Instruction through the Medicine

There are many patterns of activity and belief associated with Peyotism that are clear carryovers from the traditional culture. Among the more striking manifestations of this are inspiration and instruction. As described in Chapter 2, the Menomini waited for inspiration and even instruction to come to them rather than actively and purposely seeking it out. The *activity* would consist of putting oneself in a position to *receive* the inspiration or instruction. In the first of the two personal documents following, inspiration is not gained by the use of peyote, but the respondent both receives and reproduces the inspiration in the context of Peyotism. In the second case the medicine itself is the direct antecedent to the experience. Both statements make clear what the Peyotist means when he says, "No one can tell you—you have to get in there and learn it for yourself— use the medicine."

Respondent 11

I'll tell you about how I got a song one time. My old aunt that I told you about died. She used me good, gave me clothes, fed me lots of times. I felt bad when she died. I walked way over from W.'s house, he used to live up at Neconish settlement, over to where she used to work. I looked at them things she used to work with. I was sad, standing there and looking at all them things, and thinking about how she used to do.

Then a wind come up. . . . I could hear it up above. I listened to that wind . . . it seemed like it was saying something . . . like it was a song. I listened hard. It was a song in my own language, about her dying. It come right into me, that song. . . . I got it all. Then I walked over to my uncle's house. All the way over there I sung that song over and over, so I wouldn't forget it. I sung it all the way.

I sat down over there, and kept thinking about that. My uncle was watching me. He kind of knew I felt bad because I was so near to my aunt. So he come over and sat down beside me. "Don't feel so bad. We all got to go when our time comes. Then someday we all come together again, be with our friends and all the peoples we knew again." I told him, "I'm alright. I got something real good." So I told him about my song, how it come to me. I sung it for him. "Good! You sing that when we have the funeral meeting." So when we had the meeting next day I waited until just the right time. Then I signaled my uncle, he was leading, that I was ready. So I sung my song, in my own language. Everybody liked it, they thought it was good. It was the first song in Menomini that anybody got.

Respondent 17

One time I was sitting in a meeting. It was on the Fourth of July; we celebrate it that way. Different tribes come in, Winnebago, Potowatami, for a visit. I was sitting there . . . all at once something . . . I could see something going on . . . the last stick, burning on the fire. . . . I see a staff there. I took a good look at it. Everybody was sitting there, but no one else seen what I see. It was made out of a bow, like a bow and arrow. It was like a Thunderbird, with the head here, tail here, and a place to hold it. Just the shape of it like the bow in the shape of a Thunderbird. Just before the meeting was over, the fire went down, and that disappeared. But it looks like something else in there, a few feathers there, like a fan. I see how it's made, for about fifteen seconds I see everything, just how it's made. Just when I got through looking at it . . . it disappeared. It was something given to me. . . . I was supposed to make them tools . . . a drumstick too. . . . I got a drawing of that, everything they use there. . . . I'm supposed to make.

Conversion

Every one of the 15 active male members,[9] during early childhood at least, had experience with a way of life oriented toward the old culture. Seven of them were initiated into the Medicine Lodge, but all of them were raised by comparatively conservative parents or parental surrogates. Every member has also had extensive experience with Western culture. Five have been practicing Catholics.

There are two major trends in these conversion statements. In one, the individual becomes unsure of the meaning of the older religious forms with which he identified and begins to drift away from them. He goes to the Catholic church; he tries being agnostic. For a time he "floats" from one group to another, just as many transitionals do that have not taken up Peyote. However, everything he tries is unsatisfactory—until he finds "a home" in the cult. (Respondent 22 is a particularly good example.)

In the other type of conversion, the individual is, like the first, at a loss as to what to identify himself with. Here, the situation is similar, but the stresses are even more acutely personal. The person has no primary group, no stable friendships, but in the cult he finds security. (Respondent 17 is a clear example.)

In both types, and in all cases, the individual is always marginal and "free floating." He is without secure identifications with any primary groups, and cannot identify with any set of symbols. He has come to doubt the old way of life, but cannot accept Catholicism and the acculturative implications and patterns that go with it. He cannot, however, turn back to the old religious forms or the old way of life. To him, the cohesive, in-group, protective support of the Peyote cult is attractive because it gives him a social body with which to identify and a basis for self-maintenance; and it helps him to resolve the conflict between the internalized patterns of the old way of life and the values and modes of satisfaction of Western culture, for in ritual, premise, and group position in the social structure of the Menomini community, the Peyote cult is a unique combination of the two cultures, even though it is native oriented in principle. Conversion to Peyotism means salvation, both in the literal religious sense, as the convert sees it, and in the broader social psychological sense, as we are speaking of it here. The convert is "saved" from dissolution, self-loss, normlessness, by acceptance of the Peyote way between two cultures. The quotations following, drawn

---

[9] The actual membership of the Menomini Peyote church was always hard to determine since people wax and wane in their interest, and some ostensible "members" never seemed to come to services. The figure 15 represents those males who attended meetings regularly during our fieldwork period. Women are also members, but are much less active in meetings. We estimate a total membership of between 80 and 110, including men, women, and children, but a considerably larger number of Menomini have at one time or another attended services. Active membership has recently (1970) dropped off.

from interviews and conversations with Menomini Peyotists, give meaning to these generalizing statements.

Respondent 22

Some years ago I had an old aunt, sixty-five years old. She got sick, and she was sick a long time, so we took her to the hospital. After awhile the doctor said, "It's no use, she's going to die, no medicine will help her." So we took her home, so she could be comforted in her last hours. The doctor said he would be out with the hearse in two days.

We were sitting around talking when suddenly somebody said, "Those Peyote people, they have a medicine. Go! Talk to them. Tell them about her. Maybe they can help." It happened that they were having a meeting just then. We went over to them. They said "Sure! Bring her over. This is where you Indians belong. This is your place. Not at the other place, here with us." So we took her over, and all that night we sat in the tepee with her. It was a rough go for us. We didn't understand the songs, we didn't understand anything. We took some medicine, to help her, and the others fed it to her all night. The next morning she was still, she was warm. Then later that day we took her home. After a little while she got up! She said she felt good. The next morning the doctor came out, with the hearse just behind. He asked where she was. We told him, "Inside, go see for yourself!" He went in. There she was, preparing breakfast. He stopped. He was surprised so much he could not talk. Then he said, "My God! What happened? What medicine did you give her?" We said "Never mind what medicine. That is the work of the Almighty." He went to his car talking to himself.

That was all I needed. I had been looking for something, somehow, somewhere. This Medicine Lodge was nothing for me. I danced, sung, had a good time, that's all. I was in school. I looked over this Catholic religion. It didn't satisfy me. People go to church, they say prayers, they cross themselves. But it wasn't in here. They didn't feel it in the heart. So I go to some more meetings. I learn more. I listen to them songs. I watch the people pray. Finally I see: "This is where we Indians belong. This is our church."

You know, other Indians and some White men come, tell us we are wrong, that we are crazy. I tell them, "Read the Bible! It tells about Noah. He builded an ark. He worked long. People came to tell him he was crazy. They laughed at him. He kept right on building, him and his little group. Finally one day the others saw that he was right, the great floods did come, and they all ran to his ark."

That is the way it is with us. People tell us we are crazy, that we do wrong. We keep right on, worshiping our own way. We pray how we feel, not the way somebody tells us to. We all pray different, from our own heart.

Respondent 17

Well, I just happen to . . . how I come across Peyote. . . . I was amongst the Winnebago, roaming around after I lost my folks . . . all alone. Of course, I had two sisters, but they in school. I didn't know where to go or what to do, kinda lost like. I come across the people that use that . . . just happened to be traveling through there. Just happened to be a family, very much respected. They invited me to visit them, they asked me how come I roaming around. I told them my bad luck story. I told them I didn't know what to do with myself. Of course, there was other ways I could do . . . drink, carry on like that . . . but I was looking for something good anyway. Of course my Dad didn't know nothing about Peyote. They just told me to watch my step . . . to follow life in a good way. I remember that, what they told me. I had it in my mind. That's what I told them people I visited. They invited me, after I told them everything, they tell me, "You stay with us, you be alright." I was even adopted. "We lost a son, we kind of like to have you," they told me. I kind of made up my mind to help them along . . . whatever they do, cut wood, drive team, take them to town.

They said one time they was going to have a doings. I didn't know nothing about it. They said, "Prayer meeting tomorrow." A big gathering . . . people come from all around. When finally they got started, they told the leader how to run it. . . . I kind of wondered, I was going to find out something . . . how that meeting going to go. The leader talked, "Whenever we have a meeting, there is some purpose; another reason, we got one kind of lost . . . don't know where to go. So I adopt him, make him a son. So we have him join us now." He ask each one to pray for me . . . take care of me as they go along.

That's the first time I use the medicine. I find out about nice people, respectable people. Of course I didn't know nothing about it. I told them about morning, "I think I'm going to follow this, find out for myself, use this medicine . . . follow it up." Then I thanked them. That's all I said. That's how I got started using this medicine, with them people. They used me good. Next morning they was glad to see me . . . they wished me good luck. "Now I have come to something good . . . something . . . very wonderful," I thought. I was glad about it. Until now that's all I have been doing. Now finally they got me to be a chairman and they consider me a very respected man. I never had no trouble of any kind.

Respondent 11

When I was a young fellow I went to these powwow [Dream Dance] and Medicine Lodge. I used to hear all the people say [in the powwow] that the Peyote people was crazy, they carried on all sorts of ways. They said when they took peyote at the meetings they writhed all together on the floor, like snakes.

One time I was at a powwow meeting. Somehow I got to thinking about what they say. So I started walking to where there was a meeting that night. My cousin was there too, and when he sees me going out he caught up and said, "You're going somewhere . . . up there?" I wondered how he knew where I was going. He knew, somehow, that I wanted to see how these peyote eaters looked when they had a meeting; what they did in there. I told him, "I'm going up there to see for myself." So then he said, "Alright, I'll come too." So we went up there together. When we got there it was just about midnight. You know that's when everything really begins at a meeting. Well, we went in and sat down after the intermission. My uncle was there, sitting right across from me. I looked around. Everybody was quiet, praying . . . no one acting crazy or writhing like snakes. . . . I wondered. Then I looked at my cousin . . . he was lookin' around too.

Pretty soon my uncle came over to me. He asked me if I wanted to try some peyote. I said "No". . . . I was scared somehow. Well, we sat there a long time. There was a lot of praying, but everybody was quiet and acted real nice. I didn't see anybody acting crazy. My uncle come over again. He told me, "Come over and sit down by me, at my side." "Alright," so I went over and sat down by him. Then he told me, "I like you nephew. I would like to see you take some peyote. It will do you good, help you. It's up to you though. You can come to the meeting, you don't have to eat peyote . . . think it over." Well, I thought about it, and decided to try some. So I asked my uncle for some. I started eating one, and when my cousin see that, he left. He was scared what was going to happen. Well, I ate just three, like you did the first time. I was scared to try more the first time. Then I sat there, and I felt alright . . . nothing bad happened. Then somebody started drumming and singing. My uncle said to me, "Now listen to this, you can hear something now!" Of course I heard singing before, but now it seemed more loud somehow. I thought, "This is good music. This is better than any I ever heard before." I heard lots of other kinds of music. I sung on the big drum [powwow] many times, and I heard White men's music, bands, and like that, but somehow this seemed more better. I kept listening. I could hear this music way up high, like it was up above my head someplace, coming down from up there. I never hear singing like that before. . . . I kept listening . . . it was something good.

That's the way I got started with the [Native American Church]. I found out who was tellin' all the stories. It wasn't the people in that tepee . . . they wasn't crazy . . . they was alright. I learned something good there . . . so I kept coming back. [Question] I stopped going to the powwow[10] then. I turned away from it. I didn't go back at all until just two years ago. [Question] No, I never go to Medicine Lodge any more, not since I went in there . . . to Peyote, and become a member. This is more interestin', somehow.

Respondent 3

We (G. and L. Spindler) spent the evening with M. and J. B. after a wiener roast in back of their house. M. entertained us with a vivid telling of the story of his conversion to Peyote. Since the telling of it took over two and one-half hours, we cannot reproduce it in his language or with the enormous and significant detail with which he furbished it. We will outline the main elements.

1. He used peyote as a child—at the persuasion of his parents, but when he went off to school, he pulled away from it so that when he returned he tried to persuade his parents against it. One night when his brother J. was

_____

[10] Menomini of all acculturative categories frequently use the term "powwow" to refer to the *ni·mihe·twan*.

giving a meeting, however, he decided to give it another try. He was curious as to its effects and cynical concerning the experiences he heard recounted by the others.

2. Seated at the meeting, held inside a house, he scorned the four buds the others took, and grabbed a whole handful, eating them "like crackers," to "show 'em" who could eat peyote. His attitude was "know-it-all."

3. Suddenly he heard a voice, "You don't know nothing, nothing at all. You don't even know enough to know where your upper teeth are." Sure enough, when he tried to feel his upper teeth with his tongue, he could not feel them at all.

4. After this, his jaws became weakened, and he was unable to chew the hard peyote any longer, so he called for the waiter and asked him to bring ten peyote all mashed up. He did, and M. was surprised to see that it filled a whole saucer. He was still cocky about his capacity and "knew it all."

5. Then he had his first vision of the evening—a railway depot with a train pulled up to the siding, and a man apparently unloading something, but carrying nothing in his arms. M. was curious to find out what it was he was carrying, and heard a voice telling him, "Take more peyote, that's the only way you'll find out anything. You don't know nothing now."

6. So he continued to take peyote, but he got restive and went outside, feeling somewhat depressed because of his ignorance. He saw angels in billowing, transparent dress.

7. When he returned to the kitchen off the main room, he felt very restless, looked out the window, saw a Western town that slowly changed to a scene in hell, and he could see the horns on the people's heads, and recognized the devil.

8. This frightened him, so he wanted to go in, but someone was singing, so out of respect for him he had to wait. He could not take his eyes off the infernal scene before him.

9. However, he returned finally, took his place, then heard someone clanking chains behind him. He knew it was the devil. He knew it was a message, and that by the Peyote Road he would find salvation.

10. His conversion followed a usual pattern, the contrast of light and dark, evil and good, his abysmal ignorance released only through Peyote. This was interpreted by M. as a lesson in humility.

Visions

Visions are facilitated in Peyotism by consumption of the sacrament, the bud of the cactus *Lophophera williamsii*, which contains nine psychotropic alkaloids, the most significant of which is mescaline, which is hallucinogenic. Considerable research has been done on peyote, mescaline, and, recently, lysergic acid, but confusion about their effects and consternation about their use has not subsided. There is no acceptable evidence to date that indicates that peyote, used as American Indians use it, is habit forming or physically deleterious in its effects.

Vision experiences are almost always a part of conversion, but many visions occur outside of this context. Of all the esoteric aspects of Peyotism, that of visions has received the most attention, and yet there are comparatively few verbatim transcriptions of vision experiences in the readily available literature. Full-blown visions with complete visual imagery are not too frequently experienced. Some of the members stated that they could not remember more than three or four in years of participation. A few claimed they had them nearly every meeting. In all cases they were regarded as events of great significance and were repeated in detail and with care. It is also clear, however, that many psychophysical experiences occur that are not regarded as having such significance. They are usually no more than fleeting impressions, a shape in the fire, a voice, a sound of rushing wind, a sensation of floating, a separation of mind and body.

The content of the "full" vision, involving a definite image, frequently accompanied by audio and kinesthetic sensation, can be categorized under the following headings: instruction and revelation, power-attaining and protection, inspiration, prophesy, and salvation. These categories are not mutually exclusive, and any one vision may express elements from all of them. The theme given greatest significance in accounts of visions is that of salvation, frequently connected with curing, thwarting of the evil power of a witch, or conversion. Contrasts of dark and light, good and evil, hope and despair, with a resolution in the salvation of the sinner through being "pulled up" by the Peyote power, are usually present.

Vision experiences are regarded as sources of instruction, as means of acquiring power, as signs of being "blessed" (having power), as reaffirmation of grace and power attained, as heavenly sanction for one's actions as a sincere Peyotist, as "messages" of importance from the Creator. Visions seem to be "what makes meetings interesting" for many participants. They are something to be "pondered" so that their meaning may become clear. They are also something to be shared with others, as one's experiences during the night-long ritual are discussed in the relaxed social atmosphere of the following Sunday with one's fellow Peyotists.

VISION AND CURING

Respondent 26

One of the old men who started us on Peyote said, "Every meeting something new happens, something different. No one can see it all." Well, he was right, absolutely right. [Do you mean you have different visions every time?] I suppose that's what a Whiteman would say. But these are not visions. They are what you see. Your eyes are open, you're not asleep. It is in your mind's eye you might say, but these things happen because the Holy Spirit from the peyote fills you. The peyote is injected by the word of God with the Holy Spirit. It stands to reason that if you partake of it you are filled with the Spirit. [How do you feel?] Well, if it is a dull meeting, like if it is just a lot of talk about something I'm not interested in, I feel sleepy, relaxed. If it is a lively meeting, like if someone sick has been brought in that we're all working on, I feel full of life, strong. I just want to get in there, trace the illness, do something for the person, use my power to cure with the others.

The peyote works wonders. Your eyes can see what you can't in everyday life. One time my brother was at a meeting. He had been sick, hadn't been feeling good for a long time. I watched him, and I was surprised to see that I could see his bones, just like an X-ray. I kept looking, watching. Pretty soon I could see his organs, all working. I could see his heart beating, his stomach working, everything. I checked up on how everything was working. I watched to see if anything was wrong. But all was fine, ticking along just right. But then I saw a sort of blue spot in his lung, about as big as a man's fist. Then I knew where his disease came from. So I took a button I had in my hand and gave it to him. He ate it. I could see it spread out through his body. It surrounded the blue spot. It pushed it out of his body. It cleaned him out. Soon he was alright again.

You know, this Rorschach [subject was taking the Rorschach at the time] is something like peyote in a way. It looks into your mind. Sees the things that aren't out in the open. It is like that with peyote. At a meeting you get to know a man in a few hours better than you would get to know him in a lifetime otherwise. Everything about him is right there for you to see.

PROPHECY IN VISION

Respondent 5

One time I got sick, then I . . . not much members around Stone Lake, not many singers there, so I want to sing too. They give me forty-four peyote. Pretty soon it started to work. Then pretty soon, I see something. It was a boat, or more a submarine. There was two of them, and one was moving all the time. I don't know what they was. . . . I watched. Then one of them turn over in the water, and you know how it is when something goes down in the water, sinks in the water, there's a whirlpool. Well, I went down in there, I didn't know how far. Sure enough, I feel it, I don't know how far . . . sure enough it come up again. . . . Well, that one what went over, that was the old country . . . that's when the war started, the old country went down, and this country started to shake. That's what I learned that time. Not long after that I seen bombs dropping, and exploding . . . shell holes all around. Then I had my little boy with me . . . carrying him in my arms right through there. I dunno where I'm going but I'm going! I come to a hill, the shells was dropping all around, and I'm going right through. So it seems like it was the war . . . coming.

This was three-four years ago. Somebody was sick. I went over there, but my wife stayed home. I was setting in there, and took twenty or twenty-two pieces, when it got to be morning. All of a sudden I see a vision, a nice room. It had three-four curtains, I never seen them kind before, hanging over each other and split in the middle. One was moving, like somebody was trying to get through. I looked away, and when I look back, the curtains is wide open. I look out, and see the ground boiling, fire coming out, up to about as close as that road over there. I begin to think, I wonder. Then the answers came right in mind. "It's coming close!" That's the answer I got. Now I don't know what that is. Now it seems like this war starting again, and they're going to use this fire . . . [atomic] bombs, you know.

Respondent 5

[How often do you have visions?] Oh Gee! I dunno . . . almost every meeting. Sometimes they come in the morning.

One time I had an experience here at my place.[11] I was kind of sick. My wife told me to boil some tea, so I said, "Well, alright." I put fifty in the little pot, boiled it good, put all that in a dipper, so it was pretty near full. . . . I strained it good when I put it in the dipper. Then when it was cooled just enough so I could drink it I took it down all at one time.

A. and D. come around then, so I asked D. to pray . . . then I took a rest, during the day. When it started to work I was going after water. I could see a real fine wire, like a cobweb, in circles, all even, right up. It seemed like they was going around, I could hear them.

Then I see a Zeppelin . . . big! Then a stool, not exactly a stool, but higher than a chair . . . then a girl, all dressed up. I dunno just what she's gonna do. Then I see another stool, then another young lady . . . both dressed up. This was all inside there, in that Zeppelin. That's the time the boys come over. They brought a drum, and was singing. Then them fan belts, them rings . . . not really fan belts, but shaped like them, some long, some short . . . every time one of them sings one of them fan belts would go off, fly off by itself.

Pretty soon I see a vision . . . the way it looks like in the war. I could see them wheels, all apart, and some stuff burning . . . burning away and smoking. Then I could picture a tavern, and there's a fight going on inside . . . and they was going at it, too! Pretty soon I hear that drum . . . Gee! I feel good! Then I see what looks like police, with blue uniform. He had a box, it looks like a candy box. I see what he's going to do with that . . . he comes to me and says, "Eat that!" I look in and there was peyote in that box. "Eat that in your own home," he says. So that's what I try to do. . . . I put a tepee ground here.

But this other part, it happened that same night, it's hard to explain. It looks like a square jar and it looks like some real fine beads was in there. I could explain that in my own language, but I can't do it so good in English. That's like I explain . . . all kinds of beads, and it looks like water all underneath. It seems like a place in there where there is seats, two of them, with glass in between, going around. It looks like them beads, you gotta catch that in your eye [gestures with forefinger to pupil]. That's what I can't explain . . . how you're supposed to catch that in your eyes. It's supposed to be good for your eyes somehow.

That's what I mean, if anybody was to tell me that, I wouldn't know what they meant. The only way you can find out is to take the medicine yourself.

---

[11] Peyotists frequently use the medicine at home when they are ill.

Peyote himself runs the whole thing . . . no one rank above another. Man power wouldn't work, you got to use peyote. The Almighty gave it to the Indian so we could know there's an Almighty somewheres. You got to pray, ask him the best way you know how. It's like maybe you wash that floor. If it's pretty dirty you need lots of water, if you get a little, it ain't enough. Same way with that peyote . . . you take a little, it does no good. [Question] I take twenty to twenty-five each time. The leader is supposed to take more. The more you take the more interesting it is.

HEAVEN

Respondent 25

[Have any of the people in your church ever seen Heaven?]
Some say they get pretty close. One old man told me how he saw a long stairway, it reached way, way up. There was pretty flowers, real nice, all along the sides. He climbed up these steps, until he got almost to the top. But there was a gate there and two angels, one on each side of the stairway. They were guarding the gate. But they wouldn't let him inside, so he never could see in there. He didn't quite make it. Maybe he didn't live just right.

[What is he—*Keseˑmanetoˑw*—like?]
I see him; I seen him there when I first eat that medicine. . . . He look like White man; tall; well, he's got some kind of white coat on, something like that, like a—I don't know what you call that. [A gown or robe?] Yes, a robe, that's it. I seen that [one] standing there; that's why I like that, this Medicine. . . . he had whiskers on . . . he didn't say nothing to me. I just saw him. [Slotkin 1952:629][12]

EPISODES

Respondent 3

You can always tell when a singer has had a lot of peyote. What you hear before midnight is just warming up. But after that, when the peyote has had its effect, the singing is different. It has a ring to it that it never has no other time. I ain't too much as a singer, but when I think I'm going to sing I take ten to fifteen peyote and keep eating them all night. There ain't many good singers here. Oh, they're alright, but nothing as good as some of the Winnebago. There was two here, they sang small, small. A baby would be bass compared to them. They sang so small, so fine. They ate lots of peyote.

Lots of times I see things that hasn't no story to them, that I know of anyhow. Many times I see these Waterbirds, in the morning, towards the end of the meeting. I even made them fly once. . . . I hollered at them and they all rushed up. I could hear their wings, too.

[12] No Peyotist described *Keseˑmanetoˑw* to the Spindlers this explicitly. All three descriptions in Slotkin's texts are of this order.

Then, too, I see a white mass, like the cleanest, whitest snow. It boils and burbles . . . seethes. Every once in awhile it throws up a black thing, that might turn out to be a mink, or an otter, or some other animal. I took that to mean I might have good luck trapping but I never took my traps out to find out.

One time I could see a big field, bigger than that one over there [about ten acres]. That field was covered with deer horns, all over. It seemed like I was looking through deer horns too. Gee! that looked good . . . real nice.

Then once when I started shakin' the rattle I saw a whole flock of wild geese. You know the whirrin' noise they make. I was flyin' with them and could even feel the wind swishing past my wings. They honked and I hollered back at them. Then they would honk again and I hollered again. All the time I was singin' my song with the drum. Then two of the men beside me joined in, but it seemed as if they was always far behind me. I had taken lots more peyote than them. They honked back at the geese, but I was always out in front of 'em. Then my song ended and the geese disappeared.

Another time when I was singin' and shakin' my rattle I saw four corners. It was in a big city and I was standin' on one. Up above me was a big clock in a tower. All the time I was singin' it seemed like my voice would pull the hands a little ways around. I threw my voice up there and hollered and the hands would move. But they would go just so fast. I couldn't make them move no faster. And when the hands had gone clear around my song was finished and the clock was gone.

Sometimes while I was singin' I saw a long, hollow tube that reached way way out. I could holler and could see my voice go down the tube. I would try to throw my voice way down to the other end and then would watch it circle round and round and come back to me. I could do more with my voice than the others because I take more medicine. When the drum stops and I stop singin' the tube goes.

Another time when someone else was drumming, I was way off in that place where people all had that religious dress on, and something around their heads. There was a big tent there and the people were all kneeling and praying and I was praying with them. I could tell it was a foreign land because the air smelled different. I could smell that air so plain! [What sort of a tent was it?] It was a sort of awning-like tent with fringes, sort of khaki color.

HEAVENLY MESSAGE

Respondent 3

I was drumming for J. He was leader that night. I had taken a lot of peyote, maybe seventy of them. When you take a lot you can drum better than the others, you can get all different tones out of the drum. I drummed, and as he began his song I could see all sorts of letters on the top of the drum. As I drummed harder they got bigger, but they kept shimmering so I couldn't read them. I kept trying to get them better and then he finished his song and I stopped drumming and they disappeared. Then he began to sing and I played the drum again. There were the letters . . . all shimmering. They got bigger, so big I couldn't see them, then small, so small I couldn't read them at all . . . when the song got small. I kept trying to get them again so I could see them better, and just when it seemed that I could read them the song ended. I kept thinking, if I had taken more medicine, maybe just four more, I could have read them. The way I see it, it was a message from the Almighty I cheated my people by not taking more medicine. You always should take as much as you can. If I had taken more I could have read the message and told my people what it was, and given them the word of God.

THE KING'S PALACE

Respondent 3

One time when I was singin' I was inside a beautiful palace, the palace of the King [points above reverently]. There was jewels inside. Such jewels as I never see on this earth. Red, blue, shining jewels sparkling so beautiful. Then there was four men, carrying something between them over their backs [a litter]. It was the King's crown on it. I knew it was because a voice said it was, and it was there on the crown in big letters, "This is the King's crown." They walked to a place in the palace where there was four corners [crosses index fingers to demonstrate]. They stopped there, and it seemed like I was walkin' with them, at the same time and was singin' my song. They turned the crown around and around, and the jewels sparkled. Then I could see the outside of the palace. I could see how big it was. It seemed like I would be both inside and outside it at the same time. Then my song ended and it all disappeared.

Respondent 17

There was one meeting. The leader was praying, when the medicine was working . . . and I was just setting there. This leader enjoyed himself praying. Of course I was sitting pretty close by him. . . . It seemed like I could see clouds on both sides, and a tepee, and we all setting there with our heads down. Seems like this prayer looks pure. Everybody setting around the tepee, all full. And of course there's another part, the caboose. I was listening to the prayer. He was praying for everybody, even for every tribe, even those sick people, even those other Indians doing different ways of worship, even way back to our forefathers . . . the prayer was just pure. The sun coming up . . . it shone in there. It seemed like we all sheep. But we're all Indians . . . all had the blanket on.

On these clouds I could see, it looks nice. It was just like I could see more over there. Seems like the angels was all set on them mountains . . . that's how it looks. Them prayers, all pure. Just then I heard something, like when he is getting through praying, it sounds like "Ph ph ph." I looked around, but everything was quiet. I look at somebody, but nobody else hear that, just myself. I thought they would notice that, but just myself. It seems like them prayers was taken somehow . . . when I hear that noise, hear that floppin'. It went by just like that . . . [snaps fingers]. I didn't ask the others. I studied that. It's just when that leader, his prayers was pure, when I see that. He ain't much of a leader, but much respected. He dunno how, but we all don't know how. Even myself, don't know it all. When I use the medicine, I go right ahead.

The reason for that . . . his prayers was answered, because he was a much respected man, his prayers go straight. That's the way I find out. . . . I just kind of see his prayers go off. That's one of the best. Others I see I didn't study very much. [How often?] I see something almost every time.

In-group Symbolism

Respondent 11

It's like I was telling you before. . . . I can't hardly tell you much. When you go to the meetings you learn. I learned many things . . . things I was glad, *glad* to know. It comes to you, *somehow* . . . nobody has to tell you, you *know*, you learn yourself, in your own heart.

[Can you give me an example?] I was a good singer, them peoples, they like to hear me sing. I like to sing for them too . . . makes them glad. I learned something about that one time. This meeting . . . I think too much about my singing. . . . I listen to it, try to throw it just right. I didn't think hardly about them other peoples. . . . I didn't think enough about praying with them. Then I was singing . . . it sounded good, I thought. . . . I was singing a song, with my mind on it, and then I see a ring. It was the sound, the song, somehow, right in front of me. It moved around, but I couldn't get into it, somehow. All the others was in it . . . they was praying. But I was left out. Then it moved away, it went, and left me behind. . . . I was scared about that. I told the leader about my trouble. He told me, "Don't worry, you will be alright." He gave me some more medicine, and told me to pray. Then I felt alright again.

Peyote Power

Respondent 3

A visitor who had taken an unusually large amount of peyote spoke at midnight.[13] He arose, put out his hand, and the fan of eagle feathers flew to it. Then he spoke of the twelve disciples, and plucked out each feather from the holder, then cast them to the ground where they stuck upright in a row. When he was through, he put out his hand again, and the twelve feathers flew back

---

[13] This report is paraphrased since, at the time the incident occurred, circumstances prevented its being recorded.

into it. He placed them back in the holder with one motion and released the fan, which flew back into its usual place in front of the chairman.

Another visitor made no speech. He merely got up, took off his shoes and socks, and walked to the fire and stood in the burning coals, saying, "He who believes in Jesus Christ will not burn," then went back to his place and put his shoes and socks back on again.

Protection

Peyotism is a source of protection for the individual in all of its manifestations since it provides insulation against cultural and personal trauma through in-group and symbolic support.

However the protective function of Peyote is more specific than this. The traditional Menomini cultural system provided protection, in the form of ritual precautions, medicines, powerful shamans, and organized associations like the Medicine Lodge, Dream Dance, and, earlier, the Thunder cult, against the machinations of witches and other evil powers. With the disintegration of many of the traditional patterns that could provide this protection, however, and with the acculturating individual's loss of faith in the efficacy of those still available, new sources of protection are needed. Individuals who are still responding to the internalized compulsives of the traditional culture, however much they may be moving away from this culture at the manifest level, are in the situation of being frightened by the old fears and symbols of fears but lacking mechanisms to combat them. The psychological situation is made more precarious by the additional burden of culture conflict, and the self-doubts and generalized anxieties created as individuals attempt to adjust to it. They impute motives to others that may, they believe, result in sorcery, as in one case quoted here. Often those to whom such motives and powers are imputed are members of the native-oriented group, especially elders. Sometimes they are transitional persons, who are even more dangerous, it is believed, because they are not constrained by the norms of the native-oriented group. Sometimes impersonal forces are perceived, like the disease "shape" described by one of the respondents following. The protective function of Peyote is implicit in many of the personal documents preceding. In the three following, this function is made very explicit.

Respondent 4

One time we had a meeting . . . the first part of the second war. There was Indian boys leaving . . . so we had a meeting for them. I had two boys went away. I had a brother, E., went too. We had meeting for them. I was leading. Along about the time when the medicine was affecting my mind . . . I was praying. It seems like I could see wings, tip to tip, down to the earth . . . , covering the earth, and we was all under this. So then, I know, our boys are protected. As I go along, studying about these wings with my prayer, it come to me they was the angel's. Then I turned around, asked the Creator, one of his guardian angels . . . to send one over there, where the war was going on, to watch over our boys. From them wings, it puts me in mind that I should pray to the angels.

That's one experience. Those wings could be eagle's too, represent the American flag. That took place all at one meeting.

Respondent 26

I'll tell you a story that this reminds me of. [The subject was cued to this response by card IV while taking the Rorschach.] Well, first I should say that the old Indian doctors could see sickness like a shadow, as it passed from one person to another. Now there was an old fellow lived back of Zoar. He said one day he saw a shadow coming from a northwest direction, a shape. It went into all the houses, just slapped the people as it went past. But some houses it didn't go into, like B.'s where there was one of our staffs above the door. Sure enough, the next day all those people were sick with deep colds, this phlegm, *"h'naek"* was bad. All had those colds but the houses it couldn't go into because of the staffs.

Now my girl had a fever. It was high. I was going to call the doctor next day. But I decided to take some peyote. I did, and gave her some. She quieted down, breathed easier. All of a sudden she screamed and jumped at me, and said, "Look! look out the window!" I did, while holding her and there was this thing. It looked like these advertisements with Jack Frost or the West Wind. I saw it there. If he touched her she'd have pneumonia. But I felt sure. I was full of the Holy Spirit. I knew he couldn't touch me, and I told him to go, and he did. Next day she was well and healthy. This thing looked like the disease shape. It has no definite form and is all shadowy.

Respondent 11

In the old times it was different. The doctors, like this *Cese·ko* I was telling you about, could fight the bad men's [witches'] power.[14] But nowadays . . . only protection. . . . I'll tell you. One time I was out working . . . cutting wood, me and my brother. All of a sudden I felt something touch me on the back, and I could hardly straighten up. I couldn't work no more. So I went home. . . . I was in such pain. I lay down but I couldn't rest, and I was weak. Of course I had some medicine, only a few pieces . . . it was scarce then [about 1921]. . . . Well, I took some peyote. I could rest whenever I took that.

Then Thursday [he became ill on Wednesday] I was getting worse. I wasn't suffering, but I was tired, I could hardly move. Well, of course I was brought up to be brave, I could sleep out in the woods alone, never get scared, but I was afraid then. It seemed like every time I took that medicine I could feel something, like somebody was around. I said to my wife, "I believe somebody is trying to hurt me. I been getting along pretty good. Maybe somebody is jealous of me." She said, "Oh? Maybe that could be." That night I was laying

---

[14] The last *Cese·ko* is reputed to have died in 1912, just two years before Peyotism was introduced to the Menomini.

in bed. I took some medicine. I could tell there was something at the door, some animal. I could see the eyes, not clear, but they were lookin' at me through the door. I knew, if I went to sleep . . . it would get me. But that medicine keeps you awake. I kept taking some, every little once in awhile. I set up in bed. If you keeps up they can't get you. If you sleep, he could come in, no matter if the door is locked tight, they got the power to open it, come in, put something in you to kill. Then that thing moved around to the side of the house . . . he knew he couldn't get in yet. I kept watching to see where he was. He come around to the front again. Well . . . all night that kept up . . . him trying to get in. He tried hard, because if they don't get you, they die. Well, it seemed like morning would never come. But next day, whoever it was, he would come, or send somebody to see how I was getting along. They can't move around themselves in daytime, just at night. But next morning lots of people come, I didn't know which one it was that was sent. I was just waitin' for Friday night, they said they was going to put up a meeting for me, all them peoples. So they come, put up the meeting right here in the house. About 11:30 . . . my Dad was singing . . . he wanted me to drum. I was up by then, but somehow I could hardly drum . . . it seemed like my arms was stiff. Then there was two fellows wanted to go home. They was up to Crandon by train to get the medicine night before. They had no sleep, so they wanted to go home, get rest. J. told them, "Don't go now, something going on out there. You might meet him coming up here." But they went out anyway . . . but then they seen a light, like a moon, right by the side of the house, so they run back in, tell my wife and mother, and they run to me and told me "It's come!" So then I was going out . . . meet it face to. But J. say "You stay right here, if he's got the power he can come in!" Then he hand me the staff and rattle. I pass it over to the leader . . . and then, just suddenly, I just slide down right on my back. I couldn't do nothing about it . . . it was like somebody had hold of my legs and just pulled me down. I lay there, I thought, "He's going to get me yet, I think." But then them peoples in there all pray. . . . I could hear them praying for me. And then I felt alright . . . he go away, that one trying to get me.

[Question] we never knew who it was. Somebody die, but it could be any place, maybe far off somewhere. [Question] If that happens to one of the people not in the Peyote way they just have to give up. They try to fight it maybe, but it wouldn't do much good.

Peyote Cures

While visions are a significant and striking aspect of Peyote behavior, the curative function of peyote is probably just as important, or more important to the individual, and visions are frequently seen as simply a part of such curing. To the members "curing" includes not only relief from or elimination of bodily ills but also therapy for despondency and anxiety, a means of absolution of sins, and a process of salvation. These meanings, attached to the notion of "curing," are a part of many of the statements preceding, and are projected, in various combinations, in those following. The curing function, in its various senses, is closely related to the protective function since in traditional belief illness was frequently, if not always, caused by sorcery, or by some supernatural force set in motion by wrongdoing against another person sometime in the past.

If a Peyote doctor is present, the treatment is performed with a ritual that is transparently native in origin. More often, at least with the Menomini, the curing is done simply through the Peyote power and the joint endeavors of the members to influence the supernatural to aid. If the cure works, it is because the individual gave himself sincerely to the absolution of his sins as well as the consumption of peyote. In this usage, peyote is a sacrament. However, it is also regarded as an herb, and is taken or eaten as such. Anything from a common cold to arthritis may be benefited by the peyote thus consumed.

Respondent 4

One time I was working here at Phlox. There was a sawmill at the time. I was working there, on the landing where they haul logs. 12:00 P.M. came . . . time to go to dinner. Then a log fell on me. . . . I couldn't hardly get home . . . took me two hours to go only a little ways. I was sick, hurt. The doctor came, looked me over . . . he want to give me quarantine. I says "No! this is not no sickness. I just got hurt working." So, then, being sick some time, about a month maybe, laying in bed, a bunch of Peyote people come along . . . asked me if they could pray for me. I says "alright" . . . so they did. After the prayer was over they went home . . . then I was alone in the house. Then I could feel something come to me. . . . I know I'm going to pass away. My breath is short, my heart jump. But I have some peyote under my pillow, about fifty pieces. . . . I ate it. No one there to help me. I took water with it. In about one hour, my mind went blank again. Then I was standing . . . like in some basement. I could see all around. Then looking back at me I could see a big chain, like a big logging chain. I didn't know how to get out. Then that quick it come to my mind. "There is a God, some-where." I say, "Help me!" I could hear something above me . . . it sounded like some person talking . . . can't hardly make it out. But as I go along getting away from them stones. . . . I go higher and higher. It took just so long, then I could see a hole above me. Then there was someone talking in that hole. That voice got closer and closer, as I got up there. As I was getting near this hole, so I could make out who it was. . . . I could tell it was some-one praying for me. When I get there, just about to get out. . . . I come to. "Father, Son, and the Holy Ghost," he was praying. Then just that quick I got up. Then I know I'm going to be Peyote member as long as I live. I know there is a God some place. Then I pray, "I be a Peyote member all my life. I try to be good. I never go back to where I was." Then I was well, my body was strong. People was surprised I got up. . . . I was in bed a long time. I could eat a little bit, as I went along. Then, in about another month, I could go back to work. That's one time Peyote helped me. This is my own experience. I was about 22 years old then.

Respondent 3

One time there was a doctor meeting. H. R. was leading it and there was a Winnebago doctor there. After I took a lot of peyote I could see a big operating table, with a body laid out on it. Only the body didn't have no arms or legs. There was a doctor working on it. Then I could hear a voice, coming from above the doctor. This voice was talking, telling the doctor what to do, giving him instructions. But it seemed as though the doctor wasn't listening. The voice, that was God's voice, was telling him what to do, telling him to put the arm where the arm belong, the leg where the leg belong, but the doctor wasn't listening. He had one leg and one arm on the right places, but he was putting the other leg where the arm was supposed to be. Somehow it was made so wherever he touched the body with the leg or arm he was putting on it would stick. He put the leg in the wrong place then, and the body started moving, waving its arm and legs. It wasn't put together right because the doctor didn't listen to his instruction. This is the way I knew the doctoring wasn't going right. It wasn't no criticism of the leader. It was the doctor's fault.

One time I was awful sick—high fever an' everything. I had taken medicine all day long and this night. I was lyin' on the floor watchin' the clock. It said 10:00 and I just kept lookin' at it and thinkin', "I'll be well by morning." It seemed like a long time to wait. Then I seemed to forget everythin'. The next thing I knew I was inside the clock! I could see the gears and the wheels movin' all around me. Then a cat come up and I knew where I was again. The cat arched his back and spat at me. I said, "Boo!" and he jumped inside a bag, then ran up the Christmas tree. I had to go outside. A quarter mile down the road a couple was quarreling. I knew it was a boy and girl without seeing them and could hear everything they saying, clear as could be, a quarter mile away.

The next morning I walked out and coughed up a lot of thick phlegm and was all well. I could even smell the apple trees for the first time, and you know that's hard to do when there are all kinds of trees around and there's no blossoms.

ATTEMPTED CURE AND PROPHETIC NOTIFICATION

Respondent 17

There's another one. . . . I kinda study that once in awhile. One meeting, they doctored a woman, but she died . . . too far gone. This woman was . . . well she and her husband was parted some way, and the woman, she joined the Native American Church, just starting to come in. She had bad luck. Her man was killed along the road, the boys dumped him in the water near Neopit. He was in the water all winter. The very next spring there was this meeting. A Winnebago doctor come, stayed here. . . . I invited him. This woman here, she wanted this Indian doctor to come down, see what he could do. Anyway, he see what he have to do. He didn't have the power to do so, but he's gonna try, ask for power. He didn't quite get started. There was some good reason . . . the Thunderbirds come all of a sudden, and these other kind [Waterbirds], we call them loons, they made all kinds of noise, hollering. At the same time, it was lightning, thundering, close by, all on account of that. They knew right away that woman was in there and they was mad. There was some meaning to all that, and we all in there knew it. Just then, that woman was taken, right after midnight, after we took water. Before she could be doctored she was taken.

A short time after they found that man, some of the fellers in the meeting. Most of them in there knew he was in the water, and two of them found him. It seemed like they was notified in there. There was some noise in there, but I didn't quite get that. somehow. But everybody was talking it over after the meeting, and some of us knew that I don't know how I could explain that . . . that . kind of notified about it.

Respondent 11

I was pretty sick, I had the flu bad. Then I went up to a meeting outside the reservation. I took peyote, and drank some water, and I was awful sick. My head was going around and I couldn't hardly walk. The next day they took care of me, and I stayed at somebody's house. But I didn't want to stay there long. Those people didn't know nothing about peyote, and I wasn't interested in what they talked about. But they paid my fare back. I was still real sick, but I took some more peyote I had in my pocket and I wasn't even hungry. I ate some more peyote while I was at their house, too, and they tried to feed me breakfast but I said I couldn't eat. I didn't want to eat. I went on the bus, and I kept eating peyote to keep me going, somehow. Then I got to the reservation and started walking to where we lived then, not here, over on the other side of the road. I walked awhile, then I got to some old people's house back in the woods. They were all sitting down at a big table, just about to eat. All of a sudden when I saw them I felt like eating. They had everything just like they used to in the old days . . . roast meat, corn, all the same. They asked me to join them. "Alright," I said, so I ate until I was full. Then I went on. "You better run so you get there," they told me. Of course the snow was this [12 inches] deep. So I run all the way. The most times I had to stop was once.

Well, then, I got home. Of course, I lay down, because I was still sick. Then the next day my folks took me to a meeting that was going on. I went in and lay down, J. W. was sitting there too. J. said they should all help me because I was pretty sick. So they give me about thirty peyote all smashed up with warm water so I could take it down good. My uncle told me. "There's nothing we can do for you. The power is all right here. If you want to live, take this." "Well alright," I said. So I took it all down. The water come right back up, but not the rest. Then later they give me thirty more peyote smashed the same way. I took it all down. Sometimes, too, I take some dry peyote, about fifteen, in there.

Well, I was lying there. My head was turning . . . dizzy. Then they were singing. . . . I listened to that. Then all of a sudden I see a big stairway in front of me. The first step was right like this [points out weathered stoop] right by me. It seemed like them steps was all glassy. They was shining, real nice, gee! they was clean and nice. The first was about like this here [indicates porch stoop again], . . . and each one got brighter it seemed like, all the way up. I could see them all, one by one. Up to the top it seemed all bright and light, real good, clear. Then I knew I would be well next day. The next day, sure enough, when I woke up, I felt good.

[What did those steps mean?] Well, it seems like to me it means that if I keeps on living good, and learning more and more, I could climb them steps one by one, somehow. That was the first time I ever see anything at a Peyote meeting.

Respondent 11

The Peyote doctors is all south. Them people going at this a long time. [How do they work?]

Like them other people. Somebody get hurt, or some kind of a sickness, they go out to different doctors, maybe they never get cured. So they come back . . . try Peyote doctors. About the last thing they can try. These doctors has different ways. One doctor, he use a silk handkerchief . . . hold up handkerchief, look at person through that handkerchief, then put it away. I never seen this, but I heard of it. Some use whistle, blow on person, all over. Then they use three long yellow feathers, they're sharp on the end. They pick that sick person, they suffer, but they hit that right spot. They know it then. In their fireplace, the coals is red hot. They go over there, pick up coals, put it in their mouth. I seen that, they done it right here. They blow it in the sick person . . . red hot after they get through, they throw it in the fire again. They go over there, suck that sickness right out. Whenever he get through he get up, go over, spit that right in fire. Oh, they do that maybe four times, they do that all meeting. The next morning, first thing, them people be up. That's the way them doctors do it.

AN UNSUCCESSFUL ATTEMPT

Respondent 4

One time we had a meeting here. There used to be a house then, where that apple tree is. They tell me a White man is coming—paralyzed for ten years —been all over the country. We got together and put up a meeting. Along toward evening they brought him and his wife. We put the man on a bed and his wife alongside of him. I was the drummer for the leader. He says, "Fix up medicine for this man. Fix some medicine for him and some tea." So we did. We fixed up one-hundred pieces, ground it up, gave it to him. We pray for him, the singing was going around, different ones singing. Along about midnight this man sat up on his bed, and he swung his legs down towards the floor, and one of his feet was moving, just like the drum was going, keeping time. So we give him some more. And this woman was beginning to get scared. She thought this man was going crazy, and this woman said, "Don't give him any more." About that time it was getting along towards morning. As the quitting time came, the man was still sitting up, but didn't walk yet. And this lady wanted to go right away. Because this man was under the peyote we told them not to go. But this lady got help somewhere and got this man out. That's the last we saw that man. He promised he'd come back. . . . He never came back. That's one explanation we had at the meeting. If he had taken more peyote, he could have walked, which he never did for ten years.

The personal statements just presented have provided us with an experiential view of Peyotism. We have interpreted those statements functionally, showing how the Peyote experience helps resolve culture conflict, provides a primary group and security, cures ills, and protects against witchcraft and other evil influences through power.

Peyotism and Personality

One of the objectives of our research was to find out how the adaptations people made to culture change influenced personality. The Peyotists, it turned out, were quite different from the native oriented, or any other Menomini sample. We used observation of behaviors in and outside of meetings, autobiographies, interviews, and projective tests to study personality. We collected these data from the fifteen most active men and the seven most active women. The differences between the Peyotists and others were consistent, and the Peyotists as a group are much like each other. This suggests that the ideology and ritual, as well as possibly the recruitment process, worked together to somehow produce a distinctive personality type. What are the features of this type?

The Peyotists are concerned with their past, with the things they have done that are wrong, and with their personal redemption or salvation. There is intense self-concern, that is reinforced by the Peyote ritual and setting. The mescaline in the peyote also has the effect of turning one in upon oneself, at least in the ritual context, aided by the hypnotic singing and drumming, staring at the chief peyote or into the fire, and being surrounded by others doing the same thing. This self-concern is not strong among the native oriented.

There is also anxiety. It is quite pervasive in things the people say. They are anxious about their identity, belonging somewhere, about "doing right," about witchcraft, their health, losing their lands to whites, and about salvation. The native oriented had potentially most of the same things to worry about, but they expressed little anxiety, either in things they said or did, or in responses to projective tests.

The Peyotists are also introspective. The introspection is often self-ruminative, that is, they think about their past lives and their future lives, and about salvation. But they are also introspective about more impersonal matters in a rather philosophical way. Peyote ideology sanctions introspection, aided by the medicine, as a means to knowledge and power. Much of the behavior at meetings is introspective in nature.

Peyotists are also less emotionally controlled than the native-oriented people. Crying when praying or speaking at meetings is sanctioned, almost required. It is in sharp contrast to the controlled composure of the native oriented. There is also evidence of a kind of looseness in the perception of ordinary reality (in contrast to "nonordinary" reality).[15] But this feature is more relevant to behavior at meetings and immediately afterwards than elsewhere. The Peyotists are not handicapped in earning a living or getting along in the everyday world.

What caused these differences? We hypothesized that people coming into Peyotism are in a psychologically ready state. They are attracted to it because they are anxious about who they are and what is happening to them. They are caught up in culture conflict and are unsure about the future. They need conflict resolution and they need friends and reassurance. The Peyote church supplies these things. They also need, as they see it, to be cleansed of sin by the power of Peyote. They are looking for redemption. As they are redeemed, their organization of emotions, their cognition and perception become, we hypothesize, virtual projections of the ritual, symbolism, and ideology of Peyotism.

It is probable that Peyotism will be less attractive to younger Native Americans. Political activism is more likely to attract them. They are less concerned with resolving culture conflict than their parents. They are struggling for identity but a different one. The accommodative character of Peyotism is not the answer for most.

There, are, however, many parallels to Peyotism among the non-Indian American population. Psychedelicism, the proliferation of religious groups and cults, some of which provide a synthesis of certain features of Eastern and Western belief, some utopian movements with redemptive features, even marijuana smoking, when it is ritualized as a communal event, all have something in common with Peyotism.

The Peyote Women

The Peyote way becomes the only way for the committed member. Most committed members are males. Women among the Menomini have the right to participate in the ritual, though this was not always the case, but most of the women are much less involved than are their husbands or fathers. No offices are held by women. A woman, usually called the "dawn woman," sometimes the wife of the leader of the meeting, sometimes the sponsor's wife, brings in the ceremonial breakfast, and often the water. Occasionally, this woman, or some other, if the spirit moves her, will pray, as does the leader, for the assemblage as a whole. More often she will merely speak, welcoming the guests and inviting them to come to the meals to be served the next day. The female members of the sponsor's

---

[15] Carlos Casteñadas' term.

One of the leaders of the Native American Church and his wife.

family, and other volunteers, help prepare these meals, frequently during the night while the ritual is taking place. When the women do come to meetings, they lie behind the men, where they not infrequently sleep, and in any event, block the cold draft, whistling under the edges of the tepee, from the men's backs. Some women, particularly the younger ones, take no peyote or only consume one or two buttons. Some drink peyote tea, or eat some of the ground and moistened peyote as it is passed around in the earlier part of the meeting. Few have visions.

The women do, however, not infrequently make secular use of the peyote in a practical manner. As one woman said:

One time I was gonna make a pillowcover. That time I took forty pieces of medicine, wonderin' how I was gonna get my pattern. My husband took me to Antigo and just past the reservation line I saw a thunderstorm coming. While I was starin' at the sky I could see a blacker cloud above us. This cloud gradually formed the shape of a bird and how it looked. It looked as if the cloud turned into a bird. So I could tell just how. I took them for a pattern. They say if you want a rainbow, just take enough medicine.

Later she said:

When my youngest girl was about a year old, she got real sick and her fever went way up and we thought she was gonna die. While she was lying there she kept pointin' up at the cupboard. Then I saw she was pointin' at the pitcher where I always keep some tea [peyote]. So I gave her some and some more later. Soon she was sweatin' good and by morning her fever was gone.

The last time I went to the hospital to have my baby I took a bunch—about nineteen buttons before I went, and told D. to pray for me, and I got along fine. They didn't give no drugs then, so it helped me. (Menomini woman, in L. Spindler, field notes).

In view of the lesser commitment of the women to the ideology and sacred practice of Peyotism, do the women exhibit the same psychological organization as the men? The strongly introspective and self-conscious rumination characteristic of the men is not as strongly developed among the women, who are more outward oriented. The women also exhibit somewhat more control over emotions than do the males, and seem to be somewhat less anxious. In general we can say that the women exhibit diminished Peyote psychological characteristics. This is what we might expect, given their lesser identification with Peyotism. The Peyote women are, however, like the men, psychologically deviant within the Menomini sample of groups. This deviation may be the result of their participation in the ritual, symbolic process, and ideology, even though this participation is relatively limited.[16]

Conclusion

In this chapter we have described and interpreted one of the adaptive strategies some of the Menomini have utilized as they have coped with the confrontation between their culture and Whiteman culture. We see Peyotism as a syncretistic movement with redemptive overtones eliciting a high degree of commitment from fully participating members. It is syncretistic because it combines and rationalizes beliefs, symbols, and behavior from divergent cultures and redemptive because it reduces self-doubt and provides an acceptable identity for those who have lost their way. It is not transformative. It does not seek to change the world. It redeems the individual whose self and self-respect have been eroded by the loss of cultural norms and values and by the loss of the support of a stable ingroup. We have tried to show how the ideology, ritual, and symbolism are a synthesis within a native-oriented framework of cultural elements from both Menomini (and broadly Indian) and Western culture, however discongruent these two cultures are. Menomini Peyotism, both as a religious-redemptive movement and as synthesis of discongruent cultural elements, is functional in the adaptive process.[17] It is a microcosmic expression of the conflict between cultures, and of one kind of solution, widespread elsewhere in this world of cataclysmic change, to the dilemma that the native oriented solved another way.

---

[16] Those who wish to pursue further the Menomini male/female differences in roles, values, and Rorschachs might read *Menomini Women and Culture Change* (L. Spindler 1962) and "Male and Female Adaptations in Culture Change," (L. Spindler and G. Spindler 1958).

[17] Students wishing bibliographic references on various kinds of religious and neo-religious movements will find "Material for a History of Studies of Crisis Cults: A Bibliographic Essay," (LaBarre 1971) very useful.

References

ABERLE, DAVID F., 1968, *The Peyote Religion among the Navaho*. Chicago: Aldine Publishing Co.

BEALS, ALAN, AND G. AND L. SPINDLER, 1973, *Culture in Process*. New York: Holt, Rinehart and Winston.

BERRY, BREWTON, 1969, *The Education of American Indians: A Survey of the Literature*. Washington, D.C.: U.S. Government Printing Office.

BENNETT, JOHN W., ed., 1973, *The New Ethnicity: Perspectives from Ethnology*. American Ethnological Society. New York: West Publishing Co.

BLAIR, E. H., trans. and ed., 1911, *The Indian Tribes of the Upper Mississippi Valley and the Region of the Great Lakes as described by Nicolas Perrot, French commandant in the northwest; Bacqueville de la Potherie, French royal commissioner to Canada; Morrell Marston, American army officer; and Thomas Forsyth, United States agent at Fort Armstrong*, 2 vols. Cleveland: Arthur H. Clark Company.

BLOOMFIELD, L., 1928, *Menomini Texts*. New York: Publications of the American Ethnological Society, vol. 12.

CASTANEDA, CARLOS, 1968, *The Teachings of Don Juan: A Yaqui Way of Knowledge*. Berkeley: University of California Press.

GOLDSCHMIDT, WALTER, AND ROBERT B. EDGERTON, 1961, "A Picture Technique for the Study of Values," *American Anthropologist*, 63:26–47.

HENNEPIN, 1689, *A Continuation of the New Discovery*. London (cited in Hoffman, 1896, p. 141).

HILGER, SISTER M. INEZ, 1960, "Some Early Customs of the Menomini Indians," *Journal de la Societe des Americanistes*, Nouvelle Serie, 49:45–68.

HOFFMAN, WALTER JAMES, 1896, *The Menomini Indians*, Fourteenth Annual Report, Bureau of Ethnology, 1892–1893, part I. Washington, D.C.: Government Printing Office.

JESUIT RELATIONS, 1896–1901, *The Jesuit Relations and Allied Documents: Travels and Explorations of the Jesuit Missionaries in New France, 1610–1791*, R. G. Thwaites, ed., 73 vols. i., lvi, and lvii. Cleveland: Burrows Brothers Company.

JONES, PETER, 1843, *History of the Ojibway Indians*. London (cited in Hoffman 1896, p. 152).

KEESING, FELIX M., 1939, *The Menomini Indians of Wisconsin*, vol. 1. Philadelphia: The American Philosophical Society.

LABARRE, WESTON, 1960, "Twenty Years of Peyote Studies," *Current Anthropology*, 1:45–60.

———, 1971, "Materials for a History of Studies of Crisis Cults: A Bibliographic Essay, *Current Anthropology*, 12:3–44.

SCHUSKY, ERNEST, 1971, *Manual for Kinship Analysis*. New York: Holt, Rinehart and Winston.

SKINNER, ALANSON, 1913, *Social Life and Ceremonial Bundles of the Menomini Indians*, Anthropological Papers of the American Museum of Natural History, vol. XIII, part I. New York.

———, 1915, *Associations and Ceremonies of the Menomini Indians*, Anthropological Papers of the American Museum of Natural History, vol. XIII, part II. New York.

————, 1920, *Medicine Ceremony of the Menomini, Iowa, and Wahpeton Dakota, etc., Indian Notes and Monographs,* Vol. IV. New York: Museum of the American Indian.

————, 1921, *Material Culture of the Menomini,* Museum of the American Indian, Heye Foundation, Indian Notes and Monographs, no. 4. New York.

SKINNER, ALANSON, AND JOHN V. SATTERLEE, 1915, *Folklore of the Menomini Indians,* Anthropological Papers of the American Museum of Natural History, vol. XIII, part III. New York.

SLOTKIN, JAMES S., 1952, *Menomini Peyotism.* Philadelphia, American Philosophical Society.

————, 1956, *The Peyote Religion: A Study in Indian-White Relations.* New York: The Free Press.

————, 1957, *The Menomini Powwow: A Study in Cultural Decay,* Milwaukee Public Museum Publications in Anthropology, no. 4.

SPINDLER, GEORGE D., 1955, *Sociocultural and Psychological Processes in Menomini Indian Acculturation,* University of California Publications in Culture and Society, vol. 5. Berkeley: University of California Press.

————, 1958, "Personal Documents in Menomini Peyotism," in *Microcard Publications of Primary Records in Culture and Personality,* B. Kaplan, ed., vol. 2, no. 12. Madison: University of Wisconsin Press.

————, 1963, "Personality, Sociocultural System, and Education among the Menomini," in *Education and Culture: Anthropological Approaches,* G. Spindler, ed. New York: Holt, Rinehart and Winston.

————, 1968, "Psychocultural Adaptation," in *The Study of Personality: An Interdisciplinary Appraisal,* E. Norbeck *et al.,* eds. New York: Holt, Rinehart and Winston.

————, AND LOUISE G. SPINDLER, 1970, "Fieldwork among the Menomini," in *Being an Anthropologist: Fieldwork in Eleven Cultures,* G. Spindler, ed. New York: Holt, Rinehart and Winston.

————, and ————, 1971, *Dreamers Without Power: The Menomini Indians.* New York: Holt, Rinehart and Winston.

SPINDLER, LOUISE S., 1958, "61 Rorschachs and 15 Expressive Autobiographic Interviews of Menomini Indian Women," in *Microcard Publications of Primary Records in Culture and Personality,* B. Kaplan, ed., vol. 2, no. 10. Madison: University of Wisconsin Press.

————, 1962, *Menomini Women and Culture Change,* American Anthropological Association, vol. 64, memoir 91. Menasha, Wisconsin: Banta and Sons.

————, 1970, "Menomini Witchcraft," in *Systems of North American Witchcraft and Sorcery,* D. Walker, ed., University of Idaho. Moscow, Idaho.

SPINDLER, LOUISE, AND GEORGE SPINDLER, 1958, "Male and Female Adaptations in Culture Change," *American Anthropologist,* 60:217–233.

SPIRO, MELFORD E., ed., 1965, *Context and Meaning in Cultural Anthropology.* New York: The Free Press.

WALKER, H. LLOYD, 1966, "An Analysis of Witchcraft in Menomini Accultruration," unpublished manuscript.

WALLACE, ANTHONY F. C., 1961, *Culture and Personality.* New York: Random House, Inc.

Further Reading on Each Culture

We have selected a few books and articles for each of the case studies included in *Native North American Cultures* that can extend your knowledge of the culture. You should also note the titles contained in the References list at the end of each of the studies.

THE HANO TEWA

DENNIS, WAYNE, 1940, *The Hopi Child*. New York: Appleton.
An observational study of child-care and child-rearing techniques among the Hopi.

DOZIER, EDWARD T., 1970, *The Pueblo Indians of North America*. New York: Holt, Rinehart and Winston. (Case Studies in Cultural Anthropology Series.)
An inclusive synthesis and interpretation of the entire Pueblo area.

EGGAN, FRED, 1950, *Social Organization of the Western Pueblos*. Chicago: The University of Chicago Press.
An excellent study of the Pueblo communities of Hopi, Hano, Zuni, Acoma, and Laguna. In addition, Eggan has provided a comparative survey or the Rio Grande Pueblos.

O'KANE, WALTER COLLINS, 1950, *Sun in the Sky*. Norman: University of Oklahoma Press.
A popular and sympathetic account of Hopi life, industries, and interests. Excellent photographs of people and mesatop communities.

PARSONS, ELSIE CLEWS, 1939, *Pueblo Indian Religion*. Chicago: The University of Chicago Press.
A classic and encyclopedic two-volume work covering all aspects of Pueblo Indian religion, social organization, and the changes brought about by contacts with other peoples.

THOMPSON, LAURA, 1950, *Culture in Crisis: A Study of the Hopi Indians*. New York: Harper & Row.
Presents the integrative aspects of Hopi culture and emphasizes the problems the Hopi have adjusting to white culture.

TITIEV, MISCHA, 1944, *Old Oraibi: A Study of the Hopi Indians of Third Mesa*. New York: Columbia University Press.
A superb analysis of the disintegration of "Old Oraibi" over factional disputes.

THE KWAKIUTL

BARNETT, HOMER G., 1968, "The Nature and Function of the Potlatch." Eugene: Department of Anthropology, University of Oregon. (Mimeographed)
Analyzes this extremely important institution, putting it into a somewhat different perspective.

BOAS, FRANZ, 1897, *Kwakiutl Ethnography*. Chicago: The University of Chicago Press. Helen Codere, editor.
Boas did the classic work on the Kwakiutl.

CODERE, HELEN, 1950, *Fighting with Property*. American Ethnological Society, Monograph No. 18.
One of the several important interpretations of the potlatch.

DRUCKER, PHILIP, 1965, *Cultures of the North Pacific Coast.* San Francisco: Chandler.
Drucker's work on the Northwest Coast is famous. In this volume he provides
a very useful summary of the culture area as a whole.

————, AND ROBERT F. HEIZER, 1967, *To Make My Name Good: A Reexamination of the Southern Kwakiutl Potlatch.* Berkeley: University of California Press.
Raises issues and considers them concerning the potlatch, still a controversial
subject among interpreters of the Northwest Coast and particularly the Kwakiutl.

HAWTHORN, AUDREY, 1967, *Art of the Kwakiutl Indian and Other Northwest Coast
Tribes.* Seattle: University of Washington Press.
Next to the potlatch, the art of the Northwest Coast and of the Kwakiutl is best
known as the trademark of the culture.

ROHNER, RONALD P., 1967, *The People of Gilford: A Contemporary Kwakiutl Village,* Bulletin 225. Ottawa: National Museum of Canada.
This is the professional monograph that stands behind the case study in this
volume.

SPRADLEY, JAMES P., 1969, *Guests Never Leave Hungry: The Autobiography of
James Sewid, a Kwakiutl Indian.* New Haven, Conn.: Yale University Press.
For a more complete understanding of any culture and its present state, it is
important to read about individual lives.

WOLCOTT, HARRY F., 1967, *A Kwakiutl Village and School.* New York: Holt, Rinehart and Winston. (Case Studies in Education and Culture Series).
One of the best studies of the functions of the school in a community where the
school represents alien forces and the teacher is an alien. Wolcott was the teacher
and describes the situation from the inside.

THE BLACKFEET

EWERS, JOHN C., 1958, *The Blackfeet: Raiders on the Northwest Plains.* Norman: University of Oklahoma Press.
Ewers did careful research through the historical and ethnographic literature and
also worked with many Blackfeet during the years he was curator of the Museum of the Plains Indian at Browning, Montana. The best single source of information about the traditional Blackfeet culture and the history of change from
the buffalo days through the mid-1940s.

GRINNELL, GEORGE BIRD, 1962, *Blackfoot Lodge Tales.* Lincoln: University of
Nebraska Press.
This is a collection of Blackfeet myths and tales as told to Grinnell during his
visits to the Piegan from 1885 to 1907. It includes his systematic but often
paternalistic description of Blackfeet life and customs.

McCLINTOCK, WALTER, 1968, *The Old North Trail.* Lincoln: University of Nebraska Press.
A reprint of the hard-to-find 1908 edition. McClintock visited the Blackfeet
in 1896. This is one of the best first-hand reports on the Blackfeet of that time.

NURGE, ETHEL, ed., 1970, *The Modern Sioux: Social Systems and Reservation Culture.*
Lincoln: University of Nebraska Press.
A collection of papers by eleven anthropologists dealing with modern Indian
life and problems in another plains area culture.

LOWIE, ROBERT, 1954, *Indians of the Plains.* New York: McGraw-Hill, for the
American Museum of Natural History.
An authoritative survey of major features of the Plains Indian culture area.

SCHULTZ, J. W., 1935, *My Life as an Indian.* New York: Fawcett World Library.
Schultz settled among the Blackfeet, married a Piegan girl and lived as a trader
and rancher among the Blackfeet for twenty-six years. After the death of his wife
in 1903 he left the reservation and wrote about his experiences. A first-hand
account of the last of the buffalo days.

SPINDLER, GEORGE AND LOUISE, 1965, "The Instrumental Activities Inventory: A Technique for the Study of the Psychology of Culture Change." *Southwestern Journal of Anthropology* 21:1–23.

Application of a picture-eliciting technique to a sample of Blood Indians, closely related to the Blackfeet described by McFee and only 40 miles north of them. Discusses different instrumental choices by economic groups, sex, etc., and delineates certain cognitive orientations related to culture change.

THE MENOMINEE

HALLOWELL, A. IRVING, 1955, *Culture and Experience*. Philadelphia: University of Pennsylvania Press (new edition, 1975).

This is a collection of some of the most important writings of Hallowell that have contributed to the understanding of psychological and cultural characteristics of the Northeast Woodlands peoples.

HICKERSON, HAROLD, 1970, *The Chippewa and Their Neighbors*. New York: Holt, Rinehart and Winston.

Provides useful ethnohistorical background on all of the peoples of the Great Lakes area.

JOHNSON, FREDERICK, ed., 1946, *Man in Northeastern North America*. Papers of the Peabody Foundation, Phillips Academy, vol. 3. Andover, Mass.

This remains the most wide-ranging statement interrelating various dimensions of knowledge of man in northeastern North America, including ethnohistorical, cultural, prehistorical, and physical anthropology.

KEESING, FELIX, 1939, *The Menomini Indians of Wisconsin*, Vol. I. Philadelphia: The American Philosophical Society.

Excellent ethnohistorical overview of the Menomini from the beginning of contact up to 1938.

LANDES, RUTH, 1969, *Ojibwa Religion and the Midewiwin*. Madison: University of Wisconsin Press.

The salient features of the ceremonial organization and belief system as represented in the Ojibwa version of the Medicine Lodge (the Menominee Mitäwin.)

SLOTKIN, JAMES S., 1957, *The Menomini Powwow*. Milwaukee Public Museum Publications in Anthropology, No. 4.

Slotkin and the Spindlers did fieldwork with the same small group of native-oriented Menominee. Slotkin provides an excellent description of the "powwow," or Nemehetween (Dream Dance), which is described more briefly in the Menominee study included in this volume.

SHAMES, DEBORAH, (coordinating editor), 1972, *Freedom with Reservation: The Menominee Struggle To Save Their Land and People*. Madison, Wis. The National Committee to Save the Menominee People and Forests. Printed by Impressions, Inc., Madison, Wis.

The Menominee's own analysis of termination and its effects upon the Menominee, the struggle for restoration, the introduction of the Restoration Bill to Congress and the hopes for the future.

SKINNER, ALANSON B., 1915, *Social Life and Ceremonial Bundles of the Menomini Indians*. Anthropological Papers of the American Museum of Natural History, vol. 13, part I.

All of Skinner's several volumes and articles are relevant to anyone who wishes to extend his or her knowledge of the Menominee since he studied them when the traditional culture was relatively intact. We selected this volume because it provides more information on the social life of the Menominee than any of his other works.

SPINDLER, GEORGE D., 1955, *Sociocultural and Psychological Processes in Menomini Acculturation*, University of California Publications in Culture and Society, vol. 5. Berkeley: University of California Press.

Provides data on the original male Menominee sample from five acculturative categories. Employs an experimental design.

SPINDLER, LOUISE S., 1962, *Menomini Women and Culture Change*, American Anthropological Association, vol. 64, memoir 91. Menasha, Wis.: Banta and Sons.

Discusses the women and their psychological adaptation and contrasts them to those of the men. Uses also concepts of social role, values, and social self for the first time in this kind of analysis.

SPINDLER, GEORGE, AND LOUISE SPINDLER, 1971, *Dreamers without Power: The Menomini Indians*. New York: Holt, Rinehart and Winston. (Case Studies in Cultural Anthropology Series).

This case study goes into detail about each of the adaptations the Menominee have made in the contemporary world. It takes a cognitive view and stresses what the Menominee say of themselves and their situation. The Peyote chapter integrates ritual, conversion and vision experiences, and psychological data.

SPINDLER, GEORGE AND LOUISE eds., 1970, *Being an Anthropologist: Fieldwork in Eleven Cultures*. New York: Holt, Rinehart and Winston.

This book contains the personal accounts of anthropologists doing fieldwork in eleven very different cultures. The Spindlers have a chapter on fieldwork with the Menominee that is very useful reading along with the study in this volume.

Useful General Reading

There is a vast literature on native Americans and their cultures and there are at least a dozen usable textbooks. The books listed below call attention to certain contemporary processes.

BROWN, DEE, 1970, *Bury My Heart at Wounded Knee*. New York: Holt, Rinehart and Winston.

This book, subtitled "An Indian History of the American West," is a compassionate history of the events and conditions leading up to Wounded Knee. Must reading.

COSTO, RUPERT, ed., 1970, *Textbooks and the American Indian*. San Francisco: Indian Historian Press, Inc.

A critical and telling analysis of bias and distortion in textbooks on American history, government and citizenship, and geography widely used in American secondary schools.

DELORIA, VINE, JR., 1969, *Custer Died for Your Sins*. London: Macmillan.

Deloria's scathing attack on "Anthros" has become a rallying cry for Indian militants and a focus for relief of anthropological guilt feelings. However, one should be careful to read past the first few chapters of this book, for he states, and gives substantial reasons for so stating, "This book has been the hardest on those people in whom I place the greatest amount of hope for the future—Congress, the anthropologists, and the churches" (page 275).

HENRY, JEANETTE, ed., 1972, *The American Indian Reader*. Book One of a Series in Educational Perspectives. San Francisco: The Indian Historian Press, Inc.

This book is on anthropology and anthropologists from an Indian point of view.

HODGE, WILLIAM, 1975, "Ethnicity as a Factor in Modern American Indian Migration: A Winnebago Case Study with References to Other Indian Situations." In *Migration and Development: Implications for Ethnic Identity and Political Conflict*, edited by H. I. SAFA and B. M. DU TOIT. The Hague: Mouton (distributed by Aldine Press, Chicago, in the United States).

In this chapter Hodge compares the adaptation of a Winnebago man in an urban context with those of a family from the "Bear Pueblo," in the light of their respective socio-structural bases.

———, 1975, *A Bibliography of Contemporary North American Indians*. New York: Interland Publishing Inc.

Contains 2600 entries cross-indexed by tribe, state, and geographical region and covering 27 different categories such as history, material culture, reservations, anthropologists and Indians, music, religion, etc. Easy to use.

LEACOCK, ELEANOR, AND NANCY OESTREICH LURIE, eds., 1971, *North American Indians in Historical Perspective*. New York: Random House.

Takes a more historical position than most textbooks and has a useful concluding chapter on the contemporary scene.

REYNOLDS, DIANE TROMBETTA, AND NORMAN T. REYNOLDS, 1974, "The Roots of Prejudice: California Indian History in School Textbooks." In G. Spindler, ed., *Education and Cultural Process: Toward an Anthropology of Education*. New York: Holt, Rinehart, and Winston.

Another and updated attack on the problems of distortion and miscommunication about American Indians and their cultures, this time on California Indians, and the elementary school texts.

WALKER, DEWARD E., JR., ed., 1972, *The Emergent Native Americans: A Reader in Culture Contact*. Boston: Little Brown.

Includes a very wide range of articles on policies of native administration, population dynamics, technoeconomic change, new religions, changing social relations, values, identities, conflict, and social problems.

Index*

Abortion, *M* 451

Acculturative classes, *K* 153, 160, 175–176; *B* 229–246, 295–302, 306–318, 321–323, 324–329, 332–346; *M* 370

Adoption, of children, *HT* 52; *K* 192

Adoption ceremony, *B* 307–308

Age, and authority, *HT* 50, 59–60; *M* 401–402, 434–435

Age classes, *K* 186–187, 210–211; *B* 270

Aggression, *K* 156–158, 179; *M* 389, 438–439

Agriculture, *B* 286–287
See also Horticulture

Alcoholism, *K* 162

Allouez, Fr., 433

Anglican church, *K* 170–172

Anxiety, *HT* 92; *M* 492–493

Arts and crafts, *HT* 39; *K* 139; *B* 325

Asch, S., 38

Assimilation doctrine, 276–278, 283

Authority, and age, *HT* 50, 59–60; *M* 401–402, 434–435

Autonomy, *M* 384–385, 389
See also Individualism

Avoidance behavior, *M* 399

Awotovi, destruction of, 23–24

Bakoos season, 217

Band, *B* 269–270; *M* 400

Band council, *K* 172–178

Barnett, H. G., 195, 207, 210

Big house (gyux), 196

Birth rites, *HT* 67–68

Blackfeet, all-tribe social interactions, 303–306; annual income, 259; before 1850, 263–265; chiefs, 340–342; Constitution and Corporate Charter, 284; dependency 1884–1935, 276–284; during 1850–1880, 265–275; future of, 347–357; Indian-orientation, 298–301; Indian-oriented social interaction, 306–314; Indian-oriented values, 324–329; interpreters, 340, 342–343; representative types, 229–246; self-government (1935–1970), 284–292; tribal council, 257; trust vs. fee patent land, 257; white-orientation, 295–298; white-oriented social interaction, 314–316; white-oriented values, 321–323

Blackfeet Forest Products Enterprises, 288

Blackfeet Indian Housing Authority, 289–290

Blackfeet Indian Reservation, 249–251, 253–260

Boas, F., 117, 193, 196, 197, 199–200, 203–204, 208, 218

Borrowing and sharing, *K* 153–154

Bourke, J. C., 22

Bravery, *B* 325

Bruner, E. M., 301

Buffalo, 265–267

Burial rites, *HT* 75; *K* 167–169; *M* 401

Calhoun, J. C., 25

Campbell, F. C., 282–283

Ceremonial associations, *HT* 36, 56, 71, 82; *K* 218–222; *B* 270–271; *M* 376–378, 416–433

Ceremonial father, *HT* 61

Ceremonial sponsors, *HT* 65–66

Cese•ko (Jugglers), *M* 407–408

Chamuscado, F. S., 14

Child rearing, *HT* 68, 78–79; *K* 179–186; *B* 324–325; *M* 440–454

Christianity, *HT* 42–44; *K* 169–172; *B* 342; *M* 464, 470–471; Pueblo Indians, 16–17

Clan, *HT* 51–58, 102–103

Clan linkage, *HT* 53–55

Codere, H., 196

Common-law marriage, *K* 205

Communications, *K* 148; *B* 251

Competency status, *B* 281

Confederacy, 201

Cooperative economic activities, *HT* 98–106

Coppers, *K* 209–210, 211

Coronado, F. V. de, 14

Cosmogony, *M* 376

Court kiva, *HT* 55–57, 83–86

Crane, L., 37

Crime, *K* 158, 162; *B* 254–255, 349

Curing, *HT* 88; *B* 312; *M* 407–408, 478–479, 487–492

---

* Italic letters before page numbers indicate the case study for which pages are given: *HT* (Hano Tewa), *K* (Kwakiutl), *B* (Blackfeet), and *M* (Menominee).

Death, *HT* 75; *K* 166–167, 211
De Vargas, D. D., 20–21
Division of labor, *HT* 3; *K* 133; *B* 267
Divorce, *HT* 64; *K* 158
Dream Dance, *M* 413, 424–430
Dreams, *M* 385, 387, 411–412, 435
Drinking, *K* 128–129, 134, 157, 160–166; *B* 349
Drucker, P., 208, 216–217, 218
Drum, sacred, *M* 424–430
Dualism (*see* Moiety system)

Economic system, *HT* 95–96; *K* 131–132, 134, 195; *B* 252, 253–260, 265–269, 278, 329, 350; *M* 393–397
Education, formal, *HT* 46, 68–69; *K* 183–186; *B* 326–327; *M* 449–454
Education, informal, *HT* 69; *K* 183–184; *M* 445–446
Eggan, F., 53–54
Egoism, *M* 492
Elimination habits, *K* 120
Emotional control, *M* 380–382, 387, 466–467, 493
Emotional inhibition, *K* 162–163
English language, *K* 175; *B* 235, 327
Equanimity under duress, *M* 387–389
Espejo, A. de, 14–15
Ethnic identity, *B* 324
Ewers, J. C., 263—265, 266–267, 316–317, 325, 329
Exchange system, *B* 268

Fagg, H. G., 259
Fear, as social control, *K* 181–182; of witchcraft, *M* 439
Fictitious marriage, *K* 193
Fieldwork techniques and experience, *K* 123–130; *B* 246–247; *M* 371–372
Fishing, commercial, *K* 144–150
Flagstaff Pow-wow, 41
Food, *K* 132–133; *B* 268
Food taboos, *HT* 70, 71; *M* 396
Four Tribes of Gilford, 201
Future-orientation, *K* 153, 154; *B* 239

Gallup Intertribal Ceremonial, 41
General Allotment Act (1887), 278
Generational relations, *HT* 39–40, 46; *B* 340–343, 355–356; *M* 401–402, 434–435, 436–438
Generosity, *K* 154–155, 195; *B* 268–269, 274, 328–329
Ghost feast, *M* 413

Gilford Island Band (*see* Kwakiutl)
Gill-net fishing, *K* 145–146
Gossip as social control, *HT* 77; *B* 271; *M* 434
Great Fast, *M* 408–410, 452
Grinnel, G. B., 272
Guardian spirit, *M* 410–411

Half-moon altar, *M* 464, 470
Hallucinations, *M* 477–485
Hamatsa dance, *K* 212, 214, 219
Hano Tewa, clan mythology, 55; curse on Hopi, 28–29, 35; history and background, 13–27; and Hopi ritual activities, 93–94; the kiva, 32; language, 26–27; life cycle, 67–76; migration legend, 28–29, 34–35, 57; as minority, 35; physical environment, 30–31; relations with Hopi, 28, 33–41; relations with Navaho and other Indians, 41–42; relations with whites, 42–46; separation and identity of, 34–40; as spokesmen for Hopi, 36–37; traditional history, 27–29; yearly cycle of, 47–48
See also Tewa
Hawaiian cousin terminology, 201
Hawthorn, A., 219
Heizer, R. F., 208, 216–217
Hilger, Sr., M. I., 410, 414
Hoffman, W. J., 400
Hopi, constitution of, 26, 79–80; migration legends, 56–57; Reservation, 26; ritual activities, 93–94; Tribal Council, 79–80
Horned Hairy Serpent, *M* 403–404
Horses, *B* 265–269, 278
Horticulture, *HT* 27, 31, 43, 95, 96, 98; *See also* Agriculture
Hospitality, *M* 390
Household, *HT* 50–51, 100–102; *B* 269
Housing, *HT* 32; *K* 120, 196; *B* 289–290, 331–346
Hudson's Bay blankets, as currency, 195
Humor, *M* 386, 389–390
Hunting, *K* 137; *B* 265–267; *M* 396–397

Illness, *HT* 74; *K* 133, 196; *M* 487–492
Indian, definition of, 254
Indian Affairs Branch (Canada), 140–141, 177
Indian-orientation, *B* 298–301, 306–314, 348–349; and status, 339–340
Indian Reorganization Act (1934), 79, 259, 283
Indian time, *K* 131

Individualism, *HT* 38–38; *K* 155–156; *B* 324–325, 328–329; *M* 384–385, 389
Industrial development, *B* 351
Inheritance, *HT* 96–97; *K* 191–192; *B* 258
Initiation rites, *M* 408–410, 452; female, *HT* 61, 71–72; male, *HT* 71, 89
Intermarriage, *HT* 34, 41–42, 59; *B* 281
Introversion, *M* 493

Johnson-O'Malley Act (1934), 284
Joking relations, *HT* 66; *M* 386, 399, 401
June Sports, *K* 144–145, 187–188

Kachina cult, *HT* 69–70, 78–79, 86–87, 89, 93
Keam, T. V., 44
Keesing, F. M., 416
Kinship behavior, *HT* 58–67
Kinship system, *HT* 33–34, 49–67, 75–76; *K* 192, 195–199, 201, 202; *M* 398–399, 401
Kiva, *HT* 32, 55–58; initiation into, 89; organization, 83–86; sharing and exchange, 103–104
Koyala (clown association), *HT* 77, 88
Kwakiutl, authority, power and friendship, 172–178; Bella Coola raid, 199–200; borrowing and sharing, 153–154; clam digging, 134–137; commercial fishing, 144–150; coppers, 209–210; daily life of, 131–144; life cycle, 179–188; nobility and commoners, 191–192; oulachon fishing, 142–144; potlatch, 207–217; potlatch period (1849–1930), 189–222; subsisting and future orientations, 153; tribes, bands, and locations, 118; winter ceremonials, 217–222
Kwakwala language, 148

Land, allotment, *B* 280–282; ownership, *B* 253–254, 257–259; rights, Hopi 56–57, *HT* 96
Language, *HT* 26–27, 35, 58; *K* 148, 181; *B* 237, 241, 263, 280, 327; *M* 387, 388, 401, 447
Latescence, *M* 387–388
Legal affairs, *HT* 80; *K* 142, 157; *B* 254–255, 259, 278
Lewis, O., 263
Lineage, *HT* 51–58
Little God Boys, *M* 405
Livestock herding, *B* 278, 280, 286–287

Magic, black, *M* 383
    See also Witchcraft
Marine Medical Mission Vacation Bible School, *K* 170
Marriage, *HT* 72–74, 102–103; *K* 141, 157, 203–207
Marriage taboos, *HT* 52, 72; *M* 398
Mead, M., 446
Medicine bags, *M* 414, 417–423, 439–444
Medicine bundle, *B* 272–273, 308
Medicine Dance, *M* 416–424
Medicine lodge, *B* 309
Medicine making, *M* 451–452
Medicine Men, *B* 285; *M* 376–378
Medicine, modern, *B* 285
Me'napos (culture hero), *M* 367, 378
Me'napos blanket, *M* 444–445
Menarche, *HT* 61, 71–72; *K* 187
Menomini, adaptation to white culture, 367–375; changes in social organization, 397–402; cosmology, 402–408; culture vs. Western culture, 372; decision-making, 433; Indian Agency "termination," 370–371; lost culture, 375–379; shaking-tent rite, 407–408; socialization, 440–454
    See also Peyotism
Menstruation taboos, *M* 412–413, 450
The Meriam Report (1928), 283
Missionaries, *HT* 42–44
Mobility, *K* 120–122; *B* 266–267; *M* 394
Mock behavior, *HT* 64–65, 73
Moiety system, *HT* 56, 85, 108; *M* 397–398, 400–401
Murder, *B* 272
Mystic Rite (*see* Medicine Dance)
Mythology, *HT* 34–35, 55; *K* 197–199, 200–201; *M* 367, 376–378; 402–405, 415–416, 424–426, 432–433

Naming ceremony, *HT* 68; *K* 210; *M* 441
Nampeyo, *HT* 39
Native American Church (*see* Peyotism)
Native Celebration (*see* June Sports)
Native-orientation, *M* 370, 380–454
Navaho, 40–41
Niman ceremony, *HT* 93
Non-interference, *K* 172, 180; *see also* Individualism
North American Indian Days, 229, 306–310
Numina, *K* 89, 195–199

Outside Kiva, *HT* 56, 57–58, 78, 83–86
Outsiders, interaction with, *HT* 32–46

Panchale dance, *HT* 91
Parsons, E. C., 43–44, 67
Passive acceptance, *K* 149
Passive resistance, *HT* 43–44
Patriotism, *B* 325
Pearson, H., 172
Pentecostal church, 169–172
Personal property, *HT* 96–97; *K* 179–180; *B* 267–269, 272–273, 274
Personality traits, *HT* 37–38, 107–109; *K* 151; *B* 272; *M* 380–393
Peyote (god), *M* 469–470
Peyotism (Menomoni), 370, 374–375, 456–496; conversion to, 473–477; cures, 487–492; egoism, 467; emotionalism, 466–467; group support, 467; ideology of, 456–462; introversion, 467; origin of, 461; parallels to, 493; and personality, 492–493; as protection, 485–487; ritual and meeting, 462–468; symbolism, 468–471; and traditional culture, 471–473; visions, 477–485; and women, 494–495
Phratry organization, *HT* 53–55; *M* 398
Physical characteristics, *HT* 33; *K* 151
Physical environment, *HT* 30–31, 96; *K* 117–118; *B* 249–250
Pictographs, *M* 376–377
Piegan Blackfeet, 262–265
Polacca (settlement), 31
Polacca, T., 37, 39
Political organization, *HT* 79–80; *K* 172–173; *B* 252, 259, 303–305, 352–353; *M* 399
Population, *HT* 32; *K* 120–122; *B* 248, 251, 281, 287
Potlatch, *K* 144, 207–217; rivalry, *K* 215–217
Pottery making, *HT* 39
Power, spiritual, *K* 172; *M* 387–389, 408–416, 428, 434–435
Preaching, *M* 449–454
Premarital sex, *HT* 72; *K* 188
Prestige, *K* 173–176; *B* 268–269, 273–275
Primogeniture, rule of, 193–194
Privileges, *K* 191–192
Prophecy, *M* 479–481, 489–491
Puberty rites (*see* Initiation rites)
Pueblo Indians, and Christian missionaries, 16–17; colonization by Spain, 15–16; effects of Spanish rule, 21–22; resistance to change, 22; secular authority during Spanish rule, 17–21; and Spanish exploration, 14–15
Pueblo Revolt (1680), 16, 19–20
Purse seining, *K* 146–147

Reincarnation, *M* 434, 440
Religion, *HT* 40, 43, 82–94; *K* 169–172;

B 272–273, 279–280, 299, 309, 342; *M* 406–408, 456–496
Religious Crimes Code, 43–44
Relocation program, 333, 350–351
Residence patterns, *HT* 50; *K* 201–203
See also Mobility
Reward, as social control, *M* 434–435
Ridicule, as social control, *HT* 77
Robbins, L. A., 291
Rorschach Projective Technique, *M* 390–392

Satterlee, J., 378
Scott, J., 38–39
Self-government, *B* 284–292
Settlement pattern, *HT* 31–32; *K* 118–119, 196; *B* 255–256
Sex roles, *K* 182–183
Sexual behavior, *K* 158; *M* 399, 444–445, 450–451
Shaman, *HT* 88; *M* 401–402, 407
See also Medicine men
Shumakoli, *HT* 56
Sibling relationship, *HT* 59–60
Sichomovi, *HT* 31
Sign language, *M* 447
Skinner, A., 378, 400, 401, 433
Slotkin, J. S., 372, 456
Social class, *K* 189–192
Social control, *HT* 76–79; *K* 153–159, 181–182; *B* 271, 325; *M* 433–440
Social dances; *HT* 82–83, 90–91; *B* 309–310
Social organization and interaction, *K* 122–123, 160–166, 189–222; *B* 269–272, 303–319; *M* 397–402
Social ostracism, *HT* 77; *K* 159
Social Security, 285
Songs and dances, *K* 212–214, 218–222; *B* 309; *M* 421, 467–468
Soul, human, *K* 172; *M* 405–406
Status, *B* 331–346
Stereotyping, racial, *B* 316–318, 338–339, 350, 354
Stern, T., 332
Subsistence-orientation, *K* 153; *B* 238, 241
Subsistence technology, *HT* 27, 31, 95–106, 108–109; *K* 131–150; *B* 265–267, 284–285; *M* 393–397
Suicide, *K* 166–167
Sumakolih (curing association), *HT* 88
Sun Dance, *B* 309
Supernatural, *HT* 86–87
See also Religion

Tanoan linguistic group, 13
Tenbroeck, P. S. G., 26

Tewa, at Hopi, 23–29; migration of, 20–21; population, 13
   See also Hano Tewa
Third generation phenomenon, 355–356
Thompson, D., 262–263
Time orientation, *B* 306
   See also Indian time
Titiev, M., 54
Tobacco, ritual use of, *M* 428, 429–430
Totem, *M* 396, 401
Tourists, contact and trade, *HT* 45; *B* 290–291, 310, 352, 354–355; *M* 394
Trader, white, *HT* 44
Trading party, *HT* 105
Traditional narrative, *K* 199–200; *M* 378–379, 446–454
Transportation, *K* 122–123
Tribal ranking, *K* 189
Tribes, *K* 199–201; *B* 257, 270
Tsetseka season, *K* 218–222

United Church, *K* 171
United States Bureau of Indian Affairs, *HT* 45–46; *B* 237, 276–278, 292, 301–302, 353–354; *M* 370–371

Value system, *HT* 38–39, 40, 91–92; *K* 153–159, 175–177, 208; *B* 245, 271, 273–275, 282, 320–330; *M* 380–393, 413, 428, 435, 436, 447, 452–454
Village Chief, *HT* 78, 83–84

Wage work, *HT* 98; *K* 137–139
Walpi, 31–32
"Wandering man," *M* 404–405
War Chief, *HT* 84, 85–86
Warfare, *HT* 57; *B* 273–274, 278
Warrior societies, *B* 270
Warrior's Dance, *M* 430–433
Water supply, *HT* 31, 96; *K* 118, 178
Wheeler-Howard Act (1934), 237
White man, contact with, *HT* 26–27, 36, 42–46, 108–109; *K* 132, 139–141, 147–148, 196; *B* 260, 281; *M* 367–375, 453–454
White-orientation, *B* 295–298, 314–316, 321–323, 332–339, 347–348
Williams, R. M., Jr., 323
Winter Solstice Association, *HT* 71, 84, 86
Wisdom, *B* 327–328
Wissler, C., 271, 272
Witch bags (*See* Medicine bags)
Witchcraft, *HT* 74, 77–78; *M* 383, 389, 414–415, 433–440
Women, role of, *HT* 33, 50, 58–63, 97; *K* 164, 193–194; *B* 267, 332; *M* 449, 493–495
Work, as value, *B* 321–323, 325–326; *M* 397
World view, *HT* 91–92; *M* 378–379, 387–393, 402–408
World War II, *B* 285

Yava, A., 37

Zoomorphism, *M* 407